Webster's Dictionary

Of The English Language

New Revised Edition

NICHOLS

Publishing Group

Imprint of Allied Publishing Group, Inc
Copyright © 2003 V. Nichols
Printed in the U.S.A.

A, a The first letter of the English alphabet; the highest grade, meaning excellent or best.

aard-vark (ärd´värk´) n. A burrowing African animal, which resembles the anteater and feeds on ants and termites.

ab-a-ca (ä´bä kä´) n. A plant from the Philippines whose leafstalks are the source of Manila hemp.

a-back (a bak´) adv. Unexpectedly; by surprise; startled; confused.

ab-a-cus (ab´a ka s) n. A frame holding parallel rods with beads, used for manual computation, by the Chinese.

a-baft (a baft´) adv. On or toward the stern, aft, or hind part of a ship.

a-ban-don (a ban´don) v. To yield utterly; to desert; to forsake; to withdraw protection, support, or help. **abandoned** adj. **abandonment** n. **abandonedly** adv.

a-base (a bs´) v. To lower in rank, prestige, position, or estimation; to cast down, to humble.

a-base-ment (a bs´ment) n. A state of depression, degradation, or humiliation.

a-bash (a bash´) v. To embarrass; to disconcert; to make ashamed or uneasy.

a-bate (a bt´) v. To deduct; to make less; to reduce in quantity, value, force, or intensity. **abater** n. **abatable** adj. **abated** adj.

ab-bre-vi-ate (a br´v t) v. To make briefer; to abridge; to shorten; to reduce to a briefer form, as a word or phrase.

ab-bre-vi-a-tion (a br´v shan) n. A shortened form of a word or phrase, used to represent the full form.

ab-di-cate (ab´di kt) v. To relinquish power or responsibility formally. **abdication** v.

ab-do-men (ab´do men) n. That part of the human body that lies between the thorax and the pelvis. **abdominal** adj.

ab-duct (ab dukt´) v. To carry away wrongfully, as by force or fraud; to kidnap; to draw aside or away. **-or** n.

a-beam (a bm´) adv. At right angles to the keel of a ship.

a-bed (a bed´) adv. In bed; on a bed; to bed.

a-bet (a bet´) v. To incite, encourage, or

assist. **abetment** n.

ab-hor (ab hor´) v. To dislike intensely; to loathe. **abhorrer** n. **abhorrence** n.

a-bide (a bd´) v. To tolerate; to bear; to remain; to last; to conform to; to comply with. **-er** n.

a-bil-i-ty (a bil´i t) n. State of being able; possession of qualities necessary; competence; skill; a particular talent.

ab-jure (ab jer´) v. To renounce solemnly or on oath; to repudiate; to forswear.

a-blaze (a blz´) adv. On fire; brilliantly lighted up; very excited; angry.

a-ble (´bl) adj. Having sufficient ability; capable or talented.

ab-lu-tion (ab lō´shan) n. The act of washing, cleansing, or purification by a liquid, usually water; specifically, a washing of the body as a part of religious rites.

ab-nor-mal (ab nor´mal) adj. Not normal; irregular; unnatural. **abnormality** n.

a-board (a brd´) adv. On board a ship or other vehicle.

a-bode (a bd´) n. A dwelling place; home.

a-bol-ish (a bol´ish) v. To put an end to; to annul. **abolisher** n. **abolishment** n. **a-bort (a bort´)** v. To terminate or cause to terminate an operation or procedure before completion. **abort** n.

a-bor-tion (a bor´shan) n. Induced termination of pregnancy before the fetus can survive; something malformed.

a-bound (a bound´) v. To have plenty; to exist in large numbers.

a-bout (a bout´) adv. Approximately; on every side, here and there.

a-bove (a buv´) adv. Higher or greater than; in or at a higher place.

a-brade (a brd´) v. To wear or rub off; to grate off; abrasive; scouring.

a-breast (a brest´) adv. or Side by side.

a-bridge (a brij´) v. To make smaller, fewer, or shorter while maintaining essential contents. **-er** n. **-able** adj.

a-broad (a brod´) adv. Widely; in many places; outside one's country; at large.

ab-ro-gate (ab´ro gt´) v. To cancel; to put an end to; to repeal. **abrogation** n. **abrogable** adj. **abrogative** adj.

ab-rupt (a brupt´) adj. Happening or coming suddenly with no warning;

very gruff. **abruptness** n. **-tly** adv.

ab-scess (ab´ses) n. An infected place in the body which becomes sore and swollen and contains pus. **-ed** adj.

ab-scind (ab sind´) v. To cut off; to sever; to pare away; to separate.

ab-scond (ab skond´) v. To remove one-self, as to flee from justice. **-er** n.

ab-sent (ab´sent) adj. Not present; away; lacking; nonexistent. **-tly** adv.

ab-so-lute (ab´so lōt´) adj. Unconditional; without restraint; perfect; complete. **absoluteness** n. **-ly** adv.

ab-solve (ab zolv´) v. To set free or release from duties, guilt, debt, or penalty.

ab-sorb (ab sôrb´) v. To take in; to take up the full attention; to engage one's whole attention. **absorbable** adj.

ab-stain (ab stn´) v. To refrain from doing something. **abstainer** n.

ab-ste-mi-ous (ab st´m us) adj. Showing moderation in the use of drink and food. **abstemiousness** n. **abstemiously** adv.

ab-stract (ab´strakt) v. To remove from, reduce, or summarize. **abstractedness** n.

ab-struse (ab strös´) adj. Hard or difficult to understand. **abstruseness** n.

ab-surd (ab serd´) adj. Contrary to reason; clearly untrue or unreasonable.

a-bun-dance (a bun´dans) n. Ample supply; plenty; amount more than enough.

a-buse (a bz´) v. To use in an improper or wrong way. n. Improper treatment.

a-but (a but´) v. To border; to touch at one end.

a-bys-mal (a biz´mal) adj. Immeasurably deep or low; profound.

a-byss (a bis´) n. A deep crack or gap in the earth. **abyssal** adj.

a-ca-cia (a k´sha) n. Thorny tree or shrub of warm climates.

a-cap-pel-la (ä´ka pel´a) adj. Singing without instrumental accompaniment.

a-cat-a-lec-tic (kat´a lek´tik) adj. Not stopping short; having the complete number or syllables, in a line of verse.

ac-cede (ak sd´) v. To consent; to agree; to arrive at a certain condition or state.

ac-cel-er-ate (ak sel´a rt´) v. To make run or work faster; to increase the

speed; to hasten or bring about sooner. **acceleration** n.

ac-cent (ak´sent) n. An effort to make one syllable more prominent than the others.

ac-cept (ak sept´) v. To take what is given; to believe to be true; to agree. **accepter** n.

ac-cept-able (ak sep´ta bl) adj. Satisfactory; proper; good enough. **acceptability** n. **acceptably** adv.

ac-cess (ak´ses) n. Admission, entrance; attack. **accessibility** n. **accessible** adj.

ac-ces-sion (ak sesh´an) n. In Computer Science, the act of obtaining data from storage; the ability to store data.

ac-ces-si-ble (ak ses´i bl) adj. Easy access or approach.

ac-ci-dent (ak´si dent) n. A happening that is not planned or expected. **accidental** adj.

ac-claim (a klm´) v. To greet with strong approval or loud applause; to hail or cheer.

ac-cli-mate (a kli´mit) v. To get used to a different climate or new surroundings.

ac-co-lade (ak´a ld´) n. Award; praise; ceremony used in conferring knighthood.

ac-com-mo-date (a kom´a dt) v. To give room or lodging; to make fit; to adjust.

ac-com-mo-dat-ing (a kom´a d´ting) adj. Ready to help; willing to please; obliging.

ac-com-pa-ni-ment (a kum´pa ni ment) n. Something that goes well with another.

ac-com-pa-ny (a kum´pa n) v. To be together with; to go along with.

ac-com-plice (a kom´plis) n. Companion who helps another break the law.

ac-com-plish (a kom´plish) v. To perform; to carry out; to complete; to do. **accomplisher** n. **accomplishable** adj.

ac-cord (a kord´) n. Harmony; agreement. v. To grant or award. **accordance** n.

ac-cord-ing-ly (a kor´ding l) adv. In a way that is proper and fitting.

ac-cor-di-on n. A musical instrument fitted with bellows and button keyboard, played by pulling out and press ing together the bellows to force air through the reeds.

ac-cost (*a* kost ´) *v*. To come close to and to speak first in an unfriendly manner.

ac-count (*a* kount ´) *n*. A description; a statement of debts and credits in money transactions; a record; a report.

ac-cred-it (*a* kred ´it) *v*. To authorize someone; to give official power.

ac-crete (*a* krt ´) *v*. To grow together or join. **accretive** *adj*.

ac-crue (*a* krö ´) *v*. To result naturally; to increase at certain times.

ac-cu-mu-late (*a* k´mya lt ´) *v*. To collect or gather over a period of time; to pile up.

ac-cu-ra-cy (ak ´*yur* a s) *n*. **-cies** Exactness; precision; the fact of being accurate or without mistakes.

ac-cu-rate (ak ´*yur* it) *adj*. Without mistakes or errors; careful and exact; correct.

ac-curs-ed (a kers ´) *adj*. Sure to end badly; under a curse; unpleasant or annoying; very bad. **accursedness** *n*. **accursedly** *adv*.

ac-cu-sa-tion (ak ´ z ´shan) *n*. A charge that a person is guilty of breaking the law.

ac-cu-sa-tive (a k´za tiv) *adj*. Relating to the direct object of a preposition or of a verb.

ac-cuse (*a* kz ´) *v*. To find fault with; to blame; to charge someone with doing wrong or breaking the law. **accuser** *n*.

ac-cus-tom (a kus ´tom) *v*. To familiarize by habit.

ace-tate (as ´i tt ´) *n*. Salt formed by union of acetic acid with a base, used in making rayon and plastics.

a-cet-y-lene (a set ´e ln ´) *n*. A highly inflammable, poisonous, colorless gas that burns brightly with a hot flame, used in blowtorches for cutting metal and welding.

ache (k) *v*. To give or have a dull, steady pain; to want much; to long for. *n*. A dull, continuous pain.

a-chieve (a chv ´) *v*. To reach or to by trying hard; to do; to succeed in doing; to accomplish.

a-chieve-ment (*a* chv ´ment) *n*. Something achieved by work, courage, or skill.

ac-id (as ´id) *n*. A chemical compound containing hydrogen that forms a salt when combined with a base; dissolves in water, has a very sour taste, makes litmus paper turn red.

a-cid-i-ty (*a* sid ´i t) *n*. Condition or quality of being acid.

acid rain *n*. Acid precipitation that falls as rain.

a-cid-u-late (a sij ´u lt ´) *v*. To become or make somewhat acid.

ack-ack (ak ´ak ´) *n*. Anti-aircraft fire.

ac-knowl-edge (ak nol ´ij) *v*. To admit the truth, existence or reality.

ac-me (ak ´m) *n*. The highest point of attain ment; peak.

ac-ne (ak ´n) *n*. A common inflammatory disease of young people in which pimples continue to appear on the face, back, and chest, occurring when oil glands in the skin become clogged and swollen.

ac-o-lyte (ak ´o lit ´) *n*. An altar boy or someone who assists a priest at Mass.

a-cous-tic (a kö ´stik) *adj*. Having to do with sound or the sense of hearing; the sense of sound; absorbing sound. **acoustical** *n*.

a-cous-tics (a kö ´stiks) *n*. The scientific study of sound; total effect of sound, especially in an enclosed space.

ac-quaint (a kwnt ´) *v*. To make familiar; to let know, to make aware; to inform.

ac-quaint-ance (a kwn ´tans) *n*. A person whom one knows but not as a close friend.

ac-quire (a kwier ´) *v*. To secure control or possession; to become the owner.

ac-quire-ment (a kw er ´ ment) *n*. The act of acquiring something, as a skill gained by learning.

ac-qui-si-tion (ak ´wi zish ´an) *n*. Something that is acquired; the act of acquiring.

ac-quis-i-tive (a kwiz ´i tiv) *adj*. Eager to gain and possess things; greedy.

ac-quit (a kwit ´) *v*. To rule that a person accused of something is not guilty; to conduct oneself; to behave. **-tal** *n*.

a-cre (´kr) *n*. A measurement of land that equals 43,560 square feet.

ac-rid (ak ´rid) *adj*. Having a sharp, bitter, or irritating taste or smell. **acridity** *n*. **acridness** *n*. **acridly** *adv*.

ac-ri-mo-ni-ous (ak´ri mo´n us) *adj.* Sharp or bitter in speech or manner. **acrimoniousness** *n.* **-ly** *adv.*

ac-ro-bat (ak´ro bat´) *n.* One who is skilled in gymnastic feats. **- ic** *adj.*

ac-ro-pho-bi-a (ak´ro f´b a) *n.* Unusual fear of heights.

a-cross (*a* kros) *adv. & prep.* From side to side; to one side from the other.

a-cros-tic (*a* kro´stik) *n.* A series of lines or a poem in which certain letters in each line form a name or motto. **acrostically** *adv.*

a-cryl-ic (*a* kril´ik) *n.* Relating to or of acrylic acid or its derivatives.

acrylic fiber *n.* A fiber which is made of chemicals, used in making fabrics.

act (akt) *n.* Doing something; a thing done; deed; an action; a showing of emotion which is not real or true; one of the main parts of a play, opera, etc. **actability** *n.* **actable** *adj.*

ac-tin-o-gen *n.* An element which is radioactive.

ac-tion (ak´shan) *n.* The process of doing or acting; an effect produced by something; a lawsuit.

ac-ti-vate (ak´ti vt) *v.* To put into action.

ac-tive (ak´tiv) *adj.* Working; full of action; busy; lively; quick. **-ness** *n.*

ac-tor (ak´tor) *n.* A person who acts in movies, plays, television shows, etc.

ac-tress (ak´tris) *n.* A female actor.

ac-tu-al (ak´chõ al) *adj.* Acting or existing in fact or reality; as it really is, true, real.

ac-tu-ate (ak´chõ t´) *v.* To put into motion or action. **actuation** *n.*

ac-u-punc-ture (ak´ pungk´chur) *n.* A traditional Chinese means of treating some illnesses or means of lessening pain by putting thin needles into certain parts of the body.

a-cute (*a* kt´) *adj.* Extremely sensitive; sharp and quick, as pain; shrewd.

ad-age (ad´ij) *n.* A proverb; a wise or true saying.

a-da-gio (*a* dä´j) *adj.* Term used in music to tell how fast a piece should be played.

ad-a-mant (ad´a mant) *adj.* Standing firm; not giving in easily; unyielding.

a-dapt (*a* dapt´) *v.* To fit or suit; to change oneself as to adjust to new con-

ditions.

ad-ap-ta-tion (ad´ap t´shan) *n.* An act of changing so as to fit or become suitable.

add (ad) *v.* To join or put something with another so that there will be more; to cause an increase. **addable** *adj.* **addible** *adj.*

ad-dax (ad´aks) *n.* An African antelope with spiral twisted horns.

ad-dict (ad´ikt) *n.* A person with a habit so strong that he cannot easily give it up. **-ion** *n.*

ad-di-tion (*a* dish´an) *n.* An adding of numbers to find their total; the act of joining one thing to another. **-ional** *adj.* **additionally** *adv.*

ad-di-tive (ad´i tiv) *n.* A substance added to another in small amounts to alter it.

ad-dle (ad´el) *v.* To become or make confused; to spoil, as eggs.

addn *abbr.* Addition.

ad-dress (*a* dres´) *v.* To direct or aim; to speak to; to give attention to. *n.* The location to which mail or goods can be sent to a person, business, or organization.

ad-duce (*a* dõs´) *v.* To offer as proof or give as a reason. **-er** *n.* **adducible** *adj.*

a-dept (ad´ept) *adj.* Highly skilled; expert. **adeptly** *adv.* **adeptness** *n.*

ad-e-qua-cy (ad´e kwa s) *n.* The state of being good enough to fill a requirement.

ad-e-quate (ad´e kwit) *adj.* Sufficient; good enough for what is needed.

ad-here (ad hr´) *v.* To stay attached; to stick and not come loose; to stay firm in support.

ad-he-sion (ad h´zhan) *n.* The act or state of sticking to something or of being stuck together.

ad-he-sive (ad h´siv) *adj.* Tending to stick and not come loose; cling; having a sticky surface.

ad-in-ter-im *adj.* In the meantime.

ad-ja-cent (*a* j´sent) *adj.* Close to or nearby.

adjacent angles *n.* Two angles with a side in common, having the same vertex.

ad-jec-tive (aj´ik tiv) *n.* A word used to describe a noun or pronoun, indicating

ad-join (*a join*) *v.* To be next to; to be in or nearly in contact with.

ad-journ (*a jern*) *v.* To close a meeting or session for a time; to move from one location to another.

ad-judge (*a juj*) *v.* To decide by judicial procedure.

ad-junct (aj ´unkt) *n.* Something less important added to something with more importance.

ad-jure (*a jer*) *v.* To ask urgently; to command solemnly.

ad-just (*a just*) *v.* To arrange or change; to make work correctly; to regulate.

ad-just-ment (*a just ´ment*) *n.* The act or process of changing; a settlement of a suit or claim.

ad-lib (ad lib ´) *v.* To improvise; to compose or make up spontaneously.

ad-min-is-ter (ad min ´i str) *v.* To direct or manage; to give or carry out instructions.

ad-min-is-tra-tion (ad min ´i str ´shan) *n.* The people who manage a school, company, or organization; the act of administering.

ad-mi-ra-ble (ad ´mer a bl) *adj.* Worthy of being admired or praised; excellent.

ad-mire (ad mer ´) *v.* To hold a high opinion; to regard with wonder, delight, and pleased approval; to regard with admiration. **admiringly** *adv.* **ad-mirer** *n.*

ad-mis-si-ble (ad mis ´i bl) *adj.* Capable of being admitted, accepted or allowed.

ad-mis-sion (ad mish ´an) *n.* The right or act of being admitted; an admitting of the truth of something; a confession.

ad-mit (ad mit ´) *v.* To take or accept as being the truth; to permit or give the right to enter.

ad-mon-ish (ad mon ´ish) *v.* To warn a person to correct a fault; to criticize in a gentle way.

ad-mo-ni-tion (ad ´mo nish ´an) *n.* A mild criticism or warning.

a-do-be (*a d ´b*) *n.* A brick or building material made from clay and straw and then dried in the sun.

ad-o-les-cent (ad ´o les ´ent) *n.* A person in the transitional period between childhood and adulthood.

a-dopt (*a dopt ´*) *v.* To legally take into one's family and raise as their own. **adoption** *n.*

a-dor-a-ble (*a dr ´a bl*) *adj.* Very likable; charming. **adorably** *adv.* -**ness** *n.*

a-dore (*a dr ´*) *v.* To love greatly; to worship or honor highly; to like very much.

a-dorn-ment (*a dorn ´ment*) *n.* Something that adorns; decoration; ornament; the act of adorning.

ad rem *adj.* Relevant to a point at issue.

ad-re-nal gland (*a dr ´nal*) *n.* A small endocrine gland that consists of a medulla and cortex, located near the kidney.

a-drift (*a drift ´*) *adv.* Drifting; floating freely without being steered; having no clear purpose or aim.

a-droit (*a droit ´*) *adj.* Skillful and clever in difficult circumstances. -**ly** *adv.*

ad-sorb (ad sorb ´) *v.* To collect and hold as molecules of gases, liquids; to become adsorbed. **adsorbable** *adj.*

ad-u-late (aj ´u lt ´) *v.* To give greater praise or flattery than is proper or deserved.

a-dult (*a dult ´*) *n.* A man or woman who is fully grown; a mature person. *adj.* Having reached full size and strength. To make impure or of less quality by adding improper ingredients.

ad-vance (ad vans ´) *v.* To move ahead; to make or become higher; to increase in value or price. *adj.* Something made or given ahead of time.

ad-vanced (ad vanst ´) *adj.* Ahead in time; beyond beginning status.

ad-van-tage (ad van ´taj) *n.* A better chance or more forcible position; a condition, thing or event that can help or benefit; the first point, after deuce scored in the game of tennis.

ad-ven-ture (ad ven ´chur) *n.* An exciting and dangerous experience that is remembered; an unusual experience.

ad-ven-tur-er (ad ven ´chur r) *n.* A person who looks for adventure; one who seeks wealth and social position.

ad-verb (ad ´verb) *n.* A word used with a verb, adjective, or another adverb to tell when, where, how, what kind, or how much.

ad·verse (ad´vers) *adj.* Opposed; not helpful; against someone or something.

ad·ver·si·ty (ad ver´si t) *n.* Bad luck or misfortune.

ad·ver·tise (ad´ver tz) *v.* To draw public attention to a product you wish to sell.

ad·vice (ad vs´) *n.* Suggestion or recommendation regarding a course of action or decision.

ad·vo·cate (ad´vo kit) *v.* To write or speak in favor of or support.

ae·gis (jis) *n.* Protection; support or sponsorship.

aer·ate (âr´t) *v.* To purify by exposing to the open air.

aer·i·al (âr´al) *adj.* Of or in the air; pertaining to aircraft. *n.* An antenna for television or radio.

aer·o·bics (â r´biks) *n.* Strenuous exercise that increases oxygen to the heart and lungs; therefore strengthening them.

aer·o·nau·tics (âr´o no tiks) *n. pl.* The science of designing and constructing aircraft.

aer·o·pause (âr´o poz´) *n.* The region in the upper atmosphere where aircraft cannot fly.

aer·o·sol (âr´o sl) *n.* A liquid substance under pressure within a metal container.

aes·thet·ic (es thet´ĭk) *adj.* Having a love for beauty.

aes·thet·ics (es thet´ĭks) *n.* The study of the nature of beauty. **aesthetically** *adv.*

a·far (a fär´) *adv.* Far off; far away.

af·fa·ble (af´a bl) *adj.* Good natured, easy to talk to; friendly. **affably** *adv.*

af·fair (a fâr´) *n.* An event or happening; matters of business or public concern.

af·fect (a fekt´) *v.* To move emotionally; to feel sympathetic or sad; to bring about a change in. **affecting** *adj.* **affected** *adj.*

af·fec·tion (a fek´shan) *n.* A tender or fond feeling towards another.

af·fec·tion·ate (a fek´sha nit) *adj.* Loving and gentle. **affectionately** *adv.*

af·fi·da·vit (af´ĭ d´vit) *n.* A written statement by a person swearing that something is the truth.

af·fil·i·ate (a fil´t´) *v.* To join in, connect, or associate with. **affiliation** *n.*

af·fin·i·ty (a fin´ĭ t) *n.* A special attraction with kinship; a natural attraction or liking.

af·firm (a ferm´) *v.* To declare positively and be willing to stand by the truth.

af·firm·a·tive (a fer´ma tiv) *adj.* Asserting the fact is true.

af·fix (af´ĭks) *n.* To attach; to fasten; to add at the end. *n.* A prefix or suffix added to a word.

af·flict (a flĭkt´) *v.* To cause suffering or pain; to cause mental suffering. **affliction** *n.*

af·flu·ent (af´lö ent) *adj.* Prosperous; rich; having all the wealth or money needed.

af·ford (a frd´) *v.* To be able to provide; to have enough money to spare.

af·fray (a fr´) *n.* Brawl or noisy fight.

af·front (a frunt´) *v.* To insult one to his face; to confront.

a·fire (a fr´) *adv.* Burning.

a·flut·ter (a flut ar) *adj.* Nervously excited.

a·foot (a fet´) *adj.* In the progress of happening; walking; on foot.

a·foul (a foul´) *adv.* Tangled; entangled in a collision.

a·fraid (a frd´) *adj.* Hesitant; filled with fear; reluctant.

a·fresh (a fresh´) *adj.* Once more; again.

aft (aft) *adv.* At, close to, near, or toward the rear of an aircraft or stern of a ship.

af·ter (af´tr) *adj.* In the rear. *prep.* following.

af·ter·ef·fect (af´tr i fekt´) *n.* An effect coming after.

af·ter·math (af´tr math´) *n.* Consequence; result.

a·gain (a gen´) *adv.* Moreover; another time; once more.

a·gainst (a genst´) *prep.* In exchange for; in preparation for.

a·gape (a gp´) *adv.* With expectation; in wonder; open-mouthed.

ag·ate (ag´ĭt) *n.* The type of quartz that has bands of colors.

age (aj) *n.* The length of time from beginning to a certain date; the time of life when a person has full legal rights; the age of 21. *v.* To grow or become old; to mature.

aged (jid) *adj.* Grown or become old. **agedness** *n.* **agedly** *adv.*

a-gen-da (*a* jen´da) *n.* Program or list of things to be done.

a-gent (jent) *n.* One who acts as the representative of another; one who acts or exerts power.

ag-gior-na-men-to *n.* Bringing up to date.

ag-glom-er-ate (*a* glom´e rt´) *v.* To collect; to form into a mass.

ag-glu-ti-nate (*a* glöt´i nt´) *v.* To join by adhesion; to cause red blood cells to clump together.

ag-glu-ti-nin *n.* A substance that causes agglutination; a group or mass formed by the union of separate elements.

ag-gran-dize (ag´ran dz´) *v.* To enlarge; to extend; to increase. **aggrandizee-ment** *n.*

ag-gra-vate (ag´ra vt´) *v.* To annoy; to make worse.

ag-gre-gate (ag´re git) *adj.* To gather together into a mass or whole.

ag-gres-sion (*a* gresh´an) *n.* Hostile action or behavior; an unprovoked assault.

a-ghast (*a* gast´) *adj.* Appalled; struck with amazement.

ag-ile (aj´l) *adj.* Marked by the ability to move quickly and easily; nimble.

ag-i-tate (aj´i tt´) *v.* To disturb; to upset; to stir or move with violence; to try to arouse the public interest. **agitation** *n.*

ag-nos-tic (ag nos´tik) *n.* One who doubts that there is a God or life hereafter.

a-go (*a* g´) *adj.* & *adv.* In the past; gone by.

a-gog (*a* gog´) *adj.* Excited; eagerly expectant.

ag-o-nize (ag´o nz´) *v.* To afflict with great anguish or to suffer. **agonized** *adj.* **-zing** *adj.*

ag-o-ny (ag´o n) *n. pl.* **-nies** Intense mental distress or physical pain; anguish.

ag-o-ra-pho-bi-a (ag´or a f´b a) *n.* Fear of open spaces.

a-gree (*a* gr´) *v.* To give assent; to consent; to share an understanding or opinion; to be beneficial or suitable; to correspond.

ag-ri-cul-ture (ag´ri kul chur) *n.* Raising of livestock; farming and cultivating the crops. **agriculturalist** *n.* **agriculturist** *n.*

a-ground (*a* ground´) *adv.* & *adv.* Stranded; on the ground; to run ashore; beached.

a-gue (´g) *n.* Fever accompanied by chills or shivering and sweating. **aguish** *adj.*

a-head (*a* hed´) *adv.* Before; in advance; to or at the front of something.

a-hoy (*a* hoi´) *interj.* A nautical call or greeting.

aid (d) *v.* To give help or assistance.

AIDS *n.* Disease that destroys the body's immunological system; Acquired Immune Deficiency Syndrome.

ail (l) *v.* To feel sick; to make ill or uneasy. **ailing** *adj.*

ai-lan-thus (lan´thus) *n.* A tree with numerous pointed leaves.

ai-ler-on (le´ron) *n.* Movable control flap on the trailing edge of an airplane wing.

ail-ment (l´ment) *n.* A mild illness.

aim (m) *v.* To direct a weapon; to direct pur pose. *n.* Intention.

aim-less (m´lis) *adj.* Lacking of pur pose.

ain't (nt) Am not, are not, is not, has not, or have not.

ai-o-li *n.* Rich garlic-flavored mayonnaise.

air (âr) *n.* An odorless, tasteless, colorless, gaseous mixture; primarily composed of nitrogen (78%) and oxygen (21%); the sky; a breeze.

air-craft (âr´kraft) *n.* A machine that flies, such as a helicopter, airplane, or glider.

air-foil (âr´foil) *n.* Part of an airplane which controls stability, lift, thrust, etc.

air lock *n.* Airtight compartment between regions of unequal pressure.

aisle (l) *n.* Passageway between rows of seats, as in a church, auditorium, or airplane.

a-jar (*a* jär´) *adv.* & *adj.* Partially opened.

a-kim-bo (*a* kim´b) *adj.* & *adv.* Bent; with a crook.

a-kin (*a* kin´) *adj.* Related, as in family; similar in quality or character.

a la carte (ä ´la kärt ´) *n.* Separate price for each item on the menu.

a-lack (a lak ´) *interj.* An exclamation expressive of sorrow.

a-lac-ri-ty (a lak ´ri t) *n.* Readiness; cheerfulness; eagerness; briskness.

a la mode (al ´a md ´) *n.* Served with ice cream, as pie; fashionable.

a-larm-ist (a lär ´mist) *n.* Someone who needlessly alarms others. **alarmism** *n.*

a-las (a las ´) *interj.* Expressive of anxiety or regret.

al-ba-core (al ´ba kr ´) *n.* Large marine fish; major source of canned tuna.

al-ba-tross (al ´ba tros ´) *n.* Large, web-footed, long- winged sea bird.

al-be-it (ol b ´it) *conj.* Although; even though.

al-bi-no (al b ´n) *n.* An animal or person with an abnormal whiteness of the skin and hair and pink colored eyes.

al-bu-men (al b ´men) *n.* White of an egg.

al-bu-min *n.* Several proteins found in the white of eggs, blood serum, milk, and plant and animal tissue.

al-che-my (al ´ke m) *n.* Traditional chemical philosophy concerned primarily with changing base metals into gold.

al-co-hol (al ´ko hol ´) *n.* Intoxicating liquor containing alcohol; ethanol; a series of related organic compounds.

al-de-hyde (al ´de hd ´) *n.* Any of a class of highly reactive compounds obtained by oxidation of alcohols.

al-der-man (o l ´dr man) *n.* Member of a municipal legislative body.

ale (l) *n.* Beverage similar to, but more bit ter than beer, made from malt by fermentation.

a-lem-bic (a lem ´bik) *n.* A glass or metal vessel formerly used in distillation.

a-lert (a lert ´) *adj.* Vigilant; brisk; watchful; active. *n.* A signal by siren of air attack.

al-fres-co (al fres ´k) *adv. & adj.* In the fresh air; outside.

al-gae (al ´j) *n. pl.* Various primitive, chiefly aquatic, one celled or multicellular plants, as the seaweed.

al-ge-bra (al ´je bra) *n.* Generalization of math in which symbols represent members of a specified set of numbers and are related by operations that hold for all numbers in the set. **-ic** *adv.*

a-li-as (1 ´as) *n. pl.* **aliases** Assumed name.

al-i-bi *n.* A form of defence, an attempt by a defendant to prove he was else where when a crime was committed; an excuse.

a-lien (l ´yen) *adj.* Owing allegiance to a government or country, not one's own; unfamiliar; repugnant; a member of another region, or country. *n.* A stranger; a foreigner.

al-ien-a-ble (l ´ye na bl) *adj.* Able to be transferred to the ownership of another.

al-ien-ate (l ´ye nt ´) *v.* To cause to become indifferent or unfriendly. **alienation** *n.*

al-ien-ist (l ´ye nist) *n.* A psychiatrist accepted by a court as an expert on mental stability.

a-lign (a ln ´) *v.* To arrange in a line; to take one side of an argument or cause.

a-lign-ment *or* **alinement** (a ln ´ment) *n.* Arrange or position in a straight line.

a-like (a lk ´) *adj.* Similar, having close resemblance. *adv.* In the same manner, way, or degree.

al-i-ment (al ´i ment) *n.* Nourishment; food. **alimentation** *n.* **alimental** *adj.*

al-i-men-ta-ry (al ´i men ´ta r) *adj.* Pertaining to nutrition or food.

alimentary canal *n.* The tube of the digestive system from the mouth to the anus, including the pharynx, esophagus, stomach, and intestines.

a-live (a lv ´) *adj.* Living; having life; in existence or effect; full of life.

a-li-yah *n.* Immigration of Jewish people to Israel.

a-liz-a-rin (a liz ´r in) *n.* A red-orange compound used in dyes.

al-ka-li (al ´ka l ´) *n. pl.* **-lies** *or* **-lis** A hydroxide or carbonate of an alkali metal, whose aqueous solution is slippery, bitter, caustic, and basic in reactions.

al-ka-line (al ´ka ln ´) *adj.* Of, relating to, or containing an alkali. **alkalinity** *n.*

al-ka-lin-ize (al ´ka li nz) *adj.* To make alkaline.

al-ka-loid (al´ka loid) *n.* Any of various nitrogen containing organic bases obtained from plants.

al-ka-lo-sis (al ka l´sis) *n.* Unusually high alkali content in the blood and tissues.

all (ol) *adj.* Total extent or total entity; being a whole number, amount, or quantity; every.

al-lay (a l´) *v.* To relieve; to lessen; to calm; to pacify. **allayer** *n.*

al-le-ga-tion (al´e g´shan) *n.* The act or result of alleging.

al-lege (a lej´) *v.* To affirm; to assert to be true; to declare without proof.

al-le-giance (a l´jans) *n.* Loyalty to one's nation, cause, or sovereign; obligations of a vassal to an overlord. **allegiant** *adj.*

al-le-go-ry (al´e gr´) *n. pl.* **-ries** A dramatic, literary, or pictorial device in which each object, character, and event symbolically illustrates a moral or religious principle. **allegoric** *adj.* **allegorical** *adj.* **allegorically** *adv.* **-rist** *n.*

al-le-gret-to (al´e gret´) *adv., Mus.* Slower than allegro but faster than andante.

al-lele (a ll´) *n.* Any of a group of possible mutational forms of a gene. **allelism** *n.*

al-ler-gen (al´r jen´) *n.* Substance which causes an allergy. **-ic** *adj.*

al-ler-gist (al´r jist) *n.* A doctor specializing in allergies.

al-ler-gy (al´r j) *n.* **-gies** Pathological or abnormal reaction to environmental substances, as foods, dust, pollens, or microorganisms.

al-le-vi-ate (a l´v t´) *v.* To make more bearable. **alleviation** *n.* **alleviator** *n.*

al-lit-er-ate (a lit´e rt´) *v.* To arrange or form words beginning with the same sound.

al-lit-er-a-tion (a lit´e r´shan) *n.* Occurrence of two or more words having the same initial sound. **-tive** *adj.*

al-lo-cate (al´o kt´) *v.* To assign; to allot.

al-lot (a lot´) *v.* To distribute or set aside as a share of something. **allotment** *n.*

al-low (a lou´) *v.* To make a provision for, to permit; to permit to have; to admit; to concede. **allowable** *adj.*

allowably *adv.*

al-low-ance (a lou´ans) *n.* The act of allowing something, a regular amount of money, food, etc.; a price discount.

al-loy (a loi´) *v.* Something that has been added to; reduced in purity or value.

al-lude (a lōd´) *v.* To refer to something indirectly. **allusion** *n.* **allusive** *adj.*

al-lure (a ler´) *v.* To entice; to tempt. *n.* Attraction; charm; enticement; the prospect of attracting. **allurement** *n.*

al-lu-sion (a lō´zhan) *n.* The act of referring to something indirectly; a hint.

al-lu-vi-um (a lō´v um) *n.* Sediment deposited by flowing water as in a river bed. **luvial** *adj.*

al-most (ol´mst) *adv.* Not quite; slightly short of.

alms (ämz) *n. pl.* Goods or money given to the poor in charity.

a-loft (a loft´) *adv.* Toward the upper rigging of a ship; in or into a high place; in the air.

a-lo-ha (a l´a) Hawaiian expression of greeting or farewell.

a-loof (a lōf´) *adj.* Indifferent; distant. **aloofness** *n.* **aloofly** *adv.*

a-loud (a loud´) *adv.* Orally; audibly.

al-pha-bet (al´fa bet´) *n.* The letters of a language, arranged in an order fixed by custom.

al-pha-bet-i-cal *adj.* Arranged in the traditional order of the letters of a language. **alphabetically** *adv.*

al-pha-bet-ize (al´fa bi tz´) *v.* To arrange in alphabetical order.

al-pha de-cay *n.* Decay of an atomic nucleus as it emits an alpha particle.

al-read-y (ol red´) *adv.* By this or a specified time.

al-so (ol´s) *adv.* Likewise; besides; in addition.

al-tar (ol´tr) *n.* An elevated structure before which religious ceremonies may be held or sacrifices offered.

al-ter (ol´tr) *v.* To make change or become different; to modify; to castrate or spay, as an animal. **alterability** *n.* **alteration** *n.*

al-ter-a-tive (ol´te r´tiv) *adj.* Tending to alter or produce alterations.

al-ter e-go *v.* An intimate friend; another aspect of oneself.

al-ter-nate (ol'tŕ nt') v. To happen or follow in turn; to occur in successive turns. **alternately** adv. **alternation** n.

al-ter-na-tive (ol ter'na tiv) n. A choice between two or more possibilities; one of the possibilities to be chosen. adj. Allowing a choice. **alternatively** adv.

al-ter-na-tor (ol'tŕ n'tŕ) n. Electric generator producing alternating current.

al-though (ol th') conj. Even though.

al-tim-e-ter (al tim'í tŕ) n. Instrument for measuring and indicating altitude.

al-ti-tude (al'tï td') n. The height of a thing above a reference level; above the earth's surface; above sea level.

al-to-geth-er (ol'to geth'r) adv. Entirely; with all included or counted.

al-tru-ism (al'trö iz'um) n. Selfless concern for the welfare of others. **altruist** n. **-ic** adj. **altruistically** adv.

al-um (al'um) n. Any one of several similar double sulfates.

a-lu-mi-na (a lö'mi na) n. Any of several forms of aluminum oxide.

a-lu-mi-num (a lö'mi num) n. A silvery-white, ductile metallic element used to form many hard, light, corrosion-resistant alloys.

a-lum-na (a lum'na) n. pl. **-nae** Female graduate or former student of a school, college, or university.

al-ways (ol'wz) adv. Continuously; forever; on every occasion; at all times.

am (am) v. First person, singular, present tense of be.

a-mal-gam (a mal'gam) n. An alloy of mercury with other metals, as with tin or silver; a blend of diverse elements. **amalgramable** adj.

a-mal-ga-mate (a mal'ga mt') v. To mix so as to make a unified whole; to blend. **amalgamation** n. **-tor** n.

a-man-dine adj. Made or garnished with almonds.

am-a-ranth (am'a ranth') n. Various weedy plants with greenish or purplish flowers; an imaginary flower that never fades.

am-a-ryl-lis (am'a ril'is) n. A bulbous plant with large, lily-like, reddish or white flowers.

am-a-teur (am'a cher') n. One who engages in an activity as a pastime rather than as a profession; one who lacks expertise. **-ish** adj. **-ism** n.

am-a-to-ry (am'a tr') adj. Of or expressive of sexual love.

a-maze (a mz') v. To astound; to affect with surprise or wonder. **amazingly** adv. **amazement** n. **amazing** adj.

am-bas-sa-dor (am bas'a dor) n. Official representative of the highest rank, accredited by one government to another.

am-bi-ance n. Environment; atmosphere.

am-bi-dex-trous (am'bi dek'strus) adj. Able to use both hands with equal facility.

am-bi-ent (am'b ent) adj. Surrounding.

am-big-u-ous (am big'u us) adj. Doubtful; uncertain. **-ness** n. **-ly** adv.

am-bi-tion (am bish'an) n. Strong desire to achieve; will to succeed; the goal or object desired.

am-bi-tious (am bish'us) adj. Challenging. **-ness** n. **ambitiously** adv.

am-biv-a-lence (am biv'a lens) n. Existence of mutually different feelings about a person or thing.

am-ble (am'bl) v. To move at a leisurely pace. **ambler** n.

am-bu-lance (am'b lans) n. Vehicle equipped to transport the injured or sick.

am-bu-la-to-ry (am'b la tr') adj. Moving about; movable; of or to do with walking.

am-bus-cade (am'bu skd') n. Ambush.

am-bush (am'besh) n. Surprise attack made from a hidden position. **ambush** v. **ambusher** n. **ambushment** n.

a-me-lio-rate (a ml'yu rt') v. To become or make better. **ameliorator** n. **amelioration** n.

a-men ('men') Used at the end of a prayer to express solemn approval.

a-me-na-ble (a m'na bl) adj. Responsive; tractable; accountable. **-ness** n.

a-mend (a mend') v. To correct; to improve; to rectify. **amendable** adj.

a-mend-ment (a mend'ment) n. Correction, reformation or improvement; the parliamentary procedure where such alteration is made.

a-mends (a mendz') n. pl. Compensation for insult or injury.

a-men-i-ty (a men'í t) n. pl. **-ties**

Agreeableness; means of comfort or convenience.

a-merce (a mers´) v. To punish. **-ment** n.

am-e-thyst (am´i thist) n. Violet or purple form of transparent corundum or quartz, used as a gemstone. **amethystine** adj.

a-mi-a-ble (´m a bl) adj. Friendly and pleasant. **amiableness** n. **amiability** n.

am-i-ca-ble (am´i ka bl) adj. Harmonious; friendly. **amicability** n. **amicableness** n.

a-mid (a mid´) prep. In the middle of; surrounded by.

a-mid-ships (a mid´ships) adv. Halfway between the bow and the stern.

a-midst (a midst´) prep. In the middle of; surrounded by; during.

a-mi-go (a m´g) n. A friend.

a-miss (a mis´) adj. Out of order or place; in an improper or wrong way.

a-mi-ty (am´it) n. Relationships that are friendly, as between two states.

am-me-ter (am´tr) n. A tool measuring electric current.

am-mo (am´) n. Ammunition.

am-mo-nia (a mn´ya) n. Colorless, pungent gas.

ammonium hydroxide (a m´n um) n. A colorless, basic aqueous solution of ammonia.

am-mu-ni-tion (am´ nish´an) n. Projectiles that can be propelled or discharged from guns; any means of defense.

am-ne-sia (am n´zha) n. The loss of memory. **amnesiac** n.

am-nes-ty (am´ni st) n. pl. **-ties** Pardon for political offenders.

a-moe-ba (a m´ba) n. pl.**-bas** or **-bae** Various minute one-celled organism shaving an indefinite, changeable form.

a-mong (a mung´) prep. In or through the midst of; between one another.

a-mon-til-la-do (a mon´ti lä´d) n. pl. **-dos** A pale, dry sherry.

a-mor-al (´mor´al) adj. Neither moral nor immoral. **amorality** n. **-ly** adv.

am-o-rous (am´r us) adj. Inclined to or indicative of sexual love. **-ness** n.

a-mor-phous (a mor´fus) adj. Lacking definite form; shapeless; general; vague.

am-or-tize (am´r tz) v. To liquidate a loan by installment payments; a loan.

a-mount (a mount´) n. Aggregate, sum or total quantity. v. To be equivalent.

a-mour (a mer´) n. A forbidden love affair.

a-mourpro-pre n. Self-respect.

am-per-age (am´pr ij) n. Strength of an electric current, expressed in amperes.

am-pere (am´pr) n. Unit of electric current equal to a flow of one amp per second.

am-per-sand (am´pr sand´) n. The character or sign that represents and (&).

am-phet-a-mine (am fet´a mn´) n. Colorless volatile liquid; a drug.

amphi prefix. Around, on both sides, all around on all sides.

am-phib-i-an (am fib´ an) n. An organism, as a frog or toad, developing from an aquatic state into an air-breathing state; aircraft that can take off and land on land or water; a vehicle that can take off or land on land or water.

am-phi-the-a-ter (am´fi th´a tr) n. A round or oval building having tiers of seats rising around an arena.

am-pho-ra (am´for a) n. pl. **-rae** or **-ras** Ancient Greek jar with two handles and a narrow neck, used to carry oil or wine.

am-ple (am´pel) adj. Sufficient; abundant; large. **ampleness** n. **amply** adv.

am-pli-tude (am´pli töd) n. Maximum value of a periodically varying quantity; greatness of size; fullness.

am-pul or **am-pule** (am´pl) n. A small, sealed vial containing a hypodermic injection solution.

am-pu-tate (am´p tt´) v. To cut off; to remove, as a limb from one's body.

am-pu-tee (am´p t´) n. A person who has had one or more limbs amputated.

a-muck (a muk´) n. In an uncontrolled manner; a murderous frenzy; out of control.

am-u-let (am´lit) n. A charm worn as protection against evil or injury.

a-muse (a mz´) v. To entertain in an agreeable, pleasing way. **-ment** n.

an (an) adj. One; one sort of; each; form of "a" used before words beginning with a vowel or with an unpronounced "h" as an elephant or honor.

a-nach-ro-nism (*a* nak'ro niz'*um*) *n.* Connecting of a thing, of a person or happening with another that came after in history; anything that seems to be out of place in history.

an-a-con-da (an'a kon'da) *n.* A large tropical American snake which kills its prey by crushing it to death in its coils.

an-a-dem (an'a dem') *n.* A wreath for the head.

a-nae-mi-a *n.* Variant of anemia.

a-nad-ro-mous *adj.* Migrating up river from the sea to breed in fresh water, as a salmon.

an-aes-the-sia (an'is th'zha) *n.* Variant of anesthesia.

an-a-gram (an'a gram') *n.* Word formed by transposing the letters of another word. **anagrammatical** *adj.* **anagramatic** *adj.*

a-nal (n'al) *adj.* Of or relating to the anus.

anal *abbr.* Analogous; analogy; analytic.

an-al-ge-sia (an'al g'z a) *n.* Inability to feel pain while awake.

analog computer (an'a log) *n.* A computer where numerical data are represented by measurable quantities as lengths, electrical signals, or voltage.

a-nal-o-gous (a nal'o gus) *adj.* Similar; corresponding in certain ways.

an-a-logue (an'a log') *n.* Something that bears resemblance to something else.

a-nal-o-gy (a nal'o j) *n. pl.* -gies Connection between things that are otherwise dissimilar; a conclusion or opinion that if two things are alike in some respects they must be alike in others.

a-nal-y-sis (a nal'i sis) *n.* Breaking up or separation of something into its parts so as to examine them and see how they fit together; result.

an-a-lyst (an'a list) *n.* A person who analyzes or who is skilled in analysis.

an-a-lyze (an'a lz') *v.* To make an analy-sis of.

an-a-pest (an'a pest') *n.* Metrical foot made up of two short syllables followed by one long one. **anapestic** *adj.*

an-ar-chic (an är'kik) *adj.* Of, like, or promoting confusion or disorder.

an-ar-chism (an'är kiz'um) *n.* Belief

that all forms of government act in an unfair way against the liberty of a person and should be done away with.

an-ar-chy (an'är k) *n.* Lack of political authority, disorder and confusion; the absence of any purpose or standard.

a-nas-to-mo-sis (a nas'to m'sis) *n.* Connection or union of branches, as of rivers, leaf veins, or blood vessels.

a-nas-tro-phe (a nas'tro f) *n.* Changing the normal syntactic order of words.

a-nath-e-ma (a nath'a ma) *n.* Curse; ban; or excommunication. **-tize** *v.*

a-nat-o-mize (a nat'o miz') *v.* To examine in great detail; to analyze; in biology, to dissect. **anatomization** *n.*

a-nat-o-my (a nat'o m) *n. pl.* -mies Structure of an organ or organism; a detailed analysis. **-ical** *adj.* **-ic** *adj.*

an-ces-try (an'ses tr) *n. pl.* -tries Line of descent; lineage ancestors collectively.

an-ces-tor (an'ses tr) *n.* A person who comes before one in a family line; someone earlier than a grandparent; forefather.

an-chor (ang'kr) *n.* Heavy metal device lowered into the water by a chain to keep a ship from drifting. *v.* To attach or fix firmly.

anchor man *n.* The main member of a team of newscasters.

an-cient (n'shent) *adj.* Anything belonging to the early history of people; very old. **ancientness** *n.* **anciently** *adv.*

and (and) *conj.* Together with; along with; as well as; added to; as a result; plus; also.

an-dan-te (an dan't) *adv. Mus.* Rather slow in tempo. **andante** *adj.*

an-dan-ti-no (an'dan t'n) *adj.* Slightly faster in tempo than andante. *Mus.*

and-i-ron (and'rn) *n.* Heavy metal support for logs or wood in a fireplace.

andr *n.* The male sex; masculine.

an-dro-gen (an'dro jen) *n.* Hormone that develops and maintains masculine characteristics. **androgenic** *adj.*

an-drog-y-nous (an droj'i nus) *adj.* Having the characteristics or nature of both male and female; having both staminate and pistillate flowers in the same cluster with the male flower suppermost. **androgynal** *n.*

an-droid *n.* In science fiction; a synthetic man made to look like a human being.

an-ec-dote (an´ik dt´) *n.* Short account of a story of some happening or about some person. **-tal** *adj.* anecdotic *adj.*

an-echo-ic (an´e k ik) *adj.* Neither having or producing echoes.

a-ne-mi-a (a n´m a) *n.* The condition in which a person's blood does not have enough red corpuscles or hemoglobin and, therefore, does not carry a normal amount of oxygen.

a-ne-mic (a n´mik) *adj.* Of or having anemia.

an-e-mom-e-ter (an´e mom´ tr) *n.* Instrument for measuring wind force and speed.

a-nem-o-ne (a nem´o n) *n.* A plant with purple, white, or red cup-shaped flowers.

a-nent (a nent´) *prep.* Regarding; concerning.

an-es-the-sia (an´is th´zha) *n.* Condition in which one has no perception of heat, touch, or pain in all or part of the body.

an-es-the-tize (a nes´thi tz´) *v.* To bring on unconsciousness by giving anesthetics; to remove the capacity to feel pain in a localized area.

an-gel (n´jel) *n.* An immortal being attendant upon God; a very kind and lovable person; a helping or guiding spirit. **agelic** *adj.*

an-gel-i-ca (an jel´i ka) *n.* A plant with aromatic seed, used as flavoring.

an-ger (ang´gr) *n.* Feeling of extreme hostility; rage; wanting to fight back.

an-gi-na (an j´na) *n.* A disease marked by painful choking spasms and attacks of suffocation pain. **anginous** *adj.*

an-gle (ang´gl) *v.* A shape made by two straight lines meeting in a point or two surfaces meeting along a line.

an-gle-worm (ang´gl werm´) *n.* Earthworm, used as fishing bait.

an-gli-cize (ang´gli sz´) *v.* To make English in form, idiom, or character.

an-gling (ang´gling) *n.* The act of fishing with a hook and line.

an-go-ra (ang gr´a) *n.* The long silky hair of the Angora rabbit or Angora goat; yarn or fabric made from the hair of an Angora goat or rabbit.

an-gry (ang´gr) *adj.* Feeling or showing anger; having a menacing aspect; inflamed.

an-guish (ang´gwish) *n.* Great suffering, from worry, grief, or pain; agony.

an-gu-lar (ang´g lr) *adj.* Having angles or sharp corners; measured by an angle or degrees of an arc; gaunt, bony, lean. **angularity** *n.* **angularly** *adv.*

an-hy-dride (an h´drd) *n.* Chemical compound formed from another by removing the water.

an-hy-drous (an h´drus) *adj.* Does not contain any water.

an-i-line (an´i lin´) *n.* Colorless, oily, poisonous liquid, used to make rubber, dyes, resins, pharmaceuticals, and varnishes.

an-i-mad-vert (an´i mad vert´) *v.* To comment with disapproval. **animadversion** *n.*

an-i-mal (an´i mal) *n.* Any being other than a human being; any four-footed creature; beast. **animalize** *v.*

an-i-mal-cule (an´i mal´kl) *n.* Microscopic or minute animal.

an-i-mate (an´i mt´) *v.* To give liveliness, life or spirit to; to cause to act; to inspire. **animatedly** *adv.* **animation** *n.*

a-ni-ma-to (ä´ni mä´t) *adv.* *Mus.* In a lively or animated manner; used as a direction. **animato** *adj.*

an-i-ma-tor *n.* One who animates, such as an artist or technician who produces an animation, as a cartoon.

an-i-mism (an´i miz´um) *n.* A belief in primitive tribes that natural objects and forces have souls. **animist** *n.* **animistic** *adj.*

an-i-mos-i-ty (an´i mos´i t) *n.* *pl.* -ties Hostility; bitterness; hatred.

an-i-mus (an´o mus) *n.* Feeling of animosity.

an-i-on (an´i´on) *n.* An ion with a negative charge that is attracted to an anode; electrolysis.

an-ise (an´is) *n.* A plant with yellowish-white flower clusters and licorice-flavored seeds; aniseed.

an-i-seed (an´i sd´) *n.* Seed used for flavoring and in medicine.

an-i-sette (an´i set´) *n.* Anise-flavored liqueur.

an-kle (ang´kl) n. Joint that connects the foot with the leg; slender section of the leg immediately above this joint.

ann abbr. Annals; annual; annuity.

an-nals (an´alz) n. pl. Descriptive record; history. **annalist** n.

an-neal (a nl´) v. To heat and then cool glass slowly to make it less brittle.

an-nex (a nks´) v. To add or join a smaller thing to a larger one. **-ation** n.

an-ni-hi-late (a n´i lt´) v. To destroy completely; totally. **annihilator** n.

an-ni-ver-sa-ry (an i ver´sa r) n. pl. **-ries** The date on which something happened at an earlier time; this event celebrated on this date each year.

an-no-tate (an´ tt´) v. To use notes to give one's opinions. **-tion** n. **-ive** adj.

an-nounce (a nouns´) v. To proclaim; to give notice. **announcement** n.

an-noy (a noi´) v. To bother; to irritate; to make slightly angry. **annoying** adj.

an-noy-ance (a noi´ans) n. A nuisance; irritation; act of annoying.

an-nu-al (an´ al) adj. Recurring or done at the same time each year; a yearly publication, as a yearbook. **-ly** adv.

an-nu-i-tant (a n´i tant) n. Person who receives an annuity.

an-nu-i-ty (a n´i t) n. pl. **-ties** Annual payment of an income or allowance.

an-nul (a nul´) v. To cancel a marriage or a law; to do away with; to put an end to. **annullable** adj. **annulment** n.

an-nu-lar (an´yu lr) adj. Shaped like or forming a ring. **annularity** n.

an-nun-ci-ate (a nun´s t´) v. To proclaim; to announce.

an-nun-ci-a-tion (a nun´s a´shan) n. An announcement; the act of announcing.

an-ode (an´d) n. Positively charged electrode. **anodic** adj. **anodically** adv.

an-o-dize (an´o dz´) v. To coat a metallic surface by electrolysis with a protective oxide.

a-noint (a noint´) v. To apply oil in a religious ceremony. **-er** n. **-ment** n.

a-nom-a-ly (a nom´a l) n. pl. **-lies** Anything irregular or abnormal. **anomalistic** adj.

a-non adv. Soon; in a short period of time.

a-non-y-mous (a non´i mus) adj. An unknown or withheld name, agency. **anonymity** n.

an-oth-er (a nuhth´r) adj. Additional; one more different, but of the same character.

ans abbr. Answer.

an-swer (an´sr) n. A written or spoken reply, as to a question; a result or solution, as to a problem. v. To respond correctly; to be responsible for. **answerable** adj.

ant n. A small insect, usually without wings; living in wood, or in or on the ground in large colonies or communities.

ant abbr. Antenna; antonym.

ant-ac-id (ant as´id) n. A substance which neutralizes or weakens acids.

an-tag-o-nism (an tag´o niz´um) n. Hostility; condition of being against; the feeling of unfriendliness toward.

an-tag-o-nize (an tag´o nz´) v. To arouse hostility; to make an enemy of someone.

Ant-arc-tic (ant ärk´tik) n. Large area of land completely covered with ice; the South Pole.

ant-eat-er (ant´´tr) n. Animal with a long snout and a long, sticky tongue, feeding mainly on ants.

an-te-ced-ent (an´ti sd´ent) adj. One event that precedes another; previous.

an-te-date (an´ti dt´) v. To precede in time; to give an earlier date than the actual date.

an-te-lope (an´te lp´) n. A slender, long-horned, swift-running, hoofed mammal.

an-te me-rid-i-em n. Time before noon, abbreviated as "A.M."

an-ten-na (an ten´a) n. pl. **-nae** Slender feelers on the head of an insect, lobster, crab, etc.; wire or set of wires used in radio and television to send and receive signals.

an-te-pe-nult (an´t p´nult) n. The third syllable from the end of a word.

an-te-ri-or (an tr´or) adj. Toward or at the front; coming before; earlier.

an-te-room (an´t röm´) n. Waiting room; a room leading to a larger more, important room.

an-them (an´them) n. Hymn of praise or loyalty; an official song of a country, school, etc.

an-ther (an´thr) n. The part of the flower where the pollen is located at the end of a stamen.

an-thol-o-gy (an thol´o j) n. A collection of stories, poems, or other writings.

an-thra-cite (an´thra st´) n. Coal with a high carbon content and low volatile matter; hard coal. **anthracitic** adj.

an-thrax (an´thraks) n. The infectious, usually fatal disease found in animals such as cattle and sheep; disease that can be transmitted to man.

an-thro-poid (an´thro poid´) n. Gorillas or chimpanzees resembling man.

an-thro-pol-o-gy (an´thro pol´oj) n. The science that studies the origin, culture, and development of man. **anthropologic** adj. **anthropological** adj. **-ically** adv.

an-thro-po-mor-phism (an´thro po mor´fiz´um) n. The ascribing of human motivation and human characteristics to something that is not human. **anthropomorphic** adj.

an-ti (an´t) n. One who opposes a group, policy, practice, or proposal.

an-ti-anx-i-ety (an´t a z´et) adj. Preventing or relieving anxiety.

antiballistic missile n. A missile designed to destroy a ballistic missile.

an-ti-bi-ot-ic (an´ti b ot´ik) n. A substance, as streptomycin or penicillin, that is produced by organisms, as fungi and bacteria, effective in the destruction of microorganisms and used widely to prevent or treat diseases.

an-ti-bod-y (an´ti bod´) n. Proteins generated in the blood that react to foreign proteins or carbohydrates of certain types, neutralizing them and producing immunity against certain microorganisms or their toxins.

an-tic (an´tik) n. Mischievous caper or act.

an-tic-i-pate (an tis´i pt) v. To look forward; to act in advance of; to foresee. **anticipation** n. **anticipator** n.

an-ti-cli-max (an´ti klī´maks) n. A letdown or decline; a commonplace conclusion; a series of significant events or happenings. **anticlimactic** adj. **anti-**

climactically adv.

an-ti-dote (an´ti dt´) n. A substance that counteracts an injury or poison.

an-ti-gen (an´ti jen) n. Substance, when introduced into the body, stimulates the production of antibodies. **antigenic** adj. **antigenicity** n.

an-ti-his-ta-mine (an´ti his´ta mn) n. A drug used to relieve the symptoms of allergies and colds by interfering with the production of histamines.

an-ti-mat-ter (an´t mat´r) n. A form of matter that is composed of antiparticles.

an-ti-mo-ni-al (an´ti m n al) adj. Containing or of antimony.

an-ti-mo-ny (an´ti m´n) n. Silver-white metallic element used in chemistry, medicine, and alloys, etc.

an-ti-par-ti-cle (an´t pär´ti kal) n. Identically matched atomic particles, but with exactly opposite electrically charged magnetic properties and spin.

an-ti-pas-to (an´ti pä´st) n. Appetizer including cheese, fish, vegetables, and smoked meat served with oil and vinegar.

an-tip-a-thy (an tip´a th) n. pl. **-thies** Feeling of repugnance or opposition. **antipathetic** adj. **antipathetical** adj.

an-ti-per-spi-rant n. Substance applied to the underarm to reduce excessive perspiration.

an-tiph-o-ny (an tif´o n) n. One that echoes or answers another; responsive chanting or singing.

an-ti-pode (an´ti pd´) n. A direct opposite.

an-ti-pro-ton (an´t pr´ton) n. The antiparticle of a proton.

an-tique (an tk´) adj. Belonging to or of ancient times. n. An object that is over 100 years old. **antique** v.

an-ti-sep-sis (an´ti sep´sis) n. Condition of being free from pathogenic bacteria and the method of obtaining this condition.

an-ti-sep-tic (an´ti sep´tik) adj. Pertaining or capable of producing antisepsis; thoroughly clean. **-ly** adj.

an-ti-so-cial (an´t s´shal) adj. Unsociable; opposed to society.

an-tith-e-sis (an tith´i sis) n. pl. **-eses** Direct opposition or contrast. **-tic** adj.

an-ti-trust (an´trust´) adj. Having to do with the regulation of trusts, monopolies, and cartels.

an-to-nym (an´to nim) n. A word opposite in meaning to another word.

an-uria (a nr´a) n. The inability to urinate.

a-nus (´nus) n. The lower opening of the alimentary canal.

an-vil (an´vil) n. A heavy block of steel or iron on which metal is formed.

anx-i-e-ty (ang zi´i t) n. A state of uncertainty; disturbance of the mind regarding uncertain events.

anx-ious (angk´shus) adj. Troubled in mind or worried about some uncertain matter or event. **-ness** n. **-iously** adv.

any (en´) adj. One; no matter which; some; every; and quantity or part.

any-body (en bod) pron. pl **-bodies** Anyone; any person.

any-how (en´hou´) adv. By any means; in any way; whatever.

any-more (en´mr´) adv. At present and from now on.

any-one (en´wun´) pron. Any person; anybody.

any-place (en´pls´) adv. Anywhere.

any-thing (en´thing´) pron. Any occurrence, object or matter.

any-time adv. At any time whatever.

any-way (en´w´) adv. Nevertheless; anyhow; in any manner; carelessly.

any-where (en´hwâr´) adv. In, at, or to any place; to any degree or extent.

a-or-ta (a´ta) n. pl. **-tas** or **-tae** The main artery that carries blood away from the heart; distributes blood to all of the body except the lungs. **-al** adj.

a-pace (a ps´) adv. Rapid in pace.

a-part (a´pärt´) adv. Separate or at a distance; in pieces; to pieces; to set aside.

a-part-heid (a´pärt´ht) n. In the Republic of South Africa, an official policy of political, social, and economic discrimination and segregation against non-whites.

a-part-ment (a´pärt´ment) n. A suite or room in a building equipped for individual living.

ap-a-thy (ap´a th) n. The lack of emotions or feelings. **apathetic** adj.

ap-a-tite (ap´a tt´) n. Mineral used as a source of phosphorus compounds.

ape (p) n. A large mammal such as a gorilla, chimpanzee, or monkey; a very clumsy, coarse person. **aped** v.

ap-er-ture (ap´r chr) n. An opening.

a-pex (´peks) n. pl. **apexes** or **apices** The highest point; tip; top.

a-pha-sia (a f´zha) n. Any partial or total loss of the ability to express ideas, resulting from brain damage. **aphasiac** n. **aphasic** adj. & n.

a-phe-li-on (a f´l on) n. The point in an orbit farthest from the sun.

aphid (´fid) n. Small insects that suck sap from plants.

aph-o-rism (af´o riz´um) n. Brief statement of truth or principal. **aphorist** n. **aphoristically** adv. **aphoristic** adj.

a-pho-tic (´f´tik) adj. Without light.

aph-ro-dis-i-ac (af´ro diz´ak´) adj. Increasing or arousing the sexual desire or potency.

a-pi-ary (´p´er) n. Place where bees are kept and raised for their honey.

a-piece (a ps´) adv. For or to each one.

a-plomb (a plom´) n. Assurance; poise; self-confidence.

apo- pref. Lack of; separation of; being away from.

a-poc-ry-phal (a pok´ri fal) adj. False; of questionable authenticity. **-ly** adv.

ap-o-gee (ap´o j´) n. The point most distant from earth in the moon's orbit.

a-pol-o-get-ic (a´pol´o jet´ik) adj. Making an expression of apology. **apological** adv. **apologetically** adv.

a-pol-o-gize (a pol´o jz´) v. To make an apology. **apologizer** n.

a-pol-o-gy (a pol´o j) n. pl. **-gies** A statement expressing regret for an action or fault; a formal justification or defense.

ap-o-plex-y (ap´o pleks) n. Sudden loss of muscular control, consciousness, and sensation resulting from a rupture or blockage of the blood vessel in the brain.

a-pos-ta-sy (a pos´ta s) n. pl. **-sies** Desertion of one's political party, religious faith, or cause.

a-pos-tate (a´pos´tt) n. One who forsakes his faith or principles.

a pos-te-ri-o-ri (a´po str´o´ri) adj., L. Inductive; reasoning from facts to principles or from effect to cause.

a-pos-tro-phe (*a pos´tro f*) *n.* The mark (') used to indicate the removal of letters or figures, the plural of letters or figures, and the possessive case; the act of turning away; addressing the usually absent person or a usually personified thing rhetorically.

a-pos-tro-phize *v.* To make use of apostrophe. **pothecaries' measure** *n. pl.* A measurement used mainly by pharmacists; a measurement of capacity.

a-poth-e-car-y (*a poth´e ker´*) *n. pl.* **-caries** A person who prepares drugs for medical uses.

apo-the-ci-um *n.* A single-celled structure in many lichens and fungi that consists of a cupped body bearing asci on the exposed flat or concave surface.

ap-o-thegm (*ap´o them´*) *n.* A short, essential, and instructive formulation or saying. **-atical** *adj.* **-atic** *adj.*

apo-the-o-sis (*a poth´´sis*) *n.* The perfect way to explain or define something or someone. **apotheosize** *v.*

ap-pall (*a pol´*) *v.* To overcome by shock or dismay; to weaken; to fail; to become pale.

ap-pa-ra-tchik *n.* A member of the Communist party.

ap-pa-ra-tus (*ap´a rat´us*) *n. pl.* **-tuses** Appliance or an instrument designed and used for a specific operation.

ap-par-ent (*a par´ent*) *adj.* Clear and opened to the eye and mind; open to view, visible. **apparently** *adv.* **apparentness** *n.*

apparent time *n.* Time of day so indicated by a sundial or the sun.

ap-pa-ri-tion (*ap´a rish´an*) *n.* An unusual or unexpected appearance; the act of being visible; a ghostly figure. **apparitional** *adj.*

ap-par-i-tor (*a par´i tor*) *n.* An official person sent to carry out the order of a judge, court, or magistrate.

ap-peal (*a pl´*) *n.* Power to arouse a sympathetic response; an earnest plea; a legal preceding where a case is brought from a lower court to a higher court for a rehearing. *v.* To make a request; to ask another person for corroboration, vindication, or decision on a matter of importance. **appealable** *adj* **appealingly** *adv.*

ap-pear (*a pr´*) *v.* To come into existence; to come into public view; to come formally before an authorized person.

ap-pease (*a pz´*) *v.* To give peace; to cause to stop or subside; to calm; to pacify. **-able** *adj.* **appeasement** *n.*

ap-pel-late (*a pel´it*) *adj.* Having the power to hear and review the decisions of the lower courts.

ap-pel-la-tion (*ap´e l´shan*) *n.* Identifying by a name or title.

ap-pel-la-tive (*a pel´a tiv*) *adj.* Having to do with the giving of names; relating to or of a common noun.

ap-pend (*a pend´*) *v.* To add an appendix or supplement, as to a book; to attach.

ap-pen-dec-to-my (*ap´en dek´to m*) *n.* The surgical removal of the appendix.

ap-pen-dix (*a pen´diks*) *n. pl.* **-dixes** A medical term that refers to an appendage or projecting part as of the vermiform appendix. Supplementary material usually found at the end of something that has been written; the vermiform appendix.

ap-per-cep-tion (*ap´r sep´shan*) *n.* The mental understanding of something perceived in terms of previous experience. **apperceptively** *adv.* **apperceptive** *adj.*

ap-per-tain (*ap´r tn´*) *v.* To belong to or connect with, as a rightful part.

ap-pe-tite (*ap´i tt´*) *n.* The craving or desire for food. **appetitive** *adj.*

ap-plaud (*a plod´*) *v.* To express or show approval by clapping the hands. **applaudable** *adj.*

ap-plause (*a ploz´*) *n.* The expression of public approval. **applausive** *adj.*

ap-pli-ca-ble (*ap´li ka bl*) *adj.* Appropriate; suitable; capable of being applied.

ap-pli-cant (*ap´li kant*) *n.* A person who applies for a job or position.

ap-plies (*a plz*) *adj.* Putting something to practical use to solve definite problems.

ap-point (*a point´*) *v.* To arrange something; to fix or set officially. **appointable** *adj.*

ap-por-tion (*ap´r shan*) *v.* To divide and share according to a plan. **-ment** *n.*

ap-pose (*a pz´*) *v.* To apply one thing to another; to put before. **apposable** *adj.*

ap-po-site (*ap´o zit*) *adj.* Highly appropriate or pertinent. **-ness** *n.* **-ly** *adv.*

ap-po-si-tion (*ap´o zish´an*) *n.* A grammatical construction where a noun or noun phrase is followed by another; the explanatory equivalent. **-al** *adj.*

ap-prais-al (*a pr´zal*) *n.* The evaluation of property by an authorized person.

ap-praise (*a prz´*) *v.* To estimate the value, worth, or status of a particular item. **appraisement** *n.* **-er** *n.* **-ing** *adj.*

ap-pre-cia-ble (*a pr´sh a bl*) *adj.* Capable of being measured or perceived, noticed, or estimated. **-ably** *adv.*

ap-pre-ci-ate (*a pr´sh t´*) *v.* To recognize the worth, quality, or significance; to value very highly; to be aware of; to realize; to increase in price or value.

ap-pre-ci-a-tion (*a pr´sh´shan*) *n.* The expression of admiration, gratitude, or approval; increase in value.

ap-pre-hend (*ap´ri hend´*) *v.* To anticipate with anxiety, dread or fear; to recognize the meaning of; to grasp; to understand.

ap-pre-hen-si-ble (*ap´ri hen´si bl*) *adj.* Capable of being apprehended.

ap-pre-hen-sion (*ap´ri hen´shan*) *n.* The act of or comprehending power to comprehend; suspicion or fear of future events.

ap-pre-hen-sive (*ap´ri hen´siv*) *adj.* Viewing the future with anxiety or fear. **-ly** *adv.*

ap-pressed (*a prest´*) *adj.* Pressed close to or lying flat against.

ap-prise (*a prz´*) *v.* To inform; to give notice.

ap-proach (*a prch´*) *v.* To come near to or draw closer; to be close in appearance.

ap-pro-ba-tion (*ap´ro b´shan*) *n.* A formal approval.

ap-pro-pri-ate (*a pr´prt´*) *v.* To take possession of; to take without permission. *adj.* Suitable for a use or occasion; fitting. **appropriately** *adv.* **appropriator** *n.*

ap-pro-pri-a-tion (*a pr´pr´shan*) *n.* Money set apart for a particular use; the act or instance of appropriating.

ap-prov-al (*a prō´val*) *n.* The act of approving; subject to acceptance or refusal.

ap-prove (*a prōv´*) *v.* To regard or express a favorable opinion; to give formal or official approval.

approx *abbr.* Approximate; approximately.

ap-prox-i-mate (*a prok´si mt´*) *adj.* Located close together; almost accurate or exact. *v.* To bring close or near to; to approach; to estimate; to be near the same.

ap-pur-te-nance (*a per´te nans*) *n.* Something that belongs with another more important thing; an accessory that is passed along with.

ap-pur-te-nant (*a per´te nant*) *adj.* Constitutes a legal attachment.

aprax-ia (*a praks´s a*) *n.* Inability to execute complex coordinate movement. **apractic** *adj.* **apraxic** *adj.*

a pri-o-ri (*´pr r´*) *adj.* Based on theory rather than personal experience; deductive.

ap-ro-pos (*ap´ro p´*) *adv.* At a good time; by the way.

apse (*aps*) *n.* A semicircular or polygonal projection of a building or church.

ap-si-dal *adj.* Relating to an apse.

apt (*apt*) *adj.* Unusually qualified or fitting; appropriate; having a tendency; suitable; quick to understand. **aptly** *adv.* **aptness** *n.*

ap-ti-tude (*ap´ti tōd´*) *n.* A natural talent or ability; quickness in learning or understanding.

aq-ua (*ak´wa*) *n.* *pl.* **aquas** Water; aquamarine.

aq-ua-cade (*ak´wa kd´*) *n.* Water entertainment, consisting of swimming and diving exhibitions, with musical accompaniment.

aq-ua-lung-er *n.* A scuba diver.

aq-ua-naut (*ak´wa not´*) *n.* A scuba diver who lives inside and outside of an underwater shelter for an extended period of time.

aq-ua-pu-ra (*ak´wa p´ro*) *n.* Very pure water.

aq-ua re-gi-a (*ak´wa r j a*) *n.* Mixture of hydrochloric and nitric acids that dissolves platinum or gold.

a-quat-ic (*a kwat´ik*) *adj.* Anything occurring on or in the water.

aq-ue-duct (ak´wi dukt´) n. A conduit for carrying a large quantity of flowing water; a bridge-like structure supporting a canal over a river.

a-que-ous hu-mor n. The clear fluid in the chamber of the eye between the cornea and lens.

aq-ui-cul-ture or aqua-cul-ture (ak-e-kel-cher) n. The cultivation of produce in natural water; hydroponics. **aquicultural** adj.

aq-ui-fer (ak´wi fr) n. The layer of underground gravel, sand, or rocks where water collects.

aq-ui-line (ak´wi ln´) adj. Resembling or related to an eagle; hooked or curved like the beak on an eagle.

a-quiv-er adj. Slang Trembling or quivering.

ar-a-besque (ar´a besk´) n. An intricate style or design of interwoven leaves, flowers, and geometric forms.

ar-a-ble (ar´a bl) adj. Land that is suitable for cultivation by plowing.

a-rach-nid (a rak´nid) n. Arthropods that are mostly air-breathing, having four pairs of legs but no antennae; an insect as a spider. **arachnidan** n. **arachnid** adj.

ara-ne-id (a r´n id) n. A breed of spider.

ar-bi-ter (är´bi tr) n. A person chosen to decide a dispute, having absolute power of determining and judging.

ar-bi-tra-ble (är´bi tra bl) adj. Subject to arbitration.

ar-bit-ra-ment (är bi´tra ment) adj. The settling of a dispute; the power or right of deciding.

ar-bi-trar-y (är´bi trer´) adj. Something based on whim or impulse.

ar-bi-tra-tor (är´bi tr´tor) n. A person chosen to settle a dispute or controversy between parties.

ar-bor (är´bor) n. A garden shelter that is shady and covered with or made of climbing plants. **arborous** adj.

ar-bo-re-al (är br´ al) adj. Resembling or related to a tree; living in trees.

ar-bo-re-tum (är´bo r´tum) n. A place for studying and exhibiting trees, shrubs, and plants cultivated for educational and for scientific purposes.

ar-bo-ri-cul-ture (är´bor i kul´chr) n. The ornamental cultivation of shrubs and trees.

ar-bo-rize v. To branch repeatedly and freely.

ar-bo-vi-rus n. Various viruses transmit-ted by arthropods, including the causative agents for yellow fever and encephalitis.

arc (ärk) n. Something that is curved or arched; the luminous discharge of electric current across a gap of two electrodes.

ar-cade (är kd´) n. An arched covered passageway supported by columns; a long arched gallery or building.

ar-cad-ed adj. Furnished with arcades or arches.

ar-ca-dia (är k´d a) n. The ancient Greek area usually ´chosen as background for poetry; region of simple quiet and pleasure.

arch (ärch) n. A structure that spans over an open area and gives support. **archly** adv. **-ness** n.

ar-chae-ol-o-gy (är´k ol´o j) n. Scientific study of ancient times and ancient peoples. **archaeological** adj. **archaeologist** n.

ar-cha-ic (är k ´ik) adj. Something that belongs to an earlier time; characteristic of an earlier language, now used only in special cases.

ar-cha-ism (är´k iz´um) n. Something that is outdated or old fashioned, as an expression or word. **archaistic** adj. **archaist** n.

arch-an-gel (ärk´n´jel) n. The highest in order of angels. **archangelic** adj.

arch-di-o-cese (ärch´d´o ss) n. The territory or district of an archbishop.

arch-en-e-my (ärch´en´e´m) n. One who is a chief enemy.

ar-che-spore n. A single cell or group of cells from which a mother spore is formed.

ar-che-type (är´ki tp´) n. An original from which other things are patterned.

ar-chi-tect (är´ki tekt´) n. A person who may design and or supervise the construction of large structures.

ar-chi-tec-ton-ic (är´ki tek ton´ik) adj. To resemble architecture in organization or structure. **-ically** adv.

ar-chi-tec-ture (är´ki tek´chr) n. The art or science of designing and building structures; a method or style of construction or building. **-al** *adj.*

ar-chi-trave (är´ki trv) *n.* In classical architecture, a horizontal piece supported by the columns of a building.

ar-chives *n. pl.* Public documents or records; the place where archives are kept. **archival** *adj.* **archivist** *n.*

arch-way (ärch´w´) *n.* A passage or way under an arch; an arch over a passage.

arc-tic (ärk´tik) *adj.* Extremely cold or frigid; relating to the territory north of the Arctic Circle.

-ard *or* **-art** *suff.* A person who is characterized by performing something excessively.

ar-dor (är´dr) *n.* Extreme warmth or passion; emotion; intense heat.

ar-du-ous (är´j us) *adj.* Taking much effort to bring forth; difficult. **arduously** *adv.*

are (är) *v.* First, second, and third person plural and second person singular of the verb "to be".

ar-e-a (âr´ a) *n.* A flat or level piece of ground. **areal** *adj.*

area-way (âr´ a w´) *n.* A sunken area in a basement that offers access, light and air.

a-re-ca *n.* Tall palm of southeast Asia that has white flowers and red or orange egg-shaped nuts.

a-re-na (a r´na) *n.* Enclosed area for public entertainment, such as football games, concerts, etc.

aren't (ärnt) *contr.* Are not.

ar-gen-tite (är´jen tt´) *n.* A lustrous ore.

ar-gil-la-ceous (är´j e ´l shes) *adj.* Resembling or containing clay.

ar-go-sy (är´go s) *n. pl.* **-sies** A fleet of ships; a large merchant ship.

ar-got (är´g) *n.* A secret, specialized vocabulary.

ar-gu-able (är´g a bl) *adj.* Open to argument. **arguably** *adv.*

ar-gue (är´g) *v.* To debate, to offer reason for or against a subject; to dispute, argue, or quarrel; to persuade or influence. **-ment** *n.* **-er** *n.*

ar-gu-men-ta-tion (är´gya men t´shan) *n.* The process or art of arguing; debating.

ar-gu-men-ta-tive (är´gya men´ta tiv) *adj.* Given to argument.

ar-gyle *or* **argyll** (är´gl) *n.* A pattern knitted with various colored, diamond-shaped designs.

a-ri-a (är´ a) *n.* A vocal piece with accompaniment sung in solo; part of an opera.

ar-id (ar´id) *adj.* Insufficient rain; dry; lacking in interest or feeling; dull. **aridity** *n.*

a-right (a rt) *adv.* Correctly; rightly.

a-rise (a rz´) *v.* To come from a source; to come to attention.

a-ris-ta (a ris´ta) *n. pl.* **-tae** *or* **-tas** Bristle-like appendage or structure.

ar-is-toc-ra-cy (ar´ stok´ra s) *n.* A government by the best individuals or by a small privileged class; a class or group viewed as superior; the hereditary privileged ruling nobility or class.

a-rith-me-tic (a rith´me tik) *adj.* Branch of math that deals with addition, subtraction, multiplication, division. **arithmetical** *adj.* **-ically** *adv.*

arithmetic mean *n.* The number received by dividing the sum of a set of quantities by the number of quantities in the set.

arithmetic progression *n.* A progression in which the difference between any term and the one before or after is constant, as 2,4,6,8, etc.

-ar-i-um *suff.* The place or thing connected to or relating with.

arm (ärm) *n.* The part between the shoulder and the wrist; upper limb of the human body. *v.* To furnish with protection against danger. **armer** *n.*

ar-ma-da (är mä´da) *n.* A fleet of warships; a large force of moving things.

ar-ma-dil-lo (är´ma dil´) *n.* A burrowing nocturnal animal with an armorlike covering of jointed, bony plates.

ar-ma-ment (är´ma ment) *n.* Military supplies and weapons; the process of preparing for battle.

ar-ma-ture (är´ma chr) *n.* The main moving part of an electric device or machine; a piece of soft iron that connects the poles of a magnet.

arm-ful (ärm´fel´) *n. pl.* **armfuls** *or* **armsful** As much as the arm can hold.

ar-mi-stice (är´mi stis) *n.* The temporary suspension of combat by mutual agreement; truce.

arm-let (ärm´lĭt) *n.* A band worn on the upper arm.

ar-moire (ärm wär) *n.* A large wardrobe or cup board.

ar-mor (är´mor) *n.* Covering used in combat to protect the body, made from a heavy metal. **armor** *v.* **armored** *adj.*

ar-my (är´m) *n. pl.* **-mies** A group of persons organized for a country's protection; the land forces of a country.

ar-ni-ca (är´nĭ ka) *n.* Plant of the genus Arnica with yellow flowers from which a form of a tincture, as a liniment, is made.

a-ro-ma (a r´ma) *n.* A distinctive fragrance or pleasant odor. **aromatical** *adj.* **-tic** *adj.*

a-round (a round´) *adv.* To or on all sides; in succession or rotation; from one place to another; in a circle or circular movement.

arouse (a rouz´) *v.* To wake up from a sleep; to stir; to excite. **arousal** *n.*

ar-peg-gi-o (är pej´´) *n.* Tones of a chord produced in succession and not simultaneously.

arr *abbr.* Arranged; arrival; arrive.

ar-raign (a rn´) *v.* To be called before a court to answer a charge or indictment; to accuse of imperfection, inadequacy, or of wrong doing. **arraignment** *n.*

ar-range (a rnj´) *v.* To put in correct order or proper sequence; to prepare for something; to take steps to organize something; to bring about an understanding or an agreement; to prepare or change a musical composition for instruments or voices other than those that it was written for.

ar-range-ment (a rnj´ment) *n.* The state of being arranged; something made by arranging things or parts together.

ar-rant (ar´ant) *adj.* Extreme; being notoriously without moderation. **-ly** *adv.*

ar-ras (ar´as) *n.* A screen or wall hanging of tapestry.

ar-ray (a r´) *v.* To place or set in order; to draw up; to decorate or dress in an impressive attire. **arrayer** *n.*

ar-rears *n. pl.* The state of being behind something, as an obligation, payment, etc.; an unfinished duty.

ar-rear-age (a rr´ĭj) *n.* The condition of

having something unpaid or overdue.

ar-rest (a rest´) *v.* To stop or to bring an end to; to capture; to seize; to hold in custody by the authority of law. **arrester** *n.* **arrestor** *n.* **arrestment** *n.*

arrest-ee *n.* A person under arrest.

ar-rest-ing (a res´ting) *adj.* Very impressive or striking; catching the attention.

ar-rhyth-mia (a rĭth´m a) *n.* The alteration in rhythm of the heartbeat, either in force or time.

ar-rhyth-mic (a rĭth´mĭk) *adj.* Lacking regularity or rhythm.

ar-riv-al (a r´val) *n.* The act of arriving.

ar-ri-ve (a rv´) *v.* To reach or get to a destination.

ar-ro-gance (ar´o gans) *n.* An overbearing manner, intolerable presumption; an insolent pride. **arrogant** *adv.* **arrogantly** *adv.*

ar-row (ar´) *n.* A weapon shot from a bow; a sign or mark to show direction.

ar-row-head (ar´hed´) *n.* The striking end of an arrow, usually shaped like a wedge.

ar-se-nal (är´se nal) *n.* A collection of weapons; a place where arms and military equipment are manufactured or stored.

ar-se-nic (är´se nik) *n.* A solid, poisonous element, steel-gray in color, used to make insecticide or weed killer.

ar-son (är´son) *n.* The fraudulent burning of property. **arsonist** *n.* **-ous** *adj.*

art (ärt) *n.* A human skill of expression of other objects by painting, drawing, sculpture, etc.; a branch of learning.

ar-te-ri-ole (är tr´ l) *n.* One of the small terminal twigs of an artery that ends in capillaries.

ar-ter-y (är´te r) *n. pl.* **-teries** A blood vessel that carries blood from the heart to the other parts of the body; a major means for transportation. **arterial** *adj.*

ar-te-sian well (är t´zhun) *n.* A well that produces water without a pump.

art form The recognized form of an artistic expression.

art-ful (ärt´fel) *adj.* Showing or performed with skill or art. **artfully** *adv.*

ar-thral-gia (är thral´je) *n.* Pain that occurs in one or more joints. **-gic** *adj.*

ar-thrit-ic (är thrit´ĭk) *n.* A person who

has arthritis. *adj.* Affected with arthritis; showing effects associated with aging.

ar-thri-tis (är thr´tis) *n.* Inflammation of joints due to infectious or metabolic causes.

ar-thro-pod (är´thrə pod´) *n.* An animal with jointed limbs and segmented body, as a spider. **arthropodal** *adj.* **arthropodan** *adj.*

ar-ti-cle (är´ti kəl) *n.* A term or clause in a contract; a paragraph or section; a condition or rule; an object, item or commodity.

ar-tic-u-lar (är tik´yu lr) *adj.* Related to or of a joint.

ar-tic-u-late (är tik´yu lit) *adj.* Able to express oneself clearly, effectively, or readily; speaking in distinct words, or syllables. **articulateness** *n.* **articulator** *n.* -**ly** *adv.*

ar-ti-fact (är´ti fakt´) *n.* Something made by man showing human modification or workmanship.

ar-ti-fice (är´ti fis) *n.* An artful or clever skill; ingenuity.

ar-ti-fi-cial (är´ti fish´al) *adj.* Not genuine; made by man; not found in nature.

ar-til-lery (är til´e r) *n.* Weapons, especially cannons; troops that are trained in the use of guns and other means of defense.

ar-ti-san (är´ti zən) *n.* A mechanic or a craftsman.

art-ist (är´tist) *n.* A person who practices the fine arts of painting, sculpture, etc.

ar-tiste (är tst´) *n.* One who is an expert in the theatrical profession.

ar-tis-tic (är tis´tik) *adj.* Relating to the characteristic of an artist or art.

art-ist-ry (är´ti str) *n.* The artistic ability, or quality of workmanship or effect.

art-work *n.* The artistic work of an artist.

as (az) *adv.* In the manner like; of the same degree or amount; similar to.

as-bes-tos (as bes´tus) *n.* A noncombustible, fibrous, mineral form of magnesium silicate that is used especially in fireproofing.

as-cend (a send´) *v.* To rise up from a lower level; to climb; to mount; to walk up. **ascendible** *adj.* -**able** *adj.*

as-cen-dant *or* **ascendent** (a sen´dənt) *adj.* Rising; moving up.

as-cent (a sent´) *n.* A way up; a slope; the act of rising.

as-cer-tain (as´r tn´) *v.* To find out for certain; to make sure. -**ment** *n.*

as-cet-i-cism (a set´i siz´um) *n.* The practice of strict self-denial through personal and spiritual discipline.

as-cot (as´kot) *n.* A scarf or broad tie that is placed under the chin.

as-cribe (a skrb´) *v.* To assign or attribute to something. **ascribable** *adj.* **ascription** *n.*

a-sex-u-al (sek´shö al) *adj.* Lacking sexual reproductive organs; without sex.

asg *abbr.* Assigned, assignment.

ash (ash) *n.* A type of tree with a hard, tough elastic wood; the grayish dust remaining after something has burned.

a-shamed (a shmd´) *adj.* Feeling guilt, disgrace, or shame; feeling unworthy or inferior. **ashamedly** *adv.*

a-shore (a shr´) *adv.* On or to the shore.

aside (a sd´) *adv.* Out of the way; to a side; to one side; something that is said in an undertone and not meant to be heard by someone.

ask (äsk) *v.* To request; to require or seek in formation. **asker** *n.*

askance (a skans´) *adv.* With a side glance; with suspicion or distrust.

askew (a sk´) *adv. or adj.* Out of line, not straight.

a-slant (a slänt´) *adv.* In a slanting direction.

a-slope (a slp´) *adv.* In a slanting or sloping position or direction.

a-so-cial (s´shal) *adj.* Selfish, not social.

as-par-a-gus (a spar´a gus) *n.* A vegetable with tender shoots, very succulent when cooked.

as-pect (as´pekt) *n.* The situation, position, view, or appearance of something.

as-per-i-ty (a sper´i t) *n. pl.* -**ties** Roughness in manner.

as-per-sion (a sper´zhən) *v.* False charges or slander; defamation; maligning.

as-phyx-i-ate (as fik´s at´) *v.* To suffocate, to prevent from breathing. **asphyxiation** *n*.

as-pic (as 'pik) *n*. A savory jelly made from fish, meat, or vegetable juices.

as-pi-rate (as 'pi rt ') *v*. To give pronunciation with a full breathing sound; to draw out using suction. **aspiration** *n*.

as-pire (a spr ') *v*. To desire with ambition; to strive towards something that is higher. **aspiringly** *adv*. **aspirer** *n*.

as-pi-rin (as 'pi rin) *n*. Medication used for the relief of pain and fever.

as-sail (a sl ') *v*. To attack violently with words or blows. **assailant** *n*.

as-sas-sin *n*. Murderer, especially one that murders a politically important person either for fanatical motives or for hire.

as-sas-si-nate *v*. To murder a prominent person by secret or sudden attack.

as-sault (a solt ') *n*. A very violent physical or verbal attack on a person.

as-say (a s ') *n*. To evaluate or to assess; to try; to attempt. **assayer** *n*.

as-sem-blage (a sem blij) *n*. A collection of things or people; artistic composition made from junk, scraps, and miscellaneous materials.

as-sem-ble (a sem bl) *v*. To put together the parts of something; to come together as a group. **assembly** *n*.

as-sent (a sent ') *v*. To agree on something.

as-sert (a sert ') *v*. To declare or state positively, to maintain; to defend.

as-sess (a ses ') *v*. To fix or assign a value to something. **assessor** *n*.

as-sess-ment (a ses 'ment) *n*. The official determination of value for tax purposes.

as-set (as 'et) *n*. A valuable quality or possession; all of the property of a business or a person that can be used to cover liabilities.

as-sev-er-ate (a sev 'e rt ') *v*. To state positively, firmly, and seriously. **asseveration** *n*.

as-sign (a sn ') *v*. To designate as to duty; to give or allot; to attribute. **-able** *adj*.

as-sign-ment (a sn 'ment) *n*. A given amount of work or task to undertake; a post, position, or office to which one is assigned.

as-sim-i-late (a sim 'i lt ') *v*. To take in,

to understand; to make similar; to digest or to absorb into the system. **-or** *n*.

as-sist (a sist ') *v*. To give support, to aid, to give help. **assistance** *n*. **assistant** *n*.

as-size (a sz ') *n*. A fixed or customary standard.

assoc *abbr*. Associate.

as-so-ci-ate (a s 'sh it) *v*. To connect or join together. *n*. A partner, colleague, or companion.

as-so-ci-a-tion (a s 's 'shan) *n*. An organized body of people having a common interest; a society. **-al** *adj*.

as-so-nance (as 'o nans) *n*. The repetition of sound in words or syllables.

as-sort (a sort ') *v*. To distribute into groups of a classification or kind.

as-sort-ed (a sort 'id) *adj*. Made up of different or various kinds.

as-suage (a swj ') *v*. To quiet, pacify; to put an end to by satisfying. **-ment** *n*.

as-sua-sive (a sw 'siv) *adj*. Having a smooth, pleasant effect or quality.

as-sume (a sŏm ') *v*. To take upon oneself to complete a job or duty; to take responsibility for; to take for granted. **assumable** *adj*. **assumably** *adv*.

as-sump-tion (a sump 'shan) *n*. An idea or statement believed to be true without proof.

as-sur-ance (a sher 'ans) *n*. A statement made to inspire confidence of mind or manner; freedom from uncertainty or selfdoubt.

as-sure (a sher ') *v*. To give the feeling of confidence; to make sure or certain.

as-sured (a sherd ') *adj*. Satisfied as to the truth or certainty. **assuredly** *adv*.

as-ter (as 'tr) *n*. A plant having white, bluish, purple, or pink daisy-like flowers.

as-ter-isk (as 'ter risk) *n*. The character (*) used to indicate letters omitted or as a reference to a footnote.

a-stern (a stern ') *adv. & adj*. Toward the rear or back of an aircraft or ship.

as though *conj*. As if.

a-stig-ma-tism (a stig 'ma tiz 'um) *n*. A defect of the lens of an eye resulting in blurred or imperfect images.

as to *prep*. With reference to or regard to; concerning; according to.

as-ton-ish (a ston 'ish) *v*. To strike with sudden fear, wonder, or surprise.

as-ton-ish-ing (*a* ston´i shing) *adj.* Causing surprise or astonishment.

as-ton-ish-ment (*a* ston´ish m*e*nt) *n.* The state of being amazed or astonished.

as-tound (*a* stound´) *v.* To fill with won-der and bewilderment. **-ing** *adj.*

as-tral (as´tral) *adj.* Resembling, or re-lated to the stars.

a-stray (*a* str´) *adv.* Away from a desir-able or proper path or development.

as-trin-gent (*a* strin´jent) *adj.* Able to draw together or to constricting tissue.

as-trol-o-gy (*a* strol´o j) *n.* The study of the supposed influences of the planets and stars and their movements and positions on human affairs. **-gical** *adj.*

as-tro-naut (as´tro not´) *n.* A person who travels in a spacecraft beyond the earth's atmosphere.

as-tro-nom-i-cal (as´tro nom´i kal) *adj.* Relating to astronomy; something inconceivable or enormously large.

as-tron-o-my (*a* stron´o m) *n.* The sci ence of the celestial bodies and their motion, magnitudes, and constitution.

as-tro-phys-ics (as´tr fiz´iks) *n.* Branch of astronomy dealing with the chemical and physical constitution of the celes tial bodies. **astrophysical** *adj.* **astro-physicist** *n.*

as-tute (*a* stöt´) *adj.* Sharp in discern-ment; very shrewd. **astutely** *adv.* **astuteness** *n.*

a-sun-der (*a* sun´dr) *adv.* Separate into parts or positions apart from each other.

asy-lum (*a* s´lum) *n.* A refuge or institu tion for the security and retreat; an institution providing help and care for the destitute or insane.

at (at) *prep.* To indicate presence, occur-rence, or condition; used as a function word to indicate a certain time.

at-a-vism (at´*a* viz´um) *n.* The reap-pearance of a hereditary characteristic that skipped several generations. **atavistic** *adj.*

a-tax-i-a (*a* tak´s *a*) *n.* Any nervous dis-order with an inability to coordinate voluntary muscular movements.

a-the-ist (´th ist) *n.* A person who does not believe in God. **-tic** *adj.* **-ical** *adj.*

ath-lete (ath´lt) *n.* A person who partic-

ipates in sports, as football, basketball, soccer,etc.

ath-let-ic (ath let´ik) *adj.* Relating to athletes; physically strong and active.

a-thwart (*a* thwort´) *adv.* Opposition to the expected or right; from one side to another.

a-tilt (*a* tilt´) *adj. & adv.* Inclined upward or tilted in some way.

at-las (at´las) *n.* A collection or book of maps.

at-mos-phere (at´mos fr´) *n.* A gaseous mass that surrounds a celestial body, as the earth; a predominant mood or feeling.

at-oll (at´ol) *n.* An island of coral that encircles a lagoon either partially or completely.

at-om (at´om) *n.* A tiny particle, small-est unit of an element.

atomic energy (*a* tom´ik) *n.* Energy that is released by changes in the nucleus of an atom.

a-ton-al (tn´al) *adj.* Marked by the deliberate avoidance of a traditional key or tonal center. **-ity** *n.* **-ly** *adv.*

a-tone (*a* tn´) *v.* To give satisfaction; to make amends.

a-tone-ment (*a* tn´ment) *n.* Amends for an injury or a wrong doing; the recon-ciliation between God and man.

a-tri-um (´tr um) *n.* One of the heart chambers; the main hall of a Roman house. **atrial** *adj.*

a-tro-cious (*a* tr´shus) *adj.* Exceedingly cruel or evil.

a-troc-i-ty (*a* tros´i t) *n. pl.* **-ties** The condition of being atrocious; an atro-cious act.

at-tach (*a* tach´) *v.* To bring together; to fasten or become fastened; to bind by personal attachments. **attachable** *adj.*

at-tain (*a* tn´) *v.* To arrive at or reach a goal. **attainability** *n.* **attainable** *adj.*

at-taint (*a* tnt´) *v.* To disgrace or stain; to achieve or obtain by effort.

at-tar (at´ar) *n.* The fragrant oil from flowers.

at-tempt (*a* tempt´) *v.* To make an effort to do something. **attempt** *n.*

at-tend (*a* tend´) *v.* To be present; to take charge of or to look after.

at-ten-tion (*a* ten´shan) *n.* Observation, notice, or mental concentration. attentive, **attentively** adv. **attentiveness** n.

at-ten-u-ate (*a* ten´*t*´) v. To lessen the force, amount or value; to become thin; to weaken. **attenuation** n.

at-test (*a* test´) v. To give testimony or to sign one's name as a witness.

at-ti-tude (at´*i* töd´) n. A mental position; the feeling one has for oneself.

at-tor-ney (*a* ter´n) n. pl. **-neys** A person with legal training who is appointed by another to transact business for him.

at-tract (*a* trakt´) v. To draw by appeal; to cause to draw near by appealing qualities.

at-trib-ute (*a* tríb´yöt´) v. To explain by showing a cause. A characteristic of a thing or person. **attributable** adj.

at-tune (*a* tn´) v. To bring something into harmony; to put in tune; to adjust.

a-typ-i-cal (tip´*i* kal) adj. Not confirming to the typical type. **atypically** adv.

au cou-rant (kö rän´) adj. Fully familiar or informed.

auc-tion (ok´shan) n. A public sale of merchandise to the highest bidder.

au-da-cious (o d´shus) adj. Bold, daring, or fearless; insolent. **-ously** adv.

au-di-ble (o´di bl) adj. Capable of being heard.

au-di-o (o´d) adj. Of or relating to sound or its high-fidelity reproduction.

au-dit (o´dit) n. Verification or examination of financial accounts or records.

au-di-to-ry (o´di tr´) adj. Related to the organs or sense of hearing.

aught (ot) n. Zero (0).

aug-ment (og ment´) v. To add to or increase; to enlarge. **augmentation** n. **augmenter** n. **augmentative** adj.

au jus (zhös´) adj. Served in the juices obtained from roasting.

au-ra (or´*a*) n. pl. **-ras, -rae** An emanation said to come from a person's or an animal's body.

au-ral (or´al) adj. Relating to the ear or the sense of hearing. **aurally** adv.

au-re-ate (or´´it) adj. Of a brilliant golden color.

au re-voir (re vwär´) Used in expressing farewell to someone.

au-ri-cle (or´i kal) n. The two upper chambers of the heart.

au-ric-u-lar (o rik´yu lr) adj. Dealing

with the sense of hearing or of being in the shape of the ear.

aus-tere (o str´) adj. Stern in manner and appearance. **austerity** n.

au-then-tic (o then´tik) adj. Real; genuine; worthy of acceptance.

au-then-ti-cate (o then´ti kt´) v. To prove something is true or genuine. **authentication** n. **authenticity** n.

au-thor (o´thor) n. A person who writes an original literary work.

au-thor-i-tar-i-an (*a* thor´i tär´ an) adj. Blind submission and absolute, unquestioned obedience to authority. **authoritarian** n. **authoritative** adj.

au-thor-i-ty n., pl. **-ties** A group or person with power; a government; an expert.

au-thor-ize (o tho rz´) v. To give authority, to approve, to justify.

au-thor-ship n. The character of being an author.

au-to-bi-og-ra-phy (o´to b og´ra f) n. pl. **-phies** The life story of a person, written by that person. **-er** n.

au-toc-ra-cy (o tok´ra s) n. Government by one person who has unlimited power. **autocrat** n. **autocratic** adj.

au-to-di-dact (o´t di dakt´) n. A person who has taught himself. **-ic** adj.

au-to-graph (o´to graf) n. A handwritten signature.

au-to-mat-ic (o´to mat´ik) adj. Operating with very little control; self-regulating.

au-ton-o-my (o ton´o m) n. Independence; self-government.

autonomic nervous system n. The part of the body's nervous system which is regulated involuntarily.

au-top-sy (o´top s) n. pl. **-sies** Postmortem examination; the examination of a body after death to find the cause of death. **autopsic** adj. **autopsical** adj.

au-to-stra-da n. An expressway in Italy.

aux-il-ia-ry (og zil´ya r) adj. Providing help or assistance to someone; giving support.

aux-il-ia-ry verb n. Verbs that accompa-ny a main verb and express the mood, voice, or tense.

a-vail (*a* vl´) v. To be of advantage or use; to use. n. The advantage toward attaining a purpose or goal.

a-vail-able (a vāl bl) *adj.* Ready or present for immediate use. **-ably** *adv.*

av-a-lanche (av´a lanch´) *n.* A large amount of rock or snow that slides down a mountainside.

a-vast (a vast´) *v.* A command to stop or cease.

a-venge (a venj´) *v.* To take revenge for some thing. **avenger** *n.*

av-e-nue (av´e n´) *n.* A street lined with trees; a way of achieving something; sometimes called an "avenue of attack".

a-ver (a ver´) *v.* To be firm and to state positively. **averment** *n.*

av-er-age (av´r ij) *n.* Something that is typical or usual, not being exceptional; common.

a-verse (a vers´) *adj.* Having a feeling of distaste or repugnance. **-ness** *n.*

a-vert (a vert´) *v.* To prevent or keep from happening; to turn aside or away from.

a-vi-ar-y (´v er´) *n.* A place where birds are kept. **aviarist** *n.*

a-vi-a-tion (´ v shan) *n.* The operation of planes and other aircraft.

a-vi-a-tor (´v ´tor) *n.* Pilot of an aircraft.

av-id (av´id) *adj.* Greedy; eager; enthusiastic. **avidly** *adv.*

av-o-ca-tion (av´o k´shan) *n.* A pleasurable activity that is in addition to the regular work a person must do; a hobby.

a-void (a void´) *v.* To stay away from; to shun; to prevent or keep from happening. **avoidable** *adj.* **avoidably** *adv.*

a-void-ance (a void´ans) *n.* The act of making something void

a-vouch (a vouch´) *v.* To assert; to guarantee. **avouchment** *n.*

a-vow (a vou´) *v.* To state openly on a subject. **avower** *n.* **-al** *n.* **-edly** *adv.*

a-wait (a wt´) *v.* To wait for something.

a-way (a w´) *adv.* At a distance; to another place; apart from.

awe (o) *n.* A feeling of wonder mixed with reverence.

a-wea-ry (a w´r) *adj.* Tired.

aw-ful (o ful) *adj.* Very unpleasant or dreadful. **awfully** *adv.*

a-while (a hwl´) *adv.* For a short time.

a-whirl (a hwerl´) *adj.* To spin around.

awk-ward (ok´ward) *adj.* Not graceful; clumsy; to cause embarrassment. **awkwardly** *adv.* **awkwardness** *n.*

awn (on) *n.* The part of a piece a grass which resembles a bristle. **awned** *adj.*

a-wry (a r´) *adv.* In a twisted or turned position.

ax-i-om (ak´s um) *n.* Statement recognized as being true; something assumed to be true without proof. **axiomatic** *adj.* **axiomatically** *adv.*

ax-is (ak´sis) *n.* *pl.* **axes** The line around an object or body that rotates or may be thought to rotate.

ax-le (ak´sel) *n.* A spindle or shaft around which a wheel or pair of wheels revolve.

ax *or* **axe (aks)** *n.* A cutting tool used to split wood. *v.* To split or chop with an ax; to remove abruptly.

a-zo-ic (a z´ik) *adj.* Time period which occurred before life first appeared on the earth.

AZT *abbr.* Azidothymidine; a drug that improves the symptoms of AIDS; (Acquired Immune Deficiency Syndrome), allowing a longer and better life. Approved early 1987 by the Federal Government for prescription use.

az-ure (azh´ur) *n.* The blue color of an unclouded sky.

B

B, b The second letter of the English alphabet; a student's grade rating of good, but not excellent.

bab-ble (bab´bl) *v.* To reveal secrets; to chatter senselessly; to talk foolishly.

babe (bb) *n.* A very young child or infant.

ba-bel (b´bel) *n.* Babbling noise of many people talking at the same time.

ba-by (b´b) *n.*, *pl.* **babies** A young child; infant. **babyish** *adj.*

bac-ca-lau-re-ate (bak´a lor´it) *n.* A degree given by universities and colleges; an address given to a graduating class.

bach-e-lor (bach´e lor) *n.* An unmarried male; the first degree one can receive from a four year university.

ba-cil-lus (ba sil´us) *n. pl.* **bacilli** A rod-like microscopic organism which can cause certain diseases.

back (bak) n. The rear part of the human body from the neck to the end of the spine, also the rear part of an animal.

back-ache (bak´k´) n. A pain in the back.

back-bite (bak´bt´) v. To gossip or speak in a nasty way about a person who is not present.

back-bone (bak´bn´) n. The spinal column or spine of the vertebrates; the strongest support, or strength.

back-drop (bak´drop´) n. A curtain or scene behind the back of a stage set.

back-ground (bak´ground´) n. The area or surface behind which objects are represented; conditions leading up to a happening; the collection of a person's complete experience, education, or knowledge.

back-ing (bak´ing) n. Support or aid; a supply in reserve.

back-lash (bak´lash´) n. A violent backward movement or reaction.

back-log (bak´log´) n. The accumulation of unfinished work; a reserve supply.

backup (bak´up´) n. One that serves as an alternative or substitute.

back-ward (bak´ward) adv. Toward the back; to or at the back; in a reverse order. **backwardness** n.

ba-con (b´kon) n. Side and back of a pig, salted and smoked.

bac-ter-ia (bak tr´ a) n. pl. The plural of bacterium.

bac-te-ri-cide (bak tr´i sd´) n. A substance that kills bacteria.

bac-te-ri-um (bak tr´ um) n. pl. -ria Any of various forms of numerous unicellular microorganisms that cause disease.

bad (bad) adj. Naughty or disobedient; unfavorable; inferior; poor; spoiled; invalid. **badly** adv.

baf-fle (baf´fl) v. To puzzle; to perplex. **baffle** n. A device that checks or regulates the flow of gas, sound, or liquids etc.

bag (bag) n. A flexible container used for holding, storing, or carrying something. **bagful** n. **baggy** adj.

ba-gasse (ba gas´) n. Plant residue.

ba-gel (b´gel) n. A hard, glazed, round roll with a chewy texture and a hole in the middle.

bag-gage (bag´ij) n. The personal belongings of a traveler.

bag-gy (bag´) adj. Loose. **baggily** adv.

bag-man (bag´man) n. A person who collects illicit payments for another.

ba-guette (ba get´) n. A gem in the shape of a long, narrow rectangle.

bail (bl) n. The security or money given to guarantee the appearance of a person for trial. **bail** v. To remove water from a boat by dipping and emptying the water overboard.

bail-iff (b´lif) n. The officer who guards prisoners and keeps order in a courtroom.

bait (bt) v. To lure; to entice. n. Food that is used to catch or trap an animal.

baize (bz) n. A coarse woolen or cotton cloth.

bake (bk) v. To cook in an oven; to harden or dry. **baker** n.

bak-sheesh (bak´shsh) n. A tip or gratuity.

bal-a-lai-ka (bal´a l ka) n. A three-stringed musical instrument.

bal-ance (bal´ans) n. Device for determining the weight of something; the agreement of totals in the debit and credit of an account.

bal-co-ny (bal´ko n) n. pl. -nies Gallery or platform projecting from the wall of a building.

bald (bold) adj. Lacking hair on the head.

bale (bl) n. A large, bound package or bundle.

ba-leen n. A whalebone.

balk (bok) v. To refuse to go on; to stop short of something. **balk** n. A rafter or crossbeam extending from wall to wall. **balky** adj.

ball (bol) n. A round body or mass; a pitched baseball that is delivered outside of the strike zone.

bal-lad (bal´ad) n. A narrative story or poem of folk origin; a romantic song.

bal-last (bal´ast) n. Heavy material placed in a vehicle to give stability and weight.

bal-let (ba l´) n. An artistic expression of dance by choreographic design.

ballistic missile n. A projectile that is

self-powered, is guided during ascent, and has a free-fall trajectory at descent.

bal-loon (ba lön´) *n.* A bag inflated with gas lighter than air which allows it to float in the atmosphere, often having a basket or compartment for carrying passengers; a bag made of rubber and used as a child's toy.

bal-lot (bal´ot) *n.* A slip of paper used in secret voting. *v.* To vote by ballot.

balm (bäm) *n.* A fragrant ointment that soothes, comforts, and heals.

ba-lo-ney (ba l´n) *n. Slang* Nonsense.

bal-sa (bol´sa) *n.* American tree that is very light in weight.

bal-sam (bol´sam) *n.* A fragrant ointment from different trees; a plant cultivated for its colorful flowers.

bal-us-ter (bal´u str) *n.* The upright post that supports a handrail.

bam-boo (bam bö´) *n.* Tropical, tall grass with hollow, pointed stems.

bam-boo-zle (bam bö´zl) *v.* To trick or deceive.

ban (ban) *v.* To prohibit; to forbid.

ba-nal (bn´al) *adj.* Trite; lacking freshness.

ba-nan-a (ba nan´a) *n.* The crescent-shaped usually yellow, edible fruit of a tropical plant.

band (band) *n.* A strip used to trim, finish, encircle, or bind; the range of a radio wave length; a group of musicians who join together to play their instruments.

band-age (ban´dij) *n.* A strip of cloth used to protect an injury. **bandage** *v.*

ban-dan-na (ban dan´a) *n.* A brightly colored cotton or silk handkerchief.

ban-deau (ban d´) *n.* A narrow band worn in the hair; a narrow brassiere.

ban-dit (ban´dit) *n. pl.* **bandits, banditti** A gangster or robber. **banditry** *n.*

ban-dy (ban´d) *adv.* Bent; crooked; curved outward.

bane (bn) *n.* A cause of destruction or ruin.

bang (bang) *n.* A sudden loud noise; short hair cut across the forehead. *v.* To move or hit with a loud noise.

ban-gle (bang´gel) *n.* A bracelet worn around the wrist or ankle.

ban-ish (ban´ish) *v.* To leave; to drive away; to remove from the mind.

ban-jo (ban´j) *n.* A stringed instrument similar to a guitar. **banjoist** *n.*

bank (bangk) *n.* A slope of land adjoining water; an establishment that performs financial transactions. **-able** *adj.*

bank-rupt (bangk´rupt) *n. pl.* **-cies** A person who is legally insolvent and whose remaining property is divided among the creditors. **bankruptcy** *n.*

ban-nock (ban´ak) *n.* Unleavened or flat cake made from barley or oatmeal.

banns (banz) *n. pl.* The announcement of a forthcoming marriage.

ban-quet (bang´kwit) *n.* An elaborate dinner or feast.

ban-yan (ban´yan) *n.* A tree from the tropics whose aerial roots grow downward to form additional roots.

bap-tize (bap tz´) *v.* To immerse or sprinkle with water during baptism.

bar (bär) *n.* A rigid piece of material used as a support; a barrier or obstacle; a counter where a person can receive drinks. **bar** *v.* To prohibit or exclude.

barb (bärb) *n.* A sharp projection that extends backward making it difficult to remove.

bar-bar-i-an (bär bâr´ an) *n.* A person or culture thought to be primitive and therefore inferior. **barbarous** *adj.* **barbaric** *adj.*

bar-be-cue (bär´be k´) *n.* An outdoor fireplace or pit for roasting meat.

bar-ber (bär´br) *n.* A person whose business is cutting and dressing hair and also shaving and trimming beards.

bard (bärd) *n.* A poet. **bardic** *adj.*

bare (bär) *adj.* Exposed to view; without coloring. **bare** *v.* **bareness** *n.*

bare-back (bär´bak´) *adv. & adj.* Riding a horse without a saddle.

bare-ly (bâr´l) *adv.* Sparsely; by a very little amount.

barf *v. Slang* To vomit.

bar-gain (bär´gin) *n.* A contract or agreement on the purchase or sale of an item; a purchase made at a favorable or good price.

barge (bärj) *n.* A flat-bottomed boat. *v.* To intrude abruptly.

bar-i-tone (bar´i tn) *n.* A male voice in the range between tenor and bass.

bark (bärk) *n.* The outer protective covering of a tree; the abrupt, harsh sound made by a dog. **barker** n.

bar-ley (bär´l) n. A type of grain used for food and for making whiskey and beer.

barn (bârn) n. A farm building used to shelter animals and to store farm equipment and products.

bar-na-cle (bär´na kl) n. A fish with a hard shell that remains attached to an underwater surface.

ba-rom-et-er (ba rom´i tr) n. An instrument that records the weight and pressure of the atmosphere.

bar-on (bar´on) n. The lowest rank of nobility in Great Britain. **baroness** n. **baronial** adj.

ba-roque (ba rk´) adj. An artistic style characterized by elaborate and ornate forms.

bar-rack (bar´ak) n. A building for housing soldiers.

bar-ra-cu-da (bar´a kö´da) n. pl. -da, -das A fish with a large, narrow body, found in the Atlantic Ocean.

bar-rage (bär´ij) n. A concentrated outpouring or discharge of missiles from small arms.

bar-ra-try (bar´a tr) n. The unlawful breach of duty by a ship's crew that results in injury to the ship's owner.

bar-rel (bar´el) n. Wooden container with round, flat ends of equal size and sides that bulge.

bar-ren (bar´en) adj. Lacking vegetation; sterile.

bar-ri-er (bar´ r) n. A structure that restricts or bars entrance.

bar-row (bar´) n. A rectangular, flat frame with handles; a wheelbarrow.

bar-ter (bär´tr) v. To trade something for something else, without the exchange of money. **barterer** n.

ba-salt (bo solt´) n. A greenish-black volcanic rock.

base (bs) n. The fundamental part; the point from which something begins; headquarters; the lowest part; the bottom. **base** v.

base-ball (bs´bol´) n. A game played with a ball and bat; the ball used in a baseball game.

base-ment (bs´ment) n. The foundation of a building or home.

bash (bash) v. To smash with a heavy blow; Slang A party.

bash-ful (bash´ful) adj. Socially shy.

ba-sic (b´sik) adj. Forming the basis; fundamental. **basically** adv.

BASIC n. A common computer programming language.

bas-il (baz´l) n. An herb used as seasoning in cooking.

ba-sin (b´sn) n. A sink; a washbowl; a round open container used for washing; an area that has been drained by a river system.

ba-sis (b´sis) n. pl. **bases** The main part; foundation.

bask (bask) v. To relax in the warmth of the sun.

bas-ket (bas´kit) n. An object made of woven material, as straw, cane, or other flexible items. **basketry** n.

bas-ket-ball (bas´kit bol) n. A game played on a court with two teams; each team trying to throw the ball through the basket ball hoop at the opponents' end of the court.

bass (bas) n. pl. **bass, basses** A fresh water fish, one of the perch family.

bas-si-net (bas´a net´) n. A basket on legs used as an infant's crib.

bas-soon (ba sön´) n. A woodwind instrument with a low-pitched sound.

baste (bst) v. To run a loose stitch to hold a piece of material in place for a short time; to moisten meat while cooking it by pouring on liquids.

bat (bat) n. A wooden stick made from strong wood; a nocturnal flying mammal.

bath (bath) n. The act of washing the body.

bathe (bth) v. To take a bath.

bat-ter-y (bat´e r) n. A group of heavy guns.

bat-tle (bat´l) n. A struggle; combat between opposing forces. v. To engage in a war or battle.

bawl (böl) v. To cry very loudly.

bay (b) n. The inlet of a body of water; a main division or compartment; an animal that is reddish brown in color.

ba-zaar (ba zär´) n. A fair where a variety of items are sold as a money-making project for charity, clubs, churches, or other such organizations.

ba-zooka (ba zö´ka) n. Weapon for firing rockets.

be (b) *v.* To occupy a position; to exist; used with the present participle of a verb to show action; used as a prefix to construct compound words, as behind, before, because, etc.

beach (bch) *n.* Pebbly or sandy shore of a lake, ocean, sea, or river.

bea·con (b´kan) *n.* A coastal guiding or signaling device.

bead (bd) *n.* A small round piece of material with a hole for threading.

beak (bk) *n.* The bill of a bird. **-ed** *ed*

beak·er (b´ker) *n.* Large, wide mouth cup for drinking; a cylindrical, glass laboratory vessel with a lip for pouring.

beam (bm) *n.* Large, oblong piece of wood or metal used in construction. *v.* To shine.

bean (bn) *n.* An edible seed or seed pod.

bear (bâr) *n.* A carnivorous mammal. **bear** *v.* To endure; to carry; to support. **bearable** *adj*

beard (bîrd) *n.* Hair growing on the chin and cheeks. **bearded** *adj.*

beast (bst) *n.* A four-legged animal. **beastly** *adj.*

beat (bt) *v.* To strike repeatedly; to defeat. *adj.* Exhausted, very tired. **beaten beat** *n.*

be·a·tif·ic (b´a tif´ik) *adj.* Giving or showing extreme bliss or joy.

be·at·i·tude (b at´ tōd´) *n.* The highest form of happiness; heavenly bliss.

beau (b) *n.* Sweetheart; dandy.

beau·ty (b´t) *n.* Quality that is pleasing to the eye. **beautiful** *adj.* **-tifully** *adv.*

be·bop (b´bop´) *n.* Slang Jazz music.

be·calm (b käm) *v.* To make quiet or calm.

be·cause (b koz´) *conj.* For a reason; since.

beck (bek) *n.* A summons; a call.

be·come (b kum´) *v.* To come, to be, or to grow. **becoming** *adj.*

bed (bed) *n.* Furniture for sleeping; a piece of planted or cultivated ground. **bedding** *n.*

be·daz·zle (b daz´l) *v.* To confuse with bright lights.

bed·lam (bed´lam) *n.* A state or situation of confusion.

be·drag·gled (b drag´ld) *adj.* Limp and wet; soiled as though pulled through mud.

bee (b) *n.* A hairy-bodied insect characterized by structures for gathering pollen and nectar from flowers.

beech (bch) *n.* A tree of light-colored bark, with edible nuts.

beef (bf) *n. pl.* **beefs, beeves** A cow, steer, or bull that has been fattened for consumption of its meat. **beefy** *adj.*

beer (br) *n.* An alcoholic beverage.

bees·wax (bz´waks) *n.* The wax from bees that is used for their honeycombs.

bee·tle (bt´l) *n.* An insect with modified, horny front wings, which cover the membranous back wings when it is not in flight.

be·fit (bi fit´) *v.* To be suitable. **-ting** *adj.*

be·fore (bi fr´) *adv.* Earlier; previously. *prep.* In front of.

be·friend (bi frend´) *v.* To be a friend to someone.

beg (beg) *v.* To make a living by asking for charity. **beggar** *n.* **beggarly** *adj.*

be·gan *v.* The past tense of begin.

be·get (bi get´) *v.* To cause or produce.

be·gin (bi gin´) *v.* To start; to come into being; to commence. **beginner** *n.*

be·gone (bi gon´) *v. interj.* Go away; depart.

be·go·nia (bi gn´ya) *n.* A tropical plant with waxy flowers and showy leaves.

be·grime (bi grm´) *v.* To soil with grime.

be·grudge (bi gruj´) *v.* To envy someone's possessions or enjoyment.

be·guile (bi gl´) *v.* To deceive; to delight; to charm.

be·gun *v.* The past participle of begin.

be·half (bi haf´) *n.* The support or interest of another person.

be·have (bi hv´) *v.* To function in a certain manner; to conduct oneself in a proper manner. **behavior** *n.*

be·held (bi held´) *v.* Past participle of behold.

be·hind (bi hnd´) *adv.* To or at the back; late or slow in arriving.

be·hold (bi hld´) *v.* To look at; to see.

be·hoove (bi hōv´) *v.* To benefit or give advantage.

beige (bzh) *n. or adj.* A light brownish, grey color.

being (b´ing) *n.* One's existence.

be-la-bor (bi l´br) v. To work on or to discuss beyond the point where it is necessary; to carry to absurd lengths.

be-lat-ed (bi l´ted) adj. Tardy; late.

bel can-to (bel´ kan´t) n. Operatic singing with rich lyricism and brilliant vocal means.

belch (belch) v. To expel stomach gas through the mouth.

bel-fry (bel´fr) n. pl. belfries The tower that contains the bell of a church.

be-lief (bi lf´) n. Something that is trusted or believed.

be-lieve (bi lv´) v. To accept as true or real; to hold onto religious beliefs.

be-lit-tle (bi lit´l) v. To think or speak in a slighting manner of someone or something.

bell (bel) n. A metal instrument that gives a metallic sound when struck.

belles let-tres (bel le´tra) n. pl. Literature that is regarded not for its value, but for its artistic quality.

bel-lig-er-ent (be lij´r ent) adj. Hostile and inclined to be aggressive.

bel-low (bel´) v. To make a deep, powerful roar like a bull.

bel-lows (bel´z) n. An instrument that produces air in a chamber and expels it through a short tube.

bel-ly (bel´) n. pl. bellies The abdomen or the stomach.

be-long (bi long´) v. To be a part of.

be-loved (bi luv´id) adj. To be dearly loved.

be-low (bi l´) adv. At a lower level or place. below prep. To be inferior to.

belt (belt) n. A band worn around the waist; a zone or region that is distinctive in a special way.

belt-way (belt´w) n. A highway that encircles an urban area.

be-muse (bi mz´) v. To bewilder or confuse; to be lost in thought. -ed adj.

bench (bench) n. A long seat for more than two people; the seat of the judge in a court of law.

bend (bend) v. To arch; to change the direct course; to deflect. bender n.

be-neath (bi nth´) adv. To or in a lower position; below; underneath.

ben-e-dict (ben´i dikt) n. A previously confirmed bachelor who was recently married.

ben-e-dic-tion (ben´i dik´shan) n. A blessing given at the end of a religious service.

ben-e-fac-tion (ben´e fak´shan) n. A charitable donation; a gift. -factor n.

ben-e-fice (ben´e fis) n. Fixed capital assets of a church that provide a living.

be-nef-i-cence (be nef´i sens) n. The quality of being kind or charitable.

ben-e-fi-cial (ben´e fish´al) adj. Advantageous; helpful. beneficially adv.

ben-e-fit (ben´e fit) n. Aid; help; an act of kindness; a social event or entertainment to raise money for a person or cause.

be-nev-o-lence (be nev´o lens) n. The inclination to be charitable. benevolent adj.

be-nign (bi nn´) adj.. Having a gentle and kind disposition; gracious; not malignant.

ben-i-son (ben´i zen) n. A blessing; benediction

bent (bent) adj. Curved, not straight. n. A fixed determination; purpose.

be-numb (bi num´) v. To dull; to make numb.

be-queath (bi kwth´) v. To give or leave to someone by leaving a will; to hand down.

be-rate (bi rt´) v. To scold severely.

be-reave (bi rv´) v. To deprive; to suffer the loss of a loved one. bereft adj.

be-ret (be r´) n. A round, woolen cap that has no brim.

berg (berg) n. A large mass of ice; iceberg.

ber-i-ber-i (ber´ ber´) n. Nervous disorder from the deficiency of vitamin B producing partial paralysis of the extremities.

berry (ber´) n. pl. berries An edible fruit, such as a strawberry or blackberry.

ber-serk (br serk´) adj. Destructively violent.

berth (berth) n. Space at a wharf for a ship or boat to dock; a built-in bunk or bed on a train or ship.

ber-yl (ber´l) n. A mineral composed of silicon, oxygen, and beryllium that is the major source of beryllium; a precious stone which is exceptionally hard.

be-seech (bi sch´) v. To ask or request earnestly.

be-side (bi sd´) prep. At the side of; next to.

be-siege (bi sj´) v. To surround with troops; to harass with requests.

be-sit v. To surround on all sides.

be-smear (bi smir´) v. To soil; to smear.

bes-om (b´zum) n. A broom made of twigs that are attached to a handle, used to sweep floors.

be-spat-ter (bi spat´r) v. To splash; to soil.

be-speak (bi spk´) v. To indicate; to speak; to foretell. **bespoken** adj.

best (best) adj. Exceeding all others in quality or excellence; most suitable, desirable, or useful. **best** v.

bes-tial (bs´chal) adj. Of or relating to an animal; brutish. **bestiality** n.

bes-ti-a-ry (bes´ch er´) n. A medieval collection of fables about imaginary and real animals, each with a moral.

be-stir (bi str´) v. To rouse into action.

be-stow (bi st´) v. To present or to give honor.

be-stride (bi strd´) v. To step over or to straddle.

bet n. An amount risked on a stake or wager. abbr. Between.

be-take (bi tk´) v. To cause oneself to make one's way; move or to go.

be-ta-tron (b´ta tron´) n. Accelerator in which electrons are propelled by the inductive action of a rapidly varying magnetic field.

be-tide (bi td´) v. To happen to; to take place.

be-to-ken (bi t´ken) v. To show by a vis-ible sign.

be-tray (bi tr´) v. To be disloyal or unfaithful; to indicate; to deceive.

be-troth (bi trth´) v. To promise to take or give in marriage. **betrothal** n.

be-trothed (bi trthd´) n. A person to whom one is engaged to marry.

bet-ter (bet´r) adj. More suitable, use-ful, desirable, or higher in quality. **bet-ter** v. To improve oneself. **-ment** n.

be-tween (bi twn´) prep. The position or time that separates; in the middle or shared by two.

be-twixt (bi twikst´) prep. & adv. Not knowing which way one should go; between.

bev-el (bev´el) n. The angle at which one surface meets another when they are not at right angles.

bev-er-age (bev´r ij) n. A refreshing liq-uid for drinking other than water.

bev-y (bev´) n. pl. bevies A collection or group; a flock of birds.

be-wail (bi wl´) v. To express regret or sorrow.

be-ware (bi wâr´) v. To be cautious; to be on guard.

be-wil-der (bi wil´dr) v. To confuse; to perplex or puzzle. **bewilderment** n.

be-witch (bi wich´) v. To fascinate or captivate completely. **bewitchery** n.

bey (b) n. The Turkish title of respect and honor.

be-yond (b ond´) prep. Outside the reach or scope of; something past or to the far side.

bez-el (bez´el) n. A flange or groove that holds the beveled edge of an object such as a gem in a ring mounting.

bi-an-nu-al (b an´ al) adj. Taking place twice a year; semiannual. **-ly** adv.

bi-as (b´as) n. A line cut diagonally across the grain of cloth; prejudice. **bias** v. To be or to show prejudice.

bib (bib) n. A cloth that is tied under the chin of small children to protect their clothing.

Bi-ble (b´bl) n. The holy book of Christianity, containing the Old and New Testaments. **Biblical** adj.

bib-li-og-ra-phy (bib l og´ra f) n. pl. -phies A list of work by a publisher or writer; a list of sources of information.

bib-u-lous (bib´ya les) adj. Inclined to drink, of or related to drinking.

bi-cen-ten-ni-al (b´sen ten´ al) adj. Happening once every 200 years. n. Anniversary or celebration of 200 years.

bi-ceps (b´seps) n. Large muscle in the front of the upper arm and at the back of the thigh.

bick-er (bik´er) v. To quarrel or argue.

bi-con-cave (b kon´kv) adj. Bowing in on two sides.

bi-cul-tur-al (b kul´chur al) adj. Having or containing two distinct cul-tures.

bi-cus-pid (b kus´pid) n. A tooth with

two roots.

bi-cy-cle (b´si kl) *n.* A two-wheeled vehicle propelled by pedals. **-cyclist** *n.*

bid (bid) *v.* To request something; to offer to pay a certain price. **bid** *n.* One's intention in a card game. **-der** *n.*

bid-dy (bid´) *n.* A young chicken; a hen. *Slang* A fussy woman.

bide (bd) *v.* To remain; to wait.

bi-det *n.* A basin for bathing the genital and anal areas.

bi-en-ni-al (b en´ el) *adj.* Occurring every two years; lasting or living for only two years. **biennially** *adv.*

bier (br) *n.* A stand on which a coffin is placed before burial.

bi-fo-cal (b f´kal) *adj.* Having two different focal lengths.

bi-fo-cals *n. pl.* Lenses used to correct both close and distant vision.

bi-fur-cate (b´fer kt) *v.* To divide into two parts.

big (big) *adj.* Very large in dimensions, intensity, and extent; grownup; bountiful; powerful. **bigness** *n.*

big-a-my (big´a m) *n. pl.* **bigamies** The act of marrying one person while still married to another. **bigamist** *n.*

bight (bt) *n.* The slack in a rope; a bend in the shoreline.

big-ot (big´ot) *n.* A person who is fanatically devoted to one group, religion, political view, or race. **bigoted** *adj.* **bigotry** *n.*

big-wig *n.* A person of authority.

bike (bk) *n.* A bicycle. **bike** **biker** *n.*

bi-ki-ni (b k´n) *n.* A scanty, two-piece bathing suit.

bi-lat-er-al (b lat´er al) *adj.* Having or relating to two sides.

bile (bl) *n.* A brownish-yellow alkaline liquid that is secreted by the liver to help digest fats. **biliary** *adj.*

bilge (bilj) *n.* Lowest inside part of the hull of a ship.

bi-lin-gual (b ling´gwal) *adj.* Able to speak two languages with equal ability.

bil-ious (bil´yus) *adj.* Undergoing gastric distress from a sluggish gallbladder or liver.

bilk (bilk) *v.* To cheat or swindle.

bill (bill) *n.* Itemized list of fees for services rendered; a document presented containing a formal statement of a case complaint or petition; the beak of a bird. **bill** *v.*

bill-board (bil´brd´) *n.* A place for displaying advertisements.

bil-liards (bil´yardz) *n.* Game played on a table with cushioned edges.

bil-lion (bil´yon) *n.* A thousand million.

bill of lading *n.* A form issued by the carrier for promise of delivery of merchandise listed.

Bill of Rights *n.* The first ten amendments to the United States Constitution.

bil-low (bil´) *n.* Large swell of water or smoke; wave. **billowy** *adj.*

bil-ly goat *n.* A male goat.

bi-met-al-lism (b met´al iz´um) *n.* The use of two metals, gold and silver, as legal tenders.

bi-month-ly (b munth´l) *adj. pl.* **-lies** Occurring every two months.

bin (bin) *n.* An enclosed place for storage.

bi-na-ry (b´na r) *adj.* Made of two different components or parts.

bind (bnd) *v.* To hold with a belt or rope; to bandage; to fasten and enclose pages of a book between covers.

bind-er (bnd´r) *n.* A notebook for holding paper; payment or written statement legally binding an agreement.

bind-er-y (bn´da r) *n. pl.* **binderies** The place where books are taken to be bound.

binge (binj) *n.* Uncontrollable self-indulgence; a spree.

bin-na-cle (bin´a kal) *n.* A place where a ship's compass is contained.

bin-oc-u-lar (bi nok´ lr) *n.* A device designed for both eyes to bring objects far away into focus.

bi-o-chem-is-try (b´ kem´i str) *n.* Chemistry of substances and biological processes.

bi-o-de-grad-able *adj.* Decomposable, by natural processes.

bio-feed-back *n.* The technique of controlling involuntary bodily functions, such as blood pressure and heartbeat.

bi-o-haz-ard *n.* Biological material that threatens humans and or their environment if infective.

biological warfare (b´o loj´i kal) *n.*

Warfare that uses organic biocides or disease-producing microorganisms to destroy crops, livestock, or human life.

bi·ol·o·gy (b ol´o j) *n.* Science of living organisms and the study of their structure, reproduction, and growth. **biological** *adj.*

bi·on·ics *n.* Application of biological principles to the study and design of engineering systems, as electronic systems.

bi·o·phys·ics (b´ fiz´iks) *n.* The physics of living organisms.

bi·op·sy (b´op s) *n. pl.* **biopsies** The examination for the detection of a disease in tissues removed from a living organism.

bi·ot·ic (b ot´ik) *adj.* Related to specific life conditions or to life itself.

bi·o·tin (b´o tin) *n.* Part of the vitamin B complex found in liver, milk, yeast, and egg yolk.

bi *pref.* Two; occurring two times; used when constructing nouns.

bi·par·ti·san (b pär´ti zan) *adj.* Support by two political parties. **bipartisanship** *n.*

bi·plane (b´pln´) *n.* A glider or airplane with wings on two levels.

bi·po·lar (b p´lar) *adj.* Having or related to two poles; concerning the earth's North and South Poles.

bi·ra·cial (b r´shal) *adj.* Composed of or for members of two races.

birch (berch) *n.* A tree providing hard, close-grained wood.

bird (berd) *n.* A warm-blooded, egg-laying animal whose body is covered by feathers.

bird-brain (berd´brn´) *n. Slang* A person who acts in a silly fashion.

bird-ie (ber´d) *n.* A stroke under par in the game of golf; a shuttlecock.

bi·ret·ta (b ret´a) *n.* Cap worn by Roman Catholic clergy, square in shape.

birl·ing *n.* A game of skill in which two lumberjacks try to balance on a floating log while spinning the log with their feet.

birth (berth) *n.* The beginning of existence. *v.* To bring forth a baby from the womb.

birth control *n.* A technique used to control or prevent the number of children born, by lessening the chances of conception.

birth-day (berth´d) *n.* The day a person is born and the anniversary of that day.

bis (bis) *adv.* Again; encore.

bis-cuit (bis´kit) *n.* Small piece of bread made with baking soda or baking powder; a cookie, or cracker.

bi-sect (b sekt´) *v.* To divide or cut into two equal parts. **bisection** *n.*

bi-sex-u-al (b sek´shö al) *adj.* Sexually relating to both sexes.

bish-op (bish´op) *n.* A Christian clergyman with high rank. **bishopric** *n.*

bis-muth (biz´muth) *n.* A white, crystalline metallic element.

bi-son (b´son) *n.* A large buffalo of northwestern America, with a dark-brown coat and short, curved horns.

bisque (bisk) *n.* A creamy soup made from fish or vegetables; unglazed clay.

bis-sex-tile (b seks´til) *adj.* Related to the extra day occurring in a leap year.

bis-tro (bis´tr) *n. pl.* **bistros** A bar or small nightclub.

bit (bit) *n.* A tiny piece or amount of something; a tool designed for boring or drilling especially, drilling for oil; metal mouthpiece of a horse bridle; in computer science, either of two characters, as the binary digits zero and one, of a language that has only two characters; a unit of information; storage capacity, as of a computer memory.

bite (bt) *v.* To cut, tear, or crush with the teeth. **bite** *n.* **bitingly** *adv.*

bit-stock (bit´stok´) *n.* A brace that secures a drilling bit.

bit-ter (bit´r) *adj.* Having a sharp, unpleasant taste. **-ly** *adv.* **bitterness** *n.*

bit-ter-sweet (bit´r swt´) *n.* A woody vine whose root, when chewed, has first a bitter, then a sweet taste.

bi-tu-mi-nous coal (bi tö´mi nus kl´) *n.* Coal that contains a high ratio of bituminous material and burns with a smoky flame.

bi-valve (b´valv´) *n.* A mollusk that has a hinged two-part shell, a clam or oyster.

biv-ou-ac (biv´ö ak´) *n.* A temporary military camp in the open air. *v.* To camp overnight in the open air.

bi-week-ly (b wk´l) n. Occurring every two weeks.

bi-year-ly (b yr´l) n. Occurring every two years.

bi-zarre (bi zär´) adj. Extremely strange or odd.

blab (blab) v. To reveal a secret by indiscreetly talking; to gossip.

blab-ber (blab´r) v. To chatter; to blab.

blab-ber-mouth (blab´r mouth´) n. Slang A person who gossips.

black (blak) adj. Very dark in color; depressing; cheerless; darkness, the absence of light. **blackness** n **-ly** adv.

black box n. The container that protects the tape recordings of airline pilots from water and fire, normally recoverable in the event of an accident.

black magic n. Witchcraft.

black-mail (blak´ml´) n. The threat of exposing a past discreditable act or crime; money paid to avoid exposure.

black market (blak´mär´kit) n. The illegal buying or selling of merchandise or items.

black-out (blak´out´) n. The temporary loss of electrical power. v. To conceal lights that might be seen by enemy aircraft; to temporarily lose consciousness.

blad-der (blad´r) n. The expandable sac in the pelvis that holds urine.

blade (bld) n. The cutting part of a knife; the leaf of a plant or a piece of grass.

blame (blm) v. To hold someone guilty for something; to find fault. **-less** n.

blanch (blänch) v. To remove the color from something, as to bleach; to pour scalding hot water over fresh vegetables.

bland (bland) adj. Lacking taste or style. **blandly** adv. **blandness** n.

blan-dish (blan´dish) v. To coax by flattery.

blank (blangk) adj. Having no markings or writing; empty; confused.

blank check n. Carte blanche; freedom of action.

blan-ket (blang´kit) n. A woven covering used on a bed.

blank verse n. A poem of lines that have rhythm but do not rhyme.

blare (blâr) v. To make or cause a loud sound.

blar-ney (blär´n) n. Talk that is deceptive or nonsense.

blast (bläst) n. A strong gust of air; the sound produced when a horn is blown.

blast-off (blast´of´) n. The launching of a space ship.

bla-tant (blt´ænt) adj. Unpleasant; offensively loud; shameless. **blatancy** n.

blath-er (blath´r) v. To talk, but not making sense.

blaze (blz) n. A bright burst of fire; a sudden outburst of anger; a trail marker; a white mark on an animal's face.

bla-zon (blz´n) v. To make known; to announce.

bleach (blch) v. To remove the color from a fabric; to become white.

bleak (blk) adj. Discouraging and depressing; barren; cold; harsh. **bleakness** n. **bleakly** adv.

bleat (blt) n. The cry of a sheep or goat.

bleed (bld) v. To lose blood, as from an injury; to extort money; to mix or allow dyes to run together.

bleed-ing heart n. A plant with pink flowers; a person who feels very sympathetic toward the underprivileged.

bleep (blp) n. A signal with a quick, loud sound.

blem-ish (blem´ish) n. A flaw or defect.

blend (blend) v. To mix together smoothly, to obtain a new substance.

bless (bles) v. To honor or praise; to confer prosperity or well-being.

bless-ing (bles´ing) n. A short prayer before a meal.

blight (blt) n. A disease of plants that can cause complete destruction.

blimp (blimp) n. A large aircraft with a nonrigid gas-filled hull.

blind (blnd) adj. Not having eyesight; something that is not based on facts.

blind n. A shelter that conceals hunters.

blink (blingk) v. To squint; to open and close the eyes quickly; to take a quick glance.

blink-er (bling´ker) n. A signaling light that displays a message; a light on a car used to indicate turns.

blintz (blints) n. A very thin pancake rolled and stuffed with cottage cheese or other fillings.

blip (blip) v. To remove; erase sounds

from a recording. *n.* The brief interruption as the result of blipping.

bliss (blis) *n.* To have great happiness or joy. **blissful** *adj.* **blissfully** *adv.*

blis-ter (blis´tr) *n.* The swelling of a thin layer of skin that contains a watery liquid.

blithe (blith) *adj.* Carefree or casual. **blithery** *adv.* **blitheness** *n.*

blitz (blits) *n.* A sudden attack; an intensive and forceful campaign.

bliz-zard (bliz´ard) *n.* A severe winter storm characterized by wind and snow.

blk *abbr.* Black, block.

bloat (blt) *v.* To swell or puff out.

blob (blob) *n.* A small shapeless mass.

bloc (blok) *n.* A united group formed for a common action or purpose.

block (blok) *n.* A solid piece of matter; the act of obstructing or hindering something. **blockage** *n.* **blocker** *n.*

block-ade (blo kd´) *n.* The closure of an area. **blockader** *n.* **blockade** *v.*

blond (blond) *adj.* A golden or flaxen color.

blood (blud) *n.* The red fluid circulated by the heart throughout the body that carries oxygen and nutrients to all parts of the body.

blood count *n.* The determination of the number of white and red corpuscles in a specific amount of blood.

blood-cur-dling (blud´kerd´ling) *adj.* Terrifying; horrifying.

blood poisoning *n.* The invasion of blood by toxin produced by bacteria; septicemia.

blood-stream (blud´strm´) *n.* The circulation of blood in the vascular system.

blood vessel *n.* Any canal in which blood circulates, such as a vein, artery, or capillary.

bloop-er (blö´pr) *n.* An embarrassing blunder made in public.

blos-som (blos´om) *n.* A flower or a group of flowers of a plant that bears fruit. *v.* To flourish; to grow; to develop.

blot (blot) *n.* A spot or stain. *v.* To dry with an absorbent material.

blotch (bloch) *n.* An area of a person's skin that is discolored. **blotchy** *adj.*

blouse (blous) *n.* A loosely fitting shirt or top.

blow (bl) *v.* To move or be in motion because of a current. **blow** *n.* A sudden hit with a hand or fist. **blower** *n.*

blowbyblow *adj.* Minutely detailed in description.

blow dry *v.* To dry one's hair with a hand-held hair dryer.

blow-hole (bl´hl´) *n.* A hole in the ice that enables aquatic mammals to come up and breathe; the nostril of a whale and other cetaceans.

blow-out (bl´out´) *n.* The sudden deflation of a tire that occurs while driving.

blow-torch (bl´torch´) *n.* A hand-held tool that generates a flame hot enough to melt soft metals.

blow-up (bl´up´) *n.* An enlargement; a photograph; an explosion of a violent temper.

blub-ber (blub´r) *n.* The fat removed from whales and other marine mammals.

blue (blö) *n.* A color the same as the color of a clear sky; the hue that is between violet and green; the color worn by the Union Army during the Civil War.

blue-print (blö´print´) *n.* A reproduction of technical drawings or plans, using white lines on a blue background.

blues (blöz) *n. pl.* A state of depression.

bluff (bluf) *v.* To deceive or mislead; to intimidate by showing more confidence than the facts can support. **bluff** *n.* A steep and ridged cliff.

blun-der (blun´dr) *n.* An error or mistake caused by ignorance. *v.* To move clumsily.

blunt (blunt) *adj.* Frank and abrupt; a dull end or edge. **bluntly** *adv.*

blur (bler) *v.* To smudge or smear; to become hazy.

blurt (blert) *v.* To speak impulsively.

blush (blush) *v.* To be embarrassed from modesty or humiliation and to turn red in the face; to feel ashamed. **blush** *n.* Make-up used to give color to the cheekbones.

blus-ter (blus´tr) *n.* A violent and noisy wind in a storm. **bluster** *v.* **blusterer** *n.*

blvd *abbr.* Boulevard

bo-a (b´a) *n.* A large nonvenomous

snake of the Boidea family which coils around prey and crushes it.

boar (br) *n.* A male pig; wild pig.

board (brd) *n.* A flat piece of sawed lumber; a flat area on which games are played. **board** *v.* To receive lodging, meals or both, usually for pay; to enter a ship, train, or plane.

boast (bst) *v.* To brag about one's own accomplishments. **-er** *n.* **boastful** *adj.*

boat (bt) *n.* A small open craft or ship.

boat-swain (b´san) *n.* Warrant or petty officer in charge of the rigging, cables, anchors, and crew of a ship.

bob (bob) *v.* To cause to move up and down in a quick, jerky movement.

bob-bin (bob´in) *n.* A spool that holds thread in a sewing machine.

bob-by (bob´) *n.* An English police officer.

bobby socks *n. pl.* An ankle sock, usually worn by teenaged girls.

bode (bd) *v.* To foretell by omen or sign.

bod-ice (bod´is) *n.* The piece of a dress that extends from the shoulder to the waist.

bod-kin (bod´kin) *n.* A small instrument with a sharp point for making holes in fabric or leather goods.

bod-y (bod´) *n.* The main part of something; the physical part of a person; a human being.

body building *n.* The development and toning of the body through diet and exercise.

body-guard (bod´ gärd´) *n.* A person hired to protect another person.

bo-gey (b g) *n.* In golf, one stroke over par for a hole.

bog-gle (bog´l) *v.* To pull away from with astonishment.

bo-gus (b´gas) *adj.* Something that is counterfeit; worthless in value.

boil (boil) *v.* To raise the temperature of water or other liquid until it bubbles; to evaporate; reduce in size by boiling. *n.* A very painful, pus-filled swollen area of the skin caused by bacteria in the skin.

bois-ter-ous (boi´str us) *adj.* Violent, rough and stormy; undisciplined.

bold (bld) *adj.* Courageous; showing courage; distinct and clear; conspicuous; confident. **boldly** *adv.* **boldness** *n.*

bold-face (bld´fs´) *n.* A style of printing type with heavy thick lines.

bole (bl) *n.* A tree trunk.

boll (bl) *n.* A rounded capsule that contains seeds, as from the cotton plant.

boll weevil *n.* A small beetle whose larvae damage cotton bolls.

bo-lo-gna (ba l´n) *n.* A seasoned, smoked sausage.

bol-ster (bl´str) *n.* A long, round pillow.

bolt (blt) *n.* A threaded metal pin designed with a head at one end and a removable nut at the other; a thunderbolt; a quick flash of lightning; a large roll of material. **bolt** *v.* To run or move suddenly.

bomb (bom) *n.* A weapon that is detonated upon impact releasing destructive material as gas or smoke. *Slang* A complete and total failure.

bom-bard (bom bärd´) *v.* To attack repeatedly with missiles or bombs. **bombarder** *n.* **bombardment** *n.*

bom-bast (bom´bast) *n.* Very ornate speech.

bombed *adj. Slang* Drunk.

bomb-er (bom´r) *n.* A military aircraft that carries and drops bombs.

bo-na fide (b´na fd´) *adj.* Performed in good faith; genuine; authentic.

bo-nan-za (ba nan´za) *n.* A profitable pocket or vein of ore; great prosperity.

bond (bond) *n.* Something that fastens or binds together; a duty or binding agreement; an insurance agreement in which the agency guarantees to pay the employer in the event an employee is accused of causing financial loss.

bond-age (bond´ij) *n.* Slavery; servitude.

bonds-man (bondz´man) *n.* One who agrees to provide bond for someone else.

bone (bn) *n.* The calcified connecting tissue of the skeleton. **bone** *v.*

bone--dry *adj.* Completely without water.

bon-er (b´nr) *n. Slang* A mistake or blunder.

bon-kers *adj. Slang* Acting in a crazy fashion.

bon-net (bon´it) *n.* A woman's hat that ties under the chin.

bon-ny (bon´) *adj.* Attractive or pleasing; pretty.

bo-nus (bō´nəs) n. pl. **-nuses** Something that is given over and above what is expected.

bon voy-age (bon voi äzh´) n. A farewell wish for a traveler to have a pleasant and safe journey.

boo (bö) n. Verbal expression showing disapproval or contempt.

boog-ie v. Slang To dance especially to rock and roll music.

book (bek) n. A group of pages fastened along the left side and bound between a protective cover; literary work that is written or printed. **Book** The Bible.

book-ing n. A scheduled engagement.

book-keep-ing (bek´k´ping) n. The business of recording the accounts and transactions of a business. **-er** n.

boom (böm) n. A deep, resonant sound; a long pole extending to the top of a derrick giving support to guide lifted objects. v. To cause to flourish or grow swiftly.

boo-mer-ang (bö´mə rang´) n. A curved, flat missile that can be thrown so that it returns to the thrower.

boon (bön) n. Something that is pleasant or beneficial; a blessing; favor.

boon-docks n. pl. Slang Back country; a rural area.

boor (ber) n. A person with clumsy manners and little refinement; rude person.

boost (böst) v. To increase; to raise or lift by pushing up from below. n. An increase in something.

boot (böt) n. A protective covering for the foot; any protective sheath or covering. computer science; to load a computer with an operating system or other software.

boo-tee (bö t´) n. A soft, knitted sock for a baby.

booth (böth) n. A small enclosed compartment or area; display area at trade shows for displaying merchandise for sale; an area in a restaurant with a table and benches.

boot-leg (böt´leg´) v. Slang. To sell, make, or transport liquor illegally.

booze (böz) n. Slang. An alcoholic drink.

bor-der (bor´dr) n. A surrounding mar-

gin or edge; a political or geographic boundary.

bore (br) v. To make a hole through or in something using a drill; to become tired, repetitious, or dull. **boredom** n.

bo-ric ac-id n. A colorless or white mixture that is used as a preservative and as a weak antiseptic.

born (born) adj. Brought into life or being; having an innate talent.

bo-ron (br´on) n. A soft, brown nonmetallic element used in nuclear reactor control elements, abrasives, and flares.

bor-ough (ber´) n. A self-governing incorporated town, found in some United States cities; an incorporated British town that sends one or more representatives to Parliament.

bor-row (bor´) v. To receive money with the intentions of returning it; to use another idea as one's own.

borscht (borsh) n. Hot or cold beet soup.

BOS abbr. Basic Operating System; the program that handles the routine functions of computer operations, such as accessing the diskdrive, displaying information on the screen, handling input and output, etc.

bos-om (bez´əm) n. The female's breasts; the human chest; the heart or center of something.

boss (bos) n. An employer or supervisor for whom one works. **boss** v. To command; to supervise. **bossy** adj.

bot-a-ny (bot´ə n) n. The science of plants. **botanical** adj. **botanist** n.

botch (boch) v. To ruin something by clumsiness; to repair clumsily. **botch-er** n.

both (bth) adj. Two in conjunction with one another.

both-er (both´r) v. To pester, harass, or irritate; to be concerned about something.

bot-tom (bot´əm) n. The lowest or deepest part of anything; the base; underside; the last; the land below a body of water. Informal The buttocks.

bottom line n. The end result; lowest line of a financial statement, showing net loss or gain.

bot-u-lism (boch´ə liz´əm) n. Food poisoning, often fatal, caused by bacteria that grows in improperly prepared food.

bough (bou) *n.* The large branch of a tree.

bouil-lon (bel´yon) *n.* A clear broth made from meat.

boul-der (bl´dr) *n.* A large round rock.

boul-e-vard (bel´a värd) *n.* A broad city street lined with trees.

bounce (bouns) *v.* To rebound or cause to rebound; to leap or spring suddenly; to be returned by a bank as being worthless or having no value.

bounc-er (boun´sr) *n.* A person who removes disorderly people from a public place.

bounc-ing (boun´sing) *adj.* Healthy; vigorous; robust; lively and spirited.

bound (bound) *n.* A leap or bounce. *v.* To limit; to be tied.

bound-a-ry (boun´da r) *n. pl.* -ries A limit or border.

bound-en (boun´dan) *adj.* Under an obligation or agreement.

bound-er (boun´dr) *n.* A vulgar person.

bound-less (bound´lis) *adj.* Without limits.

boun-te-ous (boun´t as) *adj.* Plentiful or generous; giving freely. **-ly** *adv.*

boun-ti-ful (boun´t fal) *adj.* Abundant; plentiful. **bountifully** *adv.*

boun-ty (boun´t) *n.* Generosity; an inducement or reward given for the return of something; a good harvest.

bou-quet (b k´) *n.* A group of cut flowers; the aroma of wine.

bour-bon (ber´bon) *n.* Whiskey distilled from fermented corn mash.

bour-geois (ber´zhwä) *n.* A member of the middle class. **bourgeois** *adj.*

bout (bout) *n.* A contest or match; the length of time spent in a certain way.

bou-tique (bö tk´) *n.* A small retail shop that sells specialized gifts, accessories, and fashionable clothes.

bou-ton-niere (böt´o nr´) *n.* A flower worn in the buttonhole of a man's jacket.

bow (bou) *n.* The front section of a boat or ship; bending of the head or waist to express a greeting or courtesy; a weapon made from a curved stave and strung taut to launch arrows; a rod strung with horsehair, used for playing stringed instruments.

bow-el (bou´al) *n.* The digestive tract located below the stomach; the intestines.

bowl (bl) *n.* A hemispherical container for food or liquids; a bowl-shaped part, as of a spoon or ladle; a bowl-shaped stadium. **bowl** *v.* To participate in the game of bowling.

bowl-er (b´ler) *n.* A person who bowls.

bow-sprit (bou´sprit) *n.* A spar that projects forward from the stem of a ship.

box (boks) *n.* A small container or chest, usually with a lid; a special area in a theater that holds a small group of people; a shrub or evergreen with leaves and hard wood that is yellow in color. *v.* To fight with the fists.

box-car (boks´kär´) *n.* An enclosed railway car used for the transportation of freight.

box office *n.* An office where theatre tickets are purchased.

boy (boi) *n.* A male youth or child.

boy-cott (boi´kot) *v.* To abstain from dealing with, buying, or using as a means of protest.

bra (brä) *n.* Brassiere.

brace (brs) *n.* A device that supports or steadies something. **brace** *v.*

brace-let (brs´lit) *n.* An ornamental band for the wrist.

brack-en (brak´an) *n.* A large species of fern with tough stems and finely divided fronds.

brack-et (brak´it) *n.* A support attached to a vertical surface that projects in order to hold a shelf or other weight. *v.* To enclose a word in brackets ( ).

bract (brakt) *n.* A leaf-like plant below a flower cluster or flower.

brad (brad) *n.* A nail that tapers to a small head.

brag (brag) *v.* To assert or talk boastfully.

brag-gart (brag´art) *n.* A person who brags.

braid (brd) *v.* To interweave three or more strands of something; to plait.

braille (brl) *n.* A system of printing for the blind, consisting of six dots, two across and four directly under the first two. Numbers and letters are represented by raising certain dots in each group of six.

brain (brn) n. The large mass of nerve tissue enclosed in the cranium, responsible for the interpretation of sensory impulses, control of the body, and coordination; the center of thought and emotion in the body.

braise (brz) v. To cook by first browning in a small amount of fat, adding a liquid such as water, and then simmering in a covered container.

brake (brk) n. A device designed to stop or slow the motion of a vehicle or machine.

bram-ble (bram´bl) n. A prickly shrub or plant such as the raspberry or blackberry bush.

bran (bran) n. The husk of cereal grains that is separated from the flour.

branch (branch) n. An extension from the main trunk of a tree. v. To divide into different subdivisions.

brand (brand) n. A trademark or label that names a product; a mark of disgrace or shame; a mark of charred or burning wood; a mark made by a hot iron to show ownership.

brand-new (brand´nō´) adj. Unused and new.

brash (brash) adj. Hasty, rash, and unthinking; insolent; impudent.

brass (bras) n. An alloy of zinc, copper and other metals in lesser amounts. Slang. A high-ranking officer in the military.

bras-siere (bra zr´) n. A woman's under- garment with cups to support the breasts.

brass tacks n. pl. The details of immediate, practical importance.

brat (brat) n. An ill-mannered child.

brat-wurst n. A fresh pork sausage.

bra-va-do (bra vä´d) n. A false showing of bravery.

brave (brv) adj. Having or displaying courage. brave n. An American Indian warrior.

bra-vo (brä´v) interj. Expressing approval.

brawl (brol) n. A noisy argument or fight.

brawn (brän) n. Well-developed and solid muscles. **brawniness** n. -y adj.

bray (br) v. To make a loud cry like a donkey.

braze (brz) v. To solder using a nonferrous alloy that melts at a lower temperature than that of the metals being joined together.

bra-zen (br´zan) adj. Made of brass; shameless or impudent.

bra-zier (br´zhr) n. A person who works with brass; a metal pan that holds burning charcoal or coals.

breach (brch) n. Ruptured, broken, or torn condition or area; a break in friendly relations. v. To break the law or obligation.

breach of promise n. The violation of a promise.

breadth (bredth) n. The distance or measurement from side to side; width.

bread-win-ner (bred´win´r) n. The one whose wages supports a household.

break (brk) v. To separate into parts with violence or suddenness; to collapse or give way; to change suddenly. Informal A stroke of good luck.

break-age (br´kij) n. Things that are broken.

breakdown (brk´doun´) n. Failure to function.

break-er (br´kr) n. A wave that breaks into foam.

break-fast (brek´fost) n. The first meal of the day.

breast (brest) n. The milk-producing glandular organs on a woman's chest; the area of the body from the neck to the abdomen.

breast-bone (brest´bn´) n. The sternum.

breast-plate (brest´plt´) n. A metal plate worn on the chest for protection.

breath (breth) n. The air inhaled and exhaled in breathing; a very slight whisper, fragrance, or breeze.

breathe (brth) v. To draw air into and expel from the lungs; to take a short rest.

breath-tak-ing (breth´t´king) adj. Astonishing; awesome. -ly adv.

breech (brch) n. The buttocks; the hind end of the body; the part of a gun or firearm located at the rear of the bore.

breeches n. plural Trousers that fit tightly around the knees.

breed (brd) v. The genetic strain of any domestic animal developed and maintained by mankind. **breeding** n.

breeze (brz) n. A slight gentle wind; something that is accomplished with very little effort. **breezy** adj.

bre-vi-a-ry (br´v er´) n. A book that contains prayers and psalms for the canonical hours.

brev-i-ty (brev´i t) n. pl. **-ties** A brief duration; conciseness.

brew (brö) v. To make beer from malt and hops by boiling, infusion, and germination.

brew-er-y (brö´a r) n. A building or plant where beer or ale is brewed.

bribe (brb) v. To influence or induce by giving a token or anything of value for a service.

brib-ery (br´ba r) n. The practice of giving or receiving a bribe.

bricabrac (brik´a brak´) n. A collection of small objects.

brick (brik) n. A molded block of baked clay, usually rectangular in shape.

brick-work (brik´wurk´) adj. Relating to a bride or a nuptial ceremony.

bride (brd) n. A women just married or about to be married.

bride-groom (brd´grōm´) n. A man just married or about to be married.

brides-maid (brdz´md´) n. A woman who attends a bride at her wedding.

bridge (brij) n. A structure that provides passage over a depression or obstacle; a card game for four players.

bridge-work (brij´werk´) n. The construction of dental work.

bri-dle (brd´al) n. A harness used to restrain or guide a horse **bridler** n.

brief (brf) n. A concise, formal statement of a client's case. adj. Short in duration. v. To summarize or inform in a short statement. **briefly** adv. **-ness** n.

bri-er (br´r) n. A woody, thorny, or prickly plant.

brig (brig) n. A prison on a ship; a twin-masted, square-rigged sailing ship.

bri-gade (bri gd´) n. A military unit organized for a specific purpose.

brig-and (brig´and) n. A person who lives as a robber; bandit.

bright (brt) adj. Brilliant in color; vivid; shining; emitting or reflecting light;

happy; cheerful; lovely. **brightness** n.

bril-liant (bril´yant) adj. Very bright and shiny; sparkling; radiant; extraordinarily intelligent.

brim (brim) n. The edge or rim of a cup.

brim-ful (brim´fel) adj. Completely full.

brim-stone (brim´stn´) n. Sulfur.

brin-dle (brin´dl) adj. Having dark streaks or flecks on a gray or tawny background.

brine (brn) n. Water saturated with salt; the water contained in the oceans and seas.

bring (bring) v. To carry with oneself to a certain place; to cause, act, or move in a special direction.

brink (bringk) n. The upper edge or margin of a very steep slope.

bri-oche (br´sh) n. A roll made from flour, eggs, butter, and yeast.

bri-quette (bri ket´) n. A small brick-shaped piece of charcoal.

brisk (brisk) adj. Moving or acting quickly; being sharp in tone or manner; energetic, invigorating or fresh. **briskly** adv.

bris-ket (bris´kit) n. The meat from the lower chest or breast of an animal.

bris-ling (bris´ling) n. A small fish that is processed like a sardine.

bris-tle (bris´al) n. Short, stiff, coarse hair. v. To react in angry defiance. **bristly** adj.

britch-es (brich´iz) n. pl.Trousers; breeches.

brit-tle (brit´l) adj. Very easy to break; fragile.

bro abbr. Brother.

broach (brch) n. A tapered and serrated tool used for enlarging and shaping a hole.

broad (brod) adj. Covering a wide area; from side to side; clear; bright. **-ly** adv.

broad-cast (brod´kast´) v. To transmit a program by television; to make widely known.

broad-cloth (brod´kloth´) n. A textured woolen cloth with a lustrous finish.

broad-en (brod´n) v. To become or make broad or broader.

broad-mind-ed (brod´mn´did) adj. Tolerant of varied views; liberal. **broadmindedness** n.

broad-side (brod´sd´) *n.* The side of a ship that is above the water line; a sheet of paper printed on both sides and then folded.

bro-cade (br kd´) *n.* A silk fabric with raised patterns in silver and gold.

broc-co-li (brok´a l) *n.* A green vegetable from the cauliflower family, eaten before the small buds open.

bro-chure (br shor´) *n.* A booklet or pamphlet.

bro-gan (br´gan) *n.* A sturdy oxford shoe.

broil (broil) *v.* To cook by exposure to direct radiant heat.

broil-er (broi´lr) *n.* A device, usually a part of a stove, that is used for broiling meat; a young chicken.

broke (brk) *adj.* Penniless; completely without money.

bro-ken (br´ken) *adj.* Separated violently into parts.

broken home *n.* A family situation in which the parents are not living together.

bro-ker (br´kr) *n.* A person who acts as a negotiating agent for contracts, sales, or purchases in return for payment.

bro-ker-age (br´kr ij) *n.* The establishment of a broker.

bro-mide (br´md) *n.* A compound of bromine with other elements; a sedative; a common place idea or notion.

bro-mine (br´mn) *n.* A nonmetallic element of a deep, red, toxic liquid that gives off a disagreeable odor.

bron-chi-al (brong´k al) *adj.* Pertaining to the bronchi or their extensions.

bron-chus (brong´kus) *n.* Either of two main branches of the trachea that lead directly to the lungs.

bron-to-saur (bron´ta sor´) *n.* A very large dinosaur.

bronze (bronz) *n.* An alloy of tin, copper, and zinc; moderate olive brown to yellow in color. **bronze** *v.* **bronze** *adj.*

Bronze Age *n.* Human culture between the Iron Age and the Stone Age.

brooch (brch) *n.* A large decorative pin.

brood (brd) *n.* The young of an animal; a family of young. *v.* To produce by incubation; to hatch; to think about at length.

brook (brek) *n.* A small fresh-water stream that contains many rocks.

bros *abbr.* Brothers.

broth (broth) *n.* The liquid in which fish, meat, or vegetables have been cooked; also called stock.

broth-el (broth´l) *n.* A house of prostitution; whorehouse.

broth-er (bruth´r) *n.* A male who shares the same parents as another person. **brotherly** *adj.* **brotherliness** *n.*

brougham (brö´am) *n.* A vehicle without a cover on the driver's seat.

brought *v.* The past tense of bring.

brow (brou) *n.* The ridge above the eye where the eyebrow grows.

brow-beat (brou´bt´) *v.* To bully; dominate; intimidate.

brown (broun) *n.* A color between yellow and red; a dark or tanned complexion.

brown-out (broun´out´) *n.* An interruption of electrical power.

brown sugar *n.* Sugar with crystals covered by a film or refined dark syrup.

browse (brouz) *v.* To look over something in a leisurely and casual way.

bruise (bröz) *n.* An injury that ruptures small blood vessels and discolors the skin without breaking it.

brunch (brunch) *n.* A combination of a late breakfast and an early lunch.

bru-net *or* **bru-nette (brö net´)** *adj.* A person with dark brown hair.

brunt (brunt) *n.* The principal shock, or force.

bru-tal (bröt´al) *adj.* Very harsh or cruel treatment. **brutality** *n.* **-ly** *adv.*

brute (bröt) *n.* A person characterized by physical power rather than intelligence; a person who behaves like an animal.

bub-ble (bub´l) *n.* A small round object, usually hollow; a small body of gas contained in a liquid. **bubble** *v.* To produce bubbles.

bu-bon-ic plague (b bon´ik plg´) *n.* The contagious and normally fatal disease that is transmitted by fleas from infected rats, characterized by fever, diarrhea, chills, and vomiting.

buck (buk) *n.* The adult male deer; the lowest grade in a military category. **buck** *v.* To throw a rider; to oppose the system. *n. Slang* A dollar.

buck-et (buk´it) *n.* A vessel used to carry liquids or solids; a pail.

buckle (buk´l) *v.* To warp, crumple, or bend under pressure. *n.* Metal clasp for fastening one part to another.

bud (bud) *n.* Something that has not developed completely; a small structure that contains flowers or leaves that have not developed.

budge (buj) *v.* To give way to; to cause to move slightly.

bud-get (buj´it) *n.* The total amount of money allocated for a certain purpose.

buff (buf) *n.* A leather made mostly from skins of buffalo, elk, or oxen, having the color of light to moderate yellow.

buf-fa-lo (buf´a l) *n.* A wild ox with heavy forequarters, short horns, and a large muscular hump. *v.* To bewilder, to intimidate.

buf-fet (ba f´) *n.* A meal placed on a side table so that people may serve themselves; a side table for serving food.

buffet (bafit) *v.* To strike sharply with the hand.

bug (bug) *n.* Any small insect; a concealed listening device. **bug** *v.* To bother or annoy.

bug-gy (bug´) *n.* A small carriage pulled behind a horse.

bu-gle (b´gal) *n.* A brass instrument without keys or valves. **bugle** *v.*

build (bild) *v.* To erect by uniting materials into a composite whole; to fashion or create; to develop or add to. **build** *n.* The form or structure of a person.

build-ing (bil´ding) *n.* A roofed and walled structure for permanent use.

builtin (bilt´in´) *adj.* Containing something within a structure.

bulb (bulb) *n.* A rounded underground plant such as a tulip that lies dormant in the winter and blooms in the spring; an incandescent light for electric lamps. **bulbous** *adj.* Resembling a bulb in shape.

bulge (bulj) *n.* A swelling of the surface caused by pressure from within. **bulge** *v.* **bulgy** *adj.*

bulk (bulk) *n.* A large mass; anything that has great size, volume, or units. **bulky** *adj.*

bulk-head (bulk´hed´) *n.* The partition that divides a ship into compartments; a retaining wall along a waterfront.

bul-let (bul´it) *n.* A cylindrical projectile that is fired from a gun.

bul-le-tin (bul´i tan) *n.* A broadcasted statement of public interest; a public notice.

bul-lion (bul´yan) *n.* Refined gold or silver in the uncoined state.

bull-ish (bul´ish) *adj.* Tending to cause or hopeful of rising prices, as in the stock market.

bul-ly (bel´) *n. pl.* **-ies** A person who is mean or cruel to weaker people.

bul-rush (bul´rush´) *n.* Tall grass as found in a marsh.

bul-wark (bul´wrk) *n.* A strong protection or support.

bum (bum) *n.* One who begs from others; one who spends time unemployed. *v.* To loaf.

bum-mer (bum´r) *Slang* Depressing.

bump (bump) *v.* To collide with, knock, or strike something. *n.* A swelling or lump on a person's body.

bump-er (bum´pr) *n.* A device on the front of vehicles that absorbs shock and prevents damage.

bump-tious (bump´shus) *adj.* Crudely self-assertive and forward; pushy.

bun (bun) *n.* Any of a variety of plain or sweet small breads; tightly rolled hair that resembles a bun.

bunch (bunch) *n.* A cluster or group of items that are the same.

bun-dle (bun´dl) *n.* Anything wrapped or held together. *Slang* A large amount of money.

bundle up. *v.* To dress warmly, usually using many layers of clothing.

bun-ga-low (bung´ga l´) *n.* A small one- story cottage.

bun-gle (bung´gl) *v.* To work or act awkwardly or clumsily. **bungler** *v.*

bun-ion (bun´yan) *n.* An inflamed, painful swelling of the first joint of the big toe.

bunk (bungk) *n.* A narrow bed that is built in; one of a tier of berths on a ship.

bun-ker (bung´kr) *n.* A tank for storing fuel on a ship; an embankment or a sand trap creating a hazard on a golf course.

bunt (bunt) v. To tap a pitched ball with a half swing. n. The center of a square sail.

bunt-ing (bun´ting) n. A hooded blanket for a baby.

buoy (bō´) n. A floating object to mark a channel or danger. v. To stay afloat.

buoy-an-cy (boi´an s) n. The tendency of an object or body to remain afloat in liquid or to rise in gas or air.

bur-den (ber´dan) n. Something that is hard to bear; a duty or responsibility; a ship's capacity for carrying cargo.

bu-reau (bur´) n. pl. **bureaus.** A low chest for storing clothes; a branch of the government or a subdivision of a department.

bu-reauc-ra-cy (b rok´r s) n. pl. **bureaucracies.** A body of nonelected officials in a government; the administration of a government through bureaus.

burg-er (ber´gr) n. Slang A hamburger.

bur-glar (ber´glr) n. A person who steals personal items from another person's home.

bur-glar-ize (ber´gla rz´) v. To commit burglary.

bur-gla-ry (ber´gla r) n. The breaking into and entering of a private home with the intent to steal.

bur-i-al (ber´ al) n. The process or act of burying.

burl (burl) n. A woody, often flat and hard, hemispherical growth on a tree.

bur-lap (ber´lap) n. A coarse cloth woven from hemp or jute.

bur-lesque (br lesk´) n. Theatrical entertainment with comedy and mocking imitations.

bur-ly (ber´l) adj. Very heavy and strong.

burn (bern) v. To be destroyed by fire; to consume fuel and give off heat. **burn** n. An injury produced by fire, heat, or steam; the firing of a rocket engine in space.

burn-er (bern´r) n. The part of a fuel-burning device where the fire is contained.

bur-nish (ber´nish) v. To make shiny by rubbing; to polish.

burnt (bernt) adj. Affected by burning.

burp (berp) n. A belch.

bur-ro (ber´) n. A small donkey.

bur-row (ber´) n. A tunnel dug in the ground by an animal.

bur-sar (ber´sr) n. The person or official in charge of monies at a college.

bur-si-tis (ber s´tis) n. An inflammation of the small sac between a tendon of the knee, elbow, or shoulder joints.

burst (berst) adj. To explode or experience a sudden outbreak; to very suddenly become visible or audible. **burst** n. A sudden explosion or outburst.

bus (bus) n. pl. **busses** A large passenger vehicle.

bush (bush) n. A low plant with branches near the ground; a dense tuft or growth; land that is covered densely with undergrowth.

bushed (busht) adj. Extremely exhausted; tired.

bush-el (bush´l) n. A unit of dry measurement which equals four pecks or 2,150.42 cubic inches; a container that holds a bushel.

bush-ing (bush´ing) n. A metal lining that reduces friction.

busi-ness (biz´nes) n. A person's professional dealings or occupation; an industrial or commercial establishment.

bust (bust) n. A sculpture that resembles the upper part of a human body; the breasts of a women. **bust** v. To break or burst; to become short of money.

bus-tle (bus´al) n. A padding that gives extra bulk to the back of a woman's skirt.

bus-y (biz´) adj. Full of activity; engaged in some form of work. **busily** adv.

busy-body (biz´ bod´) n. An inquisitive person who interferes with someone else's business.

but (but) conj. On the contrary to; other than; if not; except for the fact.

bu-tane (b´tn) n. A gas produced from petroleum, used as a fuel, refrigerant and aerosol propellant.

butch-er (buch´r) n. One who slaughters animals and dresses them for food.

but-ler (but´lr) n. A male servant of a household.

butt (but) *n.* The object of ridicule; the thick, large or blunt end of something.

butt *v.* To hit with horns or the head; to be joined end to end.

butte (bt) *n.* A small mountain with steep, precipitous sides with a smaller summit area than a mesa.

but-ter (but´r) *n.* A yellow substance churned from milk.

but-tocks (but´ox) *n. pl.* The two round fleshy parts of the rump.

but-ton (but´on) *n.* A small disk that interlocks with a button hole to close a piece of garment.

but-tress (bu´tris) *n.* A support made of either brick or stone.

butyl alcohol *n.* Chemically related form of alcohol that contains the butyl radical, used in manufacturing perfumes, lacquers and other organic compounds.

bux-om (buk´som) *adj.* Lively; full of life; happy; pleasantly plump. **buxomness** *n.*

buy (b) *v.* To purchase in exchange for money. *n.* Anything that is bought.

buy-er (b´r) *n.* A person who buys from a store or an individual.

buzz (buz) *v.* To make a low vibrating sound, as a bee.

buz-zard (buz´rd) *n.* A broad-winged vulture from the same family as the hawk.

buzz-er (buz´r) *n.* An electrical signaling device that makes a buzzing sound.

by (by) *prep. & adv.* Up to and beyond; to go past; not later than; next to; according to; in proximity to.

bye (b) *n.* A position in which a contestant has no opponent after pairs are drawn for a tournament, and, therefore, advances to the next round.

bye-bye *Slang* Farewell.

by-gone (b´gon´) *adj.* Gone by; past.

by-law (b´lo) *n.* A rule or law governing internal affairs of a group or organization.

byproduct (b´prod´ukt) *n.* Material that is left over when something is manufactured but also has a market value of its own.

byte (bt) *n.* In computer science, a sequence of adjacent binary digits operated on as a unit.

by-way (b´wa) *n.* A secondary field of study; a side road; an unfrequented path.

C

C, c (s) The third letter of the English alphabet; the Roman numeral for 100.

cab (kab) *n.* A taxi cab; the compartment where a person sits to drive a large truck or machinery.

ca-bal (ka bal´) *n.* A group that conspires against a government or other public institution.

cab-a-ret (kab´a r´) *n.* A restaurant that provides dancing and live entertainment.

ca-ble (k´bl) *n.* A heavy rope made from fiber or steel; a bound group of insulated conductors; a cablegram.

ca-ca-o (ka k´) *n.* Any tree of the chocolate family; the dried seed of the cacao tree from which chocolate and cocoa are made.

cach-a-lot (kash´a lot´) *n.* A sperm whale.

cache (kash) *n.* A safe place to hide and conceal goods. **cache** *v.*

ca-chet (ka sh´) *n.* A mark of distinction or authenticity; a seal on a letter or an important document showing that it is official.

ca-coph-o-ny (ka kof´a n) *n.* A harsh and disagreeable sound. **-honous** *adj.*

cad (kad) *n.* An ungentlemanly man.

ca-dav-er (ka dav´r) *n.* The body of a person who has died; pale and gaunt.

ca-dence (kd´ens) *n.* A rhythmic movement or flow.

ca-den-za (ka den´za) *n.* An elaborate ornamental section for a soloist near the end of a concerto.

ca-det (ka det´) *n.* A student in training at a naval or military academy.

cadge (kaj) *v.* To beg or to receive by begging; to mooch. **cadger** *n.*

cad-re (ka´dra) *n.* The group of trained personnel that forms the heart of an organization.

ca-du-ce-us (ka dö´s us) *n.* The symbol of the medical profession, a winged staff entwined with two serpents entwined around it.

cae-su-ra (si zher´a) *n.* A pause or break in a line of verse or poetry.

caf-feine (ka fn´) n. A stimulant found in coffee, tea, and dark colas.

caf-tan (kaf´tan) n. A loose-fitting, full-length garment worn in the Near East.

ca-gey (k´j) adj. Shrewd, wary, or cautious.

cais-son (k´san) n. A waterproof structure that is used for construction work underwater.

ca-jole (ka jl´) v. To wheedle or coax someone into doing something.

cal-a-mine (kal´a mn´) n. A pink powder of zinc oxide and ferric oxide mixed with mineral oils to form a lotion for skin irritations such as poison ivy.

ca-lam-i-ty (ka lam´i t) n. pl. **-ies** Misfortune or great distress. **-itous** adj.

cal-car-e-ous (kal kâr´ us) adj. Having the characteristics of or made up of calcium, calcium carbonate, or lime stone.

cal-ci-fy (kal´si´f) v. To become or make chalky or stony. **calcification** n.

cal-ci-mine (kal´si mn´) n. A tinted or white liquid that contains water, glue, coloring matter, and zinc oxide.

cal-cine (kal´sn) v. To heat to a high temperature without melting, but causing loss of moisture and reduction. **calcination** n.

cal-ci-um (kal´s um) n. The alkaline element that is found in teeth and bones; the element symbolized by Ca.

calcium chloride n. A deliquescent salt, white in color, used in its dry state as a dehumidifying agent and in its moist state for controlling ice and dust on roads.

cal-cu-late (kal´k lt) v. To figure by a mathematical process, to evaluate; to estimate. **-lable** adj. **calculative** adj.

cal-cu-lat-ed (kal´k l´tid) adj. Worked out beforehand with careful estimation.

cal-cu-lat-ing (kal´k l´ting) adj. Shrewd consideration of self-interest.

cal-cu-la-tor (kal´k l´tr) n. A machine with a keyboard for automatic mathematical operation.

cal-cu-lus (kal´k lus) n. pl. **-es** A stone in the gallbladder or kidneys; the mathematics of integral and differential calculus.

cal-en-dar (kal´an dr) n. A system for showing time divisions by years, months, weeks, and days; the twelve months in a year.

cal-en-der (kal´an dr) n. A machine that makes paper and cloth smooth and glossy.

cal-ends (kal´endz) n. The first day of the new moon.

cal-i-ber (kal´i br) n. The inner diameter of a tube or gun; the quality or worth of something.

cal-i-per (kal´i pr) n. An instrument with two curved, hinged legs, used to measure inner and outer dimensions.

ca-liph (k´lif) n. A religious and secular head in Islam. **caliphate** n.

cal-is-then-ics (kal´is then´iks) n. Exercises that develop muscular tone and promote good physical condition.

call (kol) v. To call out to someone; to name or designate; to telephone; to pay a short visit; to demand payment; in card games, to demand the opponent show his cards; to stop officially.

cal-lig-ra-phy (ka lig´ra f) n. The art of writing with a pen using different slants and positions.

cal-li-o-pe (ka l´o p´) n. A keyboard musical instrument that is fitted with steam whistles.

cal-lous (kal´us) adj. Having calluses; to be without emotional feelings. **callously** adv.

calm (kom) adj. Absence of motion; having little or no wind, storms, or rough water.

cal-o-mel (kal´o mel´) n. A white, tasteless compound used as a purgative.

cal-o-rie (kal´a r) n. pl. **-ries** A measure ment of the amount of heat or energy produced by food. **caloric** adj.

cal-o-rim-e-ter (kal o rim´i tr) n. An instrument for measuring heat.

ca-lum-ni-ate pl. **-nies** To slander; to malign.

cal-um-ny (kal´am n) n. pl. **-nies** A state ment that is malicious, false, and damaging to someone's reputation.

calve (kav) v. To give birth to a calf.

ca-lyx (ka´liks) n. pl. **calyces** The outer cover of a flower.

cam (kam) n. A curved wheel used to produce a reciprocating motion.

ca-ma-ra-de-rie (kä'mə rä'də r) n. Good will among friends.

cam-ber (kam'br) n. A slight curve upward in the middle.

cam-bric (km'brik) n. A cotton fabric or white linen.

came (km) n. A grooved lead bar that is used to hold together the panes of glass in latticework or stained glass windows. v. Past tense of come.

cam-el (kam'el) n. An animal used in desert regions, having either one or two humps on its back.

ca-mel-lia (kə ml'yə) n. A shrub with shiny green leaves and various colored flowers.

ca-mel-o-pard (kə mel'o pärd) n. A giraffe.

cam-er-a (kam'er ə) n. An apparatus for taking photographs in a lightproof enclosure with an aperture and shuttered lens through which the image is focused and recorded on photosensitive film.

cam-i-sole (kam'i sl) n. A woman's short, sleeveless undergarment.

cam-ou-flage (kam'ə fläzh') v. To disguise by creating the effect of being part of the natural surroundings.

camp (kamp) n. A temporary lodging or makeshift shelter.

cam-paign (kam pn') n. An organized operation designed to bring about a particular political, commercial, or social goal.

cam-pa-ni-le (kam'pə n'l) n. pl. -iles A freestanding bell tower that is associated with a church.

camp-er (kam'pr) n. A person who camps in makeshift shelters for recreation; a vehicle specially equipped for casual travel and camping.

cam-phor (kam'fr) n. A crystalline compound used as an insect repellent.

camp-site n. The area used for camping.

cam-pus (kam'pus) n. The buildings and grounds of a college, school, or university.

cam-shaft (kam'shaft) n. The shaft of an engine that is fitted with cams.

ca-nal (kə nal') n. A man-made water channel for irrigating land.

ca-nal-ize (kə nal'z) v. To convert into canals; to make new canals.

can-cel (kan'sel) v. To invalidate or annul; to cross out; to neutralize; in mathematics, to remove a common factor from the numerator and the denominator of a fraction; in computer science, to abort or stop a procedure or program.

can-cer (kan'ser) n. A malignant tumor that invades healthy tissue and spreads to other areas; the disease marked by such tumors. **cancerous** adj.

can-de-la-bra (kan'de lä'brə) n. pl. **candelabrum** A decorative candlestick with several branching arms for candles.

can-did (kan'did) adj. Free from bias, malice, or prejudice; honest and sincere.

can-di-date (kan'di dt) n. A person who is, aspires to or is nominated or qualified for a membership, award, or office. **candidacy** n. **candidature** n.

can-dor (kan'dr) n. Straightforwardness; frankness of expression.

cane (kn) n. A pithy or hollow, flexible, jointed stem of bamboo or rattan that is split for basketry or wickerwork; a walking stick.

can-ker (kang'kr) n. An ulcerated sore in the mouth.

canned (kand) adj. Preserved and sealed under pressure.

can-ner-y (kan'e r) n. pl. -ies A company that processes canned meat, vegetables, and other foods.

can-ny (kan') adj. Thrifty; careful; cautious; shrewd. **cannily, canniness** n.

ca-noe (kə nö') n. A lightweight, slender boat with pointed ends which moves by paddling.

cant (kant) n. The external angle of a building. v. To throw off by tilting.

can't (kant) Can not.

can-ta-bi-le (kän tä'bi l') n. A lyrical, flowing style of music.

can-ta-loupe (kan'ta lp') n. A sweettasting, orange-colored muskmelon.

can-tan-ker-ous (kan tang'kr us) adj. Bad-tempered and argumentative.

can-ta-ta (kan tä'ta) n. A drama that is sung but not acted.

can-ter (kan'tr) n. An easy lope just a little slower than a gallop, but faster than a trot.

can-ti-lev-er (kan´ti lev´r) n. A long structure, such as a beam, supported only at one end.

can-ton (kan´ton) n. A small area of a country divided into parts. **-al** adj.

can-tor (kan´tr) n. The chief singer in a synagogue.

can-vas (kan´vas) n. A heavy fabric used in making tents and sails for boats; a piece of canvas that is used for oil paintings.

can-vass (kan´vas) v. To travel through a region to solicit opinions or votes; to take a poll or survey. **canvasser** n.

can-yon (kan´yun) n. A deep and narrow gorge with steep sides.

ca-pa-ble (k´pa bl) adj. Having the ability to perform in an efficient way; qualified.

ca-pa-cious (ka p´shus) adj. Having a lot of room or space.

ca-pac-i-tance (ka pas´i tans) n. The property of a body or circuit which allows it to store an electrical charge. .

ca-pac-i-ty (ka pas´i t) n. pl. **-ies** The ability to contain, receive, or absorb; having the aptitude or ability to do something; the maximum production or output; in computer science, the total amount of data or information that can be processed, stored, or generated.

ca-par-i-son (ka par´i san) n. An ornamental covering for a horse, saddle, or harness.

cap-il-lary (kap´i ler´) n. pl. **-ies** Any of the small vessels that connect the veins and arteries. adj. Having a hairlike bore; very fine or small in size.

cap-i-tal-ism (kap´i ta liz´um) n. The economic system in which the means of distribution and production are privately owned and operated for private profit.

capitalist (kap´i ta list) n. A person who invests in a business. **capitalistic** adj.

cap-i-ta-tion (kap´i t´shan) n. A census or tax of equal amount for each person.

ca-pit-u-late (ka pich´u lt´) v. To surrender under terms of an agreement.

ca-price (ka prs´) n. A sudden change of action or mind without adequate reason; a whim. **capricious** adj.

cap-stan (kap´stan) n., Naut. A drum-like apparatus rotated to hoist weights by winding in a cable on a ship or boat.

cap-su-lated (kap´sa l´ted) adj. Formed or in a capsule-like state. **-tion** n.

cap-sule (kap´sul) n. A small gelatinous case for a dose of oral medicine; a fatty sac that surrounds an organ of the body, as the kidney, and protects it; a summary in a brief form.

cap-tion (kap´shan) n. A subtitle; a description of an illustration or picture.

cap-tious (kap´shus) adj. Deceptive; critical.

cap-ti-vate (kap´ti vt´) v. To hold the attention, fascinate, or charm a person or group of people. **captivation** n.

cap-tive (kap´tiv) n. A person being held as a prisoner.

cap-ture (kap´cher) v. To take something or someone by force. **-er** n.

car (kär) n. An automobile; an enclosed vehicle, as a railroad car.

ca-rafe (ka raf´) n. A glass bottle for serving wine or water.

car-a-mel (kar´a mel) n. A chewy substance primarily composed of sugar, butter, and milk.

car-a-mel-ize (kar´a ma lz) v. To make into caramel.

car-at (kar´at) n. The unit of weight for gems that equals 200 milligrams.

car-bide (kär´bd) n. A carbon compound with a more electropositive element.

car-bo-hy-drate (kär´b h´drt) n. A group of compounds, including starches, celluloses, and sugars that contain carbon, hydrogen, and oxygen.

car-bon (kär´bon) n. A nonmetallic element that occurs as a powdery noncrystalline solid; the element symbolized by C.

car-bon-ate (kär´bo nt´) v. To add or charge with carbon dioxide gas, as in a beverage.

car-bon di-ox-ide n. An odorless, colorless, nonflammable gas, removed from the atmosphere by the photosynthesis of plants and returned by the respiration of animals.

car-bon mon-ox-ide n. An odorless, colorless gas that is formed by the incomplete oxidation of carbon, burns with a blue flame, and is highly poisonous when inhaled.

car-bun-cle (kär´bung kl) *n.* An infection of the skin and deeper tissue which is red, inflamed, full of pus, and painful.

car-cass (kär´kas) *n.* The dead body of an animal; something that no longer has life.

car-ci-no-ma (kär´si n´ma) *n.* A malignant tumor; cancer. -**matous** *adj.*

car-di-ac (kär´d ak´) *adj.* Relating to the heart.

car-di-gan (kär´digan) *n.* A sweater with an opening down the front.

car-di-o-gram (kär´d o gram´) *n.* The curve recorded by a cardiograph and is used in the diagnosis of heart defects.

car-di-ol-o-gy (kär´d ol´o j) *n.* The study of the heart, its diseases, and treatments.

car-di-o-pul-mo-nary *adj.* Relating to the heart and lungs.

car-di-o-vas-cu-lar (kär´d vas´k lr) *adj.* Involving and relating to the heart and the blood vessels.

care (kâr) *n.* A feeling of concern, anxiety, or worry; guardianship or custody. *v.* To show interest or regard.

ca-reen (ka rn´) *v.* To lurch or twist from one side to another while moving rapidly.

ca-reer (ka rr´) *n.* The profession or occupation a person takes in life.

care-ful (kâr´ful) *adj.* Exercising care; cautious; watchful.

ca-ress (ka res´) *v.* To gently show affection by touching or stroking.

car-go (kär´g) *n.* Freight; the goods and merchandise carried on a ship, plane, or other vehicle.

car-ies (kâr´z) *n.* The decay of a bone or tooth.

car-il-lon (kar´i lon) *n.* A set of tuned bells in a tower, that are usually played by a keyboard.

car-mine (kär min) *n.* A vivid red color; crimson; deep purplish red.

car-nage (kär´nij) *n.* A bloody slaughter; war; massacre.

car-nal (kär´nal) *adj.* Relating to sensual desires. **carnality** *n.* **carnally** *adv.*

car-na-tion (kär n´shan) *n.* A fragrant perennial flower in a variety of colors.

car-ne-lian (kär nl´yan) *n.* A clear red

chalcedony that is used as a gem.

car-ni-vore (kär´ni vr´) *n.* A flesh-eating animal. **carnivorous** *adj.*

car-ol (kar´ol) *n* A song to celebrate joy or praise. **caroler** *n.* **carol** *v.*

ca-rouse (ka rouz´) *v.* To be rowdy and to be in a drunken state. **carouser** *n.*

car-pal (kär´pal) *adj.* Pertaining to the wrist and the bones in the wrist.

car-pel (kär´pel) *n., Bot.* A seed vessel or pistil.

car-pen-ter (kär´pen tr) *n.* A person who builds and repairs wooden structures.

car-port (kär´port) *n.* A roof attached to the side of a building to give shelter for a vehicle.

car-riage (kar´ij) *n.* A horse-drawn vehicle for passengers.

car-rot (kar´ot) *n.* An orange vegetable that is a root.

car-rou-sel (kar´a sel´) *n.* A merry-go-round.

car-tel (kär tel´) *n.* A group of independent companies that have organized to control prices, production, etc.

car-ti-lage (kär´ti lij) *n.* A tough, elastic substance of connective tissue attached to the surface of bones near the joints.

car-tog-ra-phy (kär tog´ra f) *n.* The art of developing charts and maps. **cartographer** *n.* **cartographic** *adj.*

car-ton (kär´ton) *n.* A container made from cardboard.

carve (kärv) *v.* To slice meat or poultry; to cut into something; to create, as sculpture.

cary-at-id (kar´ at´id) *n.* A supporting column sculptured in the form of a female figure.

cas-cade (kas kd´) *n.* A waterfall that flows over steep rocks.

casing (k´sing) *n.* A protective covering or container; the framework of a window or door.

ca-sein (k´sn) *n.* A dairy protein that is used in foods and in manufacturing adhesives and plastics.

cash-ier (ka shr´) *n.* An employee who handles cash as part of his job description; an officer in a bank in charge of receiving or distributing money.

cash-mere (kazh´mr) *n.* The wool from the Kashmir goat; the yarn made from this wool.

ca-si-no (ka sēn') *n. pl.* **-nos** A public establishment open especially for gambling.

cask (kask) *n.* A large wooden vessel or barrel; the quantity that a cask will hold.

cas-ket (kas'kit) *n.* A coffin; a small chest or box.

casque (kask) *n.* A helmet. **casqued** *adj.*

cas-se-role (kas'e rl') *n.* A dish in which the food is baked and also served; food cooked and served in this manner.

cas-sette (ka set') *n.* A cartridge of magnetic tape used in tape recorders to play and record.

cast-a-way (kast'a w') *adj.* Thrown away. *n.* One who is shipwrecked or discarded.

cas-tel-lat-ed (kas'te l'tid) *adj.* Adorned by battlements and turrets.

cas-ti-gate (kas'ti gt') *v.* To punish or criticize severely.

cast-ing (kas'ting) *n.* The act of one that casts.

cast-off *adj.* Discarded; thrown away.

cas-trate (kas'trt) *v.* To remove the testicles; to remove the ovaries; to spay.

ca-su-al (kazh'ö al) *adj.* Informal; occurring by chance. **-ly** *adv.* **-ness** *n.*

ca-su-al-ty (kazh'ö al t) *n. pl* **-ies** One who is injured or killed in an accident. *Milit.* A soldier who is killed, wounded, taken prisoner by the enemy, or missing in action.

cat (kat) *n.* A small domesticated animal, a pet; any of the animals in the cat family, such as the lion, lynx, tiger, etc.

cat-a-clysm (kat'a kliz'um) *n.* A sudden and violent disaster.

cat-a-combs *n.* An underground passage with small rooms for coffins.

cat-a-falque (kat'a falk') *n.* The structure that supports a coffin during a state funeral.

cat-a-log (kat'a log) *n.* A publication containing a list of names, objects, etc.

cat-a-lyst (kat'a list) *n., Chem.* Any substance that alters and decreases the time it takes a chemical reaction to occur.

cat-a-ma-ran (kat'a ma ran') *n.* A boat with twin hulls.

ca-tarrh (ka tär') *n., Pathol.* Inflam-

mation of the nose and throat. **catarrhal** *adj.*

ca-tas-tro-phe (ka tas'tro f) *n.* A terrible and sudden disaster; a calamity.

catch (kach) *v.* To take; to seize or capture; to reach in time; to intercept; to become entangled or fastened. **catch** *n.*

catch-all (kach'ol') *n.* A container or bag for odds and ends.

catch-er (kach'er) *n.* A person who catches; in baseball. *Slang* The position behind the batter.

cat-e-gor-i-cal (kat'a gor'i kal) *adj.* Absolute; certain; related to or included in a category without qualification.

cat-e-go-rize (kat'a go rz') *v.* To place in categories.

cat-e-go-ry (kat'a gr') *n. pl.* **-ries** A general group to which something belongs.

ca-ter (k'tr) *v.* To provide a food service; to bring directly to a location. **caterer** *n.*

cat-er-pil-lar (kat'a pil'er) *n.* The very fuzzy, worm-like, brightly-colored spiny larva of a moth or butterfly.

ca-the-dral (ka th'dral) *n.* A large and important church, containing the seat of a bishop.

cath-e-ter (kath'i tr) *n., Med.* A thin, flexible tube that is inserted into body cavities for drainage and to draw urine from the bladder.

cath-ode (kath'd) *n.* The negatively charged electrode which receives positively charged ions during electrolysis.

cathode ray tube *n.* The vacuum tube on which images are found, used in a computer screen.

cat-i-on (kat''on) *n.* A positively charged ion that is attracted in electrolytes to a negative electrode. **-ic** *adj.*

cat-nap (kat'nap') *n.* A short nap.

CAT scan *n.* A cross-sectional picture produced by a scanner, used to x-ray the body by using computerized axial tomography.

cat-tle (kat'al) *n. pl.* Farm animals raised for meat and dairy products.

cat-ty (kat') *adj.* Malicious or spiteful.

cau-cus (ko'kus) *n.* A meeting of a political party to make policy decisions and to select candidates.

caulk (kok) *v.* To seal seams and edges

against leakage of water and air.

cause (koz) v. To produce a result, consequence, or effect. n. A goal, principle; a reason; motive.

cau-se-rie (k´za r´) n. A short informal conversation or chat.

cause-way (koz´w´) n. A paved highway through a marsh tract; raised road over water.

cau-ter-ize (ko´ta rz´) v. To sear or burn with a hot instrument. **cauterization** n.

cau-ter-y (ko´ta r) n. A very hot instrument used to destroy tissue that does not seem normal.

cau-tion (ko´shan) n. A warning, careful planning. **cautionary** adj.

cau-tious (ko´shus) adj. Very careful.

cav-al-ry (kav´al r) n. pl. **-ies** Army troops trained to fight on horseback or in armored vehicles. **cavalryman** n.

cave (kv) n. An underground tomb or chamber with an opening at the ground surface.

ca-ve-at (k´v at´) n. A formal legal notice to stop the proceedings until both sides have a hearing; a warning or caution.

ca-vern (kav´ern) n. A very large underground cave. **cavernous** adj.

cav-i-ar or **cav-iare** (kav´ är´, kav´ är´) n. The eggs of large fish, eaten as an appetizer.

cav-i-ty (kav´i t) n. pl **-ies** A decayed place in a tooth; a hollow or hole.

CD Compact disk; civil defense; certificate of deposit.

cease (ss) v. To come to an end or put an end to; to stop.

cease-fire (ss´f er) v. To stop fighting, usually as a result of a truce.

cease-less (ss´lis) adj. Endless.

ce-cum or **cae-cum** (se´kum) Anat. The pouch where the large intestine begins.

ce-dil-la (si dil´a) n. A diacritical mark placed under the letter c in the French vocabulary to indicate a modification or alteration of the usual phonetic sound.

cel-e-brate (sel´e brt´) v. To observe with ceremonies, rejoicing, or festivity.

cel-leb-ri-ty (se leb´ri t) n. pl. A famous person.

ce-les-ta (se les´ta) n. A musical instrument which produces bell-like tones when the keyboard and metal plates are struck by hammers.

ce-les-tial (se les´chel) adj. Heavenly; spiritual.

cel-i-bate (sel´a bit) n. A person who remains unmarried because of religious vows; one who is sexually abstinent.

cell (sel) n. A prison; a small room; the smallest unit of any organism that is capable of independent function, is composed of a small mass of cytoplasm, usually encloses a central nucleus, and is surrounded by a membrane or a rigid cell wall; a cavity of an ovary or pericarp that is seed-bearing. *Electr.* The part of a battery that generates the electricity; in computer science, the location in memory that holds a single unit of information; a byte.

cel-lar (sel´er) n. An underground area, beneath a building, used for storage.

cel-lo (chel´) n. A base instrument of the violin family.

cel-lo-phane (sel´o fn´) n. A transparent material made from treated cellulose that has been processed in thin, clear strips.

cel-lu-lar (sel´ya lr) adj. Consisting of cells.

cel-lu-lite n. A fatty deposit under the skin.

cel-lu-lose (sel´ya ls´) n. A carbohydrate that is insoluble in ordinary solvents and forms the fundamental material for the structure of plants.

cem-e-ter-y (sem´i ter´) n. pl. **-ies** The place for burying the dead.

cen-ser (sen´sr) n. A vessel or container for burning incense.

cen-sor (sen´sr) n. A person who examines films and printed materials to determine what might be objectionable. **censorship** n.

cen-sure (sen´shur) n. An expression of criticism and/or disapproval.

cen-sus (sen´sus) n. An official count of the population.

cent (sent) n. One; one hundredth of a dollar.

cen-te-nar-i-an (sen´te när´ an) n. A

person who has reached the age of 100 or more.

cen-ter (sen´tr) *n.* The place of equal distance from all sides; the heart; in sports, a person who holds the middle position, as in the forward line.

cen-tral (sen´tral) *adj.* In, near, or at the center; of primary importance. **centrally** *adv.* **-centralize** *v.*

cen-trif-u-gal (sen trif´ gal) *adj.* Moving or directing away from a center location.

cen-tu-ry (sen´cha r) *n. pl.* **-ies** A period consisting of 100 years.

ce-ram-ic (se ram´ik) *adj.* Of or relating to a brittle material made by firing a nonmetallic mineral, such as clay.

ce-re-al (sr´ al) *n.* An edible grain eaten as a breakfast food.

cer-e-bel-lum (ser´e bel´um) *n. pl.-bellums* The part of the brain responsible for the coordination of voluntary muscular movements.

cerebral hemorrhage *n.* The rupture of an artery in the brain, which allows blood to escape.

cer-e-brum (ser´e brum) *n. pl.* **-brums** *or* **-bra** The brain structure that is divided into two cerebral hemispheres and occupies most of the cranial cavity.

cer-e-mo-ni-al (ser´e m´n al) *adj.* Marked by or relating to a ceremony.

cer-e-mo-ny (ser´e m´n) *n. pl.* **-ies** A ritual or formal act performed in a certain manner.

ce-rise (se rs´) *n.* The color of deep purplish red.

cer-tain (sr´tan) *adj. pl.* **-ties** Being very sure of something; without any doubt; inevitable; not mentioned but assumed. **certainly** *adv.* **certainty** *n.*

cer-tif-i-cate (sr tif´i kt´) *n.* A document stating the truth or accuracy of something; a document that certifies fulfillment of duties or requirements, as of a course of study.

cer-tif-i-ca-tion (ser´ti fi k´shan) *n.* A certified statement.

cer-ti-fy (sr´ti f´) *v.* To testify in writing that something is true or a fact.

cer-vi-cal (sr´vi kal) *adj.* Relating to the neck of the cervix.

ce-si-um (s´z um) *n.* An electrometal,

white in color, from the alkali group, used in photoelectric cells.

ces-sa-tion (se s´shan) *n.* The act of stopping or ceasing.

ces-sion (sesh´on) *n.* The act of giving up territory or rights to another.

chafe (chf) *v.* To become sore by rubbing; to irritate.

cha-grin (sha grin´) *n.* A feeling of distress caused by disappointment, failure, or humiliation. **chagrin** *v.*

chain (chn) *n.* A connection of several links; anything that confines or restrains. **gang** Prisoners that are chained together. **reaction.** Series of events that directly affect one another.

chair-man (châr´man) *n. pl.* **-men** The person presiding over a committee, board, or other meeting. **chairmanship** *n.*

chaise (shz) *n.* A one-horse vehicle for two people.

cha-let (sha l´) *n.* A cottage that has a gently sloping and overhanging roof.

chal-ice (chal´is) *n.* A drinking goblet or cup.

chal-lah *or* **cha-lah** (käl e) *n.* A loaf of braided bread eaten by Jews on holidays and the Sabbath.

chal-lenge (chal´inj) *n.* A demand for a contest; a protest. *v.* To call into question.

chal-lis (shal´) *n.* A lightweight printed cloth in rayon, cotton, or wool.

cham-pagne (sham pn´) *n.* A white sparkling wine.

cham-pi-on (cham´p an) *n.* The holder of first place in a contest; one who defends another person.

cham-pi-on-ship (cham´p an ship´) *n.* The competition that determines a winner.

chance (chans) *n.* The random existence of something happening; a gamble or a risk.

chan-cel (chan´sel) *n.* The area of a church that contains the altar and choir.

chan-cel-lor (chan´se lr) *n.* The chief director or minister of state in certain countries in Europe. **chancellorship** *n.*

chan-cer-y (chan´se r) *n.* The office for the safekeeping of official records.

chan-cre (shang´kr) *n.* A lesion that is

the first indication of syphilis.

chanc-y (chan´s) *adj.* Risky; dangerous.

chan-de-lier (shan´de lr´) *n.* A light fixture with many branches for lights that is suspended from the ceiling.

chan-dler (chand´lr) *n.* A person who makes and sells candles. **chandlery** *n.*

change (chnj) *v.* To become or make different; to alter; to put with another; to use to take the place of another; to freshen a bed by putting clean coverings on. *n.* Coins; money given back when the payment exceeds the bill.

chan-nel (chan´el) *n.* The deepest part of a stream, river, or harbor; the course that anything moves through or past; a groove.

chant (chant) *n.* A melody in which all words are sung on the same note. *v.* To celebrate with a song. **chanter** *n.*

cha-os (k´os) *n.* Total disorder. **chaotic** *adj.* **chaotically** *adv.*

chap (chap) *n.* *Slang* A fellow; a man. *v.* To dry and split open from the cold and wind.

chap-el (chap´el) *n.* A place to worship, usually contained in a church.

chap-er-on or **chap-er-one** (shap´e rn´) *n.* An older woman who supervises younger people. **chaperone** *v.*

chap-let (chap´lit) *n.* A garland for the head; a string of beads.

chap-ter (chap´tr) *n.* One division of a book; a branch of a fraternity, religious order, or society.

char-ac-ter (kar´ik tr) *n.* A quality or trait that distinguishes an individual or group; a person that is portrayed in a play; a distinctive quality or trait. *adj.* Distinctive; peculiar.

cha-rades *n.pl* A game in which the syllables of words are acted out by each player.

chard (chärd) *n.* An edible white plant with large, succulent leaves.

charge (chärj) *v.* To give responsibility; to ask a price; to accuse; to impute something to; to command; to record a debt owed. *n.* Management; custody; supervision; an expense or price. *Slang* A thrill. **-able** *adj.*

charg-er *n.* An apparatus for recharging a battery.

char-i-ot (char´ot) *n.* An ancient horse-drawn vehicle used to fight battles.

char-i-ty (char´i t) *n.* Money or help given to aid the needy; an organization, fund, or institution whose purpose is to aid those in need.

cha-ri-va-ri (sha riv´a r´) *n.* A mock serenade to newlyweds, performed with horns, tin pans, etc.

charm (chärm) *n.* The ability to delight or please; a small ornament that has a special meaning, usually worn on a bracelet.

char-nel (chär´nel) *n.* A special room or building that contains the bones or bodies of the dead.

chart (chärt) *n.* A map, graph, or table that gives information in a form that is easy to read.

char-ter (chär´tr) *n.* An official document that grants certain privileges and rights. *v.* To lease or hire a vehicle or aircraft.

char-y (châr´) *adj.* Wary; cautious; not wasting time, resources, or money.

chase (chs) *v.* To follow quickly; to pursue; to run after. **chase** *n.* **chaser** *n.*

chasm (kaz´um) *n.* A very deep crack in the earth's surface.

chas-sis (shas´) *n.* The rectangular framework that supports the body and engine of a motor vehicle.

chaste (chst) *adj.* Morally pure; modest; not guilty of participating in sexual intercourse.

chas-tise (chas tz´) *v.* To severely reprimand; to punish by beating.

chas-u-ble (chaz´ bl) *n.* The vestment without sleeves worn over the alb by a priest when celebrating Mass.

chat (chat) *v.* To converse in a friendly manner.

chat-tel (chat´el) *n.* An item of movable personal property.

chauf-feur (sh´fr) *n.* A person who is hired to drive an automobile for another person.

chau-vin-ism *n.* The unreasonable belief in the superiority of one's own group. .

cheap (chp) *adj.* Inexpensive; low in cost; of poor quality. **cheaply** *adv.*

cheap-en (ch´pen) *v.* To lessen the value; to make cheap.

cheat (cht) *v.* To deprive of by deceit; to break the rules. **cheater** *n.*

cheer-ful (chr´fúl) *adj.* Having good spirits.

cheese (chz) *n.* A food made from the curd of milk that is seasoned and aged.

chef (shef) *n.* A male cook who manages a kitchen; the head cook.

che-la (k´la) *n.* The pincerlike claw of an arachnid.

chem-i-cal (kem´i kal) *adj.* Of or related to chemistry. **chemically** *adv.*

chem-ist (kem´ist) *n.* A person who is versed in chemistry.

chem-is-try (kem´i str) *n.* The scientific study of the composition, structure, and properties of substances and their reactions.

che-mo-ther-a-py (kem´o ther´a p) *n.* The treatment of a disease, such as cancer, with chemicals. **-apeuti** *adj.*

cher-ish (cher´ish) *v.* To treat with love; to hold dear.

che-root (she röt´) *n.* A cigar that is cut square at both ends.

cher-ry (cher´) *n.* *pl.* **-ies** A fruit tree bearing a small, round, deep, or purplish red fruit with a small, hard stone.

chest (chest) *n.* The part of the upper body that is enclosed by the thorax; the ribs; a box usually having a hinged lid, used for storage.

chew (chö) *v.* To crush or grind with the teeth; to masticate. *n.* The act of chewing.

chi-a-ro-scu-ro (k är´o sker´) *n.* The distribution of shade and light in a picture.

chick (chik) *n.* A young chicken or bird. *Slang* A young woman.

chic-le (chik´el) *n.* The milky juice of a tropical tree; the principal ingredient of chewing gum.

chic-o-ry (chik´o r) *n.* *pl.* **-ies** An herb with blue flowers used in salads, the dried, roasted roots of which are used as a coffee substitute.

chide (chd) *v.* To scold or find fault.

chief (chf) *n.* The person of highest rank.

chief-tain (chf´tan) *n.* The head of a group, clan, or tribe.

chif-fon (shi fon´) *n.* A sheer fabric made from rayon or silk. *adj.* In cooking, having a fluffy texture.

chig-ger (chig´r) *n.* A mite that attaches itself to the skin and causes intense itching.

chil-blain (chil´bln´) *n.* An inflammation of the hands and feet caused by exposure to cold.

child (chld) *n.* *pl.* **children** A young person of either sex; adolescent; a person between infancy and youth.

chill (chil) *v.* To be cold, often with shiv-ering; to reduce to a lower temperature. *n.* A feeling of cold.

chin (chin) *n.* The lower part of the face. *v.* To lift oneself up while grasping an overhead bar until the chin is level with the bar.

chine (chn) *n.* The spine or backbone of animals.

chink (chingk) *n.* A narrow crack.

chintz (chints) *n.* A printed cotton fabric which is glazed.

chintz-y (chint´s) *adj.* Cheap.

chip (chip) *n.* A small piece that has been broken or cut from another source; a disk used in the game of poker; *in computer science,* an integrated circuit engraved on a silicone substrate. **chip** *v.*

chi-ro-prac-tic (k´ro prak´tik) *n.* A method of therapy in which the body is manipulated to adjust the spine.

chirp (cherp) *n.* The high-pitched sound made by a cricket or a small bird.

chis-el (chiz´el) *n.* A tool with a sharp edge which is used to shape and cut metal, wood, or stone.

chit (chit) *n.* A voucher indicating the amount owed for food or drink; a lively girl.

chit-chat (chit´chat´) *n.* Casual conversation or small talk.

chi-tin (k´tin) *n.* The substance that forms the hard outer cover of insects.

chit-ter-lings, *n. pl.* The small intestines of a pig, used as food.

chiv-al-ry (shiv´al r) *n.* *pl.* **-ies** The brave and courteous qualities of an ideal knight.

chive (chv) *n.* A herb used as flavoring in cooking.

chlo-ride (klr´d) *n.* A compound of chlorine with a double positive element.

chlo-rine (klr´n) *n.* A greenish-yellow compound used to purify water, bleach, and disinfectant.

choice (chois) *n.* To select or choose; the opportunity, right, or power to choose.

choir (kwr) *n.* An organized group of singers that usually perform in a church.

chok-er (ch´kr) *n.* A necklace that fits tightly around the neck.

cho-les-ter-ol (ka les´te rl´) *n.* A fatty crystalline substance that is derived from bile and is present in most gallstones, the brain, and blood cells.

choose (chöz) *v.* To select or pick out; to prefer; to make a choice. **choosy** or **chosen** *adj.*

chop (chop) *v.* To cut by making a sharp downward stroke; to cut into bits or small pieces.

cho-ral (kr´al) *adj.* Pertaining to, written for, or sung by a choir or chorus.

cho-rale (ko ral´) *n.* A Protestant hymn with a simple melody, sung in unison.

chore (chr) *n.* A daily task; a task that becomes unpleasant or burdensome.

cho-re-a (ko r´a) *n.* An acute nervous disease especially of children, marked by irregular and uncontrollable movement of muscles.

cho-re-og-ra-phy (kr´ og´ra f) *n.* The creation of a dance routine.

chor-is-ter (kor´i str) *n.* A choirboy or a member of a choir.

chor-tle (chor´tl) *v.* To chuckle with glee, especially in triumph or joy.

cho-rus (kr´us) *n. pl.* -**ses** A group of people who sing together; the repeated verses of a song.

chose (shz) *v.* The past tense of choose.

cho-sen (ch´zen) *adj.* Selected or preferred above all.

Christ (krst) *n.* Jesus; The Messiah; God's son who died to save Christians from sin.

chris-ten (kris´n) *v.* To baptize; to give a Christian name at baptism; to use for the first time. **christening** *n.*

chro-mat-ic (kr mat´ik) *adj.* Relating to color.

chro-mo-some (kro´mo sm´) *n.* One of several small bodies in the nucleus of a cell, containing genes responsible for the determination and transmission of hereditary characteristics.

chron-ic (kron´ik) *adj.* Frequently recurring; continuing for long periods

of time; affected by a disease for a long time. **-ally** *adv.*

chron-i-cle (kron´i kal) *n.* A record of events written in the order in which they occurred.

chrys-a-lis (kris´a lis) *n. pl.*- **ses** The enclosed pupa from which a moth or butterfly develops.

chuck-le (chuk´ul) *v.* To laugh quietly with satisfaction. **chuckler** *n.*

church (cherch) *n.* A building for Christian worship; a congregation of public Christian worship.

churl (cherl) *n.* A rude or rustic person. **churlish** *adj.* **churlishness** *n.*

ci-der (s´dr) *n.* The juice from apples.

ci-gar (si gär´) *n.* Rolled tobacco leaves used for smoking.

cig-a-rette (sig´a ret´) *n.* or **cig-a-ret** A small amount of tobacco rolled in thin paper used for smoking.

cinch (sinch) *n.* The strap for holding a saddle. *v.* To assure. *Slang* Something easy to do.

cinc-ture (singk´chr) *n.* A belt or cord to put around the waist. *v.* To encircle or surround with a cincture.

cin-der (sin´dr) *n.* A piece of something that is partially burned. **cindery** *adj.*

cin-e-ma (sin´a ma) *n. pl.* -**mas** A motion picture; a motion picture theatre; the business of making a motion picture.

cin-e-mat-o-graph (sin´e mat´o graf´) *n.* A movie projector or camera.

cin-e-ma-tog-ra-phy (sin´e ma tog´ra f) *n.* The art of photographing a motion picture.

cin-na-mon (sin´a mon) *n.* The aromatic inner bark of a tropical Asian tree, used as a spice, reddish brown in color.

ci-pher (s´fr) *n.* The symbol for the absence of quantity; O; secret writing that has a prearranged key or scheme.

cir-cuit (ser´kit) *n.* The closed path through which an electric current flows.

circuit court *n.* The lowest court of record, located in various counties or districts over which its jurisdiction extends.

cir-cu-lar (ser´klr) *adj.* Moving in a circle or round-like fashion; relating to something in a circle; having free motion, as the air.

cir-cu-late (ser´k lt´) v. To pass from place to place or person to person; to distribute in a wide area. **circulation** n.

cir-cum-cise (ser´kum sz´) v. To remove the foreskin on the male penis.

cir-cum-fer-ence (ser kum´fr ens) n. The perimeter or boundary of a circle.

cir-cum-flex (ser´kum fleks´) n. A mark indicating the quality or sound of vowels as they appear in words.

cir-cum-scribe (ser´kum skrb´) v. To confine something within drawn boundaries; to surround.

cir-cum-stance (ser´kum stans´) n. A fact or condition that must be considered when making a decision.

cir-cum-stan-tial (ser´kum stan´shal) adj. Incidental; not essential; dependent on circumstances.

cir-cum-stan-ti-ate (ser´kum stan´sh t) adj. Providing support or circumstantial evidence.

cir-cum-vent (ser´kum vent´) v. To outwit or gain advantage; to avoid or go around. **circumvention** n. **circumven-tive** adj.

cir-rho-sis (si r´sis) n. A liver disease that is ultimately fatal. **cirrhotic** adj.

cis-tern (sis´trn) n. A man-made tank or artificial reservoir for holding rain water.

cit-a-del (sit´a del) n. A fortress commanding a city; a stronghold.

ci-ta-tion (s t´shan) n. An official summons from a court; a quotation used in literary or legal material; an honor.

cite (st) v. To bring forward as proof; to summon to action; to rouse; to summon to appear in court. **citeable** adj.

cit-i-zen (sit´i zen) n. A resident of a town or city; a native or naturalized person entitled to protection from a government.

citric acid n. A colorless acid found in lime, lemon, and other juices.

cit-ron (si´tran) n. A fruit resembling a lemon, but less acidic and larger in size.

cit-rus (sit´rus) n. pl. **citrus**, **citruses** Any of a variety of trees bearing fruit with thick skins, as limes, oranges, lemons, and grapefruits.

civ-ic (siv´ik) adj. Relating to or of a cit-

izen, city, or citizenship.

civ-il (siv´il) adj. Relating to citizens; relating to the legal proceedings concerned with the rights of private individuals.

ci-vil-ian (si vil´yen) n. A person not serving in the military, as a firefighter, or as a policeman.

civ-i-li-za-tion (siv´i li z´shan) n. A high level of social, cultural, and political development.

civil rights n. pl. Rights guaranteed to citizens; the rights provided by the 13th and 14th amendments of the United States Constitution.

claim (klm) v. To ask for one's due; to hold something to be true; to make a statement that something is true **claimant** n.

clair-voy-ance (klâr voi´ans) n. The ability to visualize in the mind distant objects or objects hidden from the senses. .

clam-my (klam´) adj. Damp, cold, and sticky. **clammily** adv. **clamminess** n.

clam-or (klam´r) n. A loud noise or outcry; protest or demand.

clan (klan) n. A large group of people who are related to one another by a common ancestor. **clannish** adj.

clan-des-tine (klan des´tin) adj. Kept or done in secrecy for a purpose.

clang (klang) v. To cause or make a loud, ringing, metallic sound.

clan-gor (klang´r) n. A loud series of clangs.

clap (klap) v. To applaud; to strike the hands together with an explosive sound.

clap-per (klap´r) n. The part of a bell that hits against the side.

clar-i-fy (klar´i f´) v. To become or make clearer. **clarification** n.

clar-i-net (klar´i t) n. A woodwind instrument with a single reed. **clarinetist** n.

clar-i-ty (klar´i t) n. The state or quality of being clear.

clash (klash) v. To bring or strike together; to collide; to conflict.

clasp (klasp) n. A hook to hold parts of objects together; a grasp or grip of the hands.

clas-sic (klas´ik) adj. Belonging in a certain category of excellence; having a lasting artistic worth.

clas-si-fy (klas´i f´) v. To arrange or assign items, people, etc., into the same class or category. **classification** n.

claus-tro-pho-bia (klo´stro f´b a) n. A fear of small or enclosed places.

clav-i-cle (klav´i kl) n. The bone that connects the breastbone and the shoulder blade.

cla-vier (kla vr´) n. An instrument with a keyboard, such as the harpsichord.

clean (kln) adj. Free from impurities, dirt, or contamination; neat in habits.

clear (klr) adj. Free from precipitation and clouds; able to hear, see, or think easily; free from doubt or confusion; free from a burden, obligation, or guilt.

cleat (klt) n. A metal projection that provides support, grips, or prevents slipping.

clef (klf) n. A symbol indicating which pitch each line and space represents on a musical staff.

clem-ent (klem´ent) adj. Merciful; mild.

cler-gy (klr´j) n. The group of men and women who are ordained as religious leaders and servants of God.

clerk (klork) n. A worker in an office who keeps accounts, records, and correspondence up to date; a person who works in the sales department of a store.

clev-er (klev´r) adj. Mentally quick; showing dexterity and skill. **-ly** adv.

cli-ent (kl´ent) n. A person who secures the professional services of another.

cli-en-tele (kl´en tel´) n. A collection of patients, customers, or clients.

cli-mac-ter-ic (kl mak´tr ik) n. A critical stage or major turning point in life.

cli-mate (kl´mit) n. The weather conditions of a certain region generalized or averaged over a period of years; the prevailing atmosphere. **climatic** adj.

cli-max (kl´maks) n. The point of greatest intensity and fullest suspense; the culmination.

climb (klm) v. To move to a higher or lower location; to advance in rank or status. **climbable** adj. **climber** n.

clinch (klinch) v. To secure; to fasten; to settle definitively. **clinch** n.

cling (kling) v. To hold fast to; to grasp

or stick; to hold on and resist emotional separation.

clin-ic (klin´ik) n. A medical establishment connected with a hospital; a center that offers instruction or counseling.

clink (klingk) v. To cause a light ringing sound.

clip (klip) v. To cut off; to curtail; to cut short. n. Something that grips, holds, or clasps articles together.

clique (klk) n. A small and exclusive group of people.

cloak (klk) n. A loose outer garment that conceals or covers.

cloche (klsh) n. A bell-shaped, close-fitting hat.

clock (klok) n. An instrument that measures time. v. To time with a watch, clock, stopwatch, etc.

clod (klod) n. A large piece or lump of earth; a stupid, ignorant person.

clog (klog) v. To choke up. n. A shoe with a wooden sole.

clone (kln) n. An identical reproduction grown from a single cell of the original.

close (kls) adj. Near, as in time, space, or relationship; nearly even, as in competition; fitting tightly. v. To shut.

clos-et (kloz´it) n. A small cabinet, compartment, or room for storage. **closet** v.

clot (klot) n. A thick or solid mass, as blood.

clothe (klth) v. To provide clothes; to cover with clothes; to wrap.

clo-ture (kl´shr) n. A parliamentary action that calls for an immediate vote.

clout (klout) n. A heavy blow with the hand. Slang The amount of influence or pull a person may have. **clout** v.

cloy (kloi) v. To make one sick or disgusted with too much sweetness.

clum-sy (klum´z) adj. Lacking coordination, grace, or dexterity; not tactful or skillful.

clus-ter (klus´tr) n. A bunch; a group.

clut-ter (klut´r) n. A confused mass of disorder.

co-ad-ju-tor (k aj u tr) n. An assistant.

co-ag-u-lant (k ag´ lant) n. A substance that causes coagulation.

co-ag-u-late (k ag´ lt´) v. To clot.

co-a-lesce (k´a les´) v. To come together

or to grow as one.

co-ali-tion (k a lish´an) *n.* A temporary alliance.

coarse (krs) *adj.* Lacks refinement; of inferior or low quality; having large particles; harsh.

coax (kks) *v.* To persuade by tact, gentleness, or flattery. **coaxingly** *adv.*

co-ax-i-al (k aks´s al) *adj.* Having common coincident axes.

cob (kob) *n.* A male swan; a corncob; a thick-set horse that has short legs.

co-balt (k´bolt) *n.* A hard, lustrous metallic element that resembles iron and nickel.

cob-ble (kob´l) *v.* To make or repair shoes; to make or put together roughly.

CO-BOL (k´bl) *n.* In Computer Science, computer programming that is simple and based on English.

coc-cyx (kok´siks) *n.* The small bone at the bottom of the spinal column.

coch-i-neal (koch´i nl´) *n.* A brilliant scarlet dye prepared from the dried, pulverized bodies of certain female insects of tropical America.

coch-le-a (kok´l a) *n.* The spiral tube of the inner ear, forming an essential part for hearing.

co-co (k´k) *n.* The fruit obtained from the coconut palm.

co-coa (k´k) *n.* The powder from the roasted husked seed kernels of the cacao.

co-coon (k kön´) *n.* The protective fiber or silk pupal case that is spun by insect larvae.

co-dex (k´deks) *n.* An ancient manuscript of the classics or Scriptures.

co-ed-u-ca-tion (k´ej e k´shan) *n.* An educational system for both men and women at the same institution. **coeducational** *adj.*

co-erce (k ers´) *v.* To restrain or dominate with force; to compel by law, authority, fear, or force.

co-e-val (k ´val) *adj.* Of the same time period. **coeval** *n.*

co-ex-ist (k´ig zist´) *v.* To exist at the same time or together; the ability to live peaceably with others in spite of differences. **-ence** *n.*

cof-fee (ko´f) *n.* A beverage prepared from ground beans of the coffee tree.

cof-fer (ko´fr) *n.* A strongbox or chest made for valuables.

cof-fin (ko´fin) *n.* A box in which a corpse is buried.

cog (kog) *n.* A tooth or one of series of a teeth on the rim of a wheel in a machine or a mechanical device.

co-gent (k´jent) *adj.* Compelling; forceful; convincing.

cog-i-tate (koj´i tt´) *v.* To think carefully about or to ponder. **cogitation** *n.*

cog-nate (kog´nt) *adj.* From a common ancestor; identical or similar in nature; related.

cog-ni-zance (kog´ni zans) *n.* Perception of fact; awareness; recognition; observation.

co-hab-it (k hab´it) *v.* To live together as husband and wife.

co-here (k hr´) *v.* To stick or hold together.

co-hort (k´hort) *n.* A group of people who are united in one effort; an accom-plice.

coif (koif) *n.* A close-fitting hat that is worn under a nun's veil.

coil (koil) *n.* A series of connecting rings. *v.* To wind in spirals.

coin (koin) *n.* A flat, rounded piece of metal used as money. *v.* To invent or make a new phrase or word.

co-in-cide (k´in sd´) *v.* To happen at the same time; to agree exactly.

co-in-ci-dence (k in´si dens) *n.* Two events happening at the same time by accident but appearing to have some connection.

col-ic (kol´ik) *n.* A sharp pain in the abdomen caused by muscular cramps or spasms, occurring most often in very young babies.

col-i-se-um (kol´i s´um) *n.* A large amphitheater used for sporting games.

col-lab-o-rate (ko lab´o rt´) *v.* To cooperate or work with another person. **collaboration** *n.* **collaborator** *n.*

col-lapse (ko laps´) *v.* To fall; to give way; to fold and assume a smaller size; to lose all or part of the air in a lung.

col-lar-bone (kol´r bn´) *n.* *,Anat.* The clavicle, located near the neck.

col-late (ko lt´) *v.* To compare in a critical fashion; to assemble in correct sequence or order.

col·lat·er·al (kə lat´r əl) *adj.* Serving to support; guaranteed by stocks, property, bonds, etc.

col·league (kol´g) *n.* Someone who works in the same profession or official body.

col·lect (kə lekt´) *v.* To gather or assemble; to gather donations or payments.

col·lide (kə līd´) *v.* To come together with a direct impact; to clash; to come into conflict.

col·lo·cate (kol´ō kt´) *v.* To compare facts and arrange in correct order.

col·lo·di·on (kə līd on) *n.* A highly flammable spray solution used to protect wounds and used for photographic plates.

col·loid (kol´oid) *n.* A glue-like substance, such as gelatin, that cannot pass through animal membranes.

col·lo·quy (kol´ō kw) *n. pl.* **-quies** A formal conversation or conference.

col·lu·sion (kə lö´zhən) *n.* A secret agreement between two or more people for an illegal purpose.

co·lon (k´lon) *n.* A punctuation mark (:) used to introduce an example or series; the section of the large intestine that extends from the cecum to the rectum. **colonic** *adj.*

col·o·ny (kol´ō n) *n. pl* **-ies** A group of emigrants living in a new land away from, but under the control of, the parent country; a group of insects, as ants.

col·o·phon (kol´ō fon´) *n.* The inscription at the end of a book that gives the publication facts.

col·or (kul´r) *n.* The aspect of things apart from the shape, size, and solidity; a hue or tint that is caused by the different degrees of light that are reflected or emitted by them.

col·or·a·tion (kul´ō r´shən) *n.* The arrangement of different colors or shades.

co·los·sal (kə los´al) *adj.* Very large or gigantic in degree or size.

col·umn (kol´um) *n.* A decorative and or supporting pillar used in construction; a vertical division of typed or printed lines on paper.

co·ma (k´ma) *n.* A deep sleep or unconsciousness caused by an illness or injury.

co·ma·tose (kom´a ts´) *adj.* Unconscious.

com·bine (kom bn´) *v.* To unite; to merge. *n.* A farm machine that harvest by cutting, threshing, and cleaning the grain.

com·bus·tion (kom bus´chən) *n.* The chemical change that occurs rapidly and produces heat and light; a burning. **combustive** *adj.*

come (kum) *v.* To arrive; to approach; to reach a certain position, state, or result; to appear; to come into view.

com·e·dy (kom´i d) *n. pl.* **-ies** A humorous, entertaining performance with a happy ending; a real life comical situation.

co·mes·ti·ble (kə mes´ti bl) *adj.* Something that is fit to eat. *adj.* Fit to eat.

com·et (kom´it) *n.* A celestial body that moves in an or bit around the sun, consisting of a solid head that is surrounded by a bright cloud with a long, vaporous tail.

com·ic (kom´ik) *adj.* Characteristic of comedy. *n.* A comedian. **Comics** Comic strips.

com·i·cal (kom´i kal) *adj.* Amusing; humorous.

com·ma (kom´a) *n.* The punctuation mark (,) used to indicate separation of ideas or a series in a sentence.

com·mem·o·rate (kə mem´o rt´) *v.* To honor the memory of; to create a memorial to.

com·mence (kə mens´) *v.* To begin; to start.

com·mence·ment (kə mens´ment) *n.* A graduation ceremony.

com·mend (kə mend´) *v.* To give praise; to applaud. **commendable** *adj.* **commendably** *adv.* **commendation** *n.*

com·men·su·rate (kə men´sr it) *adj.* Equal in duration, extent, or size.

com·ment (kom´ent) *n.* A statement of criticism, analysis, or observation.

com·merce (kom´rs) *n.* The exchanging of products or materials; buying and selling.

com·mer·cial (kə mer´shal) *adj.* Of or relating to a product; supported by advertising. *n.* An advertisement on radio or television.

com·mis·er·ate (ko miz´e rat) v. To display or feel sympathy for someone. **commiserative** adj. **-ation** n.

com·mis·sar·y (kom´i ser´) n. pl. **-ies** A store that sells food and supplies on a military base.

com·mit·tee (ko mit´) n. A group of persons appointed or elected to perform a particular task or function.

com·mon (kom´on) adj. Having to do with, belonging to, or used by an entire community or public; vulgar; unrefined.

common denominator n. A number that can be evenly divided by all the denominators of a set of fractions.

common fraction n. A fraction with both the denominator and numerator being whole numbers.

common law n. The unwritten system of law that is based on judicial decisions, customs, and usages.

com·mu·ni·ca·ble (ko·mú·ni ka bl) adj. Capable of being transmitted, as with a disease.

com·mu·ni·cate (ko m´ni kt´) v. To make known; to cause others to partake or share something.

com·mu·ni·ca·tion (ko m´ni k´shan) n. The act of transmitting ideas through writing or speech; the means to transmit messages between person or places.

com·mu·nism (kom´ niz´um) n. A system of government in which goods and production are commonly owned; the theory of social change and struggle toward communism through revolution.

com·mute (ko mt´) v. To travel a long distance to one's job each day; to exchange or to substitute.

com·muter (ko m´tr) n. One who travels a long distance on a regular basis.

com·pact (kom pakt´) adj. Packed together or solidly united; firmly and closely united.

com·pac·tor n. A device for compressing trash into a small mass for disposal.

com·pan·ion (kom pan´yon) n. An associate; a person employed to accompany or assist another; one hired to travel or live with another. **compan-**

ionship n.

com·pan·ion·a·ble (kom pan´yo na bl) adj. Friendly; sociable.

com·pa·ra·ble (kom´par a bl) adj. Capable of comparison; worthy of comparison; similar. **comparability** n. **comparably** adv.

com·pare (kom pâr´) v. To speak of or represent as similar or equal to; to note the similarities or likenesses of.

com·par·i·son (kom par´i son) n. Likeness; similarity. Gram. Modification of a verb or adjective that indicates the positive, comparative, or superlative degree.

com·pass (kum´pas) n. An instrument used to determine geographic direction; an enclosed area or space; the extent of reach of something; range or area; scope.

compasses A device shaped like a V that is used for drawing circles.

com·pas·sion (kom pash´on) n. Sympathy for someone who is suffering or distressed in some way. **-ate** adj.

com·pat·i·ble (kom pat´i bl) adj. Able to function, exist, or live together harmoniously.

com·pa·tri·ot (kom p´tr ot) n. A person of the same country.

com·peer (kom pr´) n. A person that is a peer or equal.

com·pel (kom pel´) v. To urge or force action.

com·pen·di·um (kom pen´dum) n. pl. **-diums** A short summary.

com·pen·sate (kom´pen st´) v. To make up for; to make amends; to pay; to neutralize or counter balance.

com·pete (kom pt´) v. To contend with others; to engage in a contest or competition.

com·pe·tent (kom´pi tent) adj. Having sufficient ability; being capable.

com·pe·ti·tion (kom´pi tish´an) n. The act of rivalry or competing; a trial of skill or ability; a contest between teams or individuals.

com·pet·i·tor (kom pet´i tr) n. One who competes against another.

com·pile (kom pl´) v. To put together material gathered from a number of sources; in Computer Science, to convert our language into machine language. **compilation** n.

com-plai-sance (kom pl´sans) n. The willingness to please, to oblige.

com-ple-ment (kom´ple ment) n. Something that perfects, completes, or adds to. **complementary** adj.

com-plete (kom plt´) adj. Having all the necessary parts; whole; project concluded.

com-plex (kom pleks´) adj. Consisting of various intricate parts. **-plexity** n.

com-plex-ion (kom plek´shan) n. The natural color and texture of the skin.

com-pli-ance (kom pl´ans) n. The act of agreeing passively to a request, rule, or demand; the tendency to yield to others. **compliant** adj. **compliancy** n.

com-pli-cate (kom´pli kt´) v. To make or become involved or complex.

com-plic-i-ty (kom plis´i t) n. An involvement or association with a crime.

com-pli-ment (kom´pli ment) n. An expression of praise or admiration.

com-pli-men-ta-ry (kom´pli men´ta r) adj. Conveying a compliment.

com-ply (kom pl´) v. To agree, to consent to, or obey a command or wish.

com-po-nent (kom p´nent) n. A constituent part.

com-port (kom prt´) v. To behave or conduct oneself in a certain way.

com-pose (kom pz´) v. To make up from elements or parts; to produce or create a song; to arrange, as to typeset.

com-posed (kom pzd´) adj. Calm.

com-pos-ite (kom poz´it) adj. Made up from separate elements or parts; combined or compounded. **Bot.** Characteristic of a plant with densely clustered flowers.

com-po-si-tion (kom´po zish´on) n. The act of putting together artistic or literary work; a short essay written for an assignment in school. **-tional** adj.

com-post (kom´pst) n. A fertilizing mixture that consists of decomposed vegetable matter.

com-po-sure (kom p´zhr) n. Tranquility; calm self-possession.

com-pote (kom´pt) n. Fruit that is preserved or stewed in syrup; a dish used for holding fruit, candy, etc.

perceive, to grasp mentally, or to understand fully; to comprise; to include.

com-pre-hen-si-ble (kom´pri hen´si bl) adj. Capable of being understood.

com-pre-hen-sive (kom´pri hen´siv) adj. Large in content or scope.

com-press (kom´pres) v. To press together into a smaller space; to condense. n. A soft pad sometimes medicated, for applying cold, heat, moisture, or pressure to a part of the body. **compressibility** adj.

com-prise (kom prz´) v. To consist of; to be made up of. **comprisable** adj.

com-pro-mise (kom´pro mz´) n. The process of settling or the settlement of differences between opposing sides, with each side making concessions.

comp-trol-ler (kon tr´lr) n. A person appointed to examine and verify accounts.

com-pul-sion (kom pul´shan) n. The act or state of being compelled; an irresistible urge or impulse to act irrationally.

com-pute (kom pt´) v. To ascertain or determine by the use of mathematics; to determine something by the use of a computer. **computability** n.

com-put-er (kom p´tr) n. A person who computes; a high speed, electronic machine which performs logical calculations, processes, stores, and retrieves programmed information.

computer language n. The various codes and information that are used to give data and instructions to computers.

con (kon) v. To study carefully. **Slang** To swindle or trick.

con-cat-e-nate (kon kat´e nt) v. To join, connect, or link together. **concatenate** adj.

con-cave (kon´kv) adj. Hollowed and curved inward. **concavely** adv.

con-ceal (kon sl´) v. To keep from disclosure, sight, or knowledge; to hide. **concealable** adj. **concealer** n.

con-cede (kon sd´) v. To grant or yield to a right or privilege; to acknowledge as true.

con-ceive (kon sv´) v. To become pregnant; to create a mental image. **conceivability** n. **conceivable** adj.

con-cen-trate (kon´sen trt´) v. To give intense thought to; to draw to a common point; to intensify by removing certain elements; to become compact.

con-cept (kon´sept) n. A generalized idea formed from particular occurrences or instances; an opinion. **conceptual** adj.

con-cep-tion (kon sep´shon) n. The union of sperm and egg; a mental thought or plan.

con-cern (kon srn´) n. Something to consider; sincere interest; something that affects one's business or affairs. v. To be interested in; to be involved with.

con-cert (kon´srt) n. A musical performance for a group of people; agreement in purpose, action, or feeling. v. To act or plan together.

con-cer-to (kon cher´t) n. pl. -tos, -ti A composition that features one or more solo instruments.

con-ces-sion (kon sesh´an) n. The act of conceding; something that has been conceded; a tract of land that is granted by a government for a particular use.

con-ces-sion-aire (kon sesh´o när´) n. The operator or holder of a concession.

con-chol-o-gy (kong kol´o j) n. The study of mollusks and shells. **conchological** adj.

con-cil-i-ate (kon sil´ t´) v. To win over or to gain a friendship. **conciliation** n.

con-cise (kon ss´) adj. Short and to the point.

con-clave (kon´klv) n. A private or secret meeting; the private meeting of the Roman Catholic cardinals to elect a new pope.

con-clude (kon klöd´) v. To close or bring to an end; to bring about an agreement; to arrive at a decision; to resolve.

con-clu-sive (kon klö´siv) adj. Putting an end to any questions or doubt.

con-coct (kon kokt´) v. To make by combining ingredients; to devise or to plan.

con-com-i-tant (kon kom´i tant) adj. Accompanying. **concomitance** n.

con-cord (kon´kord) n. Accord; harmony; friendly and peaceful relationships.

con-cor-dance (kon kor´dans) n. A condition of concord or agreement; the alphabetical index of major words used by an author, listed in the order of use in a book.

con-cor-dant (kon kor´dant) adj. Exist in agreement; harmonious. **-ly** adv.

con-course (kon´krs) n. A large, open space for the assembling or passage of crowds.

con-cres-cence (kon kres´ens) n. Increase by the addition of particles; growing together.

con-cu-bine (kong´k bn´) n. A woman living with a man and not being legally married to him. **cobcubinage** n.

con-cur (kon kr´) v. To agree or express approval; to cooperate; to happen at the same time; to coincide.

con-cur-rent (kon kr´ant) adj. Referring to an event that happens at the same time as another; acting together.

con-cus-sion (kon kush´on) n. A sudden and violent jolt; a violent injury to an organ, especially the brain.

con-demn (kon dem´) v. To find to be wrong; to show the guilt; to announce judgment upon; to officially declare unfit for use.

con-dense (kon dens´) v. To make more concentrated or compact; to change something from a liquid state to a solid state or from a gaseous to a liquid state.

con-di-ment (kon´di ment) n. A relish, spice, or sauce used to season food.

con-di-tion (kon dish´on) n. The mode or state of existence of a thing or person; a circumstance that is found to be necessary to the occurrence of another; a provision in a contract or will that leaves room for modification or changes at a future date. Slang A sickness or ailment. **condition** v.

con-di-tion-al (kon dish´a nal) adj. Tentative; depending on a condition; implying or expressing a condition. Gram. A mood, clause, tense, or condition. **conditionality** n. **conditionally** adv.

con-di-tioned (kon dish´ond) adj. Prepared for a certain process or action by past experience.

con-done (kon dn´) v. To overlook; to

forgive; to disregard. **condoner** n.

con-dor (kon´dor) v. One of the largest flying birds, with a bare head and a white downy neck.

con-du-cive (kon dö´siv) adj. Contributing towards or promotion; helpful.

con-duct (kon dukt´) v. To lead and direct a performance of a band or orchestra; to guide or show the way; to lead; to direct or control the course of; to transmit heat, electricity, or sound. n. Behavior. **conductibility** n. **conduction** n. **conductible** adj.

con-duit (kon´dwit) n. A pipe used to pass electric wires or cable through; a channel or pipe that water passes through.

cone (kn) n. A solid body that is tapered evenly to a point from a base that is circular; a wafer that is cone-shaped and used for holding ice cream.

con-fab-u-late (kon fab´ lt´) v. To chat or speak informally. **confabulation** n. **confabulator** n. **confabulatory** adj.

con-fed-er-ate (kon fed´r it) n. An ally or friend; a person who supports the Confederacy. **confederate** v.

con-fer (kon fer´) v. To consult with another; to hold a conference; to give or grant. **conferment** n. **conferral** n. **conferrer** n.

con-fer-ence (kon´fr ens) n. A formal meeting for discussion; a league of churches, schools, or athletic teams.

con-fess (kon fes´) v. To disclose or admit to a crime, fault, sin, or guilt; to tell a priest or God of one's sins. **confessedly** adv.

con-fes-sion (kon fesh´on) n. The act of confessing.

con-fes-sion-al (kon fesh´o nal) n. The small enclosure where a priest hears confessions.

con-fet-ti (kon fet´) n. pl. Small pieces of paper thrown during a happy occasion.

con-fide (kon fd´) v. To entrust a secret to another. **confider** n. **confiding** adj.

con-fi-dence (kon´fi dens) n. A feeling of selfassurance; a feeling of trust in a person; reliance; good faith. **-dent** adj.

con-fi-den-tial (kon´fi den´shal) adj. Hold as a secret; having another's entrusted confidence.

con-fig-u-ra-tion (kon fig´ r´shan) n. An arrangement of parts or things; the arrangement of elements. **configuration** adv.

con-fine (kon fn´) v. To keep within a certain boundary or limit. **confines** n. **confinement** n. **confiner** n.

con-firm (kon frm´) v. To establish or support the truth of something; to make stronger; to ratify and bind by a formal approval. **confirmable** adj.

con-fir-ma-tion (kon´fr m´shan) n. The act of confirming to show proof; a religious rite that admits a person to full membership in a church.

con-fis-cate (kon´fi skt´) v. To seize for public use; to officially seize. **confiscation** n.

con-flate (kon´flt) v. To combine two different ideas into a whole. **-flation** n.

con-flict (kon flikt´) n. A battle; clash; a disagreement of ideas, or interests. **conflict** v. **conflictive** adj.

con-flu-ence (kon´flö ens) n. The flowing together of two streams or rivers; the point where the two join. **-ent** n.

con-form (kon form´) v. To be similar in form or character; to adhere to prevailing customs or modes. **-able** adj.

con-for-ma-tion (kon´for m´shan) n. The manner in which something is shaped, structured, or arranged.

con-found (kon found´) v. To amaze, confuse, or perplex; to confuse one thing for another.

con-front (kon frunt´) v. To put or stand face to face with defiance. **-ation** n.

con-fuse (kon fz´) v. To mislead or bewilder; to jumble or mix up. **confusedness** n. **confusingly** adv.

con-fu-sion (kon f´zhan) n. The state of being confused.

con-fute (kon ft´) v. To prove to be invalid or false. **confutable** adj. **confutation** n.

con-geal (kon jl´) v. To jell; to solidify; to change from a liquid to a solid form.

con-gen-ial (kon jn´yal) adj. Having similar character habits, or tastes; sociable; friendly. **congeniality** n. **congenially** adv.

con-gen-i-tal (kon jen´i tal) adj. Existing from the time of birth, but not from heredity.

con-gest (kon jest´) *v.* To enlarge with an excessive accumulation of blood; to clog. **congestion** *n.* **congestive** *adj.*

con-glom-er-ate (kon glom´r it) *n.* A business consisting of many different companies; gravel that is embedded in cement material.

con-grat-u-late (kon grach´u lt) *v.* To acknowledge an achievement with praise. **congratulator** *n.* **-latory** *adj.*

con-gre-gate (kong´gre gt) *v.* To assemble together in a crowd.

con-gre-ga-tion (kong´gre g´shan) *n.* A group of people meeting together for worship.

Con-gress (kong´gris) *n.* The United States legislative body, consisting of the Senate and the House of Representatives. **Congressional** *adj.*

con-gru-ent (kong´grö ent) *adj.* A-greeing to conform; in mathematics, having exactly the same size and shape.

con-ic *or* **con-i-cal** (kon´ik) *adj.* Related to and shaped like a cone.

conj *abbr.* Conjunction.

con-jec-ture (kon jek´chr) *n.* A guess or conclusion based on incomplete evidence.

con-join (kon join´) *v.* To unite; join together.

con-ju-gal (kon´ju gal) *adj.* Pertaining to the relationship or marriage of husband and wife.

con-ju-gate (kon´ju git) *adj.* To change the form of a verb; to join in pairs.

con-junct (kon jungkt´) *adj.* Combined; joined together.

con-junc-tion (kon jungk´shan) *n.* The act of joining; the state of being joined. *Gram.* A word used to join or connect other words, phrases, sentences, or clauses.

con-junc-ti-va (kon´jungk t´va) *n. pl.* **-vas, -vae** The membrane lining of the eyelids.

con-junc-tive (kon jungk´tiv) *adj.* Connective; joining. *Gram.* Serving as a conjunction.

con-junc-ti-vi-tis (kon jungk´ti v´tis) *n., Pathol.* Inflammation of the membrane that lines the eyelids.

con-jure (kon´jr) *v.* To bring into the mind; to appeal or call on solemnly; to practice magic.

con-nect (ko nekt´) *v.* To join; to unite; to associate, as to relate. **connectedly** *adv.* **connector** *n.* **connecter** *n.*

con-nive (ko nv´) *v.* To ignore a known wrong, therefore implying sanction; to conspire; to cooperate in secret.

con-nois-seur (kon´o ser´) *n.* A person whose expertise in an area of art or taste allows him to be a judge; an expert.

con-no-ta-tion (kon´o t´shan) *n.* The associative meaning of a word in addition to the literal meaning. **-tative** *adj.*

con-note (ko nt´) *v.* To imply along with the literal meaning.

con-nu-bi-al (ko nö´b al) *adj.* Having to do with marriage or the state of marriage.

con-quer (kong´kr) *v.* To subdue; to win; to overcome by physical force.

con-science (kon´shens) *n.* The ability to recognize right and wrong regarding one's own behavior.

con-sci-en-tious (kon´sh en´shus) *adj.* Honest; scrupulous; careful.

con-scious (kon´shus) *adj.* Aware of one's own existence and environment; aware of facts or objects.

con-script (kon´skript) *n.* One who is drafted or forced to enroll for a service or a job.

con-se-crate (kon´se krt´) *v.* To declare something to be holy; to dedicate to sacred uses. **consecration, -crator** *n.*

con-sec-u-tive (kon sek´tiv) *adj.* Following in uninterrupted succession. **consecutively** *adv.* **consecutiveness** *n.*

con-sen-sus (kon sen´sus) *n.* A general agreement; a collective opinion.

con-sent (kon sent´) *v.* To agree; an acceptance. **consenter** *n.*

con-se-quence (kon´se kwens´) *n.* The natural result from a preceding condition or action; the effect.

con-se-quent (kon´se kwent´) *adj.* Following as a natural result or effect. **consequently** *adv.*

con-se-quen-tial (kon´se kwen´shal) *adj.* Having or showing self-importance. **-ly** *adv.*

con-serv-a-tive (kon sr´va tiv) *adj.* Opposed to change; desiring the preservation of the existing order of things; moderate; cautious; wanting to conserve. **conservatively** adv.

con-ser-va-to-ry (kon sr´va tr´) n. pl. **-ries** A school of dramatic art or music; a greenhouse.

con-sider (kon sid´r) v. To seriously think about; to examine mentally; to believe or hold as an opinion; to deliberate.

con-sid-er-a-ble (kon sid´r a bl) adj. Large in amount or extent; important; worthy of consideration. **-ly** adv.

con-sid-er-a-tion (kon sid´e r´shan) n. The taking into account of circumstance before forming an opinion; care and thought; a kind or thoughtful treatment or feeling.

con-sign (kon sn´) v. To commit to the care of another; to deliver or forward, as merchandise; to put aside, as for specific use. **consignee** n. **-able** adj.

con-sist (kon sist´) v. To be made up of.

con-sis-ten-cy (kon sis´ten s) n. pl. **-cies** Agreement or compatibility among ideas, events, or successive acts; the degree of texture, viscosity, or density.

con-sole (kon sl´) v. To give comfort to someone. **solable** adj. **consolation** n.

con-sol-i-date (kon sol´i dt´) v. To combine in one or to form a union of; to form a compact mass. **consolidation** n.

con-so-nant (kon´so nant) n. A sound produced by complete or partial blockage of the air from the mouth, as the sound of b, f, k, s, t; the letter of the alphabet that represents such a sound. adj. In agreement. **-al** adj. **-ly** adv.

con-sort (kon´sort) n. A spouse; companion or partner. v. To unite or keep in company.

con-sor-ti-um (kon sor´sh um) n. pl. **-tia** An association with banks or corporations that require vast resources.

con-spic-u-ous (kon spik´ us) adj. Noticeable.

con-spir-a-cy (kon spir´a s) n. pl.**-ies** A plan or act of two or more persons to do an evil act.

con-spire (kon spr´) v. To plan a wrong act in secret; to work or act together.

con-sta-ble (kon´sta bl) n. A peace officer.

con-stant (kon´stant) adj. Faithful; unchanging; steady in action, purpose, and affection. Math A quantity that remains the same throughout a given problem.

con-ster-na-tion (kon´str n´shan) n. Sudden confusion or amazement.

con-sti-pa-tion (kon´sti p´shan) n. A condition of the bowels characterized by difficult or infrequent evacuation.

con-stit-u-en-cy (kon stich´ö en s) n. pl. **-cies** A group of voters that is represented by an elected legislator.

con-stit-u-ent (kon stich´ö ent) adj. Having the power to elect a representative. n. A necessary element or part.

con-sti-tu-tion (kon´sti tö´shan) n. The fundamental laws that govern a nation; structure or composition. **constitutional** adj.

con-strain (kon strn´) v. To restrain by physical or moral means. **-trained** adj.

con-straint (kon strnt´) n. The threat or use of force; confinement; restriction.

con-strict (kon strikt´) v. To squeeze, compress, or contract. **constriction** n. **constrictive** adj. **constrictively** adv.

con-struct (kon strukt´) v. To create, make, or build. **constructor** n. **constructer** n.

con-struc-tive (kon struk´tiv) adj. Useful; helpful; building, advancing, or improving; resulting in a positive conclusion. **constructively** adv. **constructiveness** n.

con-strue (kon strö´) v. To interpret; to translate; to analyze grammatical structure.

con-sul (kon´sul) n. An official that resides in a foreign country and represents his or her government's commercial interests and citizens. **consular** adj. **consulship** n.

con-sul-ate (kon´su lit) n. The official premises occupied by a consul.

con-sult (kon sult´) v. To seek advice or information from; to compare views. **consultant** n. **consultation** n.

con-sume (kon söm´) v. To ingest; to eat or drink; to destroy completely; to absorb; to engross.

con-sum-mate (kon´su mt´) v. To conclude; to make a marriage complete by the initial act of sexual intercourse.

con-sump-tion (kon sump´shan) n. Fulfillment; the act of consuming; the quantity consumed; tuberculosis.

con-sump-tive (kon sump´tiv) adj. Tending to destroy or waste away; affected with or pertaining to pulmonary tuberculosis. **consumptively** adv. **consumptiveness** n.

con-ta-gion (kon t´jon) n. The transmitting of a disease by contact. **contagious** adj. **contagiously** adv.

con-tain (kon tn´) v. To include or enclose; to restrain or hold back. **containable** adj.

con-tam-i-nate (kon tam´i nt´) v. To pollute or make inferior by adding undesireable elements; to taint; to infect; to make dirty or to soil. **contaminant** n. **-tion** n.

con-temn (kon tem´) v. To scorn or despise.

con-tem-plate (kon´tem plt´) v. To look over; to ponder; to consider thoughtfully. **contemplative**, **-templation** n.

con-tem-po-ra-ne-ous (kon tem´po r´n us) adj. Occurring or living at the same time;

con-tempt (kon tempt´) n. The act of viewing something as mean, vile, or worthless scorn; legally, the willful disrespect or disregard of authority. **contemptible** adj.

con-temp-tu-ous (kon temp´chö us) adj. Feeling or showing contempt.

con-tend (kon tend´) v. To dispute; to fight; to debate; to argue. **contender** n.

con-tent (kon´tent) n. Something contained within; the subject matter of a book or document; the proportion of a specified part. adj. Satisfied. **contentment** n. **contentedly** adv. **-ed** adj.

con-test (kon´test) n. A competition; strife; conflict. v. To challenge. **contestable** adj. **contestant** n. **contester** n.

con-text (kon´tekst) n. A sentence, phrase, or passage so closely connected to a word or words that it affects their meaning; the environment in which an event occurs.

con-ti-nent (kon´ti nent) n. One of the seven large masses of the earth Asia, Africa, Australia, Europe, North America, South America and Antarctica.

con-ti-nen-tal (kon´ti nen´tal) adj. Of or characteristic of a continent.

continental divide n. A divide separating rivers or streams that flow to opposite sides of a continent.

con-ti-nu-i-ty (kon´ti nö´i t) n. pl. **-ties** The quality of being continuous.

con-tin-u-ous (kon tin´ us) adj. Uninterrupted. **continuously** adv.

con-tort (kon tort´) v. To severely twist out of shape.

con-tor-tion-ist (kon tor´sha nist) n. An acrobat who exhibits unnatural body positions.

con-tour (kon´ter) n. The outline of a body, figure, or mass.

con-tra-band (kon´tra band´) n. Illegal or prohibited traffic; smuggled goods.

con-tra-cep-tion (kon´tra sep´shan) n. The voluntary prevention of impregnation.

con-tract (kon´trakt) n. A formal agreement between two or more parties to perform the duties as stated.

con-trac-tion (kon trak´shan) n. The act of contracting; a shortening of a word by omitting a letter or letters and replacing them with an apostrophe (').

con-trac-tile adj. Having the power to contract.

con-tra-dict (kon´tra dikt´) v. To express the opposite side or idea; to be inconsistent.

con-tral-to (kon tral´t) n. pl. **-tos** The lowest female singing voice.

con-trap-tion (kon trap´shan) n. A gadget.

con-tra-pun-tal (kon´tra pun´tal) adj. Relating to counterpoint. **-ly** adv.

con-trar-y (kon´trer) adj. Unfavorable; incompatible with another.

con-trast (kon trast´) v. To note the differences between two or more people, things, etc. **contrastable** adj.

con-tra-vene (kon´tra vn´) v. To be contrary; to violate; to oppose; to go against.

con-trib-ute (kon trib´t) v. To give something to someone; to submit for publication. **contribution** n. **-utor** n.

con-trite (kon trt´) adj. Grieving for sin or shortcoming. **contritely** adv. **contrition** n.

con-trol (kon trl´) v. To have the authority or ability to regulate, direct, or dominate a situation. **controllable** *adj.*

con-trol-ler (kon trl lr) *n.* The chief accounting officer of a business, also called the comptroller.

con-tro-ver-sy (kontrø vrs) *n.* A dispute; a debate; a quarrel -**versial** *adj.*

con-tro-vert (kon´trō vert´) *v.* To contradict; to deny.

con-tu-me-ly (kon´te me l) *n. pl* -**lies** Rude treatment. **contumelious** *adj.*

co-nun-drum (ko nun´drum) *n.* A riddle with an answer that involves a pun; a question or problem with only a surmise for an answer.

con-va-lesce (kon´va les´) *v.* To grow strong after a long illness. **convalescence** *n.* **convalescent** *adj.*

con-vec-tion (kon vek´shən) *n.* The transfer of heat by the movement of air, gas, or heated liquid between areas of unequal density. **convectional** *adj.*

con-vene (kon vn´) *v.* To meet or assemble formally. **convenable** *adj.* -**er** *n.*

con-ven-ience (kon vn´yəns) *n.* The quality of being convenient or suitable.

con-ven-tion-al (kon ven´sha nal) *adj.* Commonplace, ordinary.

con-verge (kon vrj´) *v.* To come to a common point. **convergence** *n.*

con-ver-sa-tion (kon´vr s´shan) *n.* An informal talk. **conversational** *adj.*

converse (kon vrs´) *v.* To involve oneself in conversation with another.

con-ver-sion (kon vr´zhən) *n.* The act or state of changing to adopt new opinions or beliefs; a formal acceptance of a different religion. **conversional** *adj.*

con-vex (kon´veks) *adj.* Curved outward like the outer surface of a ball. **convexity** *n.*

con-vey (kon v´) *v.* To transport; to pass information on to someone else; to conduct.

con-vey-ance (kon v´ans) *n.* The action of conveying, the legal transfer of property or the document effecting it.

con-vict (kon vikt´) *v.* To prove someone guilty. *n.* A prisoner.

con-vic-tion (kon vik´shan) *n.* The act of being convicted.

con-vince (kon vins´) *v.* To cause to believe without doubt. -**vincingly** *adv.*

con-vo-ca-tion (kon´vo k´shan) *n.* A formal or ceremonial assembly or meeting.

con-voke (kon vk´) *v.* To call together for a formal meeting.

con-voy (kon´voi) *n.* A group of cars, trucks, etc., traveling together. *v.* To escort or guide.

con-vulse (kon vuls´) *v.* To move or shake violently. **convulsive** *adj.*

con-vul-sion (kon vul´shan) *n.* A violent involuntary muscular contraction.

cool (köl) *adj.* Without warmth; indifferent or unenthusiastic. *Slang* First-rate; composure.

cool-ant (kō´lant) *n.* The cooling agent that circulates through a machine.

coon (kön) *n. Informal* A raccoon.

coop (köp) *n.* A cage or enclosed area to contain animals, as chickens.

coop (k´op) *n.* A cooperative.

co-op-er-ate (k op´e rt´) *v.* To work together toward a common cause. **cooperation** *n.*

co-op-er-a-tive (k op´e r´tiv) *adj.* Willing to cooperate with others. **cooperatively** *adv.* **cooperativeness** *n.*

coopt (k opt´) *v.* To elect or choose as a new member.

cop (kop) *n. Informal* A police officer.

cope (kp) *v.* To strive; to struggle or contend with something. *n.* The long cape worn by a priest on special ceremonial occasions.

cop-ier (kop´ r) *n.* A machine that makes copies of original material.

co-pi-lot (k´p´lot) *n.* The assistant pilot on an aircraft.

co-pi-ous (k´p´əs) *n.* Large in quantity; abundant.

cop-per (kop´r) *n.* A metallic element that is a good conductor of electricity and heat, reddish-brown in color.

cop-ra (kop´ra) *n.* Dried coconut meat that yields coconut oil.

cop-ter (kop´tr) *n. Slang* A helicopter.

cop-u-la (kop´la) *n., Gram.* A word or words which connect a subject and predicate.

cop-u-late (kop´ lt´) *v.* To have sexual intercourse. **copulation** *n.*

copy (kop´) *v. pl.*-**ies** To reproduce an original. *n.* A single printed text. -**ist** *n.*

coq au vin *n.* Chicken cooked in wine.

co-quette (k ket´) *n.* A woman who flirts.

cor-al (kor´al) n. The stony skeleton of a small sea creature, often used for jewelry.

co-re-spon-dent (k´ri spon´dent) n. A person charged with having committed adultery with the defendant in a divorce case.

cor-ne-a (kor´n a) n. The transparent membrane of the eyeball. corneal adj.

cor-net (kor net´) n. A three valved, brass musical instrument. cornetist n.

corn-meal n. Meal made from corn.

corn-row v. To braid the hair in rows very close to the head.

corn-stalk n. A stalk of corn.

corn-y (kor´n) adj. Slang Trite or mawkishly old-fashioned.

co-rol-la (ko rol´a) n. The petals of a flower.

cor-ol-lary (kor´o ler´) n. pl. -ies Something that naturally or incidentally follows or accompanies.

cor-o-nar-y (kor´o ner´) adj. Of or relating to the two arteries that supply blood to the heart muscles.

coronary thrombosis n. A blockage of the coronary artery of the heart.

cor-po-rate (kor´pr it) adj. Combined into one joint body; relating to a corporation.

cor-po-ra-tion (kor´po r´shan) n. A group of merchants united in a trade guild; any group or persons that act as one.

cor-po-re-al (kor pr´ al) adj. Of a physical nature.

corpse (korps) n. A dead body.

cor-pu-lence n. The excessive accumulation of body fat; obesity. -pulent adj.

cor-pus delicti (kor´pus di lik´t) n. The essential evidence pertaining to a crime.

cor-rect (ko rekt´) v. To make free from fault or mistakes.

cor-rel-a-tive (ko rel´a tiv) adj. Having a mutual relation.

cor-ri-gen-dum (kor´i jen´dum) n. pl. -da An error in print that is accompanied by its correction.

cor-ri-gi-ble (kor´i ji bl) adj. Able to correct; capable of being corrected.

cor-rob-o-rate (ko rob´o rt´) v. To support a position or statement with evidence. corroboration n. -rative adj.

cor-rode (ko rd´) v. To eat away through chemical action. corrosive n. corrodi-ble adj. corrosion n.

cor-rupt (ko rupt´) adj. Dishonest; evil. v. To become or make corrupt.

cor-sage (kor säzh´) n. A small bouquet of flowers worn on a woman's shoulder, lapel or wrist.

cor-sair (kor´sár) n. A pirate; a fast moving vessel.

cor-tege (kor tezh´) n. A ceremonial procession; a funeral procession.

cor-tex (kor´teks) n. pl. -tices The external layer of an organ, especially the gray matter that covers the brain; the bark of trees and the rinds of fruits.

cor-ti-sone (kor´ti sn´) n. A hormone produced by the adrenal cortex, used in the treatment of rheumatoid arthritis.

co-run-dum (ko run´dum) n. An aluminum oxide used as an abrasive.

or-us-cate (kor´u skt´) v. To sparkle.

co-ry-za (ko r´za) n. An acute inflammation of the upper respiratory system.

co-sign v. To sign a document jointly.

co-sig-na-to-ry (k sig´na tr´) n. pl. -ies One who jointly cosigns a document.

cos-met-ic (koz met´ik) n. A preparation designed to beautify the face.

cos-me-tol-o-gy n. The study of cosmetics and their use. cosmetologist n.

cos-mog-o-ny (koz mog´o n) n. The creation of the universe.

cos-mo-naut n. A Soviet astronaut.

cos-mo-pol-i-tan (koz´mo pol´i tan) adj. Being at home anywhere in the world.

cos-mop-o-lite (koz mop´o lt) n. A cosmopolitan person.

cos-mos (koz´mos) n. An orderly and harmoniously systematic universe.

cos-set (kos´it) v. To pamper; pet.

cost (kost) n. The amount paid or charged for a purchase. costly adj.

cos-tive (kos´tiv) adj. Affected with or causing constipation.

cot-tage (kotij´) n. A small house, usually for vacation use.

cough (kof) v. To suddenly expel air from the lungs with an explosive noise.

could (ked) v. Past tense of can.

could·n't (ked´ent) Could not.

cou·lomb (kö´lom) n. The unit of quantity used to measure electricity; the amount conveyed by one amphere in one second.

coun·cil (koun´sil) n. A group of people assembled for consultation or discussion; an official legislative or advisory body. **councilman** n. **councilor** n.

coun·sel (koun´sel) n. Advice given through consultation; a lawyer engaged in the management or trial of a court case.

coun·te·nance (kount´te nans) n. The face as an indication of mood or character; bearing or expression that would suggest approval or sanction.

coun·ter·act (koun´tr akt´) v. To oppose and, by contrary action, make ineffective.

coun·ter·bal·ance (koun´tr bal´ans) n. A force or influence that balances another; a weight that balances another.

coun·ter·claim (koun´tr klm´) n. A contrary claim made to offset another.

coun·ter·cul·ture n. A culture with values opposite those of traditional society.

coun·ter·es·pi·o·nage (koun´tr es´p o näzh´) n. Espionage aimed at discovering and thwarting enemy espionage.

coun·ter·in·tel·li·gence (koun´tr in tel´i jens) n. An intelligence agency function designed to block information, deceive the enemy, prevent sabotage, and gather military and political material and information.

coun·ter·ir·ri·tant (koun´tr ir´i tant) n. An irritation that diverts attention from another.

coun·ter·of·fen·sive (koun´tr o fen´ siv) n. A military offensive designed to thwart an enemy attack.

coun·ter·pane (koun´tr pn´) n. A covering.

coun·ter·part (koun´tr pärt´) n. One that matches or complements another.

coun·ter·pro·duc·tive adj. Tending to hinder rather than aid in the attainment of a goal.

coun·ter·ten·or n. An adult tenor with a very high range, higher than that of the average tenor.

coun·ter·vail (koun´tr vl´) v. To counteract.

ccoun·try (kun´tr) n. pl. **-ies** A given area or region; the land of one's birth, residence, or citizenship; a state, nation, or its territory.

coup (kö) n. A brilliant, sudden move that is usually highly successful.

cou·ple (kup´l) n. A pair; something that joins two things together; a few. v. To join in marriage or sexual union.

cou·plet (kup´lit) n. Two rhyming lines of poetry in succession.

cour·age (ker´ij) n. Mental or moral strength to face danger without fear.

cou·ri·er (ker´ r) n. A messenger; a person who carries contraband for another.

court (krt) n. The residence of a sovereign or similar dignitary; a sovereign's family and advisors; an assembly for the transaction of judicial business; a place where trials are conducted; an area marked off for game playing. v. To try to win favor.

cour·te·ous (kr´t us) adj. Marked by respect for and consideration of others.

cour·te·sy (kr´ti s) n. pl. **-ies** Courteous behavior; general allowance despite facts.

court·house (krt´hous´) n. A building for holding courts of law.

cour·ti·er (kr´t r) n. One in attendance at a royal court.

cov·e·nant (kuv´e nant) n. A formal, binding agreement; a promise or pledge.

cov·et (kuv´it) v. To wish for enviously; to crave possession of that which belongs to someone else.

cov·ey (kuv´) n. A small group of birds, especially quail or partridges.

coy (koi) adj. Quieting or shy, or pretending to be so. **coyness** n.

coz·en (kuz´en) v. To swindle, cheat, deceive, win over, or induce to do something by coaxing or trickery. **cozener** n.

co·zy (k´z) adj. Comfortable and warm; snug. n. A cover placed over a teapot to retain the warmth. **cozily** adv.

crab n. Any one of numerous chiefly marine crustaceans with a short, broad shell, four pairs of legs, and one pair of pincers; sideways motion of a airplane headed into a crosswind. **crabs** *n.* festation with crab lice. **crabbed** *adj.* Morose or peevish; difficult to read or understand.

crag (krag) *n.* A steep, jagged rock or cliff. **cragged** *adj.* **craggy** *adj.*

cra-ni-um (kr´n *um*) *n. pl.* **crania** The skull, especially the part in which the brain is enclosed. **cranial** *adj.*

crank-y (krang´k) *adj.* Grouchy, irritable.

crass (kras) *adj.* Insensitive and unrefined.

cra-vat (kr*a* vat´) *n.* A necktie.

crave (krv) *v.* To desire intensely.

cra-ven (kr´ven) *adj.* Completely lacking courage.

crav-ing *n.* An intense longing or desire.

craw (kro) *n.* The crop of a bird; the stomach of a lower animal.

craw-fish (kro´fish´) *n.* A crayfish.

creak (krk) *n.* A squeaking or grating noise. **creaky** *adj.* **creakily** *adv.*

crease (krs) *n.* A line or mark made by folding and pressing a pliable substance.

cre-ate (kr t´) *v.* To bring something into existence; to give rise to.

cre-a-tion (kr ´shan) *n.* The act of creating; something that is created; the universe.

cre-ative (kr ´tiv) *adj.* Marked by the ability to create; inventive; imaginative.

cre-ator (kr ´tr) *n.* One that creates. **Creator.** God.

crea-ture (kr´chr) *n.* Something created; a living being.

cre-dence (krd´ens) *n.* Belief.

cre-den-za (kri den´za) *n.* A buffet or sideboard, usually without legs.

cred-i-ble (kred´i bl) *adj.* Offering reasonable grounds for belief. **-ibility** *n.*

cred-u-lous (krej´u lus) *adj.* Gullible; ready to believe on slight or uncertain evidence. **credulously** *adv.* **-ness** *n.*

creed (krd) *n.* A brief authoritative statement of religious belief.

creek (krk) *n.* A narrow stream.

creel (krl) *n.* A wicker basket for holding fish.

creep (krp) *v.* To advance at a slow pace; to go timidly or cautiously; to

grow along a surface, clinging by means of tendrils or aerial roots.

cre-mate (kr´mt) *v.* To reduce to ashes by burning.

cre-o-sote (kr´o st´) *n.* An oily liquid mixture obtained by distilling coal tar, used especially as a wood preservative.

crept *v.* The past tense of creep.

cre-pus-cu-lar (kri pus´k lr) *adj.* Of, resembling, or relating to twilight.

cre-scen-do (kri shen´d) *adv.* In music, gradually increasing in loudness.

cres-cent (kres´ent) *n.* The shape of the moon in its first and fourth quarters, defined with a convex and a concave edge.

cress (kres) *n.* Any of numerous plants with sharp-tasting edible leaves.

crest (krest) *n.* A tuft or comb on the head of a bird or animal; the top line of a mountain or hill.

cre-tin (kr´tin) *n.* One afflicted with cretinism; a person with marked mental deficiency.

cre-tin-ism (krt´e niz´um) *n.* A condition marked by physical stunting and mental deficiency.

cre-vasse (kr*e* vas´) *n.* A deep crack or crevice.

crev-ice (krev´is) *n.* A narrow crack.

crew-el (krö´el) *n.* Slackly twisted worsted yarn, used in embroidery.

cri-er (kr´r) *n.* One who calls out public notices.

crime (krm) *n.* An act or the commission of an act that is forbidden by law.

crimp (krimp) *v.* To cause to become bent or crinkled; to pinch in or together.

crim-son (krim´zon) *n.* A deep purplish color. *v.* To make or become crimson.

cringe (krinj) *v.* To shrink or recoil in fear.

crin-kle (kring´kl) *v.* To wrinkle.

crin-o-line (krin´o lin) *n.* An open-weave fabric used for lining and stiffening garments.

cri-sis (kr´sis) *n. pl.* **crises** An unstable or uncertain time or state of affairs, the outcome of which will have a major impact; the turning point for better or worse in a disease or fever.

crisp (krisp) *adj.* Easily broken; brittle;

brisk or cold; sharp; clear. *v.* To make or become crisp. **crisply** *adv.* **crispness** *n.* **crispy** *adj.*

cri-te-ri-on (kr tr´ on) *n. pl.* **criteria** A standard by which something can be judged.

crit-ic (krit´ik) *n.* A person who is critical; a person who examines a subject and expresses an opinion as to its value; a person who judges or evaluates art or artistic creations, as a theatre critic.

crit-i-cal (krit´i kal) *adj.* Very important, as a critical decision; tending to criticize harshly.

crit-i-cism (krit´i siz´um) *n.* The act of criticizing, usually in a severe or negative fashion.

crit-i-cize (krit´i sīz´) *v.* To be a critic; to find fault with; to judge critically; to blame.

croak (krk) *n.* A hoarse, raspy cry such as that made by a frog. *v.* To utter a croak. *Slang* To die.

crock (krok) *n.* An earthenware pot or jar most often used for cooking or storing food.

crone (krn) *n.* A witch-like, withered old woman.

crook (krek) *n.* A bent or hooked implement; a bend or curve; a person given to dishonest acts. *v.* To bend or curve.

croon (krön) *v.* To sing in a gentle, low voice; to make a continued moaning sound.

crop (krop) *n.* A plant which is grown and then harvested for use or for sale; a riding whip. *v.* To cut off short; to appear unexpectedly.

cro-quette (kr ket´) *n.* A small patty or roll of minced food that is breaded and deep fried.

cross-bar (kros´bär´) *n.* A horizontal bar or line.

crotch (kroch) *n.* The angle formed by the junction of two parts, such as legs or branches.

crotch-et (kroch´it) *n.* A peculiar opinion or preference.

crouch (krouch) *v.* To bend at the knees and lower the body close to the ground.

croup (kröp) *n.* A spasmodic laryngitis, especially of children, marked by a loud, harsh cough and difficulty in breathing.

crou-pi-er (krö´p r) *n.* One who collects and pays bets at a gambling table.

crou-ton (krö´ton) *n.* A small piece of toasted or fried bread.

crow (kr) *n.* A large, black bird.

cru-cial (krö´shal) *adj.* Extremely important; critical.

cru-ci-ble (krö´si bl) *n.* A vessel used for melting and calcining materials at high temperatures; a hard test of someone.

cru-ci-fy (krö´si f´) *v.* To put to death by nailing on a cross; to treat cruelly; to torment.

crude (kröd) *adj.* Unrefined; lacking refinement or tact; haphazardly made. *n.* Unrefined petroleum. **crudely** *adv.*

cruel (krö´el) *adj.* Inflicting suffering; causing pain. **cruelly** *adv.* **cruelty** *n.*

crum-ple (krum´pel) *v.* To bend or crush out of shape; to cause to collapse; to be crumpled.

crush (krush) *v.* To squeeze or force by pressure so as to damage or injure; to reduce to particles by pounding or grinding; to put down or suppress.

crus-ta-cean (kru st´shan) *n.* Any one of a large class of aquatic arthropods, including lobsters and crabs, with a segmented body and paired, jointed limbs.

crux (kruks) *n.* An essential or vital moment; a main or central feature.

cry (kr) *v.* To shed tears; to call out loudly; to utter a characteristic call or sound; to proclaim publicly.

crypt (kript) *n.* An underground chamber or vault primarily used to bury the dead.

cryp-tic (krip´tik) *adj.* Intended to be obscure; serving to conceal.

cryp-tog-ra-phy (krip tog´ra f) *n.* The writing and deciphering of messages in secret code.

cub (kub) *n.* The young of the lion, wolf, or bear; an awkward child or youth.

cube (kb) *n.* A regular solid with six equal squares, having all its angles right angles.

cube root *n.* A number whose cube is a given number.

cubic (k´bik) *adj.* Having the shape of a cube; having three dimensions; having the volume of a cube with the edges of a specified unit.

cu-bi-cle (k´bi kl) *n.* A small partitioned area.

cu-bit (k´bit) *n.* An ancient unit of measurement that equals approximately eighteen to twenty inches.

cuffs *n.* Handcuffs.

cui-sine (kwi zn´) *n.* A style of cooking and preparing food; the food prepared.

cu-li-nar-y (k´li ner´) *adj.* Relating to cooking.

cull (kul) *v.* To select the best from a group.

cul-mi-nate (kul´mi nt´) *v.* To reach or rise to the highest point. **-ation** *n.*

cu-lotte (kö lot´) *n.* A woman's full pants made to look like a skirt.

cul-pa-ble (kul´pa bl) *adj.* Meriting blame.

cul-prit (kul´prit) *n.* A person guilty of a crime.

cult (kult) *n.* A group or system of religious worship. **cultic** *adj.* **cultist** *n.*

cul-ti-vate (kul´ti vt´) *v.* To improve land for planting by fertilizing and plowing; to improve by study; to encourage. **-able** *adj.* **cultivation** *n.*

cul-vert (kul´vrt) *n.* A drain that runs under a road or railroad.

cum-ber-some *adj.* Clumsy; unwieldy due to weight or size.

cum-mer-bund (kum´r bund´) *n.* A wide sash worn by men in formal attire.

cu-ne-i-form (k n´i form´) *n.* Wedge-shaped characters used in ancient Babylonian, Assyrian, and Sumerian writing.

cun-ning (kun´ing) *adj.* Crafty; sly in the use of special resources. **-ly** *adv.*

cu-pid-i-ty (k pid´i t) *n.* An excessive desire for material gain.

cu-po-la (k´po la) *n.* A rounded roof; a small vaulted structure that usually rises above a roof.

cur (ker) *n.* A mongrel; a dog of mixed breeds.

cu-rate (kr´it) *n.* A member of the clergy that assists the priest.

cu-ra-tor (k r´tr) *n.* A person in charge of a zoo, museum, or other places with exhibits.

curd (kerd) *n.* The coagulated portion of milk used for making cheese.

cure (kr) *n.* Recovery from a sickness; a medical treatment; the process of preserving food with the use of salt, smoke, or aging.

cu-ret-tage *n.* Surgical cleaning and scraping by means of curette.

cu-ri-o (kr´ ´) *n.* An unusual or rare object.

cu-ri-ous (kr´ us) *adj.* Questioning; inquisitive; eager for information

curl (kerl) *v.* To twist into curves; shape like a coil. *n.* A ringlet of hair. **-er** *n.*

cur-mudg-eon (kr muj´on) *n.* An ill-tempered person.

cur-rant (ker´ant) *n.* A small seedless raisin.

cur-ren-cy (ker´en s) *n. pl.* **-cies** Money in circulation.

cur-rent (ker´ent) *adj.* Belonging or occurring in the present time. *n.* Water or air that has a steady flow in a definite direction.

cur-ric-u-lum (ku rik´ lum) *n. pl.* **-la, -lums** The courses offered in a school.

cur-ry (ker´) *v.* To groom a horse with a brush. *n.* A pungent spice used in cooking.

curse (kers) *n.* A prayer or wish for harm to come to someone or something. **cursed** *adj*

cursor *n.* In computer science, the flashing square, underline, or other indicator on the CRT screen of a computer that shows where the next character will be deleted or inserted.

cur-sive (kr´siv) *n.* A flowing writing in which the letters are joined together.

curt (krt) *adj.* Abrupt; rude. **curtly** *adv*

cur-tail (kr´tl´) *v.* To shorten; to make less as if by cutting away some part. **curtailment** *n.*

curt-sy (kert´s) *n. pl* **-sies** A respectful gesture made by bending the knees and lowering the body. **curtsy** *v.*

cush-ion (kesh´on) *n.* A pillow with a soft filling. *v.* To absorb the shock or effect.

cus-pid (kus´pid) *n.* A pointed canine tooth.

cus-pi-dor (kus´pi dor´) *n.* A spittoon.

cuss (kus) *v.* To use profanity.

cus-tard (kus´trd) *n.* A mixture of milk, eggs, sugar, and flavoring that is baked.

cus-to-di-an (ku st´d *a*n) *n.* One who has the custody or care of something or someone.

cus-to-dy (kus´to d) *n. pl.* **-dies** The act of guarding; the care and protection of a minor; a caretaker; care or custody of anything.

cus-tom (kus´tom) *n.* An accepted practice of a community or people; the usual manner of doing something. **customs** The tax one must pay on imported goods.

cute (kt) *adj.* Attractive in a delightful way.

cy-a-nide (s´a nd) *n., Chem.* A compound of cyanogen with a metallic element; a poison.

cyc-la-men (sik´la men) *n.* A plant with red, white, or pink flowers.

cy-cle (s´kl) *n.* A recurring time in which an event occurs repeatedly; a bicycle or motorcycle. **cyclical** *adj.* **-cally** *adv.*

cy-clist (s´klist) *n.* A person who rides a cycle.

cy-clom-e-ter *n.* A device for recording the revolutions of a wheel and the distance traversed by the wheeled vehicle; an instrument that measures circular arcs.

cy-clo-tron (s´klo tron´) *n.* Machine that obtains high-energy electrified particles by whirling at a high speed in a strong magnetic field.

cyl-in-der (sil´in dr) *n.* A long, round body that is either hollow or solid.

cyn-ic (sin´ik) *n.* One who believes that all people have selfish motives. **cynical** *adj.*

cy-no-sure (s´no shör´) *n.* A person or object that attracts admiration and interest.

cyst (sist) *n.* A closed abnormal sac or vesicle which may develop in a structure or cavity of the body. **cystic** *adj.*

cystic fibrosis *n.* A congenital disease, usually developing in childhood and resulting in disorders of the lungs and pancreas.

cys-ti-tis (si st´tis) *n.* An inflammation of the bladder.

cy-tol-o-gy (s tol´o j) *n.* The scientific study of cell formation, function, and structure. **cytological** *adj.* **-logic** adj.

cy-to-tax-on-o-my *n.* Classification of plants and animals according to characteristics of the chromosomes. **cyto-taxonomic** *adj.*

cy-to-trop-ic *Biol.* Having an attraction for cells, as various viruses; or pertaining to the propensity of cells to be drawn toward or to move away from each other, singly or in groups.

cy-tot-ro-pism *n.* The tendency of cells to move.

czar (zär) *n.* An emperor or king or one of the former emperors or kings of Russia. *Slang* One who has authority. **czardom** *n.*

D

D, d (d) The fourth letter of the English alphabet; the Roman numeral for 500.

dab (dab) *v.* To touch quickly with light, short strokes.

dab-ble (dab´l) *v.* To play in a liquid, as water, with the hands; to work in or play with in a minor way. **dabbler** *n.*

dad (dad) *n. Informal* Father.

dad-dy (dad´) *n. pl.* **-dies** *Informal* Father.

daf-fo-dil (daf´o dil) *n.* A bulbous plant with solitary yellow flowers.

daft (daft) *adj.* Insane; crazy; foolish.

da-querre-o-type (da ger´ o tp´) *n.* A very early photographic process which used silver-coated metallic plates that were sensitive to light.

dai-ly (d´l) *adj., pl.* **-lies** To occur, appear, or happen everyday of the week. *n.* A newspaper which is published daily.

dain-ty (dn´t) *adj.* **-ties** Having or showing refined taste; delicately beautiful. **daintily** *adv.* **daintiness** *n.*

dai-qui-ri (d´ki r) *n.* A cocktail made with rum and lime juice.

dair-y (dâr´) *n. pl.* **-ies** A commercial establishment which processes milk for resale.

dale (dl) *n.* A small valley.

dal-ly (dl´) *v.* To waste time; to dawdle; to flirt. **dallier** *n.* **dalliance** *n.*

dam-age (dam´ij) *n.* An injury to person

or property; in law, the compensation given for loss or in jury. **-able** adj.

dam-ask (dam´ask) n. An elaborately patterned, reversible fabric, originally made of silk.

dam-sel (dam´zel) n. A maiden; a young unmarried woman.

dance (dans) v. To move rhythmically to music using improvised or planned steps and gestures. **dance** n. **dancer** n.

dan-dle (dan´dl) v. To move a child or infant up and down on the knees or in the arms with a gentle movement. **dandler** n.

dan-ger (dn´jr) n. An exposure to injury, evil, or loss.

dan-ger-ous (dn´jr us) adj. Unsafe. **dangerously** adv. **dangerousness** n.

dan-gle (dang´gl) v. To hang loosely and swing to and fro; to have an unclear grammatical relation in a sentence.

dank (dangk) adj. Uncomfortably damp; wet and cold. **dankly** adv.

dan-seuse (dän soez´) n. pl. **-seuses** A female ballet dancer.

dap-per (dap´r) adj. Stylishly dressed.

dap-ple (dap´l) v. To make variegated or spotted in color.

dark-en v. To become or make dark or darker. **darkish** adj. **darkly** adv.

dar-ling (där´ling) n. A favorite person; someone who is very dear; a person tenderly loved.

darn (därn) v. To mend a hole by filling the gap with interlacing stitches. **darner** n.

dart (därt) n. A pointed missile either shot or thrown. **darts** pl. The game of throwing darts at a usually round target.

dash (dash) v. To break or shatter with a striking violent blow; to move quickly; to rush; to finish or perform a duty in haste.

das-tard (das´trd) n. A coward; a sneak. **dastardliness** n. **dastardly** adj.

da-ta (d´ta) n. pl. The figures or facts from which conclusions may be drawn.

data bank n. In computer science, the location in a computer where information is stored.

data processing n. In computer science, the business of handling and storing information using computers and other available machines.

date (dt) n. A particular point in time; a day, month, or year; the exact time at which something happens; a social engagement; a person's partner on such an occasion.

date-line (dt ln´) n. The line or phrase at the beginning of a periodical giving the date and place of publication; the 180th meridian on a map or globe which is where a day begins.

da-tum (d´tum) n. pl. **-ta** A single piece of information.

daub (dob) v. To coat or smear with grease, plaster, or an adhesive substance.

daugh-ter (do´tr) n. The female offspring of a man or woman; a female descendant.

daughter--in--law n. One's son's wife.

daunt (dont) v. To intimidate or discourage.

dav-it (dav´it) n. A small crane on the side of a ship, for lifting its boats.

daw-dle (dod´l) v. To waste; to take more time than is needed. **dawdler** n.

dawn (don) n. The beginning of a new day; to begin to understand, expand, or develop.

daylight saving time n. The period of the year, beginning in the spring, when clocks are moved ahead by one hour.

daze (dz) v. To bewilder or stun with a heavy blow or shock. **dazedly** adv.

dead (ded) adj. Without life; no longer in existence or use; dormant; quiet; in law, no longer in force.

dead-eye n. A sharpshooter.

dead-line (ded´ln´) n. A time limit when something must be finished.

deaf (def) adj. Totally or partially unable to hear; refusing or unwilling to listen.

deal (dl) v. To distribute or pass out playing cards; to be occupied or concerned with a certain matter; to discuss, consider, or take affirmative action. n. An indefinite amount; a business transaction. **dealer** n.

deal-ing (d´ling) n. Slang Involved in the buying and selling of illegal drugs.

dean (dn) n. The head administrator of a college, high school, or university.

dear (dr) adj. Greatly cherished; loved.

dearly *adv.* dearness *n.*

death (deth) *n.* Termination; the permanent cessation of all vital functions.

deb *n.* A debutante.

de-ba-cle (di bä´kl) *n.* A sudden downfall, failure, or collapse.

de-bark (di bärk´) *v.* To disembark.

de-base (di bes´) *v.* To lower in character or value; demean. **debasement** *n.* **debaser** *n.*

de-bate (di bt´) *v.* To discuss or argue opposing points; to consider; to deliberate. **debate**. **debatable** *adj.*

de-bauch (di boch´) *v.* To lead away from morals; to corrupt. **-chery** *n.*

de-ben-ture (di ben´chr) *n.* A voucher given as an acknowledgment of debt.

de-bil-i-tate (di bil´i tt´) *v.* To make feeble or weak. **debilitation** *n.*

deb-it (deb´it) *n.* A debt or item recorded in an account *v.* To enter a debt in a ledger; to charge someone with a debt.

de-brief (d brf´) *v.* To interrogate or question in order to obtain information.

de-bris (de br´) *n.* Scattered or discarded remains or waste.

debt (det) *n.* That which someone owes as money, services, or goods; an obligation to pay or render something to another.

debt-or (det´r) *n.* A person owing a debt to another.

de-bug *v.* To find and remove a concealed electronic listening device; in computer science, to remove errors in a computer program.

de-bunk (di bungk´) *v. Informal* To expose false pretensions.

de-but (d b´) *n.* A first public appearance; the formal introduction to society; the beginning of a new career.

deb-u-tante (deb´ tänt´) *n.* A young woman making her debut in society.

de-cade (dek´d) *n.* A period of ten years; a set or group of ten.

dec-a-dence (dek´a dens) *n.* A process of decay or deterioration; a period or condition of decline, as in morals.

caf-fein-at-ed *adj.* Having the caffeine removed.

deca-gon (dek´a gon´) *n. Geom.* A polygon with ten sides and ten angles. **decagonal** *adj.* **decagonally** *adv.*

dec-a-gram (dek´a gram´) *n.* In the metric system, a measure of weight equal to 10 grams.

de-cal (d´kal) *n.* A design or picture transferred by decalcomania.

dec-a-li-ter *or* **dek-a-li-ter** (dek´a l´tr) *n.* In the metric system, a measure of capacity equal to 10 liters.

deca-logue *or* **dec-a-log** (dek´a log´) *n.* The Ten Commandments.

deca-me-ter *or* **deka-me-ter** (dek´a m´ tr) *n.* In the metric system, a measure of length equal to 10 meters.

de-camp (di kamp´) *v.* To break camp; to leave or depart suddenly.

de-cant (di cant´) *v.* To pour off liquid without disturbing the sediments; to pour from one container to another.

de-cant-er (di kan´tr) *n.* A decorative stoppered bottle for serving wine or other liquids.

de-cap-i-tate (di kap´i tt´) *v.* To cut off the head; to behead **decapitation** *n*

de-cath-lon (di kath´lon) *n.* An athletic event with ten different track and field events in all of which each contestant participates.

de-cay (di k´) *v.* To decline in quantity or quality; to rot. *Phys.* To diminish or disintegrate by radioactive decomposition.

de-cease (di ss´) *v.* To die. **decedent** *n.*

de-ceit (di st´) *n.* Deception; the quality of being deceptive; falseness. **-ful** *adj.*

de-ceive (di sv´) *v.* To mislead by falsehood; to lead into error; to delude.

de-cen-ni-al (di sen´ al) *adj.* Happening once every 10 years; continuing for ten years.

de-cep-tion (di sep´shan) *n.* The act of deceiving; the factor state of being deceived; anything which deceives or deludes.

de-cep-tive (di sep´tiv) *adj.* Having the tendency or power to deceive. **-ly** *adv.* **-ness** *n.*

deci-are (des´ âr´) *n.* In the metric system, one tenth of an are.

deci-bel (des´i bl´) *n.* A measurement of sound; one tenth of a bel.

de-cide (di sd´) *v.* To settle; to determine, as a controversy or contest; to determine the conclusion or issue of; to make up one's mind.

de-cid-ed *adj.* Definite or unquestionable; exhibiting determination. **ly** *adv.*

de-cid-u-ous (di sij´ō us) *adj., Biol.* Shedding or falling off at maturity or at a certain season, such as fruit, leaves, petals, antlers, or snake skins.

deci-gram (des´i gram´) *n.* In the metric system, the tenth part of a gram.

deci-li-ter (des´i l´tr) *n.* In the metric system, the tenth part of a liter.

de-cil-lion (di sil´yon) *n.* The cardinal number written as one followed by thirty-three zeros; a thousand nonillions.

dec-i-mal (des´i mal) *n.* A proper fraction based on the number 10 and indicated by the use of a decimal point; every decimal place indicating a multiple of a power of 10; a number with a decimal point; a decimal fraction or one of its digits. **decimally** *adv.*

decimal point *n.* A period placed to the left of a decimal fraction.

dec-i-mate (des´i mt´) *v.* To destroy or kill a large proportion of something; to select by lot and kill one out of every ten.

deci-meter (des´i m´tr) *n.* In the metric system, the tenth part of a meter.

de-ci-pher (di s´fr) *v.* To determine the meaning of something obscure, as a poor handwriting; to translate from code or cipher into plain text; to decode. **-able** *adj.*

de-ci-sion (di sizh´an) *n.* The act of deciding; a judgment or conclusion reached by deciding.

de-ci-sive (di s´siv) *adj.* Ending uncertainty or dispute; conclusive; characterized by firmness; unquestionable; unmistakable.

de-claim (di klm´) *v.* To speak or deliver loudly and rhetorically; to give a formal speech; to attack verbally.

de-clas-si-fy (d klas´i f´) *v.* To remove the security classification of a document.

de-clen-sion (di klen´shan) *n.* A descent; a sloping downward; a decline; a deviation, as from a belief. *Gram.* The inflection of nouns, pronouns, and adjectives according to case, number, and gender

de-cline (di kln´) *v.* To reject or refuse

something; to grow frail gradually, as in health.

de-cliv-i-ty (di klv´i t) *n.* *pl.* **-ties** A steep downward slope or surface.

de-coct (di kokt´) *v.* To extract by boiling; to condense. **decoction** *n.*

de-code (d kd´) *v.* To convert from a coded message into plain language.

de-com-pose (d´kom pz´) *v.* To decay; to separate into constituent parts.

de-con-trol (d´kon trl´) *v.* To free from the control of, especially from governmental control.

de-cor (d kor´) *n.* The style of decorating a room, office, or home.

dec-o-rate (dek´o rt´) *v.* To adorn or furnish with fashionable or beautiful things; to confer a decoration or medal upon.

dec-o-rous (dek´r us) *adj.* Marked by decorum; seemly; proper. **-ly** *adv.* **decorousness** *n.*

de-co-rum (di kr´um) *n.* Proper behavior; good or fitting conduct.

de-crease (di krs´) *v.* To grow or cause to grow gradually less or smaller; to diminish. *n.* The process or act of decreasing or the resulting state; a decline.

de-cree (di kr) *n.* An authoritative and formal order or decision; a judicial judgment.

dec-re-ment (dek´re ment) *n.* The process or act of decreasing; the amount lost by gradual waste or diminution. **decremental** *adj.*

de-crep-it (di krep´it) *adj.* Broken down or worn out by old age or excessive use. **-ly** *adv.* **decrepitude** *n.*

de-cre-scen-do (d´kri shen´d) *n.* *pl.* **-dos** *Mus.* A gradual decrease in force or loudness. **decrescendo** *adj. & adv.*

de-crim-i-nal-ize *v.* To remove the criminal classification of; to no longer prohibit.

de-cry (di kr´) *v.* To express strong disapproval openly; to denounce.

de-duce (di dōs´) *v.* To derive a conclusion by reasoning. **deducible** *adj.*

de-duct (di dukt´) *v.* To subtract or take away from. **ductible** *adj.*

de-duc-tion (di duk´shan) *n.* The act of deducing or subtracting; an amount that is or may be deducted; the process or act of deducting.

deed (dd) n. Anything performed or done; a notable achievement or feat; in law, a legal document, especially one relating to the transference of property. **deedless** adj.

deem (dm) v. To judge or consider.

deep-en (d´pen) v. To become or make deep or deeper.

deep-freeze v. To quick-freeze. Slang An appliance for storing frozen foods.

deep-six v. Slang To throw overboard; to get rid of; to toss out.

deer (dr) n. pl. deer A hoofed ruminant mammal having deciduous antlers, usually in the male only, as the elk, moose, and reindeer.

de-es-ca-late (d es´ka lt) v. To decrease or be decreased gradually, as in intensity, scope, or effect.

de-face (di fs´) v. To spoil or mar the appearance or surface of something.

de fac´to (d dak´t) adj. Really or actually exercising authority.

de-fal-cate (di fal´kt) v. To embezzle; to misuse funds. **defalcation** n.

de-fame (di fm´) v. To slander or libel.

de-fault (di folt´) v. To neglect to fulfill an obligation or requirement, as to pay money due or to appear in court; to forfeit by default. n. The failure to participate or compete in a competition.

de-feat (di ft´) v. To win a victory; to beat; to prevent the successful outcome of; to frustrate; to baffle; in law, to make void; to annul.

de-fend (di fend´) v. Protect.

de-fen-dant (di fen´dant) n. The person charged in a criminal or civil lawsuit.

de-fense (di fens´) n. The action of defending.

de-fer (di fer´) v. To delay or postpone.

de-fi-ance (di f´ans) n. The instance or act of defying; a challenge. **defiant** adj.

de-fi-cient (di fish´ent) adj. Lacking in a necessary element.

de-fog v. To remove fog from, as from the inside of an automobile. -fogger n.

de-fo-li-ant (d f´l ant) n. A chemical sprayed or dusted on plants or trees to cause the leaves to drop off. -foliate v.

de-fraud (di frod´) v. To cheat; to swindle.

de-fray (di fr´) v. To provide for or to

make payment on something. **defray-able** adj.

de-frost (di frost´) v. To cause to thaw out; to remove the ice or frost from.

deft (deft) adj. Skillful and neat in one's actions.

de-funct (di fungkt´) adj. Dead; deceased.

de-fuse v. To remove the detonator or fuse from; to remove or make less dangerous, tense, or hostile.

de-fy (di f´) v. pl. -fies To confront or resist boldly and openly; to challenge someone to do something or not do something; to dare.

de-gauss (d gous´) v. To neutralize the magnetic field of something.

de-grade (d grd´) v. To reduce in rank, status, or grade; to demote; to reduce in quality or intensity. **degraded** adj.

de-hu-man-ize (d h´ma nz´) v. To deprive of human qualities, especially to make mechanical and routine.

de-hu-mid-i-fy (d´h mid´i f´) v. To remove the moisture from. -fier n.

de-hy-drate (d h´drt) v. To cause to lose moisture or water. **dehydration** n.

de-ice (d s´) v. To rid of or keep free of ice.

de-i-fy (d´i f´) v. To glorify or idealize; to raise in high regard; to worship as a god.

deign (dn) v. To think it barely worthy of one's dignity; to condescend.

de-ject (di jekt´) v. To lower the spirits; to dishearten. -ion n. **dejectedness** n.

de-jec-tion (di jek´shan) n. The state or condition of being dejected; depression; melancholy.

de ju-re (d jer´) adv. By right; legally or rightfully.

dek-a-gram n. See decagram.

dek-a-liter n. See decaliter.

dek-a-meter n. See decameter.

dek-are or dec-are n. In the metric system, a thousand square meter or 10 ares.

dek-a-stere or dec-a-stere n. In the metric system, a measure of volume equal to 10 steres.

de-lay (di l´) v. To put off until a later time; to defer; to cause to be late or detained; to linger; to waste time; to procrastinate. n. The time period that someone is delayed.

de-lec-ta-tion (d´lek t´shan) n. Enjoyment or pleasure.

del-e-ga-tion (del´e g´shan) n. The act of delegating or the state of being delegated; a person or group of people appointed to represent others.

de-lete (di lt´) v. To cancel; to take out.

del-e-te-ri-ous (del´i tr´ us) adj. Causing moral or physical injury; harmful. **deleteriously** adv. **deleteriousness** n.

del-i n. Slang Delicatessen.

de-lib-er-ate (di lib´e rt´) v. To say or do something intentionally; to plan in advance. adj. Premeditated; to be leisurely or slow in manner or motion.

del-i-ca-cy (del´i ka s) n. pl. -cies A select or choice food; the quality or state of being delicate.

de-li-cious adj. Extremely enjoyable and pleasant to the taste. n. A variety of red, sweet apples.

de-light (di lt´) n. A great joy or pleasure. v. To give or take great pleasure; to rejoice; to gratify or please highly. **delighted** adj

de-lim-it (di lim´it) v. To give or prescribe the limits of.

de-lin-eate (di lin´ t) v. To represent by a drawing; to draw or trace the outline of something; to sketch; to represent in gestures or words.

de-lin-quent (di ling´kwent) adj. Neglecting to do what is required by obligation or law; falling behind in a payment. **delinquent** n. A juvenile who is out of control, misbehaving in ways that violate the law.

del-i-quesce (del´i kwes´) v., Chem. To become liquid by absorbing atmospheric moisture; to melt. **-scent** adj.

de-lir-i-um (di lr´ um) n. A temporary or sporadic mental disturbance associated with fever, shock, or intoxication and marked by excitement, incoherence, and hallucination; uncontrolled excitement and emotion. **delirium tre-mens** (di lr´ umtr´menz) n. Acute delirium resulting from chronic and excessive use of alcohol.

delta ray n. An electron ejected from matter ionizing radiation.

de-lude (di lōd´) v. To mislead the mind

or judgment; to deceive; to cause to be deceived.

del-uge (del´j) v. To flood with water; to overwhelm; to destroy. n. A great flood.

de-lu-sion (di lō´zhan) n. A false, fixed belief held in spite of contrary evidence.

de luxe or **de-luxe** (de leks´) adj. High elegance or luxury.

delve (delv) v. To search for information with careful investigation.

de-mag-ne-tize (d mag´ni tz´) v. To remove the magnetic properties of.

dem-a-gogue (dem´a gog´) n. A person who leads the populace by appealing to emotions and prejudices. **demagoguery** n.

de-mar-cate (di mär´kt) v. To set boundaries or limits; to separate or limit.

de-mean (di mn´) v. To behave or conduct oneself in a particular manner; to degrade; to humble oneself or another. **demeanor** n.

de-ment-ed (di men´tid) adj. Insane.

de-men-tia (di men´sha) n. An irreversible deterioration of intellectual faculties.

de-mer-it (d mer´it) n. A fault; a defect; a mark against one's record, especially for bad conduct in school.

dem-i-john (dem´i jon´) n. A large, narrow-necked bottle usually enclosed in wicker.

de-mil-i-ta-rize (d mil´i ta rz´) v. To remove the military characteristics from.

dem-i-mon-daine (dem´ mon dn´) n. A woman who belongs to the demimonde.

dem-i-monde (dem´ mond´) n. A class of women who are supported by wealthy protectors or lovers.

de-mise (di mz´) n. Death; in law, a transfer of an estate by lease or will.

dem-i-tasse (dem´i tas´) n. A small cup of very strong coffee; the name of the cup used to hold this beverage.

dem-o n. pl. **-os** Slang A demonstration to show product use and purpose.

de-mo-bi-lize (d m´bi lz´) v. To disband; to release from the military service.

de-moc-ra-cy (di mok´ra s) n. pl. **-cies**

A form of government exercised either directly by the people or through their elected representatives; rule by the majority; the practice of legal, political, or social equality.

de-mog-ra-phy (di mog´ra f) n. Study of the characteristics of human population, such as growth, size, and vital statistics. **demographic** adj.

de-mol-ish (di mol´ish) v. To tear down; to raze; to completely do away with; to end. **demolisher** n. **demolition** n.

dem-o-li-tion (dem´o lish´an) n. The process of demolishing, especially destruction with explosives.

de-mon-e-tize (de mon´i tīz´) v. To deprive the currency of its standard value; to withdraw currency from use.

de-mon-ol-o-gy (d´mo nol´o j) n. The belief or study in demons.

de-mon-stra-ble (di mon´stra bl) adj. Obvious or apparent. **-strability** n.

dem-on-strate (dem´on strt´) v. To show or prove by reasoning or evidence; to make a public protest. **demonstration** n.

de-mor-al-ize (di mor´a lz´) v. To undermine the morale or confidence of someone; to degrade; to corrupt. **demoralization** n.

de-mote (di mt´) v. To reduce in rank, grade, or position. **demotion** n.

de-mul-cent (di mul´sent) n. A soothing substance.

de-mur (di mr´) v. To take issue; to object.

de-mure (di mr) adj. Reserved and modest; coy. **demurely** adv.

de-murrer (di mr´r) n. In law, a plea to dismiss a lawsuit on the grounds that the plaintiff's statements are insufficient to prove claim.

de-na-ture (d n´chr) v. To change the nature or natural qualities of, especially to make unfit for consumption. **denaturant** n.

den-drite (den´drt) n. Physiol. The branching process of a nerve cell which conducts impulses toward the cell body. **dendritic** adj.

den-drol-o-gy (den drol´o j) n. The botanical study of trees.

den-gue (deng´g) n., Pathol. An infectious tropical disease transmitted by mosquitoes, characterized by severe joint pains and fever.

de-ni-al (di n´al) n. A refusal to comply with a request; refusal to acknowledge the truth of a statement; abstinence; self-denial.

den-i-grate (den´i grt´) v. To slander; to defame.

de-nom-i-nate (di nom´i nt´) v. To give a name to; to designate.

de-nom-i-na-tion (di nom´i n´shan) n. The name of a group or classification.

de-nom-i-na-tor (di nom´i n´tr) n. In mathematics, the term for the bottom half of a fraction, which indicates the number of equal parts into which the unit is divided; a common characteristic or trait.

de-no-ta-tion (d´n t´shan) n. The meaning of a word, or the object or objects designated by a word; an indication, as a sign.

de-note (di nt´) v. To make known; to point out; to indicate; to signify; to designate; to mean, said of symbols or words.

de-noue-ment (d´nō mon´) n. The final solution of a novel, play, or plot.

de-nounce (di nouns´) v. To attack or condemn openly and threateningly; to accuse formally; to announce the ending of something in a formal way.

dense (dens) adj. Compact; thick; close; slow to understand; stupid. **-ly** adv.

den-si-ty (den´si t) n. pl. **-ties** The state or quality of being dense or close in parts; the quantity or amount of something per unit measure, area, volume, or length.

den-tal (den´tal) adj. Pertaining to the teeth; of or pertaining to dentistry.

dental hygienist n. A licensed dental professional who provides preventive dental care, as cleaning and instruction on how to care for teeth at home.

den-ti-frice (den´ti fris) n. A preparation in powder or paste form for cleaning the teeth.

den-tine or **den-tin** (den´tin) n. The hard, calcified part of the tooth beneath the enamel, containing the pulp chamber and root canals.

den-tist (den´tist) n. A licensed person whose profession is the diagnosis,

den-ti-tion (den tish´an) n. The kind, number, and arrangement of teeth, as in humans and other animals; the process of cutting teeth.

de-nun-ci-a-tion n. Open disapproval of a person or action; an accusation; warning or threat.

de-ny (di n´) v. To declare untrue; to refuse to acknowledge or recognize; to withhold; to refuse to grant. **deny one-self** To refuse oneself something desired; self-denial.

de-o-dor-ant (d ´dr ant) n. A product designed to prevent, mask, or destroy unpleasant odors.

de-o-dor-ize (d ´do rz´) v. To destroy, modify, or disguise the odor of them. **deodorizer** n.

de-ox-i-dize (d ok´si dz´) v. To remove the oxygen from; to reduction from the state of an oxide. **deoxidation** n. **deoxidizer** n.

de-ox-y-ri-bo-nu-cle-ic acid (d ok´sir´b nō kl´ik as´id) n. A nucleic acid which forms a principal constituent of the genes and is known to play a role of importance in the genetic action of the chromosomes, also known as DNA.

de-part (di pärt´) v. To leave; to go away; to deviate. **life** To die.

de-part-ment (di pärt´ment) n. The distinct division or part of something, as in a business, college, or store. *Informal* An area of special activity or knowledge. **departmental** adj.

de-par-ture (di pär´chr) n. The act of taking leave or going away; a divergence; a deviation; the act of starting out on a new course of action or going on a trip.

de-pend (di pend´) v. To rely on; to trust with responsibilities; to be determined or conditioned.

de-pend-a-ble (di pen´da bl) adj. Capable of being depended upon; trustworthy.

de-pend-ence or **de-pend-ance (di pen´dens)** n. The quality or state of being dependent; trust or reliance; the state of being contingent on or determined by something else.

de-pict (di pikt´) v. To represent in a sculpture or a picture; to describe or represent in words.

dep-i-late (dep´i lt´) v. To remove the hair from. **depilation** n. **depilator** n.

de-pil-a-to-ry (di pil´a tr´) n. pl.-ries A chemical which removes hair, usually in cream or liquid form.

de-plane (d pln´) v. To disembark or leave an aircraft.

de-plete (di plt´) v. To exhaust, empty, or use up a supply of something.

de-plor-a-ble (di plr´a bl) adj. Grievous; lamentable; very bad; wretched.

de-plore (di plr´) v. To have, show, or feel great disapproval of something.

de-ploy (di ploi´) v. To spread out; to place or position according to plans. **deployment** n.

de-po-lit-i-cize v. To remove the political status or aspect from.

de-po-nent (di p´nent) n. A person who testifies under oath giving sworn testimony, especially in writing.

de-pop-u-late (dpop´lt´) v. To quickly remove or lower the population greatly, as by massacre or disease. **depopulation** n.

de-port (di prt´) v. To banish or expel someone from a country; to behave in a specified manner.

de-port-ment (di prt´ment) n. One's conduct; behavior.

de-pose (di pz) v. To remove from a powerful position or office; in law, to declare or give testimony under oath.

de-pos-it (di poz´it) v. To put, place, or set something down; to entrust money to a bank; to put down in the form of a layer, as silt; to give as security or partial payment.

dep-o-si-tion (dep´o zish´an) n. The act of deposing, as from an office; that which is deposited; in law, written testimony given under oath.

de-pos-i-to-ry (di poz´i tor´) n. pl. -ries A place where anything is deposited for safe-keeping.

de-prave (di prv´) v. To render bad or worse; in morals, to corrupt or pervert.

dep-re-cate (dep´re kt´) v. To express regret for or disapproval of; to belittle.

de-pre-ci-ate (di pr sh t´) v. To lessen in value or price.

de‑pre‑ci‑a‑tion *n.* A loss in efficiency or value resulting from age or usage; the decline in the purchasing value of money. **‑tor** *n.*

de‑press (di pres´) *v.* To make gloomy; to lower the spirits of; to lessen in energy or vigor; to press down; to lower; to diminish in value or price.

de‑pres‑sion (di presh´an) *n.* The state of being or the act of depressing; a severe decline in business, accompanied by increasing unemployment and falling prices. *Psych.* A condition of deep dejection characterized by lack of response to stimulation and withdrawal.

de‑prive (di prv´) *v.* To take something away from; to keep from using, acquiring, or enjoying. **deprivable** *adj.*

dep‑u‑ta‑tion (dep´ t´shan) *n.* A person or persons who are acting for another or others; the act of deputing or the state of being deputed.

de‑pute (de pt´) *v.* To appoint as a deputy, an agent, or other figure of authority; to delegate; to transfer.

dep‑u‑tize (dep´ tz´) *v.* To act as a deputy; to appoint as a deputy.

dep‑u‑ty (dep´ t) *n. pl.* **‑ties** The person designated or authorized to act for in the absence of, or to assist another, generally a sheriff; a member of a legislative body in certain countries.

de‑rail (d rl´) *v.* To run off the rails; to cause a train to run off the rails.

de‑range (di rnj´) *v.* To disturb the arrangement or normal order of; to unbalance the reason; to make insane. **derangement** *n.*

de‑reg‑u‑late (d rg´ lt) *v.* To decontrol or remove from regulation or control.

der‑e‑lict (der´e likt) *adj.* Neglectful of obligations; remiss. n. Abandoned or deserted, as a ship at sea; a vagrant; a social outcast.

der‑e‑lic‑tion (der´e lik´shan) *n.* Voluntary neglect, as of responsibility; the fact or state of being abandoned.

de‑ride (di rd´) *v.* To ridicule; to treat with scornful mirth. **derider** *n.* **derision** *n.* **deridingly** *adv.* **derisive** *adj.*

de ri‑gueur (de ri ger´) *adj.* Prescribed or required by manners, custom, or fashion.

der‑i‑va‑tion (der´i v´shan) *n.* The act of or process of deriving; the process used to form new words by the addition of affixes to roots, stems, or words.

de‑riv‑a‑tive (di riv´a tiv) *adj.* Of or relating to something derived.

de‑rive (di rv´) *v.* To receive or obtain from a source. *Chem.* To produce a compound from other substances by chemical reaction.

der‑mal *or* **der‑mic** *adj.* Relating to or of the skin.

der‑ma‑ti‑tis (der´ma t´tis) *n., Pathol.* An inflammation of the skin.

der‑ma‑tol‑o‑gy (der´ma tol´o j) *n.* The medical study of the skin and the diseases related to it. **dermatologist** *n.*

de‑ro‑gate (der´o gt´) *v.* To take or cause to take away from; to distract; to cause to become inferior. **‑gation** *n.*

de‑rog‑a‑to‑ry (di rog´a tr´) *adj.* Having the effect of belittling; lessening.

der‑ri‑ere (der´ âr) *n.* The buttocks.

der‑rin‑ger (der´in jr) *n.* A short‑barreled, large‑bored, pocket‑sized pistol.

des‑cant (des´kant) *v.* To play or sing a varied melody.

de‑scend (di send´) *v.* To move from a higher to a lower level; to pass through inheritance; to come from a particular family. *Astron.* Moving toward the horizon.

de‑scend‑ent (di sen´dant) *n.* One who descends from another individual; an offspring.

de‑scen‑dant *or* **de‑scen‑dent (di sen´dent)** *adj.* Proceeding downward; descending from an ancestor.

de‑scent (di sent´) *n.* A slope; lowering or decline, as in level or status.

de‑scribe (di skrb´) *v.* To explain in written or spoken words; to draw or trace the figure of. **describable** *adj.*

de‑scrip‑tion (di skrip´shan) *n.* The technique or act of describing; an account or statement that describes. **descriptive** *adj.*

de‑scry (di skr´) *v.* To catch sight of; to discover by observation. **descrier** *n.*

des‑e‑crate (des´e krt´) *v.* To violate something sacred, turning it into something common or profane. **‑cration** *n.*

de‑seg‑re‑gate (d seg´re gt´) *v.* To

remove or eliminate racial segregation in.

de-sen-si-tize (d sen´si tz´) v. To make less sensitive; to eliminate the sensitivity of an individual, tissue, or organ, as to an allergen. **desensitizer** n. **-ation** n.

de-sert (di srt´) v. To abandon or forsake. *Mil.* To be absent without leave with the plan of not returning, AWOL.

desert n. A dry, barren region incapable of supporting any considerable population or vegetation without an artificial water supply.

de-ser-tion (di zr´shan) n. The act of deserting or leaving; in law, the willful abandonment of one´s spouse, children,or both.

de-serve (di zrv´) v. To be worthy of or entitled to.

de-served adj. Merited; earned. **deserving** adj. **deservingly** adv.

des-ic-cant (des´i kant) n. A silica gel used to absorb moisture; any material used to absorb moisture.

des-ic-cate (des´i kt´) v. To preserve by drying, such as food; dehydrate. **desiccation** n. **des-id-er-a-tum** (di sid er´tum) n. pl. **-ta** A desired and necessary thing.

des-ig-nate (dez´ig nt´) v. To assign a name or title to; to point out; to specify; to appoint or select, as to an office. **designation** n.

de-sign-ing (di z´ning) adj. Of or relating to the art or act of making designs; scheming or plotting; crafty. **designingly** adv.

de-sir-a-ble (di zr´a bl) adj. Pleasing, attractive, or valuable; worthy of desire. **desirability** n. **desirableness** n.

de-sire (di zr´) v. To long for; to wish; to crave; to request or ask for; to have sexual appetite.

de-sir-ous (di zr´us) adj. Having a craving or strong desire.

de-sist (di zist´) v. To stop doing something; to cease from an action.

desk (desk) n. A table or piece of furniture usually with drawers or compartments and a top for writing; a stand or table to hold reading materials; a department in a newspaper office, as the copy desk.

des-o-late (des´o lit) adj. Made unfit for

habitation; useless; forlorn; forsaken.

des-o-la-tion (des´o la´shan) n. A wasteland; the condition of being ruined or deserted; loneliness.

de-spair (di spâr´) v. To lose or give up hope; to abandon all purpose. **despair** n. **despairing** adj. **despairingly** adv.

des-per-a-do (des´pe rä´d) n. pl. **-does** or **-dos** A dangerous, desperate, or violent criminal.

des-per-ate (des´pr it) adj. Rash, violent, reckless, and without care, as from despair; intense; overpowering.

des-per-a-tion (des´pe r´shan) n. The state of being desperate.

des-pi-ca-ble (des´pi ka bl) adj. Deserving scorn or contempt.

de-spise (di spz´) v. To regard with contempt; to regard as worthless. **-er** n.

de-spite (di spt´) prep. Notwithstanding; in spite of.

de-spoil (di spoil´) v. To rob; to strip of property or possessions by force. **despoilment** n.

de-spond (di spond´) v. To lose hope, courage, or spirit. **despondently** adv.

de-spon-den-cy (di spon´den s) n. A dejection of spirits from loss of courage or hope.

des-pot (des´pot) n. An absolute ruler; a tyrant. **despotic** adj. **despotically** adv.

des-sert (di zrt´) n. A serving of sweet food, as pastry, ice cream, or fruit, as the last course of a meal.

des-ti-na-tion (des´ti n´shan) n. The point or place to which something or someone is directed; the purpose or end for which something is created or intended.

des-tine (des´tin) v. To be determined in advance; to design or appoint a distinct purpose.

des-ti-ny (des´ti n) n. pl. **-nies** The inevitable loss or fate to which a person or thing is destined; fate; a predetermined course of events.

des-ti-tute (des´ti töt´) adj. Utterly impoverished; not having; extremely poor.

de-stroy (di stroi´) v. To ruin; to tear down; to demolish; to kill; to make useless or ineffective.

de-struct (di strukt´) n. *Aeros.* The deliberate destruction of a defective or dangerous missile or rocket after launch.**destruction** n. **destructive** adj.

des-ue-tude (des'wi tōd') n. A condition or state of disuse.

de-sul-fur-ize (d sul'f rz') v. To remove sulfur from. **desulfurizer** n.

des-ul-to-ry (des'ul tr') adj. Something that occurs by chance; lacking continuity; aimless.

de-tach (di tach') v. To unfasten, disconnect, or separate; to extricate oneself; to withdraw.

de-tached (di tacht') adj. Separate; apart.

de-tach-ment (di tach'ment) n. The process of separating. Milit. A shipment of military equipment or personnel from a larger unit for special duty.

de-tail (di tl) n. A part or item considered separately. Milit. Military personnel selected for a particular duty.

de-tain (di tn') v. To stop; to keep from proceeding; to delay.

de-tect (di tekt') v. To find out or perceive; to expose or uncover, as a crime. **detectible** adj. **detection** n. -or n.

de-tec-tive (di tek'tiv) n. A person whose work is to investigate crimes, discover evidence, and capture criminals.

de-tent (di tent') n. A pawl.

de-ten-tion (di ten'shan) n. The act of or state of being detained; in law, a time or period of temporary custody which precedes disposition by a court.

de-ter (di ter') v. To prevent or discourage someone from acting by arousing fear, uncertainty, intimidation, or other strong emotion.

de-ter-gent (di ter'jent) n. A cleansing agent which is chemically different from soap. **detergency** n. **-gence** n.

de-te-ri-o-rate (di tr' o rt') v. To worsen; to depreciate. **deterioration** n.

de-ter-mi-nate (di ter'mi nit) adj. Definitely fixed or limited; conclusive. Bot. The terminating in a bud or flower, as each axis of an inflorescence.

de-ter-mine (di ter'min) v. To settle or decide conclusively or authoritatively; to limit to extent or scope; to fix or ascertain; to give direction or purpose to; in law, to come to an end. **deter-**

minable adj. **determination** n.

de-ter-mined (di ter'mind) adj. Showing or having a fixed purpose; resolute; firm.

de-ter-rent (di ter'ent) n. Something which deters. adj. Serving to deter.

de-test (di test') v. To dislike strongly. **detestable** adj. **detestably** adv.

de-throne (d thrn') v. To remove from the throne, to depose, as a king.

det-o-nate (det'o nt') v. To explode suddenly and violently. **detonation** n.

det-o-na-tor (det'o n'tr) n. The device, such as a fuse or percussion cap, used to detonate an explosive.

de-tour (d'ter) n. A road used temporarily instead of a main road; a deviation from a direct route or course of action.

de-tox-i-fy (d tok'si f) v. To free oneself from dependence on drugs or alcohol.

de-tract (di trakt') v. To take away from; to diminish; to divert. **detraction** n. **detractor** n. **detractive** adj.

de-train (d trn') v. To leave or cause to leave a railroad train. **detrainment** n.

det-ri-ment (de'tri ment) n. Damage; injury; loss; something which causes damage, injury, or loss. **-al** adj.

de-tri-tus (di tr'tus) n. Loose fragments or particles formed by erosion, glacial action, and other forces; debris.

deu-te-ri-um (dō tr' um) n. The isotope of hydrogen which contains one more neutron in its nucleus than hydrogen does.

de-val-u-ate (d val' t') v. To reduce or lessen the value of. **devaluation** n.

dev-as-tate (dev'a stt') v. To destroy; to ruin; to overwhelm; to overpower.

de-vel-op (di vel'up) v. To bring out or expand the potentialities; to make more elaborate; to enlarge; to advance from a lower to a higher stage or from an earlier to a later stage of maturation. Photog. To process an image upon a sensitized plate that has been exposed to v. The action of light. **developer** n.

de-vi-ant adj. Anything which deviates from a norm, especially from an accepted standard. **deviance** n.

de-vi-ate (d'v t') v. To turn away from a specified prescribed behavior or course.

de-vice (di vs´) *n.* Something constructed and used for a specific purpose, as a machine; a crafty or evil scheme or plan; an ornamental design; a motto or an emblem.

dev-il *or* **Devil** (dev´il) *n.* The devil to pay; trouble to be expected as a consequence of something.

devil's advocate *n.* One who argues about something with which he or she may not disagree, as for the sake of argument.

de-vi-ous (d´v us) *adj.* Leading away from the straight, regular, or direct course; rambling; straying from the proper way. *Slang* Underhanded.

de-vise (di vz´) *v.* To form in the mind; to contrive; to plan; to invent; in law, to transmit or give by will. *n.* The act of bequeathing lands; a clause in a will conveying real estate.

de-vi-see (di v z´) *n.* In law, the person to whom a devise is made.

de-vi-sor (di v´zr) *n.* In law, the person who devises property.

de-vi-tal-ize (d vt´a lz´) *v.* To make weak; to destroy the vitality. **devitalization** *n.*

de-void (di void´) *adj.* Empty; utterly lacking; without.

de-voir (de vwär´) *n.* The act or expression of courtesy or respect; duty or responsibility.

de-volve (di volv´) *v.* To pass duty or authority on to a successor.

de-vote (di vt´) *v.* To apply time or one-self completely to some activity, purpose, or cause. **devotement** *n.*

de-vot-ed (di v´tid) *adj.* Feeling or showing devotion; set apart, as by a vow; consecrated. **devotedly** *adv.*

dev-o-tee (dev´o t´) *n.* An enthusiastic supporter; one who is deeply devoted to anything; one marked by religious ardor.

de-vo-tion (di v´shan) *n.* A strong attachment or affection, as to a person or cause; zeal or ardor in the performance of religious duties or acts; the state or act of being devoted.

de-vour (di your´) *v.* To destroy or waste; to eat up greedily; to engulf.

de-vout (di vout´) *adj.* Extremely and earnestly religious; showing sincerity; displaying piety or reverence. **devoutly** *adv.* **devoutness** *n.*

dew (dö) *n.* Moisture condensed from the atmosphere in minute drops onto cool surfaces; something which is refreshing or pure.

dew point *n.* The temperature at which condensation of vapor occurs.

dex-ter-i-ty (dek ster´i t) *n.* Proficiency or skill in using the hands or body; cleverness.

dex-ter-ous *or* **dex-trous** (dek´strus) *adj.* Skillful or adroit in the use of the hands, body, or mind. **dexterously** *adv.*

dex-trose (dek´strs) *n.* Sugar found in animal and plant tissue and derived synthetically from starches.

di-a-be-tes (d´a b´tis) *n.* A metabolic disorder that is characterized by deficient insulin secretion, leading to excess sugar in the urine and blood, extreme hunger, and thirst.

di-a-bet-ic (d´a bet´ik) *adj.* Pertaining to, or affected with diabetes.

di-a-bol-ic *or* **di-a-bol-i-cal** (d´a bol´ik) *adj.* Wicked; proceeding from the devil; satanic or infernal. **-ally** *adv.*

di-a-crit-ic (d´a krit´ik) *n.* A mark near or through a phonetic character or combination of characters, used to indicate a special phonetic value or to distinguish words otherwise graphically identical. **diacritical** *adj.*

di-a-dem (d´a dem´) *n.* A crown or headband worn to symbolize or indicate royalty or honor.

di-aer-e-sis (d er´i sis) *n.* Variation of dieresis.

di-ag-no-sis (d´ag n´sis) *n. pl.* **diagnoses** An analysis and examination to identify a disease; the result of diagnosis. **diagnose** *v.* **diagnostic** *adj.* **diagnostician** *n.*

di-ag-o-nal (d ag´o nal) *adj.* In mathematics, joining two opposite corners of a polygon which are not adjacent. **diagonal** *n.* A diagonal or slanting plane or line.

di-a-gram (d´a gram´) *n.* A sketch, plan, drawing, or outline that is designed to demonstrate or to clarify the similarity among parts of a whole or to illustrate how something works.

di-a-lec-tic (d´a lek´tik) *n.* The act or

practice of argument or exposition in which the conflict between contradictory facts or ideas is resolved. **dialect** adj. **dialectic** adj.

di-a-logue or **di-a-log** (dī'a log') n. A conversation involving two or more persons; a conversational passage in a literary work.

di-al-y-sis (dī al'i sis) n. pl. **dialyses** The separation of substances in solution, which is accomplished by passing them through membranes or filters. **dialysis** Med. A procedure used to cleanse the blood of impurities and wastes when the kidneys are unable to perform this function.

di-am-e-ter (dī am'i tr) n. In mathematics, a straight line which passes through the center of a circle or sphere and stops at the circumference or surface; a measurement of that distance.

diametric (dī a me'trik) or **di-a-met-ri-cal** adj. Along, or relating to, a diameter; exactly opposite; contrary. **diametrically** adv.

di-a-pa-son (dī a pā'zon) n. The full range of a voice or an instrument; in a pipe organ, either of two principal stops which form the tonal basis for the entire scale.

di-aph-a-nous (dī af'a nus) adj. Of such fine texture as to be transparent or translucent; delicate. **-nously** adv.

di-a-phragm (dī'a fram') n., Anat. The muscular wall that separates the abdominal and thoracic cavities. Photog. The disk with an adjustable aperture that can control the amount of light passing through the lens of a telescope or camera; a contraceptive device usually made of rubber or rubber-like material and shaped like a cap to cover the uterine cervix.

di-ar-rhe-a or **di-ar-rhoe-a** (dī ar'a) n. A disorder of the intestines that causes excessively frequent, loose bowel movements.

di-a-ry (dī'a r) n. pl. **diaries** A daily record, especially a personal record of one's activities, experiences, or observations; a journal; a book for keeping such records.

di-as-to-le (dī as'to lī) n., Physiol. The normal rhythmic dilatation and relaxation of the heart cavities during which they fill with blood.

di-as-tro-phism (dī as'tro fiz'um) n., Geol. Any of the processes through which the earth's crust, as mountains and continents are formed.

di-a-ther-my (dī a thr'm) n. pl. **diathermies** Med. The generation of heat in the body tissues by high-frequency electromagnetic waves.

di-a-tom (dī'a tom) n. Any of various tiny planktonic algae whose walls contain silica.

di-a-tom-ic (dī a tom'ik) adj. Having two atoms in a molecule.

di-a-ton-ic (dī a ton'ik) adj., Mus. Relating to a standard major or minor scale of eight tones without the chromatic intervals.

di-a-tribe (dī'a trb') n. A bitter, often malicious criticism or denunciation.

dib-ble (dib'l) n. A gardener's pointed tool used to make holes in soil, especially for planting bulbs or seedlings.

di-chot-o-my (d kot'o m) n., pl. **dichotomies** A division into two mutually exclusive subclasses. Bot. The branching of something in which each successive axis forks into two equally developed branches.

di-chro-mate (d kr'mt) n., Chem. A chemical compound with two chromium atoms per anion.

di-chro-mat-ic (d'kr mat'ik) adj., Zool. Having two color phases within the species apart from the changes due to age or sex. Pathol. Having the ability to see only two of the three primary colors.

dick-er (dik'r) v. To haggle or work towards a deal or bargain.

di-cot-y-le-don (d kot'a ld'on) n. A plant which has two seed leaves.

dic-tate (dik'tt) v. To read or speak aloud for another to record or transcribe; to give commands, terms, rules, or other orders with authority. n. A directive or guiding principle.

dic-ta-tor (dik't tr) n. A person having absolute authority and supreme governmental powers; one who dictates.

dic-ta-to-ri-al (dik'ta tr' al) adj. Tending to dictate; relating to or characteristic of a dictator. **-ally** adv.

dic·tion (dik´shan) *n.* The selection and arrangement of words in speaking and writing; the manner of uttering speech sounds.

dic·tion·ar·y (dik´sha ner´) *n. pl.* **-ies** A reference book containing alphabetically arranged words together with definitions and usages.

dic·tum (dik´tum) *n. pl.* **-ta** *or* **-tums** An authoritative or positive utterance; a pronouncement; a saying that is popular.

did (did) *v.* Past tense of do.

di·dac·tic *or* **didactical** (d dak´ti kal) *adj.* Being inclined to teach or moralize excessively.

did·dle *v.* To cheat; to swindle; to waste valuable time.

did·n't (did´ant) Did not.

di·do (d´dÅ) *n. pl.* didos *or* didoes *Informal* A mischievous caper; an antic.

die (dÄ) *v.* To expire; to stop living; to cease to exist; to fade away.

diel·drin (dÄl´drin) *n.* A highly toxic and persistent chemical which is used as an insecticide.

di·e·lec·tric (d´i lek´trik) *n., Elect.* A nonconductor of electricity.

di·er·e·sis (d er´i sis) *n. pl.* diereses The mark over a vowel indicating that it is to be pronounced in a separate syllable.

die·sel (d´zel) *n.* A diesel engine, or a vehicle driven by a diesel engine.

di·et (dÄ´it) *n.* A regulated selection of food and drink, especially one followed for medical or hygienic reasons; something that is taken or provided regularly; an assembly or provided regularly; an assembly or legislature.

di·e·tet·ics (d´i tet´iks) *n.* The study of diet and of the regulations of a diet. **dietetical, dietetic** *adj.* **-ically** *adv.*

di·eth·yl·stil·bes·trol *n.* A synthetic estrogen used especially to treat menstrual disorders.

dif·fer (dif´r) *v.* To have different opinions; to disagree.

dif·fer·ence (dif´r ens) *n.* The quality, state, or degree of being different or unlike.

dif·fer·ent (dif´r ent) *adj.* Not the same; separate; other; marked by a differ-ence; unlike; differing from the ordinary. **differently** *adv.*

dif·fer·en·tia (dif´e ren´sh a) *n. pl.* **-tiae** A specific difference; something that distinguishes a species from others of the same genus.

differential calculus *n.* In mathematics, the difference or variation of a function with respect to changes in independent variables.

dif·fer·en·ti·ate (dif´e ren·sh t´) *v.* To show, state, or distinguish the difference; to become or make different.

dif·fi·cult (dif´i kult´) *adj.* Hard to do, deal with, or accomplish; hard to please.

dif·fi·cul·ty (dif´i kul´t) *n. pl.* **-ties** The quality or state of being difficult; something that requires great effort; conflicts or problems.

dif·fi·dent *adj.* Lacking confidence in oneself; timid. **diffidence** *n.* **-ly** *adv.*

dif·frac·tion (di frak´shan) *n., Phys.* A modification of light rays, especially a beam of light as it passes an aperture or obstacle.

dif·fuse (di fz´) *v.* To pour out and spread freely in all directions; to scatter.

di·gest (di jest´) *v.* To change ingested food into usable form; to mentally assimilate; to endure; to tolerate patiently; to decompose or soften with moisture or heat. **digestibility** *n.* **digestible, digestive** *adj.*

dig·it (dij´it) *n.* A toe or finger; the Arabic numerals 0 through 9.

dig·i·tal (dij´i tal) *adj.* Pertaining to or like the fingers or digits; expressed in digits, especially for computer use; reading in digits, as a clock.

digital computer *n.* In computer science, a computer using data that is represented as digits to perform operations.

dig·i·tal·is (dij´i tal´is) *n.* The foxglove plant; a drug prepared from dried leaves of foxglove, used as a heart stimulant.

dig·ni·fied (dig´ni fd´) *adj.* Showing or possessing dignity; poised.

dig·ni·fy (dig´ni f´) *v.* To give dignity or distinction to something.

dig·ni·tary (dig´ni ter´) *n. pl.* **-ies** A

person of high rank, notability, and influence.

dig-ni-ty (dig´ni t) *n. pl.* **-ties** The quality or state of being excellent; the quality of being poised or formally reserved in appearance and demean or; a high rank, office, or title.

di-graph (d´graf) *n.* A pair of letters, as the ea in seat or oa in boat, that represents a single sound. **digraphic** *adj.*

di-gress (di gres´) *v.* To turn away or aside from the main subject in a discourse; to wander. **digression** *n.* **digressive** *adj.*

dike (dk) *n.* An embankment made of earth, built to hold and control flood waters, also known as a levee.

di-lap-i-dat-ed (di lap´i d´tid) *adj.* Being in a state of decay or disrepair.

di-late (d lt´) *v.* To become or make enlarged; to expand. **dilatable** *adj.*

dil-a-to-ry (dil´a tr´) *adj.* Tending to cause delay; characterized by delay; slow; tardy.

di-lem-ma (di lem´a) *n.* A predicament requiring a choice between equally undesirable alternatives.

dil-et-tante (dil´i tan t´) *n. pl.* **-tantes** One who has an amateurish and superficial interest in something.

dil-i-gent (dil´i jent) *adj.* Showing painstaking effort and application in whatever is undertaken; industrious. **diligence** *n.* **diligently** *adv.*

dill (dil) *n.* An aromatic herb with aromatic leaves and seeds used as seasoning.

dil-ly *n. pl.* **-lies** *Slang* Someone or something that is extraordinary.

dil-ly-dal-ly (dil´dal´) *v.* To waste time with indecision or hesitation.

di-lute (di lt´) *v.* To weaken, thin, or reduce the concentration of by adding a liquid.

dime (dm) *n.* A United States coin worth ten cents or one tenth of a dollar.

di-men-sion (di men´shan) *n.* A measurable extent, as length, thickness, or breadth. **dimensions** *pl.* The magnitude or scope of something. **dimensional** *adj.*

di-min-ish (di min´ish) *v.* To become or make smaller or less; to reduce in power, rank, or authority; to decrease;

to taper. **diminishable** *adj.* **-ment** *n.*

dim-in-ished (di min´isht) *adj.* Reduced; lessened.

di-min-u-en-do (di min´en´do) *adv.* Gradually lessening in volume.

di-min-u-tive (di min´tiv) *adj.* Very small; tiny.

dim-mer (dim´r) *n.* A rheostat used to reduce the intensity of an electric light.

dim-wit (dim´wit) *n. Slang* A simpleminded or stupid person.

din (din) *n.* A loud, confused, harsh noise.

dine (dn) *v.* To eat dinner.

din-er (d´nr) *n.* A dining car on a train; a restaurant usually shaped like a railroad car.

din-ghy (ding´g) *n. pl.* **-ghies** A small rowboat; an inflatable rubber raft.

din-ky (ding´k) *adj., Informal* Insignificant or small.

din-ner (din´r) *n.* The last meal of the day, taken usually between the hours of 5:00 and 7:00 P.M.; a banquet or formal meal.

di-no-saur (d´no sor´) *n., Paleon.* A group of extinct reptiles from the Mesozoic period, some of which were the largest land animals known to exist.

dint (dint) *n.* Means; force; effort. *v.* To drive with force.

di-oc-ese (d´o ss´) *n.* The territory under the jurisdiction of a bishop.

di-ode (d´d) *n.* An electron tube which permits electrons to pass in only one direction, used as a rectifier.

diph-the-ri-a (dif thr´a) *n., Pathol.* An acute, contagious disease that is caused by bacillus and is characterized by formation of a false membrane in the throat and other air passages causing weakness and fever.

diph-thong (dif´thong) *n., Phon.* A blend of a single speech sound, which begins with one vowel sound and moves to another in the same syllable, such as oi in oil, oi in coil or oy in toy.

di-plo-ma (di pl´ma) *n.* A document issued by a college, school, or university testifying that a student has earned a degree or completed a course of study.

di-plo-ma-cy (di pl´ma s) *n. pl.* **diplo-**

macies The art or practice of conducting international negotiations; skill and tact in dealing with people.

dip-lo-mat (dip´lo mat´) *n.* A person employed in diplomacy. **-matic** *adj.*

dip-so-ma-ni-a (dip´so m´n a) *n.* An insatiable craving for alcohol.

dip-ter-ous (dip´tr us) *adj.* Pertaining to or of animals having a single pair of wings such as the fly, gnat, and mosquito.

dip-tych (dip´tik) *n.* A pair of painted or carved panels which are hinged together.

dir *abbr.* Director.

dire (dr) *adj.* Dreadful or terrible in consequence. **direly** *adv.* **direfully** *adv.*

di-rect (d rekt´) *v.* To control or regulate the affairs of; to command or order; to direct or tell someone the way; to cause something to move in a given or direct course; to indicate the destina-tion of a letter; to supervise or instruct the performance of a task; to move or *v.* Lie in a straight line; to do something immediate. *adj.* Without compromise; absolute; in the exact words of a person, as a direct quote.

direct current *n.* An electrical current which flows in only one direction.

di-rec-tion (di rek´shɑn) *n.* The act of directing; an order or command; the path or line along which something points, travels, or lies.

di-rec-tive (di rek´tiv) *n.* A regulation or order from someone with authority.

di-rec-tor (di rek´tr) *n.* A person who manages or directs; one of a group of persons who supervises the affairs of an institute, corporation or business.

di-rec-to-ry (di rek´to r) *n. pl.* **-ries** A booklisting data, alphabetically or classified, containing the names and addresses of a specific group, persons, organizations, inhabitants, or businesses.

dirge (drj) *n.* A slow mournful song; a funeral hymn.

dir-i-gi-ble (dir´i ji bl) *n.* A lighter-than-air plane which may be steered by means of its own motive power.

dirk (drk) *n.* A dagger.

dirn-dl (drn´dl) *n.* A lady's full-skirted dress with a gathered waistband.

dis-a-ble (dis bl) *v.* To make powerless or to incapacitate; to disqualify legally.

dis-a-buse (dis´a bz´) *v.* To free from delusion, misunderstanding, or misconception.

dis-ad-van-tage (dis´ad van´tij) *n.* A circumstance that is unfavorable; cause of loss or damage; detriment.

dis-af-fect (dis´a fekt´) *v.* To weaken or destroy the affection or loyalty of.

dis-a-gree (dis´a gr´) *v.* To vary in opin-ion; to differ; to argue; to quarrel; to be unfavorable or unacceptable.

dis-al-low (dis´a lou´) *v.* To refuse to allow; to reject as invalid or untrue.

dis-ap-pear (dis´a pr´) *v.* To vanish; to drop from sight. **disappearance** *n.*

dis-ap-point (dis´a point´) *v.* To fail to satisfy the desires, hopes, or expectations of.

dis-ap-pro-ba-tion (dis´ap ro b´shɑn) *n.* Disapproval; condemnation.

dis-ap-prove (dis´a prv´) *v.* To refuse to approve; to reject; to condemn.

dis-arm (dis ärm´) *v.* To make harmless; to deprive or take away the weapons or any means of attack or defense. **disarmament** *n.*

dis-ar-range (dis´a rnj´) *v.* To disturb the order of something. **disarrangement** *n.*

dis-ar-ray (dis´a r´) *n.* A state of confusion or disorder; an upset or turmoil.

dis-as-sem-ble (dis´a sem´bl) *v.* To take a part.

dis-as-so-ci-ate (dis´a s´sht´) *v.* To break away from or to detach oneself from an association. **disassociation** *n.*

dis-as-ter (di zas´tr) *n.* An event that causes great ruin or distress; a sudden and crushing misfortune. **-astrous** *adj.*

dis-a-vow (dis´a vou´) *v.* To disclaim or deny any responsibility for or knowledge of.

dis-band (dis band´) *v.* To disperse; to break up. **disbandment** *n.*

dis-bar (dis bär´) *v.* In law, to be expelled officially from the legal profession.

dis-be-lieve (dis´bi lv´) *v.* To refuse to believe in something. **disbelief** *n.*

dis-burse (dis brs´) *v.* To pay out. **disburser** *n.* **disbursement** *n.* **-bursal** *n.*

disc *or* **disk (disk)** *n., Informal* A

phonograph record.

dis-cern (di srn´) v. To detect visually; to detect with senses other than that of vision; to comprehend mentally; to perceive as separate and distinct. **discernment** n.

dis-ci-ple (di s´pl) n. One who accepts and assists in spreading the doctrines of another. Disciple One of Christ's followers.

dis-ci-pline (dis´i plin) n. Training which corrects, molds, or perfects the mental faculties or moral character; behavior which results from such training; obedience to authority or rules; punishment meant to correct poor behavior. **discipline** v. To train or develop by teaching and by control; to bring order to; to penalize. **disciplinary** adj.

dis-claim (dis klm´) v. To disavow any claim to or association with. **disclaimer** n.

dis-close (dis sklz´) v. To make known; to bring into view. **disclosure** n.

dis-co pl. **-cos** A discotheque.

dis-color (dis kul´r) v. To alter or change the color of. **discoloration** n.

dis-com-fit (dis kum´fit) v. To defeat in battle; to make upset or uneasy.

dis-com-fort (dis kum´frt) n. Physical or mental uneasiness; pain; an inconvenience. v. To make uncomfortable.

dis-com-mode (dis´ko md´) v. To inconvenience.

dis-com-pose (dis kom pz´) v. To disrupt the composure or serenity of; to unsettle; to destroy the order of. **composure** n.

dis-con-cert (dis´kon srt´) v. To upset; to discompose; to perturb. **-ingly** adv.

dis-con-nect (dis´ko nekt´) v. To sever or break the connection of or between. **dis-con-nect-ed** adj. Not connected.

dis-con-so-late (dis kon´so lit) adj. Without consolation; dejected; cheerless; sorrowful.

dis-con-tent (dis´kon tent´) n. Lack of contentment; dissatisfaction. v. To make unhappy. **discontentedly** adv. **discontented** adj.

dis-con-tin-ue (dis´kon tin´) v. To come or bring to an end; to break the continuity of; to interrupt; to stop trying,

taking, or using. **discontinuance** n.

dis-cord (dis´kord) n. Lacking accord or harmony; a harsh combination of musical sounds.

dis-co-theque (dis´k tek´) n. A nightclub where music is provided for dancing.

dis-coun-te-nance (dis koun´te nans) v. To look upon with disfavor; to make uneasy.

dis-cour-age (di skr´ij) v. To deprive or be deprived of enthusiasm or courage; to hinder by disfavoring. **discouragement** n.

dis-course (dis´krs) n. A conversation; a formal and lengthy discussion of a subject. v. To write or converse extensively.

dis-cour-te-ous (dis kr´t us) adj. Lacking consideration or courteous manners.

dis-cov-er (di skuv´r) v. To make known or visible; to observe or learn of for the first time. **discoverable** adj.

dis-cred-it (dis kred´it) v. To mar the reputation of or disgrace someone or something; to injure the reputation of. n. Loss of credit or reputation; doubt; disbelief.

dis-creet (di skrt´) adj. Tactful; careful of appearances; modest. **-ly** adv.

dis-crep-an-cy (di skrep´an s) n. pl. discrepancies A difference in facts; an instance of being discrepant.

dis-crete (di skrt´) adj. Separate; made up of distinct parts.

dis-cre-tion (di skresh´shan) n. The quality or act of being discreet; the ability to make responsible choices; power to decide; the result of separating or distinguishing.

dis-cur-sive (di skr´siv) adj. Covering a wide field of subjects in a quick manner; rambling from subject to subject. **discursively** adv. **discursiveness** n.

dis-cuss (di skus´) v. To investigate by argument or debate; to consider or examine something through discourse. **discussible** adj. **discussion** n.

dis-dain (dis dn´) v. To treat contemptuously; to look upon with scorn.

dis-ease (di zz´) n. A condition of the living animal, plant body, or one of its parts which impairs normal functioning; a condition of ill health. **-ed** *adj.*

dis-em-bark (dis´em bärk´) *v.* To go or put ashore from a ship; unload.

dis-em-body (dis´em bod´) *v.* To release or free the soul or physical existence.

dis-en-chant (dis´en chant´) *v.* To free from false beliefs or enchantment. **dis-enchantingly** *adv.* **disenchanting** *adj.*

dis-en-cum-ber (dis´en kum´br) *v.* To relieve of hardships; unburden.

dis-en-fran-chise (dis´en fran´chz) *v.* To disfranchise. **-ment** *n.*

dis-en-gage (dis´en gj´) *v.* To free from something that holds or otherwise engages; to set free. **disengagement** *n.*

dis-en-tan-gle (dis´en tang´gl) *v.* To relieve of entanglement, confusion, etc. **-ment** *n.*

dis-es-teem (dis´e stm´) *v.* To regard with little esteem. *n.* Lack of esteem.

dis-fa-vor (dis f´vr) *n.* Disapproval; the state of being disliked. **disfavor** *v.*

dis-fig-ure (dis fig´r) *v.* To mar, deface, or deform the appearance of something or someone. **disfigurement** *n.*

dis-fran-chise (dis fran´chz) *v.* To deprive of a legal right or privilege, especially the right to vote. **disfranchisement** *n.*

dis-grace (dis grs´) *n.* The state of having lost grace, favor, respect, or honor; something that disgraces. *v.* To bring reproach or shame to; to humiliate by a superior showing; to cause to lose favor or standing. **disgracefulness** *n.* **disgraceful** *adj.*

dis-grun-tle (dis grun´tl) *v.* To make dissatisfied or discontented.

dis-guise (dis gz´) *v.* To alter the customary appearance or character of in order to prevent recognition.

dis-gust (dis gust´) *v.* To affect with nausea, repugnance, or aversion; to cause one to become impatient or lose attention. *n.* A marked aversion to something distasteful; repugnance. **disgusted** *adj.* **disgusting** *adj.* **-ful** *adj.*

dis-ha-bille (dis´a bl´) *n.* The state of being carelessly dressed; undress.

dis-har-mo-ny (dis här´mo n) *n.* Lack of harmony or agreement; discord.

dis-heart-en (dis här´ton) *v.* To cause to lose spirit or courage; to discourage, demoralize, or dispirit.

di-shev-el (di shev´el) *v.* To mess up or disarrange; to throw into disorder or disarray.

dis-hon-est (dis on´ist) *adj.* Lack of honesty; arising from or showing fraud or falseness. **dishonesty** *n.* **-ly** *adv.*

dis-hon-or (dis on´r) *n.* The deprivation of honor; disgrace; the state of one who has lost honor; a cause of disgrace; failure to pay a financial obligation. *v.* To bring disgrace on something or someone; to fail to pay.

dis-il-lu-sion (dis´i lö´zhэn) *v.* To deprive of illusion; to disenchant.

dis-in-cline (dis´in kln´) *v.* To make or to be unwilling; to be or cause to be not interested.

dis-in-fect (dis´in fekt´) *v.* To cleanse and make free from infection, especially by destroying harmful microorganisms; to sterilize. **disinfection** *n.*

dis-in-gen-u-ous (dis´in jen´ us) *adj.* Lacking frankness, sincerity, or simplicity; crafty; not straightforward.

dis-in-her-it (dis´in her´it) *v.* To deliberately deprive of inheritance; to depose of previously held privileges.

dis-in-te-grate (dis in´te grt´) *v.* To break or reduce into separate elements, parts, or small particles; to destroy the unity or integrity of; to explode; to undergo a change in structure, as an atomic nucleus. **disintegrator** *n.*

dis-in-ter (dis´in tr) *v.* To exhume or dig up something buried; to bring to light, disclose, uncover, or expose.

dis-in-ter-est-ed *adj.* The state of being unbiased, impartial, unselfish, or not interested; free from selfish motive or interest.

dis-join (dis join´) *v.* To end the joining of; to become detached; to disconnect.

disk *or* **disc** (disk) *n.* A thin, flat, circular object; in computer science, a round, flat plate coated with a magnetic substance on which data for a computer is stored; a fairly flat, circular, metal object used to break up soil; the implement employing such tools.

disk operating system *n.* In computer science, the software which controls the disk drives and disk accessing; abbreviated as DOS.

disk pack *n.* In computer science, a

computer storage device which has several magnetic disks to use and store as a unit.

dis-like (dis lk´) v. To regard with aversion or disapproval. n. Distaste.

dis-lo-cate (dis´l kt´) v. To put out of place or proper position. Med. To displace a bone from a socket or joint.

dis-lodge (dis loj´) v. To remove or drive out from a dwelling or position; to force out of a settled position.

dis-loy-al (dis loi´al) adj. Not loyal; untrue to personal obligations or duty. **disloyally** adv. **disloyalty** n.

dis-mal (diz´mal) adj. Causing gloom or depression; depressing; lacking in interest or merit. **dismally** adv.

dis-man-tle (dis man´tl) v. To strip of dress or covering or to strip of furniture and equipment; to take apart.

dis-may (dis m´) v. To deprive or be deprived of courage or resolution through the pressure of sudden fear or anxiety. **dismayingly** adv.

dis-mount (dis mount´) v. To get down from; to remove from a seat, setting, or support; to take apart; to disassemble.

dis-o-bey (dis´o b´) v. To refuse or fail to obey; to be disobedient. **-bedient** adj.

dis-o-blige (dis´o blj´) v. To act contrary to the wishes of; to neglect or refuse to act in accordance with the wishes of; to offend; to inconvenience. **disobligingly** adv.

dis-or-gan-ize (dis or´ga nz´) v. To destroy or break up the organization, unity, or structure of. **-ization** n.

dis-own (dis n´) v. To refuse to acknowledge or claim as one's own.

dis-pa-rate (dis´pr it) adj. Altogether dissimilar; unequal. **disparately** adv.

dis-pas-sion-ate (dis pash´o nit) adj. Free from bias or passion. **-ly** adv.

dis-patch or des-patch (di spach´) v. To send off to a particular destination or on specific business; to dispose of quickly; to kill summarily. n. The act of dispatching; a message sent with speed; a message; A news story sent to a newspaper.

dis-pel (di spel´) v. To drive off or away.

dis-pense (di spens´) v. To give out; to distribute; to administer; to let go or exempt. **with** To get rid of; to forgo.

dis-perse (di sprs´) v. To break up or scatter in various directions; to spread or distribute from a common source; to distribute. **dispersible** adj. **dispersion** n.

di-spir-it (di spir´it) v. To deprive of or be deprived of spirit; to discourage or be discouraged.

dis-place (dis pls´) v. To change the position of; to take the place of; to discharge from an office; to cause a physical displacement of.

dis-please (dis plz´) v. To cause the disapproval or annoyance of; to cause displeasure.

dis-pose (di spz´) v. To put in place; to finally settle or come to terms. To get rid of; to attend to or settle; to transfer or part with, as by selling.

dis-pos-sess (dis´po zes´) v. To deprive of possession or ownership of land, possessions, or property.

dis-pro-por-tion (dis´pro pr´shan) n. Lack of proportion, symmetry or proper relation.

dis-prove (dis prv´) v. Prove to be false or erroneous. **disproof** n. **disprovable** adj.

dis-pu-ta-tion (dis´p t´shan) n. The act of disputing; a debate.

dis-pute (di spt´) v. To debate or argue; to question the validity of; to strive against or to resist. n. A verbal controversy; a quarrel. **disputable** adj. **disputably** adv.

dis-qual-i-fy (dis kwol´i f´) v. To deprive of the required properties or conditions; to deprive of a power or privilege; to make ineligible for a prize or further competition. **disqualification** n.

dis-quiet (dis kw´it) v. To take away the tranquillity of; to trouble. **disquieting** adj.

dis-qui-si-tion (dis´kwi zish´on) n. A formal inquiry into or discussion of a subject.

dis-re-gard (dis´ri gärd´) v. To ignore; to neglect; to pay no attention to; to treat without proper attention.

dis-re-pair (dis´ri pâr´) n. The state of being in need of repair, usually due to neglect.

dis-re-pute (dis´ri pt´) n. A state of

being held in low esteem; loss of a good reputation; disgrace.

dis-re-spect (dis'ri spekt') n. Lack of respect or reverence. **disrespect** v.

dis-robe (dis rb') v. To undress.

dis-rupt (dis rupt') v. To throw into disorder or confusion; upset; to cause to break down. **disruption** n. **-ive** adj.

dis-sat-is-fy (dis sat'is f) v. To fail to satisfy; to disappoint. **-isfaction** n.

dis-sect (di sekt') v. To cut into pieces; to expose the parts of something, such as an animal, for examination; to analyze in detail.

dis-sem-ble (di sem'bl) v. To conceal or hide the actual nature of; to put on a false appearance; to conceal facts. **dissembler** n.

dis-sem-i-nate (di sem'i nt') v. To scatter or spread, as if by sowing, over a wide area. **dissemination** n.

dis-sen-sion (di sen'shan) n. Difference of opinion; discord; strife.

dis-sent (di sent') v. To differ in opinion or thought. n. Difference of opinion; refusal to go along with an established church.

dis-ser-ta-tion (dis'r t'shan) n. A formal written discourse or thesis, especially one submitted for a doctorate.

dis-serv-ice (dis sr'vis) n. An ill turn; an ill service, injury, or harm.

dis-sev-er (di sev'r) v. To sever; to divide; to separate. **disseverance** n.

dis-si-dent (dis'i dent) adj. Strong and open difference with an opinion or group. **dissident** n. **dissidence** n.

dis-sim-i-lar (di sim'i lr) adj. Different; not the same; unlike. **dissimilarity** n.

dis-si-mil-i-tude (dis'si mil'i tōd') n. Lack of resemblance; unlikeness.

dis-sim-u-late (di sim' lt') v. To conceal under a false appearance; to dissemble.

dis-si-pate (dis'i pt') v. To disperse or drive away; to squander or waste; to separate into parts and scatter or vanish; to become dispersed; to lose irreversibly.

dis-so-ci-ate (di s'sh t') v. To break from the association with another. **dissociation** n.

dis-so-lute (dis'o lōt) adj. Loose in morals; lacking moral restraint. **dissolutely** adv.

dis-so-lu-tion (dis'o lō'shan) n. The act or process of changing from a solid to a fluid form; the separation of body and soul; death.

dis-solve (di zolv') v. To pass into solution, such as dissolving sugar in water; to overcome, as by emotion; to fade away; to become decomposed; to terminate.

dis-so-nance (dis'o nans) n. Lack of agreement; a conflict. Mus. A harsh or disagreeable combination of sounds; discord. **dissonant** adj. **-nantly** adv.

dis-suade (di swd') v. To alter the course of action; to turn from something by persuasion or advice. **dissuader** n.

dis-taff (dis'taf) n. A staff rotation for holding the flax, tow, or wool in spinning; the female side of a family; women in general.

dis-tal (dis'tal) n. Relatively remote from the point of attachment or origin.

dis-tant (dis'tant) adj. A part or separate by a specified amount of time or space; situated at a great distance; coming from, going to, or located at a distance; remotely related.

dis-taste (dis tst') v. To feel aversion to; to have an offensive taste; dislike. **distasteful** adj. **distastefully** adv.

dis-tend (di stend') v. To expand from internal pressure. **distensible** adj. **distention** n.

dis-tinct (di stingkt') adj. Distinguished from all others; clearly seen; unquestionable.

dis-tinc-tion (di stingk'shan) n. The act of distinguishing; a difference; a special honor or recognition.

dis-tinc-tive (di stingk'tiv) adj. Serving to give style or distinction to.

dis-tin-guish (di sting'gwish) v. To recognize as being different; to discriminate; to make something different or noticeable. **distinguishable** adj. **distinguished** adj.

dis-tort (di stort') v. To twist or bend out of shape; to twist the true meaning of; to give a misleading account of. **distortion** n.

dis-tract (di strakt') v. To draw or divert one's attention away from something; to cause one to feel conflicting emotions.

dis-tinc-tion (di stingk´shan) n. Act of distinguishing or separating; a contrast; that which marks superiority by quality.

dis-tin-guish (di sting´gwish) v. To set apart or separate from others; to recognize the individuality of; to divide by quality.

dis-tort (di stort´) v. To twist out of natural shape; to change from the real meaning.

dis-tract (di strakt´) v. To draw from another object or subject.

dis-trac-tion (di strak´shan) n. The act of distracting; extreme confusion of the mind brought on by grief or pain.

dis-trait (di str) adj. Absent-minded.

dis-traught (di strot´) adj. Deeply agitated with doubt or anxiety; crazed.

dis-tress (di stres´) n. To cause suffering of mind or body. n. Pain or suffering; severe physical or mental strain; a very painful situation. adj. Goods or merchandise sold as a loss.

dis-trib-u-tar-y (di strib´ ter) n. A branch of the rive not flowing from the main stream and does not join the main stream at any point.

dis-trib-ute (di strib´t) v. To divide among many; to deliver or give out; to classify. **distribution** n. **-utive** adj.

dis-trict (dis´trikt) n. An administrative or political section of a territory.

district attorney n. The public prosecuting officer of a judicial district.

dis-trust (dis trust´) n. Suspicion; doubt. v. To doubt; to suspect. **distrustful** adj.

dis-turb (di strb´) v. To destroy the tranquillity or composure of; to unsettle mentally or emotionally; to interrupt or interfere with; to bother. **-turbance** n.

dis-u-nite (dis´ nt´) v. To divide or separate.

dis-u-ni-ty n. Discord; unrest.

dis-use (dis s´) n. The state of not using; out of use.

dith-er (dith´r) n. A state of nervousness or indecision; commotion.

dit-to (dit´) n. pl. **dittos** An exact copy; the same as stated before. **ditto mark** The pair of marks " used to substitute for the word ditto. **ditto** adv.

dit-ty (dit´) n. pl. **-ties** A short, simple song.

di-u-ret-ic (d´ ret´ik) adj. Tending to cause an increase in the flow of urine. n. A drug given to increase the amount of urine produced.

di-ur-nal (d er´nal) adj. Having a daily cycle or recurring every day; of, relating to, or occurring in the daytime; opening in the daytime and closing at night.

di-van (di van´) n. A long, backless and armless sofa or couch.

div-er (d´vr) n. A person who dives; a person who stays underwater for prolonged periods by having air supplied either from the surface or from compressed air tanks.

di-verge (di vrj´) v. Tomove or extend in different directions from a common point; to differ in opinion or manner. **divergent** adj.

di-vers (d´vrz) adj. Various; several.

di-verse (di vers´) adj. Unlike in characteristics; having various forms or qualities. **diversely** adv. **diverseness** n.

di-ver-si-fy (di ver´si f´) v. To give variety to something; to engage in varied operations; to distribute over a wide range of types or classes. **diversification** n.

di-ver-sion (di ver´zhan) n. The act of diverting from a course, activity or use; something that diverts or amuses.

di-ver-si-ty (di ver´si t) n. pl. **diversities** A difference; variety; unlikeness.

di-vert (di vert´) v. To turn from a set course; to give pleasure by distracting the attention from something that is burdensome or oppressive. **diversionary** adj. **diversion** n.

di-vest (di vest´) v. To undress or strip, especially of clothing or equipment; to deprive or dispossess of property, authority, or title.

div-i-dend (div´i dend´) n. An individual share of something distributed; a bonus; a number to be divided; a sum or fund to be divided and distributed.

di-vi-sive (di v´siv) adj. Tending to create dissension or disunity. **-ness** n.

di-vi-sor (di v´zr) n. In mathematics, the number by which a dividend is to be divided.

di-vorce (di vrs´) n. The legal dissolution of a marriage; the complete separation of things.

div-ot (div'ot) n. A square of turf or sod; a piece of turf torn up by a golf club while making a shot.

di-vulge (di vulj') v. To reveal or make known; to disclose; to reveal a secret.

diz-zy (diz') adj. Having a whirling sensation in the head with loss of proper balance; mentally confused; caused by or marked by giddiness; extremely rapid. **dizzily** adv.

do (dō) v. To bring to pass; to bring about; to perform or execute; to put forth; to exert; to bring to an end

do-cent (dōsent) n. A teacher at a college or university; a guide or lecturer in a museum.

doc-ile (dos'il) adj. Easily led, taught, or managed.

dock-et (dok'it) n. A brief written summary of a document; an agenda; an identifying statement about a document placed on its cover.

dock-yard (dok'yärd) n. A shipyard; a place where ships are repaired or built.

doc-tor (dok'tr) n. A person who is trained and licensed to practice medicine, such as a physician, surgeon, dentist, or veterinarian; a person holding the highest degree offered by a university. **doctor** v. To restore to good condition; to practice medicine; to administer medical treatment; to tamper with; to alter for a desired end.

doc-tor-ate (dok'tr it) n. The degree, status, or title of a doctor.

doc-trine (dok'trin) n. Something taught as a body of principles; a statement of fundamental government policy especially in international relations. **doctrinal** adj.

doc-u-ment (dok' ment) n. An official paper that is utilized as the basis, proof, or support for something. **document** v. To furnish documentary evidence of; to prove with, support by, or provide by documents.

doc-u-men-ta-ry (dok' men'ta r) adj. Relating to or based on documents; an artistic way of presenting facts.

dod-der (dod'r) v. To tremble, shake, or totter from weakness or age. **dodder** n., Bot. A parasitic, twining vine.

dodge (doj) v. To avoid by moving sud-

denly; to evade a responsibility by trickery or deceit; to shift suddenly.

does-n't (duz'ent) Does not.

dog-ma (dog'ma) n. A rigidly held doctrine proclaimed to be true by a religious group; a principle or idea considered to be the absolute truth.

do-jo n. A school of instruction in the Japanese martial arts.

dol-drums (dl'drumz) n. pl. A period of listlessness or despondency. Naut. The ocean region near the equator where there is very little wind.

dole-ful adj. Filled with grief or sadness.

dol-lar (dol'r) n. A coin, note, or token representing one dollar; the standard monetary unit of the U.S.

dol-lop (dol'op) n. A lump or blob of a semiliquid substance; an indefinite amount or form.

dol-men (dl'man) n. A prehistoric monument made up of a huge stone set on upright stone.

do-lor-ous (dol'r us) adj. Marked by grief or pain; sad; mournful. **-ly** adv.

dol-phin (dol'fin) n. Any of various small cetaceans with the snout in the shape of a beak and the neck vertebrae partially fused.

dolt (dlt) n. A stupid person.

do-main (d mn') n. A territory under one government; a field of activity or interest.

dome (dm) n. A roof resembling a hemisphere; something suggesting a dome.

dom-i-cile (dom'i sl') n. A dwelling place, house, or home.

dom-i-nant (dom'i nant) adj. Having the most control or influence; most overwhelming; in genetics, producing a typical effect even when paired with an unlike gene for the same characteristic. **dominance** n.

dom-i-no-the-o-ry n. The theory that if a certain event occurs, a series of similar events will follow.

don (don) v. To put something on; to dress.

done (dun) adj. Completely finished or through; doomed to failure, defeat, or death; cooked adequately.

do-nee (d n') n. A recipient of a gift.

done for adj. Mortally stricken; doomed; left with no opportunity for recov-

don-key (dong´k) n. pl. **-keys** The domesticated ass. *Informal* A stubborn person.

do-nor (d´nr) n. One who gives, donates, or contributes.

don't (dnt) Do not.

dor-mant (dor´mənt) adj. Asleep; a state of inactivity or rest. **dormancy** n.

dor-sal (dor´sal) adj., *Anat.* Of, relating to, or situated on or near the back.

DOS abbr. Disk operating system.

dose (ds) n. The measured quantity of a therapeutic agent to be taken at one time or at stated intervals. *Med.* The prescribed amount of radiation to which a certain part of the body is exposed. **dosage** n. **dose** v.

dos-si-er (dos´ ´) n. A complete file of documents or papers giving detailed information about a person or affair.

dote (dt) v. To show excessive affection or fondness; to exhibit mental decline, especially as a result of senility. **-er** n.

dou-ble (dub´l) adj. twice as much; composed of two like parts.

doubt (dout) v. To be uncertain or mistrustful about something; to distrust.

dour (der) adj. Stern and forbidding; morose and ill-tempered.

douse (dous) v. To plunge into liquid; to throw water on; to drench; to extinguish.

dove (duv) n. Any of numerous pigeons; a gentle, innocent person. **dovish** adj.

dow-a-ger (dou´a jr) n. A widow holding a title or property from her dead husband; a dignified, elderly woman.

dow-dy (dou´d) adj. Not neat or tidy; old- fashioned. **dowdier** adj.

dow-el (dou´el) n. A round wooden pin which fits tightly into an adjacent hole to fasten together the two pieces.

dowse (douz) v. To search for with a divining rod to find underground water or minerals.

dox-ol-o-gy (dok sol´ə j) n. pl. **-gies** A hymn or verse in praise of God.

doz-en (duz´en) n. Twelve of a kind; a set of twelve things.

drab (drab) adj. Of a light, dull brown or olive brown color; commonplace or dull.

draft (draft) n. A current of air; a sketch or plan of something to be made; a note for the transfer of money; the depth of water a ship draws with a certain load.

drake (drk) n. A male duck.

dram (dram) n. A small drink; a small portion.

drank v. Past tense of drink.

dras-tic (dras´tik) adj. Acting extremely harsh or severe. **drastically** adv.

draught (draft) n. & v. A variation of draft.

draw-back (dro´bak´) n. An undesirable feature.

drawl (drol) v. To speak slowly with prolonged vowels.

dray (dr) n. A low, heavy cart without sides, used for hauling.

dread (dred) v. To fear greatly; to anticipate with alarm, anxiety, or reluctance. n. A great fear. **dreadful** adj.

drea-ry (drr´) adj. Bleak and gloomy; dull. **drearily** adv. **dreariness** n.

dregs (dreg) n. p. The sediment of a liquid; the least desirable part.

drench (drench) v. To wet thoroughly; to throw water on. **drencher** n.

drew v. Past tense of draw.

drive (drv) v. To propel, push, or press onward; to repulse by authority; to force into a particular act or state.

driv-el (driv´el) v. To slobber; to talk nonsensically.

driz-zle (driz´el) n. A fine, quiet, gentle rain.

droop (dröp) v. To hang or bend downward; to become depressed.

drop-sy (drop´s) n., *Med.* A diseased condition in which large amounts of fluid collect in the body tissues and cavities.

drought or **drouth** (drout) n. A prolonged period of dryness; a chronic shortage of something.

drove (drv) n. A herd being driven in a body; a crowd. v. Past tense of drive.

drown (droun) v. To kill or die by suffocating in a liquid; to cause not to be heard by making a loud noise; to drive out.

drowse (drouz) v. To doze. **drowse** n.

drows-y (drou´z) adj. Sleepy; tending to induce sleep. **drowsiness** n.

drub (drub) v. To hit with a stick; to

abuse with words; to defeat decisively.
drudge (druj) n. A person who does tiresome or menial tasks. **drudge** v.
drug (drug) n. A substance used in the treatment of disease or illness; a narcotic. v. To take drugs for narcotic effect; to mix or dose with drugs.
dry-ad (dr´ad) n. A wood nymph.
du-al (dö´al) adj. Made up or composed of two parts; having a double purpose.
dub (dub) v. To equip with a new sound track.
du-bi-e-ty (dö b i t) n. A feeling of doubt.
du-bi-ous (dö´b us) adj. Causing doubt; unsettled in judgment; reluctant to agree; question as to quality or validity; verging on impropriety.
du-bi-ta-ble (dö´bi ta bl) adj. Doubtful; liable to be doubted.
duct (dukt) n. A bodily tube especially one carrying a secretion; a tubular passage through which something flows.
duc-tile (duk´til) adj. Capable of being drawn into a fine strand or wire; easily influenced or persuaded.
dud (dud) n. Milit. A bomb of gun shell that fails to explode. adj. Useless.
du-et (dö et´) n. A musical composition for two performers or musical instruments.
dul-cet (dul´sit) adj. Melodious; pleasing to the ear; having an agreeable, soothing quality.
dul-ci-mer (dul´si mr) n. A musical stringed instrument played with two small picks or by plucking.
du-ly (dö´l) adv. In a proper or due manner.
dumb (dum) adj. Unable to speak; temporarily speechless. Informal Stupid.
dunce (duns) n. A slow-witted person.
dune (dn) n. A ridge or hill of sand blown or drifted by the wind.
dun-geon (dun´jon) n. A dark, confining, underground prison chamber.
dunk (dungk) v. To dip a piece of food into liquid before eating; to submerge someone in a playful fashion.
du-o (dö´) n. pl. -os An instrument duet; two people in close association.
du-o-de-num (d´o d´num) n. pl. -dena The first portion of the small intestine, extending from the lower end of

the stomach to the jejunum. -nal adj.
du-pli-cate (dö´pli kit) adj. Identical with another; existing in or consisting of two corresponding parts. n. Either of two things which are identical; an exact copy of an original. v. To make an exact copy of.
du-ra-ble (der´a bl) adj. Able to continue for a prolonged period of time without deterioration.
du-ra-tion (de r´shan) n. The period of time during which something exists or lasts.
du-ress (de res´) n. Constraint by fear or force; in law, coercion illegally applied; forced restraint.
dur-ing (dur´ing) Throughout the time of; within the time of.
dwin-dle (dwin´dl) v. To waste away; to become steadily less.
dying (d´ing) n. Coming to the end of life; about to die. Ceasing to exist. n. The process or act of ceasing to exist
dy-nam-e-ter (di nam´i tr) n. Instrument for determining the telescopes magnifying power.
dy-nam-ic (d nam´ik) adj. Marked by energy and productive activity or change; of or relating to energy, motion, or force.
dy-nam-ics (d nam´iks) n., Phys. The part of physics which deals with force, energy, and motion and the relationship between them.
dys-lex-i-a n. An impairment in one's ability to read. **dyslexic** adj.
dys-lo-gis-tic (dislo jis´tik) adj. Conveying disapproval or censure.
dys-pep-sia (dis pep´sha) n. Indigestion. Impaired or a problem with digestion
dys-tro-phy (dis´tro f) n. Atrophy of muscle tissue; any of various neuromuscular disorders, especially muscular dystrophy.

E

E, e The fifth letter of the English alphabet. Mus. The third tone in the natural scale of C.
each (ch) adj. Everyone of two or more considered separately. **each** adv. To or for each; apiece.

each other *pron.* Each in reciprocal action or relation; one another.

ea-ger (´gr) *adj.* Marked by enthusiastic interest or desire; having a great desire or wanting something. **eagerly** *adv.*

ear (r) *n., Anat.* The hearing organ in vertebrates, located on either side of the head; any of various organs capable of detecting vibratory motion; the ability to hear keenly; attention or heed; something that resembles the external ear. **be all ears** Listen closely. **play by ear** Without reference to written music.

ear-lock (r läk) *n.* A curl of hair in front of the ear.

ear-ly (ûr´l) *adj.* Occurring near the beginning of a period of time; a development or a series; distant in past time; before the usual or expected time; occurring in the near future. **earlier** *adj.* **earliest** *adj.*

earn (ûrn) *v.* To receive payment in return for work done or services rendered; to gain as a result of one's efforts. **earner** *n.*

earth (ûrth) *n.* The third planet from the sun and the planet on which there is life; the outer layer of the world; ground; soil; dirt.

earth-ly (ûrth-l) *adj.* Belonging to this earth.

ea-sel (´zel) *n.* A frame used by artists to support a canvas or picture.

ease-ment (z-ment) *n.* Land owned by another for a specific limited use.

east (st) *n.* The direction opposite of west; the direction in which the sun rises. **easterly, -ward, -wards** *adv.*

Easter (´str) *n.* A Christian festival which celebrates the resurrection of Christ.

easy (´z) *adj.* Capable of being accomplished with little difficulty; free from worry or pain; not hurried or strenuous; something readily and spontaneously obtainable. **easily** *adv.*

eat (t) *v.* To chew and swallow food; to erode; to consume with distress or agitation; to take a meal.

ebb (eb) *n.* The return of the tide towards the sea; a time of decline. *v.* To recede, as the tide does; to fall or flow back.

eb-o-nite (eb-nt) *n.* Hard rubber.

eb-o-ny (eb´o n) *n. pl.* **-nies** The dark, hard, colored wood from the center of the ebony tree of Asia and Africa. *adj.* Resembling ebony; black.

ebul-lience (bel-yen) *n.* The enthusiastic expression of thoughts.

e-bul-lient (i bul´yent) *adj.* Filled with enthusiasm. **ebullience** *n.* **-liently** *adv.*

eb-ul-li-tion (eb´u lish´an) *n.* The process of boiling or bubbling; a sudden release of emotion.

ec-cen-tric (ik sen´trik) *adj.* Differing from an established pattern or accepted norm; deviating from a perfect circle; not located at the geometrical center. *n.* An odd or erratic person; a disk or wheel with its axis not situated in the center. **eccentrically** *adv.* **-tricity** *n.*

ec-lec-tic (i klek´tik) *adj.* Having components from diverse sources or styles. Selecting what appears to be the best in various methods, styles, or doctrines

e-clipse (i klips´) *n.* A total or partial blocking of one celestial body by another. *v.* To fall into obscurity or decline; to cause an eclipse of; to overshadow.

ec-logue *n.* A short pastoral poem in the form of a dialogue.

ec-o-cide *n.* The deliberate destruction of the natural environment, caused by pollutants.

e-col-o-gy (i kol´o j) *n.* The branch of science concerned with the interrelationship of organisms and their environments; the relationship between living organisms and their environments. **ecologic** *adj.* **ecologist** *n.*

ec-o-nom-ic (´ko nom´ik) *adj.* The science relating to the development, production, and management of material wealth; relating to the necessities of life.

ec-o-nom-i-cal (´ko nom´i kal) *adj.* Not wasteful; frugal; operating with little waste. Careful, prudent and efficient use of resources **economically** *adv.*

ec-o-nom-ics (´ko nom´iks) *n. pl.* The science which treats production, distribution, and consumption of commodities.

e-con-o-my (i kon´o m) *n. pl.* **-mies** Careful management of money, materials, and resources; a reduction in expenses; a system or structure for the management of resources and production of goods and services.

ec-ru (ek´rō) n. A light yellowish brown, as the color of unbleached linen.

ec-sta-sy (ek´sta s) n. pl. **-sies** The state of intense joy or delight. **-tic** adj.

ec-u-men-i-cal (ek´ men´i kal) adj. Worldwide or general in extent, application, or influence; promoting unity among Christian churches or religions. **ecumenically** adv. **ecumenism** n.

ec-ze-ma (ek´se ma) n. A noncontagious inflammatory skin condition, marked by itching and scaly patches.

e-del-weiss (d´el vs´) n. An Alpine plant having woolly leaves and small flowers.

edge (ej) n. The thin, sharp, cutting side of a blade; keenness; sharpness; the border where an object or area begins or ends; an advantage. v. To furnish with an edge or border; to sharpen; to move gradually.

ed-i-ble (ed´i bl) adj. Safe or fit for consumption. **edibility** n. **edible** n.

e-dict (´dikt) n. A public decree; an order or command officially proclaimed.

ed-i-fy (ed´i f) v. To benefit and enlight-en, morally or spiritually. **edification** n. **edifier** n.

ed-it (ed´it) v. To prepare and correct for publication; to compile for an edition; to delete or change. **editor** n.

e-di-tion (i dish´an) n. The form in which a book is published; the total number of copies printed at one time; one similar to an original version.

ed-i-to-ri-al (ed´i tr´al) n. An article in a newspaper or magazine which expresses the opinion of a publisher or editor. adj. Of or relating to an editor or an editor's work; being or resembling an editorial.

ed-u-cate (ej´u kt´) v. To supply with training or schooling; to supervise the mental or moral growth of. **-cator** n.

e-duce (i dōs´) v. To call forth or bring out; to develop from given facts.

ef-face (i fs´) v. To remove or rub out. **effacer** n. **effacement** n.

ef-fect (i fekt´) n. Something produced by a cause; the power to produce a desired result; the reaction something has on an object; a technique which produces an intended impression. **take effect** To become operative. **effecter** n.

ef-fec-tive (i fek´tiv) adj. Producing an expected effect or proper result.

ef-fem-i-nate (i fem´i nit) adj. Having a more woman-like quality or trait than a man. **effeminacy** n. **-nately** adv.

ef-fer-ent (ef´r ent) adj., Physiol. Carrying away or outward from a central organ or part. **efferent** n. **-ly** adv.

ef-fete (i ft´) adj. Exhausted of effectiveness or force; worn-out; decadent. **effetely** adv., **effeteness** n.

ef-fi-ca-cious (ef´i k´shus) adj. Producing an intended effect. **efficaciously** adv., **efficaciousness** n.

ef-fi-cient (i fish´ent) adj. Adequate in performance with a minimum of waste or effort; giving a high ratio of output.

ef-fi-gy (ef´i j) n. pl. **-gies** A life-size sculpture or painting representing a crude image or dummy of a hated person.

ef-flo-res-cence (ef´lo res´ens) n. A time of flowering; a slow process of development; the highest point.

ef-flu-ence (ef´lö ens) n. An act of flowing out; something that flows out or forth.

ef-flu-vi-um (i flö´v um) n. pl. **-via** or **-viums** An unpleasant vapor from something. **effluvial** adj.

ef-fort (ef´rt) n. Voluntary exertion of physical or mental energy; a difficult exertion; a normally earnest attempt or achievement; something done through exertion. Phys. A force applied against inertia. **effortless** adj.

ef-fron-ter-y (i frun´te r) n. pl. **-ies** Shameless boldness; impudence.

ef-ful-gent adj. Shining brilliantly; radiant.

ef-fu-sion (i f´zhan) n. An instance of pouring forth; an unrestrained outpouring of feeling. **effuse** v. **effusive** adj.

egg (eg) n. The hard-shelled reproductive cell of female animals, especially one produced by a chicken, used as food. v. To incite to action.

eg-lan-tine (eg´lan tin´) n. The sweetbrier, a type of rose.

e-go (**'g**) *n.* The self thinking, feeling, and acting distinct from the external world. *Physiol.* The conscious aspect that most directly controls behavior and is most in touch with reality.

e-go-cen-tric (**'g** sen´trik) *adj.* Thinking, observing, and regarding oneself as the object of all experiences. **egocentric** *n.*

e-go trip *n. Slang* Something which satisfies the ego.

e-gre-gious (i gr´jus) *adj.* Outstandingly or remarkably bad; flagrant. **egregiously** *adv.* **egregiousness** *n.*

e-gress (´gres) *n.* The act of coming out; emergence; a means of departing; exit.

e-gret (´grit) *n.* Any of several species of white wading birds having long, drooping plumes.

eight (t) *n.* The cardinal number which follows seven. **ball** The black ball with the number eight in the game of pool. **ball** In a bad spot. **eighth** *adj.*

ei-ther (´thr) *adj.* One or the other. *conj.* Used before the first of two or more alternatives linked by or. *adj.* One or the other of two. *adv.* Likewise; also.

e-jac-u-late (i jak´ lt0´) *v.* To eject abruptly, to utter suddenly and briefly; to exclaim. **ejaculation** *n.* **-latory** *adj.*

e-ject (i jekt´) *v.* To throw out; to expel. **ejection** *n.* **ejector** *n.*

eke out *v.* To obtain with great effort; to make do.

e-lab-o-rate (i lab´o rt´) *adj.* Planned or carried out with great detail; very complex; intricate. *v.* To work out or complete with great detail; to give more detail. **elaborateness** *n.* **-ration** *n.*

e-lapse (i laps´) *v.* To slip or glide away; to pass away silently.

e-las-tic (i las´tik) *adj.* Complying with changing circumstances; capable of easy adjustment. **elastically** *adv.* **elasticity** *n.*

e-late (i lt´) *v.* To make proud of.

el-bow (el´b) *n.* A sharp turn, as in a river or road, which resembles an elbow. *Anat.* The outer joint of the arm between the upper arm and forearm. *v.* To push or shove aside with the elbow.

e-lect (i lekt´) *v.* To choose or select by vote, as for an office; to make a choice. *adj.* Singled out on purpose; elected but not yet inaugurated. *n.* One chosen or set apart, especially for spiritual salvation.

e-lec-tric or **e-lec-tri-cal** (i lek´tri kal) *adj.* Relating to electricity; emotionally exciting. **electrically** *adv.*

e-lec-tri-cian (i lek trish´an) *n.* A person whose job it is to install or maintain electric equipment.

e-lec-tric-i-ty (i lek tris´i t) *n., Phys., Chem.* A force that causes bodies to attract or repel each other, responsible for a natural phenomena as lightning; electric current as a power source; emotional excitement.

e-lec-tro-car-di-o-graph (i lek´tr kär´do graf´) *n.* An electric instrument which detects and records the heartbeat.

e-lec-tro-cute (i lek´tro kt´) *v.* To kill or execute by the use of electric current.

e-lec-trode (i lek´trd) *n.* A conductor by which an electric current enters or leaves.

e-lec-tro-dy-nam-ics (i lek´tr d nam´iks) *n., Phys.* The study of the interactions of moving electric charges.

e-lec-tro-mag-net (i lek´tr mag´nit) *n.* A magnet consisting of a soft iron core magnetized by an electric current passing through a wire which is coiled around the core.

e-lec-trom-e-ter (i lek trom´i tr) *n.* An instrument for detecting or measuring electric potential or differences between two conductors.

e-lec-tron (i lek´tron) *n., Elect.* A subatomic particle with a negative electric charge found outside of an atoms nucleus.

e-lec-tro-stat-ic (i lek´tro stat´ik) *adj.* Pertaining to static electric charges.

el-e-gance (el´e gans) *n.* Refinement in appearance, movement, or manners.

el-e-gy (el´i j) *n. pl.* **-gies** A poem expressing sorrow and lamentation for one who is dead.

el-e-ment (el´e ment) *n.* A constituent part. *Chem. & Phys.* A substance not separable into less complex substances by chemical means. **elements** *pl.* The conditions of the weather.

el-e-men-ta-ry (el´e men´ta r) adj. Fundamental, essential; referring to elementary school; introducing fundamental principles.

el-e-phant (el´e fant) n. A large mammal having a long, flexible trunk and curved tusks.

el-e-vate (el´e vt´) v. To lift up or raise; to promote to a higher rank.

elf (elf) n. pl. **elves** An imaginary being with magical powers, often mischievous; a small, mischievous child.

e-lic-it (i lis´it) v. To bring or draw out; to evoke.

e-lide (i ld´) v. To omit, especially to slur over in pronunciation, as a vowel, consonant, or syllable. **elision** n.

e-lim-i-nate (i lim´i nt´) v. To get rid of, remove; to leave out; to omit; to excrete, as waste. **elimination** n. **eliminator** n. **eliminative** adj. **-natory** adj.

e-lite (i lt´) n. The most skilled members of a group; a small, powerful group; a type size yielding twelve characters to the inch.

e-lix-ir (i lik´sr) n., Phar. A sweetened aromatic liquid of alcohol and water, used as a vehicle for medicine; a medicine regarded as a cureall; a sovereign remedy.

ell (el) n. An extension of a building at right angles to the main structure.

el-lipse (i lips´) n., Geom. A closed curve, somewhat oval in shape.

e-lo-cu-tion (el´o k´shan) n. The art of effective public speaking.

e-lope (i lp´) v. To run away, especially in order to get married, usually without parental permission. **elopement** n.

el-o-quent (el´o kwent) adj. Having the power to speak fluently and persuasively; vividly expressive. **eloquence** n. **eloquently** adv.

else (els) adj. Different; other; more; additional. adv. In addition; besides.

else-where (els´hwâr´) adv. To or in another place.

e-lu-ci-date (i l´si dt´) v. To make clear, clarify; to explain. **elucidator** n.

e-lude (i ld´) v. To evade or avoid; to escape understanding.

e-ma-ci-ate (i m´sh t´) v. To become or cause to become extremely thin from

the loss of appetite. **emaciation** n.

em-a-nate (em´a nt´) v. To come or give forth, as from a source. **emanation** n.

e-man-ci-pate (i man´si pt´) v. To liberate; to set free from bondage.

e-mas-cu-late (i mas´k lt´) v. To castrate; to deprive of masculine vigor.

em-balm (em bäm´) v. To treat a corpse with preservatives in order to protect from decay.

em-bank (em bangk´) v. To support, protect, or defend with a bank of earth or stone.

em-bar-go (em bär´g) n. pl. **-goes** A prohibition or restraint on trade, as a government order forbidding the entry or departure of merchant vessels, for example the oil embargo of 1973.

em-bark (em bärk´) v. To board a ship; to set out on a venture. **-ation** n.

em-bar-rass (em bar´as) v. To cause to feel self-conscious; to confuse; to burden with financial difficulties. **embarrassment** n.

em-bas-sy (em´ba s) n. pl. **-sies** The headquarters of an ambassador.

em-bat-tle (em bat´l) v. To prepare or arrange for battle.

em-bed (em bed´) v. To fix or enclose tightly in a surrounding mass.

em-bel-lish (em bel´ish) v. To adorn or make beautiful with ornamentation; to decorate; to heighten the attractiveness by adding ornamental details.

em-bez-zle (em bez´l) v. To take money or other items fraudulently. **embezzlement** n.

em-bit-ter (em bit´r) v. To make bitter; to create feelings of hostility.

em-bla-zon (em bl´zon) v. To decorate in bright colors.

em-blem (em´blem) n. A symbol of something; a distinctive design. **emblematic** adj. **emblematical** adj.

em-bod-y (em bod´) v. To give a bodily form to; to personify. **embodiment** n.

em-bold-en (em bl´den) v. To encourage; to make bold.

em-bo-lism (em´bo liz´um) n., Med. The blockage of a blood vessel, as by an air bubble or a detached clot.

em-bon-point n. Plumpness; stoutness.

em-boss (em bos´) v. To shape or decorate in relief; to represent in relief.

em-bou-chure (äm´bŭ shŭr´) *n., Mus.* The part of a wind instrument which is applied to the lips to produce a musical tone.

em-bow-er (em bou´r) *v.* To enclose, cover, or shelter.

em-brace (em brs´) *v.* To clasp or hold in the arms; to hug; to surround; to take in mentally or visually. *n.* The act of embracing; a hug.

em-bra-sure (em br´zhr) *n., Arch.* A flared opening in a wall, as for a door or window.

em-bro-cate (em´brŏ kt´) *v.* To moisten and rub an injured part of the body with a liquid medicine. **-cation** *n.*

em-broi-der (em broi´dr) *v.* To decorate with ornamental needlework; to add fictitious details. **embroidery** *n.*

em-broil (em broil´) *v.* To involve in contention or violent actions; to throw into confusion. **embroilment** *n.*

em-bry-o (em´br´) *n. pl.* **-os** An organism in its early developmental stage, before it has a distinctive form; in the human species, the first eight weeks of development, especially before birth or germination; a rudimentary stage.

em-cee (em´s´) *n. Informal* A master of ceremonies. **emcee** *v.*

e-mend (i mend´) *v.* To correct or remove faults. **emendation** *n.* **-er** *n.*

em-er-ald (em´r ald) *n.* A bright-green, transparent variety of beryl, used as a gemstone.

e-merge (i mrj´) *v.* To rise into view; to come into existence. **emergence** *n.*

e-mer-gen-cy (i mr´jen s) *n. pl.* **-cies** A sudden and unexpected situation requiring prompt action.

e-mer-i-tus (i mer´i tŭs) *adj.* Retired from active duty but retaining the honorary title held immediately before retirement

em-er-y (em´e r) *n.* A grainy, mineral substance having impure corundum, used for polishing and grinding.

e-met-ic (e met´ik) *adj.* A medicine used to induce vomiting. **emetic** *n.*

em-i-grate (em´i grt´) *v.* To move from one country or region to settle elsewhere. **emigrant** *n.* **emigration** *n.*

e-mi-gre (em´i gr´) *n.* A refugee.

em-i-nent (em´i nent) *adj.* High in esteem, rank, or office; conspicuous; outstanding.

em-i-nent do-main *n.* The right of a government to take or control property for public use.

e-mir (e mr´) *n.* A Moslem prince.

em-is-sar-y (em´i ser´) *n. pl.* **-ies** A person sent out on a mission.

e-mit (i mit´) *v.* To send forth; to throw or give out. **emission** *n.*

e-mol-lient (i mol´yent) *n.* A substance for the soothing and softening of the skin.

e-mol-u-ment (i mol´ment) *n.* Profit; compensation, as a salary or perquisite.

e-mote (i mt´) *v.* To show emotion, as in acting.

e-mo-tion (i m´shan) *n.* A strong surge of feeling; any of the feelings of fear, sorrow, joy, hate, or love; a particular feeling, as love or hate.

em-pa-thy (em´pa th) *n., Physiol.* Identification with and understanding the feelings of another person. **empathetic** *adj.*

em-pen-nage (äm´pe näzh´) *n.* The rear section or tail of an aircraft.

em-per-or (em´pr r) *n.* The ruler of an empire.

em-pha-sis (em´fa sis) *n. pl.* **-ses** Significance or importance attached to anything.

em-phat-ic (em fat´ik) *adj.* Expressed or spoken with emphasis. **emphatically** *adv.*

em-pire (em´pr) *n.* The territories or nations governed by a single supreme authority.

em-pir-i-cal *or* **em-pir-ic** (em pir´i kal) *adj.* Depending on or gained from observation or experiment rather than from theory and science. **-cally** *adv.*

em-place-ment *n.* A platform for guns or military equipment.

em-ploy (em ploi´) *v.* To engage the service or use of; to devote time to an activity. **employable** *adj.* **employer** *n.* **employment** *n.*

em-po-ri-um (em pr´um) *n. pl.* **-riums** *or* **-ria** A large store which carries general merchandise.

em-pow-er (em pou´r) *v.* To authorize;

to delegate; to license.

em-press (em´pris) n. A woman who rules an empire; an emperor's wife or widow.

emp-ty (emp´t) adj. Containing nothing; vacant; lacking substance. v. To empty. **emptily** adv. **emptiness** n.

em-py-re-an (em´pi re´an) n. Pertaining to the highest part of heaven; the sky.

e-mu (´m) n. A swift-running Australian bird related to the ostrich.

em-u-late (em´ lt´) v. To strive to equal, especially by imitating. **emulation** n.

e-mul-sion (i mul´shan) n., Chem. A suspended mixture of small droplets, one within the other. Photog. A light-sensitive coating on photographic paper, film, or plates.

en-a-ble (en bl) v. To supply with adequate power, knowledge, or opportunity; to give legal power to another.

en-act (en akt´) v. To make into law; to decree. **enactment** n.

en-am-or (en am´r) v. To inflame with love; to charm.

en-camp (en kamp´) v. To form or stay in a camp. **encampment** n.

en-cap-su-late (en kap´su lt´) v. To enclose or encase in a capsule.

en-ceph-a-li-tis (en sef a ´l tis) n., Pathol. Inflammation of the brain.

en-chain (en chn´) v. To put in chains.

en-chant (en chant´) v. To put under a spell; to bewitch; to charm; to delight greatly.

en-cir-cle (en sr´kl) v. To form a circle around; to move around. -ment n.

en-clave (en´klv) n. A country surrounded by a foreign country; a cultural group living within a larger group.

en-close (en klz´) v. To surround on all sides; to put in the same envelope or package with something else. **enclo-sure** n.

en-co-mi-ast (en´k m ast) n. A person who praises.

en-co-mi-um (en k´m um) n. pl. -mium or -mia High praise.

en-com-pass (en kum´pas) v. To surround; to form a circle; to enclose.

en-core (äng´kr) n. An audience's demand for a repeated performance; a performance in response to an encore. v. To call for an encore.

en-coun-ter (en koun´tr) n. An unplanned or unexpected meeting or conflict. v. To come upon unexpectedly; to confront in a hostile situation.

en-cour-age (en kr´ij) v. To inspire with courage or hope; to support. **encouragement** n. **encouragingly** adv.

en-croach (en krch´) v. To intrude upon the rights or possessions of another. **encroacher** n. **encroachment** n.

en-crust (en krust´) v. To cover with a crust; to crust. **encrustation** n.

en-cum-ber (en kum´br) v. To hinder or burden with difficulties or obligations.

en-cy-clo-pe-di-a (en s´klo p´da) n. A comprehensive work with articles covering a broad range of subjects. -ic adj.

en-cyst (en sist´) v. To become enclosed in a sac. **encystment** n.

end (end) n. A part lying at a boundary; the terminal point at which something concludes; the point in time at which something ceases; a goal; a fragment; a remainder; in football, either of the players in the outer most position on the line of scrimmage. v. To come or bring to a termination; to ruin or destroy; to die.

en-dan-ger (en dn´jr) v. To expose or put into danger or imperil.

en-dear (en dr´) v. To make beloved or dear.

en-deav-or (en dev´r) n. An attempt to attain or do something. **endeavor** v.

en-dem-ic (en dem´ik) adj. Peculiar to a particular area or people.

en-dive (en´dv) n. A herb with crisp succulent leaves, used in salads; a plant related to the endive.

en-do-cri-nol-o-gy (en´d kri nol´oj) n. The area of science or study of the endocrine glands and various secretions.

en-dog-e-nous (en doj´e nus) adj., Biol. Originating or growing from within.

en-dor-phin (en´dor fen) n. Hormones with tranquilizing and pain-killing capabilities, secreted by the brain.

en-dorse (en dors´) v. To write one's signature on the back of a check, so as to obtain the cash indicated on the front, or on the back of a car title, so as to show transfer of ownership. -**dorsee** n.

en-do-scope (en´do skp´) n., Med. An

instrument used to examine a bodily canal or hollow organ. **endoscopic** *adj.*

en-dow (en dou´) *v.* To supply with a permanent income or income-producing property; to bestow upon.

en-dure (en dûr´) *v.* To undergo; to sustain; to put up with; to tolerate; to bear.

en-e-ma (en´e ma) *n.* The injection of a liquid into the rectum for cleansing; the liquid injected.

en-e-my (en´e m) *n. pl.* **-mies** One who seeks to inflict injury on another; a foe; a hostile force or power.

en-er-gy (en´r j) *n. pl.* **-gies** Capacity or tendency for working or acting; vigor; strength; vitality of expression. *Phys.* The capacity for doing work; usable heat or electric power.

en-er-vate (en´r vt) *v.* To deprive of vitality or strength; to weaken. **-ion** *n.*

en-fee-ble (en f´bl) *v.* To weaken; to make feeble. **enfeeblement** *n.*

en-fold (en fld´) *v.* To enclose; to wrap in layers; to embrace.

en-force (en frs´) *v.* To compel obedience; to impose by force or firmness. **enforceable** *adj.* **enforcement** *n.*

en-fran-chise (en fran´chz) *v.* To grant with civil rights, as the right to vote; to give a franchise to. **-chisement** *n.*

en-gage (en gj´) *v.* To employ or hire; to secure or bind, as by a contract; to pledge oneself, especially to marry; to undertake conflict; to participate. *Mech.* To interlock.

en-gen-der (en jen´dr) *v.* To give rise to; to exist; to cause.

en-gine (en´jin) *n.* A machine which converts energy into mechanical motion; a mechanical instrument; a locomotive.

en-gorge (en gorj´) *v.* To swallow greedily. *Pathol.* To fill an artery with blood.

en-graft (en graft´) *v.*, *Bot.* To join or fasten, as if by grafting.

en-grave (en grv´) *v.* To carve a surface; to carve, cut, or etch into a stone, metal, or wood for printing; to print from plates made by such a process. **engraver** *n.*

en-grav-ing (en gr´ving) *n.* The act or technique of one that engraves; the impression printed from an engraved plate.

en-gross (en grs´) *v.* To occupy the complete attention of; to copy or write in a large, clear hand. **engrossingly** *adv.*

en-gulf (en gulf´) *v.* To enclose completely; to submerge; to swallow.

en-hance (en hans´) *v.* To make greater; to raise to a higher degree. **-ment** *n.*

e-nig-ma (e nig´ma) *n.* One that baffles; anything puzzling; a riddle.

en-jamb-ment *or* **en-jambe-ment** (en jam´ment) *n.* Construction of a sentence from one line of a poem to the next, allowing related words to fall on different lines.

en-join (en join´) *v.* To command to do something; to prohibit, especially by legal action. **enjoiner** *n.*

en-joy (en joi´) *v.* To feel joy or find pleasure in; to have the use or possession of. **enjoyable** *adj.* **enjoyably** *adv.*

en-large (en lärj´) *v.* To make larger; to speak or write in greater detail. **enlargement** *n.* **enlarger** *n.*

en-light-en (en lt´en) *v.* To give a broadening or revealing knowledge; to give spiritual guidance or light to. **-ment** *n.*

en-list (en list´) *v.* To secure the help or active aid of. *Milit.* To sign-up for service with the armed forces. **ment** *n.*

en-liv-en (en l´ven) *v.* To make livelier, cheerful or vigorous. **enlivener** *n.*

en masse (än mas´) *adv.,* *Fr.* All together; grouped.

en-mesh (en mesh´) *v.* To catch in a net; to entangle.

en-mi-ty (en´mi t) *n. pl.* **-ties** Deep hatred; hostility.

en-no-ble (en n´bl) *v.* To make noble or honorable in quality or nature; to confer the rank of nobility. **-blement** *n.*

en-nui (än w´) *n.* Boredom; weariness.

e-nor-mi-ty (i nor´mi t) *n. pl.* **-ties** Excessive wickedness; an outrageous offense or crime.

e-nor-mous (i nor´mus) *adj.* Very great in size or degree. **enormously** *adv.*

e-nough (i nuf´) *adj.* Adequate to satisfy demands or needs. *adv.* To a satisfactory degree.

en-quire (en kwr´) *v.* Variation of inquire.

en-rage (en rj´) *v.* To put or throw into a rage.

en-rap-ture (en rap´chr) v. To enter into a state of rapture; to delight.

en-rich (en rich´) v. To make rich or richer; to make more productive.

en-roll *or* **en-rol** (en rl´) v. To enter or write a name on a roll, register, or record; to place one's name on a roll, register, or record. **enrollment** n. **enrollment** n.

en-sconce (en skons´) v. To settle securely; to shelter.

en-sem-ble (än säm´bl) n. A group of com- plementary parts that are in harmony; a coordinated outfit of clothing; a group of people performing together; music for two or more performers.

en-shrine (en shrn´) v. To place in a shrine; to hold sacred. -ment n.

en-shroud (en shroud´) v. To cover with a shroud.

en-si-lage (en´si lij) n. The process of storing and preserving green fodder in a silo; fodder that has been stored.

en-slave (en slv´) v. To make a slave of; to put in bondage. **enslavement** n.

en-snare (en snär´) v. To catch; to trap.

en-sue (en sö´) v. To follow as a consequence.

en-sure (en shür´) v. To make certain of.

en-tail (en tl´) v. To have as a necessary accompaniment or result; to restrict the inheritance of property to a certain line of heirs. **entailment** n.

en-tan-gle (en tang´gl) v. To tangle; to complicate; to confuse. -ment n.

en-tente (än tänt´) n., Fr. A mutual agreement between governments for cooperative action; the parties to an entente.

en-ter (en´tr) v. To go or come into; to penetrate; to begin; to become a member of or participant in; in law, to make a record of.

en-ter-prise (en´tr priz´) n. A large or risky undertaking; a business organization; boldness and energy in practical affairs.

en-ter-tain (en´tr tn´) v. To harbor or give heed to; to accommodate; receive as a guest; to amuse. **entertainer**, -ment n.

en-thrall (en throl´) v. To fascinate; to captivate. **enthrallment** n.

en-throne (en thrn´) v. To place on a throne. **enthronement** n.

en-thu-si-asm (en thö´z az´um) n. Intense feeling for a cause; eagerness. **enthusiast** n. **enthusiastic** adj.

en-tice (en ts´) v. To attract by arousing desire. **enticer** n. **enticement** n.

en-tire (en ter´) adj. Having no part left out; whole; complete. **entirely** adv.

en-ti-tle (en t´tl) v. To give a name to; to furnish with a right. **entitlement** n.

en-ti-ty (en´ti t) n. pl. -ties The fact of real existence; something that exists alone.

en-tomb (en tömb´) v. To place in a tomb.

en-to-mol-o-gy (en´to mol´o j) n. The study of insects. **entomologist** n.

entomologic adj. **entomological** adj.

en-trails (en´trlz) n. pl. Internal organs of man or animals.

en-trance (en trans´) n. The act of entering; the means or place of entry; the first appearance of an actor in a play. v. To fascinate; enchant.

en-trap (en trap´) v. To catch in a trap.

en-treat (en trt´) v. To make an earnest request of or for.

en-trench (en trench´) v. To dig a trench, as for defense; to fix or sit firmly.

en-tre-pre-neur (än´tre pre nr´) n., Fr. A person who launches or manages a business venture. **entrepreneurial** adj.

en-trust (en trust´) v. To transfer to another for care or performance; to give as a trust or responsibility.

en-try (en tr´) n. pl. -tries An opening or place for entering; an item entered in a book, list, or register.

en-twine (en twn´) v. To twine about or together.

e-nu-mer-ate (i nö´me rt´) v. To count off one by one. **enumeration** n.

e-nun-ci-ate (i nun´s t´) v. To pronounce with clarity; to announce; proclaim.

en-ven-om (en ven´om) v. To make poisonous; to embitter.

en-vi-a-ble (en´v a bl) adj. Highly desirable. **enviably** adv.

en-vi-ron-ment (en v´ron ment) n. Surroundings; the combination of external conditions which affect the development and existence of an individual, group, or organism. **environ-**

mental *adj.* **environmentalist** *n.*

en-vi-rons (en v′ronz) *n. pl.* A surrounding region; a place; outskirts, especially of a city.

en-vis-age (en viz′ij) *v.* To have or form a mental image of; to visualize.

en-voy (en′voi) *n.* A messenger or agent; a diplomatic representative who is dispatched on a special mission.

en-vy (en′v) *n. pl.* **-vies** A feeling of discontent or resentment for someone else's possessions or advantages; any object of envy. *v.* To feel envy because of or toward.

en-zyme (en′zm) *n., Biochem.* Proteins produced by living organisms that function as biochemical catalysts in animals and plants. **enzymatic** *adj.*

e-o-li-an (′l an) *adj., Geol.* Caused by or transmitted by the wind.

e-on (′on) *n.* An indefinite period of time.

ep-au-let *or* **ep-au-lette** (ep′e let′) *n.* A shoulder ornament, as on a military uniform.

e-pergne (i prn′) *n.* An ornamental center- piece for holding flowers or fruit, used on a dinner table.

e-phed-rine (i fed′rin) *n., Chem.* A white, odorless alkaloid used to relieve nasal congestion.

e-phem-er-al (i fem′r al) *adj.* Lasting a very short time. **ephemerally** *adv.*

ep-ic (ep′ik) *n.* A long narrative poem celebrating the adventures and achievements of a hero. **epic** *adj.*

ep-i-cen-ter (ep′i sen′tr) *n.* The part of the earth's surface directly above the focus of an earthquake.

ep-i-cure (ep′i kr′) *n.* One having refined tastes, especially in food and wine.

ep-i-dem-ic (ep′i dem′ik) *adj.* Breaking out suddenly and affecting many individuals at the same time in a particular area, especially true of a contagious disease; anything that is temporarily widespread, as a fad.

ep-i-der-mis (ep′i dr′mis) *n., Anat.* The outer, nonvascular layer of the skin.

ep-i-glot-tis (ep′i glot′is) *n. Anat.* The leaf-shaped, elastic cartilage at the base of the tongue that covers the windpipe during the act of swallowing.

epiglottal *adj.*

ep-i-gram (ep′i gram′) *n.* A clever, brief, pointed remark or observation; a terse, witty poem or saying. **epigrammatic** *adj.*

ep-i-graph (ep′i graf′) *n.* An inscription on a tomb, monument, etc.; a motto or quotation placed at the beginning of a literary work.

e-pig-ra-phy (i pig′ra f) *n.* The study and interpretation of inscriptions.

ep-i-lep-sy (ep′i lep′s) *n. pathol.* A nervous disorder marked by attacks of unconsciousness with or without convulsions.

ep-i-logue *or* **ep-i-log** (ep′i log′) *n.* A short speech given by an actor to the audience at the end of a play; an appended chapter placed at the end of a novel or book, etc.

e-pis-co-pa-cy (i pis′ko pa s) *n. pl.* **-cies** The government of a church by bishops; an episcopate.

ep-i-sode (ep′i sd′) *n.* A section of a poem, novel, etc., that is complete in itself; an occurrence; an incident.

ep-i-taph (ep′i taf′) *n.* An inscription, as on a tomb or gravestone, in memory of a deceased person.

ep-i-the-li-um (ep′i th′l um) *n. pl.* **-liums** *or* **- lia** *Biol.* The thin, membranous tissue consisting of one or more layers of cells, forming the covering of the outer bodily surface and most of the internal surfaces and organs. **epithelial** *adj.* **epithelioid** *adj.*

ep-i-thet (ep′i thet′) *n.* A term, word, or phrase used to characterize a person or thing; an abusive phrase or word.

e-pit-o-me (i pit′o m) *n.* A concise summary, as of a book; an extreme or typical example.

e-pit-o-mize (i pit′o mz′) *v.* To be a perfect example.

ep-och (ep′ok) *n.* A point in time marking the beginning of a new era.

ep-ox-y (e pok′s) *n. pl.* **-ies** *Chem.* A durable, corrosion-resistant resin used especially in surface glues and coatings.

eq-ua-ble (ek′wa bl) *adj.* Not changing or varying; free from extremes; evenly proportioned; uniform; not easily upset.

e-qual (´kwal) *adj.* Of the same measurement, quantity, or value as another; having the same privileges or rights.

e-qual-i-ty *n.* The state of being equal.

e-qual-ize (´kwa lz´) *v.* To become or make equal or uniform. **-ization** *n.*

e-qua-nim-i-ty (´kwa nim´i t) *n.* Composure.

e-quate (i kwt´) *v.* To consider or make equal.

e-qua-tion (i kw´zhan) *n.* The act or process of being equal; a mathematical statement expressing the equality of two quantities, usually shown as (=).

e-qua-tor (i kw´tr) *n.* The great imaginary circle around the earth; a line lying in a plane perpendicular to the earth's polar axis.

e-qui-an-gu-lar (kwi a gye ler) *adj. Geom.* Having all angles equal.

e-qui-lat-er-al (´kwi lat´r al) *adj.* Having all sides equal.

e-qui-lib-ri-um (-kwe´lib-r-em) *n. pl.* **-ums** *Phys.* The state of balance between two opposing forces or influences; any state of compromise, adjustment, or balance.

e-qui-nox (´kwi noks´) *n.* Either of the two times a year when the sun crosses the celestial equator and the days and nights are equal in time. **-noctial** *adj.*

e-quip (i kwip´) *v.* To furnish or fit with whatever is needed for any undertaking or purpose; to dress for a certain purpose or reason.

e-quip-ment (i kwip´ment) *n.* The state or act of being equipped; the material one is provided with for a special purpose.

e-qui-poise (´kwi poiz´) *n.* A state of balance.

eq-ui-ta-ble (ek´wi ta bl) *adj. pl.* **-ties** Being impartial in treatment or judgment. **equitableness** *n.* **equitably** *adv.*

eq-ui-ta-tion (ek´wi t´shan) *n.* The art or act of horse riding.

eq-ui-ty (ek´wi t) *n. pl.* **-ties** Fairness or impartiality; the value of property beyond a mortgage or liability; in law, justice based on the concepts of fairness and ethics.

e-quiv-a-lent (i kwiv´a lent) *adj.* Being equal or virtually equal, as in effect or meaning.

e-quiv-o-cal (i kwiv´o kal) *adj.* Ambiguous; questionable. **equivocally** *adv.*

e-quiv-o-cate (i kwiv´o kt´) *v.* To use intentionally evasive or vague language. **equivocation** *n.* **equivocator** *n.*

-er *n. suff.* A thing or person that performs the action of the root verb; a person concerned with a trade or profession, as a banker, teacher, etc.; one who lives in or comes from a certain area, as a northerner, midwesterner, etc.; used to form the comparative usage degree of adverbs and adjectives.

e-ra (r´a) *n.* An extended period of time that is reckoned from a specific date or point in the past and used as the basis of a chronology.

e-rad-i-cate (i rad´i kt´) *v.* To destroy utterly; to remove by the roots.

e-rase (i rs´) *v.* To remove something written. *Slang* To kill. **erasable** *adj.* **eraser** *n.* **erasure** *n.*

ere (âr) *prep.* Prior to; before.

e-rect (i rekt´) *adj.* In a vertical position; standing up straight. *v.* To construct; build. *Physiol.* The state of erectile tissue, as through an influx of blood. **erectness** *n.* **erector** *n.* **erection** *n.*

er-e-mite (er´em mt´) *n.* A hermit.

er-go (ür´g) *conj.* & *adv.* Consequently; therefore.

er-got (ür´got) *n.* The disease of rye and other cereal plants; a drug used to contract involuntary muscles and to control hemorrhage.

e-rode (i rd) *v.* To wear away gradually by constant friction; to corrode; to eat away.

e-rot-ic (i rot´ik) *adj.* Pertaining to or promoting sexual desire. **-ically** *adv.*

err (ür) *v.* To make a mistake; to sin.

er-rand (er´and) *n.* A short trip to carry a message or to perform a specified task, usually for someone else.

er-rant (er´ant) *adj.* Wandering or traveling about in search of adventure; straying from what is proper or customary. **errantry** *n.*

er-rat-ic (i rat´ik) *adj.* Lacking a fixed course. *Med.* Irregular; inconsistent.

er-ra-tum (i r´tum) *n. pl.* **-ta** An error in writing or printing.

er-ro-ne-ous (e r´n us) *adj.* To have or

contain an error. **erroneously** adv.

er-ror (er´ or) n. Something said, believed, or done incorrectly; a mistake; the state of being wrong or mistaken; in baseball, a misplay by a team member who is not batting.

er-satz (er´zäts) adj. A substitute that is usually inferior; artificial.

er-u-dite (er´ dt´) adj. Scholarly.

er-u-di-tion (er´ dish´an) n. Great learning.

e-rupt (i rupt´) v. To burst forth violently and suddenly; to explode with steam, lava, etc., as a volcano or geyser; to break out in a skin rash or pimples.

e-ryth-ro-cyte (i rith´ro st´) n. A disk-shaped blood cell that contains hemoglobin and is responsible for the red color of blood.

es-ca-late (es´ka lt´) v. To intensify, increase, or enlarge. **escalation** n.

es-ca-la-tor (es´ka l´tr) n. A moving stairway with steps attached to an endless belt.

es-cal-lop (e skol´op) n. & v. Variation of scallop.

es-ca-pade (es´ka pd) n. Reckless or playful behavior; a prankish trick.

es-cape (e skp´) v. To break free from capture, confinement, restraint, etc; to fade from the memory; to enjoy temporary freedom from unpleasant realities. **escape** n. **escapee** n. **escaper** n.

es-cape-ment (e skp´ment) n., Mech. A device used in timepieces to control the movement of the wheel and supply energy impulses to a pendulum or balance; a typewriter mechanism that controls the horizontal movement of the carriage.

es-carp-ment n. A steep slope or drop; a long cliff formed by erosion.

-escense n. suff. To give off light in a certain way, as florescence.

-escent adj. suff. To give off light in a special way, as hosphorescent; beginning to be.

es-chew (es chö´) v. To shun or avoid.

es-cort (es´kort) n. A group or individual person accompanying another so as to give protection or guidance; a male who accompanies a female in public.

es-cri-toire (es´kri twär´) n. A writing desk.

es-crow (es´kr) n. In law, a written deed, contract, or money placed in the custody of a third party until specified conditions are met.

es-cutch-eon (e skuch´on) n. A shield-shaped surface with an emblem bearing a coat of arms; a protective plate, as for a keyhole.

-ese n. & adj., suff. An inhabitant or native of; in the language or style of.

e-soph-a-gus (i sof´a gus) n. pl. -gi Anat. The muscular, membranous tube through which food passes on the way from the mouth to the stomach. **esophageal** adj.

es-o-ter-ic (es´o ter´ik) adj. Confidential; kept secret; understood or meant for only a particular and often very small group.

es-pe-cial (e spesh´al) adj. Having a very special place; apart or above others; exceptional. **especially** adv.

es-pi-o-nage (es´p o näzh´) n. The act or practice of spying to obtain secret intelligence.

es-pla-nade (es´pla nd´) n. A flat, open stretch of land along a shoreline.

es-pou-sal (e spou´zal) n. Support or adoption, as of a cause; a wedding.

es-pouse (e spouz´) v. To make something one's own; to take as a spouse; to marry; to give in marriage.

es-pres-so (e spres´) n. pl. -sos A strong coffee brewed by steam pressure from darkly-roasted beans.

es-prit (e spr´) n. Spirit; wit; mental liveliness.

es-py (e sp´) v. To catch a quick view or sight of.

-esque adj. suff. Resembling.

es-quire (e skwer´) n. The title of courtesy or respect; sometimes written as Esq. behind a man's last name.

-ess n. suff. Female.

es-say (es´) n. A short composition that deals with a single topic and expresses the author's viewpoint on a subject; an effort or attempt. **essayer** n. **essayist** n.

es-sence (es´ ens) n. The real nature in which something consists; the most important element; an immaterial spirit; being.

es-sen-tial (e sen´shal) adj. Necessary;

indispensable; containing, of, or being an essence. **essential** n. **essentiality** n. **essentialness** n. **essentially** adv.

est abbr. Established; estimate.

-est adj. & adv., suff. Used to form the superlative degree of adverbs and adjectives.

es-tab-lish (e stab'lish) v. To make permanent, stable, or secure; to install; to create or find; to cause to be accepted or recognized; to prove.

es-tab-lish-ment (e stab'lish ment) n. The state of being established; a place of business or residence; those collectively who occupy positions of influence and status in a society.

es-tate (e stt') n. A usually large or extensive piece of land containing a large house; in law, the nature, degree, and extent of ownership or use of property.

es-teem (e stm') v. To regard with respect.

es-ter (es'tr) n., Chem. Any of a class of organic compounds formed by the reaction of an acid with an alcohol.

es-thet-ic (es thet'ik) adj. Variation of aes- thetic.

es-ti-ma-ble (es'ti ma bl) adj. Worthy of respect or admiration. **-ness** n. **-ly** adv.

es-ti-mate (es'ti mt') v. To form or give an approximate opinion or calculation. n. A preliminary opinion or statement of the approximate cost for certain work.

es-ti-val (es'ti val') adj. Pertaining to or of summer.

es-ti-vate (es'ti vt') v. To pass the summer in a state of dormancy.

es-trange (e stranj') v. To arouse hatred or indifference where there was once love and caring; to disassociate or remove oneself.

es-tro-gen (es'tro jen) n., Biochem. Any of various steroid hormones that regulate female reproductive functions and secondary sex characteristics.

etch (ech) v. To engrave or cut into the surface by the action of acid; to sketch or outline by scratching lines with a pointed instrument. **etcher** n.

e-ter-nal (i tr'nal) adj. Existing without beginning or end; unending; meant to last indefinitely. **eternal** n. **eternality**

n. **eternalness** n. **eternally** adv.

e-ter-ni-ty (i tr'ni t) n. pl. **-ties** Existence without beginning or end; forever; the immeasurable extent of time; the endless time after a person dies.

eth-a-nol (eth'a nl') n., Chem. The alcohol obtained after the distillation of certain fermented sugars or starches; the intoxicant in liquors, wines, and beers; alcohol.

e-ther ('thr) n., Chem. A highly flammable liquid compound with a characteristic odor, used as a solvent and an anesthetic; the clear upper regions of space.

e-the-re-al (i thr' al) adj. Very airy and light; highly refined; delicate; heavenly.

eth-ic (eth'ik) n. pl. **-ics** The system of moral values; the principle of right or good conduct.

eth-i-cal (eth'i kal) adj. Relating to or of ethics; conforming to right principles of conduct as accepted by a specific profession, as medicine. **-ly** adv.

eth-nic (eth'nik) adj. Relating to or of a national, cultural, or racial group.

eth-nol-o-gy (eth nol'o j) n. pl. **-gies** The branch of anthropology that is concerned with the study of ethnic and racial groups, their cultures, origins, and distribution.

eth-yl-ene (eth'i ln') n., Chem. A colorless, flammable gas refined from natural gas and petroleum and used as a fuel.

ethyl ether n. Chem. Ether.

e-ti-ol-o-gy ('t ol'o j) n. The science and study of causes or origins. Med. The theory of the cause of a particular disease.

et-i-quette (et'i kit) n. The prescribed rules, forms and practices, established for behavior in polite society or in official or professional life.

-ette n. suff. Small; female.

et-y-mol-o-gy (et'i mol'o j) n. pl. **-gies** The history of a word as shown by breaking it down into basic parts, tracing it back to the earliest known form, and indicating its changes in form and meaning; the branch of linguistics that deals with etymologies.

et-y-mon (et'i mon') n. pl. **-mons** or

-ma The earlier form of a word in the same language or in the ancestral language.

eu-gen-ics (jen´iks) n. The science of im- proving the physical and mental qualities of human beings through genetics.

eu-lo-gy (´lo j) n. pl. **-gies** A speech that honors a person or thing, usually delivered at a funeral; high praise.

eu-nuch (´nuk) n. A castrated man.

eu-phe-mism (´fe miz´um) n. A substitution for a word or expression that is thought to be too strong, blunt, or painful for another person.

eu-pho-ny (´fo n) n. pl. **-nies** The agreeable sound of spoken words. **euphonious** adj. **euphoniously** adv.

eu-pho-ri-a (fr´ a) n. A very strong feeling of elation or well-being.

eu-re-ka (r´ka) An expression of triumph or achievement.

eu-ro-pi-um (r´p um) n. Chem. A soft, silvery-white, rare-earth element used in nuclear research symbolized by Eu.

Eu-sta-chian tube (st´shan tōb) n. Anat. The passage between the middle ear and the pharynx that equalizes the air pressure between the tympanic cavity and the atmosphere.

eu-tha-na-sia (u´tha n´zha) n. The act or practice of putting to death painlessly a person suffering from an incurable disease; also called mercy killing.

e-vac-u-ate (i vak´ ´shan) v. To leave a threatened area, town, building, etc.; to empty; to remove the contents. Physiol. To discharge or eject, as from the bowels. **evacuation** n. **-ator** n.

e-vac-u-ee (i vak´ ´) n. A person who is evacuated from a hazardous place.

e-vade (i vd´) v. To baffle; to elude; to get away from by using cleverness or tricks. To take refuge

e-val-u-ate (i val´ t´) v. To examine carefully; to determine the value of; to appraise. **evaluation** n. **evaluator** n.

e-va-nesce (ev´a nes´) v. To disappear; to fade away.

ev-a-nes-cent (ev´a nes´ent) adj. Vanishing or passing quickly; fleeting. **evanescence** n. **evanescently** adv.

e-van-ge-list or **Evangelist** (i van´je list) n. One of the four writers of the New Testament Gospels Matthew, Mark, Luke, or John; a zealous Protestant preacher or missionary.

e-vap-o-rate (i vap´o rt´) v. To convert into vapor; to remove the liquid or moisture from fruit, milk, etc., so as to concentrate or dry it. **evaporative** adj. **evaporator** n.

e-va-sion (i v´zhan) n. The act or means of evading.

e-va-sive (i v´siv) adj. Being intentionally vague; equivocal. **evasively** adv.

eve (v) n. The evening before a special day or holiday; the period immediately preceding some event; evening.

e-ven (´ven) adj. Having a flat, smooth, and level surface; having no irregularities; smooth; on the same line or plane; equally matched; not owing or having anything owed to one; exactly divisible by 2; opposed to odd. **even** Informal To end with neither profit or loss, as in business. **to get even** One's full measure of revenge. **evenly** adv.

eve-ning (v´ning) n. The time between sunset and bedtime.

e-vent (i vent´) n. A significant occurrence; something that takes place; the actual or possible set of circumstances; a real or contingent situation; the final outcome; one of the parts of a sports program.

e-ven-tide (´ven td´) n. Evening.

e-ven-tu-al (i ven´chö al) adj. Happening or expected to occur in due course of time.

e-ven-tu-al-i-ty (i ven´chö al i t) n. pl. **-ties** A likely or possible occurrence; the conceivable outcome.

e-ven-tu-ate (i ven´chö t´) v. To result ultimately; to come out eventually.

ev-er (ev´r) adv. At any time; on any occasion; by any possible chance or conceivable way; at all times; throughout the entire course of time.

ev-er-more (ev´r mr´) adv. Poet. For and at all time to come; always.

e-vert (i vrt´) v. To turn inside out or outward.

eve-ry (ev´r) adj. Without exceptions; the utmost; all possible. **then** From time to time; occasionally. **every other** Each alternate. **way** Informal In every way or direction and with very little order.

eve·ry·bod·y (ev´r bod´) *pron.* Every person.

eve·ry·day (ev´r d´) *adj.* Happening every day; daily; suitable for ordinary days.

eve·ry·one (ev´r wun´) *pron.* Everybody; every person.

eve·ry·place *adv.* Everywhere.

eve·ry·thing (ev´r thing´) *pron.* All things; whatever exists; whatever is needed, relevant, or important; the essential thing; the only thing that really matters.

eve·ry·where (ev´r hwâr´) *adv.* In, at, or to everyplace.

e·vict (i vikt´) *v.* To put out or expel a tenant by legal process. **evictor** *n.* **eviction** *n.*

ev·i·dence (ev´i dens) *n.* Signs or facts on which a conclusion can be based. *v.* To indicate clearly. **evidence** Clearly present; evident.

ev·i·dent (ev´i dent) *adj.* Easily understood or seen; obvious. **evidently** *adv.*

e·vil (´vil) *adj.* Morally bad or wrong; causing injury or any other undesirable result; marked by misfortune or distress; low in public esteem.

e·vince (i vins´) *v.* To demonstrate or indicate clearly; to give an outward sign of having a quality or feeling.

e·vis·cer·ate (i vis´e rt´) *v.* To remove the vital part of something; to remove the entrails. **evisceration** *n.*

e·voke (i vk´) *v.* To call or summon forth; to draw forth or produce a reaction; to summon up the spirits by or as by incantations. **evocation** *n.* **evocative** *adj.*

ev·o·lu·tion (ev´o lö´shan) *n.* The gradual process of development or change. *Biol.* The theory that all forms of life originated by descent from earlier forms.

e·volve (i volv´) *v.* To develop or change gradually. *Biol.* To be developed by evolutionary processes; to develop or work out.

ex- *pref.* Out of; former.

ex *n.* The letter x. *Slang* A former spouse. *abbr.* Example; exchange.

ex·ac·er·bate (ig zas´r bt´) *v.* To make more severe or worse; to aggravate.

ex·act (ig zakt´) *adj.* Perfectly complete and clear in every detail; accurate in every detail with something taken as a model; similar. *v.* To be extremely careful about accuracy and detail; to force unjustly for the payment of something; to insist upon as a strict right or obligation; to call for or require. **-ion** *n.* **exactness** *n.* **-ly** *adv.*

ex·act·ing (eg zak´ting) *adj.* Making severe demands; rigorous; involving constant attention, hardwork, etc.

ex·act·i·tude (ig zak´ti töd´) *n.* The quality of being exact.

ex·ag·ger·ate (ig zaj´e rt´) *v.* To look upon or to represent something as being greater than it really is; to make greater in intensity or size than would be normal or expected.

ex·alt (ig zolt´) *v.* To raise in character, honor, rank, etc.; to praise or glorify; to increase the intensity of. **-alted** *adj.*

ex·am (ig zam´) *n. Slang* An examination.

ex·am·i·na·tion (ig zam´i n´shan) *n.* A test of skill or knowledge; the act of examining or the state of being examined; medical testing and scrutiny.

ex·am·ine (ig zam´in) *v.* To observe or inspect; to test by questions or exercises, as to fitness or qualification.

ex·am·ple (ig zam´pl) *n.* One that is representative as a sample; one worthy of imitation; an object or instance of punishment, reprimand, etc..

ex·as·per·ate (ig zas´p rt´) *v.* To make frustrated or angry; to irritate.

ex·ca·vate (eks´ka vt´) *v.* To dig a hole or cavity; to form or make a tunnel, hole, etc., by digging, scooping, or hollowing out; to remove or uncover by digging; to unearth. **excavation** *n.* **excavator** *n.*

ex·ceed (ik sd´) *v.* To surpass in quality or quantity; to go beyond the limit; to be superior. **exceeding** *adj.*

ex·cel (ik sel´) *v.* To surpass or to do better than others.

ex·cel·lent (ek´se lent) *adj.* The best quality; exceptionally good.

ex·cel·si·or (ik sel´s r) *n.* Long, firm woodshavings used in packing to protect delicate materials. *adj.* Upward; higher.

ex·cept (ik sept´) *prep.* With the omission or exclusion of; aside from; not including; leaving out. **exception** *n.*

ex·cep·tion·al (ik sep´sha nal) *adj.* Being an exception to the rule; unusual; well above average. **-ally** *adv.*

ex·cerpt (ik srpt´) *n.* A passage from a book, speech, etc. *v.* To select and cite.

ex·cess (ik ses´) *n.* The amount or condition of going beyond what is necessary, usual, or proper; overindulgence, as in drink or food. **excessive** *adj.*

exch. *abbr.* Exchange

ex·change (iks chnj) *v.* To give in return for something else; to trade; to return as unsatisfactory and get a replacement. *n.* The substitution of one thing for another.

ex·cise (ik sz´) *n.* The indirect or internal tax on the production, consumption, or sale of a commodity, such as liquor or tobacco, that is produced, sold, and used or transported within a country. *v.* To remove surgically.

ex·cit·a·ble (ik s´ta bl) *adj.* To be easily excited. **excitably** *adv.* **excitability** *n.*

ex·cite (ik st´) *v.* To stir up strong feeling, action, or emotion; to stimulate the emotions of; to bring about; to induce.**excitation** *n.* **excitement** *n.* **excitedly** *adv.*

ex·claim (ik sklm´) *v.* To cry out abruptly; to utter suddenly, as from emotion; to speak loudly.

ex·cla·ma·tion (ek´skla m´shan) *n.* An abrupt or sudden forceful utterance.

exclamation point *n.* A punctuation mark, (!) used after an interjection or exclamation.

ex·clude (ik sklöd´) *v.* To keep out; to omit from consideration; to put out. To bar from participation, inclusion or consideration.

ex·clu·sive (ik sklö´siv) *adj.* Intended for the sole use and purpose of a single individual or group; intended for or **exclusiveness** *n.* **exclusivity** *n.*

ex·co·ri·ate (ik skr´ t´) *v.* To tear the skin or wear off; to censure harshly.

ex·cre·ment (ek´skre ment) *n.* Bodily waste, especially feces. **-mental** *adj.*

ex·cre·ta (ik skr´ta) *n. pl.* Excretions from the body such as sweat, urine, etc.

ex·crete (ik skrt´) *v.* To throw off or eliminate waste matter by normal discharge from the body. **excretion** *n.*

ex·cru·ci·at·ing (ik skrö´sh ´ting) *adj.* Intensely painful; agonizing. **-ly** *adv.*

ex·cul·pate (ek´skul pt´) *v.* To free from wrong doing; to prove innocent of guilt. **exculpation** *n.* **exculpatory** *adj.*

ex·cur·sion (ik skür´zhan) *n.* A short trip, usually made for pleasure; a trip available at a special reduced fare. *Phys.* The oscillating movement between two points; also, half of this total distance. **excursionist** *n.*

ex·cur·sive (ik skür´siv) *adj.* To go in one direction and then another; rambling; digressive.

ex·cuse (ik skz´) *v.* To ask forgiveness or pardon for oneself; to grant pardon or forgiveness; to overlook or accept; to apologize for; to justify; to allow one to leave; to release. *n.* Areas on, justification, or explanation. **excuse** *In-formal* An inferior example for some-thing. **excusable** *adj.*

exec *abbr.* Executive; executor.

ex·e·cra·ble (ek´si kra bl) *adj.* Extremely bad; detestable; revolting.

ex·e·crate (ek´si krt´) *v.* To detest; to feel or express detestation for; to abhor. **execration** *n.* **execrator** *n.*

ex·e·cute (ek´se kt´) *v.* To carry out; to put into effect; to validate, as by signing; to carry out what has been called for in a will; to put to death by the legal authority.

ex·ec·u·tive (ig zek´ tiv) *n.* A manager or administrator in an organization; the branch of the government responsible for activating or putting the laws of a country into effect and for carrying out plans or policies.

ex·ec·u·tor (ig zek´yu tr) *n.* The person appointed to carry out the reading and execution of a will. One who executes something. **executorial** *adj.*

ex·e·ge·sis (ek´si j´sis) *n. pl.* **-ses** An interpretation or explanation of a text. **exegetic** *adj.* **exegetically** *adv.*

ex·em·plar (ig zem´plr) *n.* Something that serves as a worthy model or imitation; a typical example.

ex·em·pla·ry (ig zem´pla r) *adj.* Serving as a model; worthy of imitation;

commendable.

ex-em-pli-fy (ig zem´pli f´) v. To show by giving examples; to be an example of.

ex-empt (ig zempt´) v. To free or excuse from an obligation or duty to which others are subject. **exemption** n.

ex-ert (ig zrt´) v. To put into action, as influence or force; to put oneself through a strenuous effort. **exertion** n.

ex-er-tion (ig-zer-shen) n. The instance or act of exerting.

ex-haust (ig zost´) v. To make extremely tired; to drain oneself of resources, strength, etc. n. The escape or discharge of waste gases, working fluid, etc.; the waste gases, etc. that escape; the device through which waste gases are released or expelled. **exhaustible** adj. **exhaustion** n.

ex-hib-it (ig zib´it) v. To display, as to put up for public view; to bring documents or evidence into a court of law.

ex-hi-bi-tion-ism n.The practice of deliberately drawing undue attention to oneself. **exhibition** n. **exhibitor** n. **exhibitionistic** adj.

ex-hil-a-rate (ig zil´a rt´) v. To elate, make cheerful, or refresh. **exhilaration** n.

ex-hort (ig zort´) v. To urge by earnest appeal or argument; to advise or recommend strongly. **exhortation** n.

ex-hume (ig zōm´) v. To dig up and remove from a grave; to disinter.

ex-i-gen-cy (ek´si jen s) n. pl. **-cies** The quality or state of being exigent. usually pl. A pressing need or necessity. A state of affairs making urgent demands.

ex-ig-u-ous (ig zig´us) adj. Extremely small; scanty. **exiguity** n.

ex-ile (eg´zl) n. The separation by necessity or choice from one's native country or home; banishment; one who has left or been driven from his or her country. v. To banish or expel from one's native country or home.

ex-ist (ig zist´) v. To have actual being or reality; to live.

ex-is-tence (ig zis´tens) n. The fact or state of existing, living, or occurring; the manner of existing. **existent** adj.

ex-is-ten-tial (eg´zi sten´shal) adj. Based on experience; of or relating to existentialism.

ex-it (eg´zit) n. A way or passage out; the act of going away or out; the departure from a stage, as in a play. **exit** v.

ex-o-bi-ol-o-gy (ek´s b ol o´ j) n. The search for and study of extra terrestrial life.

ex-o-dus (ek´so dus) n. A going forth; a departure of large numbers of people, as that of Moses and the Israelites as described in Exodus, the second book of the Old Testament.

ex-og-e-nous (ek soj´e nus) n., Biol. That which is derived from external causes.

ex-on-er-ate (ig zon´e rt´) v. To free or clear one from accusation or blame; to relieve or free from responsibility.

ex-or-bi-tant (ig zor´bi tant) adj. Beyond usual and proper limits, as in price or demand. **exorbitance** n. **exorbitantly** adv.

ex-or-cise (ek´sor sz´) v. To cast out or expel an evil spirit by prayers or incantations; to free from an evil spirit. **exorciser** n. **exorcism** n. **exorcist** n.

ex-o-sphere (ek´s sfr´) n. Meteor. The outer fringe region of a planet or the earth's atmosphere starting about 400 miles up.

ex-o-ther-mic (ek´s ther´mik) adj. Releasing rather than absorbing heat.

ex-ot-ic (ig zot´ik) adj. Belonging by nature or origin to another part of the world; foreign; strangely different and fascinating.

exp abbr. expenses; export; express.

ex-pand (ik spand´) v. To increase the scope, range, volume, or size; to open up or spread out; to develop in form or details.

expandable adj. **expander** n.

ex-panse (ik spans´) n. A wide, open stretch.

ex-pan-sion (ik span´shan) n. The act of or state of being expanded; the amount of increase in range, size, or volume.

ex-pan-sive (ik span´siv) adj. Capable of expanding or inclined to expand; characterized by expansion; broad and extensive; open and generous; outgoing. **expansively** adv. **-ness** n.

ex par-te (eks pär´t) adj. & adv. In law, giving only one side or point of view.

ex-pa-ti-ate (ik sp´sh t´) v. To elaborate; to talk or write at length. **-ation** n.

ex-pa-tri-ate (eks pa´tr t´) v. To leave one's country and reside in another; to send into exile; to banish. **expatriate** n. **expatriation** n.

ex-pect (ik spekt´) v. To look forward to something as probable or certain; to look for as proper, right, or necessary. Slang To presume or suppose.

ex-pec-tan-cy (ik spek´tan s) n. pl. -cies The action or state of expecting; expectation; an object or amount of expectation.

ex-pec-ta-tion (ek´spek t´shan) n. The state or act of expecting; something that is expected and looked forward to. **expectations** pl. Something expected in the future.

ex-pec-to-rate (ik spek´to rt) v. To spit.

ex-pe-di-en-cy (ik sp´d en s) n. pl.-cies The state or quality of being expedient. Adherence to expedient methods or means

ex-pe-di-ent (ik sp´d ent) adj. Promoting narrow or selfish interests; pertaining to or prompted by interest rather than by what is right. **expediently** adv.

ex-pe-dite (ek´spi dt´) v. To speed up the progress or process of something; to do with quick efficiency. **-diter** n.

ex-pe-di-tion (ek´spi dish´an) n. A journey of some length for a definite purpose; the person or group and equipment that engage in such a journey; promptness.

ex-pe-di-tious (ek´spi dish´us) adj. Quick; speedy. **expeditiously** adv.

ex-pel (ik spel´) v. To drive or force out, as to dismiss from a school. **-lable** adj.

ex-pend (ik spend´) v. To consume; to pay out or use up. **expendable** adj.

ex-pend-i-ture (ik spen´di chr) n. An amount spent; the act or process of expending; something that is expended; disbursement.

ex-pense (ik spens´) n. The outlay or consumption of money; the amount of money required to buy or do something. **expenses** pl. The funds that have been allotted or spent to cover incidental costs; the charges incurred by an employee while at or pertaining to work. Informal The reimbursement for such charges incurred.

ex-pen-sive (ik spen´siv) adj. Costing a lot of money; high-priced or beyond the buyer's means.

ex-pe-ri-ence (ik spr´ens) n. The actual participation in something or the direct contact with; the knowledge or skill acquired from actual participation or training in an activity or event; one's total judgments or reactions based on one's past.

ex-per-i-ment (ik sper´i ment) n. The act or test performed to demonstrate or illustrate a truth; the conducting of such operations. **experimental** adj. **experimentally** adv. **experimentation** n. **experimenter** n.

ex-pert (ik spŭrt´) n. A person having great knowledge, experience, or skill in a certain field. adj. Skilled as the result of training or experience. **expertly** adv. **expertness** n.

ex-per-tise (ek´spr tz´) n. A specialized knowledge, ability, or skill in a particular area.

ex-pire (ik spr´) v. To come to an end; to breathe out, as from the mouth; to exhale.

ex-plain (ik spln´) v. To make understandable; to clarify; to give reasons for; to account for; to give an explanation for. **explainable** adj. **explanatory** adj. **explainer** n. **explanation** n.

ex-ple-tive (ek´sple tiv) n. An exclamation, often profane. adj. A word added merely to fill out a sentence.

ex-pli-ca-ble (ek´spli ka bl) adj. Capable of explanation.

ex-pli-cate (ek´spli kt´) v. To clear up the meaning of. **explication** n.

ex-plic-it (ik splis´it) adj. Plainly expressed; specific; unreserved in expression; straightforward. **explicitly** adv. **-ness** n.

ex-plode (ik spld´) v. To burst or blow up violently with a loud noise; to increase rapidly without control; to show to be false.

ex-ploit (ek´sploit) n. A deed or act that is notable. v. To use to the best advantage; to make use of in a selfish or unethical way. **exploitable** adj. **ex-**

ploitative *adj.*

ex-plore (ik splr´) *v.* To examine and investigate in a systematic way; to travel through unfamiliar territory. **-ation** *n.* **explorer** *n.* **exploratory** *adj.*

ex-plo-sion (ik spl´zhan) *n.* A sudden, violent release of energy; the sudden, violent outbreak of personal feelings.

ex-plo-sive (ik spl´siv) *adj.* Marked by or pertaining to an explosion. *n.* A chemical preparation that explodes. **explosively** adv.

ex-po-nent (ik sp´nent) *n.* A person who represents or speaks for a cause or group; in mathematics, a number or symbol that indicates the number of times an expression is used as a factor.

ex-port (ik sprt´) *v.* To carry or send merchandise or raw materials to other countries for resale or trade. *n.* A commodity exported. **exportable** *adj.* **exportation** *n.* **exporter** *n.*

ex-pose (ik spz´) *v.* To lay open, as to criticism or ridicule; to lay bare and uncovered; to reveal the identity of someone; to deprive of the necessities of heat, shelter, and protection. *Photog.* To admit light to a sensitized film or plate. **exposer** *n.*

ex-po-si-tion (ek´spo zish´an) *n.* A statement of intent or meaning; a detailed presentation of subject matter; a commentary or interpretation; a large public exhibition. **expository** *adj.*

ex post fac-to (eks´ pst´fak´t) *adj.* L. After the fact and retroactive.

ex-pos-tu-late (ik spos´cha lt´) *v.* To reason earnestly with someone about the inadvisability of his or her actions in an effort to correct or dissuade that person. **expostulatory** *adj.*

ex-po-sure (ik sp´zhr) *n.* The act or state of being exposed; an indication of which way something faces. *Photog.* The act of exposing a sensitive plate or film; the time required for the film or plate to be exposed.

ex-pound (ik spound´) *v.* To give a detailed statement of something; to explain the meaning at length.

ex-pres-sive (ik spres´iv) *adj.* Of or characterized by expression; serving to indicate or express; full of expression. **expressively** adv. **-ness** *n.*

ex-pro-pri-ate (eks pr´prt´) *v.* To transfer or take property from the owner for public use; to deprive a person of property or ownership. **expropriation** *n.*

ex-pul-sion (ik spul´shan) *n.* The act of expelling or the state of being expelled.

ex-punge (ik spunj´) *v.* To delete or remove; to erase. **expunger** *n.*

ex-pur-gate (ek´spr gt´) *v.* To remove obscene or objectionable material from a play, book, etc., before it is available to the public. **expurgation** *n.* **-gator** *n.*

ex-qui-site (ek´skwi zit) *adj.* Delicately or intricately beautiful in design or craftsmanship; highly sensitive; keen or acute, as in pain or pleasure. **-ly** *adv.*

ex-tant (ek´stant) *adj.* Still in existence; not lost or destroyed; surviving.

ex-tem-po-re (ik stem´po r) *adj.* Extemporaneously.

ex-tem-po-rize (ik stem´po rz´) *v.* To make, do, or perform with little or no advance preparation; to improvise to meet circumstances. **-porization** *n.*

ex-tend (ik stend´) *v.* To stretch or open to full length; to make longer, broader, or wider; to continue; to prolong; to put forth or hold out, as the hand; to exert to full capacity; to offer something.

ex-tent (ik stent´) *n.* The degree, dimension, or limit to which anything is extended; the area over which something extends; the size.

ex-ten-u-ate (ik sten´t´) *v.* To minimize the seriousness of something as a crime or fault; to lessen or try to lessen the seriousness of something by making excuses **extenuation** *n.*

ex-te-ri-or (ik str´r) *adj.* Pertaining to or of the outside; the external layer; the outside surface.

ex-ter-mi-nate (ik str´mi nt´) *v.* To annihilate; to destroy completely; to get rid of completely. **-nation** *n.*

ex-tern or **externe** (ek´strn) *n.* A person that is associated with but not officially residing in a hospital or an institution.

ex-ter-nal (ik str´nal) *adj.* For, of, or on the outside; acting from the outside; pertaining to foreign countries; outside; exterior. **externals** *pl.* Outward or superficial circumstances. **-ly** adv.

ex-tinct (ik stingk´) adj. Inactive; no longer existing; extinguished; gone out of use; no longer active. **extinction** n.

ex-tin-guish (ik sting´gwish) v. To put an end to; to put out; to make extinct. **extinguishable** adj. **extinguisher** n.

ex-tir-pate (ek´stir pt´) v. To pull up by the roots; to destroy wholly, completely. To remove or cut out by surgery. **extirpation, extirpator** n. **-pative** adj.

ex-tol also **ex-toll** v. To praise highly.

ex-tort (ik stort´) v. To obtain money from a person by threat, oppression, or abuse of authority. **extortion** n.

ex-tra (ek´stra) adj. Over and above what is normal, required, or expected.

ex-tract (ik strakt´) v. To pull or draw out by force; to obtain in spite of resistance; to obtain from a substance as by pressure or distillation; in mathematics, to determine the root of a number. n. A passage taken from a larger work; a concentrated substance used in cooking. **extractable** adj.

ex-trac-tion (ik strak´shan) n. The process or act of extracting; that which is extracted; one's origin or ancestry.

ex-tra-cur-ric-u-lar (ek´stra ka rik´lr) adj. Pertaining to or of activities not directly a part of the curriculum of a school or college; outside the usual duties.

ex-tra-dite (ek´stra dt´) v. To obtain or surrender by extradition.

ex-tra-di-tion (ek´stra dish´an) n. The legal surrender of an alleged criminal to the jurisdiction of another country, government, or state for trial.

ex-tra-dos (ek´stra dos´) n. pl. **-dos , -doses** The exterior or upper curve of an arch.

ex-tra-mu-ral (ek´stra mr´al) adj. Taking place outside of an educational building or institution; involving teams from different schools.

ex-tra-or-di-nar-y Beyond what is usual or common; remarkable.

ex-trav-a-gant (ik strav´a gant) adj. Overly lavish in expenditure; wasteful; exceeding reasonable limits; immoderate.

ex-trav-a-gan-za (ik strav´a gan´za) n. A lavish, spectacular, showy entertainment.

ex-treme (ik strm´) adj. Greatly exceeding; going far beyond the bounds of moderation **extremely** adv.

ex-trem-ist n. A person who advocates or resorts to extreme measures or holds extreme views. **extremism** n.

ex-tri-cate (ek´stri kt´) v. To free from hindrance, entanglement, or difficulties; to disengage. **extrication** n.

ex-tro-vert or **extravert** (ek´str vrt´) Psychol. A person who is more interested in people and things outside himself than in his own private feelings and thoughts.

ex-trude (ik ströd´) v. To push or thrust out; to shape by forcing through dies under pressure; to project or protrude.

ex-u-ber-ant (ig zö´br ant) adj. Full of high spirits, vitality, vigor, and joy; plentiful; abundant. **exuberance** n

ex-ult (ig zult´) v. To be jubilant; to rejoice greatly. **exultant** adj. **exulta-tion** n.

eye n. An organ of sight consisting of the cornea, iris, pupil, retina, and lens; a look; gaze; the ability to judge, perceive, or discriminate. **storm** Meteor. The central area of a hurricane or cyclone. **wind** Naut. The direction from which the wind blows. **eye** To get someone's attention. **eye** To be in complete agreement.

eye-ball n. The ball of the eye, enclosed by the socket and eyelids and connected at the rear to the optic nerve.

F

F, f (ef) The sixth letter of the English alphabet; in music, the fourth tone in the scale of C major; a failing grade.

fa-ble (f´bl) n. A brief, fictitious story embodying a moral and using persons, animals, or inanimate objects as characters; a falsehood; a lie. **fabulist** adj. **fabled** adj.

fab-ric (fab´rik) n. A cloth produced by knitting, weaving, or spinning fibers; a structure or framework, as the social fabric.

fab-u-lous (fab´ya lus) adj. Past the limits of belief; incredible. Slang Very successful or pleasing. **fabulously** adv.

fa-cade (fa säd´) n. Arch. The face or front of a building; an artificial or false appearance.

fac-et (fas´it) n. One of the flat, polished surfaces cut upon a gemstone; the small, smooth surface on a bone or tooth; a phase, aspect, or side of a person or subject.

fa-ce-tious (fa s´shus) adj. Given to or marked by playful jocularity; humorous. **facetiously** adv. **facetiousness** n.

face value n. The apparent value of something; the value printed on the face of a bill or bond.

fa-cial (f´shal) adj. Near, of, or for the face; a massage or other cosmetic treatment for the face. **facially** adv.

fac-ile (fas´il) adj. Requiring little effort; easily achieved or performed; arrived at without due care, effort, or examination; superficial.

fa-cil-i-tate (fa sil´i tt´) v. To make easier. **facilitation** n. **facilitator** n.

fa-cil-i-ty (fa sil´i t) n. pl. -ies Ease in performance, moving, or doing something; something that makes an operation or action easier.

fac-ing (f´sing) n. The lining or covering sewn to a garment; any outer protective or decorative layer applied to a surface.

fac-sim-i-le (fak sim´l l) n. An exact copy, as of a document; the method of transmitting drawings, messages, or such by an electronic method.

fact (fakt) n. Something that actually occurred or exists; something that has real and demonstrable existence; actuality.

fac-tion (fak´shan) n. A group or party within a government that is often self-seeking and usually in opposition to a larger group; conflict within a party; discord. **factional** adv.

fac-tious (fak´shus) adj. Given to dissension; creating friction; divisive. **factiously** adv.

fac-ti-tious (fak tish´us) adj. Produced artificially; lacking authenticity or genuineness.

fac-to-ry (fak´to r) n. pl. -ies An establishment where goods are manufactured; a plant.

fac-to-tum (fak t´tum) n. An employee who performs all types of work.

fac-tu-al (fak´chö al) adj. Containing or consisting of facts, literal and exact.

fac-ul-ty (fak´ul t) n. pl. -ies A natural ability or power; the inherent powers or capabilities of the body or mind; the complete teaching staff of a school or any other educational institution.

fad (fad) n. A temporary fashion adopted with wide enthusiasm. **faddish** n.

fade (fd) v. To lose brightness, brilliance, or loudness gradually; to vanish slowly; to lose freshness, vigor, or youth; to disappear gradually.

fa-ience (f äns´) n. Earthenware that is decorated with a colorful opaque glaze.

fail-ing (f´ling) n. A minor fault; a defect.

faille (fl) n. A ribbed material of cotton, silk, or rayon.

faint (fnt) adj. Having little strength or vigor; feeble; lacking brightness or clarity; dim. n. A sudden, temporary loss of consciousness; a swoon.

faith (fth) n. A belief in the value, truth, or trustworthiness of someone or something; belief and trust in God, the Scriptures, or other religious writings; a system of religious beliefs.

fa-kir (fa kr) n. A Moslem or Hindu religious mendicant, performing feats of endurance or magic.

fal-la-cious (fa l´shus) adj. Containing or based on fundamental errors in reasoning; deceptive; misleading.

fal-la-cy (fal´a s) n. pl. -ies A deception; an error.

fal-li-ble (fal´i bl) adj. Capable of making an error; liable to be deceived or misled; apt to be erroneous. **-bility** n.

fall-off n. A decrease in something.

Fal-lo-pi-an tube (fa l´p an töb´) n. One of a pair of long, slender ducts serving as a passage for the ovum from the ovary to the uterus.

fal-low (fal´) n. Ground that has been plowed but left unseeded during the growing season. **fallow** adj. Light yellowish-brown in color. **fallowness** n.

false (fols) adj. Contrary to truth or fact; incorrect; deliberately untrue or deceptive; treacherous; unfaithful; not natural or real; artificial; in music, an incorrect pitch. *adv.* Faithless in manner. **falsely** *adv.* **falseness** *n.* **falsity** *n.*

false-hood (fols´hed) *n.* The act of lying; an intentional untruth.

false ribs *n. pl.* Ribs that are not united directly with the sternum. In man there are five on each side.

fal-set-to (fol set´) *n.* A high singing voice, usually male, that is artificially high.

fal-si-fy (fol´si f´) *v.* To give an untruthful account of; to misrepresent; to alter or tamper with in order to deceive; to forge. **falsification** *n.* **falsifier** *n.*

fal-ter (fol´tr) *v.* To be uncertain or hesitant in action or voice; to waver; to move with unsteadiness. **falteringly** *adv.* **-ing** *adj.*

fame (fm) *n.* Public esteem; a good reputation.

fa-mil-iar (fa mil´yr) *adj.* Unconstrained or informal; being well-acquainted with; common; having good and complete knowledge of something. **familiar** *n.* A close friend or associate. **familiarly** *adv.*

fa-mil-iar-ize (fa mil´ya rz´) *v.* To make oneself or someone familiar with something. **familiarization** *n.*

fam-i-ly (fam´i l) *n. pl.* **families** Parents and their children; a group of people connected by blood or marriage and sharing common ancestry.

fam-ine (fam´in) *n.* A widespread scarcity of food; a drastic shortage of, or scarcity of, anything; severe hunger; starvation.

fa-mous (f´mus) *adj.* Well-known; renowned. *Slang* Excellent; admirable. **famously** *adv.* **famousness** *n.*

fa-nat-ic (fa nat´ik) *n.* One who is moved by a frenzy of enthusiasm or zeal. **fanatical** *adj.* **fanatically** *adv.* **fanaticism** *n.*

fan-ci-er (fan´s r) *n.* A person having a special enthusiasm for or interest in something.

fan-ci-ful (fan´si ful) *adj.* Existing or produced only in the fancy; indulging in fancies; exhibiting invention or whimsy in design. **fancifully** *adv.* **fancifulness** *n.*

fan-fare (fan´fâr) *n.* A short, loud trumpet flourish; a spectacular public display.

fang (fang) *n.* A long, pointed tooth or tusk an animal uses to seize or tear at its prey; one of the hollow, grooved teeth with which a poisonous snake injects its venom.

fan-ta-sia (fan´zha) *n.* A composition structured according to the composer's fancy and not observing any strict musical form.

fan-ta-sied *v.* To create mental fantasies; to imagine or indulge in fantasies.

fan-tas-tic (fan tas´tik) *adj.* Existing only in the fancy; wildly fanciful or exaggerated; impulsive or capricious; coming from the imagination; unreal. *Slang* Superb; wonderful. **fantastically** *adv.*

fare (fâr) *v.* To be in a specific state; to turn out. *n.* A fee paid for hired transportation; food or a variety of foods.

fare-well (fâr´wel´) *n.* Good-by; a departure. *adj.* Closing; parting.

farfetched (fär´fecht´) *adj.* Neither natural nor obvious; highly improbable.

farflung (fär´flung´) *adj.* Widely distributed over a great distance.

fa-ri-na (fa r´na) *n.* A fine meal obtained chiefly from nuts, cereals, potatoes, or Indian corn, used as a breakfast food or in puddings.

far-i-na-ceous (far´i n´shus) *adj.* Made from, rich in, or composed of starch; mealy.

faroff (fär´of´) *adj.* Distant; remote.

farout *adj. Slang* Very unconventional.

farreaching (fär´r´ching) *adj.* Having a wide range, effect, or influence.

far-row (far´) *n.* A litter of pigs.

farsight-ed (fär´s´tid) *adj.* Able to see things at a distance more clearly than things nearby; having foresight; wise.

far-ther (fär´thr) *adv.* To or at a more distant point. *adj.* More remote or distant.

fas-ci-nate (fas´i nt´) *v.* To attract irresistibly, as by beauty or other qualities; to captivate; to hold motionless; to spellbind. **fascinating** *adj.* **fascinatingly** *adv.* **fascination** *n.*

fas-ten (fas´en) *v.* To join something else; to connect; to securely fix something; to shut or close.

fas-tid-i-ous (fa stid´ us) *adj.* Exceedingly delicate or refined; hard to please in matters of taste. **fastidiously** *adv.* **-ness** *n.*

fa-tal (ft´ al) *adj.* Causing death; deadly; destined; inevitable; bringing ruin or disaster; destructive; decisively important; fateful; brought about by fate. **fatally** *adv.*

fa-tal-ism (ft´a liz´um) *n.* The belief that events or things are predetermined by fate and cannot be altered. **fatalist** *n.* **fatalistic** *adj.* **fatalistically** *adv.*

fa-tal-i-ty (fa tal´i t) *n. pl.* **-ies** A death caused by a disaster or accident; the capability of causing death or disaster; the quality or state of being subject to or determined by fate.

fate (ft) *n.* The force or power held to predetermine events; fortune; inevitability; the final result or outcome; unfortunate destiny; doom. **fated** *adj.*

fa-ther (fä´thr) *n.* The male parent; any male forefather; ancestor.

fa-tigue (fa tg´) *n.* The state or condition of extreme tiredness or weariness from prolonged physical or mental exertion.

fa-tu-i-ty (fa tö´i t) *n.* Stupidity; foolishness.

fat-u-ous (fach´ö us) *adj.* Silly and foolish in a self-satisfied way. **-ly** *adv.*

fau-cet (fo´sit) *n.* A fixture with an adjustable valve to draw liquids from a pipe or cask.

fault (folt) *n.* An impairment or defect; a weakness; a minor offense or mistake.

fau-na (fo´na) *n. pl.* **faunas** or **faunae** Animals living within a given area or environment. **faunal** *adj.*

fauv-ism (f´viz um) *n.* An art movement noted for the use of very flamboyant colors and bold, often distorted forms.

faux pas (f pä´) *n.* A false step; a social blunder.

fa-vor-a-ble (f´vr a bl) *adj.* Beneficial; advantageous; building up hope or confidence; approving; promising.

fa-vor-ite (fo´vr it) *n.* Anything regarded with special favor or preferred above all others; in sports, the contestant considered to be the most likely winner.

fa-vour (f´vr) *n. & v.* British variety of favor.

fawn (fon) *n.* A young deer less than a year old; a light yellowish-brown color. **fawn** *v.* To show cringing fondness; to displays lavish affection. **fawningly** *adv.*

fay (f) *n.* A fairy or elf.

faze (fz) *v.* To worry; to disconcert.

fe-al-ty (f´ al t) *n. pl.* **-ies** The obligation of allegiance owed to a feudal lord by his vassal or tenant; faithfulness; loyalty.

fear (fr) *n.* The agitated feeling caused by the anticipation or the realization of danger; an uneasy feeling that something may happen contrary to one's hopes.

fea-si-ble (f´zi bl) *adj.* Capable of being put into effect or accomplished; practical. **feasibility** *n.* **feasibly** *adv.*

feast (fst) *n.* A delicious meal; a banquet.

feat (ft) *n.* A notable act or achievement.

fea-ture (f´chr) *n.* The appearance or shape of the face; the main presentation at a movie theater; a special article in a magazine or newspaper that is given special prominence.

feb-ri-fuge (feb´ri fj´) *n.* A medicine used to reduce fever.

fe-brile (f´bril) *adj.* Feverish.

fe-ces (f´sz) *n.* Waste that is excreted from the bowels; excrement. **fecal** *adj.*

fe-cund (f´kund) *adj.* Fruitful; productive.

fe-cun-date (f´kun dt´) *v.* To make fertile.

fed *v.* Past tense of feed. **fed** *abbr.* Federal, federated.

fed-er-al (fed´r al) *adj.* Of, relating to, or formed by an agreement between two or more states or groups in which each retains certain controlling powers while being united under a central authority; of or pertaining to the United States central government.

fe-do-ra (fi dr´a) *n.* A soft hat with a low crown creased lengthwise and a brim that can be turned up or down.

fed up *adj.* Extremely annoyed or disgusted.

fee (f) *n.* A fixed charge, compensation, or payment for something; a charge for professional services; an inherited estate in land.

fee-ble (f´bl) *adj.* Very weak; lacking in strength; lacking force; ineffective.

fee-ble-mind-ed (fē'bl mīn'dĭd) *adj.* Mentally deficient; intellectually subnormal.

feel (fēl) *v.* To examine, explore, or perceive through the sense of touch.

feet *n.* The plural of foot.

feign (fān) *v.* To make a false show of; to dream up a false story and tell it as the truth; to fabricate; to imitate so as to deceive.

feint (fānt) *n.* A deceptive or misleading movement intended to draw defensive action away from the real target.

fe-lic-i-tate (fĭ lĭs'ĭ tāt') *v.* To congratulate; to wish happiness. **felicitation** *n.*

fe-lic-i-tous (fĭ lĭs'ĭ tus) *adj.* Most appropriate; well chosen; pertinent or effective in manner or style. **-ly** *adv.*

fe-lic-i-ty (fĭ lĭs'ĭ tē) *n. pl.* **felicities** Happiness; bliss; an instance or source of happiness; an agreeably pertinent or effective style.

fe-line (fē'līn) *adj.* Of or relating to cats, including wild and domestic cats; resembling a cat, as in stealth or agility. **felinity** *n.* **feline** *n.* **felinely** *adv.*

fell (fĕl) *v.* Past tense of fall; to strike or cause to fall down; to finish a seam with a flat, smooth strip made by joining edges, then folding under and stitching flat. **fell** *n.* Timber cut down during one season; an animal's hide; pelt. **fell** *adj.* Cruel and fierce; lethal.

fel-low (fĕl') *n.* A boy or man; an associate, comrade; the counterpart; one of a pair. *Informal* A boyfriend.

fel-low-ship (fĕl'shĭp') *n.* A friendly relationship; the condition or fact of having common interests, ideals, or experiences; the status of being a fellow at a college or university, also the financial grant made to a fellow.

fel-on (fĕl'on) *n.* A person who has committed a felony; an inflammation in the terminal level at the cuticle of a finger or toe.

fel-o-ny (fĕl'o n) *n. pl.* **-ies** A serious crime, such as rape, murder, or burglary, punishable by a severe sentence.

felt (fĕlt) *v.* Past tense of feel. *n.* An unwoven fabric made from pressed animal fibers, as wool or fur; a piece of fabric or material made of felt.

fe-male (fē'ml) *n.* The sex that produces

ova or bears young; a plant with a pistil but no stamen, which is capable of being fertilized and producing fruit.

female *adj.* Of or relating to the sex that produces ova or bears young; suitable to this sex having a bore, slot, or hollow part designed to receive a projecting part, as a plug or prong.

fe-mur (fē'mr) *n. pl.* **femurs** *or* **femo-ra** The bone extending from the pelvis to the knee. **femoral** *adj.*

fen (fĕn) *n.* A low, marshy land; a bog.

fend (fĕnd) *v.* To ward off or to keep off; to offer resistance.

fen-es-tra-tion (fĕn'ĭ str'shan) *n.* The design and position of doors and windows in a building.

fe-ral (fr'al) *adj.* Not tame nor domesticated; returned to a wild state; existing in a untamed state.

ferdelance (fer'de lans') *n.* A large, venomous snake of tropical America, with gray and brown markings.

fer-ment (fer ment') *n.* Any substance or agent producing fermentation, as yeast, mold, or enzyme; excitement; unrest; agitation. **fermentability** *n.*

fern (fern) *n.* Any of a number of flowerless, seedless plants, having fronds with divided leaflets and reproducing by spores. **-y** *adj.*

fe-ro-cious (fe r'shus) *adj.* Extremely savage, fierce, cruel, or bloodthirsty. *Slang* Very intense. **ferociously** *adv.* **ferocity** *n.*

fer-rule (fer'ul) *n.* A cap or ring used near or at the end of a stick, as a walking cane, to reinforce it or prevent splitting.

fer-ry (fer') *n. pl.* **-ies** A boat or other craft used to transport people, vehicles, and other things across a body of water.

fer-tile (fer'tĭl) *adj., Biol.* Having the ability to reproduce; rich in material required to maintain plant growth. **fertility** *n.*

fer-ti-lize (fer'tĭ līz') *v.* To make fertile; to cause to be productive or fruitful; to begin the biological reproduction by supplying with sperm or pollen; to make fertile by spreading or adding fertilizer. **fertilization** *n.*

fer-ti-liz-er (fer'tĭ l'zr) *n.* A material

that fertilizes, such as nitrates or manure which enriches soil.

fer-ule (fer´ul) n. A flat stick sometimes used to punish children. **ferule** v.

fer-vent (fer´vent) adj. Passionate; ardent; very hot. **fervency** n. **-ness** n.

fer-vid (fer´vid) adj. Fervent to an extreme degree; impassioned; very hot; burning. **fervidly** adv. **fervidness** n.

fer-vor (fer´vr) n. Great emotional warmth or intensity.

fes-cue (fes´k) n. A type of tough grass, often used as pasturage.

fes-tal (fes´tal) adj. Pertaining to or typical of a festival, holiday, or feast.

fes-ter (fes´tr) v. To develop or generate pus; to be a constant source of irritation or resentment.

fes-ti-val (fes´ti val) n. A particular holiday or celebration; a regularly occurring occasion.

fes-tive (fes´tiv) adj. Relating to or suitable for a feast or other celebration.

fet-a n. A white Greek cheese made of goat's or ewe's milk and preserved in brine.

fe-tal (ft´al) adj. Relating to or like a fetus.

fetch (fech) v. To go after and return with; to draw forth; to elicit; to bring as a price; to sell for; to strike a blow.

fete (ft) n. A festival or feast; a very elaborate outdoor celebration. **fete** v.

fet-id (fet´id) adj. Having a foul odor; stinking. **fetidly** adv. **fetidness** n.

fet-lock (fet´lok´) n. A tuft of hair that grows just above the hoof at the back of the leg of a horse.

fe-tol-o-gy n. The medical study of a fetus.

fe-tus (f´tus) n. The individual unborn organism carried within the womb from the time major features appear; specifically in humans, the unborn young after the eighth week of development.

feud (fd) n. A bitter quarrel between two families, usually lasting over a long period of time. **feud** v.

feu-dal-ism n. The political, social, and economic organization produced by the feudal system. **feudalist** n. **feudalistic** adj.

fe-ver (f´vr) n. Abnormally high body temperature and rapid pulse; a craze; a heightened emotion or activity.

fey (f) adj. Seemingly spellbound; having clairvoyance; acting as if under a spell.

fez (fez) n. A red felt, black-tasseled hat worn by Egyptian men.

fi-an-ce (f an s´) n. A man to whom a woman is engaged to be married.

fi-an-cee (f an s´) n. A woman to whom a man is engaged to be married.

fi-as-co (f as´k) n. pl. **fiascoes** A complete or total failure.

fi-at (f´at) n. A positive and authoritative order or decree.

fib (fib) n. A trivial lie. **fibber** n.

fi-ber (f´br) n. A fine, long, continuous piece of natural or synthetic material made from a filament of asbestos, spun glass, textile, or fabric; internal strength; character.

fiber-glass (f´br glas´) n. A flexible, nonflammable material of spun glass used for textiles, insulation, and other purposes.

fiber optics n. pl. Light optics transmitted through very fine, flexible glass rods by internal reflection.

fib-ril-la-tion (fi bri l´shan) n., Pathol. The rapid and uncoordinated contraction of the muscle fibers of the heart.

fi-brin (f´brin) n., Biochem. An insoluble protein that promotes the clotting of blood.

fi-brin-o-gen (f brin´o jen) n., Biochem. A complex blood plasma protein that is converted to fibrin during the process of blood clotting.

fi-broid (f´broid) adj. Made up or resembling fibrous tissue.

fib-u-la (fib´ la) n., Anat. The outer and smaller bone of the lower limb or hind leg, in humans located between the knee and ankle.

-fic adj. & suffix Making; causing; rendering.

-fication n. & suffix Making; production.

fich-u (fish´ö) n. A lightweight, triangular scarf, worn about the neck and fastened loosely in front.

fick-le (fik´l) adj. Inconstant in purpose or feeling; changeable. **fickleness** n.

fic-tion (fik´shan) n. Something that is

created or imaginary; a literary work that is produced by the imagination and not based on fact. **fictitious** adj.

fi-del-i-ty (fi del´i ti) n. pl. -ies Faithfulness or loyalty to obligations, vows, or duties. Elect. The degree to which a phonograph, tape recorder, or other electronic equipment receives and transmits input signals without distortion.

fidg-et (fij´it) v. To move nervously or restlessly. **fidgets** pl n. The condition of being nervous or restless. **fidgeter** n. -iness n. **fidgety** adj.

fie (f) An expression of disgust or impatience in response to an unpleasant surprise.

fierce (frs) adj. Savage and violent in nature. Slang Very difficult or disagreeable. **fiercely** adv. **fierceness** n.

fier-y (fr´) adj. Containing or composed of fire; brightly glowing; blazing; hot and inflamed; full of spirit or intense with emotion.

fife (ff) n. A small, shrill-toned instrument similar to a flute.

Fifth Amendment n. An amendment to the United States Constitution, ratified in 1791, guaranteeing due process of law and that no person shall be forced to testify against himself.

fig (fig) n. A tree or shrub bearing a sweet, pear-shaped, edible fruit; the fruit of the fig tree.

fight (ft) v. To struggle against; to quarrel.

fig-ment (fig´ment) n. An invention or fabrication.

fig-ure (fig´r) n. A symbol or character that represents a number; anything other than a letter; the visible form, silhouette, shape, or line of something.

fig-u-rine (fig´yu rn) n. A small sculptured or molded figure; a statuette.

fil-a-ment (fil´a ment) n. A very thin, finely spun fiber, wire, or thread; a fine wire enclosed in an electric lamp bulb which is heated electrically to incandescence.

fil-bert (fil´brt) n. The edible nut of the hazel tree or the tree it grows on.

filch (filch) v. To steal. **filcher** n.

fi-let (fi l´) n. A filet of meat or fish; lace or net with a pattern of squares.

fi-let mi-gnon (fi l min yon´) n. A small, tender cut of beef from the inside of the loin.

fil-i-al (fil´al) adj. Of or relating to a son or daughter; pertaining to the generation following the parents. **filially** adv.

fil-i-bus-ter (fil´i bus´tr) n. An attempt to prolong, prevent, or hinder legislative action by using delaying tactics such as long speeches. **filibuster** v. **filibusterer** n.

fil-i-gree (fil´i gr´) n. Delicate, lace-like ornamental work made of silver or gold intertwisted wire. **filigree** adj.

fil-ing (f´ling) n. often **filings** Particles removed by a file.

fil-lip (fil´ip) n. A snap of the finger that has been pressed down by the thumb and then suddenly released; something that arouses or excites. **fillip** v.

fil-ly (fil´) n. A young female horse.

film (film) n. A thin covering, layer, or membrane.

fil-ter (fil´tr) n. A device, as cloth, paper, charcoal, or any other porous substance, through which a liquid or gas can be passed to separate out suspended matter.

filth (filth) n. Anything that is dirty or foul; something that is considered offensive.

filth-y (fil´th) adj. Highly unpleasant; morally foul; obscene. **filthily** adv.

fil-trate (fil´trt) v. To pass or cause to pass through something. n. Anything which has passed through the filter.

fin (fin) n. A thin membranous extension of the body of a fish or other aquatic animal, used for swimming and balancing. Slang A five dollar bill.

fi-na-gle (fi n´gl) v. Slang To get something by trickery or deceit.

fi-nal (fn´al) adj. Pertaining to or coming to the end; last or terminal. **finality** n.

finals n. pl. Something decisively final, as the last of a series of athletic contests; the final academic examination.

fi-nal-ist (fn´a list) n. A contestant taking part in the final round of a contest.

fi-nal-ize (fn´a lz´) v. To put into final and complete form. **finalization** n.

fi-nance (fi nans´) n. The science of

monetary affairs. **finances** *pl.* Monetary resources; funds. To supply the capital or funds for something; to sell or provide on a credit basis. **financial** *v.* **financially** *adj.*

finch (finch) *n.* A small bird, as a grosbeak, canary, or goldfinch, having a short stout bill.

find (fnd) *v.* To come upon unexpectedly; to achieve; to attain; to ascertain; to determine; to consider; to regard; to recover or regain something; to detect the true identity or nature of something or someone.

find-ing (fn´ding) *n.* Something that is found or discovered. **findings** *pl.* Conclusions or statistics that are the result of a study, examination, or investigation.

fi-ne (f´na) *n., Mus.* The end.

fine arts *n. pl.* The arts of drawing, painting, sculpture, architecture, literature, music, and drama.

fin-er-y (f´ne r´) *n. pl.* **fineries** Elaborate jewels and clothes.

fi-nesse (fi nes´) *n.* A highly refined skill; the skillful handling of a situation.

fin-i-al (fin´ al) *n.* The ornamental projection or terminating part, as on a lamp shade.

fin-ick-y (fin´i k) *adj.* Hard to please; choosy. **finickiness** *n.*

fin-is (fin´is) *n.* The end.

fin-ish (fin´ish) *v.* To bring to an end; to conclude; to reach the end; to consume all. *Slang* To kill, defeat, or destroy. **finish** *n.* The last stage or conclusion of anything; the perfection or polish in manners, speech, or education; the surface quality or appearance of paint, textiles, or other materials. **finish** *adj.* Having a glossy polish. **finisher** *n.*

fi-nite (f´nt) *adj.* Having bounds or limits; of or relating to a number which can be determined, counted, or measured. **finitely** *adv.* **-ness** *n.*

fink (fingk) *n., Slang* A person that breaks a strike; an unsavory person.

fin-nan had-die (fin´an had´) *n.* Smoked haddock.

fin-ny (fin´) *adj.* Having or suggesting fins or fin-like extensions.

fir (fr) *n.* An evergreen tree with flat needles and erect cones.

fire (fr) *n.* The chemical reaction of burning, which releases heat and light. **fire** *v.* To have great enthusiasm; to ignite or cause to become ignited; to bake in a kiln; to discharge a firearm or explosive; to let a person go from a job; to dismiss.

fire extinguisher *n.* A portable apparatus that contains fire extinguishing chemicals, which are ejected through a short nozzle and hose.

firm (ferm) *adj.* Relatively solid, compact, or unyielding to pressure or touch; steadfast and constant; strong and sure. **firm** *n.* A partnership of two or more persons for conducting a business. **firm** *v.* To become or make firm or firmer. **firmly** *adv.* Unwaveringly; resolutely. **firmness** *n.*

fir-ma-ment (fer´ma ment) *n.* The expanse of the heavens; the sky.

firn (firn) *n.* Snow that is partially consolidated by thawing and freezing but has not converted to glacial ice.

first (ferst) *adj.* Preceding all others in the order of numbering; taking place or acting prior to all others; earliest; ranking above all in importance or quality; foremost. **first** *adv.* Above or before all others in time, order, rank, or importance; for the very first time. **first** *n.* The ordinal number that matches the number 1 in a series, 1st; the transmission gear producing the lowest driving speed in an automotive vehicle.

first aid *n.* The emergency care given to a person before full treatment and medical care can be obtained.

First Amendment *n.* The amendment to the Constitution of the United States which forbids Congress from interfering with religious freedom, free speech, free press, the right to assemble peaceably, or the right to petition the government, ratified in 1791.

first-hand (ferst´hand´) *adj.* Coming directly from the original source. **first-hand** *adv.*

firstrate (ferst´rt´) *adj.* Of the finest rank, quality, or importance.

firth (ferth) *n.* A narrow inlet or arm of the sea.

fis-cal (fis′kəl) *adj.* Relating to or about the finances or treasury of a nation or a branch of government; financial. **fiscally** *adv.*

fish (fish) *n. pl.* **fish** or **fishes** A cold-blooded, vertebrate aquatic animal having fins, gills for breathing, and usually scales; the flesh of fish used as food. **like a fish out of water** Not at ease or comfortable. **fish** *v.* To try to catch fish; to seek or find one's way; to grope; to try and obtain something in an artful or indirect way. **fishing** *n.*

fish-er-y (fish′e r) *n. pl.* **fisheries** The business of catching, processing, or selling fish; a fish nursery or hatchery.

fish-y (fish′) *adj.* Resembling fish, as in taste or odor; improbable; highly suspicious.

fis-sile (fis′ĭl) *adj.* Capable of being separated or split. *Physics* Fissionable. **fissility** *n.*

fis-sion (fish′ən) *n.* The process or act of splitting into parts. *Physics* The exploding of the nucleus of an atom that leads to the formation of more stable atoms and the release of large quantities of energy.

fis-sure (fish′r) *n.* A narrow opening, crack, or cleft in a rock. **fissure** *v.*

fist (fist) *n.* The hand closed tightly with the fingers bent into the palm. *Slang* The hand.

fist-ful *n. pl.* **-fuls** A hand full.

fis-tu-la (fis′che lə) *n. pl.* **-las** or **-lae** *Pathol.* A duct or other passage formed by the imperfect closing of a wound or abscess and leading either to the body surface or to another hollow organ. **fistulous** *adj.*

fit (fit) *v.* To be the proper size and shape; to be in good physical condition; to possess the proper qualifications; to be competent; to provide a time or place for something; to belong. *adj.* Adapted or adequate for a particular circumstance or purpose. *Med.* A convulsion; an impulsive and irregular exertion or action. **fitter** *n.* **fitness** *n.*

fitch (fich) *n.* The polecat of the Old World or its fur.

fit-ting (fit′ing) *adj.* Suitable or proper. **fitting** *n.* The act of trying on clothes for fit or alteration; a piece of equipment or an appliance used in an adjustment.

five (fv) *n.* The cardinal number equal to 4 + 1; any symbol of this number, as 5; anything with five units, parts, or members. **five** *adj. & pron.*

fix (fiks) *v.* To make stationary, firm, or stable; to direct or hold steadily; to place or set definitely; to make rigid; to arrange or adjust; to prepare, as a meal. **fix** *n.* A position of embarrassment or difficulty. *Naut.* The position of a ship determined by bearings, observations, or radio. *Slang* The injection of a narcotic, such as heroin.

fix-a-tion (fiks′shən) *n.* The act or state of being fixed; a strong, often unhealthy preoccupation. **fixate** *v.*

fix-ture (fiks′chr) *n.* Anything that is fixed or installed, as a part or appendage of a house; any article of personal property affixed to reality to become a part of and governed by the law of real property.

fizz (fiz) *n.* A hissing or bubbling sound; effervescence; tiny gas bubbles. **fizz** *v.*

flab *n.* Excessive, loose, and flaccid body tissue. **flabby** *adj.* **flabbiness** *n.*

flab-ber-gast (flab′r gast) *v.* To astound; to amaze.

flac-cid (flak′sid) *adj.* Lacking resilience or firmness. **flaccidity** *n.*

flac-on (flak′on) *n.* A small, stoppered decorative bottle.

flag (flag) *n.* A piece of cloth, usually oblong, bearing distinctive colors and designs to designate a nation, state, city, or organization. *Bot.* Any of various iris or cattail plants with long blade-shaped leaves. **flag** *v.* To mark or adorn with flags for identification or ornamentation; to grow weak or tired.

flag-on (flag′on) *n.* A vessel or container with a handle, spout, and hinged lid, used for holding wines or liquors.

fla-grant (fl′grant) *adj.* Obvious; glaring; disgraceful; notorious; outrageous. **flagrance** *n.* **flagrancy** *n.*

flair (flâr) *n.* An aptitude or talent for something; a dashing style.

flak (flak) *n.* Antiaircraft fire; abusive or excessive criticism.

flake (flk) *n.* A small, flat, thin piece

which has split or peeled off from a surface. *Slang* Oddball; eccentric.

flakily *adv.* **flakiness** *n.* **flaky** *adj.*

flam-boy-ant (flam boi´ant) *adj.* Extravagantly ornate; showy; florid; brilliant and rich in color. **flamboyance** *n.* **flamboyancy** *n.* **-antly** *adv.*

flame (flm) *n.* A mass of burning vapor or gas rising from a fire, often having a bright color and forming a tongue-shaped area of light; something that resembles a flame in motion, intensity, or appearance; a bright, red-yellow color; violent and intense emotion or passion. *Slang* A sweetheart.

flame-out (flm´out´) *n.* The combustion failure of a jet aircraft engine while in flight.

flange (flanj) *n.* A projecting rim or collar used to strengthen or guide a wheel or other object, keeping it on a fixed track. **flange** *v.*

flank (flangk) *n.* The fleshy part between the ribs and the hip on either side of the body of an animal or human being; the lateral part of something. *Mil.* The extreme right or left side of an army. **flank** *v.* To be stationed at the side of something.

flan-nel (flan´el) *n.* A woven fabric made of wool, cotton, or synthetic blend. **flannels** *pl.* Trousers made of flannel.**flannelly** *adj.*

flannelette *n.* Cotton flannel.

flare (flâr) *v.* To blaze up or burn with a bright light; to break out suddenly or violently, as with emotion or action; to open or spread outward. **flare** *n.*

flash (flash) *v.* To burst forth repeatedly or suddenly into a brilliant fire or light; to occur or appear briefly or suddenly. *n.* A short and important news break or transmission.

flash-back (flash´bak´) *n.* The interruption in the continuity of a story, motion picture, drama, or novel to give a scene that happened earlier.

flash card *n.* A card printed with numbers or words and displayed briefly as a learning drill.

flash flood *n.* A violent and sudden flood occurring after a heavy rain.

flash point *n.* The lowest temperature at which the vapor of a combustible liq-

uid will ignite or burn.

flash-y (flash´) *adj.* Showing brilliance for a moment; tastelessly showy; gaudy. **flashily** *adv.* **flashiness** *n.*

flask (flask) *n.* A small container made of glass and used in laboratories.

flat (flat) *adj.* Extending horizontally with no curvature or tilt; stretched out level, prostrate or prone; lacking flavor or zest; deflated. *Mus.* Below the correct pitch. *n.* An apartment that is entirely on one floor of a building. **flat broke** Having little or no money. **to fall flat** to fail to achieve. **flat** *adv.* **flat-bed** *n.* A truck that has a shallow rear platform without sides.

flat-ten (flat´en) *v.* To make flat; to knock down. **flattener** *n.*

flat-ter (flat´r) *v.* To praise extravagantly, especially without sincerity; to gratify the vanity of; to portray favorably; to show as more attractive. **flatterer** *n.* **flattering** *adj.*

flat-ter-y (flat´e r) *n.* Excessive, often insincere compliments.

flat-u-lent (flach´u lent) *adj.* Marked by or affected with gases generated in the intestine or stomach; pretentious without real worth or substance. **-lence** *n.*

flat-ware (flat´wâr´) *n.* Tableware that is fairly flat and designed usually of a single piece, as plates; table utensils, as knives, forks, and spoons.

flaunt (flont) *v.* To display showily. **flaunter** *n.* **flauntingly** *adv.*

flau-tist (flo´tist) *n.* A flutist.

fla-vor (fl´vr) *n.* A distinctive element in the taste of something; a distinctive, characteristic quality; a flavoring. *v.* To impart flavor to. **flavorful** *adj.*

fla-vor-ing (fl´vr ing) *n.* A substance, as an extract or something else that is used to increase the flavor.

flaw (flo) *n.* A defect or blemish that is often hidden and that may cause failure under stress; a weakness in character; a fault in a legal paper that may nullify it. **flaw** *v.*

flaw-less *adj.* Without flaws or defects; perfect. **flawlessly** *adv.* **flawlessness** *n.*

flay (fl) *v.* To remove the skin of; to scold harshly.

flea (fl) *n.* A small, wingless, bloodsucking, parasitic jumping insect; a parasite of warm-blooded animals.

flea market *n.* A place where antiques and used items goods are sold.

fleck (flek) *n.* A tiny spot or streak; a small flake or bit. *v.* To mark with flecks.

fledg-ling *or* **fledge-ling (flej´ling)** *n.* A young bird with newly acquired feathers; a person who is inexperienced; a beginner.

flee (fl) *v.* To run away; to move swiftly away.

fleece (fls) *n.* A coat of wool covering a sheep; the soft wool covering a sheep. *v.* To shear the fleece from; to swindle; to cover with fleece. **fleecer** *n.* **fleeciness** *n.* **fleecily** *adv.*

fleet (flt) *n.* A number of warships operating together under the same command; a number of vehicles, as taxicabs or fishing boats, operated under one command. *adj.* Moving rapidly or nimbly. **fleetly** *adv.* **fleetness** *n.*

flesh (flesh) *n.* Soft tissue of the body of a human or animal, especially skeletal muscle; the meat of animals as distinguished from fish or fowl.

flesh-ly (flesh´l) *adj.* Of or pertaining to the body; sensual; worldly.

flesh-y (flesh´) *adj.* Of, resembling, or suggestive of flesh; firm and pulpy.

flew *v.* Past tense of fly.

flex (fleks) *v.* To bend the arm repeatedly; to contract a muscle.

flex-i-ble (flek´si bl) *adj.* Capable of being bent or flexed; pliable; responsive to change; easily yielding.

flick (flik) *n.* A light, quick snapping movement or the sound accompanying it. **flick** *v.* To strike or hit with a quick, light stroke; to cause to move with a quick movement. *Slang* A movie.

flick-er (flik´r) *v.* To burn or shine unsteadily, as a candle. **flicker** *n.* A wavering or unsteady light.

fli-er *or* **fly-er (fl´r)** *n.* One who or that which flies, especially an aviator; a daring or risky venture; a printed advertisement or handbill for mass distribution.

flight (flt) *n.* The act or manner of flying; a scheduled airline trip; a group that flies together; a swift or rapid passage or movement, as of time; a group of stairs leading from one floor to another; an instance of fleeing.

flight attendant *n.* A person employed to assist passengers on an aircraft.

flight-y (fl´t) *adj.* Inclined to act in a fickle fashion; marked by irresponsible behavior, impulse, or whim; easily excited, skittish.

flim-flam (flim´flam´) *n.* *Slang* A swindle; trick; hoax. **flimflam** *v.*

flim-sy (flim´z) *adj.* Lacking in physical strength or substance; unconvincing.

flinch (flinch) *v.* To wince or pull back, as from pain; to draw away. **flincher** *n.*

fling (fling) *v.* To throw or toss violently; to throw oneself completely into an activity. *n.* An act of casting away; a casual attempt; a period devoted to self-indulgence; unrestraint.

flint (flint) *n.* A hard quartz that produces a spark when struck by steel; an implement used by primitive man; an alloy used in lighters to ignite the fuel.

flip (flip) *v.* To turn or throw suddenly with a jerk; to strike or snap quickly and lightly. *Slang* To go crazy; to become upset or angry; to react enthusiastically. **flip** *n.*

flip-pant (flip´ant) *adj.* Marked by or showing disrespect, impudence, or the lack of seriousness. **flippancy** *n.*

flip-per (flip´r) *n.* A broad flat limb, as of a seal, adapted for swimming; a paddle-like rubber shoe used by skin divers and other swimmers.

flip side *n.* The reverse or opposite side.

flirt (flert) *v.* To make teasing romantic or sexual overtures; to act so as to attract attention; to move abruptly; to dart. *n.* A person who flirts; a snappy, quick, jerky movement. **flirtation** *n.*

flit (flit) *v.* To move rapidly or abruptly.

flit-ter *v.* To flutter. **flitter** *n.*

float (flt) *n.* An act or instance of floating; something that rides on the surface of or in a liquid; a device used to buoy the baited end of a fishing line; a platform anchored near a shore line, for use by swimmers or boats; a vehicle with a platform used to carry an exhibit in a parade; a drink consisting of ice cream floating in a beverage.

float *v.* To be, or cause to be, suspended within or on the surface of a liquid;

to be or cause to be suspended in or move through the air as if supported by water; to drift randomly from place to place; to move lightly and easily; to place a security on the market. **floating rib** *n.* One of the four lower ribs in the human being that are not attached to the other ribs.

flock (flok) *n.* A group of animals of all the same kind, especially birds, sheep, geese, etc., living and feeding together; a group under the direction of a single person, especially the members of a church; a large number. **flock** *v.* To travel as if in a flock.

floe (fl) *n.* A large, flat mass of floating ice or a detached part of such a mass.

flog (flog) *v.* To beat hard with a whip or stick.

flood (flud) *n.* The great deluge depicted in the Old Testament; an overflow of water onto land that is normally dry; an overwhelming quantity. **flood** *v.* To overwhelm with or as if with a flood; to fill abundantly; to supply the carburetor of an engine with an excessive amount of fuel; in football, to send more than one pass receiver into the same defensive area.

flood-gate (flud´gt´) *n.* A valve for controlling the flow or depth of a large body of water.

floor (flr) *n.* The level base of a room; the lower inside surface of a structure; the right, as granted under parliamentary rules, to speak to a meeting or assembly; an area dividing a building into stories. **floor** *v.* To cover or furnish with a floor; to knock down; to overwhelm; to puzzle; to press the accelerator of a vehicle to the floorboard.

flop (flop) *v.* To fall down clumsily; to move about in a clumsy way. *Slang* To completely fail; to go to bed. **flop** *n.*

flop house (flop´hous´) *n.* A cheap, run-down hotel.

flop-py (flop´) *adj.* Flexible and loose.

floppy disk *n.* In computer science, a flexible plastic disk coated with magnetic material, used to record and store computer data.

flo-ra (flr´a) *n.* Plants growing in a specific region or season.

flo-ral (flr´al) *adj.* Of or pertaining to flowers.

flo-res-cence (fl res´ens) *n.* A state or process of blossoming. **florescent** *adj.*

flor-id (flr´id) *adj.* Flushed with a rosy color or redness; ornate. **floridness** *n.*

flo-rist (flr´ist) *n.* One who grows or sells flowers and also artificial ones made of silk or silk-like fibers.

floss (flos) *n.* A loosely-twisted embroidery thread; a soft, silky fiber, such as the tassel on corn; dental floss. *v.* To clean between the teeth with dental floss.

flo-ta-tion (fl t´shan) *n.* The act or state of floating.

flo-til-la (fl til´a) *n.* A fleet of small vessels; a group resembling a small fleet.

flot-sam (flot´sam) *n.* Any goods remaining afloat after a ship has sunk.

flounce (flouns) *n.* A gathered piece of material attached to the upper edge of another surface, as on a curtain. *v.* To move with exaggerated tosses of the body.

floun-der (floun´dr) *v.* To struggle clumsily, as to gain footing; to act or speak in a confused way. *n.* Any of various edible marine flatfish.

flour (flour) *n.* A soft, fine, powder-like food made by grinding the meal of grain, such as wheat. **flour** *v.* To coat or sprinkle with flour.

flour-ish (fler´ish) *v.* To thrive; to fare well; to prosper and succeed. *n.* A decorative touch or stroke, especially in handwriting; a dramatic act or gesture; a musical fanfare, as of trumpets.

flout (flout) *v.* To have or show open contempt for. **floutingly** *adv.*

flow (fl) *v.* To move freely, as a fluid; to circulate, as blood; to proceed or move steadily and easily; to be abundant in something; to hang in a loose, free way. **flow** *n.*

flow chart *n.* A chart or diagram showing the sequence and progress of a series of operations on a specific project.

flow-er (flou´r) *n.* A cluster of petals, bright in color, near or at the tip of a seed-bearing plant; blossoms; the condition of highest development; the peak; the best example or representative of something. *v.* To produce flowers; to bloom; to develop fully.

fl oz *abbr.* Fluid ounce.

flu (flō) *n. Informal* Influenza.

flub (flub) *v.* To bungle or botch; to make a mess of. **flub** *n.*

fluc-tu-ate (fluk'chŏ t') *v.* To shift irreg-ularly; to change; to undulate. **fluctuation** *n.*

flue (flō) *n.* A conduit or passage through which air, gas, steam, or smoke can pass.

flu-ent (flō'ent) *adj.* Having an understanding of a language and its use; flowing smoothly and naturally; flowing or capable of flowing. **fluency** *n.* **fluently** *adv.*

flu-id (flō'id) *n.* A substance, as water or gas, capable of flowing. *adj.* Changing readily, as a liquid. **fluidity** *n.* **fluidness** *n.*

fluke (flōk) *n.* A flatfish, especially a flounder; an unexpected piece of good luck.

flung *v.* Past tense of fling.

flunk (flungk) *v. Slang* To fail in, as a course or an examination; to give a failing grade to.

flu-o-res-cence (flō'o res'ens) *n., Chem. & Phys.* Emission of electromagnetic radiation, esp. of visible light, result-ing from and occurring during the absorption of radiation from another source; the radiation emitted.

fluor-i-date *v.* To add a sodium compound to water in order to prevent tooth decay.

flu-o-ride (flō'o rd') *n.* A compound of fluorine with another element or a radical.

flu-o-rine (flō'o rn') *n.* A pale yellow, corrosive, and extremely reactive gaseous element, symbolized by F.

fluor-o-scope (fler'o skp') *n.* A device for observing shadows projected upon a fluorescent screen of an optically opaque object, as the human body, which may be viewed by transmission of x-rays through the object.

flur-ry (flur') *n. pl.* -ies A sudden gust of wind; a brief, light fall of snow or rain, accompanied by small gusts; a sudden burst of excitement or commotion.

flush (flush) *v.* To flow or rush out suddenly and abundantly; to become red in the face; to blush; to glow with a reddish color; to purify or wash out with a brief, rapid gush of water; to cause to flee from cover, as a game animal or bird. *n.* Glowing freshness or vigor; a hand in certain card games, as poker, in which all the cards are the same suit. *adj.* Having a heightened reddish color; abundant; affluent; prosperous; having surfaces that are even; arranged with adjacent sides close together; having margins aligned with no indentations; direct as a blow. *adv.* In an even position with another surface.

flus-ter (flus'tr) *v.* To make or become nervous or confused.

flute (flōt) *n.* A high-pitched, tubular woodwind instrument equipped with finger holes and keys; a decorative groove in the shaft of a column; a small grooved pleat, as in cloth. **flut-ist** *n.* A flute player.

flut-ter (flut'r) *v.* To flap or wave rapidly and irregularly; to fly as with a light, rapid beating of the wings; to beat erratically, as one's heart; to move about in a restless way. **flutter** *n.*

flux (fluks) *n.* A flowing or discharge; a constant flow or movement; a state of constant fluctuation or change.

foal (fl) *n.* The young animal, as a horse, especially one under a year old. *v.* To give birth to a foal.

foam (fm) *n.* A mass of bubbles produced on the surface of a liquid by agitation; froth; a firm, spongy material used especially for insulation and upholstery. *v.* To cause to form foam. **foam at the mouth** To be very angry. **foam** *n.* **foaminess** *n.* **foamy** *adj.*

fob (fob) *n.* A chain or ribbon attached to a pocket watch and worn dangling from a pocket; an ornament or seal worn on a fob. *v.* To dispose of by fraud, deceit, or trickery; to put off by excuse.

fo-cus (f'kus) *n. pl.* cuses *or* ci A point in an optical system at which rays converge or from which they appear to diverge; the clarity with which an optical system delivers an image; adjustment for clarity; a center of activity or interest To produce a

fod-der (fod'r) *n.* A coarse feed for livestock, made from chopped stalks of corn and hay.

foe (f) *n.* An enemy in war; an opponent or adversary.

foe-tal (ft'al) *adj.* Variation of fetal.

foe-tus (f'tus) *n.* Variation of fetus.

fog (fog) *n.* A vapor mass of condensed water which lies close to the ground; a state of mental confusion or bewilderment. **fog** *v.* To obscure or cover with, as if with fog. **fogginess** *n.* **foggy** *adj.*

fo-gy *or* **fo-gey** (f g) *n.* A person with old-fashioned attitudes and ideas.

foi-ble (foi'bl) *n.* A minor flaw, weakness, or failing.

foil (foil) *v.* To prevent from being successful; to thwart. **foil.** *n.* A very thin, flexible sheet of metal; one that serves as a contrast; a fencing sword having a light, thin, flexible blade and a blunt point.

foist (foist) *v.* To pass off something as valuable or genuine.

fold (fld) *v.* To double or lay one part over another; to bring from an opened to a closed position; to put together and intertwine; to envelop; to blend in by gently turning one part over another. *Slang* To give in; to fail in business. **fold** *n.* A line, layer, pleat or crease formed by folding; a folded edge; an enclosed area for domestic animals; a flock of sheep; a people united by common aims and beliefs; a church and its members.

fol-de-rol (fol'de rol') *n.* Nonsense; a pretty but useless ornament.

fo-li-age (f'l ij) *n.* The leaves of growing plant sand trees; a cluster of flowers and branches.

fo-li-o (f'l ') *n.* A large sheet of paper folded once in the middle; a folder for loose papers; a book that consists of folios; a page number.

folk (fk) *n. pl.* **folk** *or* **folks** An ethnic group of people forming a nation or tribe; people of a specified group. A person's parents, family, or relatives.

fol-li-cle (fol'i kl) *n.* A small anatomical

cavity or sac.

fol-low (fol') *v.* To proceed or come after; to pursue; to follow the course of; to obey; to come after in time or position; to ensue; to result; to attend to closely; to understand the meaning of.

fol-ly (fol') *n. pl.* **-ies** Lack of good judgment; an instance of foolishness; an excessively costly and often unprofitable undertaking.

fo-ment (f ment') *v.* To rouse; to incite; to treat therapeutically with moist heat. **foment** *n.* **fomentation** *n.*

fond (fond) *adj.* Affectionate liking; cherished with great affection; deeply felt. **fondly** *adv.*

fon-dant (fon'dant) *n.* A sweet, soft preparation of sugar used in candies and icings; a candy made chiefly of fondant.

fon-dle (fon'dl) *v.* To stroke, handle, or caress affectionately and tenderly.

font (font) *n.* A receptacle in a church that holds baptismal or holy water; an assortment of printing type of the same size and face.

food (fd) *n.* A substance consisting essentially of carbohydrates and protein used to sustain life and growth in the body of an organism; nourishment, as in solid form; something that sustains or nourishes. **thought.** Something to think about, something to ponder.

fool (fl) *n.* One lacking good sense or judgment; one who can easily be tricked or made to look foolish. *v.* To dupe; to act in jest; to joke. *Slang* To amuse oneself.

foot (fet) *n. pl.* **feet** The lower extremity of the vertebrate leg upon which one stands; a unit of measurement equal to 12 inches; a basic unit of verse meter that consists of a group of syllables; the end lower or opposite to the head; the lowest part. **foot** *v.* To go on foot; to walk or run; to pay the bill. **on foot** Walking rather than riding.

foot-hold (fet'hld') *n.* A place providing support for the foot, as in climbing; a position usable as a base for advancement.

foot-note (fet'nt') *n.* A note of reference, explanation, or comment usually below the text on a printed page; a commentary.

fop (fop) *n.* A man unduly concerned with his clothes or appearance; a dandy. **foppery** *n.* **foppish** *adj.*

for (for) *prep.* Used to indicate the extent of something; used to indicate the number or the amount of; considering the usual characteristics of; on behalf of someone; to be in favor of. **for** *conj.* Because; in as much as; with the purpose of.

for-ay (for´) *n.* A raid to plunder.

for-bade *or* **for-bad** *v.* Past tense of forbid.

for-bear (for´bâr´) *v.* To refrain from; to cease from. **forbearance** *n.*

for-bid (fr bid´) *v.* To command someone not to do something; to prohibit by law; to prevent.

for-bid-ding (fr bid´ing) *adj.* Very diffi-cult; disagreeable.

force (frs) *n.* Energy or power; strength; the use of such power; intellectual influence; a group organized for a certain purpose. *Physics* Something that changes the state of rest, or the body motion, or influence. **force** *v.* To compel to do something or to act; to obtain by coercion; to bring forth, as with effort; to move or drive against resistance; to break down by force; to press or impose, as one's will. **in force** In large numbers; in effect. **forceable** *adj.* **forceful** *adj.* **forcefully** *adv.*

for-ceps (for´seps) *n. pl.* **forceps** An instrument resembling a pair of tongs used for manipulating, grasping or extracting, especially in surgery.

for-ci-ble (fr´si bl) *adj.* Accomplished or achieved by force; marked by force.

fore (fr) *adj. & adv.* Situated in, at, or toward the front; forward. **fore** *n.* The front of something. **fore** *interj.* A cry, used by a golfer, to warn others that a ball is about to land in their direction.

fore-arm (fr ärm´) *v.* To prepare in advance, as for a battle. **forearm** *n.* The part of the arm between the elbow and the wrist.

fore-bear *or* **for-bear** (fr´bâr´) *n.* An ancestor.

fore-bode (fr bd´) *v.* To give an indica-

tion or warning in advance; to have a premonition of something evil. **fore-boding** *n.*

fore-cast (fr´kast´) *v.* To estimate or calculate in advance, esp. to predict the weather. **forecast** *n.* **forecaster** *n.*

fore-close (fr klz´) *v.* To recall a mortgage in default and take legal possession of the mortgaged property; to exclude; to shut out. **foreclosure** *n.*

fore-fa-ther (fr´fo´Thr) *n.* An ancestor.

fore-fin-ger (fr´fing´gr) *n.* The finger next to the thumb.

fore-foot (fr´fet´) *n.* A front foot of an animal, insect, etc.

fore-go (fr g´) *v.* To go before; to precede in time, place, etc.

fore-go-ing *adj.* Before; previous.

fore-gone (fr gon´) *adj.* Already finished or gone.

fore-ground (fr´ground´) *n.* The part of a picture or landscape represented as nearest to the viewer.

for-eign (for´in) *adj.* Situated outside one's native country; belonging to; located in or concerned with a country or region other than one's own; involved with other nations; occurring in a place or body in which it is not normally located.

for-eign-er *n.* A person from a different place or country; an alien.

fore-knowl-edge (fr´nol´ij) *n.* Prior knowledge of something; knowledge beforehand.

fore-lock (fr´lok´) *n.* A lock of hair growing from the front of the scalp and hanging over the forehead.

fore-man (fr´man) *n.* The person who oversees a group of people; the spokesperson for a jury. **forewoman** *n.*

fore-most (fr´mst´) *adj. & adv.* First in rank, position, time, or order.

fore-noon (fr´ nön´) *n.* The period between sunrise and noon.

fo-ren-sic (fo ren´sik) *adj.* Of, relating to, or used in courts of justice or formal debate.

forensic medicine *n.* A science dealing with the application of medicine in legal problems.

fore-or-dain (fr´or dn´) *v.* Appoint or dispose of in advance; predestine.

fore-part (fr´port´) *n.* The first or earliest part of a period of time.

fore-see (fr sē´) v. To know or see beforehand. **foreseeable** adj. **foreseer** n.

fore-shad-ow (fr shad´) v. To represent or warn of beforehand.

fore-sight (fr´sīt´) n. The act or capacity of foreseeing; the act of looking forward; concern for the future; prudence. **foresighted** adj. **foresightedness** n.

fore-skin (fr´skin´) n. A fold of skin that covers the glans of the penis.

for-est (for´ist) n. A large tract of land covered with trees; something resembling a forest, as in quantity or density. v. To cover with trees. **forested** adj. **forestland** n.

fore-stall (fr stol´) v. To exclude, hinder, or prevent by prior measures.

fore-taste (for tst´) v. To sample or indicate beforehand. **foretaste** n.

fore-tell (fr tel´) v. To tell about in advance; to predict. **foreteller** n.

for-ev-er (for ev´r) adv. For eternity; without end.

fore-warn (fr worn´) v. To warn in advance.

fore-word (fr´werd´) n. An introductory statement preceding the text of a book.

for-feit (for´fit) n. Something taken away as punishment; a penalty; something that is placed in escrow and redeemed on payment of a fine; a forfeiture. **forfeit** v. To lose or give up the right to by committting some offense or error. **forfeiter** n.

forge (frj) n. A furnace where metals are heated and wrought; a smithy; a workshop that produces wrought iron.

for-get (fr get´) v. To lose the memory of; to fail to become mindful or aware of at the right time. **forgetful** adj. **forgetable** adj. **forgetfulness** n.

for-give (fr giv´) v. To pardon; to give up resentment of; to cease to feel resentment against. **forgiveness** n. **forgivable** adj.

for-ked (forkt´) adj. Shaped like or having a fork.

for-lorn (for lorn´) adj. Abandoned or left in distress; hopeless; being in a poor condition. **forlornly** adv. **-ness** n.

form (form) n. The shape or contour of something; a body of a living being; the basic nature of something; the way

in which something exists; variety; style or manner as established by custom or regulation or etiquette; performance according to established criteria; fitness with regard to training or health; procedure of words, as in a ceremony; a document having blanks for insertion of information; style in musical or literary composition; the design or style of a work of art. **form** v. To construct or conceive in the mind.

form suffix Having the form or shape of; cuneiform.

for-mal (for´mal) adj. Of or pertaining to the outward aspect of something; relating or concerned with the outward form of something; adhering to convention, rule, or etiquette; based on accepted conentions.

for-mat (for´mat) n. A general style of a publication; the general form or layout of a publication. v. In computer science, to produce data in a specified form.

for-ma-tion (for m´shan) n. The act or process of forming or the state of being formed; the manner in which something is formed; a given arrangement, as of troops, as a square or in a column.

form-a-tive (for´ma tiv) adj. Forming or having the power to form; of or pertaining to formation, growth, or development.

for-mer (for´mr) adj. Previous; preceding in place; being the first of two persons or things mentioned or referred to.

for-mer-ly adv. Previously.

for-mi-da-ble (for´mi da bl) adj. Extremely difficult; exciting fear by reason of size or strength. **-dably** adv.

for-mu-la (for´m la) n. pl. **formulas** or **formulae** A prescribed method of words or rules for use in a ceremony or procedure; a nutritious food for an infant in liquid form. Math. A combination or rule used to express an algebraic or symbolic form. Chem. A symbolic representation of the composition of a chemical compound.

for-mu-late (for´m lt´) v. To state or express as a formula. **formulation** n.

for-ni-ca-tion (for´ni k´shan) n.

Voluntary sexual intercourse between two unmarried people. **fornicate** v.

for-sake (for skā') v. To abandon or renounce; to give up.

for-sooth (for sōth') adv. In truth; certainly.

for-swear (for swâr') v. To renounce emphatically any oath; to forsake; to swear falsely; to perjure oneself.

for-syth-i-a (for sith' a) n. An Asian shrub cultivated for its early-blooming, bright, yellow flowers.

fort (frt) n. A fortified structure or enclosure capable of defense against an enemy; a permanent army post.

forte (frt) n. An activity one does with excellence; a person's strong point; the part of a sword blade between the middle and the hilt.

forth (frth) adv. Out into plain sight, as from seclusion; forward in order, place, or time.

forth-com-ing (frth'kum'ing) adj. Ready or about to appear or occur; readily available.

forth-right (frth'rt') adj. Straightforward; direct; frank. **forthrightly** adv.

forth-with (frth'with') adv. At once; promptly; immediately.

for-ti-tude (for'ti tōd') n. Strength of mind inadversity, pain, or peril, allowing a person to withstand fear.

fort-night (fort'nt') n. A period of two weeks.

FORTRAN (for'tran) n. In computer science, a programming language for problems that are expressed in algebraic terms.

for-tress (for'tris) n. A fort.

for-tu-i-tous (for tō'i tus) adj. Occurring by chance; lucky; fortunate. **fortuitously** adv.

for-tu-nate (for'chu nit) adj. Brought about by good fortune; having good fortune.

for-tune (for'chan) n. A hypothetical force that, unpredictably, determines events and issues favorably and unfavorably; success that results from luck; possession of material goods; a very large amount of money.

for-ward (for'wrd) adv. At, near, or toward a place or a time in advance; overstepping the usual bounds in an insolent or presumptuous way; extremely unconventional, as in political opinions; socially advanced. **forward** n. A player in football at the front line of offense or defense. **forward** v. To send forward or ahead; to help advance onward. **forwardly** adv.

fos-sil (fos'īl) n. The remains of an animal or plant of a past geologic age preserved in the rocks of the earth's surface; one that is outdated. **fossilization** n. **fossilize** v.

foun-da-tion (foun d'shan) n. The act of founding or establishing; the basis on which anything is founded; an institution supported by an endowment; a cosmetic base for makeup.

foun-dry (foun'dr) n. pl. **ries** An establishment where metal is cast.

fount (fount) n. A fountain; an abundant source.

four (fr) n. The cardinal number that equals 3 + 1; anything consisting of four units. **four** adj. & pron.

four-score (fr'skr') adj. Being four times twenty; eighty.

fowl (foul) n. pl. **fowl** or **fowls** A bird used as food or hunted as game, as the duck, goose, etc.; the edible flesh of a fowl. To hunt or catch wild fowl.

fox (foks) n. A wild mammal having a pointed snout, upright ears, and a long bushy tail; the fur of a fox; a sly or crafty person. **fox** v. To outwit; to trick.

fox-hole (foks'hl') n. A shallow pit dug by a soldier as cover against enemy fire.

foy-er (foi'r) n. The public lobby of a hotel, theater, etc.; an entrance hall.

fra-cas (fr'kas) n. A noisy quarrel or disturbance; fight or dispute.

frac-tion (frak'shan) n. A small part; a disconnected part or fragment of anything; in mathematics, an indicated quantity less than a whole number that is expressed as a decimal. **Chem.** A component of a compound separated from a substance by distilling. **-al** adj.

frac-ture (frak'chr) n. The act of breaking; the state of being broken. **Med.** The breaking or cracking, as in a bone.

frag-ile (fraj'īl) adj. Easily damaged or broken; frail; tenuous; flimsy. **fragilely** adv.

frag-ment (frag´ment) n. A part detached or broken; some part unfinished or incomplete. **fragment** v. To break into fragments. **fragmentation** n.

frag-rant (fr´grant) adj. Having an agreeable, usually sweet, odor. **fragrance** n.

frail (frl) adj. Delicate; weak; easily damaged. **frailly** adv. **frailness** n.

fran-gi-ble (fran´ji bl) adj. Breakable.

fran-tic (fran´tik) adj. Emotionally out of control with worry or fear. **frantically** adv.

fra-ter-nal (fra ter´nal) adj. Pertaining to or relating to brothers; pertaining to or befitting a fraternity.Biol. Of or relating to a twin or twins that developed from separately fertilized ova.

frat-er-nize (frat´er nz´) v. To associate with others in a friendly way; to mingle intimately with the enemy, often in violation of military law.

fraud (frod) n. A deliberate and willful deception perpetrated for unlawful gain; a trick or swindle; an impostor; a cheat.

fraud-u-lent (fro´ju lent) adj. Marked by or practicing fraud. **fraudulence** n.

fraught (frot) adj. Full of or accompanied by something specified.

fray (fr) n. A brawl, or fight; a heated argument or dispute. v. To wear out by rubbing; to irritate one's nerves.

fraz-zle (fraz´el) v. Slang To wear out; to completely fatigue. **frazzle** n.

free (fr) adj. Not imprisoned; not under obligation; independent; possessing political liberties; not affected by a specified circumstance or condition; exempt; costing nothing; not being occupied or used; too familiar; forward; liberal, as with money. **free** adv. In a free way; without charge. **free** v. To set at liberty; to release or rid; to untangle. **freely** adv. **freeness** n.

free-dom (fr´dom) n. The condition or state of being free; independence; possession of political rights; boldness of expression; liberty; unrestricted access or use.

freight (frt) n. A service of transporting commodities by air, land or water; the price paid such transportation; a train that transports goods only. **freight** v.
To carry as cargo.

freight-er (fr´tr) n. A ship used for transporting cargo.

fren-zy (fren´z) n. pl. **frenzies** A state of extreme excitement or violent agitation; temporary insanity or delirium.

fre-quent (fr´kwent) adj. Happening or appearing often or time after time. **frequent** v. To go to a place repeatedly. **frequenter** n. **frequentness** n. **frequently** adv.

fres-co (fres´k) n. pl. **frescoes** or **frescos** The art of painting on moist plaster with water-based paint; a picture so painted.

fresh (fresh) adj. Newly-made, gathered, or obtained; not spoiled, musty, or stale; different; pure and clean; having just arrived; refreshed; revived. Slang Impudent; disrespectful.

fri-a-ble (fr´a bl) adj. Easily crumbled or pulverized brittle. **friableness** n.

fri-ar (fr´r) n. A member of a mendicant Roman Catholic order.

fric-as-see (frik´a s´) n. A dish of meat or poultry stewed in gravy. **fricassee** v.

fric-tion (frik´shan) n. The rubbing of one surface or object against another; a conflict or clash. Phys. A force that retards the relative motion of two touching objects.

frig-ate (frig´it) n. A square-rigged warship of the 17th to mid 19th centuries; U.S. warship smaller than a cruiser but larger than a destroyer.

fright (frt) n. Sudden violent alarm or fear; a feeling of alarm. Slang Something very unsightly or ugly.

fright-en (frt´en) v. To fill with fear; to force by arousing fear. **-ening** adj.

frig-id (frij´id) adj. Very cold; lacking warmth of feeling or emotional warmth; sexually unresponsive. **frigidity** n. **frigidly** adv.

frill (fril) n. A decorative ruffled or gathered border. Slang A superfluous item. **frilly** adj.

fringe (frinj) n. An edging that consists of hanging threads, cords, or loops.

frip-per-y (frip´e r) n. pl.**fripperies** Showy and often cheap; nonessential; a pretentious display.

friv-o-lous (friv´o lus) adj. Trivial; insignificant; lacking importance; not serious; silly. **-ness** *n.* **frivolously** *adv.*

frizz (friz) *v.* To form into small, tight curls. **frizz.** *n.* **frizziness** *n.* **frizzy** *adj.*

fro (fr) *adv.* Away from; back, as running to and fro.

frock (frok) *n.* A smock or loosefitting robe; a robe worn by monks.

frog (frog) *n.* Any of various small, smooth- skinned, web-footed, largely aquatic, tailless, leaping amphibians.

frol-ic (frol´ik) *n.* Merriness; a playful, carefree occasion. *v.* To romp about playfully; to have fun. **frolicker** *n.* **frolicsome** *adj.*

fron-tier (frun tr´) *n.* Part of an international border or the area adjacent to it; an unexplored area of knowledge. **frontiersman** *n.*

fron-tis-piece (frun´tis ps´) *n.* An illustration that usually precedes the title page of a book or periodical.

froth (froth) *n.* A mass of bubbles on or in a liquid, resulting from agitation or fermentation; a salivary foam, as of an animal, resulting from disease or exhaustion; anything unsubstantial or trivial. **froth** *v.* To expel froth. **frothily** *adv.* **frothiness** *n.* **frothy** *adj.*

frou-frou (frö´frö´) *n.* A rustling sound, as of silk; a frilly dress or decoration.

fro-ward (fr´wrd) *adj.* Obstinate.

frown (froun) *v.* To contract the brow as in displeasure or concentration; to look on with distaste or disapproval.

frus-trate (frus´trt) *v.* To keep from attaining a goal or fulfilling a desire; to thwart; to prevent the fruition of; to nullify.

fu-gi-tive (f´ji tiv) *adj.* Fleeing or having fled, as from arrest or pursuit. **fugitive** *n.* One who flees or tries to escape.

fugue (fg) *n.* *Mus.* A musical composition in which the theme is elaborately repeated by various voices or instruments; a psychological disturbance in which actions are not remembered after returning to a normal state.

ful-crum (fel´krum) *n. pl.* **fulcrums** or **fulcra** The point on which a lever turns.

ful-mi-nate (ful´mi nt) *v.* To condemn severely; to explode. **fulmination** *n.*

ful-some (fel´som) *adj.* Offensively in-

sincere; going over the bounds of good taste and behavior. **fulsomely** *adv.*

fum-ble *n.* To search for or attempt something awkwardly. *Sports* To drop the ball; misshandle the ball.

fume (fm) *n.* An irritating smoke, gas, or vapor. **fume** *v.* To treat with or subject to fumes; to show or feel anger or distress.

fu-mi-gate (f´mi gt´) *v.* To subject to fumes in order to exterminate vermin or insects. **fumigation** *n.* **fumigator** *n.*

func-tion (fungk´shan) *n.* The characteristic activity of a person or thing; specific occupation, duty, or role; an official ceremony; something depending upon or varying with another. *Math.* a quantity whose value is dependent on the value of another. **function** *v.* To serve or perform a function as required or expected.

fund *n.* Money in hand or stored; a stock of money. **fund** *v.* To finance; provide funds to.

fun-da-men-tal (fun´da men´tal) *adj.* Basic or essential; of major significance; anything serving as the primary origin; most important. **fundamental** *n.* **fundamentally** *adv.*

fu-ner-al (f´nr al) *n.* The service performed in conjunction with the burial or cremation of a dead person.

fun-gus (fung´gus) *n. pl.* **fungi** or **fungus-es** Any of the spore-bearing plants which have no chlorophyll, such as yeasts, molds, mildews, and mushrooms.

fu-nic-u-lar (f nik´lr) *n.* A cable railway along which cable cars are drawn up a mountain, especially one with ascending and descending cars that counterbalance one another.

fur-bish (fer´bish) *v.* To make bright, as by rubbing; to polish; to renovate.

fur-fur-al (fer´fer al) *n.* A colorless, oily liquid with a penetrating odor, derived from oat or rice hulls, or corncobs; used as an organic solvent in the manufacture of synthetic resins.

fu-ri-ous (fr´us) *adj.* Extremely angry; marked by rage or activity. **-ly** *adv.*

furl (ferl) *v.* To roll up and secure to something, as a pole or mast; to curl or fold.

fur-long n. The measure of length, equal to one-eighth of a mile or 220 yards.

fur-nace (fer´nis) n. A large enclosure designed to produce intense heat.

fur-nish (fer´nish) v. To outfit or equip, as with fittings or furniture; to supply or provide with something necessary, useful, or wanted.

fu-ror (fr´or) n. Violent anger; rage; great excitement; commotion; an uproar; an outburst of public excitement.

fur-row (fer´) n. A long, narrow trench in the ground, made by a plow or other tool; a deep wrinkle in the skin, especially of the forehead.

fur-tive (fer´tiv) adj. Done in secret; surreptitious; obtained underhandedly; stolen.

fu-ry (fr´) n. pl. **furies** Uncontrolled anger; turbulence; as in storms or waves; unrestrained energy; extreme violence; a spiteful woman.

fuse n. Electrical safety device. **fuse** v. To become intermingled and blended; melting together; to cast. Mil. A mechanism or electronic device used to explode a bomb, missile or shell.

fu-sil-lage (f´se lij) n. The central section of an airplane, containing the wings and tail assembly.

fu-sion (f´zhən) n. The act or procedure of melting together by heat; a blend produced by fusion; a nuclear reaction in which nuclei of a light element combine to form more massive nuclei, with the release of huge amounts of energy.

fuss n. Excessive show of anxious activity, over trifles; a disturbance or commotion. **fuss** v. To give excess attention to; to worry.

fus-tian (fus´chən) n. A sturdy, stout cotton cloth. **fustian** adj. Pompous, pretentious language.

fus-tic (fus´ik) n. The wood of a large tropical tree; a member of the mulberry family, providing a yellow dye; any of several other dyewoods.

fu-tile (ft´il) adj. Ineffectual; being of no avail; without useful result; serving no useful purpose.

fu-ture (fy-cher) adj. Time yet to come; an expectation of progressive development.

fu-tures (fy-chers) n. Commodities or stocks purchased or sold on the basis of delivery at a future date.

fuzz (fuz) n. A mass of fine, loose particles, fibers, or hairs.

fuzz-y adj. To be covered with fuzzy; unclear.

FYI abbr. For your information.

G

G, g (j) The seventh letter of the English alphabet. Mus. The fifth tone in the scale of C major. Slang One thousand dollars; a grand. Physiol. A unit of force equal to that due to the earth's gravity.

gab-ble (gab´l) v. To speak rapidly or incoherently. **gabble** n.

gad (gad) v. To wander about restlessly with little or no purpose. **gadder** n.

gad-a-bout (gad´a bout´) n. Slang A person who goes about seeking excitement and or fun.

gad-get (gaj´it) n. Slang A small device or tool used in performing miscellaneous jobs, especially in the kitchen.

gaff (gaf) n. A sharp iron hook used for landing fish. Naut. A spar on the top edge of a fore-and-aft sail. Slang Abuse or harsh treatment. v. To deceive.

gage (gj) n. Something that is given as security for an action to be performed; a pledge; anything, as a glove, thrown down as a challenge to fight.

gag-gle (gag´l) n. A flock of geese; a group; a cluster.

gai-e-ty (g´i t) n. pl. **-ies** The state of being happy; cheerfulness; fun, festive activity.

gain (gn) v. To earn or acquire possession of something; to succeed in winning a victory; to develop an increase of; to put on weight; to secure as a profit; to improve progress; to draw nearer to.

gain-ful (gn´ful) adj. Producing profits; lucrative. **gainfully** adv. **-ness** n.

gain-say (gn´s´) v. To deny; to contradict; dispute. **gainsayer** n.

gait (gt) n. A way or manner of moving on foot; one of the foot movements in which a horse steps or runs.

ga-la (g´la) n. A festive celebration.

ga-lac-tose (ga lak´ts) n. The sugar typically occurring in lactose.

gal-ax-y (gal´ak s) n. pl. -ies Astron. Any of the very large systems of stars, nebulae, or other celestial bodies that constitute the universe; a brilliant, distinguished group or assembly. **Galaxy** The Milky Way.

gale (gl) n., Meteor. A very powerful wind stronger than a stiff breeze; an outburst, as of hilarity.

ga-le-na (ga l´na) n. A metallic, dull gray mineral that is the principal ore of lead.

gal-i-ma-ti-as n. A confused mixture of words.

gall (gol) n., Physiol. The bitter fluid secreted by the liver; bile; bitterness of feeling; animosity; impudence; something that irritates. v. To injure the skin by friction; to chafe. **galling** adj. **gallingly** adv.

gal-lant (gal´ant) adj. Dashing in appearance or dress; majestic; stately; chivalrously attentive to women; courteous. **-ly** adv.

gal-lant-ry (gal´an tr) n. pl. -ries Nobility and bravery; a gallant act.

gall-blad-der or **gall bladder** n. The small sac under the right lobe of the liver that stores bile.

gal-le-on (gal´ on) n. A large three-masted sailing ship.

gal-ler-y (gal´e r) n. pl. -ries A long, narrow passageway, as a corridor, with a roofed promenade, especially an open-sided one extending along an inner or outer wall of a building; a group of spectators, as at a golf tournament; a building where statues, paintings, and other works of art are displayed; a room or building where articles are sold to the highest bidder; an underground passage in a mine.

gal-li-nule (gal e nip er) n. A wading bird with dark iridescent plumage.

gal-li-vant (gal´i vant´) v. To roam about in search of amusement or pleasure.

gal-lon (gal´on) n. A liquid measurement used in the U.S., equal to 4 quarts; in Great Britain, a liquid measurement which equals 4 imperial quarts; a dry measurement that equals 1/8 bushel.

gal-lop (gal´op) n. A horse's gait that is faster than a canter and characterized by regular leaps during which all four feet are off the ground at once.

gal-lows (gal´z) n. A framework of two or more upright beams and a cross-beam, used for execution by hanging.

gall-stone (gol´stn´) n., Pathol. A small, hard concretion of cholesterol crystals that sometimes form in the gall bladder or bile passages.

ga-lore (ga lr´) adj. In great numbers; abundant; plentiful.

ga-losh (ga losh´) n. pl. **galoshes** Waterproof overshoes which are worn in bad weather.

gal-va-nism (gal´va niz´um) n. Electricity that is produced by chemical action. Med. A therapeutic application of continuous electric current from voltaic cells.

gal-va-nize (gal´va nz´) v. To stimulate or shock muscular action by an electric current; to protect iron or steel with rust resistant zinc. Slang To infuse with energy. **galvanization** n. **-nizer** n.

gal-va-nom-e-ter (gal´va nom´i tr) n., Electr. An apparatus for detecting the presence of an electric current and for determining its strength and direction.

gam-bit (gam´bit) n. In chess, an opening in which a piece is sacrificed for a favorable position; a maneuver that is carefully planned.

gam-ble (gam´bl) v. To take a chance on an uncertain outcome as a contest or a weekly lottery venture. n. Any risky venture.

gam-bol (gam´bol) v. To frolic, skip, or leap about in play.

game (gm) n. A contest governed by specific rules; a way of entertaining oneself; amusement; a calculated way to do something; animals, fish, or birds that are hunted for sport or food. **game** v. **gamer** adj. **gamest** adj. **gamely** adv. **gameness** n.

gam-ete (gam´t) n., Biol. Either of two mature reproductive cells, an ovum or sperm, which produce a zygote when united.

gam-in (gam´in) n. A homeless child

who wanders about the streets of a town or city.

gamma globulin *n.*, *Biochem.* A globulin that is present in blood plasma and contains antibodies effective against certain infectious diseases.

gamma ray *n.*, *Phys.* Electromagnetic radiation that has energy greater than several hundred thousand electron volts.

gam-mon (gam´on) *n.* A cured ham; in the game of backgammon, a double victory in which a player removes all his pieces before the other player removes any.

gam-ut (gam´ut) *n.* The whole range or extent of anything.

gam-y (g´m) *adj.* Having the strong flavor of game, especially when slightly tainted; scandalous. **gaminess** *n.*

gan-der (gan´dr) *n.* A male goose. *Slang* A quick glance; a look or peek.

gang (gang) *n.* A group of persons who are organized and work together or socialize regularly; a group of adolescent hoodlums or criminals. **on** To attack as a group.

gan-gling (gang´gling) *adj.* Tall and thin; lanky.

gan-gli-on (gang´gl an) *n.* *pl.* **-glia** *Physiol.* A collection of nerve cells located outside the spinal cord or brain. **ganglionic** *adj.*

gang-plank (gang´plangk´) *n.* A temporary board or ramp used to board or leave a ship.

gan-grene (gang´grn) *n.*, *Pathol.* The death and decay of tissue in the body caused by a failure in the circulation of the blood supply. **gangrenous** *adj.*

gan-try (gan´tr) *n.* *pl.* **-ies** *Aeros.* A bridge-like framework support, especially a movable vertical structure with platforms, that is used in assem-bling or servicing rockets before they are launched.

gap (gap) *n.* An opening or wide crack, as in a wall; a cleft; a deep notch or ravine in a mountain ridge, offering passage.

gape (gp) *v.* To open the mouth wide, as in yawning; to stare in amazement with the mouth wide open; to become widely separated or open. **gaper** *n.*

ga-rage (ga razh´) *n.* A building or structure in which motor vehicles are stored, repaired, or serviced. **garage** *v.*

gar-ble (gär´bl) *v.* To mix up or confuse; to change or distort the meaning of with the intent to mislead or misrepre-sent. **-er** *n.*

gar-den (gär´den) *n.* A place for growing flowers, vegetables, or fruit; a piece of ground commonly used as a public resort. *v.* To work in or make into a garden. **gardener** *n.*

gar-de-nia (gär d´nya) *n.* A tropical shrub with glossy evergreen leaves and fragrant white flowers.

gar-gan-tu-an (gär gan´chö an) *adj.* Of enormous size; immense.

gar-gle (gär´gl) *v.* To force air from the lungs through a liquid held in the back of the mouth and throat. **gargle** *n.*

gar-goyle (gär´goil) *n.* A waterspout made or carved to represent a grotesque animal or human figure, projecting from a gutter to throw rain away from the side of a building.

gar-ish (gâr´ish) *adj.* Too showy and bright; gaudy. **-ly** *adv.* **garishness** *n.*

gar-land (gär´land) *n.* A wreath, chain, or rope of flowers or leaves. *v.* To decorate with or form into a garland. *Naut.* A ring of rope attached to a spar to aid in hoisting or to prevent chafing.

gar-lic (gär´lik) *n.* A plant related to the onion with a compound bulb which contains a strong odor and flavor, used as a seasoning.

gar-ment (gär´ment) *n.* An article of clothing.

gar-ner (gär´nr) *v.* To gather and store; to accumulate.

gar-net (gär´nit) *n.* A dark-red silicate mineral used as a gemstone and as an abrasive.

gar-nish (gär´nish) *v.* To add something to, as to decorate or embellish; to add decorative or flavorful touches to food or drink.

gar-nish-ment (gär´nish ment) *n.* The act of garnishing; the legal proceeding that turns property belonging to a debtor over to his creditor.

gar-ni-ture (gär´ni chr) *n.* Anything that is used to garnish.

gar-ret (gar´it) *n.* A room in an attic.

gar-ri-son (gar´i son) *n.* The military force that is permanently placed in a fort or town; a military post.

gar-rote *or* **gar-rotte** (ga rt´) *n.* The former Spanish method of execution by strangulation with an iron collar tightened by a screw-like device.

gar-ru-lous (gar´a lus) *adj.* Given to continual talkativeness; chatty.

gar-ter (gär´tr) *n.* A band or strap that is worn to hold a stocking in place.

gash (gash) *n.* A long, deep cut. **gash** *v.*

gas-ket (gas´kit) *n., Mech.* A rubber seal, disk, or ring used between matched machine parts or around pipe joints to prevent the escape of fluid or gas.

gas-o-line *or* **gas-o-lene** (gas´o ln´) *n.* A colorless, highly flammable mixture of liquid hydrocarbons made from crude petroleum and used as a fuel and a solvent.

gasp (gasp) *v.* To inhale suddenly and sharply, as from fear or surprise; to make labored or violent attempts to breathe.

gas-tric (gas´trik) *adj.* Of or pertaining to the stomach.

gastric juice *n., Biochem.* The digestive fluid secreted by the stomach glands, containing several enzymes.

gastric ulcer *n., Pathol.* An ulcer formed on the stomach lining, often caused by excessive secretion of gastric juices.

gas-tron-o-my (ga stron´o m) *n.* The art of good eating. **gastronome** *n.* **-ic** *adj.*

gas-tro-pod (gas´tro pod´) *n.* One of the large class of aquatic and terrestrial mollusks, including snails, slugs, limpets, having a single shell and a broad, muscular organ of locomotion. **gastropodan** *n.*

gat (gat) *n. Slang* A pistol; short for Gatling gun.

gate (gt) *n.* A movable opening in a wall or fence, commonly swinging on hinges, that closes or opens; a valve-like device for controlling the passage of gas or water through a conduit or dam; the total paid admission receipts or number in attendance at a public performance.

gath-er (gath´r) *v.* To bring or come together into one place or group; to harvest or pick; to increase or gain; to accumulate slowly; to fold or pleat a cloth by pulling it along a thread. **gather** *n.* gathering *n.*

gauche (gsh) *adj.* Socially awkward; clumsy; boorish. **gauchely** *adv.* **gaucheness** *n.*

gaud-y (go´d) *adj.* Too highly decorated to be in good taste. **gaudiness** *n.*

gauge *or* **gage** (gj) *n.* A standard measurement.

gaunt (gont) *adj.* Thin and bony; haggard; gloomy or desolate in appearance.

gauze (goz) *n.* A loosely-woven, transparent material used for surgical bandages; any thin, open-mesh material; a mist.

gave *v.* Past tense of give.

gav-el (gav´el) *n.* A mallet used by a presiding officer or by a person in charge to call for order or attention.

ga-vi-al (g´v al) *n.* A large crocodile found in India, with long, slender jaws.

gawk (gok) *v.* To gape; to stare stupidly.

gay (g) *adj.* Merry; happy and carefree; brightly ornamental or colorful; homosexual. *n.* A homosexual. **gayness** *n.*

gaze (gz) *v.* To look steadily or intently at something in admiration or wonder; to stare.

ga-zette (ga zet´) *n.* A newspaper; an official publication. *v.* To publish or announce in a gazette.

gaz-et-teer (gaz i tr´) *n.* A dictionary consisting of geographical facts.

gear (gr) *n., Mech.* A toothed wheel which interacts with another toothed part to transmit motion; an assembly of parts that work together for a special purpose; equipment. *v.* To regulate, match, or suit something.

geck-o (gek´) *n. pl.* **-os** *or* **-oes** Any of various small lizards of warm regions having toes with adhesive pads enabling them to climb up or down vertical surfaces.

gel (jel) *n., Chem.* A colloid that is in a more solid than liquid form. *v.* To change into or take on the form of a gel.

geld (geld) *v.* To castrate or spay, especially a horse.

geld-ing (gel´ding) n. A gelded animal.

gel-id (jel´id) adj. Very cold; frigid.

gem (jem) n. A cut and polished precious or semiprecious stone; one that is highly treasured. v. To set or decorate with or as with gems.

gen-der (jen´dr) n., Gram. Any of two or more categories, as feminine, masculine, and neuter, into which words are divided and which determine agreement with or selection of modifiers or grammatical forms; the quality of being of the male or female sex.

gene (jn) n., Biol. A functional hereditary unit which occupies a fixed location on a chromosome and controls or acts in the transmission of hereditary characteristics.

ge-ne-al-o-gy (j´n ol´o j) n. pl.-ies A record, table, or account showing the descent of a family, group, or person from an ancestor; the study of ancestry. **genealogical** adj. -**gically** adv.

gen-er-al (jen´r al) adj. Pertaining to, including, or affecting the whole or every member of a group or class; common to or typical of most; not being limited to a special class; miscellaneous; not detailed or precise. n. Milit. An officer in the United States Army, Air Force, or Marine Corps ranking above a colonel.

general assembly n. A legislative body. **Assembly** The supreme deliberative body of the United Nations.

gen-er-al-i-ty (jen´e ral´i t) n. pl. -ies The state or quality of being general; an inadequate, inexact or vague statement or idea.

gen-er-al-ize (jen´r a lz´) v. To draw a general conclusion from particular facts, experiences, or observations.

gen-er-ate (jen´e rt´) v. To cause to be; to produce; to bring into existence, especially by a chemical or physical process.

gen-er-a-tion (jen´e r´shan) n. A group of individuals born at about the same time; the average time interval between the birth of parents and that of their offspring.

gen-er-a-tor (jen´e r´tr) n., Mech. A machine that changes mechanical energy into electrical energy.

ge-ner-ic (je ner´ik) adj. Relating to or indicating an entire class or group; general; pertaining to a genus or class of related things; of or relating to a class of product, or merchandise that does not bear a trademark or trade name.

gen-er-ous (jen´r us) adj. Sharing freely; abundant; overflowing. **generosity** n.

gen-e-sis (jen´i sis) n. pl. -ses The act or state of originating. **Genesis** The first book of the Old Testament.

ge-net-ic (je net´ik) adj. Of or pertaining to the origin or development of something; of or relating to genetics. **genetically** adv.

genetic code n., Biochem. The biochemical basis of heredity that specifies the amino acid sequence in the synthesis of proteins and on which heredity is based.

gen-ial (je n´al) adj. Cheerful, kind, pleasant and good-humored in disposition or manner. **geniality** n. **-ly** adv.

ge-nie (j´n) n. A supernatural creature, capable of taking on human form, who does one's bidding.

gen-i-tal (jen´i tal) adj. Of or pertaining to the reproductive organs or the process of reproduction.

genitals (jen´i talz) n., pl. The external sexual organs. **genitalia** n.

gen-i-to-u-ri-nar-y (jen´i t yer´iner´) adj., Anat. Of or pertaining to the genital and urinary organs or their functions.

gen-ius (jn´yus) n. pl. -ses Exceptional intellectual ability or creative power; a strong, natural talent; a person who exerts powerful influence over another.

gen-o-cide (jen´o sd´) n. The systematic extermination or destruction of a political, racial, or cultural group. **cidal** adj.

gen-teel (jen tl´) adj. Refined or well-bred; elegant; polite; stylish or fashionable. **genteelly** adv. **genteelness** n.

gen-til-i-ty (jen til´i t) n. The quality of being genteel; the members of the upper class; well-born or well-bred persons collectively.

gen-tle (jen´tl) adj. Not harsh, severe, rough, or loud; easily handled or managed; docile; not sudden or steep; from a good family of high social standing. *Meteor.* A soft, moderate breeze. *v.* To tame. **-ly** *adv.*

gen-try (jen´tr) *n.* People of good family or high social standing; the aristocracy; in England, the social class that is considered the upper ranks of the middle class.

gen-u-flect (jen´ flekt´) *v.* To bend down on one knee, as in worship.

gen-u-ine (jen´ in) *adj.* Real; authentic; not counterfeit or spurious; not hypocritical; sincere. **genuinely** *adv.* **genuineness** *n.*

ge-nus (j´nus) *n. pl. n., Biol.* A group or category of plants and animals usually including several species.

ge-o-cen-tric (j´ sen´trik) *adj.* Of or relating to the earth's center; formulated on the assumption that the earth is the center of the universe. **-ally** *adv.*

ge-o-chem-is-try (j´ kem´i str) *n.* A branch of chemistry that deals with the chemical composition of the earth's crust. **geochemical** *adj.* **geochemist** *n.*

ge-ode (j´d) *n. Geol.* A hollow rock having a cavity lined with crystals.

geodesic line *n.* In mathematics, the shortest line that connects two points on a given surface.

ge-od-e-sy (j od´i s) *n.* The geologic science dealing with the determination of the shape, area, and curvature of the earth. **geodesist** *n.* **geodetic** *adj.*

ge-og-ra-phy (j og´ra f) *n. pl.* **-hies** The science that deals with the earth's natural climate, resources, and population. **geographer** *n.* **geographic** *adj.* **geographical** *adj.* **-phically** *adv.*

ge-ol-o-gy (j ol´o j) *n. pl.* **-ies** The science that deals with the history, origin, and structure of the earth. **geologic** *adj.* **geological** *adj.* **geologically** *adv.*

ge-o-met-ric (j´ me´trik) *adj.* According to or pertaining to the rules and principles of geometry; increasing in a geometric progression.

geometric progression *n.* A sequence of numbers, as 4, 8, 16, 32 where each term is the product of a constant factor and the term that precedes it.

ge-om-e-try (j om´i tr) *n. pl.* **ies** The branch of mathematics that deals with

the measurement, properties, and relationships of lines, angles, points, surfaces and solids.

ge-o-phys-ics (j´ fiz´iks) *n. pl.* The study of the earth as the product of complex physicochemical forces that act upon it internally from outer space, with reference to exploration of the less accessible regions.

ge-o-pol-i-tics (j´ pol´i tiks) *n. pl.* The study of the influence of economic and geographical factors on the politics and policies of a nation or region.

ge-o-ther-mal (j´ ther´mal) *adj.* Relating to the internal heat of the earth.

ger-i-at-rics (jer´ a´triks) *n. pl.* The medical study that deals with the structural changes, diseases, physiology, and hygiene of old age. **geriatric** *adj.*

germ (jerm) *n.* A small red or organic structure from which a new organism may develop; a microorganism which causes disease. *Biol.* A reproductive cell.

ger-mane (jr mn) *adj.* Relevant to what is being considered or discussed.

ger-ma-ni-um (jr m´n um) *n.* A grayish-white element widely used in electronics and optics, symbolized by Ge.

germ cell *n.* An egg or sperm cell.

ger-mi-cide (jer´mi sd´) *n.* An agent used to destroy microorganisms or disease germs.

ger-mi-nal (jer´mi nal) *adj.* Of or relating to a germ or germ cell; of or in the earliest stage of development.

ger-mi-nate (jer´mi nt´) *v.* To begin to grow, develop, or sprout. **-nation** *n.*

germ plasm *n., Biol.* The part of the protoplasm of a germ cell containing the chromosomes and genes.

ger-on-tol-gy (jer´on tol´o j) *n.* The study of the processes and phenomena of aging. **gerontological** *adj.* **gerontologic** *adj.*

ger-ry-man-der (jer´i man´dr) *v.* To divide a voting area so as to advance unfairly the interests of a political party; to adjust or adapt to one's advantage.

ger-und (jer´und) *n., Gram.* A verb form that is used as a noun.

gest (jest) *n.* A notable deed or feat.

ges-ta-tion (je st´shan) n. The carrying of a developing offspring in the uterus; pregnancy. **gestate** v. **gestational** adj.

ges-tic-u-late (je stik´lt´) v. To make expressive gestures, as in speaking.

ges-ture (jes´chr) n. A bodily motion, especially with the hands in speaking, to emphasize some idea or emotion. v. To make gestures. **-er** n.

ge-sund-heit (ge zen´ht) A phrase used to wish good health to a person who has just sneezed.

get (get) v. To come into possession of, as by receiving, winning, earning or, buying. **ahead.** To attain success. **by** To revenge oneself on. **by** To manage; to survive.

get-a-way (get´a w´) n. The act of or instance of escaping by a criminal; a start, as of a race.

gey-ser (g´zr) n. A natural hot spring that intermittently ejects hot water and steam.

ghast-ly (gast´l) adj. Horrible; terrifying; very unpleasant or bad; ghostlike in appearance; deathly pale.

ghat (gät) n. A broad flight of steps that leads down to the edge of a river; a mountain pass, range, or chain.

ghet-to (get´) n. A run-down section of a city in which a minority group lives because of poverty or social pressure.

ghost (gst) n. The spirit of a dead person which is believed to appear to or haunt living persons; a spirit; a ghostwriter; a false, faint secondary television image.

ghost-writer n. A person hired to write for another person and to give credit for the writing to that other person.

ghoul (gōl) n. A person who robs graves; in Moslem legend, an evil spirit which plunders graves and feeds on corpses. **ghoulish** adj. **ghoulishly** adv.

gi-ant (j´ant) n. A legendary man-like being of supernatural size and strength; one of great power, importance, or size.

gib-ber (jib´r) v. To talk or chatter incoherently or unintelligibly.

gib-bet (jib´it) n. A gallows. v. To execute by hanging on a gibbet.

gib-bon (gib´on) n. A slender, long-armed Asian ape.

gib-bous (gib´us) adj. The moon or a planet which is seen with more than half but not all of the apparent disk illuminated. **-ly** adv. **gibbousness** n.

gibe (jb) v. To ridicule or make taunting remarks. **gibe** n. **giber** n.

gib-let (jib´lit) n. or **giblets** The heart, liver, and gizzard of a fowl.

gid-dy (gid´) adj. Affected by a reeling or whirling sensation; dizzy; frivolous and silly; flighty. **giddily** adv. **giddiness** n.

gift (gift) n. Something that is given from one person to another; a natural aptitude; a talent.

gig (gig) n. A light, two-wheeled carriage drawn by one horse. Naut. A speedy, light rowboat; a spear with forks or prongs used for fishing. Slang A job, especially an engagement to play music. Milit., Slang A demerit; a punishment to military personnel.

gi-gan-tic (j gan´tik) adj. Of tremendous or extraordinary size; huge. **gigantically** adv.

gig-gle (gig´l) v. To laugh in high-pitched, repeated, shortsounds. **-gler** n.

gig-o-lo (jig´o l´) n. A man who is supported by a woman not his wife; a man who is paid to be an escort or dancing partner.

gild (gild) v. To coat with a thin layer of gold; to brighten or adorn. **gilded** adj.

gill (gil) n., Zool. The organ, as of fishes and various other aquatic invertebrates, used for taking oxygen from water. n. A liquid measure that equals 1/4 pint.

gilt (gilt) adj. Covered with or of the color of gold. n. A thin layer of gold or a gold-colored substance which is applied to a surface.

gim-bal (jim´balz) n. A three ringed device that keeps an object supported on it level, as the compass of a ship.

gim-crack (jim´krak´) n. A cheap and useless object of little or no value.

gim-let (gim´lit) n. A small, sharp tool with a bar handle and a pointed, spiral tip used for boring holes.

gim-mick (gim´ik) n. A tricky feature that is obscured or misrepresented; a tricky device, especially when used dishonestly or secretly; a gadget.

gin (jin) n. An aromatic, clear, alcoholic

liquor distilled from grain and flavored with juniper berries; a machine used to separate seeds from cotton fibers. *v.* To remove the seeds from cotton with a gin.

gin-ger (jin'jr) *n.* A tropical Asian plant with a pungent aromatic root, used in medicine and cooking.

gin-ger-ly (jin'jr lē) *adv.* Doing something very cautiously. **gingerliness** *n.*

ging-ham (ging'am) *n.* A cotton fabric woven in solid colors and checks.

gin-gi-vi-tis (jin'ji vi'tis) *n.*, *Pathol.* Inflammation of the gums.

gin-seng (jin'seng) *n.* A herb native to China and North America with an aromatic root believed to have medicinal properties.

gi-raffe (ji raf') *n. pl.* **-fes** *or* **-fe** The tallest of all mammals, having an extremely long neck and very long legs, found in Africa.

gird (gerd) *v.* To surround, encircle, or attach with or as if with a belt.

gird-er (ger'dr) *n.* A strong, horizontal beam, as of steel or wood, which is the main support in a building.

gir-dle (ger'dl) *n.* A cord or belt worn around the waist; a supporting undergarment worn by women to give support and to shape.

girl (gerl) *n.* A female child or infant; a young, unmarried woman; any woman of any age; one's sweetheart. **girlish** *adj.* **girlishly** *adv.* **girlishness** *n.*

girl Friday *n.* A woman employee responsible for a variety of tasks.

girl friend *n.* A female friend; a regular or frequent female companion of a boy or man.

girth (gerth) *n.* The circumference or distance around something; a strap that encircles an animal's body to secure something on its back, as a saddle.

gis-mo (jis m) *n. Slang* A part or device whose name is unknown or forgotten; a gadget.

gist (jist) *n.* The central or main substance, as of an argument or question.

give (giv) *v.* To make a present of; to bestow; to accord or yield to another; to put into the possession of another; to convey to another; to donate or contribute; to apply; to devote; to yield as

to pressure; to collapse; to furnish or provide; to deliver in exchange; to pay. **away** To hand over the bride to the bridegroom at a wedding ceremony. **out** To collapse; to be exhausted. **give-up** To surrender; to submit oneself. **giver** *n.*

giv-en (giv'n) *adj.* Bestowed; presented; specified or assumed.

given name *n.* The name bestowed or given at birth or baptism.

giz-zard (giz'rd) *n.* The second stomach in birds, where partly digested food is finely ground.

gla-brous (gl'brus) *adj. Biol.* Having no hair or down; having a smooth surface.

gla-cier (gl'shr) *n.* A large mass of compacted snow that moves slowly until it either breaks off to form icebergs or melts when it reaches warmer climates.

glad (glad) *adj.* Displaying, experiencing, or affording joy and pleasure; being happy; being willing to help; grateful. *n.* Short for gladiolus.

glad-den (glad'n) *v.* To make glad.

glade (gld) *n.* A clearing in a forest or woods.

glad-i-a-tor (glad' 'tr) *n.* An ancient Roman slave, captive, or paid free man who entertained the public by fighting to the death; one who engages in an intense struggle or controversy. **gladiatorial** *adj.*

glad-some (glad'som) *adj.* Giving cheer; showing joy **-ly** *adv.* **-ness** *n.*

glam-our *or* **glam-or** (glam'r) *n.* Alluring fascination or charm. **-ous** *adj.*

glance (glans) *v.* To take a brief or quick look at something; to obliquely strike a surface at an angle and be deflected; to give a light, brief touch; to brush against.

gland (gland) *n., Anat.* Any of various body organs which excrete or secrete substances.

glare (glâr) *v.* To stare fiercely or angrily; to shine intensely; to dazzle. *n.* An uncomfortably harsh or bright light.

glass (glas) *n.* A hard, amorphous, brittle, usually transparent material which hardens from the molten state, preceded by rapid cooling to prevent crystallization; any substance made of or resembling glass; a mirror, tumbler, windowpane, lens, or other material made *n.* of glass. **glasses** A pair of eyeglasses used as an aid to vision; glassware. **glass** *adj.*

glau·co·ma (glo k′ma) *n., Pathol.* A disease of the eye characterized by abnormally high pressure within the eyeball and partial or complete loss of vision.

glaze (glz) *n.* A thin, smooth coating as on ceramics. *v.* To become covered with a thin glassy coating of ice; to coat or cover with a glaze; to fit with glass, as to glaze a window.

gleam (glm) *n.* A momentary ray or beam of light. *v.* To shine or emit light softly; to appear briefly. **gleamy** *adj.*

glean (gln) *v.* To collect or gather facts by patient effort; to collect part by part; to pick bits of a crop left by a reaper. **gleanings** *pl.* **gleaner** *n.*

glee (gl) *n.* Joy; merriment; an unaccompanied song for male voices.

glen (glen) *n.* A small, secluded valley.

glib (glib) *adj.* Spoken easily and fluently; superficial. **glibly** *adv.* **glibness** *n.*

glide (gld) *v.* To pass or move smoothly with little or no effort; to fly without motor power.

glid·er (gl′dr) *n.* One that glides; a swing gliding in a metal frame. *Aeron.* An aircraft without an engine, constructed to soar on air currents.

glim·mer (glim′r) *n.* A faint suggestion; an indication; a dim unsteady light. *v.* To give off a faint or dim light.

glimpse (glimps) *n.* A momentary look.

glis·sade (gli säd′) *n.* A gliding ballet step; a controlled slide in either a sitting or standing position, used to descend a steep, snowy, or icy incline. **glissade** *v.* **glissader** *n.*

glis·san·do (gli sän′d) *n. pl.* **-di** A rapid passing from one tone to another by a continuous change of pitch.

glit·ter (glit′r) *n.* A brilliant sparkle; small bits of light-reflecting material used for decoration. *v.* To sparkle with brilliance.

gloat (glt) *v.* To express, feel, or observe with great malicious pleasure or self-satisfaction.

glob (glob) *n.* A drop of something; a rounded, large mass of something.

glob·al (gl′bal) *adj.* Spherical; involving the whole world. **-alize** *v.* **-ly** *adv.*

globe (glb) *n.* A spherical object; anything that is perfectly rounded; the earth; anything like a sphere, as a fishbowl; a spherical representation of the earth, usually including geographical and political boundaries.

globetrotter *n.* One who travels all over the world.

glob·u·lin (glob′ lin) *n., Biochem.* Any of a class of simple proteins found widely in blood, milk, tissue, muscle and plant seeds.

gloom (glöm) *n.* Partial or total darkness; depression of the mind or spirits. **gloomily** *adv.* **gloominess** *n.* **-y** *adj.*

glo·ri·fy (glr′i f′) *v.* To worship and give glory to; to give high praise.

glo·ri·ous (glr′ us) *adj.* Magnificent; resplendent; delightful; illustrious; full of glory. **gloriously** *adv.*

glory (glr′) *n. pl.* **-ies** Distinguished praise or honor; exalted reputation; adoration and praise offered in worship; a wonderful asset; the height of one's triumph, achievement, or prosperity. *v.* To rejoice with jubilation.

gloss (glos) *n.* The sheen or luster of a polished surface; a deceptively or superficially attractive appearance; a note that explains or translates a difficult or hard to understand expression. *v.* To cover over by falsehood in an attempt to understand or ignore.

glos·sa·ry (glos′a r) *n. pl.* **-ries** A list of words and their meanings.

gloss·y (glos′) *adj.* Having a bright sheen; lustrous; superficially attractive. *n.* A photo print on smooth, shiny paper **glossily** *adv.*

glot·tis (glot′is) *n. pl.* **-ises** *or* **-ides** *Anat.* The opening or cleft between the vocal cords at the upper part of the larynx.

glow (gl) *v.* To give off heat and light, especially without a flame; to have a bright, warm, ruddy color. *n.* A warm feeling of emotion.

glow-worm (gl′werm′) *n.* A European beetle; the luminous larva or grub-like female of an insect which displays phosphorescent light; the firefly.

glu-cose (glō´ks) *n., Chem.* A substance less sweet than cane sugar, found as dextrose in plants and animals and obtained by hydrolysis; a yellowish to colorless syrupy mixture of dextrose, maltose, and dextrins with a small amount of water, used especially in confectionery and baking.

glue (glō) *n.* Any of various adhesives in the form of a gelatin, made from animal substances, as bones or skins, and used to stick and hold items together. **gluey** *adj.*

glum (glum) *adj.* Moody and silent. **glumly** *adv.* **glumness** *n.*

glut (glut) *v.* To feed or supply beyond capacity; to provide with a supply that exceeds demand. *n.* An overabundance.

glu-ten (glōt´en) *n.* A mixture of plant proteins that is used as an adhesive and as a substitute for flour. **glutenous** *adj.*

glut-ton (glut´n) *n.* Someone who eats immoderately; one who has a large capacity for work or punishment. **gluttonous** *adj.* **gluttonously** *adv.*

glyc-er-ol (glis´e rl´) *n., Chem.* A sweet, oily, syrupy liquid derived from fats and oils and used as a solvent, sweetener, antifreeze, and lubricant.

gly-co-side (gl´ko sd´) *n., Chem.* Any of a group of carbohydrates which, when decomposed, produce glucose or other sugar.

gnarl (närl) *n.* A hard, protruding knot on a tree. **gnarled** *adj.*

gnash (nash) *v.* To grind or strike the teeth together, as in a rage or pain.

gnat (nat) *n.* A small, winged insect, specially one that bites or stings.

gnaw (no) *v.* To bite or eat away with persistence; to consume or wear away.

gneiss (ns) *n.* A banded, coarse-grained rock with minerals arranged in layers.

gnome (nm) *n.* In folklore, a dwarf-like creature who lives underground and guards precious metals and treasures.

go (g) *v.* To proceed or pass along; to leave; to move away from; to follow a certain course of action; to function; to function correctly; to be in operation; to be awarded or given; to have recourse; to resort to; to pass, as of time; to be abolished or given up *v.* ; To pass to someone, as by a will. *n.* An attempt; a try. **on** To abandon. **for,** To try; to try to obtain. **places** To be on the road to success. **under** To suffer destruction or defeat.

goahead (g´a hed´) *n.* Permission; a signal to move ahead or proceed.

goal (gl) *n.* A purpose; the terminal point of a race or journey; in some games, the area, space, or object into which participants must direct play in order to score.

goat (gt) *n.* A horned, cud-chewing mammal related to the sheep; a lecherous man. *Slang* One who is a scapegoat.

goat-ee (g t´) *n.* A short, pointed beard on a man's chin.

gob-ble (gob´l) *v.* To eat and swallow food greedily; to take greedily; to grab.

gob-ble-dy-gook (gob´l d gek´) *n. Informal* Wordy and often unintelligible language.

gob-bler (gob´lr) *n.* A male turkey.

gob-let (gob´lit) *n.* A drinking glass, typically with a base and stem.

gob-lin (gob´lin) *n.* In folklore, an ugly, grotesque creature said to be mischievous and evil.

god (god) *n.* Someone considered to be extremely important or valuable; an image, symbol, or statue of such a being.

God (god) *n.* The Supreme Being; the ruler of life and the universe.

god-father (god´fä Thr) *n.* A man who sponsors a child at his or her baptism or other such ceremony.

god-less (god´lis) *adj.* Not recognizing a god.

god-ly (god´l) *adj.* Filled with love for God.

god-mother (god´muth r) *n.* A woman who sponsors a child at his or her baptism or other such ceremony.

god-send (god´send´) *n.* Something received unexpectedly that is needed or wanted.

goget-ter (g´get´r) *n.* An enterprising, aggressive person.

gog-gle (gog´l) *n. pl.* **-gles** Spectacles or eyeglasses to protect the eyes against dust, wind, sparks, and other debris. *v.* To gaze or stare with bulging eyes.

go-ing (gō'ing) *n.* The act of moving, leaving, or departing; the condition of roads or ground that affects walking, riding, and other movement; a condition influencing activity or progress. **on** Actions or behavior, used to express disapproval.

goi-ter (goi'tr) *n., Pathol.* Any abnormal enlargement of the thyroid gland, visible as a swelling in the front of the neck.

gold (gld) *n.* A soft, yellow, metallic element that is highly ductile and resistant to oxidation; used especially in coins and jewelry; a precious metal; a bright, vivid yellow; money; the element symbolized by Au.

golden anniversary *n.* The 50th anniversary.

gold mine *n.* A mine which produces gold ore; any source of great riches or profit.

gold standard *n.* The monetary system based on gold of a specified weight and fineness as the unit of value and exchange.

golf (golf) *n.* A game played outdoors with a hard ball and various clubs, on a grassy course with 9 or 18 holes. **golf** *v.* **golfer** *n.*

gon-ad (g'nad) *n., Anat.* The male or female sex gland where the reproductive cells develop; an ovary or testis. **gonadal** *adj.* **gonadial** *adj.* **-adic** *adj.*

gon-do-la (gon'do la) *n.* A long, narrow, flat-bottomed boat propelled by a sin-gle oar and used on the canals of Venice.

gone (gon) *adj.* Past; bygone; dead; beyond hope; marked by faintness or weakness.

gon-fa-lon (gon'fa lon) *n.* A banner hung from a crosspiece and cut so as to end in streamers.

gong (gong) *n.* A heavy metal disk which produces a deep resonant tone when struck.

gon-o-coc-cus (gon'o kok'us) *n. pl.* **-cocci** The bacterium which causes gonorrhea.

gon-or-rhe-a (gon'o r'a) *n., Pathol.* A contagious venereal infection trans-

mitted chiefly by sexual intercourse. **gonorrheal** *adj.*

goo-ber (gō'br) *n., Regional* A peanut.

good (ged) *adj.* Having desirable or favorable qualities or characteristics; morally excellent; virtuous; well-behaved; tractable; proper; excellent in degree or quality; unspoiled; fresh; healthy; striking or attractive. **goods** Merchandise or wares; personal belongings; cloth; fabric. **good** Forever; permanently. **better** *adj.* **best** *adj.*

goodby or goodbye (ged'b') *interj.* Used to express farewell. *n.* A farewell; a parting word; an expression of farewell. *adj.* Final.

goodhu-mored *adj.* Having a cheerful temper or mood; amiable. -**ly** *adv.*

goodna-tured (ged'n'chrd) *adj.* Having an easy going and pleasant disposition.

good will *n.* A desire for the well-being of others; the pleasant feeling or relationship between a business and its customers.

good-y (ged') *n. pl.* -**ies** Something that is good to eat; a prissy person.

goof (gōf) *n. Slang* A stupid or dullwitted person; a mistake. *v.* To blunder; to make a mistake.

gook (gek) *n. Slang* A slimy, sludgy, or dirty substance.

goon (gōn) *n. Slang* A thug or hoodlum hired to intimidate or injure someone; a person hired to break strikes; a stupid person.

goose bumps *n. pl.* A prickling sensation of the skin caused by fear or cold, also known as goose pimples and goose skin.

gore (gr) *v.* To stab or pierce. *n.* Blood that has been shed; a triangular or tapering piece of cloth as in a sail or skirt.

gorge (gorj) *n.* A deep, narrow ravine; deep or violent disgust. *v.* To eat or devour something greedily. **gorger** *n.*

gor-geous (gor'jus) *adj.* Beautiful; dazzling; extremely beautiful; magnificent. **gorgeously** *adv.* -**ness** *n.*

go-ril-la (go ril'a) *n.* A large African jungle ape, having a massive, stocky body, long arms, and tusklike canine teeth.

go-ry (gr') *adj.* Covered or stained with

blood; resembling gore; marked by much bloodshed or violence.

gos-ling (goz´ling) n. A young goose.

gos-pel or **Gos-pel** (gos´pel) n. The teachings of Christ and the apostles; any information which is accepted as unquestionably true; any of the first four books of the New Testament

gos-sa-mer (gos´a mr) n. The fine film or strands of a spider's web floating in the air; anything sheer, delicate, light, or flimsy.

gos-sip (gos´ip) n. Idle, often malicious talk; a person who spreads sensational or intimate facts. v. To spread or engage in gossip. **gossiper** n. **-y** adj.

got v. Past tense of get.

gouge (gouj) n. A chisel with a scoop-shaped blade used for woodcarving; a groove or hole made with or as if with a gouge v. To make a hole or groove with a gouge; to cheat, as to charge exorbitant prices.

gou-lash (gö´läsh) n. A stew made from beef or veal and vegetables seasoned chiefly with paprika.

gourd (grd) n. A vine fruit related to the pumpkin, squash, and cucumber and bearing inedible fruit with a hard rind; the dried, hollowed-out shell can be used as a drinking utensil.

gour-mand (ger´mand) n. A person who takes excessive pleasure in eating.

gour-met (ger´m) n. Someone who appreciates and understands fine food and drink.

gout (gout) n., Pathol. A disease caused by a defect in metabolism and characterized by painful inflammation of the joints.

gov-ern (guv´rn) v. To guide, rule, or control by right or authority; to control or guide the action of something; to restrain. **-able** adj. **governance** n.

gov-ern-ess (guv´r nis) n. A woman employed in a private household to train and instruct children.

gov-ern-ment (guv´rn ment) n. The authoritative administration of public policy and affairs of a nation, state or city; the system or policy by which a political unit is governed; any governed territory, district, or area.

gov-er-nor (guv´r nr) n. One who governs, as the elected chief executive of any state in the United States; an official appointed to exercise political authority over a territory. Mech. A device that automatically controls the speed of a machine.

govt abbr. Government.

gown (goun) n. A woman's dress, especially for a formal affair; any long, loose-fitting garment; a robe worn by certain officials, scholars, and clergymen.

grab (grab) v. To snatch or take suddenly; to take possession of by force or by dishonest means. Slang To capture the attention of someone or something.

grab bag n. A bag or container full of miscellaneous unidentified articles from which one may draw an object at random.

gra-ben (grä´ben) n., Geol. An elongated depression in the earth, caused by the downward faulting of a portion of the earth's crust.

grace (grs) n. Seemingly effortless beauty, ease, and charm of movement, proportion, or form; a charming quality or characteristic; an extension of time that is granted after a set date, as for paying a debt. **graceful** adj. **gracefully** adv. **gracefulness** n.

gra-cious (gr´shus) adj. Marked by having or showing kindness and courtesy; full of compassion; merciful. **graciously** adv.

grack-le (grak´l) n. Any of various New World blackbirds having long tails and iridescent blackish plumage.

grade (grd) n. A step or degree in a process or series; a group or category; a level of progress in school, usually constituting a year's work; a letter or number indicating a level of achievement in school work; the degree to which something slopes, as a road, track or other surface. Milit. Rank or rating.

grade school n. Elementary school, usually from kindergarten to grade 6 or grade 8.

gra-di-ent (gr´d ent) n. A slope or degree of inclination. Phys. A rate of change in variable factors, as temperature or pressure.

grad-u-al (graj´ əl) adj. Moving or changing slowly by degrees; not steep or abrupt. **-ly** adv. **gradualness** n.

grad-u-ate (graj´ō t´) v. To receive or be granted an academic diploma or degree upon completion of a course of study; to divide into categories, grades or steps. n. A person who holds an academic degree; a container or beaker marked in units or degrees, used for measuring liquids.

graduate student n. A student who has received a college degree and who is working toward an advanced or higher degree.

grad-u-a-tion (graj´ō ´shan) n. The state of graduating; a commencement ceremony; issuing of diplomas or degrees.

graf-fi-to (graf´t) n. pl. **graffiti** An inscription or drawing made on a public wall, subway train, rock, or any other surface.

graft (graft) v. To insert a shoot from a plant into another living plant so that the two will grow together as a single plant. Surg. To transplant a piece of tissue or an organ. n. Living tissue or skin used to replace damaged or destroyed tissue or skin; the act of acquiring or getting personal profit or advantage by dishonest or unfair means through one's public position.

graham flour n. Whole wheat flour.

grail (grl) n. The legendary cup used by Christ at the Last Supper; also called the Holy Grail.

grain (grn) n. A small, hard seed or kernel of cereal, wheat, or oats; the seeds or fruits of such plants as a group; a very small amount; a small, hard particle, as a grain of sand; the side of a piece of leather from which the hair has been removed; the characteristic markings or pattern of this side; texture; basic nature. **against the grain.** Contrary to one's inclinations or temperament. **grainer** n.

grain alcohol n. Ethanol.

grain elevator n. A building used to store grain.

grain-y (gr´n) adj. Having a granular texture; resembling the grain of wood.

gram (gram) n. A metric unit of mass and weight equal to 1/1000 kilogram and nearly equal to one cubic centimeter of water at its maximum density.

gram-mar (gram´r) n. The study and description of the classes of words, their relations to each other, and their arrangement into sentences; the inflectional and syntactic rules of a language. **-ian** n. **grammatical** adj. **grammatically** adv.

gran-a-ry (gr´na r) n. pl. **ries** A building for storing threshed grain; an area or region where grain grows in abundance.

grand (grand) adj. Large in size, extent, or scope; magnificent; of high rank or great importance; lofty; admirable; main or principal; highly satisfactory; excellent. Slang A thousand dollars.

grand-child (gran´chld´) n. The child of one's son or daughter.

grand-dad (gran´dad) n. The father of one's mother or father.

grand-daughter (gran´do´tr) n. The daughter of one's son or daughter.

gran-deur (gran´jer) n. The quality or condition of being grand; splendor; magnificence.

grand-fa-ther (gran´fä´thr) n. The father of one's father or mother; an ancestor.

gran-dil-o-quent (gran dil´o kwens) adj. Speaking in or characterized by a pompous or bombastic style.

gran-di-ose (gran´d s´) adj. Impressive and grand; pretentiously pompous; bombastic. **-ly** adv. **grandiosity** n.

grand mal (gran´mal´) n., Pathol. A form of epilepsy characterized by severe convulsions and loss of consciousness.

grand-moth-er (gran´muth´r) n. The mother of one's father or mother; a female ancestor.

grand opera n. A form of opera having a serious and complex plot with music the complete text set to music.

grand-par-ent (gran´pâr´ent) n. A parent of one's mother or father.

grand-son (gran´sun´) n. A son of one's son or daughter.

grand-stand (gran´stand´) n. A raised stand of seats, usually roofed, for spectators at a race track or sports event.

gran·ite (gran´it) n. A hard, coarse-grained igneous rock composed chiefly of quartz, mica, and feldspar, which is used for building material and in sculpture.

gran·ite·ware (gran´it wâr´) n. Ironware utensils coated with hard enamel.

gran·ny or **gran·nie** (gran´) n. A grandmother; an old woman; a fussy person.

grant (grant) v. To allow; to consent to; to admit something as being the truth; in law, to transfer property by a deed. n. That which is granted. **grantee** n. -er n. **grantor** n.

gran·u·lar (gran´ lr) adj. Composed or seeming to be composed or containing grains or granules. **granularity** n.

gran·u·late (gran´ lt´) v. To make or form into granules or crystals; to become or cause to become rough and grainy. -tion n.

gran·ule (gran´l) n. A very small grain or particle.

grape (grp) n. Any of numerous woody vines bearing clusters of smooth-skinned, juicy, edible berries, having a dark purplish blue, red, or green color, eaten raw or dried and used in making wine.

grape·fruit (grp´frōt´) n. A tropical, large, round citrus fruit with a pale yellow rind and tart, juicy pulp; the tree bearing this fruit.

grape sugar n. Dextrose.

grape·vine (grp´vn´) n. A climbing vine that produces grapes; a secret or informal means of transmitting information or rumor from person to person.

graph (graf) n. A diagram representing the relationship between sets of things.

graph·ic or **graph·i·cal** (graf´ik) adj. Describing in full detail; of or pertaining to drawings or blueprints, as in architecture.

graph·ite (graf´t) n. A soft black form of carbon having a metallic luster and slippery texture, used in lead pencils, lubricants, paints, and coatings. **graphitic** adj.

graph·ol·o·gy (gra fol´o j) n. The study of handwriting for the purpose of analyzing a person's character or personality.

grap·nel (grap´nel) n. A small anchor with several flukes at the end.

grap·ple (grap´l) n. An instrument with iron claws used to fasten an enemy ship alongside for boarding. v. To struggle or contend with; to fasten, seize or drag as with a grapple.

grasp (grasp) v. To seize and grip firmly; to comprehend; to understand. n. The power to seize and hold. **able** adj.

grasp·ing (gras´ping) adj. Urgently desiring material possessions; greedy. **graspingly** adv. **graspingness** n.

grass (gras) n. Any of numerous plants having narrow leaves and jointed stems; the ground on which grass is growing. Slang Marijuana.

grate (grt) v. To reduce, shred or pulverize by rubbing against a rough or sharp surface; to make or cause to make a harsh sound. n. A rasping noise. n. A framework or bars placed over a window or other opening; an iron frame to hold burning fuel in a fireplace or furnace. -er n. **grating** adj.

grate·ful (grte ful) adj. Thankful or appreciative for benefits or kindnesses; expressing gratitude. **gratefully** adv.

grat·i·fy (grat´i f´) v. To give pleasure or satisfaction to; to fulfill the desires of; to indulge. **gratification** n.

grat·ing (gr´ting) n. A grate.

grat·is (grat´is) adv. & adj. Without requiring payment; free.

grat·i·tude (grat´i tōd´) n. The state of appreciation and gratefulness; thankfulness.

gra·tu·i·tous (gra tō´i tus) adj. Given or obtained without payment; unjustified; unwarranted. **gratuitously** adv.

gra·tu·i·ty (gra tō´i t) n. pl. -ies A gift, as money, given in return for a service rendered; a tip.

gra·va·men (gra v´men) n. pl. -mens or -mina In law, the part of an accusation or charge weighing most heavily against the accused.

grave (grv) n. A burial place for a dead body, usually an excavation in the earth. adj. Very serious or important in nature; filled with danger; critical. v. To sculpt or carve; to engrave. Mus. Solemn and slow.

grav-el (grav'el) n. Loose rock fragments often with sand. *Pathol.* The deposit of sand-like crystals that form in the kidneys; also known as kidney stones.

grave-stone (grv'stn') n. A stone that marks a grave; a tombstone.

grave-yard (grv'yärd') n. An area set aside as a burial place; a cemetery.

graveyard shift n. Slang A work shift that usually begins at midnight.

gra-vim-e-ter (gra vim'i tr) n. An implement for determining specific gravity.

grav-i-tate (grav'i tt') v. To be drawn as if by an irresistible force; to sink or settle to a lower level.

grav-i-ta-tion (grav'i t'shan) n. *Physics* The force or attraction any two bodies exert towards each other. **gravitational** adj. **gravitative** adj.

grav-i-ty (grav'i t) n. pl. **-ies** The gravitational force manifested by the tendency of material bodies to fall toward the center of the earth; gravitation in general; weight; importance; seriousness.

gra-vy (gr'v) n. pl. **-ies** The juices exuded by cooking meat; a sauce made by seasoning and thickening these juices. Slang Money or profit which is easily acquired.

gray or **grey** (gr) A neutral color between black and white; gloomy; dismal; having gray hair; characteristic of old age. **-ish** adj.

gray-beard (gr'brd') n. Slang An old man.

gray matter n. The grayish-brown nerve tissue of the spinal cord and brain, consisting mainly of nerve cells and fibers; brains.

graze (grz) v. To feed upon growing grasses or herbage; to put livestock to feed on grass or pasturage; to brush against lightly in passing; to abrade or scrape slightly.

gra-zier (gr'zhr) n. One who grazes cattle.

grease (grs) n. Melted or soft animal fat; any thick fatty or oily substance, as a lubricant. v. To lubricate or coat with grease. **greasiness** n. **greasy** adj.

grease paint n. Makeup used for theatre performances.

great (grt) adj. Very large in size or volume; prolonged induration or extent; more than ordinary; considerable; remarkable; impressive; eminent; renowned; very good or first-rate; a generation removed from a relative. **greatly** adv. **greatness** n.

great-heart-ed (grt'här'tid) adj. Noble or generous in spirit; magnanimous.

great seal n. The chief seal of a government.

grebe (grb) n. Any of various swimming and diving birds having partially webbed feet, very short tails, and a pointed bill.

greed (grd) n. Selfish desire to acquire more than one needs or deserves.

green (grn) adj. Of the color between yellow and blue in the spectrum; not fully matured or developed; lacking in skill or experience. A grassy plot or lawn, especially an area of closely mowed grass at the end of a golf fairway. **greenish** adj. **greenness** n.

green-back (grn'bak') n. A U.S. legal tender currency note.

green-er-y (gr'ne r) n. pl. **-ies** Green foliage or plants.

green thumb n. A special skill for making plants thrive.

greet (grt) v. To address someone in a friendly way; to welcome; to meet or receive in a specified manner. **-er** n.

greet-ing (gr'ting) n. A word of salutation on meeting.

gre-gar-i-ous (gri gâr'us) adj. Habitually associating with others as in groups, flocks, or herds; enjoying the company of others; sociable. **-ously** adv. **gregariousness** n.

grem-lin (grem'lin) n. A mischievous elf said to cause mechanical trouble in airplanes.

gre-nade (gri nd') n. A small explosive device detonated by a fuse and thrown by hand or projected from a rifle.

gren-a-dine (gren'a dn') n. A syrup made from pomegranates or red currants and used as a flavoring in mixed drinks.

grew v. Past tense of grow.

grey (gr) n. & adj. Variation of gray.

grey-hound (gr'hound') n. One of a

breed of slender, swift running dogs with long legs.

grid (grid) n. An arrangement of regularly spaced bars; the system of intersecting parallel lines that divide maps, charts, and photographs, used as a reference for locating points.

grid-dle (grid´l) n. A flat pan used for cooking.

grid-i-ron (grid´īrn) n. A metal frame work used for broiling meat, fish, and other foods; a football field.

grief (grf) n. Deep sadness or mental distress caused by a loss, remorse, or bereavement.

griev-ance (gr´vans) n. A real or imagined wrong which is regarded as cause for complaint or resentment; a complaint of unfair treatment.

grieve (grv) v. To cause or feel grief or sorrow.

griev-ous (gr´vus) adj. Causing grief, sorrow, anguish, or pain; causing physical suffering.

grif-fin or **grif-fon** (grif´on) n. In Greek mythology, a fabulous beast with a lion's body, an eagle's head, and wings.

grill (gril) n. A cooking utensil made from parallel metal bars; a gridiron; food cooked on a grill; a restaurant where grilled foods are a specialty. v. To broil on a grill.

grille or **grill** (gril) n. A grating with open metalwork used as a decorative screen or room divider.

grim (grim) adj. Stern or forbidding in appearance or character; unyielding; relentless; grisly; gloomy; dismal. **-ly** adv. **grimness** n.

grim-ace (grim´as) n. A facial expression of pain, disgust, or disapproval.

grime (grm) n. Dirt, especially soot clinging to or coating a surface.

grin (grin) v. To smile broadly. **grin** n.

grind (grnd) v. To reduce to fine particles; to sharpen, polish, or shape by friction; to press or rub together; to work or study hard.

grinders (grn´drs) n. , pl. Slang The teeth.

grind-stone (grnd´stn´) n. A flat, circular stone which revolves on an axle and is used for polishing, sharpening, or grinding.

grip (grip) n. A firm hold; a grasp; the ability to seize or maintain a hold.

gripe (grp) v. To cause sharp pain or cramps in the bowels; to anger; to annoy; to complain.

grippe (grip) n. Influenza. **grippy** adj.

gris-ly (griz´l) adj. Ghastly; gruesome.

grist (grist) n. Grain that is to be ground; a batch of such grain.

gris-tle (gris´l) n. Cartilage of meat.

grist-mill n. A mill for grinding grain.

grit (grit) n. Small, rough granules, as of sand or stone; having great courage and fortitude. v. To clamp the teeth together. **gritty** adj.

grits (grits) n. pl. Coarsely ground hominy; coarse meal; eaten primarily in the southern states of the U.S.

griz-zle (griz´l) v. To become or cause to become gray.

grizzly bear n. A large, grayish bear of western North America. **grizzlies** pl., n., Slang Grizzly bears.

groan (grn) n. To utter a deep, prolonged sound of or as of disapproval or pain. **groan** n. **groaningly** adv.

groat (grt) n. A former British coin worth four pence; any grain without its hull; a tiny sum.

gro-cer (gr´sr) n. A storekeeper who deals in foodstuffs and various household supplies.

gro-cer-y (gr´ser´) n. pl. -ies A store in which foodstuffs and household staples are sold.

grog (grog) n. Any alcoholic liquor, especially rum, mixed with water.

grog-gy (grog´) adj. Dazed, weak, or not fully conscious, as from a blow or exhaustion; drunk. **-gily** adv. **-giness** n.

groin (groin) n., Anat. The crease or fold where the thigh meets the abdomen. Archit. The curved edge of a building formed by two intersecting vaults.

grom-met (grom´it) n. A reinforcing eyelet through which a rope, cord, or fastening may be passed. Naut. A ring of rope or metal used to secure the edge of a sail.

groom (grm) n. A male person hired to tend horses; a stableman; a bridegroom. v. To make neat in appearance;

to prepare for a particular position, as for a political office.

groove (gröv) n. A long, narrow channel or indentation; a fixed, settled habit or routine; a rut. **groove** v.

groovy (grö´v) adj. Slang Wonderful; delightful.

grope (grp) v. To feel about with or as with the hands, as in the dark; to look for uncertainly or blindly. **-ingly** adv.

gros-beck (grs´bk) n. Any of several colorful birds related to the finch, with a stout, short beak.

gros-grain (gr´grn´) n. A heavy, horizontally corded silk or rayon fabric, woven as a ribbon.

gross (grs) adj. Exclusive of deductions; of or relating to the total amount received; excessively large or fat; lacking refinement.

gro-tesque (gr tesk´) adj. Distorted, incongruous or ludicrous in appearance or style; bizarre; outlandish. **grotesqueness** n. **grotesquely** adv.

grot-to (grot´) n. pl. **-toes** or **-tos** A cave or cave-like structure.

grouch (grouch) n. An habitually irritable or complaining person. **-ily** adv.

ground (grand) n. The surface of the earth; soil sand, and other natural material at or near the earth's surface; the connecting of an electric current to the earth through a conductor.

ground hog n. A woodchuck.

ground-less (ground´lis) adj. Without foundation or basis.

ground rule n. A basic rule; the rule in sports that modifies play on a particular field, course, or court.

ground zero n. The point on the ground vertically beneath or above the point of detonation of an atomic bomb.

group (grp) n. A collection or assemblage of people, objects, or things having something in common.

grou-per (gr´pr) n. A large fish related to the seabass.

grouse (grous) n. pl. **grouse** Any of a family of game birds characterized by mottled, brownish plumage and rounded bodies. To complain; to grumble.

grout (grout) n. A material used to fill cracks in masonry or spaces between tiles. **grout** v. **grouter** n.

grove (grv) n. A small group of trees, lacking undergrowth.

grov-el (gruv´l) v. To lie or crawl face downward, as in fear; to act with abject humility. **groveler** n. **grovellingly** adv.

grow (gr) v. To increase in size, develop, and reach maturity; to expand; to increase; to come into existence. **grow on;** To become increasingly acceptable, necessary, or pleasing to. **-er** n.

growl (groul) v. To utter a deep, guttural, threatening sound, as that made by a hostile or agitated animal. **growl** n.

grown-up (grn´up) n. A mature adult.

growth (grth) n. The act or process of growing; a gradual increase in size or amount. Pathol. An abnormal formation of bodily tissue, as a tumor.

grub (grub) v. To dig up by the roots; to lead a dreary existence; to drudge. n. The thick, worm-like larva of certain insects, as of the June beetle. Slang Food; to scrounge.

grub-by (grub´) adj. Sloppy, unkempt. **grubbily** adv. **grubbiness** n.

grudge (gruj) n. A feeling of ill will, rancor, or deep resentment. v. To be displeased, resentful, or envious of the possessions or good fortune of another person. **grudger** n. **grudgingly** adv.

gru-el (grö´el) n. A thin liquid made by boiling meal in water or milk.

gru-el-ing or **gru-el-ling** (grö´e ling) adj. Extremely tiring; exhausting.

grue-some (grö´som) adj. Causing horror or fright. **-ly** adv. **gruesomeness** n.

gruff (gruf) adj. Brusque and rough in manner; harsh in sound; hoarse.

grum-ble (grum´bl) v. To complain in low, throaty sounds; to growl. **grumble** n. **grumbler** n. **grumbly** adj.

grump-y (grum´p) adj. Irritable and moody; ill tempered.

grun-gy (gren.j) adj. Slang Dirty, rundown, or inferior in condition or appearance.

grunt (grunt) n. The deep, guttural sound of a hog. A discontented grumble used to show dissatisfaction.

gua-no (gwä´n) n. The excrement of sea birds, used as a fertilizer.

guar-an-tee (gar´an t´) n. The promise or assurance of the durability or quality of a product; something held or given as a pledge or security. v. To assume responsibility for the default or debt of; to certify; to vouch for.

guar-an-tor (gar´an tor´) n. One who gives a guarantee or guaranty.

guar-an-ty (gar´an t´) n. pl. A pledge or promise to be responsible for the debt, duty, or contract of another person in case of default; something that guarantees.

guard (gärd) v. To watch over or shield from danger or harm; to keep watch as to prevent escape, violence, or indiscretion. n. A defensive position, as in boxing or fencing; in football, one of two linesmen on either side of the center; in basketball, one of the two players stationed near the middle of the court; a device or piece of equipment that protects against damage, loss, or harm.

guards-man (gärdz´man) n. A member of the U.S. National Guard.

gua-va (gwä´va) n. A tree or shrub of the myrtle family bearing small, pearshaped, edible, yellow-skinned fruit.

gub-ba (gub ba) n. Slang The neck area, especially of children and babies.

gu-ber-na-to-ri-al (gö´br natr´ al) adj. Of or pertaining to a governor.

guern-sey (gern´z) n. pl. -seys A breed of brown and white dairy cattle.

guess (ges) v. To make a judgment or form an opinion on uncertain or incomplete knowledge; to suppose; to believe.

guest (gest) n. One who is the recipient of hospitality from another; a customer who pays for lodging.

guff (guf) n. Slang Nonsense or empty talk.

guf-faw (gu fo´) n. A loud burst of laughter.

guid-ance (gd´ans) n. The act, process, or result of guiding.

guide (gd) n. One who leads or directs another, as in a course of action; a person employed to conduct others on trips through museums and sightseeing tours.

guided missile n., Mil. An unmanned missile that can be controlled by radio signals while in flight.

guide-line (gd ln) n. Any suggestion, statement, or outline of policy or procedure to be used.

guild (gild) n. An association of persons of the same trade or occupation.

guilt (gilt) n. The condition or fact of having committed a crime or wrong doing; the feeling of responsibility for having done something wrong.

guin-ea (gin´) n. Formerly, a British gold coin worth one pound and five pence.

gui-tar (gi tor´) n. A musical instrument with six strings, played by plucking or strumming the strings with a pick or the fingers.

gull (gul) n. A long-winged, web-footed sea bird, usually white and gray with a hooked upper mandible. n. A gullible person; one who is easily tricked.

gul-let (gul´it) n., Pathol. The passage from the mouth to the stomach; esophagus; the throat; the pharynx; the throat or something that resembling it; a narrow valley.

gul-li-ble (gul´i bl) adj. Easily cheated or fooled.

gul-ly (gul´) n. pl. -ies A ditch or channel cut in the earth by running water; a ravine; a ditch.

gulp (gulp) n. The act of swallowing a large mouthful of some form of liquid.

gum (gum) n. The tissue which covers the base of the teeth and parts of the jaw in which the teeth are set; chewing gum. v. A sticky substance which comes from certain plants and trees and thickens when exposed to air; to become sticky or clogged with gummy material; to stick together with a gumlike substance; **gum up** to ruin or spoil.

gump-tion (gump´shan) n. Slang Boldness; initiative; enterprise.

gun-fight (gun´ft) n. A fight using guns.

gung ho adj. Slang Extremely enthusiastic.

gunk (gungk) n. A greasy, sticky, obnoxious material, having an odor about it.

gun-pow-der (gun´pou´dr) n. An explosive powder used in blasting, fireworks, and guns.

gunshy (gun´sh) adj. Afraid of loud noises, as gunfire; wary.

gun-wale *or* **gun-nel** (gun´l) *n.* The upper edge of a ship's side.

gup-py (gup´ē) *n. pl.* **-ies** A small, tropical freshwater fish, popular in home aquariums.

gu-ru (gŏ´rō) *n.* A spiritual teacher of Hinduism.

gust (gust) *n.* A blast of wind; a sudden rush of water, sound, or fire.

gus-ta-to-ry (gus´ta t´r) *adj.* Of or pertaining to the sense of taste or the act of tasting.

gut (gut) *n.* The intestinal canal from the stomach to the anus; an intestine; the entrails. *v.* To plunder; to destroy; to remove.

gut-less (gut´lis) *adj. Slang* Lacking courage.

guts-y (guts´) *n. Slang* Courageous; bold; challenging; having nerve to do something.

gut-ta-per-cha (get e per che) *n.* The milky juice of various Malaysian trees used for electrical inulation and in dentistry.

gut-ter (gut´r) *n.* A ditch or curb along the side or middle of the road to carry off water; a channel at the eaves or on the roof of a building for drainage of rain water. *Slang* To play or come from the gutter; a derogatory usage

gut-tur-al (gut´r al) *adj.* Pertaining to the throat; having a harsh, muffled, or grating quality. **guttural** *n.* **-ally** *adv.*

guz-zle (guz´l) *n.* To drink excessively or quickly; to gulp down. To drink excessively

gym (jim) *n. Informal* A gymnasium.

gym-na-si-um (jim n´z um) *n. pl.* **-ums** *or* **-sia** A room or building equipped for indoor sports; a building for athletic exercises or contests.

gym-nast (jim´nast) *n.* A person who teaches or practices gymnastics.

gym-nas-tics (jim nas´tiks) *n. pl.* A sport or physical exercises, especially those performed with special apparatus in a gym. **gymnast** *n.* **gymnastic** *adj.*

gy-ne-col-o-gist (gne kol´o jist) *n.* A person who specializes in the study and field of gynecology.

gy-ne-col-o-gy (g´ne kol´o j) *n.* The branch of medicine dealing with the female reproductive organs, female

diseases, and female organs. **gynecological** *adj.* **gynecologic** *adj.* **-gist** *n.*

gyp (jip) *v. Informal* To swindle, cheat, or defraud. *n.* A fraud. **gypper** *n.*

gyp-sum (jip´sum) *n.* A mineral, hydrous calcium sulfate, used to make plaster of Paris, gypsum plaster, and plasterboard.

gyp-sy (jip´s) *n.* A wanderer; a person who leads a vagrant life style; a nomadic.

gypsy moth *n.* A moth whose larvae defoiates trees.

gy-rate (j´rt) *v.* To rotate , revolve or move around a fixed point or axis; to move or turn in a spiral motion. **gyrator** *n.* **gyratory** *adj.*

gy-ro-com-pass (j´r kum´pas) *n.* A compass that has a motor driven gyroscope so mounted that its axis of rotation maintains a constant position with reference to the true or geographic north.

gyro horizon *n.* A flight instrument containing a gyroscope which shows any deviation of the plane from a flight position parallel to the horizon.

gy-ro-plane (ji´ro pln) *n.* Any aircraft, such as a helicopter that has a windmill wings that rotate about an vertical axis.

gy-ro-scope (j´ro skp´) *n.* A spinning wheel or disk whose spin axis maintains its angular orientation when not subjected to external torques.

gy-ro-sta-bi-liz-er (jro st´bi lzr)*n.* Device consisting of a rotating gyroscope and used to stabilize a ship by counteracting the rolling motion cause by the ocean.

gy-ro-stat (jro stat) *n.* A modification of the gyroscope, consisting of a rotat-ing wheel pivoted within a rigid case, used to illustrate the dynamics of peo-ple.

gyve (gv) *n.* To chain; to shackle, especially the legs.

H

H, h (ch) The eighth letter of the English alphabet.

ha-be-as cor-pus (hb *askorpus*) *n.* In law, a writ commanding a person to appear before a judge or court for the purpose of releasing that person from

hab-er-dash-er (habr dashr) *n.* A person who deals in men's clothing and men's furnishings.

hab-it (habit) *n.* Involuntary pattern of behavior acquired by frequent repetition; manner of conducting oneself; an addiction.

hab-it-a-ble (habi ta bel) *adj.* Suitable for habitation. **habitability** *n.*

hab-i-tat (habi tat) *n.* The region in which an animal or plant lives or grows; the place of residence of a person or group.

hab-i-ta-tion (habi tshan) *n.* A place of residence.

hab-it-form-ing (habit for-mng) *adj.* Producing physiological addiction.

ha-ci-en-da (häs enda) *n.* A large estate or ranch in Spanish-speaking countries; the main building of a hacienda.

hack (hak) *v.* To cut with repeated irregular blows; to manage successfully. *n.* A tool used for hacking; a rough, dry cough; a taxi driver.

had-dock (hadok) *n.* A food fish that is usually smaller than the related cod and is found on both sides of the Atlantic.

had-n't (hadnt) Had not.

haft (haft) *n.* A handle of a weapon or tool.

hag (hag) *n.* A malicious, ugly old woman; a witch. **haggish** *adj.*

hag-gard (hagrd) *n.* A worn-out, exhausted, and gaunt look, as from hunger or fatigue.

hag-gle (hagl) *v.* To argue or bargain on price or terms. **haggler** *n.*

hai-ku (hkö) *n.* An unrhymed Japanese verse form with three short lines.

hail (hl) *n.* Precipitation of small, hard lumps of ice and snow; a hailstone; an exclamation, greeting, acclamation; *v.* To pour down as hail; to call loudly in greeting or welcome; to shout with enthusiasm; to signal in order to draw the attention of.

hail-stone (hlstn) *n.* A hard pellet of frozen snow & ice.

hair (hâr) *n.* One of the pigmented filaments that grow from the skin of most mammals; a covering of such structures, as on the human head and on the skin; a slender margin.

hair--raising (hârrzing) *adj.* Causing fear or horror. **hairraiser** *n.*

hake (hk) *n.* A marine food fish related to the cod.

hal-cy-on (hals on) *adj.* Calm and tranquil; peaceful; prosperous.

hale (hl) *adj.* Healthy and robust; free from defect. *v.* To compel to go.

half (haf) *n. pl.* **halves** One of two equal parts into which a thing is divisible; part of a thing approximately equal to the remainer; one of a pair. Being one of two equal parts; being partial or incomplete.

half step *n.*, *Mus.* A semitone.

halfwit (hafwit) *n.* A mentally disturbed person; a feeble-minded person.

hal-i-but (hal but) *n.* Any of the edible flat fishes of the North Atlantic or Pacific waters.

hal-ite (halt) *n.* Large crystal or masses of salt; saltrock.

hal-i-to-sis (hali tsis) *n.* A condition of having bad breath.

hal-le-lu-jah (hale löya) Used to express joy, praise, or jubilation.

hall-mark (holmärk) *n.* An official mark placed on gold and silver products to attest to their purity; an indication of quality or superiority; a distinctive characteristic.

hal-low (hal) *v.* To sanctify; to make holy; to honor.

ha-lo (hl) *n.* A ring of colored light surrounding the head; an aura of glory.

hal-o-gen (halo jen) *n.* Any of the group of nonmetallic elements including flourine, chlorine, bromine, iodine, and astatine.

hal-ter (holtr) *n.* A rope or strap for leading or tying an animal; a noose for hanging a person; a woman's upper garment tied behind the neck and across the back.

halve (hav) *v.* To divide into two equal parts; to lessen by half. *Informal* Share equally.

hal-yard (halyrd) *n.* A rope for hoisting or lowering a sail, flag, or yard.

ham (ham) *n.* The meat of a hog's thigh; the back of the knee or thigh.

ham-let (hamlit) *n.* A small rural village or town.

ham-mock (hamok) *n.* A hanging bed or couch of fabric or heavy netting, suspended from supports at each end.

ham-per (hampr) *v.* To interfere with movement or progress of. *n.* A large, usually covered, receptacle used to store dirty laundry.

ham-string (hamstring) *n.* Either of two tendons located at the back of the human knee; the large tendon at the back of the hock of four-footed animals. *v.* To cripple by cutting the hamstring; to frustrate.

hand (hand) *n.* The part of the arm below the wrist, consisting of the palm, four fingers and a thumb; a unit of measure, four inches, used especially to state the height of a horse; a pointer on a dial, as of a clock, meter, or gauge; the cards dealt to or held by a player in one round of a game; a manual laborer, worker, or employee. *v.* To give, offer, or transmit with the hand; direct with the hands.

hand-ball (handbol) *n.* A court game in which the players bat a small rubber ball against the wall with their hands.

hand-book (handbek) *n.* A small guide or reference book giving information or instructions.

hand-i-cap (hand kap) *n.* A race or contest in which advantages or penalties are given to individual contestants to equalize the odds; any disadvantage that makes achievement unusually difficult; physical disability; an obstacle. *v.* To give a handicap to.

han-dle (handl) *v.* To touch, pick up, or hold with the hands; to represent; to trade or deal in. **handler** *n.*

hand-made *adj.* Made by hand or by a hand process.

hand-maid *or* **hand-maid-en** *n.* A female maid or personal servant.

hand-out (handout) *n.* Free food, clothing, or cash given to the needy; a folder distributed free of charge; a flyer; a press release for publicity.

hand-pick (handpik) *v.* To select with care.

hand-set (handset) *n.* A telephone receiver and transmitter combined in a single unit.

hand-shake (handshk) *n.* The act of

clasping hands by two people, as in greeting, agreement, or parting.

hand-work (handwerk) *n.* Work done by hand.

hand-writ-ing (handrting) *n.* Writing performed with the hand, especially cursive; the type of writing of a person. **wall** An omen of one's unpleasant fate.

handy-man (hand man) *n.* A person who does odd jobs.

hang (hang) *v.* To be attached to from above and unsupported from below; to fasten or be suspended so as to swing freely; to be put to death by hanging by the neck; to fasten or attach something as a picture to a wall. **hangout** To spend one's time in a particular place. **up** To end a telephone conversation by replacing the receiver on its cradle.

han-gar (hangr) *n.* A building for housing aircraft.

han-ger (hangr) *n.* A device from which something may be hung or on which something hangs.

hang-nail (hangnl) *n.* The small piece of skin that hangs loose from the side or root of a fingernail.

hangup *n. Slang* A psychological or emotional problem; an obstacle.

han-ker (hangkr) *v.* To have a yearning or craving for something. **hankerer** *n.*

Ha-nuk-kah *or* **Ha-nu-kah (hänu ka)** *n.* An eight-day Jewish holiday remembering the rededication of the Temple in Jerusalem.

hap-haz-ard (haphazrd) *adj.* Occurring by accident; happening by chance or at random; hit-or-miss.

hap-less *adj.* Unfortunate; unlucky. **haplessly** *adv.* **haplessness** *n.*

hap-pen (hapn) *v.* To occur or come to pass; to take place; to discover by chance; to turn up or appear by chance.

hap-pen-ing (hape ning) *n.* A spontaneous event or performance; an important event.

hap-py (hap) *adj.* Enjoying contentment and well-being; glad, joyous, satisfied or pleased. **happily** *adv.* **happiness** *n.*

happy--go--lucky (hap g luk) *adj.* Carefree and unconcerned.

ha-rangue (hä rang) *n.* A long, extravagant, speech; a lecture.

ha-rass (haras) *v.* To disturb or annoy

constantly; to torment persistently. **harassment** *n.* **harasser** *n.*

har-bin-ger (härbinjr) *n.* A person that initiates or pioneers a major change; something that foreshadows what is to come.

har-bor (härbr) *n.* A place of refuge or shelter; a bay or cove; an anchorage for ships. *v.* To provide shelter; to entertain, as a feeling or thought.

hard (härd) *adj.* Difficult to perform, endure, or comprehend; solid in texture or substance; resistant to cutting or penetration; containing salts which make lathering with soap difficult; high in alcoholic content.

hard-back *adj.* Text bound between hard covers as opposed to paper covers.

hard--boiled (härdboild) *adj.* Boiled or cooked in the shell to a hard or solid state.

hard copy *n.* In computer science, the printed information or data from a computer.

hard disk *n.* In computer science, magnetic storage consisting of a rigid disk of aluminum coated with a magnetic recording substance; contained within a removable cartridge or mounted in the hard disk of a microcomputer.

hard-en (härden) *v.* To make or become hard or harder; to make or become physically or mentally tough; to make or become callous or unsympathetic.

hard hat (härdhat) *n.* A protective head covering made of rigid material, worn by construction workers.

har-di-hood (härd hed) *n.* Resolute courage; audacious boldness; vitality; vigor.

hard-ly (härdl) *adj.* *Slang* Very little; almost certainly not. *adv.* Forcefully; painfully; barely.

hard--nosed *adj.* Stubborn; hardheaded; unyielding.

hard-ship (härdship) *n.* A painful, difficult condition.

har-dy (härd) *adj.* Bold and robust; able to survive very unfavorable conditions, as extreme cold; daring.

hare (här) *n.* Various mammals related to the rabbits but having longer ears and legs.

hare-lip (härlip) *n.* A congenital deformity in which the upper lip is split.

hark (härk) *v.* To listen closely. **back** To retrace one's steps; to go back to earlier times.

har-le-quin (härle kwin) *n.* A jester; a clown. *adj.* Patterned with vividly colored diamond shapes.

harm (härm) *n.* Emotional or physical damage or injury. *v.* To cause harm to. **harmful** *adj.* **harmfully** *adv.*

harm-less (härmlis) *adj.* Without harm; not harmful.

har-mon-ic (här monik) *adj.* Relating to musical harmony; in harmony; concordant.

har-mon-i-ca (här mon ka) *n.* A small, rectangular musical instrument having a series of tuned metal reeds that vibrate with the player's breath.

har-mo-ni-ous (här mn us) *adj.* Pleasing to the ear; characterized by agreement and accord; having components agreeably combined. *-ly adv.*

har-mo-ny (härmo n) *n. pl.* *-ies* Complete agreement, as of feeling or opinion; an agreeable combination of component parts; pleasing sounds; a combination of musical tones into chords. *-ize v.* **harmonizer** *n.*

har-ness (härnis) *n.* The working gear, other than a yoke, of a horse or other draft animal. **harnesser** *n.*

harp (härp) *n.* A musical instrument having a triangular upright frame with strings plucked with the fingers. *v.* To play a harp. **harpon** To write or talk about excessively.

har-poon (här pön) *n.* A barbed spear used in hunting whales and large fish.

harp-si-chord (härpsi kord) *n.* A piano-like instrument whose strings are plucked by using quills or leather points.

har-py (härp) *n. pl.* *-pies* A vicious woman; a predatory person.

har-ri-dan (hari dan) *n.* A mean, hateful old woman.

har-ri-er (har r) *n.* A slender, narrow-winged hawk that preys on small animals; a hunting dog; a cross-country runner.

har-row (har) *n.* A tool with sharp teeth for breaking up and smoothing soil. *v.*

To pulverize soil with a harrow.

har-ry (har´y) *v.* To harass.

harsh (härsh) *adj.* Disagreeable; extremely severe. **harshly** *adv.* **-ness** *n.*

hart (härt) *n.* A fully grown male deer after it has passed its fifth year.

har-um--scar-um (hâr*u*m skar*u*m) *adj.* Reckless; irresponsible.

har-vest (härvist) *n.* The process or act of gathering a crop; the season or time for gathering crops. *v.* To reap; to obtain as if by gathering. **harvester** *n.*

hash (hash) *n.* A fried or baked mixture of chopped meat and potatoes. *v.* To chop up into small pieces. *Slang* To make a mess of; to discuss at great length.

hasp (hasp) *n.* A clasp or hinged fastener that passes over a staple and is secured by a pin, bolt, or padlock.

has-sle (hasl) *n. Slang* A quarrel or argument. **hassle** *v.*

has-sock (has*o*k) *n.* A firm upholstered cushion used as a footstool.

haste (hst) *n.* Speed; swiftness of motion or action; excessive eagerness to act. **haste** *v.* To hurry.

has-ten (hsen) *v.* To act or move with haste or speed.

hast-y (hst) *adj.* Rapid; swift; made or done with excessive speed.

hat (hat) *n.* A covering for the head with a crown and brim.

hatch (hach) *n.* A small opening or door, as in a ship's deck. *v.* To bring forth, as young from an egg; to devise; to produce; to contrive something.

hatch-et (hachit) *n.* A small ax with a short handle.

hatch-way (hachw) *n.* An opening covered by a hatch in a ship's deck.

hate (ht) *v.* To feel hostility or animosity toward; to dislike intensely. **hatefully** *adv.* **hatefulness** *n.* **hater** *n.*

hat-ter (hatr) *n.* A person who makes, sells, or repairs hats.

haugh-ty (hot) *adj.* Arrogantly proud; disdainful. **haughtily** *adv.* **-ness** *n.*

haul (hol) *v.* To pull or draw with force; to move or transport, as in a truck or cart. *n.* The distance over which someone travels or something is transported; an amount collected at one time.

haunch (honch) *n.* The hip; the buttock and upper thigh of a human or animal; the loin and leg of a four-footed animal.

haunt (hont) *v.* To appear to or visit as a ghost or spirit; to visit frequently; to linger in the mind. **haunting** *adj.*

hau-teur (h ter) *n.* A disdainful arrogance.

have (hav) *v.* To hold or own, as a possession or as property. **have to** Need to; must. **have had it** Suffered or endured all that one can tolerate.

hav-er-sack (havr sak) *n.* A bag for carrying supplies on a hike or march.

hav-oc (havok) *n.* Mass confusion; widespread destruction; devastation.

haw (ho) *n.* A hesitating sound made by a speaker who is groping for words. *v.* To hesitate in speaking; to falter in speaking.

haw-ser (hozr) *n.* A heavy cable or rope for towing or securing a ship.

hay (h) *n.* Alfalfa or grass that has been cut and dried for animal food.

hay fever *n.* An acute allergy to certain airborne pollens, marked by severe irritation of the upper respiratory tract and the eyes.

hay-wire (hwr) *adj. Slang* Broken; emotionally out of control; crazy.

haz-ard (hazrd) *n.* A risk; chance; an accident; an anger or source of danger. *v.* To take a chance on; to venture.

haze (hz) *n.* A fog-like suspension of dust, smoke, and vapor in the air; a confused or vague state of mind. *v.* To harass with disagreeable tasks. **-er** *n.*

ha-zel (hzel) *n.* A small tree or shrub bearing edible brown nuts with smooth shells; a light brown or yellowish brown.

haz-y (hz) *adj.* Lacking clarity; vague.

head (hed) *n.* The upper part of a human or animal body, containing the brain, the principal nerve centers, the eyes, ears, nose and mouth.

head-ache (hedk) *n.* A pain or ache in the head. *Slang* A bothersome problem.

head-first (hedferst) *adv.* With the head in a forward position; headlong.

head-ing (heding) *n.* A title or caption that acts as a front, beginning, or upper part of anything; the direction or

course of a ship or aircraft.

head-line (hedlin) n. A title, caption, or summarizing words of a newspaper story or article printed in large type. v. To provide with a headline; to serve as the star performer. **headliner** n.

head-long (hedlong) adv. Headfirst; not having deliberate. **headlong** adj.

head-piece (hedps) n. A helmet, cap or other covering for the head; a headset.

head-quar-ters (hedkwortrz) n., pl. The official location from which a leader directs a military unit.

head-set (hedset) n. A pair of headphones.

head start n. An early or advance start; an advantage.

head-strong (hedstrong) adj. Not easily restrained; obstinate.

head-y (hed) adj. Tending to intoxicate; affecting the senses; headstrong. **headily** adv. **headiness** n.

heal (hl) v. To restore to good health; to mend. **healable** adj. **healer** n.

health (helth) n. The overall sound condition or function of a living organism at a particular time; freedom from disease or defect. **-ful** adj. **-fully** adv.

health-y (helth) adj. In a state of or having good health; characteristic of a sound and good condition. **healthily** adv. **healthiness** n.

heap (hp) n. A haphazard assortment of things, a large number or quantity. v. To throw or pile into a heap.

hear (hr) v. To perceive by the ear; to listen with careful attention; to be informed of; to listen to officially or formally, as in a court of law. **hearer** n. **hear-ing (hring)** n. One of the five senses; the range by which sound can be heard; an opportunity to be heard; in law, a preliminary examination of an accused person.

hearing aid n. An electronic device used to amplify the hearing of partially deaf persons.

heark-en (härken) v. To listen carefully.

hear-say (hrs) n. Information heard from another; common talk; rumor.

hearse (hrs) n. A vehicle for conveying a dead body to the place of burial.

heart (härt) n. The hollow, primary muscular organ of vertebrates which circulates blood throughout the body; the emotional center, such as in love, hate, consideration, or compassion; the most essential part of something; a suit of playing cards marked with a red heart n. T-shaped design. **heart**. By memory.

heart-ache (härk) n. Emotional grief; sorrow; mental anguish.

heart attack n. An acute malfunction or interrupted heart function.

heart-beat (härtb) n. A pulsation of the heart, consisting of one contraction and one relaxation.

heart-en (härten) v. To give courage to.

heart-felt (härtfelt) adj. Deeply felt; sincere.

hearth (härth) n. The floor of a fireplace, furnace; the stone that forms the front of a fireplace.

heart-land (härtland) n. A strategically important central region, one regarded as vital to a nation's economy or defense.

heart-less (härtlis) adj. Having no sympathy; lacking compassion.

heart-rend-ing (härtrending) adj. Causing great distress, suffering emotional anguish.

heart-warm-ing adj. A feeling of warm sympathy.

heart-y (härt) adj. Marked by exuberant warmth; full of vigor; nourishing; substantial. **heartily** adv. **heartiness** n.

heat (ht) n. A quality of being hot or warm; a degree of warmth; depth of feeling; a period of sexual ardor in female animals. Slang Pressure or stress. v. To make or become warm or hot. **heater** n.

heat exhaustion n. A reaction to intense heat, a mild form of heat stroke.

heath (hth) n. An open tract of uncultivated wasteland covered with low-growing shrubs and plants.

hea-then (hthen) n. A person or nation that does not recognize the God of Christianity, Judaism, or Islam; in the Old Testament, a Gentile; non-Jew. **heathen** adj. **heathenish** adj.

heath-er (hether) n. A shrub that grows in dense masses and has small evergreen leaves and small pinkish flowers. **heather** adj. **heathery** adj.

heat stroke (hĭstrk) n. A state of collapse or exhaustion, accompanied by fever and marked by clammy skin, caused by excessive heat.

heave (hēv) v. To raise or lift, especially forcibly; to hurl or throw. *Naut.* To push, pull, or haul, as by a rope. *Slang* To vomit. n. The act of throwing.

heaves (hēvz) n. A disease of horses affecting the lungs and marked by coughing and difficult breathing.

heav·en (hĕv'ən) n. The sky; the region above and around the earth; the abode of God, the angels, and the blessed souls of the dead; a state or place of blissful happiness. **heavenly** *adj.*

heav·y (hĕv'ē) *adj.* Of great weight; very thick or dense; forceful; powerful; rough and violent, as stormy weather; of great significance; grave; painful, as bad news; oppressive. **heavily** *adv.*

heavy·set (hĕv'ē sĕt') *adj.* Having a stocky build.

heck·le (hĕk'əl) v. To badger or annoy, as with questions, comments, or gibes.

hec·tic (hĕk'tĭk) *adj.* Intensely active, rushed, or excited; marked by a persistent and fluctuating fever caused by a disease, such as tuberculosis; feverish; flushed.

he'd (hēd) *conj.* He had; he would.

hedge (hĕj) n. A boundary or fence formed of shrubs or low-growing trees; a means to guard against financial loss; a deliberately ambiguous statement. **hedge** v. **hedger** n.

hedge·hop (hĕj'hŏp') v. To fly an aircraft close to the ground, as in spraying crops.

he·don·ism (hēd'n nĭz'əm) n. The doctrine devoted to the pursuit of pleasure; the philosophy that pleasure is the principal good in life. **hedonist** n. **hedonistic** *adj.*

heed (hēd) v. To pay attention; to take notice of something. n. Attention.

heel (hēl) n. The rounded back part of the human foot under and behind the ankle; the part of a shoe supporting or covering the heel; a lower or bottom part; the crusty ends of a loaf of bread. v. To follow along at one's heels.

heft (hĕft) n. *Slang* Weight; bulk. v. To gauge or estimate the weight of by lift-

ing; to lift up. **hefty** (hĕf'tē) *adj.* Bulky; heavy; sizable.

he·gem·o·ny (hĭ jĕm'ə nē) n. Dominance or leadership, as of one country over another.

he·gi·ra (hĭ jī'rə) n. A journey or departure to flee an undesirable situation.

heif·er (hĕf'ər) n. A young cow, particularly one that has not produced a calf.

height (hīt) n. The quality of being high; the highest or most advanced point; the distance from the base of something; the apex; the distance above a specified level; altitude; the distance from head to foot.

height·en (hīt'n) v. To increase or become high in quantity or degree; to raise or lift.

Heimlich maneuver n. An emergency maneuver used to dislodge food from a choking person's throat; the closed fist is placed below the rib cage and pressed inward to force air from the lungs upward.

hei·nous (hā'nəs) *adj.* Extremely wicked, hateful or shockingly evil. **heinously** *adv.* **heinousness** n.

heir (âr) n. A person who inherits another's property or title.

heir·ess n. A female heir, especially to a large fortune.

heir·loom (âr'lōōm') n. A family possession handed down from generation to generation; an article of personal property acquired by legal inheritance.

heist (hīst) v. *Slang* To take from; to steal. n. A robbery.

hel·i·cal (hĕl'ĭ kəl) *adj.* Of or pertaining to the shape of a helix. **helically** *adv.*

hel·i·cop·ter (hĕl'ĭ kŏp'tər) n. An aircraft propelled by rotors which can take off vertically rather than needing an approach or a rolling start.

he·li·um (hē'lē əm) n. An extremely light, nonflammable, odorless, gaseous element, symbolized by He.

he'll (hēl) He will.

helm (hĕlm) n. A wheel or steering apparatus for a ship; a position or place of control or command.

hel·met (hĕl'mĭt) n. A protective covering for the head made of metal, leather, or plastic.

helms·man (hĕlmz'mən) n. One who

guides a ship.

hel-ot *n.* A serf; a slave. **helotry** *n.*

help (help) *v.* To assist or aid. *n.* Assistance; relief; one that assists; one hired to help. **helper** *n.* **helpful** *adj.* **helpfully** *adv.*

help-ing (helping) *n.* A single serving of food.

help-less (helplis) *adj.* Without help; powerless; lacking strength.

hel-ter--skel-ter (heltr skeltr) *adv.* In a confused or hurried manner; in an aimless way. *adj.* Rushed and confused. *n.* Great confusion; a tumult.

helve (helv) *n.* A handle on a tool such as an axe or hatchet.

hem (hem) *n.* A finished edge of fabric folded under and stitched. *interj.* A sound made as in clearing the throat, used especially to attract attention or to fill a pause in speech. *v.* To fold under and stitch down the edge of; to confine and surround.

he--man (hman) *n. Slang* A man marked by strength; a muscular man.

he-ma-tol-o-gy (hema tolo j) *n.* The branch of biological science that deals with blood and blood-generating organs.

hem-i-sphere (hemi sfr) *n.* A half sphere that is divided by a plane passing through its center; either symmetrical half of an approximately spherical shape; the northern or southern half of the earth divided by the equator or the eastern or western half divided by a meridian. **hemispherical** *adj.*

he-mo-glo-bin (hmo glbin) *n.* The respiratory pigment in the red blood cells of vertebrates containing iron and carrying oxygen to body tissues.

he-mo-phil-i-a (hmo fil a) *n., Pathol.* An inherited blood disease characterized by severe, protracted, sometimes spontaneous bleeding. **hemophiliac** *n.*

hem-or-rhage (hemr ij) *n.* Bleeding, especially excessive bleeding.

hem-or-rhoid (hemo roid) *n., Pathol.* A painful mass of dilated veins in swollen anal tissue.

he-mo-stat (hmo stat) *n.* An agent that stops bleeding; a clamp-like instrument for preventing or reducing bleeding.

hemp (hemp) *n.* An Asian herb; the female plant from which hashish and marijuana are produced; the tough fiber of the male plant from which coarse fabrics and rope are made.

hem-stitch *n.* An ornamental stitch, made by pulling out several threads and tying the remaining threads together in groups.

hen (hen) *n.* A mature female bird, especially an adult female domestic fowl.

hence-forth (hensforth) *adv.* From this time on.

hench-man (henchman) *n.* A loyal and faithful follower; one who supports a political figure chiefly for personal gain.

hen-peck (henpek) *v.* To domineer over one's husband by persistent nagging.

hep-a-rin (hepa rin) *n., Biochem* A substance found especially in liver tissue having the power to slow or prevent blood clotting.

he-pat-ic (hi patik) *adj.* Of or like the liver.

hep-a-ti-tis (hepa ttis) *n., Pathol.* Inflammation of the liver causing jaundice.

her-ald (herald) *n.* A person who announces important news; one that comes before as a sign of what is to follow.

he-ral-dic (he raldik) *adj.* An official whose duty is to grant royal proclamations. *v.* To announce.

herb (erb) *n.* A soft-stemmed plant without woody tissue that usually withers and dies each year; an often pleasant-smelling plant.

herb-age (erbij) *n.* Grass or vegetation used especially for grazing; the succulent edible parts of plants.

her-bar-i-um (her bår um) *n. pl. -ium or -ia* A collection of dried plant specimens that are scientifically arranged for study; a place housing a herbarium.

her-bi-cide (erbi sd) *n.* A chemical agent used to kill weeds. **-cidal** *adj.*

her-bi-vore (herb vr) *n.* A herbivorous animal.

her-cu-le-an (hrk lan) *adj.* Of unusual size, force, or difficulty; having great strength.

herd (hrd) *n.* A number of cattle or other animals of the same kind, kept or staying together as a group; a large crowd of people. *v.* To bring together in a herd. **herder** *n.*

here-af-ter (hr aftr) *adv.* From now on; at some future time. *n.* Existence after death.

here-by (hr b) *adv.* By means or by virtue of this.

he-red-i-tar-y (he redi ter) *adj.* Passing or transmitted from an ancestor to a legal heir; having an inherited title or possession; transmitted or transmissible by genetic inheritance. **-tarily** *adv.*

he-red-i-ty (heredi t) *n.* The genetic transmission of physical traits from parents to offspring.

here-in (hr in) *adv.* In or into this place.

here-of (hr uv) *adv.* Relating to or in regard to this.

her-e-sy (heri s) *n. pl.* **-sies** A belief in conflict with orthodox religious beliefs; any belief contrary to set doctrine.

her-e-tic (heri tik) *n.* A person holding opinions different from orthodox beliefs, especially religious beliefs.

here-to (hr tö) *adv.* To this matter, proposition, or thing.

here-to-fore (hrto fr) *adv.* Up to the present time; previously.

here-un-to (hrun tö) *adv.* Here to; to this.

here-up-on (hru pon) *adv.* Immediately following or resulting from this.

here-with (hr with) *adv.* Together or along with this; hereby.

her-i-ta-ble (heri ta bl) *adj.* Something capable of being inherited.

her-i-tage (heri tij) *n.* Property that is inherited; something handed down from past generations; a legacy.

her-maph-ro-dite (hr mafro dt) *n.* A person having both male and female reproductive organs. **-ditic** *adj.*

her-mit (hrmit) *n.* A person who lives in seclusion, often for religious reasons.

her-mit-age (hrmi tij) *n.* The dwelling place or retreat of a hermit; a secluded hideaway.

her-ni-a (hrn a) *n.* The protrusion of a bodily organ, as the intestine, through an abnormally weakened wall that usu-ally surrounds it; a rupture.

he-ro (hr) *n. pl.* **-roes** A figure in mythology and legend renowned for exceptional courage and fortitude.

her-o-in (her in) *n.* A highly addictive narcotic derivative of morphine.

her-o-ine (her in) *n.* A woman of heroic character; the principal female character in a story or play.

her-o-ism (her izum) *n.* Heroic behavior.

her-pes (hrpz) *n., Pathol.* A viral infection, characterized by small blisters on the skin or mucous membranes. **herpetic** *adj.*

her-pe-tol-o-gy (hrpi tolo j) *n.* The scientific study and treatment of reptiles and amphibians. **herpetologic** *adj.* **herpetological** *adj.* **-gically** *adv.*

her-ring (hering) *n.* A valuable food fish of the North Atlantic, the young of which are prepared as sardines, the adults are pickled, salted, or smoked.

her-ring-bone (hering bn) *n.* A pattern utilizing rows of short slanted parallel lines with connected rows slanting in the opposite direction.

hertz (hz) *n.* A unit of frequency equalling one cycle per second.

he's (hz) He has; he is.

hes-i-tant (hezi tant) *adj.* Given to hesitating; lacking decisiveness. **-tancy** *n.*

hes-i-tate (hezi tt) *v.* To pause or to be slow before acting, speaking, or deciding; to be uncertain. **hesitatingly** *adv.*

het-er-o-dox (hetr o doks) *adj.* Not in accord with established beliefs or religious doctrine; holding unorthodox opinions or beliefs.

het-er-o-sex-u-al (hetr o sekshö al) *adj.* Of or having sexual desire to the opposite sex; involving different sexes. **heterosexual** *n.* **heterosexuality** *n.*

hew (h) *v.* To make or shape with or as if with an axe; to adhere strictly; to con-form.

hex (heks) *n.* One held to bring bad luck; a jinx. *v.* To put under an evil spell; to bewitch.

hex-a-gon (heksa gon) *n.* A polygon having six sides and six angles. **hexagonal** *adj.*

hex-am-e-ter (heksami tr) *n.* A line of verse containing six metrical feet.

hey-day (hd) n. A time of great power, prosperity or popularity; a peak.

hi-a-tus (h t*u*s) n. A slight gap, break, or lapse in time from which something is missing; a break.

hi-ba-chi (h bäch) n. pl. **-chis** A deep, portable charcoal grill used for cooking food.

hi-ber-nate (hbr nt) v. To pass the winter in an inactive, dormant, sleep-like state.

hi-bis-cus (h bisk*u*s) n. A chiefly tropical shrub or tree, bearing large colorful flowers.

hick (hik) n. *Slang* A clumsy, unsophisticated country person. adj. Typical of hicks.

hick-o-ry (hik*o* r) n. pl. **-ries** A North American tree with a smooth or shaggy bark, hard edible nuts, and heavy, tough wood.

hi-dal-go (hi dalg*o*) n. pl. **-goes** A Spanish nobleman of lesser nobility.

hide (hd) v. To put, or keep out of sight; to keep secret; to obscure from sight; to seek shelter. n. The skin of an animal.

hide-bound (hdbound) adj. Obstinately narrow-minded or inflexible.

hid-e-ous (hid us) adj. Physically repulsive; extremely ugly. **hideously** adv.

hi-er-ar-chy (he rärk) n. pl. **-chies** An authoritative body or group of things or persons arranged in successive order; a ranked series of persons or things.

hi-er-o-glyph-ic (hr *o* glifik) n. A pictorial symbol representing an idea, object, or sound. **hieroglyphically** adv.

high (h) adj. Extending upward; located at a distance above the ground; more than normal in degree or amount.

high-bred (hbred) adj. Highborn; descending from superior breeding stock.

high fidelity n., *Elect.* The reproduction of sound with minimal distortion, as on records or tapes.

high--rise n. An extremely tall building.

high school n. A secondary school of grades nine through twelve or grades ten through twelve. **high** n. **schooler** n.

high seas n. pl. The open waters of an ocean or sea that are beyond the territorial jurisdiction of any one nation.

highspirited (hspiri tid) adj. Unbroken in spirit; proud.

highstrung (hstrung) adj. Very nervous and excitable.

high tech n. An interior design that incorporates industrial materials or motifs; high technology.

high technology n. The technology that involves highly advanced or specialized systems or devices.

high tide n. The highest level reached by the incoming tide each day.

hi-jack (hjak) v. *Slang* To seize illegally or steal while in transit; to coerce or compel someone; to commandeer a vehicle, especially an airplane in flight.

hike (hk) v. To walk for a lengthy amount of time usually through rugged terrain or woods; to pull up clothing with a sudden motion. **hike** n. **hiker** n.

hi-lar-i-ous (hi lär us) adj. Boisterously happy or cheerful. **hilariously** adv.

hill (hil) n. A rounded, elevation of the earth's surface, smaller than a mountain; a pile or heap; a small pile or mound, as of soil. v. To surround or cover with hills, as potatoes.

hill-ock (hilok) n. A small or low hill or mound. **hillocky** adj.

hill-side n. The side or slope of a hill.

hill-top n. The summit or top of a hill.

hilt (hilt) n. The handle of a dagger or sword. **hilt** Fully; completely; thoroughly.

him (him) The objective case of the pronoun he.

him-self (him self) That identical male one; a form of the third person, singular masculine pronoun.

hind (hnd) adj. Located at or toward the rear part; posterior.

hin-der (hindr) v. To interfere with the progress or action of. **hinderer** n.

hind-most (hndmst) adj. Farthest to the rear or back.

hin-drance (hindr*a*ns) n. The act of hindering or state of being hindered.

hind-sight (hndst) n. Comprehension or understanding of an event after it has happened.

hinge (hinj) n. A jointed device which allows a part, as a door or gate, to swing or turn on another frame. *v.* To attach by or to equip with a hinge or hinges.

hint (hint) *n.* An indirect indication or suggestion. *v.* To make something known by a hint.

hip (hip) *n.* The part of the human body that projects outward below the waist and thigh; the hip joint. The bright, red seed case of a rose. *adj. Slang* Said to be aware of or informed about current goings on.

hip-bone (hipbn) *n.* The large, flat bone which forms a lateral half of the pelvis.

hip joint *n.* The joint between the hip-bone and the thighbone.

hip-pie *or* **hip-py** (hip) *pl.* **-ies** A young person who adopts unconventional dress and behavior along with the use of drugs to express withdrawal from middle class life and indifference to its values.

hip-po-pot-a-mus (hipo pota mus) *n.* A large, aquatic mammal, native to Africa, having short legs, a massive, thick-skinned hairless body, and a broad wide-mouthed muzzle.

hire (hr) *v.* To obtain the service of another for pay. **hirer** *n.*

his (hiz) *adj.* The possessive case of the pronoun he.

hir-sute (hersöt) *adj.* Covered with hair.

his-ta-mine (hista mn) *n., Biochem.* A white, crystalline substance that occurs in plant and animal tissue, found to reduce high blood pressure and to have a contracting action on the uterus and believed to cause allergic reactions.

his-tol-o-gy (hi stolo j) *n. pl.* **-ies** The study of the minute structures of animal and plant tissues as seen through a microscope. **-gical** *adj.* **histologist** *n.*

his-to-ri-an (hi str an) *n.* A person who specializes in the writing or study of history.

his-tor-i-cal (hi stori kal) *adj.* Relating to or taking place in history; serving as a source of knowledge of the past; historic. **historically** *adv.* **-ness** *adj.*

his-to-ry (histo r) *n. pl.* **-ries** Past events, especially those involving human affairs; an account or record of past events that is written in chronological order, especially those concern-

ing a particular nation, people, activity, or knowledge; the study of the past and its significance.

hitch (hich) *v.* To fasten or tie temporarily, with a hook or knot. *Slang* To unite in marriage; to obtain a ride by hitchhiking. *n.* A delay or difficulty. *Milit.* A period of time in the armed forces.

hith-er (hithr) *adv.* To this place. *adj.* Situated toward this side.

hith-er-to (hithr tö) *adv.* Up to now.

hive (hv) *n.* A natural or man-made structure serving as a habitation for honeybees; a beehive.

hives (hvz) *n. pl.* Any of various allergic conditions marked by itching welts.

hoar (hr) *adj.* Having white or gray hair; grayish or white, as with frost.

hoard (hrd) *n.* The accumulation of something stored away for safekeeping or future use. *v.* To amass and hide or store valuables, money, or supplies.

hoarse (hrs) *adj.* Having a husky, gruff, or croaking voice. **-ly** *adv.* **-ness** *n.*

hoars-en (hrs) *v.* To become or make hoarse.

hoar-y *adj.* Ancient; aged; gray or white with age.

hoax (hks) *n.* A trick or deception. *v.* To deceive by a hoax. **hoaxer** *n.*

hob (hob) *n.* The projection at the side or interior of a fireplace used to keep things warm; an elf or hobgoblin.

hob-ble (hobl) *v.* To limp or walk with a limp; to progress irregularly or clumsily; to fetter a horse or other animal. *n.* A hobbling gait or walk.

hob-by (hob) *n. pl.* **-bies** An activity or interest undertaken for pleasure during one's leisure time.

hob-nob (hobnob) *n.* To associate in a friendly manner; to be on familiar terms.

ho-bo (hb) *n. pl.* **hoboes** *or* **hobos** A vagrant who travels aimlessly about; a tramp.

hock (hk) *n.* The joint of the hind leg of a horse, ox, or other animal which corresponds to the ankle in man.

ho-cus-po-cus (hkus pkus) *n.* Any deception or trickery, as misleading gestures; nonsense words or phrases used in conjuring or sleight of hand.

hodge-podge (hojpoj) *n.* A jumbled

mixture or collection.

Hodgkin's disease n., Pathol. A disease characterized by progressive enlargement of the lymph nodes, lymphoid tissue, and spleen, generally fatal.

hoe (h) n. A tool with a long handle and flat blade used for weeding, cultivating, and loosening the soil. **hoer** n.

hoe-cake (hkk) n. A thin, flat cake made of cornmeal.

hoe-down (hdoun) n. Slang A lively country square dance; party.

hoi pol-loi (hoi po loi) n. The common people; the masses.

hoist (hoist) v. To haul or raise up. n. A machine used for raising large objects.

hold (hld) v. To take and keep as in one's hand; to grasp; to possess; to put or keep in a particular place, position, or relationship; to suppress; to keep under control. n. A cargo storage area inside a ship or aircraft.

hold-ing (hlding) n. Property, as land, money, or stocks.

holdover n. Something that remains from an earlier time.

hole (hl) n. A cavity or opening in a solid mass or body. **hole** v.

hol-i-day (hol i d) n. A day set aside by law to commemorate a special person or event; a day set aside for religious observance; a day free from work; any day of rest.

hol-ler (holr) v. To shout loudly; to yell.

hol-low (hol) adj. Having a cavity or space within; concaved or sunken; lacking significance or substance; not genuine; empty; meaningless.

hol-ly (hol) n. pl. -ies A tree or shrub that bears glossy spiny leaves and bright-red berries.

hol-o-caust (holo kost) n. A widespread or total destruction, especially by fire.

hol-o-graph (holo graf) n. A handwritten document, as a letter or will, signed by the person who wrote it. **holographic** adj.

hol-ster (hlstr) n. A leather case designed to hold a pistol or gun.

ho-ly (hl) adj. Regarded with or characterized by divine power; sacred.

hom-age (homij) n. Great respect or honor, especially when expressed pub-

licly.

home (hm) n. The place where one resides; a place of origin; one's birthplace or residence during the formative years; a place one holds dear because of personal feelings or relationships; a place of security and comfort.

home economics n. The principles of home management.

home-ly (hml) adj. Having a simple, familiar, everyday character; having plain or ugly features; unattractive.

ho-me-op-a-thy (hm opa th) n. A system of treating a disease with minute doses of medicines that produce the symptoms of the disease being treated.

ho-me-o-sta-sis (hm o stsis) n., Biol. A state of equilibrium that occurs between different but related functions or elements.

home-sick (hmsik) adj. Longing or yearning for home and family. -**ness** n.

home-spun (hmspun) adj. Something made, woven, or spun at home; anything that is simple and plain.

home-work (hmwerk) n. Work done at home, especially school assignments.

hom-i-cide (homi sd) n. The killing of one person by another; a person killed by another.

ho-mog-e-nize (ho moje nz) v. To process milk by breaking up fat globules and dispersing them uniformly.

hom-o-graph (homo graf) n. A word that is identical to another in spelling, but different from it in origin and meaning.

hom-o-nym (homo nim) n. A word that has the same sound and often the same spelling as another but a different meaning and origin.

hom-o-phone (homo fn) n. One of two or more words that have the same sound but different spelling, origin, and meaning.

Ho-mo sa-pi-ens (hm spenz) n. The scientific name for the human race.

ho-mo-sex-u-al (hmo sekshô al) adj. Having sexual attraction or desire for persons of the same sex.-**ality** n.

hon-cho n. pl. -chos The main person in charge; the boss; the manager.

hone (hn) n. A fine-grained stone used to sharpen cutting tools, such as knives or razors. *v.* To perfect something; to sharpen.

hon-est (onist) *adj.* Not lying, cheating, or stealing; having or giving full worth or value. **honestly** *adv.* **honesty** *n.*

hon-ey (hun) *n. pl.* **hon-eys** A sweet, sticky substance made by bees from the nectar gathered from flowers; sweetness. *Slang* Dear; darling.

honey-moon (hun mōn) *n.* A trip taken by a newly-married couple.

honk (hongk) *n.* The harsh, loud sound made by a goose; the sound made by an automobile horn. **honk** *v.* **honker** *n.*

hon-or (onr) *n.* High regard or respect; personal integrity; reputation; privilege; used as a title for mayors and judges. *v.* To accept something as valid. **honorer** *n.*

honor-able (onr a bl) *adj.* Worthy of honor.

hon-or-ar-y (ono rer) *adj.* Relating to an office or title bestowed as an honor, without the customary powers, duties, or salaries.

hood (hed) *n.* A covering for the head and neck, often attached to a garment; the movable metal hinged cover of an automobile engine. **hooded** *adj.*

-hood *suff.* The quality or state of; sharing a given quality or state.

hood-lum (hōdlum) *n.* A young, tough, wild, or destructive fellow.

hoof (hef) *n. pl.* **hooves** The horny covering of the foot in various mammals, as horses, cattle, and oxen. To dance; to walk. **hoof** Alive; not butchered. **hoofed** *adj.*

hook (hek) *n.* A curved or bent piece of metal used to catch, drag, suspend, or fasten something; in golf, a stroke that sends the ball curving to the left; in boxing, to strike with a short, swinging blow; in hockey, to check illegally with the hockey stick. *Slang v.* To cause to become dependent or addicted. *Naut., Slang* An anchor. **crook** In one way or another. **and sinker** Unreservedly; entirely. **with** To marry; to form an association.

hook-worm (hekwerm) *n.* A parasitic intestinal worm with hooked mouth parts.

hook-y (hek) *n. Slang* Truant. **hooky**

To be out of school without permission.

hoop-la (hōplä) *n. Slang* Noise and excitement.

hoose-gow (hösgou) *n. Slang* A jail.

hoot (hōt) *n.* The loud sound or cry of an owl. *n. Slang* A very insignificant amount. Not caring. **hooter** *n.* **hoot** *v.*

hope (hp) *v.* To want or wish for something with a feeling of confident expectation. **hope** To continue hoping for something even when it may be in vain.

hope-ful (hpful) *adj.* Manifesting or full of hope. *n.* A young person who shows signs of succeeding. **hopefully** *adv.*

hope-less (hplis) *adj.* Totally without hope; despairing; having no grounds for hope.

horde (hrd) *adj.* A large crowd.

hore-hound (hrhound) *n.* A whitish, bitter, aromatic plant, whose leaves yield a bitter extract used as a flavoring in candy.

ho-ri-zon (ho rzon) *n.* The line along which the earth and sky seem to meet; the bounds or limit of one's knowledge, experience or interest.

hor-i-zon-tal (hori zontal) *adj.* Parallel to the horizon. **horizontal** *n.* **-ly** *adv.*

horn (horn) *n.* A hard, bone-like, permanent projection on the heads of certain hoofed animals, as cattle, sheep, or deer. *Mus.* Any of the various brass instruments, formerly made from animal horns. **in** To join in a conversation or other activities without being invited. **horny** *adj.*

hor-o-scope (horo skp) *n.* A chart or diagram of the relative positions of the planets and signs of the zodiac at a certain time, as that of a person's birth; used to predict the future.

hor-ri-ble (hor bl) *adj.* Shocking; inducing or producing horror. *Informal* Excessive; inordinate. **horribly** *adv.*

hor-rid (horid) *adj.* Horrible. **-ly** *adv.*

hor-ri-fy (hor f) *v.* To cause a feeling of horror; to dismay or shock.

hor-ror (horr) *n.* The painful, strong emotion caused by extreme dread, fear, or repugnance. *Informal* Something that is disagreeable or ugly.

hors d'oeuvre (or derv) *n.* An appetizer

served with cocktails before dinner.

horse sense n. Slang Common sense.

hor-ti-cul-ture (hort kulchr) n. The art or science of raising and tending fruits, vegetables, flowers, or ornamental plants.

hose (hz) n. A sock; a stocking; a flexible tube for carrying fluids or gases under pressure. v. To wash; to water; to squirt with a hose.

ho-sier-y (hzhe r) n. Stockings and socks.

hosp abbr. Hospital.

hos-pice (hospis) n. A lodging for travelers or the needy.

hos-pi-ta-ble (hospi ta bl) adj. Treating guests with warmth and generosity; receptive.

hos-pi-tal (hospi tal) n. An institution where the injured or sick receive medical, surgical, and emergency care.

hos-pi-tal-i-ty (hospi tali t) n. Hospitable treatment, disposition, or reception.

host (hst) n. One who receives or entertains guests; one who provides a room or building for an event or function. Biol. A living organism, as a plant or an animal, on or in which a parasite lives. **host** v.

hos-tage (hostij) n. A person held as security that promises will be kept or terms met by a third party.

hos-tel (hostel) n. A low-priced, supervised lodging for young travelers.

host-ess (hstis) n. A woman who entertains socially; a woman who greets patrons at a restaurant and escorts them to their tables.

hos-tile (hostl) adj. Of or relating to an enemy; antagonistic. **hostilely** adv.

hos-til-i-ty (ho stili t) n. pl. **-ies** A very deep-seated opposition or hatred; war.

hot (hot) adj. Having heat that exceeds normal body temperature; sexually excited or receptive; electrically charged, as a hot wire. Slang Recently and or illegally obtained.

hot air n. Slang Idle talk.

hot cake n. A pancake.

hot dog n. A cooked frankfurter, served in a long roll. Slang A person who enjoys showing off.

hot-el (h tel) n. A business that provides

lodging, meals, entertainment, and other services for the public.

hound (hound) n. Any of several kinds of long-eared dogs with deep voices which follow their prey by scent; a person unusually devoted to something; a fan. v. To pursue or drive without letting up; to nag continuously.

hour (our) n. A measure of time equal to 60 minutes; one 24th of a day; the time of day or night. **hours** pl. A specific or certain period of time.

hour-ly (ourl) adj. Something that happens or is done every hour.

house (hous) n. A building that serves as living quarters for one or more families; home; the shelter or refuge for a wild animal; a business firm; a legislative body of the U.S. government. v. To provide work space.

how (hou) adv. In what manner or way; to what effect; in what condition or state; for what reason; with what meaning.

how-dy interj. A word used to express a greeting.

how-ev-er (hou evr) adv. In whatever manner or way. conj. Nevertheless.

how-it-zer (houit sr) n. A short cannon that fires projectiles at a high trajectory.

howl (houl) v. To utter a loud, sustained, plaintive sound, as the wolf.

howl-er (hoilr) n. One that howls; a ridiculous or stupid blunder.

how-so-ev-er (hous evr) adv. To what ever degree or extent.

hub (hub) n. The center of a wheel; the center of activity.

hue (hu) n. A gradation of color running from red through yellow, green, and blue to violet; a particular color; a shade. **hued** adj.

hug (hug) v. To embrace; to hold fast; to keep, cling, or stay close to.

huge (hj) adj. Of great quantity, size, or extent. **hugely** adv. **hugeness** n.

hu-la (hōla) n. A Hawaiian dance characterized by beautiful rhythmic movement of the hips and gestures with the hands.

hulk (hulk) n. A heavy, bulky ship; the body of an old ship no longer fit for service.

hulk-ing *adj.* Unwieldy or awkward.

hull (hul) *n.* The outer cover of a fruit or seed; the framework of a boat; the external covering of a rocket, spaceship, or guided missile.

hul-la-ba-loo (hula ba lō) *n.* A confused noise; a great uproar.

hum (hum) *v.* To make a continuous low-pitched sound; to be busily active; to sing with the lips closed. **hummer** *n.*

hu-man (hmən) *adj.* Of, relating to, or typical of man; having or manifesting human form or attributes. **-ly** *adv.*

hu-mane (h mn) *adj.* To be marked by compassion, sympathy, or consideration for other people or animals.

hu-man-i-ty (h mani t) *n. pl.* **-ies** The quality or state of being human; humankind.

hum-ble (humbl) *adj.* Marked by meekness or modesty; unpretentious; lowly. *v.* To make humble. **humbleness** *n.*

hu-mer-us (hmr us) *n. pl.* **meri** The long bone of the upper arm or fore limb that extends from the shoulder to the elbow.

hu-mid (hmid) *adj.* Containing or characterized by a large amount of moisture; damp.

hu-mid-i-fy (h mid f) *v.* To make humid or more moist. **humidifier** *n.*

hu-mid-i-ty (h midi t) *n.* A moderate amount of wetness in the air; dampness.

hu-mi-dor (hmi dor) *n.* A container used to keep cigars in which the air is kept properly humidified by a special device.

hu-mil-i-ate (h mil t) *v.* To reduce one's dignity or pride to a lower position.

hu-mor (hmr) *n.* Something that is or has the ability to be comical or amusing. *Physiol.* Fluid contained in the body such as blood or lymph. **humorist** *n.* **humorousness** *n.*

hump (hump) *n.* The rounded lump or protuberance, as on the back of a camel. **hump** To be past the difficult or most critical state.

hunch (hunch) *n.* A strong, intuitive feeling about a future event or result. *v.* To bend into a crooked position or posture.

hun-dred (hundrid) *n. pl.* **-dreds** or **- dred** The cardinal number equal to 10 X 10. **hundredth** *adj. & adv.*

hun-ger (hunggr) *n.* A strong need or desire for food; a craving for food. **hunger** *v.* **hungrily** *adv.* **hungry** *adj.*

hunt (hunt) *v.* To search or look for food; to pursue with the intent of capture; to look in an attempt to find.

hur-dle (hrdl) *n.* A portable barrier used to jump over in a race; an obsta-cle one must overcome. *v.* To leap over. **-er** *n.*

hurl (hrl) *v.* To throw something with great force; in baseball, to pitch.

hur-rah (hu rä) Used to express approval, pleasure, or exultation.

hur-ri-cane (her kn) *n.* A tropical cyclone with winds exceeding 74 miles per hour, usually accompanied by rain, thunder, and lightning.

hur-ry (her) *v.* To move or cause to move with haste. *n.* The act of hurrying. **hurriedly** *adv.* **hurriedness** *n.*

hurt (hrt) *v.* To experience or inflict with physical pain; to cause physical or emotional harm to; to damage.

hus-band (huzband) *n.* A man who is married.

hush (hush) *v.* To make or become quiet; to calm; to keep secret; to suppress. *n.* A silence.

husk (husk) *n.* The dry or membranous outer cover of certain vegetables, fruits, and seeds, often considered worthless.

husk-y (husk) *adj.* Having a dry cough or grating sound; burly a robust. **huskily** , *n. pl.* **-ies** A heavy-coated working dog of the arctic region.

hus-sy (hus) *n. pl* **-ies** A saucy or mischievous girl; a woman with doubtful morals.

hus-tle (husel) *v.* To urge or move hurriedly along; to work busily and quickly. *Slang* To make energetic efforts to solicit business or make money. **hustle** *n.* **hustler** *n.*

hut (hut) *n.* An often small and temporary dwelling made of simple construction; a shack.

hutch (huch) *n.* A compartment or chest for storage.

hy-a-cinth (ha sinth) *n.* A bulbous plant that has a cluster of variously colored, highly fragrant, bell-shaped flowers.

hy-brid (hbrid) *n.* An offspring of two dissimilar plants or of two animals of different races, breeds, varieties, or species; something made up of mixed origin or makeup.

hy-drant (hdrɑnt) *n.* A pipe with a valve and spout which supplies water from a main source.

hy-drau-lic (h drolik) *adj.* Operated, moved, or effected by the means of water; hardening or setting underwater.

hy-dro-gen (hdro jen) *n.* A colorless, normally odorless, highly flammable gas that is the simplest and lightest of the elements, symbolized by H. **hydrogenous** *adj.*

hydrogen bomb *n.* A bomb that is extremely destructive, with an explosive power obtained from the rapid release of atomic energy.

hy-dro-plane (hdro pln) *v.* To skim over water with only the hull more or less touching the surface.

hy-giene (hjn) *n.* The science of the establishment and maintenance of good health and the prevention of disease. **hygienic** *adj.* **-ically** *adv.* **-ist** *n.*

hy-men (hmen) *n.* The thin membrane that partly closes the external vaginal orifice.

hymn (him) *n.* A song of praise giving thanks to God; a song of joy. **hymn** *v.*

hype *v.* *Slang* To put on; to stimulate; to promote or publicize extravagantly.

hy-per-ten-sion (hpr tenshɑn) *n.* The condition of abnormally high blood pressure.

hy-phen (hfen) *n.* A punctuation mark (-) used to show connection between two or more words. **hyphen** *v.*

hy-phen-ate (hfe nt) *v.* To separate or join with a hyphen. **hyphenation** *n.*

hyp-no-pae-di-a (hip'n pd a *n.* Pertaining to a mental condition similar to light hypnosis but caused by something other then hypnotism.

hyp-no-pom-pic (hip no pom' pik) *adj.* The state of drowsiness associated with awakening from a sleep.

hyp-no-sis (hip nsis) *n.* *pl.* **hypnoses** A state that resembles sleep but is brought on or induced by another per-

son whose suggestions are accepted by the subject; considerable loss of will power.

hyp-not-ic (hip notik) *adj.* Inducing sleep. *n.* An agent, such as a drug, which induces sleep; a sedative; a person under the influence of hypnotism.

hyp-no-tize (hipno tz) *v.* To induce hyp-nosis; to be dazzled by; to be over-come by suggestion.

hy-po (hp) *n.* *pl.* **hypos** A hypodermic needle or syringe.

hy-po-chon-dri-a (hpo kondr a) *n.* A mental depression accompanied by imaginary physical ailments.

hypodermic syringe (hpo drmik) *n.* A syringe and hypodermic needle used for injecting a substance into one's body.

hy-pog-na-thous (h pog' na thus) *n.* Having the lower jaw of greater length than the upper; protruding; a condition in man.

hy-po-pla-si-a (hpo pl'zha) *n.* A condition in which the growth of an organ or part is arrested causing it to be under-sized.

hy-po-tax-is (h po tak'sis) *n.* The arrangement of sentence parts whereby one construction, usually a clause, is dependent upon another.

hy-poth-e-sis (h poth 'i sis *n.* Proposition put forth as a basis for reasoning; supposition formulated from proved data and presented as a temporary explanation of an occurrence, as in the sciences, in order to establish a basis for further research; an assumption or guess.

hy-po-thet-i-cal (hpo thet'i kal) *n.* An idea or a statement unsupported by fact or evidence; assumed; theorized; not actual.

hy-po-ton-ic (hpo ton'ik) *n.* An inadequate degree of tone or tension, as the muscles.

hy-pox-i-a (h pok's a) *n.* A condition of insufficient oxygen in the body tissues, due to an improper functioning of the respiratory mechanisms or an absence of environmental oxygen.

hyp-som-e-ter *n.* An insturment used for measuring altitude by determining the boiling point of a liquid at a given height; a triangulation instrument used to obtain the height of trees.

hy-son n. A green China tea.

hys-sop n. An aromatic herb of the mint family, with blue flowers.

hys-ter-ec-to-my (histe rekto m) n. **pl. -ies** Surgery on a female which partially or completely removes the uterus.

hys-ter-e-sis (histe r´sis) n. The lag in the effect on a substance of a changing magnetizing force; the influence of a previous treatment of a gel upon its present behavior.

hys-ter-ia (hi str a) n. A psychological condition characterized by emotional excess and or unreasonable fear. **-ic** n.

hys-ter-ic (hi ster´ik) n. A person suffering from hysteria. n. pl. A fit of uncontrollable laughter or crying; hysteria.

I

I, i The ninth letter of the English alphabet; the Roman numeral for one.

I pron. The person speaking or writing.

i-at-ro-gen-ic (a´tro jen´ik) adj. Induced inadvertently by a physician or his treatment. **iatrogenically** adv.

ib or ibid L. Ibidem, in the same place.

ice (s) n. Solidly frozen water; a dessert of crushed ice which is flavored and sweetened; frozen surface of water *Informal* Extreme coldness of manner. v. To change into ice; to cool or chill; to cover with icing. **icily** adv. **-ness** n.

ice age n., *Geol.* A time of widespread glaciation.

ice cap (s´kap´) n. An extensive perennial covering of ice and snow that covers a large area of land.

ich-thy-ol-o-gy (ik´th ol´o j) n. The zoological study of fishes. **ichthyologic-ic** adj. **-gical** adj. **ichthyologist** n.

i-ci-cle (´si kl) n. A hanging spike of ice formed by dripping water that freezes.

i-con or i-kon (´kon) n. A sacred Christian pictorial representation of Jesus Christ, the Virgin Mary, or other sacred figures.

i-con-o-clast (kon´o klast´) n. One who opposes the use of sacred images; one who attacks traditional or cherished beliefs. **iconoclasm** n. **-clastic** adj.

id n. *Psychol..* The unconscious part of the psyche associated with instinctual needs and drives.

i-de-a (d´a) n. Something existing in the mind; conception or thought; an opinion; a plan of action.

i-de-al (d´al) n. A concept or imagined state of perfection; highly desirable; perfect; an ultimate objective; an honorable principle or motive. *adj.* Conforming to absolute excellence. **ideally** adv.

i-dem (´dem) pron. The same; used to indicate a previously mentioned reference.

i-den-ti-cal (den´ti kal) adj. Being the same; exactly equal or much alike; designating a twin or twins developed from the same ovum. **identically** adv.

i-den-ti-fi-ca-tion (den´ti fi k´shan) n. The act of identifying; the state of being identified; a means of identity.

i-den-ti-ty (den´ti t) n. pl. **-ties** The condition or state of being a specific person or thing and recognizable as such; the condition or fact of being the same as something else.

id-e-o-gram or id-e-o-graph (id´o gram´, id´o graf´) n. A pictorial symbol used in a writing system to represent an idea or thing, as Chinese characters; a graphic symbol, as $ or %.

i-de-ol-o-gy (d ol´o j) n. pl. **-gies** A body of ideas that influence a person, group, culture, or political party.

ides (dz) n. pl. In the ancient Roman calendar, the fifteenth day of March, May, July, and October or the thirteenth day of the other months.

id-i-o-cy (id´o s) n. pl. **-cies** A condition of an idiot.

id-i-om (id´om) n. A form of expression having a meaning that is not readily understood from the meaning of its component words; the dialect of people or a region; a kind of language or vocabulary. **-atic** adj. **-atically** adv.

id-i-o-syn-cra-sy (id´o sing´kra s) n. pl. **-sies** A peculiarity, as of behavior. **idiosyncratic** adj. **-cratically** adv.

i-di-ot (id´ot) n. A mentally deficient person; an extremely foolish or stupid person. **idiotic** adj. **idiotically** adv.

i-dle (d´l) adj. Doing nothing; inactive;

moving lazily; slowly; running at a slow speed or out of gear; unemployed or inactive. **-ness** *n.* **idler** *n.* **idly** *adv.*

i-dol (d´ol) *n.* A symbol or representation of a god or deity that is worshiped; a person or thing adored.

i-dol-a-try (do´a tr) *n.* The worship of idols; blind adoration; devotion. **idolater** *n.* **idolatrous** *adj.*

i-dol-ize (d´o lz´) *v.* To admire with excessive admiration or devotion; to worship as an idol. **idolization** *n.* **-er** *n.*

i-dyll *or* **i-dyl** (d´l) *n.* A poem or prose piece about country life; a scene, event, or condition of rural simplicity; a romantic interlude. **idyllic** *adj.*

if-fy (if´) *adj.* *Slang* Marked by unknown qualities or conditions.

ig-ne-ous (ig´n us) *adj., Geol.* Relating to fire; formed by solidification from a molten magma.

ig-nite (ig nt´) *v.* To start or set a fire; to render luminous by heat.

ig-ni-tion (ig nish´an) *n.* An act or action of igniting; a process or means for igniting the fuel mixture in an engine.

ig-no-ble (ig n´bl) *adj.* Dishonorable in character or purpose; not of noble rank.

ig-no-min-i-ous (ig´no min´ us) *adj.* Marked by or characterized by shame or disgrace; dishonorable. **ignominy** *n.*

ig-no-ra-mus (ig´no r´mus) *n.* A totally ignorant person.

ig-no-rant (ig´nr ant) *adj.* Lacking education or knowledge; not aware; lacking comprehension. **ignorance** *n.*

ig-nore (ig nr´) *v.* To pay no attention to; to reject. **ignorable** *adj.*

i-gua-na (i gwä´na) *n.* A large, dark-colored tropical American lizard.

il-e-i-tis (il´ ´tis) *n.* Inflammation of the ileum.

il-e-um (il´ um) *n. pl.* **ilea** The lower part of the small intestine between the jejunum and the large intestine.

ill (il) *adj.* Not healthy; sick; destructive in effect; harmful; hostile; unfriendly; not favorable; not up to standards. *adv.* In an ill manner; with difficulty; scarcely. *n.* Evil; injury or harm; something causing suffering.

I'll *contr.* I will; I shall.

ill--ad-vised (il´ad vzd´) *adj.* Done without careful thought or, sufficient advice.

ill--bred (il´bred´) *adj.* Ill-mannered; impolite; rude.

il-le-gal (i l´gal) *adj.* Contrary to law or official rules. **illegality** *n.* **illegally** *adv.*

il-leg-i-ble (i lej´i bl) *adj.* Not readable; not legible. **illegibly** *adv.* **illegibility** *n.*

il-le-git-i-mate (il´i jit´i mit) *adj.* Against the law; unlawful; born out of wedlock. **illegitimacy** *n.* **-mately** *adv.*

ill--fat-ed (il´f´tid) *adj.* Destined for misfortune; doomed; unlucky.

ill--got-ten (il´got´en) *adj.* Obtained in an illegal or dishonest way.

il-hu-mored *adj.* Irritable; cross.

il-lic-it (i lis´it) *adj.* Not permitted by custom or law; unlawful. **illicitly** *adv.*

il-lit-er-ate (i lit´r it) *adj.* Unable to read and write; uneducated. **illiteracy** *n.*

ill--man-nered *adj.* Lacking or showing a lack of good manners; rude.

ill-ness (il´nis) *n.* Sickness; a state of being in poor health.

il-log-i-cal (i loj´i kal) *adj.* Contrary to the principles of logic; not logical. **illogicality** *n.* **illogically** *adv.*

il-lu-mi-nate (i lö´mi nt´) *v.* To give light; to make clear; to provide with understanding; to decorate with pictures or designs. **illumination** *n.*

il-lu-sion (i lö´zhan) *n.* A misleading perception of reality; an overly optimistic idea or belief; misconception.

il-lus-trate (il´a strt´) *v.* To explain or clarify, especially by the use of examples; to clarify by serving as an example; to provide a publication with explanatory features.

il-lus-tra-tion (il´a str´shan) *n.* The act of illustrating; an example or comparison used to illustrate.

il-lus-tra-tive (i lus´tr tiv) *adj.* Serving to illustrate.

il-lus-tri-ous (i lus´tr us) *adj.* Greatly celebrated; renowned. **-ness** *n.*

ill will *n.* Unfriendly or hostile feelings; malice.

im-age (im´ij) *n.* A representation of the form and features of someone or something; an optically formed representation of an object made by a mirror or lens; a mental picture of something imaginary. v. To make a likeness of; to reflect; to depict vividly.

im-age-ry (im´ij r) n. pl. **-ies** Mental pictures; existing only in the imagination.

im-ag-in-a-ble (i maj´i na bl) adj. Capable of being imagined. **-bly** adv.

im-ag-i-na-tion (i maj´i n´shan) n. The power of forming mental images of unreal or absent objects; such power used creatively; resourcefulness. **imaginative** adj. **imaginatively** adv.

im-ag-ine (i maj´in) v. To form a mental picture or idea of; to suppose; to guess.

i-ma-go (i m´g) n. pl. **-goes** or **-gines** An insect in its sexually mature adult stage.

i-mam (i mäm´) n. A prayer leader of Islam; rulers that claim descent from Muhammad.

im-bal-ance (im bal´ans) n. A lack of functional balance; defective coordination.

im-be-cile (im´bi sil) n. A mentally deficient person. **imbecilic** adj.

im-bibe (im bb´) v. To drink; to take in.

im-bri-cate (im´bri kit) adj. With edges over-lapping in a regular arrangement, as roof tiles or fish scales.

im-bro-glio (im brl´y) n. pl. **-glios** A complicated situation or disagreement; a confused heap; a tangle.

im-bue (im b´) v. To saturate, as with a stain or dye.

im-i-ta-ble (im´i ta bl) adj. Capable or worthy of imitation.

im-i-tate (im´i tt) v. To copy the actions or appearance of another; to adopt the style of; to duplicate; to appear like.

im-i-ta-tion (im´i t´shan) n. An act of imitating; something copied from an original.

im-mac-u-late (i mak´ lit) adj. Free from sin, stain, or fault; impeccably clean.

im-ma-nent (im´a nent) adj. Existing within; restricted to the mind; subjective. **immanence** n. **immanency** n.

im-ma-ture (im´a ter´) adj. Not fully grown; undeveloped; suggesting a lack of maturity. **immaturely** adv. **immaturity** n.

im-meas-ur-a-ble (i mezh´r a bl) adj. Not capable of being measured.

im-me-di-ate (i m´d it) adj. Acting or happening without an intervening object, agent, or cause; directly perceived; occurring at once; close in time, location, or relation.

im-me-mo-ri-al (im´e mr´ al) adj. Beyond the limits of memory, tradition, or records.

im-mense (i mens´) adj. Exceptionally large.

immensely adv. **immensity** n.

im-merse (i mrs´) v. To put into a liquid; to baptize by submerging in water; to engross; to absorb. **immersible** adj. **immersion** n.

im-mi-grant (im´i grant) n. One who leaves his country to settle in another.

im-mi-grate (im´i grt´) v. To leave one country and settle in another. **-ion** n.

im-mi-nent (im´i nent) adj. About to happen. **imminence** n.

im-mo-bile (i m´bil) adj. Not moving or incapable of motion. **immobility** n.

im-mo-bi-lize (i m´bi lz´) v. To render motionless. **immobilization** n.

im-mod-er-ate (i mod´r it) adj. Exceeding normal bounds. **immoderately** adv.

im-mod-est (i mod´ist) adj. Lacking modesty; indecent; boastful.

im-mor-al (i mor´al) adj. Not moral.

im-mo-ral-i-ty (im´o ral´i t) n. pl. **-ies** Lack of morality; an immoral act or practice.

im-mor-tal (i mor´tal) adj. Exempt from death; lasting forever, as in fame. n. A person of lasting fame. **immortality** n.

im-mov-a-ble (i mö´va bl) adj. Not capable of moving or being moved.

im-mune (i mn´) adj. Not affected or responsive; resistant, as to a disease.

im-mu-nize (im´nz´) v. To make immune.

im-mu-nol-o-gy (im´ nol´o j) n. The study of immunity to diseases.

im-mu-no-sup-pres-sive (i m´n sa pre´siv) adj. Acting to suppress a natural immune response to an antigen.

im-mure (i mr´) v. To confine by or as if by walls; to build into a wall.

im-mu-ta-ble (i m´ta bl) adj. Unchanging or unchangeable. **immutability** n.

imp (imp) n. A mischievous child; the

im-pact (im´pakt) n. A collision; the

impetus or force produced by a collision; an initial, usually strong effect. v. To pack firmly together; to strike or affect forcefully.

im-pac-tion (im pak′ shen) n. Something wedged in a part of the body.

im-pair (im pâr′) v. To diminish in strength, value, quantity, or quality. **impairment** n.

im-pa-la (im pal′a) n. A large African antelope, the male of which has slender curved horns.

im-pale (im pl′) v. To pierce with a sharp stake or point; to kill by piercing in this fashion. **impalement** n.

im-pal-pa-ble (im pal′pa bl) adj. Not perceptible to touch; not easily distinguished. **impalpability** n. -**bly** adv.

im-part (im pärt′) v. To grant; to bestow; to make known; to communicate.

im-par-tial (im pär′shal) adj. Not partial; unbiased. **impartiality** n. -**ly** adv.

im-pass-a-ble (im pas′a bl) adj. Impossible to travel over or across.

im-passe (im′pas) n. A road or passage having no exit; a difficult situation with no apparent way out; a deadlock.

im-pas-sioned (im pash′and) adj. Filled with passion.

im-pas-sive (im pas′iv) adj. Unemotional; showing no emotion; expressionless.

im-pa-tient (im p′shent) adj. Unwilling to wait or tolerate delay; expressing or caused by irritation at having to wait; restlessly eager; intolerant. **impatience** n. **impatiently** adv. **impeach** To charge with misconduct in public office before a proper court of justice; to make an accusation against. **impatience** n. **impatiently** adv. **impeachable** adj. **impeachment** n.

im-pe-cu-ni-ous (im′pe k′n us) adj. Having no money. -**ness** n.

im-ped-ance (im pd′ans) n. A measure of the total opposition to the flow of an electric current, especially in an alternating current circuit.

im-pede (im pd′) v. To obstruct or slow down the progress of.

im-pel (im pel′) v. To spur to action; to provoke; to drive forward; to propel.

im-pend (im pend′) v. To hover threateningly; to be about to happen.

im-pen-e-tra-ble (im pen′i trabl) adj. Not capable of being penetrated; not capable of being seen through or understood; unfathomable.

im-pen-i-tent (im pen′i tent) adj. Not sorry; unrepentant. **impenitence** n.

im-per-a-tive (im per′a tiv) adj. Expressing a command or request; empowered to command or control; compulsory.

im-per-cep-ti-ble (im′per sep′ta bl) adj. Not perceptible by the mind or senses; extremely small or slight.

im-per-fect (im per′fikt) adj. Not perfect; of or being a verb tense which shows an uncompleted or continuous action or condition. n. The imperfect tense. -**ly** adv.

im-per-fec-tion (im′pr fek′shan) n. The quality or condition of being imperfect; a defect.

im-pe-ri-al-ism (im pr′ a liz′um) n. The national policy or practice of acquiring foreign territories or establishing dominance over other nations.

im-per-il (im per′il) v. To put in peril; endanger.

im-pe-ri-ous (im pr′ us) adj. Commanding; domineering; urgent. **imperiousness** n.

im-per-ish-a-ble (im per′i sha bl) adj. Not perishable. **imperishably** adv.

im-per-ma-nent (im per′ma nent) adj. Not permanent; temporary. **impermanence** n.

im-per-me-a-ble (im per′m a bl) adj. Not permeable. **impermeability** n.

im-per-mis-si-ble (im′pr mis′a bl) adj. Not permissible; not allowed.

im-per-son-al (im per′so nal) adj. Having no personal reference or connection; showing no emotion or personality.

im-per-son-ate (im per′so nt) v. To assume the character or manner of. **impersonation** n. **impersonator** n.

im-per-ti-nent (im per′ti nent) adj. Overly bold or disrespectful; not pertinent; irrelevant. **impertinence** n.

im-per-turb-a-ble (im′pr ter′ba bl) adj. Unshakably calm.

im-per-vi-ous (im per′v us) adj. Incapable of being penetrated or affected. **imperviously** adv. **imperviousness** n.

im·pe·ti·go (im´pi t´g) n. A contagious skin disease marked by pustules.

im·pet·u·ous (im pech´ us) adj. Marked by sudden action or emotion; impulsive. **impetuosity** n. **impetuously** adv.

im·pe·tus (im´pi tus) n. A driving force; an incitement; a stimulus; momentum.

im·pi·e·ty (im´p´i t) n. pl. -ies The quality of being impious; irreverence.

im·pinge (im pinj´) v. To strike or collide; to impact; to encroach. **impingement** n.

im·pi·ous (im´p us) adj. Not pious; irreverent; disrespectful. **impiously** adv.

imp·ish (im´pish) adj. Mischievous. **impishly** adv. **impishness** n.

im·pla·ca·ble (im plak´a bl) adj. Not capable of being placated or appeased. **implacability** n. **implacably** adv.

im·plant (im plant´) v. To set in firmly; to fix in the mind; to insert surgically.

im·ple·ment (im´ple ment) n. A utensil or tool. v. To put into effect; to carry out; to furnish with implements.

im·pli·cate (im´pli kt´) v. To involve, especially in illegal activity; to imply.

im·pli·ca·tion (im´pli k´shan) n. The act of implicating or state of being implicated; the act of implying; an indirect expression; something implied.

im·plic·it (im plis´it) adj. Contained in the nature of someone or something but not readily apparent; understood but not directly expressed; complete; absolute.

im·plode (im pld´) v. To collapse or burst violently inward. **implosion** n.

im·plore (im plr´) v. To appeal urgently to. **implorer** n. **imploringly** adv.

im·ply (im pl´) v. To involve by logical necessity; to express indirectly; to suggest.

im·po·lite (im´po lt´) adj. Rude.

im·pol·i·tic (im pol´i tik) adj. Not expedient; tactless.

im·port (im prt´) v. To bring in goods from a foreign country for trade or sale; to mean; to signify; to be significant. n. Something imported; meaning; significance; importance. **importer** n.

im·por·tant (im por´tant) adj. Likely to determine or influence events; significant; having fame or authority.

im·por·ta·tion (im´pr t´shan) n. The act or business of importing goods; something imported.

im·por·tu·nate (im por´cha nit) adj. Persistent in pressing demands or requests.

im·por·tune (im´por tōn´) v. To press with repeated requests. **importunity** n.

im·pose (im pz´) v. To enact or apply as compulsory; to obtrude or force oneself or a burden on another; to take unfair advantage; to impose.

im·pos·si·ble (im pos´i bl) adj. Not capable of existing or happening; unlikely to take place or be done; unacceptable; difficult to tolerate or deal with. **impossibility** n.

im·post (im´pst) n. A tax or duty.

im·pos·tor or **im·pos·ter** (im pos´tr) n. One who assumes a false identity or title for the purpose of deception.

im·pos·ture (im pos´chr) n. Deception by the assumption of a false identity.

im·po·tent (im´po tent) adj. Without strength or vigor; having no power; ineffectual; incapable of sexual intercourse. **impotence** n. **impotency** n.

im·pound (im pound´) v. To confine in or as if in a pound; to seize and keep in legal custody; to hold water, as in a reservoir.

im·pov·er·ish (im pov´r ish) v. To make poor; to deprive or be deprived of nat·ural richness or fertility. **impoverishment** n.

im·prac·ti·ca·ble (im prak´ti ka bl) adj. Incapable of being done or put into practice. **impracticableness** n. **impracticability** n.

im·prac·ti·cal (im prak´ti kal) adj. Unwise to put into effect; unable to deal with practical or financial matters efficiently.

im·pre·cise (im´pri ss´) adj. Not precise.

im·preg·nate (im preg´nt) v. To make pregnant; to fertilize, as an ovum; to fill throughout; to saturate. **impregnation** n.

im·pre·sa·ri·o (im´pri sär´´) n. pl. -os A theatrical manager or producer, especially the director of an opera company.

im·press (im pres´) v. To apply or produce with pressure; to stamp or mark with or as if with pressure; to fix firmly in the mind; to affect strongly and usually favorably. *n.* The act of impressing; a mark made by impressing; a stamp or seal for impressing. **impressible** *adj.* **impresser** *n.*

im-pres-sion (im presh´an) *n.* A mark or design made on a surface by pressure; an effect or feeling retained in the mind as a result of experience; an indistinct notion or recollection; a satiric or humorous imitation; the copies of a publication printed at one time.

im-pres-sion-a-ble (im presh´a na bl) *adj.* Easily influenced.

im-pres-sive (im pres´iv) *adj.* Making a strong impression; striking.

im-pri-ma-tur (im´pri mä´tr) *n.* Official permission to print or publish; authorization.

im-print (im print´) *v.* To make or impress a mark or design on a surface; to make or stamp a mark on; to fix firmly in the mind. *n.* A mark or design made by imprinting; a lasting influence or effect; a publisher's name, often with the date and place of publication, printed at the bottom of a title page.

im-pris-on (im priz´on) *v.* To put in prison. **imprisonment** *n.*

im-prob-a-ble (im prob´a bl) *adj.* Not likely to occur or be true. **-bility** *n.*

im-promp-tu (im promp´tö) *adj.* Devised or performed without prior planning or preparation.

im-prop-er (im prop´r) *adj.* Unsuitable; indecorous; incorrect. **-erly** *adv.*

improper fraction *n.* A fraction having a numerator larger than or the same as the denominator.

im-pro-pri-e-ty (im´pro pri´t) *n. pl.* **-ies** The quality or state of being improper; an improper act or remark.

im-prove (im pröv´) *v.* To make or become better; to increase something's productivity or value. **improvable** *adj.*

im-prove-ment (im pröv´ment) *n.* The act or process of improving or the condition of being improved; a change that improves.

im-prov-i-dent (im prov´i dent) *adj.* Not providing for the future. **improvi-**

dence *n.*

im-pro-vise (im´pro vz´) *v.* To make up, compose, or perform without preparation; to make from available materials. **improvisation** *n.* **-viser** *n.*

im-pru-dent (im präd´ent) *adj.* Not prudent; unwise. **imprudence** *n.* **imprudently** *adv.*

im-pu-dent (im´p dent) *adj.* Marked by rude boldness or disrespect.

im-pugn (im pn´) *v.* To attack as false; to cast doubt on.

im-pulse (im´puls) *n.* A driving force or the motion produced by it; a sudden spontaneous urge; a motivating force; a general tendency. *Physiol.* A transfer of energy from one neuron to another.

im-pul-sive (im pul´siv) *adj.* Acting on impulse rather than thought; resulting from impulse; uncalculated. **-ly** *adv.*

im-pu-ni-ty (im p´ni t) *n.* Exemption from punishment.

im-pure (im pr´) *adj.* Not pure; unclean; unchaste or obscene; mixed with another substance; adulterated; deriving from more than one source or style.

im-pute (im pt´) *v.* To attribute something as a mistake, to another; to charge.

in ab-sen-tia *adv.* In the absence of.

in-ac-ces-si-ble (in´ak ses´i bl) *adj.* Not accessible. **inaccessibility** *n.* **-ly** *adv.*

in-ac-tive (in ak´tiv) *adj.* Not active or inclined to be active; out of current use or service. **inactively** *adv.* **inactivity** *n.*

in-ad-e-quate (in ad´e kwit) *adj.* Not adequate. **inadequacy** *n.* **-ly** *adv.*

in-ad-ver-tent (in´ad vr´tent) *adj.* Unintentional; accidental; inattentive.

in-al-ien-a-ble (in l´ya na bl) *adj.* Not capable of being given up or transferred. **inalienably** *adv.* **inalienability** *n.*

in-ane (i nn´) *adj.* Without sense or substance. **inanely** *adv.* **inanity** *n.*

in-an-i-mate (in an´i mit) *adj.* Not having the qualities of life; not animated. **inanimately** *adv.* **inanimateness** *n.*

in-a-ni-tion (in´a nish´an) *n.* Exhaustion, especially from malnourishment.

in-ap-pre-cia-ble (in´a pr´sh a bl) *adj.* Too slight to be significant. **-y** *adv.*

in-ar-tic-u-late (in´är tik´ lit) *adj.* Not uttering or forming intelligible words or syllables; unable to speak; speechless; unable to speak clearly or effectively; unexpressed. **inarticulately** *adv.* **inarticulateness** *n.*

in-as-much as (in´az much´ az´) *conj.* Because of the fact that; since.

in-au-gu-ral (in o´gr əl) *adj.* Of or for an inauguration.

in-au-gu-rate (in o´gr ət´) *v.* To put into office with a formal ceremony; to begin officially. **inauguration** *n.*

inbe-tween *adj.* Intermediate. *n.* An intermediate or intermediary.

in between *adj.* & *prep.* Between.

in-cal-cu-la-ble (in kal´kyə lə bl) *adj.* Not calculable; indeterminate; unpredictable; very large. **incalculably** *adv.*

in-can-des-cent (in´kan des´ent) *adj.* Giving off visible light when heated; shining brightly; ardently emotional or intense.

in-can-ta-tion (in´kan t´shan) *n.* A recitation of magic charms or spells; a magic formula for chanting or reciting.

in-ca-pac-i-tate (in´kə pas´i tt´) *v.* To render incapable; to disable; in law, to disqualify. **incapacitation** *n.*

in-ca-pac-i-ty (in´kə pas´i tē) *n. pl.* **-ies** Inadequate ability or strength; a defect; in law, a disqualification.

in-car-cer-ate (in kär´sə rt´) *v.* To place in jail. **incarceration** *n.*

in-car-na-tion (in´kär n´shan) *n.* The act of incarnating or state of being incarnated; the embodiment of God in the human form of Jesus; one regarded as personifying a given abstract quality or idea.

in-cen-di-ary (in sen´d er´) *adj.* Causing or capable of causing fires; of or relating to arson; tending to inflame; inflammatory.

in-cense (in´sens) *v.* To make angry. *n.* A substance, as a gum or wood, burned to produce a pleasant smell; the smoke or odor produced.

in-cen-tive (in sen´tiv) *n.* Something inciting one to action or effort; a stimulus.

in-cep-tion (in sept´) *n.* A beginning; an origin.

in-cer-ti-tude (in ser´ti tōd´) *n.* Uncertainty; lack of confidence; instability.

in-ces-sant (in ses´ant) *adj.* Occurring

without interruption; continuous.

in-cest (in´sest) *n.* Sexual intercourse between persons so closely related that they are forbidden by law to marry. **incestuous** *adj.*

inch (inch) *n.* A unit of measurement equal to 1/12th of a foot. *v.* To move slowly.

in-cho-ate (in k´it) *adj.* In an early stage; incipient. **inchoately** *adv.*

in-ci-dence (in´si dens) *n.* The extent or rate of occurrence.

in-ci-dent (in´si dent) *n.* An event; an event that disrupts normal procedure or causes a crisis.

in-ci-den-tal (in´si den´tal) *adj.* Occurring or likely to occur at the same time or as a result; minor; subordinate. *n.* A minor attendant occurrence or condition. **-ly** *adv.*

in-cin-er-ate (in sin´e rt´) *v.* To burn up.

in-cin-er-a-tor *n.* One that incinerates; a furnace for burning waste.

in-cip-i-ent (in sip´ ent) *adj.* Just beginning to appear or occur. **incipience** *n.* **-ly** *adv.*

in-cise (in sz´) *v.* To make or cut into with a sharp tool; to carve into a surface; to engrave.

in-ci-sion (in sizh´an) *n.* The act of incising; a cut or notch, especially a surgical cut.

in-ci-sive (in s´siv) *adj.* Having or suggesting sharp intellect; penetrating; cogent and effective; telling. **incisively** *adv.* **-ness** *n.*

in-ci-sor (in s´zr) *n.* A cutting tooth at the front of the mouth.

in-cite (in st´) *v.* To provoke to action. **incitement** *n.*

in-clem-ent (in klem´e nt) *adj.* Stormy or rainy; unmerciful. **inclemency** *n.*

in-cli-na-tion (in´klĭ n´shan) *n.* An attitude; a disposition; a tendency to act or think in a certain way; a preference; a bow or tilt; a slope.

in-cline (in kln´) *v.* To deviate or cause to deviate from the horizontal or vertical; to slant; to dispose or be disposed; to bow or nod. *n.* An inclined surface.

in-clude (in klōd´) *v.* To have as a part or member; to contain; to put into a group or total. **-clusion** *n.* **-clusive** *adj.*

in-cog-ni-to (in kog´ni t´) adv. & adj. With one's identity hidden.

in-co-her-ent (in´k hr´ent) adj. Lacking order, connection, or harmony; unable to think or speak clearly or consecutively. **incoherence** n. **-ly** adv.

in-com-bus-ti-ble (in´kom bus´ti bl) adj. Incapable of burning. **incombustible** n.

in-come (in´kum) n. Money or its equivalent received in return for work or as profit from investments.

income tax n. A tax on income earned by an individual or business.

in-com-ing (in´kum´ing) adj. Coming in or soon to come in.

in-com-men-su-rate (in´ko men´shr it) adj. Not commensurate; disproportionate; inadequate. **-ly** adv.

in-com-mode (in´ko md´) v. To inconvenience; to disturb.

in-com-pa-ra-ble (in kom´pr a bl) adj. Incapable of being compared; without rival.

in-com-pat-i-ble (in´kom pat´a bl) adj. Not suited for combination or association; inconsistent. **incompatibility** n.

in-com-pe-tent (in kom´pi tent) adj. Not competent. **incompetence** n. **incompetency** n. **incompetent** n.

in-com-plete (in´kom plt´) adj. Not complete. **incompletely** adv. **-ness** n.

in-con-gru-ous (in kong´grö us) adj. Not corresponding; disagreeing; made up of diverse or discordant elements; unsuited to the surrounding or setting. **incongruity** n. **incongruously** adv.

in-con-se-quen-tial (in´kon se kwen´shal) adj. Without importance; petty. **inconsequentially** adv.

in-con-sid-er-a-ble (in´kon sidr a bl) adj. Unimportant; trivial. **inconsiderably** adv.

in-con-sid-er-ate (in´kon sid´r it) adj. Not considerate; thoughtless. **-ly** adv.

in-con-sol-a-ble (in´kon s´la bl) adj. Not capable of being consoled.

in-con-spic-u-ous (in´kon spik´ us) adj. Not readily seen or noticed.

in-con-stant (in kon´stant) adj. Likely to change; unpredictable; faithless; fickle. **inconstancy** n. **-stantly** adv.

in-con-ti-nent (in kon´ti nent) adj. Not restrained; uncontrolled; unable to

contain or restrain something specified; incapable of controlling the excretory functions. **incontinence** n.

in-con-tro-vert-i-ble (in´kon tro vr´ta bl) adj. Unquestionable; indisputable.

in-con-ven-ience (in´kon vn´yens) n. The quality or state of being inconvenient; something inconvenient. v. To cause inconvenience to; to bother.

in-con-ven-ient (in´kon vn´yent) adj. Not convenient. **inconveniently** adv.

in-cor-po-rate (in kor´po rt´) v. To combine into a unified whole; to unite; to form or cause to form a legal corporation; to give a physical form to; to embody. **incorporation** n. **-rator** n.

in-cor-po-re-al (in´kor pr´ al) adj. Without material form or substance.

in-cor-ri-gi-ble (in kor´i ji bl) adj. Incapable of being reformed or corrected.

incorrigibility n. **incorrigible** n.

in-cor-rupt-i-ble (in´ko rup´ti bl) adj. Not capable of being corrupted morally; not subject to decay.

in-crease (in krs´) v. To make or become greater or larger; to have offspring; to reproduce. n. The act of increasing; the amount or rate of increasing. **increasingly** adv.

in-cred-i-ble (in kred´i bl) adj. Too unlikely to be believed; unbelievable; extraordinary; astonishing. **-bly** adv.

in-cred-u-lous (in krej´u lus) adj. Skeptical; disbelieving; expressive of disbelief. **incredulity** n. **-lously** adv.

in-cre-ment (in´kre ment) n. An increase; something gained or added, especially one of a series of regular additions. **incremental** adj.

in-crim-i-nate (in krim´i nt´) v. To involve in or charge with a wrongful act, as a crime. **incrimination** n. **incriminatory** adj.

in-cu-bus (in´k bus) n. pl. **-buses** or **-bi** An evil spirit believed to seize or harm sleeping persons; a nightmare; a nightmarish burden.

in-cul-cate (in kul´kt) v. To impress on the mind by frequent repetition or instruction. **inculcation** n. **inculcator** n.

in-cul-pate (in kul´pt) v. To incriminate.

in-cum-bent (in kum´bent) adj. Lying or resting on something else; imposed as an obligation; obligatory; currently in office. *n.* A person who is currently in office. **incumbency** *n.* **-bently** *adv.*

in-cu-nab-u-lum (in´k nab´ lum) *n. pl.* **-la** A book printed before 1501.

in-cur (in ker´) *v.* To become liable or subject to, especially because of one's own actions. **incurrence** *n.*

in-cu-ri-ous (in ker´ us) *adj.* Lacking interest; detached.

in-cur-sion (in ker´zhan) *n.* A sudden hostile intrusion into another's territory.

in-cus (ing´kus) *n. pl.* **incudes** An anvil-shaped bone in the middle ear of mammals.

in-debt-ed (in det´id) *adj.* Obligated to another, as for money or a favor; beholden.

in-de-cent (in d´sent) *adj.* Morally offensive or contrary to good taste. **indecency** *n.*

in-de-ci-pher-a-ble (in´di s´fr a bl) *adj.* Not capable of being deciphered or interpreted.

in-de-ci-sion (in´di sizh´an) *n.* Inability to make up one's mind; irresolution.

in-de-ci-sive (in´di s´siv) *adj.* Without a clearcut result; marked by indecision. **indecisively** *adv.* **indecisiveness** *n.*

in-dec-o-rous (in dek´r us) *adj.* Lacking good taste or propriety. **indecorously** *adv.*

in-deed (in dd´) *adv.* Most certainly; without doubt; in reality; in fact. *interj.* Used to express surprise, irony, or disbelief.

in-de-fat-i-ga-ble (in´di fat´i ga bl) *adj.* Tireless. **indefatigably** *adv.*

in-de-fin-a-ble (in´di f´na bl) *adj.* Not capable of being defined. **-ness** *n.*

in-def-i-nite (in def´i nit) *adj.* Not decided or specified; vague; unclear; lacking fixed limits. **indefinitely** *adv.* **indefiniteness** *n.*

in-del-i-ble (in del´i bl) *adj.* Not able to be erased or washed away; permanent. **in-del-i-cate** (in del´i kit) *adj.* Lacking sensitivity; tactless. **indelicacy** *n.*

in-dem-ni-fy (in dem´ni f´) *v.* To secure against hurt, loss, or damage; to make compensation for hurt, loss, or damage. **indemnification** *n.* **-fier** *n.*

in-dem-ni-ty (in dem´ni t) *n. pl.* **-ties**

Security against hurt, loss, or damage; a legal exemption from liability for damages; compensation for hurt, loss, or damage.

in-dent (in dent´) *v.* To set in from the margin, as the first line of a paragraph; to notch the edge of; to serrate; to make a dent or depression in; to impress; to stamp. *n.* An indentation.

in-den-ta-tion (in´den t´shan) *n.* The act of indenting or the state of being indented; an angular cut in an edge; a recess in a surface.

in-den-ture (in den´chr) *n.* A legal deed or contract; a contract obligating one party to work for another for a specified period of time. *v.* To bind into the service of another.

in-de-pend-ent (in´di pen´dent) *adj.* Politically self-governing; free from the control of others; not committed to a political party or faction; not relying on others, especially for financial support; providing or having enough income to enable one to live without working. *n.* One who is independent, especially a candidate or voter not committed to a political party.

indepth (in-depth) *adj.* Thorough; detailed.

in-de-scrib-a-ble (in´di skr´ba bl) *adj.* Surpassing description; incapable of being described. **indescribably** *adv.*

in-de-ter-mi-nate (in´di tr´mi nit) *adj.* Not determined; not able to be determined; unclear or vague. **indeterminacy** *n.* **-ly** *adv.*

in-dex-a-tion (in deks´a shen) *n.* The linkage of economic factors, as wages or prices, to a cost-of-living index so they rise and fall within the rate of inflation.

index finger *n.* The finger next to the thumb.

index of refraction *n.* The quotient of the speed of light in a vacuum divided by the speed of light in a medium under consideration.

in-di-cate (in´di kt´) *v.* To point out; to show; to serve as a sign or symptom; to signify; to suggest the advisability of; to call for. **indication** *n.* **-cator** *n.*

in-dic-a-tive (in dik´a tiv) *adj.* Serving to indicate; of or being a verb mood used to express actions and conditions that are objective facts. *n.* The indicative mood; a verb in the indicative mood.

in-dict (in dt´) *v.* To accuse of an offense; to charge; to make a formal accusation against by the findings of a grand jury. **indictable** *adj.* **indicter** *n.* **indictment** *n.*

in-dif-fer-ent (in dif´r ent) *adj.* Having no marked feeling or preference; impartial; neither good nor bad. **indifference** *n.*

in-dig-e-nous (in dij´e nus) *adj.* Living or occurring naturally in an area; native.

in-di-gent (in´di jent) *adj.* Impoverished; needy. **indigence** *n.*

in-di-ges-tion (in´di jes´chan) *n.* Difficulty or discomfort in digesting food.

in-dig-nant (in dig´nant) *adj.* Marked by or filled with indignation. **-ly** *adv.*

in-dig-na-tion (in´dig n´shan) *n.* Anger aroused by injustice, unworthiness, or unfairness.

in-dig-ni-ty (in dig´ni t) *n. pl.* **-ies** Humiliating treatment; something that offends one's pride.

in-di-go (in´di g´) *n. pl.* **-gos** *or* **-goes** A blue dye obtained from a plant or produced synthetically; a dark blue.

in-di-rect (in´di rekt´) *adj.* Not taking a direct course; not straight to the point. **indirection** *n.* **indirectly** *adv.*

in-dis-creet (in´di skrt´) *adj.* Lacking discretion. **-ly** *adv.* **indiscretion** *n.*

in-dis-pen-sa-ble (in´di spen´sa bl) *adj* Necessary; essential. **-sability** *n.*

in-dite (in dt´) *v.* To write; to compose; to put down in writing. **inditer** *n.*

in-di-um (in´d um) *n.* A soft, silver-white, metallic element used for mirrors and transistor compounds, symbolized by In.

in-di-vid-u-al (in´di vij´ö al) *adj.* Of, for, or relating to a single human being. **indivdually** *adv.*

in-di-vis-i-ble (in´di viz´i bl) *adj.* Not able to be divided.

in-doc-tri-nate (in dok´tri nt´) *v.* To instruct in a doctrine or belief; to train to accept a system of thought uncritically. **-ion** *n.*

in-do-lent (in´do lent) *adj.* Disinclined to exert oneself; lazy. **indolence** *n.*

in-dom-i-ta-ble (in dom´i ta bl) *adj.* Incapable of being subdued or defeated.

in-du-bi-ta-ble (in dö´bi ta bl) *adj.* Too evident to be doubted. **-bly** *adv.*

in-duce (in dös´) *v.* To move by persuasion or influence; to cause to occur; to infer by inductive reasoning. **-er** *n.*

in-duct (in dukt´) *v.* To place formally in office; to admit as a new member; to summon into military service.

in-duc-tance (in duk´tans) *n.* A circuit element, usually a conducting coil, in which electromagnetic induction generates electromotive force.

in-duc-tion (in duk´shan) *n.* The act of inducting or of being inducted; reasoning in which conclusions are drawn from particular instances or facts; the generation of electromotive force in a closed circuit by a magnetic field that changes with time; the production of an electric charge in an uncharged body by bringing a charged body close to it.

in-dulge (in dulj´) *v.* To give in to the desires of, especially to excess; to yield to; to allow oneself a special pleasure. **indulger** *n.*

in-dus-tri-al (in dus´tr al) *adj.* Of, relating to, or used in industry. **-ally** *adv.*

in-dus-tri-ous (in dus´tr us) *adj.* Working steadily and hard; diligent. **industriously** *adv.* **industriousness** *n.*

in-dus-try (in´du str) *n. pl.* **-tries** The commercial production and sale of goods and services; a branch of manufacture and trade; industrial management as distinguished from labor; diligence.

in-e-bri-ate (in´br at´) *v.* To make drunk; to intoxicate. **inebriant** *n.* **inebriated** *n.*

in-ef-fa-ble (in ef´a bl) *adj.* Beyond expression; indescribable. **-fably** *adv.*

in-ef-fi-cient (in´i fish´ent) *adj.* Wasteful of time, energy, or materials. **inefficiency** *n.*

jn-e-luc-ta-ble (in´i luk´ta bl) *adj.* Not capable of being avoided or overcome.

in-ept (in ept´) *adj.* Awkward or incompetent; not suitable. **ineptitude** *n.* **in-**

eptness n. **ineptly** adv.

in·e·qual·i·ty (in′i kwol′i t) n. pl. **-ies** The condition or an instance of being unequal; social or economic disparity; lack of regularity; in mathematics, an algebraic statement that a quantity is greater than or less than another quantity.

in·eq·ui·ty n. pl. **-ies** Injustice; unfair.

in·ert (in ert′) adj. Not able to move or act; slow to move or act; sluggish; displaying no chemical activity. **-ly** adv.

in·er·tia (in er′sha) n. The tendency of a body to remain at rest or to stay in motion unless acted upon by an external force; resistance to motion or change. **inertial** adj.

in·ev·i·ta·ble (in ev′i ta bl) adj. Not able to be avoided or prevented. **inevitability** n.

in·ex·o·ra·ble (in ek′sr a bl) adj. Not capable of being moved by entreaty; unyielding.

in·ex·pe·ri·ence (in′ik spr′ ens) n. Lack of experience.

in·ex·pli·ca·ble (in eks′pli ka bl) adj. Not capable of being explained.

in·ex·tre·mis adv. At the point of death.

in·ex·tri·ca·ble (in eks′tri ka bl) adj. Not capable of being untied or untangled; too complex to resolve. **inextricably** adv.

in·fal·li·ble (in fal′i bl) adj. Not capable of making mistakes; not capable of failing; never wrong. **infallibility** n.

in·fa·mous (in′fa mus) adj. Having a very bad reputation; shocking or disgraceful.

in·fa·my (in′fa m) n. pl. **-ies** Evil notoriety or reputation; the state of being infamous; a disgraceful, publicly known act.

in·fan·cy (in′fan s) n. pl. **-ies** The condition or time of being an infant; an early stage of existence; in law, minority.

in·fant (in′fant) n. A child in the first period of life; a very young child; in law, a minor.

in·fan·ti·cide (in fan′ti sd′) n. The killing of an infant.

infantile paralysis n. Poliomyelitis.

in·farct (in färkt′) n. An area of dead tissue caused by an insufficient supply of blood. **infarcted** adj. **infarction** n.

in·fat·u·ate (in fach′ t′) v. To arouse an extravagant or foolish love in. **infatuated** adj. **infatuation** n.

in·fect (in fekt′) v. To contaminate with disease-causing microorganisms; to transmit a disease to; to affect as if by contagion.

in·fec·tion (in fek′shan) n. Invasion of a bodily part by disease-causing microorganisms; the condition resulting from such an invasion; an infectious disease.

in·fe·lic·i·tous (in fi′lis et es) adj. Not happy; unfortunate; not apt, as in an expression. **infelicity** n. **-tously** adv.

in·fer (in fer′) v. To conclude by reasoning; to deduce; to have as a logical consequence; to lead to as a result or conclusion.

in·fer·ence (in′fr ens) n. A conclusion based on facts and premises.

in·fe·ri·or (in fr′ r) adj. Located under or below; low or lower in order, rank, or quality. **inferior** n. **inferiority** n.

in·fer·nal (in fer′nal) adj. Of, like, or relating to hell; damnable; abominable. **-ly** adv.

in·fer·no (in fer′n) n. A place or condition suggestive of hell.

in·fest (in fest′) v. To spread in or over so as to be harmful or offensive. **-ion** n.

in·fi·del (in′fi del) n. One who has no religion; an unbeliever in a religion, especially Christianity.

in·fil·trate (in fil′trt) v. To pass or cause to pass into something through pores or small openings; to pass through or enter gradually or stealthily. **infiltration** n.

in·fi·nite (in′fi nit) adj. Without boundaries; limitless; immeasurably great or large; in mathematics, greater in value than any specified number, however large; having measure that is infinite. **infinitely** adv.

in·fin·i·tes·i·mal (in′fin i tes′i mal) adj. Immeasurably small. **-mally** adv.

in·fin·i·ty (in fin′i t) n. pl. **-ies** The quality or state of being infinite; unbounded space, time, or amount; an indefinitely large number.

in·firm (in ferm′) adj. Physically weak, especially from age; feeble; not sound

in-fir-ma-ry (in fer′ma r) n. pl. -ries
An institution for the care of the sick or disabled.

in-flame (in flm′) v. To set on fire; to arouse to strong or excessive feeling; to intensify; to produce, affect or be affected by inflammation.

in-flam-ma-ble (in flam′a bl) adj. Tending to catch fire easily; easily excited.

in-flam-ma-tion (in′fla m′shan) n. Localized redness, swelling, heat, and pain in response to an injury or infection.

in-flate (in flt′) v. To fill and expand with a gas; to increase unsoundly; to puff up; to raise prices abnormally. **inflatable** adj.

in-fla-tion (in fl′shan) n. The act or process of inflating; a period during which there is an increase in the monetary supply, causing a continuous rise in the price of goods.

in-flect (in flekt′) v. To turn; to veer; to vary the tone or pitch of the voice, especially in speaking; to change the form of a word to indicate number, tense, or person.

in-flex-i-ble (in flek′si bl) adj. Not flexible; rigid; not subject to change; unalterable. **inflexibility** n. **inflexibly** adv.

in-flict (in flikt′) v. To cause to be suffered; to impose. **-er** n. **-or** n. **-ion** n.

in-flo-res-cence (in′flo res′ens) n. A characteristic arrangement of flowers on a stalk. **-scent** adj.

in-flu-ence (in′flo ens) n. The power to produce effects, especially indirectly or through an intermediary; the condition of being affected; one exercising indirect power to sway or affect. v. To exert influence over; to modify. **influential** adj.

in-flu-en-za (in′flo en′za) n. An acute, infectious viral disease marked by respiratory inflammation, fever, muscular pain, and often intestinal discomfort; the flu.

in-flux (in′fluks′) n. A stream of people or things coming in.

in-form-ant (in for′mant) n. One who discloses or furnishes information which should remain secret.

in-for-ma-tive (in for′ma tiv) adj. Providing information; instructive.

in-frac-tion (in frak′shan) n. A violation of a rule.

in-fra-red (in′fra red′) adj. Of, being, or using electromagnetic radiation with wave lengths longer than those of visible light and shorter than those of microwaves.

in-fra-son-ic (in′fra son′ik) adj. Producing or using waves or vibrations with frequencies below that of audible sound.

in-fra-struc-ture (in′fra struk′chr) n. An underlying base or foundation; the basic facilities needed for the functioning of a system.

in-fringe (in frinj′) v. To break a law; to violate; to encroach; to trespass. **infringement** n.

in-fu-ri-ate (in fr′ t′) v. To make very angry or furious; to enrage.

in-fuse (in fz′) v. To introduce, instill or inculcate, as principles; to obtain a liquid extract by soaking a substance in water.

-ing suff Used in forming the present participle of verbs and adjectives resembling participles; activity or action; the result or a product of an action.

in-gen-ious (in jn′yus) adj. Showing great ingenuity; to have inventive ability; clever. **ingeniously** adv. **ingeniousness** n.

in-ge-nu-i-ty (in′je nö′ t) n. pl. -ies Cleverness; inventive skill.

in-gen-u-ous (in jen′ us) adj. Frank and straightforward; lacking sophistication.

in-gest (in jest′) v. To take or put food into the body by swallowing. **ingestion** n.

in-glo-ri-ous (in glr′ us) adj. Not showing courage or honor; dishonorable.

in-got (ing′got) n. A mass of cast metal shaped in a bar or block.

in-grate (in′grt) n. A person who is ungrateful.

in-gra-ti-ate (in gr′sh t′) v. To gain favor or confidence of others by deliberate effort or manipulation. **ingratiatingly** adv. **ingratiation** n.

in-grat-i-tude (in grat′i töd′) n. Lack of

gratitude.

in-gre-di-ent (in grʹd ent) n. An element that enters into the composition of a mixture; a part of anything.

in-gress (inʹgres) n. A going in or entering of a building. **ingression** n. **ingressive** adj.

in-grown (inʹgrn´) adj. Growing into the flesh; growing abnormally within or into.

in-hab-it (in habʹit) v. To reside in; to occupy as a home.

in-ha-la-tion (inʹha lʹshan) n. The act of inhaling.

in-here (in herʹ) v. To be an essential or permanent feature; to belong.

in-her-ent (in hrʹent) adj. Forming an essential element or quality of something.

in-her-it (in herʹit) v. To receive something, as property, money, or other valuables, by legal succession or will. *Biol.* To receive traits or qualities from one's ancestors or parents. **inheritable** adj. **inheritor** n.

in-hib-it (in hibʹit) v. To restrain or hold back; to prevent full expression. **inhibitable** adj. **inhibitor** n. **-iter** n.

in-hi-bi-tion (inʹi bishʹan) n. The act of restraining, especially a self-imposed restriction on one's behavior; a mental or psychological restraint.

in-hu-man (in hʹman) adj. Lacking pity, emotional warmth, or kindness; monstrous; not being of the ordinary human type.

in-hu-mane (inʹh mn´) adj. Lacking compassion or pity; cruel.

in-hu-man-i-ty (inʹh manʹi t) n. pl. **-ties** The lack of compassion or pity; an inhumane or cruel act.

in-im-i-cal (i nimʹi kal) adj. Harmful opposition; hostile; malign.

in-im-i-ta-ble (i nimʹi ta bl) adj. Incapable of being matched; unique. **inimitably** adv.

in-iq-ui-ty (i nikʹwi t) n. pl. **-ies** The grievous violation of justice; wickedness; sinfulness. **iniquitous** adj.

i-ni-tial (i nishʹal) adj. Of or pertaining to the beginning. n. The first letter of a name or word. v. To mark or sign with initials.

in-i-ti-ate (i nishʹt´) v. To begin or start;

to admit someone to membership in an organization, fraternity, or group; to instruct in fundamentals. adj. Initiated. **initiator** n.

in-i-ti-a-tive (i nishʹa tiv) n. The ability to originate or follow through with a plan of action; the action of taking the first or leading step. *Govt.* The power or right to propose legislative measures.

in-ject (in jektʹ) v. To force a drug or fluid into the body through a blood vessel or the skin with a hypodermic syringe; to throw in or introduce a comment abruptly.

in-jure (inʹjr) v. To cause physical harm, damage, or pain.

in-ju-ry (in jeʹr) n. pl. **-ies** Damage or harm inflicted or suffered.

in-jus-tice (in jusʹtis) n. The violation of another person's rights; an unjust act; a wrong.

ink (ingk) n. Any of variously colored liquids or paste, used for writing, drawing, and printing. **inker** n.

in-laid (inʹld´) adj. Ornamented with wood, ivory, or other materials embedded flush with the surface.

inlaw (inʹlo´) n. A relative by marriage.

in-let (inʹlet) n. A bay or stream that leads into land; a passage between nearby islands.

in-mate (inʹmt´) n. A person who dwells in a building with another; one confined in a prison, asylum, or hospital.

in-nards (inʹrdz) n., pl. The internal organs or parts of the body; the inner parts of a machine.

in-ner (inʹr) adj. Situated or occurring farther inside; relating to or of the mind or spirit.

in-no-cent (inʹo sent) adj. Free from sin, evil, or moral wrong; pure; legally free from blame or guilt; not maliciously intended; lacking in experience or knowledge; naive. **innocence** n. **innocent** n. **innocently** adv.

in-noc-u-ous (i nokʹ us) adj. Having no harmful qualities or ill effect; harmless.

in-no-vate (inʹo vt´) v. To introduce or begin something new. **innovative** adj.

in-nu-en-do (inʹ enʹd) n. pl. **-dos** or **-does** An indirect or oblique comment, suggestion or hint.

in-nu-mer-a-ble (i nŏ´mr *a* bl) *adj.* Too numerous or too much to be counted; countless.

in-oc-u-late (i nok´ lt) *v.* To introduce a mild form of a disease or virus to a person or animal in order to produce immunity.

in-op-er-a-ble (in op´r *a* bl) *adj.* Unworkable; incapable of being treated or improved by surgery.

in-op-er-a-tive (in op´r *a* tiv) *adj.* Not working; not functioning.

in-op-por-tune (in op´r tŏn´) *adj.* Inappropriate; untimely; unsuitable. **inopportunely** *adv.*

in-or-gan-ic (in´or gan´ik) *adj.* Not having or involving living organisms, their remains, or products.

in-pa-tient (in´p shent) *n.* A patient admitted to a hospital for medical treatment.

in-put (in´pet´) *n.* The amount of energy delivered to a machine; in computer science, information that is put into a data processing system. *Elect.* The voltage, current, or power that is delivered to a circuit.

in-quest (in´kwest) *n.* A legal investigation into the cause of death.

in-quire (in kwr´) *v.* To ask a question; to make an investigation. **inquirer** *n.*

in-quir-y (in kwr´) *n. pl.* **-ies** The act of seeking or inquiring; a request or question for information; a very close examination; an investigation or examination of facts or evidence.

in-quis-i-tive (in kwiz´i tiv) *adj.* Curious; probing; questioning. **inquisitively** *adv.*

in-sane (in sn´) *adj.* Afflicted with a serious mental disorder impairing a person's ability to function; the characteristic of a person who is not sane. **insanely** *adv.* **insanity** *n.*

in-san-i-tar-y (in san´i ter´) *adj.* Not sanitary; not hygienic and dangerous to one's health.

in-scribe (in skrb´) *v.* To write, mark, or engrave on a surface; to enter a name in a register or on a formal list; to write a short note on a card. *Geom.* To enclose one figure in another so that the latter encloses the former. **-er** *n.*

in-scru-ta-ble (in skrŏ´ta bl) *adj.* Difficult to interpret or understand; incomprehensible. **inscrutability** *n.* **inscrutableness** *n.* **inscrutably** *adv.*

in-se-cure (in´si kr´) *adj.* Troubled by anxiety and apprehension; threatened; not securely guarded; unsafe; liable to break, fail, or collapse. **-ly** *adv.* **-ity** *n.*

in-sem-i-nate (in sem´i nt´) *v.* To introduce semen into the uterus of; to make pregnant; to sow seed. **insemination** *n.*

in-sen-si-ble (in sen´si bl) *adj.* Deprived of consciousness; unconscious; incapable of perceiving or feeling; unmindful; unaware. **insensibility** *n.* **insensibly** *adv.*

in-sen-ti-ent (in sen´sh ent) *adj.* Without sensation or consciousness.

in-sep-a-ra-ble (in sep´r *a* bl) *adj.* Incapable of being separated or parted. **inseparability** *n.* **inseparably** *adv.*

in-sert (in sert´) *v.* To put in place; to set. In printing, something inserted or to be inserted. **insertion** *n.*

in-set (in set´) *v.* To set in; to implant; to insert.

in-side (in´sd´) *n.* The part, surface, or space that lies within. **insides** The internal parts or organs. **inside** *adj.*

in-sid-i-ous (in sid´ us) *adj.* Cunning or deceitful; treacherous; seductive; attractive but harmful. **insidiously** *adv.*

in-sight (in´st´) *n.* Perception into the true or hidden nature of things. **insightful** *adj.*

in-sig-ni-a (in sig´n *a*) *n. pl.* **-nia** or **-nias** A badge or emblem used to mark membership, honor, or office.

in-sin-cere (in´sin sr´) *adj.* Not sincere; hypocritical. **insincerely** *adv.* **-ity** *n.*

in-sin-u-ate (in sin´ t´) *v.* To suggest something by giving a hint; to introduce by using ingenious and sly means. **insinuating** *n.*

in-sip-id (in sip´id) *adj.* Lacking of flavor; tasteless; flat; dull; lacking interest. **insipidly** *adv.* **insipidness** *n.*

in-sist (in sist´) *v.* To demand or assert in a firm way; to dwell on something repeatedly, as to emphasize. **insistence** *n.* **insistent** *adj.* **insistently** *adv.*

in-so-far (in´so fär´) *adv.* To such an extent.

in-sole (in´sl) *n.* The fixed inside sole of

a shoe or boot; a removable strip of material put inside a shoe for protection or comfort.

in-sol-u-ble (in sol´ bl) *adj.* Incapable of being dissolved; not soluble; not capable of being solved. **insolubility** *n.*

in-sol-vent (in sol´vent) *adj.* In law, unable to meet debts; bankrupt.

in-som-ni-a (in som´n a) *n.* The chronic inability to sleep. **insomniac** *n.*

in-spect (in spekt´) *v.* To examine or look at very carefully for flaws; to examine or review officially. **-tion** *n.*

in-spi-ra-tion (in´spi r´shan) *n.* The stimulation within the mind of some idea, feeling, or impulse which leads to creative action; a divine or holy presence which inspires; the act of inhaling air. **-al** *adj.* **inspirationally** *adv.*

in-spire (in spir´) *v.* To exert or guide by a divine influence; to arouse and create high emotion; to exalt; to inhale; breathe in. **inspirer** *n.* **inspiringly** *adv.*

in-sta-bil-i-ty (in sta bil´i t) *n. pl.* **-ties** Lacking stability.

in-stall-ment *or* **in-stal-ment** (in stol´ ment) *n.* One of several payments due in specified amounts at specified intervals.

in-stance (in´stans) *n.* An illustrative case or example; a step in proceedings. *v.* To illustrate.

in-stant (in´stant) *n.* A very short time; a moment; a certain or specific point in time. *adj.* Instantaneously; immediate; urgent.

in-stead (in sted´) *adv.* In lieu of that just mentioned.

in-step (in´step´) *n., Anat.* The arched upper part of the human foot.

in-still *or* **in-stil** (in stil´) *v.* To introduce by gradual instruction or effort; to pour in slowly by drops. **instillation** *n.* **instiller** *n.*

in-stinct (in´stingkt) *n.* The complex and normal tendency or response of a given species to act in ways essential to its existence, development, and survival. **-ive** *adj.*

in-sti-tute (in´sti tōt´) *v.* To establish or set up; to find; to initiate; to set in operation; to start. *n.* An organization set up to promote or further a cause; an institution for educating.

in-sti-tu-tion (in´sti tō´shan) *n.* The principle custom that forms part of a society or civilization; an organization which performs a particular job or function, such as research, charity, or education; a place of confinement such as a prison or mental hospital.

in-struct (in strukt´) *v.* To impart skill or knowledge; to teach; to give orders or direction. **instructive** *adj.*

in-struc-tion (in struk´shan) *n.* The act of teaching or instructing; important knowledge; a lesson; an order or direction.

in-stru-ment (in´stru ment) *n.* A mechanical tool or implement; a device used to produce music; a person who is controlled by another; a dupe; in law, a formal legal document, deed, or contract.

in-stru-men-tal (in´stru men´tal) *adj.* Acting or serving as a means; pertaining to, composed for, or performed on a musical instrument.

in-stru-men-tal-ist (in´stru men´ta list) *n.* A person who plays or performs with a musical instrument.

in-sub-or-di-nate (in´su bor´di net) *adj.* Not obedient; not obeying orders. **insubordinately** *adv.* **insubordination** *n.*

in-sub-stan-tial (in´sub stan´shal) *adj.* Unreal; imaginary; not solid or firm; flimsy.

in-suf-fi-cient (in´su fish´ent) *adj.* Inadequate; not enough. **-ciently** *adv.*

in-su-lar (in´su lr) *adj.* Of or related to an island; typical or suggestive of life on an island; narrow-minded; limited in customs, opinions, and ideas. **insularity** *n.*

in-su-late (in´su lt´) *v.* To isolate; to wrap or surround with nonconducting material in order to prevent the passage of heat, electricity, or sound into or out of; to protect with wrapping or insulation. **insulator** *n.*

in-su-lin (in´su lin) *n., Biochem.* The hormone released by the pancreas, essential in regulating the metabolism of sugar; a preparation of this hormone removed from the pancreas of a pig or an ox, used in the treatment of diabetes.

in-sult (in´sult) v. To speak or to treat with insolence or contempt; to abuse verbally. n. An act or remark that offends someone. **insulter** n. **insulting** adj. **insultingly** adv. **insuperability** n. **insuperably** adv.

in-sur-ance (in sher´ans) n. Protection against risk, loss, or ruin; the coverage an insurer guarantees to pay in the event of death, loss, or medical bills; a contract guaranteeing such protection on future specified losses in return for annual payments; any safeguard against n. risk or harm. **insurability** n.

in-sure (in´sher´) v. To guarantee against loss of life, property, or other types of losses; to make certain; to ensure; to buy or issue insurance. **insurability** n. **insurable** adj.

in-sur-mount-a-ble (in´sr moun´ta bl) adj. Incapable of being overcome.

in-sur-rec-tion (in´su rek´shan) n. An open revolt against an established government. **insurrectionary** n. **insurrectional** adj.

in-sus-cep-ti-ble (in´su sep´ta bl) adj. Immune; incapable of being infected.

in-tact (in takt´) adj. Remaining whole and not damaged in any way. **-ness** n.

in-tan-gi-ble (in tan´ji bl) adj. Incapable of being touched; vague or indefinite to the mind. **intangibility** n. **intangibleness** n.

in-te-ger (in´ti jr) n. Any of the numbers 1, 2, 3, etc., including all the positive whole numbers and all the negative numbers and zero; a whole entity.

in-te-gral (in´te gral) adj. Being an essential and indispensable part of a whole; made up, from, or formed of parts that constitute a unity.

in-te-grate (in´te grt´) v. To make into a whole by joining parts together; to unify; to be open to people of all races or ethnic groups. **integration** n. **integrative** adj.

in-teg-ri-ty (in teg´ri t) n. Uprightness of character; honesty; the condition, quality, or state of being complete or undivided.

in-tel-lect (in´te lekt´) n. The power of the mind to understand and to accept knowledge; the state of having a strong or brilliant mind; a person of notable intellect.

in-tel-lec-tu-al (in´te lek´chö al) adj. Pertaining to, possessing, or showing intellect; inclined to rational or creative thought. n. A person who pursues and enjoys matters of the intellect and of refined taste. **intellectually** adv.

in-tel-lec-tu-al-ize (in´te lek´chö a lz´) v. To examine objectively so as not to become emotionally involved. **intellectualization** n. **intellectualizer** n.

in-tel-li-gence (in tel´i jens) n. The capacity to perceive and comprehend meaning; information; news; the gathering of secret information, as by military or police authorities; information so collected.

in-tel-li-gent (in tel´i jent) adj. Having or showing intelligence. **-gently** adv.

in-tel-li-gi-ble (in tel´i ji bl) adj. Having the capabilities of being understood; understanding.

in-tend (in tend´) v. To have a plan or purpose in mind; to design for a particular use.

in-tense (in tens´) adj. Extreme in strength, effect, or degree; expressing strong emotion, concentration, or strain; profound. **-ly** adv. **-ness** n.

in-ten-si-fy (in ten´si f´) v. To become or make more intense or acute. **-ication** n.

in-ten-si-ty (in ten´si t) n. pl. **-ies** The quality of being intense or acute; a great effect, concentration, or force.

in-ten-sive (in ten´siv) adj. Forceful and concentrated; marked by a full and complete application of all resources.

in-tent (in tent´) n. A purpose, goal, aim, or design. **intently** adv. **intentness** n.

in-ten-tion (in ten´shan) n. A plan of action; either immediate or ultimate.

in-ten-tion-al adj. Deliberately intended or done. **intentionality** n. **-ly** adv.

in-ter (in ter´) v. To place in a grave; bury. **interment** n.

inter- pref. Mutually; with each other; together; among or between.

in-ter-act (in´tr akt´) v. To act on each other or with each other. **-ion** n. **interactive** adj.

in-ter-cede (in´tr sd) v. To argue or plead on another's behalf. **-ceder** n.

in-ter-cept (in´tr sept´) v. To interrupt

the path or course of; to seize or stop. **intercept** *n.* **interception** *n.*

in-ter-ces-sion (in´tr sesh´an) *n.* An entreaty or prayer on behalf of others. **intercessor** *n.* **intercessional** *adj.*

in-ter-change (in´tr chnj´) *v.* To put each in the place of another; to give and receive in return. *n.* The intersection of a highway which allows traffic to enter or turn off without obstructing other traffic. **-able** *adj.*

in-ter-col-le-gi-ate (in´tr ko l´jit) *adj.* Involving or pertaining to two or more colleges.

in-ter-com (in´tr kom´) *n. Informal* A two-way communication system, as used in different areas of a home or business.

in-ter-com-mu-ni-cate (in´tr ko m´ni kt´) *v.* To communicate with each other.

in-ter-con-ti-nen-tal (in´tr kon´ti nen´tal) *adj.* Pertaining to or involving two or more continents.

in-ter-course (in´tr krs´) *n.* Mutual exchange between persons or groups; communication; sexual intercourse.

in-ter-dict (in´tr dikt´) *v.* To forbid or prohibit by official decree. **interdiction** *n.* **interdictory** *adj.*

in-ter-est (in´tr ist) *n.* Curiosity or concern about something; that which is to one's benefit; legal or financial right, claim, or share, as in a business; a charge for a loan of money, usually a percent of the amount borrowed.

in-ter-est-ed (in´tr i stid) *adj.* Having or displaying curiosity; having a right to share in something. **interestedly** *adv.*

in-ter-face (in´tr fs´) *n.* A surface forming a common boundary between adjacent areas; in computer science, the software or hardware connecting one device or system to another. **interface** *v.* **interfacial** *adj.*

in-ter-fere (in´tr fr´) *v.* To come between; to get in the way; to be an obstacle or obstruction. **interference** *n.*

in-ter-ga-lac-tic (in´tr ga lak´tik) *adj.* Between galaxies.

in-ter-im (in´tr im) *n.* A time between events or periods. *adj.* Temporary.

in-te-ri-or (in tr´ r) *adj.* Of, or contained in the inside; inner; away from

the coast or border; inland; private; not exposed to view.

in-ter-ject (in´tr jekt´) *v.* To go between other parts or elements; to add something between other things. **-jector** *n.*

in-ter-jec-tion (in´tr jek´shan) *n.* A word used as an exclamation to express emotion, as *Oh! Heavens! Super!*

in-ter-lace (int er´ls) *v.* To join by weaving together; to intertwine; to blend.

in-ter-lin-e-ar (in´tr lin´ r) *adj.* Situated or inserted between lines of a text.

in-ter-loc-u-tor (in´tr lok´ tr) *n.* One who takes part in a conversation.

in-ter-loc-u-to-ry (in´tr lok´ tr´) *adj.* Having the nature of a dialogue; in law, pronounced while a suit is pending and temporarily in effect.

in-ter-lope (in´tr lp´) *v.* To intrude or interfere in the rights of others.

in-ter-lude (in´tr lōd´) *n.* A period of time that occurs in and divides some longer process; light entertainment between the acts of a show, play, or other more serious entertainment.

in-ter-me-di-ar-y (in´tr m d´er´) *n. pl.* **-ies** A mediator. *adj.* Coming between; intermediate.

in-ter-me-di-ate (in´tr m´d it) *adj.* Situated or occurring in the middle or between. **intermediately** *adv.*

in-ter-min-gle (in´tr ming´gl) *v.* To blend or become mixed together.

in-ter-mit-tent *adj.* Ceasing from time to time; coming at intervals.

in-tern *or* **in-terne** (in´tern) *n.* A recent graduate of medical school.

in-ter-nal (in ter´nal) *adj.* Of or pertaining to the inside; pertaining to the domestic affairs of a country; intended to be consumed by the body from the inside.

internal medicine *n.* The branch of medicine that studies and treats the nonsurgical diseases.

in-ter-na-tion-al (in´tr nash´a nal) *adj.* Pertaining to or involving two or more nations. **internationally** *adv.*

in-ter-nec-ine (in´tr n´sn) *adj.* Mutually destructive to both sides; involving struggle within a group.

in-tern-ee (in ter´ n´) *n.* A person who is confined or interned.

in-ter-play (in´tr pl´) *n.* Action, movement, or influence between or among people.

in-ter-po-late (in ter´po lt´) v. To insert between other things or elements; to change something by introducing additions or insertions. **-lation** n.

in-ter-pose (in´tr pz´) v. To put between parts; to put in or inject a comment into a conversation or speech; to intervene. **interposer** n. **interposition** n.

in-ter-pret (in ter´prit) v. To convey the meaning of something by explaining or restating; to present the meaning of something, as in a picture; to take words spoken or written in one language and put them into another language. **interpretation** n.

in-ter-ra-cial (in´tr r´shal) adj. Between, among, or affecting different races.

in-ter-reg-num (in´tr reg´num) n. pl. -nums An interval between two successive reigns; a break in continuity.

in-ter-re-late (in´tr ri lt´) v. To have or to put into a mutual relationship. **interrelation** n. **interrelationship** n.

in-ter-ro-gate (in ter´o gt´) v. To question formally. **interrogation** n. **interrogator** n.

in-ter-rog-a-tive (in´te rog´a tiv) adj. Asking or having the nature of a question. n. A word used to ask a question.

in-ter-rupt (in´te rupt´) v. To break the continuity of something; to intervene abruptly while someone else is speaking or performing. **interrupter** n. **ion** n. **interruptive** adj.

in-ter-scho-las-tic (in´tr sko las´tik) adj. Conducted between or among schools.

in-ter-sect (in´tr sekt´) v. To divide by cutting through or across; to form an intersection; to cross.

in-ter-sec-tion (in´tr sek´shan) n. A place of crossing; a place where streets or roads cross; in mathematics, the point common to two or more geometric elements.

in-ter-sperse (in´tr spers´) v. To scatter among other things. **interspersion** n.

in-ter-state (in´tr stt´) adj. Between, involving, or among two or more states.

in-ter-stel-lar (in´tr stel´r) adj. Among or between the stars.

in-ter-stice (in ter´stis) n. The small space between things; an intervening space.

in-ter-twine (in´tr twn´) v. To unite by twisting together. **intertwinement** n.

in-ter-ur-ban (in´tr er´ban) adj. Between or among connecting urban areas.

in-ter-val (in´tr val) n. The time coming between two points or objects; a period of time between events or moments. Mus. The difference in pitch between two tones.

in-ter-vene (in´tr vn) v. To interfere or take a decisive role so as to modify or settle something; to interfere with force in a conflict. **intervention** n.

in-ter-view (in´tr v´) n. A conversation conducted by a reporter to elicit information from someone; a conversation led by an employer who is trying to decide whether to hire someone. **interview** v. **interviewer** n.

in-ter-weave (in´tr wv´) v. To weave together; to intertwine.

in-tes-tate (in tes´tt) adj. Having made no valid will; not disposed of by a will.

in-tes-tine or intestines (in tes´tin) n., Anat. The section of the alimentary canal from the stomach to the anus. **intestinal** adj. **intestinally** adv.

in-ti-mate (in´ti mit) adj. Characterized by close friendship or association. **intimately** adv. **intimacy** n. **ness** n.

in-tim-i-date (in tim´i dt´) v. To make timid or fearful; to frighten; to discourage or suppress by threats or by violence.

in-to (in´t) prep. To the inside of; to a form or condition of; to a time in the midst of.

in-tol-er-ant (in tol´r ant) adj. Not able to endure; not tolerant of the rights or beliefs of others. **intolerance** n. **intolerantly** adv.

in to-to (in t´t) L. Totally.

in-tox-i-cate (in tok´si kt´) v. To make drunk; to elate or excite. **-cation** n.

intra- prefix Within.

in-tra-cel-lu-lar (in´tra sel´ lr) adj. Within a cell or cells.

in-tra-cra-ni-al (in´tra cra´ni al) adj. Within the skull.

in-tra-mu-ral (in´tra mr´al) adj. Taking place within a school, college, or institution; competition limited to a school community.

in-tra-mus-cu-lar (in´tra mus´k lr) *adj.* Within a muscle.

in-tra-state (in´tra stt´) *adj.* Within a state.

in-tra-ve-nous (in´tra v´nus) *adj.* Within a vein. **intravenously** *adv.*

in-trep-id (in trep´id) *adj.* Courageous; un- shaken by fear; bold. **-ly** *adv.*

in-tri-cate (in´tri kit) *adj.* Having many perplexingly entangled parts or elements; complex; difficult to solve or understand.

in-trigue (in trg´) *v.* To arouse the curiosity or interest; to fascinate; to plot; to conspire; to engage in intrigues. *n.* A secret or illicit love affair; a secret plot or plan.

in-tro-duce (in´tro dös´) *v.* To present a person face to face to another; to make acquainted; to bring into use or practice for the first time; to bring to the attention of.

in-tro-vert (in´tro vert´) *n., Psychol.* A person who directs his interest to him self and not to friends or social activities. **introverted** *adj.*

in-trude (in tröde´) *v.* To thrust or push oneself in; to come in without being asked or wanted.

in-tu-it (in tö´it) *v.* To understand through intuition.

in-tu-i-tion (in´to ish´an) *n.* The direct knowledge or awareness of something without conscious attention or reasoning; knowledge that is acquired in this way.

in-un-date (in´un dt´) *v.* To overwhelm with abundance or excess, as with water.

in-ure (in r´) *v.* To become used to accepting something which is undesirable.

in-vade (in vd´) *v.* To enter by force with the intent to conquer or pillage; to pen-etrate and overrun harmfully; to vio-late; to encroach upon. **invader** *n.*

in-va-lid (in´va lid) *n.* A chronically sick, bedridden, or disabled person.

in-val-id (in val´id) *adj.* Disabled by injury or disease; not valid; unsound.

in-val-i-date (in val´i dt´) *v.* To nullify; to make invalid. **invalidation** *n.* **or** *n.*

in-val-u-able (in val´ a bl) *adj.* Priceless; of great value; to be of great help or use. **invaluably** *adv.* **invaluable-ness** *n.*

in-var-i-a-ble (in vâr´ a bl) *adj.* Constant and not changing. **-ness** *n.*

in-va-sion (in v´zhan) *n.* The act of invading; an entrance made with the intent of overrunning or occupying. **invasive** *adj.*

in-veigh (in v´) *v.* To angrily protest.

in-vent (in vent´) *v.* To devise or create by original effort or design. **-or** *n.*

in-ven-tion (in ven´shan) *n.* The act or process of inventing; a new process, method, or device conceived from study and testing.

in-ven-tive (in ven´tiv) *adj.* Skillful at invention or contrivance; ingenious. **inventively** *adv.* **inventiveness** *n.*

in-ven-to-ry (in´ven tr´) *n. pl.* **-ies** A list of items with descriptions and quantities of each; the process of making such a list.

in-verse (in vers´) *adj.* Reversed in order or sequence; inverted. *n.* Something opposite.

in-ver-sion (in ver´zhan) *n.* The act of inverting or the state of being inverted; that which is inverted.

in-vert (in vert´) *v.* To turn upside down; to reverse the position, condition, or order of something. **inverter** *n.* **invertible** *adj.*

in-ver-te-brate (in ver´te brit) *adj.* Lacking a backbone or spinal column.

in-vest (in vest´) *v.* To use money for the purchase of stocks or property in order to obtain profit or interest; to place in office formally; to install; to make an investment.

in-ves-ti-gate (in ves´ti gt´) *v.* To search or inquire into; to examine carefully. **investigative** *adj.* **investigation** *n.*

in-ves-ti-ture (in ves´ti chr) *n.* The ceremony or act of investing or installing someone in a high office.

in-vig-o-rate (in vig´o rt´) *v.* To give strength or vitality to. **invigoration** *n.*

in-vin-ci-ble (in vin´si bl) *adj.* Incapable of being defeated. **invincibility** *n.* **invincibly** *adv.*

in-vi-o-la-ble (in v´o la bl) *adj.* Secure from profanation; safe from assault.

inviolability *n.* **inviolably** *adv.*

in-vi-o-late (in v´o lit) *adj.* Not violated. **inviolately** *adv.* **inviolateness** *n.*

in-vis-i-ble (in viz´i bl) *adj.* Not capable of being seen; not visible; not open to view; hidden.

in-vi-ta-tion (in´vi t´shan) *n.* The act of inviting; the means or words that request someone's presence or participation.

in-vite (in vt´) *v.* To request the presence or participation of; to make a formal or polite request for; to provoke; to entice; to issue an invitation.

in-vit-ing *adj.* Tempting; attractive.

in-vo-ca-tion (in´vo k´shan) *n.* An appeal to a deity or other agent for inspiration, witness, or help; a prayer used at the opening of a ceremony or service.

in-voice (in´vois) *n.* An itemized list of merchandise shipped or services rendered, including prices, shipping instructions, and other costs; a bill.

in-voke (in vk´) *v.* To call upon for aid, support, or inspiration; to conjure.

in-vol-un-tar-y (in vol´un ter) *adj.* Not done by choice or willingly. *n., Physiol.* Muscles which function without an individual's control. **involuntariness** *n.*

in-volve (in volv´) *v.* To include as a part; to make a participant of; to absorb; to engross.

in-vul-ner-a-ble (in vul´nr a bl) *adj.* To be immune to attack; impregnable; not able to be physically injured or wounded. **invulnerability** *n.* **-bly** *adv.*

in-ward (in´wrd) *adj.* Situated toward the inside, center, or interior; of or existing in the mind or thoughts. **inwardness** *n.*

i-o-dine (´o dn) *n.* A grayish-black, corrosive, poisonous element, symbolized by I; a solution made up of iodine, alcohol, and sodium iodide or potassium iodide which is used as an antiseptic.

i-on (´on) *n., Physics.* An atom or group of atoms which carries a positive or negative electric charge as a result of having lost or gained one or more electrons.

i-on-ize (´o nz´) *v.* To convert completely or partially into ions. **ionization** *n.*

ip-so fac-to (ip´s fak´t) *adv., L.* By that very fact or act.

i-ras-ci-ble (i ras´i bl) *adj.* Easily provoked to anger; quick-tempered. **irascibly** *adv.* **irascibility** *n.* **-ness** *n.*

i-rate (´rt) *adj.* Raging; angry. **-ly** *adv.*

ir-i-des-cent (ir´i des´ent) *adj.* Displaying the colors of the rainbow in shifting hues and patterns. **-cence** *n.*

i-ris (´ris) *n. pl.* **irises** *or* **irides** The pigmented part of the eye which regulates the size of the pupil by contracting and expanding around it.

irk (erk) *v.* To annoy or to weary.

iron curtain *n.* An impenetrable political and ideological barrier between the Soviet bloc and the rest of the world.

i-ron-ic (ron´ik) *adj.* Marked by or characterized by irony. **ironical** *adj.* **ironically** *adv.*

i-ro-ny (´ro n) *n. pl.* **-ies** A literary device for conveying meaning by saying the direct opposite of what is really meant.

ir-ra-di-ate (i r´d t´) *v.* To subject to ultraviolet light, radiation, or similar rays. **irradiation** *n.* **irradiator** *n.*

ir-ra-tion-al (i rash´a nal) *adj.* Unable to reason; contrary to reason; absurd; in mathematics, a number which is not expressible as an integer or a quotient of integers. **irrationality** *n.* **irrationally** *adv.*

ir-rec-on-cil-a-ble (i rek´on s´la bl) *adj.* Not able or willing to be reconciled. **irreconcilability** *n.* **-bly** *adv.*

ir-re-deem-a-ble (ir´i d´ma bl) *adj.* Not capable of being recovered, bought back, or paid off; not convertible into coin.

ir-re-duc-i-ble (ir´i dö´si bl) *adj.* Not having the capabilities of reduction, as to a smaller amount. **irreducibility** *n.* **irreducibly** *adv.*

ir-ref-ra-ga-ble (i ref´ra ga bl) *adj.* Cannot be refuted or disproved. **irrefragably** *adv.*

ir-re-fut-able (i ref´ ta bl) *adj.* Cannot be disproved **irrefutability** *n.* **y** *adv.*

ir-reg-u-lar (i reg´ lr) *adj.* Not according to the general rule or practice; not straight, uniform, or orderly; uneven. *n.* One who is irregular. **irregularity**

n. **irregularly** *adv.*

ir-rel-e-vant (i rel′e vant) *adj.* Not pertinent or related to the subject matter. **irrelevantly** *adv.* **irrelevance** *n.*

ir-re-li-gious *adj.* Lacking in religion; opposed to religion. **irreligiously** *adv.*

ir-re-mis-si-ble (ir′i mis′a bl) *adj.* Unpardonable, as for sin. **irremissibly** *adv.*

ir-re-mov-a-ble (ir′i mö′va bl) *adj.* Not removable. **irremovably** *adv.*

ir-rep-a-ra-ble (i rep′r a bl) *adj.* Unable to be set right or repaired **irreparability** *n.* **irreparably** *adv.*

ir-re-place-a-ble (ir′i pl′sa bl) *adj.* Unable to be replaced.

ir-re-press-i-ble (ir′i pres′i bl) *adj.* Impossible to hold back or restrain. **irrepressibly** *adv.*

ir-re-proach-a-ble (ir′i pr′cha bl) *adj.* Blameless; not meriting reproach.

ir-re-sist-i-ble (ir′i zis′ti bl) *adj.* Completely fascinating; impossible to resist.

ir-res-o-lute (i rez′o löt′) *adj.* Lacking resolution; indecisive; lacking firmness of purpose. **irresolutely** *adv.* **irresoluteness** *n.*

ir-re-spec-tive (ir′i spek′tiv) *adj.* Regardless of.

ir-re-spon-si-ble (ir′i spon′si bl) *adj.* Lacking in responsibility; not accountable. **irresponsibility** *n.* **-bly** *adv.*

ir-re-triev-a-ble (ir′i tr′va bl) *adj.* Unable to be retrieved or recovered.

ir-rev-er-ence (i rev′r ens) *n.* A lack of reverence; a disrespectful action.

ir-re-vers-i-ble (ir′i ver′si bl) *adj.* Impossible to reverse. **irreversibility** *n.*

ir-rev-o-ca-ble (i rev′o ka bl) *adj.* Unable or incapable of being turned in the other direction; incapable of being repealed, annulled or undone.

ir-ri-gate (ir′i gt′) *v.* To water the land or crops artificially; as by means of ditches or sprinklers; to refresh with water. *Med.* To wash out with a medicated fluid or water. **irrigation** *n.* **irrigator** *n.* **irrigational** *adj.*

ir-ri-ta-ble (ir′i ta bl) *adj.* Easily annoyed; ill-tempered. *Pathol.* To respond abnormally to stimuli. **irritability** *n.*

ir-ri-tate (ir′i tt′) *v.* To annoy or bother; to provoke; to be sore, chafed, or inflamed.

ir-rupt (i rupt′) *v.* To burst or rush in; to invade. **irruption** *n.* **irruptive** *adj.*

is (iz) *v.* Third person, singular, present tense of the verb to be.

-ish *suffix* Of or belonging to a nationality or ethnic group; characteristic of; the approximate age of; the approximate time of; somewhat.

is-land (′land) *n.* A piece of land smaller than a continent, completely surrounded by water.

isle (l) *n.* A small island.

ism (iz′um) *n. Slang* A distinctive cause, doctrine, or theory.

-ism *suffix* Practice; process; a manner of behavior characteristic of person or thing; a system of principles.

is-n't (iz′ont) Is not.

i-so-late (′so lt′) *v.* To set apart from the others; to put by itself; to place or be placed in quarantine.

i-so-la-tion-ism (′so l′sha niz′um) *n.* A national policy of avoiding political or economic alliances or relations with other countries. **isolationist** *n.*

i-so-mer (′so mr) *n.* A compound having the same kinds and numbers of atoms as another compound but differing in chemical or physical properties due to the linkage or arrangement of the atoms.

i-sos-ce-les triangle (sos′e lz′) *n.* A triangle which has two equal sides.

i-so-therm (′so therm′) *n.* A line on a map linking points that have the same temperature. **isothermal** *adj.*

i-so-tope (′so tp′) *n.* Any of two or more species of atoms of a chemical element which contain in their nuclei the same number of protons but different numbers of neutrons.

i-so-trop-ic (′so trop′ik) *adj.* Having the same value in all directions. **isotropy** *n.*

is-sue (ish′ö) *n.* The act of giving out; something that is given out or published; a matter of importance to solve.

i-tal-ic (i tal′ik) *adj.* A style of printing type in which the letters slant to the right. **Italics** *pl.* Italic typeface.

i-tal-i-cize (i tal′i sz′) *v.* To print in italics.

itch (ich) *n.* A skin irritation which causes a desire to scratch; a contagious skin disease accompanied by a desire to scratch; a restless desire or craving. **itchiness** n. **itchy** adj.

-ite *suffix* A native or inhabitant of; an adherent of; a sympathizer or follower; a descendant of; a rock or mineral.

i-tem ('tem) n. A separately-noted unit or article included in a category or series; a short article, as in a magazine or newspaper.

i-tem-ize ('te mz') v. To specify by item; to list. **itemizer** n. **itemization** n.

i-tin-er-ar-y (tin'e rer') n. pl. **-ies** A scheduled route of a trip.

it'll (it'ăl) It will; it shall.

its (its) adj. The possessive case of the pronoun it.

it's (its) It is; it has.

I've n. I have

i-vy ('v) n. pl. **-ies** A climbing plant having glossy evergreen leaves and aerial rootes.

-ization n. *suffix* The process, action, or result of doing a specified thing.

-ize *suffix* To cause to become or resemble.

iz-zard (iz'rd) n. The letter Z

J

J, j (j) The tenth letter of the English alphabet.

jab (jab) v. To poke or thrust sharply with short blows; a rapid punch.

jab-ber (jabr) v. To speak quickly or without making sense.

jab-ot (zha b) n. A ruffle or decoration on the front of a blouse, dress, or shirt.

jack-al (jakæl) n. An African or Asian dog- like, carnivorous mammal.

jack-a-napes (jakæ nps) n. An impudent person.

jack-ass (jakas) n. A male donkey or ass; a stupid person or one who acts in a stupid fashion.

jack-et (jakit) n. A short coat worn by men and women; an outer protective cover for a book; the skin of a cooked potato.

jack--o--lan-tern (jakø lantrn) n. A

lantern made from a hollowed out pumpkin which has been carved to resemble a face.

jack-pot (jakpot) n. Any post, prize, or pool in which the amount won is cumulative.

jack rabbit n. A large American hare with long back legs and long ears.

jade (jd) n. A hard, translucent, green gemstone; an old, worn-out unmanageable horse; a mean old woman; hussy. adj. Worn-out; exhausted.

jag (jag) n. A very sharp projection or point. *Slang* A binge or spree.

jag-ged adj. Having jags or sharp notches; serrated. **jaggedly** adv. **-ness** n.

jag-uar (jagwär) n. A large, spotted, feline mammal of tropical America with a tawny coat and black spots.

jai alai (hl) n. A game similar to handball in which players catch and throw a ball with long, curved, wicker baskets strapped to their arms.

jail (jl) n. A place of confinement for incarceration.

jail-er (jlr) n. The officer in charge of a jail and its prisoners.

ja-lop-y (jæ lop) n. pl. **-ies** *Slang* An old, rundown automobile.

ja-lou-sie (jalø s) n. A window, blind, or door having adjustable horizontal slats.

jam (jam) v. To force or wedge into a tight position; to apply the brakes of a car suddenly; to be locked in a position; to block; to crush. *Mus.* To be a participant in a jazz session. *Slang* To be in a difficult situation or to be crowded together, as of people, cars; a difficult situation. n. A preserve of whole fruit boiled with sugar.

jamb (jam) n. The vertical sidepiece of a door.

jam-bo-ree (jambø r) n. A large, festive gathering.

jam session n. An informal gathering of a group of jazz musicians.

jan-gle (janggl) v. To make a harsh unmusical sound. n. A discordant sound. **jangle** n. **jangler** n.

jan-i-tor (jani tr) n. A person who cleans and cares for a building. **janitorial** adj.

jape (jp) v. To joke; to make fun of or

mock by words or actions. **jape** n.
japer n. **japery** n.

jar (jär) n. A deep, cylindrical vessel
with a wide mouth; a harsh sound. v.
To strike against or bump into; to
affect one's feelings unpleasantly.

jar-di-niere (järd nr) n. A decorative
pot or stand for flowers or plants.

jar-gon (järgən) n. The technical or
specialized vocabulary used among
members of a particular profession.

jas-mine or **jes-sa-mine** (jazmin) n. A
shrub with fragrant yellow or white
flowers.

jas-per (jaspr) n. An opaque red,
brown, or yellow variety of quartz,
having a high polish.

ja-to (jt) n. A takeoff of an airplane
which is assisted by an auxiliary rocket engine.

jaun-dice (jändis) n. Pathol. A diseased condition of the liver due to the
presence of bile pigments in the blood
and characterized by yellowish stain-
ing of the eyes, skin, and body fluids.
jaundiced To be affected with jaun-
dice.

jaunt (jänt) n. A short journey for pleasure.

jaun-ty (jänt) adj. Having a buoyantly
carefree and self-confident air or matter about oneself. **jauntily** adv. **jaun-
tiness** n.

jaw (jä) n. Anat. Either of the two bony
structures forming the framework of
the mouth and the teeth. Slang To talk
excessively.

jaw-bone (jäbn) n. One of the bones of
the jaw, especially the lower jaw.

jay (j) n. Any of various corvine birds of
brilliant coloring, as the blue jay.

jay-walk (jwäk) v. Slang To cross a
street carelessly, violating traffic regulations and or signals. **jaywalker** n.

jazz (jaz) n. A kind of music which has
a strong rhythmic structure and often involving
frequent syncopation and often involving
ensemble and solo improvisation.
Slang Lying and exaggerated talk; idle
and foolish talk; liveliness. Jazz up To
make more interesting; to enliven.
jct abbr. Junction.

jeal-ous (jelus) adj. Suspicious or fearful of being replaced by a rival; resent-

ful or bitter in rivalry; demanding
exclusive love. **jealously** adv. **jealous-
ness** n. **jealousy** n.

jean (jn) n. A strong, twilled cotton
cloth. **jeans** Pants made of denim.

jeer (jr) v. To speak or shout derisively.
jeer n. **jeerer** n. **jerringly** adv.

Je-ho-vah (ji hvæ) n. God, in the
Christian translations of the Old
Testament.

je-june (ji jön) adj. Lacking in substance or nourishment; immature.

je-ju-num (ji jönm) n. pl. -na Ant.
The part of the small intestine which
extends from the duodenum to the
ileum.

jel-ly (jel) n. pl. -ies Any food preparation made with pectin or gelatin and
having a somewhat elastic consistency; a food made of boiled and sweetened fruit juice and used as a filler or
spread.

jeop-ard-ize v. To put in jeopardy; to
expose to loss or danger.

jeop-ard-y (jepr d) n. Exposure to loss
or danger.

jer-bo-a (jr bæ) n. Any of a type of
small, nocturnal rodent of Asia and
Africa with long hind legs.

jer-e-mi-ad (jermad) n. A lament or
prolonged complaint.

jerk (jrk) v. To give a sharp twist or pull
to. n. A sudden movement, as a tug or
twist. Physiol. An involuntary contraction of a muscle resulting from a
reflex action. Slang An annoying or
foolish person. **jerky** adv.

jer-kin (jrkin) n. A close-fitting jacket,
usually sleeveless.

jest (jest) n. An action or remark intended to provoke laughter; a joke; a playful mood.

Jesus (jzs) n. The founder of Christian-
ity, son of Mary and regarded as the
Christian faith as Christ the son of
God, the Messiah; also referred to as
Jesus Christ or Jesus of Nazareth.

jet (jet) n. A sudden spurt or gush of liquid or gas emitted through a narrow
opening; a jet airplane; a hard, black
mineral which takes a high polish and
is used in jewelry; a deep glossy black.

jet lag n. Mental and physical fatigue
resulting from rapid travel through

several time zones.

jet stream n. A high-velocity wind near the troposphere, generally moving from west to east often at speeds exceeding 250 mph.; a high-speed stream of gas or other fluid expelled from a jet engine or rocket.

jet-ti-son (jeti sən) v. To throw cargo over-board; to discard a useless or hampering item.

jet-ty (jet) n. pl. -ies A wall made of piling rocks, or other material which extends into a body of water to protect a harbor or influence the current; a pier.

jew-el (jōl) n. A precious stone used for personal adornment; a person or thing of very rare excellence or value. v. To furnish with jewels. **jewelry** n.

jib (jib) n. Naut. A triangular sail set on a stay extending from the head of the foremast to the bowsprit. v. To swing or shift from one side of a vessel to the other.

jig (jig) n. Any of a variety of fast, lively dances; the music for such a dance. Mech. A device used to hold and guide a tool.

jig-ger (jigr) n. A small measure holding 1 1/2 oz. used for measuring liquor. Naut. A small sail in the stern of a sailing craft. Slang Any small item which does not have a particular name.

jig-gle (jigl) v. To move or jerk lightly up and down. n. A jerky, unsteady movement.

jig-saw n. A saw having a slim blade set vertically, used for cutting curved or irregular lines.

jigsaw puzzle n. A puzzle consisting of many irregularly shaped pieces which fit together and form a picture.

jilt (jilt) v. To discard a lover. n. A woman or girl who discards a lover.

jim-my (jim) n. pl. -ies A short crow-bar, often used by a burglar. v. To force open or break into with a jimmy.

jim-son-weed (jimsən wd) n. A tall, coarse, foul-smelling, poisonous annual weed with large, trumpet-shaped purplish or white flowers.

jin-gle (jinggl) v. To make a light clinking or ringing sound. n. A short, catchy song or poem, as one used for adver-

tising.

jin-go-ism n. Extreme nationalism which is marked by a belligerent foreign policy. **jingoist** n. **jingoistic** adj.

jinn (jin) n. pl. **jin-ni** In the Moslem legend, a spirit with supernatural powers.

jinx (jingks) n. Slang A person or thing thought to bring bad luck; a period of bad luck.

jit-ney (jitn) n. A vehicle carrying passengers for a small fee.

jit-ter (jitr) v. Slang To be intensely nervous.

jit-ter-bug (jitr bug) n. Slang A lively dance or one who performs this dance.

jit-ters n. Nervousness.

jive (jv) n. Slang Jazz or swing music and musicians.

job (job) n. Anything that is done; work that is done for a set fee; the project worked on; a position of employment. **jobless** adj.

job-ber (jobr) n. One who buys goods in bulk from the manufacturer and sells them to retailers; a person who works by the job; a pieceworker.

job-name n. Science. A code that is assigned to a specific job instruction in a computer program, for the operator's use.

jock-ey (jok) n. A person who rides a horse as a professional in a race; one who works with a specific object or device.

joc-u-lar (jok lr) adj. Marked by joking; playful. **jocularity** n. **jocularly** adv.

joc-und (jokænd) adj. Cheerful; merry; suggestive of high spirits and lively mirthfulness. **jocundity** n. -ly adv.

jog (jog) n. A slight movement or a slight shake; the slow steady trot of a horse, especially when exercising or participating in a sport; a projecting or retreating part in a surface or line. v. To shift direction abruptly; to exercise by running at a slow but steady pace.

jog-gle (jogl) v. To move or shake slight-ly.

john (jon) n. Slang Toilet; a prostitute's client.

john-ny-cake (jon kk) n. A thin bread made with cornmeal.

join (join) v. To bring or put together so

as to form a unit; to become a member of an organization; to participate.

joint (joint) *n*. The place where two or more things or parts are joined; a point where bones are connected. *Slang* A disreputable or shabby place of entertainment. *adj*. Marked by cooperation, as a joint effort.

join-ture (joinchr) *n*. *Law* A settlement of property arranged by a husband which is to be used for the support of his wife after his death.

joist (joist) *n*. Any of a number of small parallel beams set from wall to wall to support a floor.

joke (jk) *n*. Something said or done to cause laughter, such as a brief story with a punch line; something not taken seriously. *v*. To tell or play jokes. **jok-ingly** *adv*.

jok-er (jkr) *n*. A person who jokes; a playing card, used in certain card games as a wild card; an unsuspected or unapparent fact which nullifies a seeming advantage.

jol-li-fi-ca-tion *n*. Merrymaking; festivity.

jol-ly (jol) *adj*. Full of good humor; merry.

jolt (jlt) *v*. To knock or shake about. *n*. A sudden bump or jar, as from a blow.

jon-quil (jongkwil) *n*. A widely grown species of narcissus related to the daffodil, having fragrant white or yellow flowers and long narrow leaves.

josh (josh) *v*. *Slang* To make good-humored fun of; to tease; to joke.

joss (jos) *n*. A Chinese idol or image.

joss stick *n*. A stick of incense burnt by the Chinese.

jos-tle (josl) *v*. To make one's way through a crowd by pushing, elbowing, or shoving.

jot (jot) *v*. To make a brief note of something. *n*. A tiny bit.

jounce (jouns) *v*. To bounce; to bump; to shake. *jounce n*. *jouncy adj*.

jour *abbr*. Journal; journalist.

jour-nal (jrnæl) *n*. A diary or personal daily record of observations and experiences; in bookkeeping, a book in which daily financial transactions are recorded. *Mech*. The part of an axle which rotates in or against a bearing.

jour-nal-ism (jrnæ lizm) *n*. The occupation, collection, writing, editing, and publishing of newspapers and other periodicals. **journalist** *n*. **-istic** *adj*.

jour-ney (jrn) *n*. A trip from one place to another over a long distance; the distance that is traveled. *v*. to make a trip; to travel a long distance.

jour-ney-man (jrn mæn) *n*. *pl*. **-men** A worker who has served an apprenticeship in a skilled trade.

joust (joust) *n*. A formal combat between two knights on horseback as a part of a medieval tournament.

jo-vi-al (jv æl) *adj*. Good-natured; good- humored; jolly. **joviality** *n*.

jowl (joul) *n*. The fleshy part of the lower jaw; the cheek. **jowly** *adj*.

joy (joi) *n*. A strong feeling of great happiness; delight; a state or source of contentment or satisfaction; anything which makes one delighted or happy. **joyless**, **joyfully** *adv*. **joylessly** *adv*.

joy-ous (joius) *adj*. Joyful; causing or feeling joy. **joyously** *adv*. **-ness** *n*.

joy stick *Slang* The control stick of an airplane or video game.

ju-bi-lant (jöb lænt) *adj*. Exultantly joyful or triumphant; expressing joy.

ju-bi-la-tion (jöb lshæn) *n*. Rejoicing; exultation.

ju-bi-lee (jöb l) *n*. A special anniversary of an event; any time of rejoicing.

judge (juj) *v*. *Law* A public officer who passes judgment in a court. *v*. To decide authoritatively after deliberation.

judg-ment or judge-ment (jujmnt) *n*. The ability to make a wise decision or to form an opinion; the act of judging. *Law* The sentence or determination of a court.

ju-di-ca-ture (jöd kchr) *n*. The function or action of administration of justice; law, courts, or judges as a whole.

ju-di-cial (jö dishæl) *adj*. Pertaining to the administering of justice, to courts of law, or to judges; enforced or decreed by a court of law. **-ly** *adv*.

ju-di-ci-ar-y (jö dish êr) *adj*. Of or pertaining to judges, courts, or judgments. *n*. The department of the government which administers the law; a system of courts of law.

ju-di-cious (jö dishus) *adj.* Having, showing, or exercising good sound judgment.

ju-do (jöd) *n.* A system or form of self-defense, developed from jujitsu in Japan in 1882, which emphasizes principles of balance and leverage.

jug (jug) *n.* A small pitcher or similar vessel for holding liquids. *Slang* A jail.

jug-ger-naut (jugr năt) *n.* Any destructive force or object.

jug-gle (jugl) *v.* To keep several objects continuously moving from the hand into the air; to practice fraud or deception.

jug-u-lar (jug lr) *adj. Anat.* Of or pertaining to the region of the throat or the jugular vein.

jugular vein *n. Anat.* One of the large veins on either side of the neck.

juice (jös) *n.* The liquid part of a vegetable, fruit, or animal. *Slang* Electric current.

juic-er (jösr) *n.* A device for extracting juice from fruit.

juic-y (jösē) *adj.* Full of; abounding with juice; full of interest; richly rewarding, especially financially. **juiciness** *n.*

ju-jit-su *or* **ju-jut-su** (jö jitsö) *n.* A Japanese system of using holds, throws, and stunning blows to subdue an opponent.

ju-lep (jlip) *n.* A mint julep.

ju-li-enne (jöl en) *n.* Cut into thin strips. *n.* A clear meat soup containing vegetables chopped or cut into thin strips.

jum-ble (jumbl) *v.* To mix in a confused mass; to throw together without order; to confuse or mix something up in the mind.

jum-bo (jumb) *n.* A very large person, animal, or thing. *adj.* Extremely large.

jump (jump) *v.* To spring from the ground, floor, or other surface into the air by using a muscular effort of the legs and feet; to move in astonishment; to leap over; to increase greatly, as prices. *Informal* To attack by surprise. *Computer Science* To move from one set of instructions in a program to another set further behind or ahead.

jump-er (jumpr) *n.* One who or that which jumps; a sleeveless dress, usual-ly worn over a blouse. *Electr.* A short wire used to bypass or join parts of a circuit.

junc-tion (jungkshæn) *n.* The place where lines or routes meet, as roads or railways; the process of joining or the act of joining.

junc-ture (jungkchr) *n.* The point where two things join; a crisis; an emergency; a point in time.

jun-gle (junggl) *n.* A densely covered land with tropical vegetation, usually inhabited by wild animals. **jungle** *adj.*

jun-ior (jönyr) *adj.* Younger in years or rank, used to distinguish the son from the father of the same first name; the younger of two. *n.* The third year of high school or college.

junior high school *n.* A school which includes the 7th, 8th, and 9th grades.

ju-ni-per (jön pr) *n.* An evergreen shrub or tree of Europe and America with dark blue berries, prickly foliage, and fragrant wood.

junk (jungk) *n.* Discarded material, as glass, scrap iron, paper, or rags; a flat-bottomed Chinese ship with battered sails; rubbish; worthless matter. *Slang* Heroin, narcotics or dope.

jun-ket (jungkit) *n.* A party, banquet, or trip; a trip taken by a public official with all expenses paid for by public funds; a custard-like dessert of flavored milk set with rennet. **junket** *v.* **junketeer** *n.*

jun-ta (hntæ) *n.* A body of men or persons, as military officers, in power following a coup d'etat.

ju-rid-i-cal *or* **ju-rid-ic** (j ridi kæl) *adj.* Of or pertaining to the law and to the administration of justice.

ju-ris-dic-tion (jris dikshæn) *n.* The lawful right or power to interpret and apply the law; the territory within which power is exercised.

ju-ror (jrr) *n.* A person who serves on a jury.

ju-ry (jr) *n. pl.* **-ies** A group of legally qualified persons summoned to serve on a judicial tribunal to give a verdict according to evidence presented.

just (just) *adj.* Fair and impartial in acting or judging; morally right; merited; deserved; based on sound reason. *adv.*

To the exact point; precisely; exactly right. **-ly** *adv.* **-ness** *n.*

jus·tice (jŭstĭs) *n.* The principle of moral or ideal rightness; conformity to the law; the abstract principle by which right and wrong are defined; a judge.

justice of the peace *n.* A local magistrate having limited jurisdiction with authority to try minor cases, administer oaths, and perform marriages.

justified margin *n.* A typing or typesetting margin with all the characters at the ends of the lines vertically aligned.

jus·ti·fy (jŭst f) *v.* To be just, right, or valid; to declare guiltless; to adjust or space lines to the proper length. **justifiable** *adj.* **justifiably** *adv.* **-fication** *n.*

jut (jŭt) *v.* To extend beyond the main portion; to project.

ju·ve·nile (jōv nl) *adj.* Young; youthful; not yet an adult. *n.* A young person; an actor who plays youthful roles; a child's book.

juvenile court *n.* A court which deals only with cases involving dependent, neglected, and delinquent children.

juvenile delinquent *n.* A person who is guilty of violations of the law, but is too young to be punished as an adult criminal; a young person whose behavior is out of control.

jux·ta·pose (jukstæ pz) *v.* To put side by side; to place together. **juxtaposed** *adj.* **juxtaposition** *n.*

K

K, k (k) The eleventh letter of the English alphabet. *Computer science.* A unit of storage capacity equal to 1024 bytes.

kaiser roll *n.* A crusty round roll.

kale (kl) *n.* A green cabbage having crinkled leaves which do not form a tight head.

ka·lei·do·scope (kæ ldø skp) *n.* A tubular instrument rotated to make successive symmetrical designs by using mirrors reflecting the changing patterns made by pieces of loose, colored glass at the end of a tube; a series of continuously changing colors; changing events or phases.

kame (km) *n.* A short ridge of gravel and sand that remains after glacial ice melts.

kan·ga·roo (kanggæ rō) *n.* *pl.* **-roo, roos** Any of various herbivorous marsupials of Australia with short forelegs, large hind limbs capable of jumping, and a large tail.

kangaroo court *n.* A self-appointed, illegal court, usually marked by incompetence or dishonesty.

ka·o·lin *or* **ka·o·line** (kø lĭn) *n.* A fine clay used in ceramics.

ka·pok (kpŏk) *n.* A silky fiber manufactured from the fruit of the silk-cotton tree and used for stuffing cushions and life preservers .

ka·put (kä pt) *adj.* *Slang* Destroyed or out of order.

kar·a·kul (karæ kl) *n.* Any of a breed of fat-tailed sheep of central Asia, having a narrow body and coarse, wiry, brown fur.

kar·at (karæt) *n.* A unit of measure for the fineness of gold.

ka·ra·te (kæ rät) *n.* A Japanese art of self-defense.

kar·ma (kärmæ) *n.* The over-all effect of one's behavior, held in Hinduism and Buddhism to determine one's destiny in a future existence.

kay·ak (kak) *n.* A watertight Eskimo boat with a light frame and a sealskin cover.

ka·zoo (kæ zō) *n.* A toy musical instrument with a paper membrane which vibrates simultaneously when a player hums into the tube.

kedge (kej) *n.* A small anchor. *v.* To pull a ship by the rope of an anchor.

keel (kl) *n.* The central main stem on a ship or aircraft, which runs lengthwise along the center line from bow to stern, to which a frame is built upwards. *v.* To capsize. **over** To fall over suddenly; to turn upside down.

keel·son (klsøn) *n.* *Naut.* A structural member fastened above and parallel to the keel to give additional strength.

keen *adj.* Having a sharp edge or point; acutely painful or harsh; intellectually acute; strong; intense. *Slang* Great. *n.* Wailing lament, especially for the dead. **keenly** *adv.* **keenness** *n.*

keep (kp) v. To have and hold; to not let go; to maintain, as business records; to know a secret and not divulge it; to protect and defend.

keep-sake (kpsk) n. A memento or souvenir.

keg (keg) n. A small barrel.

keg-ler (keglr) n. A bowler.

kelp (kelp) n. Any of a large brown seaweed.

kel-pie (kelp) n. A sheep dog originally bred in Australia.

ken-nel (keni) n. A shelter for or a place where dogs or cats are bred, boarded, or trained. **kennel** v.

ke-no (kn) n. A game of chance resembling bingo; a lottery game.

kep-i (kp) n. A French military cap having a flat, round top and a visor.

ker-a-tin (kerǝ tin) n. A fibrous protein which forms the basic substance of nails, hair, horns, and hooves. **keratinous** adj.

ker-chief (krchif) n. A piece of cloth usually worn around the neck or on the head; scarf; a handkerchief.

ker-nel (krnl) n. A grain or seed, as of corn, enclosed in a hard husk; the inner substance of a nut; the central, most important part.

ker-o-sene or **ker-o-sine** (kerǝ sn) n. An oil distilled from petroleum or coal and used for illumination.

kes-trel (kestrl) n. A small falcon, with gray and brown plumage.

ketch (kech) n. A small sailing vessel with two masts.

ketch-up (kechp) n. A thick, smooth sauce made from tomatoes.

ket-tle (ketl) n. A pot.

ket-tle-drum (ketl drum) n. A musical instrument with a parchment head which can be tuned by adjusting the tension.

key-board (kbrd) n. A bank of keys, as on a piano, typewriter, or computer terminal. v. To set by means of a keyed typesetting machine; to generate letters by means of a word processor.

key-note (knt) n. Mus. The first and harmonically fundamental tone of a scale; main principle or theme.

keynote address n. An opening speech that outlines issues for discussion.

key-punch n. A machine operated from a keyboard that uses punched holes in tapes or cards for data processing systems.

key-stone (kstn) n. The wedge-shaped stone at the center of an arch that locks its parts together; an essential part.

key-stroke n. A stroke of a key, as of a typewriter.

kg abbr. Kilogram.

khan (kän) n. An Asiatic title of respect; a medieval Turkish, Mongolian or Tartar ruler. **khanate** n.

kib-itz (kibits) v. Slang To look on and offer meddlesome advice to others.

kid (kid) n. A young goat; leather made from the skin of a young goat. Slang A child; youngster v. To mock or tease playfully; to deceive for fun; to fool. **kidder** n.

kid-nap (kidnap) v. To seize and hold a person unlawfully, often for ransom.

kid-ney (kidn) n. pl. **-neys** Either of two organs situated in the abdominal cavity of vertebrates whose function is to keep proper water balance in the body and to excrete wastes in the form of urine.

kidvid n. Slang Television programming for children.

kiel-ba-sa n. A uncooked, smoked Polish sausage.

kill (kil) v. To put to death; to nullify; to cancel; to slaughter for food. **kill** n.

killer whale n. A black and white carnivorous whale, found in the colder waters of the seas.

kill-joy (kiljoi) n. One who spoils the enjoyment of others.

kiln (kil) n. An oven or furnace for hardening or drying a substance, especially one for firing ceramics, pottery, etc.

ki-lo (kil) n. A kilogram.

kil-o-bit n. In computer science, one thousand binary digits.

ki-lo-cy-cle (kilǝ skl) n. A unit equal to one thousand cycles; one thousand cycles per second.

kil-o-gram (kilǝ gram) n. A measurement of weight in the metric system equal to slightly more than one third of a pound.

kil-o-ton (kilǝ tun) n. One thousand tons; an explosive power equal to that of one thousand tons of TNT.

kil-o-watt (kilo wot) n. A unit of power equal to one thousand watts.

kilt (kilt) n. A knee-length wool skirt with deep pleats, usually of tartan, worn especially by men in the Scottish Highlands.

kil-ter (kiltr) n. Good condition; proper or working order.

ki-mo-no (kə mnə) n. A loose Japanese robe with a wide sash; a loose robe worn chiefly by women.

kin (kin) n. One's relatives by blood.

kin-der-gar-ten (kindr gärtn) n. A school or class for young children from the ages of four to six.

kin-der-gart-ner (kindr gärtnr) n. A child who attends kindergarten.

kin-dling (kindling) n. Easily ignited material, such as sticks, wood chips, etc., used to start a fire.

kin-dred (kindrid) n. A person's relatives by blood. adj. Having a like nature; similar.

kin-e-mat-ics (kin matiks) n. The branch of dynamics that deals with motion, considered apart from force and mass. **kinematical** adj.

kin-e-scope (kini skp) n. A cathoderay tube in a television set which translates received electrical impulses into a visible picture on a screen; a film of a television on broadcast.

ki-net-ic (ki netik) adj. Of, pertaining to, or produced by motion.

kink (kingk) n. A tight twist or knotlike curl; a sharp, painful muscle cramp; a mental quirk. v. To form or cause to form a kink.

kink-a-jou (kingkæ jö) n. A tropical American mammal having large eyes, brown fur, and a long, prehensile tail.

kip (kip) n. The untanned skin of a calf, a lamb and or an adult of any small breed.

kip-per (kipr) n. A salted and smoked herring or salmon. v. To cure by salting, smoking, or drying.

kir-tle (krtl) n. A woman's long skirt.

kis-met (kizmit) n. Fate; appointed lot.

kitch-en (kichn) n. A room in a house or building used to prepare and cook food.

kite (kt) n. A light-weight framework of wood and paper designed to fly in a steady breeze at the end of a string; any of various predatory birds of the hawk family having long, usually forked tails.

kith or kin (kith) n. Acquaintances or family.

kitsch (kich) n. Anything that is pretentious and in poor taste.

kit-ten (kitn) n. A young cat.

kit-ty--cor-nered (kit kärnr) adj. Diagonally; catty-cornered.

ki-wi (kw) n. A flightless bird of New Zealand having vestigial wings and a long, slender bill; a vine, native to Asia, which yields a fuzzy-skinned, edible fruit; the fruit of this vine.

ki abbr. Kiloliter.

klep-to-ma-ni-a (kleptə mn æ) n. Obsessive desire to steal or impulse to steal, especially without economic motive.

klutz (klutz) n. Slang A stupid or clumsy person. **klutziness** n. **klutzy** adj.

knack (nak) n. A natural talent; aptitude.

knack-wurst or knock-wurst n. A thick or short, heavily-seasoned sausage.

knap-sack (napsak) n. A supply or equipment bag, as of canvas or nylon, worn strapped across the shoulders.

knave (nv) n. Tricky or dishonest person.

knead (nd) v. To work dough into a uniform mass; to shape by or as if by kneading.

knee (n) n. The joint in the human body which connects the calf with the thigh.

knell (nel) v. To sound a bell, especially when rung for a funeral; to toll. n. An act or instance of knelling; a signal of disaster.

knick-ers (nikrz) n. Short, loose- fitting pants gathered at the knee.

knick-knack (niknak) n. A trinket; trifling article.

knish (nsh) n. Baked or fried dough stuffed with meat, cheese, or potatoes.

knit (nit) v. To form by intertwining thread or yarn by interlocking loops of a single yarn by means of needles; to fasten securely; to draw together; to furrow the brow. **knit** n.

knob (nob) n. A rounded protuberance;

a lump; a rounded mountain; a rounded handle. **knobbed** adj. **knobby** adj.

knock (nok) v. To hit or strike with a hard blow; to criticize; to collide; to make a noise, as that of a defective engine. **out** To render unconscious.

knoll (nl) n. A small, round hill; a mound.

knot (not) n. An intertwining of string or rope; a fastening made by tying together lengths of material, as string; a unifying bond, especially of marriage; a hard node on a tree from which a branch grows. Naut. A unit of speed, also called a nautical mile, which equals approximately 1.15 statute miles per hour. **knottiness** n. **knotty** adj.

knout (nout) n. A whip or scourge for flogging criminals. **knout** v.

know (n) v. To perceive directly as fact or truth; to believe to be true; to be certain of; to be familiar with or have experience of. **-able** adj. **-ledge** n.

ko-a-la (k älæ) n. An Australian marsupial which has large hairy ears, and gray fur, and feeds on eucalyptus leaves.

Ko-ran (k rän) n. The sacred book of Islam, accepted as containing the revelations made to Mohammed by Allah through the angel Gabriel.

ko-sher (kshr) adj. Serving food prepared according to Jewish dietary laws. Slang Appropriate; proper.

kow-tow (koutou) v. To show servile deference.

krem-lin (kremlin) n. The citadel of Moscow which houses the major Soviet government offices; the Soviet government.

kryp-ton (kripton) n. A white, inert gaseous chemical used mainly in fluorescent lamps, symbolized by Kr.

ku-dos (köds) n. Acclaim or prestige resulting from notable achievement or high position.

kung fu n. A Japanese art of self-defense similar to karate.

kw abbr. Kilowatt.

kwash-i-or-kor n. Severe malnutrition, especially in children, caused by protein deficiency.

kwh abbr. Kilowatt-hour.

ky-pho-sis n. Abnormal curving of the spine.

L

L, l (el) n. The twelfth letter of the English alphabet; the Roman numeral for fifty.

lab (lab) n. Laboratory.

la-bel (lbl) n. Something that identifies or describes. **label** To attach a label to.

la-bi-al (lb al) adj. Pertaining to or of the labia or lips.

la-bi-um (lb m) n. pl. **labia** Any of the four folds of the vulva.

la-bor (lbr) n. Physical or manual work done for hire. Med. The physical pain and efforts involved in childbirth. v. To work; to progress with great effort. **laborer** n.

lab-o-ra-to-ry (labrø tr) n. pl. **-ies** A place equipped for conducting scientific experiments, research, or testing; a place where drugs and chemicals are produced.

lab-y-rinth (lab rinth) n. A system of winding, intricate passages; a maze. **labyrinthine** adj.

lac (lak) n. The resinous secretion left on certain trees by the lac insect and used in making paints and varnishes.

lace (ls) n. A delicate open-work fabric of silk, cotton, or linen made by hand or on a machine; a cord or string used to fasten two edges together. v. To fasten or tie together; to interlace or intertwine. **lacy** adj.

lac-er-ate (las rt) v. To open with a jagged tear; to wound the flesh by tearing.

lach-ry-mal or **lac-ri-mal** Relating to or producing tears; relating to the glands that produce tears.

lack (lak) n. The deficiency or complete absence of something. v. To have little of something or to be completely without.

lack-ey (lak) n. A male servant of very low status.

lack-lus-ter (laklustr) adj. Lacking sheen; dull.

lac-quer (lakr) n. A transparent varnish which is dissolved in a volatile solution and dries to give surfaces a glossy finish.

la-crosse (la kras) *n.* A game of American Indian origin played with a ball and long-handled rackets, by two teams often men each, to advance the ball into the opponents' goal.

lac-tate (laktt) *v.* To secrete or to milk.

lac-tose (lakts) *n. Biochem.* A white, odorless, crystalline sugar that is found in milk.

lad (lad) *n.* A boy or young man.

lad-der (ladr) *n.* An implement used for climbing up or down in order to reach another place or area.

lad-en (ldn) *adj.* Heavily burdened; oppressed; weighed down; loaded.

lad-ing (lding) *n.* Cargo; freight.

la-dle (ldl) *n.* A cup-shaped vessel with a deep bowl and a long handle, used for dipping or conveying liquids.

la-dy (ld) *n. pl.* **ladies** A woman showing refinement, cultivation, and often high social position; the woman at the head of a household; an address or term of reference for any woman.

lady--in--waiting (ld in wting) *n. pl.* **ladies** A lady appointed to wait on a queen or princess.

la-dy-like (ld lk) *adj.* Having the characteristics of a lady; delicate; gentle.

lag (lag) *v.* To stray or fall behind; to move slowly; to weaken gradually. *n.* The process or act of retardation or falling behind; the amount or period of lagging.

la-gniappe (lan yap) *n.* A small gift which is given to a purchaser by a storekeeper. *Informal* Anything given as an extra bonus.

la-goon (la gōn) *n.* A body of shallow water separated from the ocean by a coral reef or sandbars. **lagoonal** *adj.*

laid Past tense of lay.

laid back *adj. Slang* Casual or relaxed in character.

lain *v.* Past tense of lie.

lais-sez--faire (lesfār) *n.* A policy stating that a government should exercise very little control in trade and industrial affairs; noninterference.

la-i-ty (li t) *n.* Laymen, as distinguished from clergy.

lake (lk) *n.* A large inland body of either salt or freshwater.

La-maze method *n.* A method of childbirth in which the mother is prepared psychologically and physically to give birth without the use of drugs.

lamb (lam) *n.* A young sheep; the meat of a lamb used as food; a gentle person.

lam-baste or lambast (lam bst) *v. Slang* To thrash or beat.

lam-bent (lambnt) *adj.* Lightly and playfully brilliant; flickering gently; softly radiant. **lambency** *n.* **-ly** *adv.*

lame (lm) *adj.* Disabled or crippled, especially in the legs or feet so as to impair free movement; weak; ineffective; unsatisfactory.

la-me (la m) *n.* A brocaded fabric woven with gold or silver thread, sometimes mixed with other fiber.

la-me duck *n. Slang* An office holder who has been defeated but continues in office until the inauguration of his or her successor.

la-ment (la ment) *v.* To express sorrow; to mourn. *n.* An expression of regret or sorrow. **lamentable** *adj.* **-ably** *adv.*

lam-i-na (lam na) *n. pl.* **-nae, -nas** A thin scale or layer. *Bot.* The blade or flat part of a leaf.

lam-i-nate (lam nt) *v.* To form or press into thin sheets; to form layers by the action of pressure and heat. **lamination** *n.*

lamp (lamp) *n.* A device for generating heat or light.

lam-poon (lam pŏn) *n.* A satirical, but often humorous, attack in verse or prose, especially one that ridicules a group, person, or institution. **lampoon** *v.* **lampoonery** *n.*

lam-prey (lampr) *n. pl.* **preys** An eel-like fish having a circular, suctorial mouth with rasping teeth and no jaw.

lance (lans) *n.* A spear-like implement used as a weapon by mounted knights or soldiers.

land (land) *n.* The solid, exposed surface of the earth as distinguished from the waters. *v.* To arrive at a destination; to catch a fish; to receive a new job.

lan-dau (landă) *n.* A four-wheeled vehicle with a closed carriage and a back seat with a collapsible top.

land-fill *n.* A system of trash and garbage disposal in which the waste is burned in low-lying land so as to build up the ground surface; a section built up by landfill.

land grant *n.* A grant of land made by a government, especially for railroads, roads, or agricultural colleges.

land-mark (landmärk) *n.* A fixed object that serves as a boundary marker.

lane (ln) *n.* A small or narrow path between walls, fences,or hedges.

lan-guage (langgwij) *n.* The words, sounds, pronunciation and method of combining words used and understood by people.

lan-guid (langgwid) *adj.* Lacking in energy; drooping; weak. **-ly** *adv.* **languidness** *n.*

lan-guish (langgwish) *v.* To become weak; to be or live in a state of depression.

lank (langk) *adj.* Slender; lean. **-y** *adv.*

lan-o-lin (lanə lin) *n.* Wool grease obtained from sheep's wool and refined for use in ointments and cosmetics.

lan-tern (lantrn) *n.* A portable light having transparent or translucent sides.

lan-yard (lanyrd) *n.* A piece of rope or line used to secure objects on ships.

la-pel (lə pel) *n.* The front part of a garment, especially that of a coat, that is turned back, usually a continuation of the collar.

lap-in (lapin) *n.* Rabbit fur that is sheared and dyed.

lap-is laz-u-li (lapis laz l) *n.* A semiprecious stone that is azure blue in color.

lap-pet (lapit) *n.* A flap or fold on a headdress or on a garment.

lapse (laps) *n.* A temporary deviation or fall to a less desirable state. **lapse** *v.*

lar-ce-ny (lärs n) *n.* *pl.* **-ies** The unlawful taking of another person's property.

lard (lärd) *n.* The soft, white, solid or semi- solid fat obtained after rendering the fatty tissue of the hog.

lar-der (lärdr) *n.* A place, such as a pantry or room, where food is stored.

large (lärj) *adj.* Greater than usual or average in amount or size. **large** To be free and not confined.

large intestine *n.* The portion of the intestine that extends from the end of the small intestine to the anus.

large--scale (lärjskl) *adj.* Larger than others of the same kind; extensive; of or relating to a scale drawing to show detail.

lar-gess *or* **lar-gesse** (lär jes) *n.* Liberal or excessive giving to an inferior; generosity.

lar-go (lärg) *adv.* *Mus.* In a very slow, broad, and solemn manner. **largo** *n.*

lar-i-at (lara t) *n.* A long, light rope with a running noose at one end to catch livestock.

lark (lärk) *n.* A bird having a melodious ability to sing; a merry or carefree adventure.

lar-va (lärvai) *n.* *pl.* **larvae** The immature, wingless, often worm-like form of a newly hatched insect; the early form of an animal that differs greatly from the adult, such as the tadpole.

lar-yn-gi-tis (larn jtis) *n.* Inflammation of the larynx.

lar-ynx (laringks) *n.* *pl.* **larynxes** The upper portion of the trachea which contains the vocal cords. **larynges** *adj.*

la-sa-gna *or* **la-sa-gne** *n.* Traditional Italian dish of wide flat noodles baked with a sauce of tomatoes, meat, and cheese.

la-ser (lzr) *n.* A device which utilizes the natural oscillations of molecules or atoms between energy levels for generating coherent electromagnetic radiation in the visible, ultraviolet, or infrared parts of the spectrum.

lass (las) *n.* A young girl or woman.

las-so (las) *n.* *pl.* **-sos, -soes** A long rope or long leather thong with a running noose used to catch horses and cattle. **lasso** *v.*

last (last) *adj.* Following all the rest; of or relating to the final stages, as of life; worst; lowest in rank. *adv.* After all others in sequence or chronology. *v.* To continue. *n.* A form in the shape of a foot used to hold a shoe while it is repaired or to shape a shoe as it is being made.

lat *abbr.* Latitude.

latch (lach) *n.* A device used to secure a gate or door, consisting of a bar that usually fits into a notch. **onto** To grab onto.

latch-et (lachit) *n.* A narrow leather strap or thong used to fasten a shoe or sandal.

latch-key (lachk) *n.* A key for opening an outside door.

late (lt) *adj.* Coming, staying, happening after the proper or usual time; having recently died. **lateness** *n.* **lately** *adv.*

lat-er-al (latr al) *adj.* Relating to or of the side. In football, an underhand pass thrown sideways or away from the line of scrimmage.

la-tex (lteks) *n.* The milky, white fluid that is produced by certain plants, such as the rubber tree; a water emulsion of synthetic rubber or plastic globules used in paints and adhesives.

lath (lath) *n.* A thin, narrow strip of wood nailed to joists, rafters, or studding and used as a supporting structure for plaster.

lathe (lth) *n.* A machine for holding material while it is spun and shaped by a tool.

lath-er (lathr) *n.* A foam formed by detergent or soap and water. **latherer** *n.* **lathery** *adj.*

lat-i-tude (lati tõd) *n.* The angular distance of the earth's surface north or south of the equator, measured in degrees along a meridian; freedom to act and to choose.

la-trine (la trn) *n.* A public toilet, as in a camp or in a barracks.

lat-ter (latr) *adj.* Being the second of two persons or two things.

lat-tice (latis) *n.* A structure made of strips of wood, metal, or other materials, interlaced or crossed, framing regularly spaced openings.

laugh (laf) *v.* To express amusement, satisfaction, or pleasure with a smile and inarticulate sounds. **laughable** *adj.*

laugh-ter (laftr) *n.* The expression, sound, or act produced by laughing.

launch (länch) *v.* To push or move a vessel into the water for the first time; to set a rocket or missile into flight. *n.* A large boat carried by a ship. **-er** *n.*

laun-der (lä|ndr) *v.* To wash clothes or other materials in soap and water; to wash and iron. **launderer** *n.* **-dress** *n.*

laun-dro-mat (lndrø mat) *n.* A place to wash and dry clothes in coin operated automatic machines.

laun-dry (lndr) *n. pl.* **-ies** An establishment where laundering is done professionally; clothes or other articles to be or that have been laundered.

la-va (läva) *n.* Molten rock which erupts or flows from an active volcano; the rock formed after lava has cooled and hardened.

lav-a-to-ry (lava tr) *n. pl.* **-ies** A room with permanently installed washing and toilet facilities.

lav-en-der (lavn dr) *n.* An aromatic plant having spikes of pale violet flowers; light purple in color. **lavender** *adj.*

lav-ish (lavish) *adj.* Generous and extra vagant in giving or spending. **lavisher** *n.* **lavishly** *adv.* **lavishness** *n.*

law (lô) *n.* A rule of conduct or action, recognized by custom or decreed by formal enactment, considered binding on the members of a nation, community, or group; a system or body of such rules.

lawn (lan) *n.* A stretch of ground covered with grass that is mowed regularly near a house, park, or building.

lax (laks) *adj.* Lacking disciplinary control; lacking rigidity or firmness. **laxity** *n.* **laxness** *n.* **laxly** *adv.*

lax-a-tive (laksa tiv) *n.* A medicine taken to stimulate evacuation of the bowels.

lay (l) *v.* To cause to lie; to place on a surface; past tense of lie.

lay-er (lr) *n.* A single thickness, coating, or covering that lies over or under another. **layered** *adj.* **layer** *v.*

lay-ette (l et) *n.* The clothing, bedding, and equipment for a newborn child.

lay-man (lman) *n.* A person not belonging to a particular profession or specialty; one who is not a member of the clergy.

lay-off (lof) *n.* A temporary dismissal of employees.

lay-out (lout) *n.* A planned arrangement of something, such as a street, room, park, or building.

la-zy (lz) *adj.* Unwilling to work; moving slowly; sluggish. **lazily** *adv.* **laziness** *n.*

la-zy-bones (lz bnz) *n.* Slang A lazy person.

lb *abbr.* Pound

lea (l) *n. poetic.* A grassy field or meadow.

leach (lch) *v.* To cause a liquid to pass through a filter; to remove or wash out by filtering.

lead (ld) *v.* To go ahead so as to show the way; to control the affairs or action of. *n.* A soft, malleable, heavy, dull gray metallic element symbolized by Pb, used in solder, paints, and bullets; a graphite stick used as the writing mate-rial in pencils; in printing, the thin strip of type metal used to provide space between printed lines. **leaden-ness** *n.* **leading** *adj.* **leaden** *adj.*

lead poisoning (led poize ning) *n.* Poisoning of a person's system by the absorption of lead or any of its salts.

leaf (lf) *n. pl.* **leaves** A flat out-growth from a plant structure or tree, usually green in color and functioning as the principal area of photo-synthesis; a single page in a book. *v.* To turn the pages of a book. **-less** *adj.* **leafy** *adj.*

leaf-let (lflit) *n.* A part or a segment of a compound leaf; a small printed hand-bill or circular, often folded.

league (lg) *n.* An association of persons, organizations, or states for common action or interest; an association of athletic com petition; an underwater measurement of distance that equals 3 miles or approximately 4.8 km.

leak (lk) *n.* An opening, as a flaw or small crack, permitting an escape or entrance of light or fluid. **leakage** *n.*

lean (ln) *v.* To rest or incline the weight of the body for support; to rest or incline anything against a large object or wall; to rely or depend on; to have a tendency or preference for; to tend towards a suggestion or action. *adj.* Having little or no fat; thin. **-ly** *adv*

lean-ing (lning) *n.* An inclination; a pre-dispositon.

lean--to (lntô) *n.* A structure of branches, sloping to the ground with a slanted support, usually an outside wall.

leap (lp) *v.* To rise or project oneself by a sudden thrust from the ground with a spring of the legs; to spring, to jump.

leaper *n.*

leap-frog (lpfrog) *n.* A game in which two players leap over each other by placing one's hands on the back of another who is bending over and leap-ing over him in a straddling position.

leap year *n.* A year containing 366 days, occurring every 4th year, with the extra day added to make 29 days in February .

learn (lrn) *n.* The process of acquiring knowledge, understanding, or mastery of a study or experience.

lease (ls) *n.* A contract for the temporary use or occupation of property or prem-ises in exchange for payment of rent.

leash (lsh) *n.* A strong cord or rope for restraining a dog or other animal.

least-wise *adv.* Slang At least; at any rate.

leath-er (lethr) *n.* An animal skin or hide with the hair removed, prepared for use by tanning.

leath-er-neck (lethr nek) *n.* Slang A United States Marine.

leave (lv) *v.* To go or depart from; to per-mit to remain behind or in a specified place or condition; to forsake; to aban-don; to bequeath, as in a will. *n.* Official permission for absence from duty.

leav-en (levn) *n.* An agent of fermenta-tion, as yeast, used to cause batters and doughs to rise; any pervasive influence that produces a significant change.

lec-i-thin (les thin) *n.* Any of a group of phosphorus containing compounds found in plant and animal tissues, commercially derived from egg yolks, corn, and soybeans, and used in the production of foods, cosmetics, phar-maceuticals, and plastics.

lec-tern (lektrn) *n.* A stand or tall desk, usually with a slanted top, on which a speaker or instructor may place books or papers.

lec-ture (lekchr) *n.* A speech on a spe-cific subject, delivered to an audience for information or instruction. *v.* To give a speech or lecture; to criticize or reprimand.

led *v. p.t. & p.p.* Past tense of lead.

ledge (lej) *n.* A narrow, shelf-like pro-jection forming a shelf, as on a wall or the side of a rocky formation.

ledg-er (lejr) *n.* A book in which sums of money received and paid out are recorded.

lee (l) *n.* The side of a ship sheltered from the wind.

leech (lch) *n.* Any of various carnivorous or bloodsucking worms; a person who clings or preys on others.

leek (lk) *n.* A culinary herb of the lily family, related to the onion, with a slender, edible bulb.

leer (lr) *n.* A sly look or sideways glance expressing desire or malicious intent.

lee-way (lw) *n.* *Naut.* The lateral drift of a plane or ship away from the correct course.

left (left) *adj.* Pertaining to or being on the side of the body that faces north when the subject is facing east.

leg (leg) *n.* A limb or appendage serving as a means of support and movement in animals and man; a part or division of a journey or trip.

leg-a-cy (lega s) *n. pl.* **-ies** Personal property, money, and other valuables that are bequeathed by will; anything that is handed down from an ancestor, predecessor, or earlier era.

le-gal (lgal) *adj.* Of, pertaining to, or concerned with the law or lawyers; something based on or authorized by law. **legality** *n.* **legalization** *n.* **-ize** *v.*

le-gal-ism (lga lizm) *n.* A strict conformity to the law, especially when stress-ing the letter and forms of the law rather than the spirit of justice. **legalist** *n.* **legalistic** *adj.*

le-ga-tion (li gshn) *n.* The official diplomatic mission in a foreign country, headed by a minister; the official residence or business premises of a diplomatic minister of lower rank than an ambassador.

le-ga-to (l gät) *adv.* *Music* Smooth and flowing with successive notes connected.

leg-end (lejnd) *n.* An unverifiable story handed down from the past; a body of such stories, as those connected with a culture or people.

leg-en-dar-y (lejn der) *adj.* Presented as, based on, or of the nature of a legend.

leg-i-ble (lej bl) *adj.* Capable of being read or deciphered. **legibility** *n.* **legibly** *adv.*

le-gion (ljn) *n.* In ancient Rome, an army unit that comprised between 4,200 and 6,000 men; any of various honorary or military organizations, usually national in character.

leg-is-late (lejis lt) *v.* To pass or make laws.

leg-is-la-tion (lejis lshn) *n.* The act or procedures of passing laws; lawmaking; an officially enacted law.

leg-is-la-tive (lejis ltiv) *adj.* Of or pertaining to legislation or a legislature; having the power to legislate.

leg-is-la-ture (lejis lchr) *n.* A body of persons officially constituted and empowered to make and change laws.

leg-ume (legm) *n.* A plant of the pea or bean family, that bears pods which split when mature; the seeds or pod of a legume used as food. **-uminous** *adj.*

leg-work *n.* *Slang* A chore, task, or gathering of information accomplished by going about on foot.

lei (l) *n. pl.* **leis** A wreath of flowers worn around the neck; the customary greeting of welcome in the state of Hawaii.

lei-sure (lzhr) *n.* The time of freedom from work or duty. **leisurely** *adv.* **leisured** *adj.*

lem-on (lemn) *n.* An oval citrus fruit grown on a tree, having juicy, acid pulp and a yellow rind that yields an essential oil used as a flavoring and as a perfuming agent. *Slang* Something, as an automobile, that proves to be defective or unsatisfactory.

lend (lend) *v.* To allow the temporary use or possession of something with the understanding that it is to be returned; to offer oneself as to a specific purpose. **-er** *n.*

length (lengkth) *n.* The linear extent of something from end to end, usually the longest dimension of a thing as distinguished from its thickness and width; the measurement of something to estimate distance. **lengthy** *adj.*

length-en (lengkthn) *v.* To make or become longer.

length-wise (lengkthwz) *adv.* & *adj.* Of

or in the direction or dimension of length; longitudinally.

le-ni-ent (ln nt) adj. Gentle, forgiving, and mild; merciful; undemanding; tolerant. **leniency** n. **lenience** n.

len-i-tive (leni tiv) adj. Having the ability to ease pain or discomfort.

lens (lenz) n. In optics, the curved piece of glass or other transparent substance that is used to refract light rays so that they converge or diverge to form an image; the transparent structure in the eye, situated behind the iris, which serves to focus an image on the retina.

lent (lent) v. Past tense of lend.

Lent (lent) n. Eccl. The period of forty days, excluding Sundays, of fasting and penitence observed by many Christians from Ash Wednesday until Easter. **Lenten** adj.

len-til (lentil) n. A leguminous plant, having broad pods and containing edible seeds.

le-o-tard (løtärd) n. A close-fitting garment worn by dancers and acrobats.

lep-er (lepr) n. One who suffers from leprosy.

lep-ro-sy (leprø s) n. pathol. A chronic communicable disease characterized by nodular skin lesions and the progressive destruction of tissue. **leprous** adj. **leprotic** adj.

les-bi-an (lezban) n. A homosexual woman. **lesbian** adj.

lese maj-es-ty (lz maji st) n. An offense against a ruler or supreme power of state.

le-sion (lzhan) n. Pathol. An injury; a wound; any well-defined bodily area where the tissue has changed in a way that is characteristic of a disease.

less (les) adj. Smaller; of smaller or lower importance or degree. prep. With the subtraction of; minus.

-less suffix. Without; lacking.

les-see (le s) n. One who leases a property.

les-son (lesøn) n. An instance from which something is to be or has been learned; an assignment to be learned or studied as by a student.

let (let) v. To give permission; to allow. n. An invalid stroke in a game such as tennis, that must be repeated because

of some interruption or hindrance of playing conditions.

let-down (letdoun) n. A decrease or slackening, as in energy or effort. Slang A disappointment.

le-thal (lthal) adj. Pertaining to or being able to cause death. **lethally** adv.

leth-ar-gy (lethr j) n. Pathol. A state of excessive drowsiness or abnormally deep sleep; laziness. **lethargic** adj.

let's (lets) Let us.

let-ter (letr) n. A standard character or sign used in writing or printing to represent an alphabetical unit or speech sound; a written or printed means of communication sent to another person.

let-ter--perfect (letr prfïkt) adj. Absolutely correct; perfect.

leu-ke-mi-a (lö km a) n. Pathol. A generally fatal disease of the blood in which white blood cells multiply in uncontrolled numbers. **leukemic** adj.

le-vee (lev) n. An embankment along the shore of a body of water, especially a river, built to prevent overflowing.

lev-el (levl) n. A relative position, rank, or height on a scale; a standard position from which other heights and depths are measured. adj. Balanced in height; even. v. To make or become flat or level. **leveler** n. **levelness** n. **-ly** adv.

lev-el--head-ed (levl hedid) adj. Showing good judgment and common sense.

lever (levr) n. A handle that projects and is used to operate or adjust a mechanism.

lever-age n. The use of a lever; the mechanical advantage gained by using a lever; power to act effectively.

lev-i-tate (levi tt) v. To rise and float in the air in apparent defiance of gravity.

lev-y (lev) v. To impose and collect by authority or force, as a fine or tax; to draft for military service; to prepare for, begin, or wage war.

lewd (löd) adj. Preoccupied with sex; lustful.

lex-i-cog-ra-phy (leks kogra f) n. The practice or profession of compiling dictionaries.

lex-i-con (leks kon) n. A dictionary; a vocabulary or list of words that relate to a certain subject, occupation, or activity.

li-a-bil-i-ty (la bili t) *n. pl.* **-ies** The condition or state of being liable; that which is owed to another.

li-a-ble (la bl) *adj.* Legally or rightly responsible.

li-ar (lr) *n.* A person who tells falsehoods.

lib *n. Slang* Liberation.

li-bel (lbl) *n. Law* A written statement in published form that damages a person's character or reputation. **libel** *v.* **libelous** *adj.*

lib-er-al (libr al) *adj.* Characterized by generosity or lavishness in giving; abundant; ample; inclining toward opinions or policies that favor progress or reform, such as religion or politics.

lib-er-al arts *n. pl.* Academic courses that include literature, philosophy, history, languages, etc., which provide general cultural information.

lib-er-ate (lib rt) *v.* To set free, as from bondage, oppression, or foreign control.

lib-er-ty (librt) *n. pl.* **-ies** The state of being free from oppression, tyranny, confinement, or slavery; freedom; in Navy terms, the permission to be absent from one's ship or duty for less that 48 hours.

li-bi-do (li bd) *n.* One's sexual desire or impulse; the psychic energy drive that is behind all human activities.

li-brar-y (lbrer) *n. pl.* **-ies** A collection of books, pamphlets, magazines, and reference books kept for reading, ref-erence, or borrowing; a commercial establishment, usually in connection with a city or school, which rents books.

lice *n.* Plural of louse.

li-cense (lsns) *n.* An official document that gives permission to engage in a specified activity or to perform a specified act. **licensee** *n.* **licenser** *n.*

li-cen-ti-ate (l sensh it) *n.* A person licensed to practice a specified profession.

li-cen-tious (l senshus) *adj.* Lacking in moral restraint; immoral. **licentiously** *adv.* **licentiousness** *n.*

li-chen (lkn) *n.* Any of various flowerless plants consisting of fungi, commonly growing in flat patches on trees and rocks. **-ed** *adj.* **lichenous** *adj.*

lic-it (lisit) *adj.* Lawful. **licitly** *adv.*

lick (lik) *v.* To pass the tongue over or along the surface of. *Slang* To beat; to thrash.

lick-e-ty--split (liki t split) *adv.* Full speed; rapidly.

lic-o-rice (likə ris) *n.* A perennial herb of Europe, the dried root of which is used to flavor medicines and candy.

lid (lid) *n.* A hinged or removable cover for a container; an eyelid. **lidless** *adj.*

lie (l) *v.* To be in or take a horizontal recumbent position; to recline. *n.* A false or untrue statement.

liege (lj) *n.* A feudal lord or sovereign. *adj.* Loyal; faithful.

lien (ln) *n.* The legal right to claim, hold, or sell the property of another to satisfy a debt or obligation.

lieu (lö) *n.* Place; stead. **of** In place of.

lieu-ten-ant (lötenant) *n.* A commissioned officer in the U.S. Army, Air Force, or Marine Corps who ranks below a captain.

life (lf) *n. pl.* **lives** The form of existence that distinguishes living organisms from dead organisms or inanimate matter in the ability to carry on metabolism, respond to stimuli, reproduce, and grow.

life-guard (lfgärd) *n.* An expert swimmer employed to protect people in and around water.

life preserver *n.* A buoyant device, as one in the shape of a ring or jacket, used to keep a person afloat in water.

life-raft *n.* A raft made of wood or an inflatable material used by people who have been forced into the water.

life--support system *n.* A system giving a person all or some of the items, such as oxygen, water, food, and control of temperature, necessary for a person's life and health while in a spacecraft or while exploring the surface of the moon; a system used to sustain life in a critical health situation.

life-time (lftm) *n.* The period between one's birth and death.

life-work (lfwrk) *n.* The main work of a person's lifetime.

life zone *n.* A biogeographic zone.

lift (lift) *v.* To raise from a lower to a higher position; to elevate; to take from; to steal. *n.* The act or process of lifting; force or power available for lifting; an elevation of spirits; a device or machine designed to pick up, raise, or carry something; an elevator. **-er** *n.*

lift-off (lǐftäf) *n.* The vertical takeoff or the instant of takeoff of an aircraft or spacecraft.

lig-a-ment (lig∂ mnt) *n.* A strong band of tissue joining bones or holding a body organ in place. **ligamentous** *adj.*

li-gate (lgt) *v.* To tie with a ligature.

lig-a-ture (lig∂ chr) *n.* Something, as a cord, that is used to bind; a thread used in surgery; something that unites or connects; a printing character that combines two or more letters.

light (lt) *n.* Electromagnetic radiation that can be seen by the naked eye; brightness; a source of light; spiritual illumination; enlightenment; a source of fire, such as a match. *adj.* Having light; bright; of less force, quantity, intensity, weight, than normal; having less calories or alcoholic content; dizzy; giddy. **light** *v.* **lightness** *n.*

light-er (ltr) *n.* A device used to light a pipe, cigar or cigarette; a barge used to load and unload a cargo ship.

light-ning (ltning) *n.* The flash of light produced by a high-tension natural electric discharge in the atmosphere. *adj.* Moving with or as if with the suddenness of lightning.

lightning bug *n.* A firefly.

lightning rod *n.* A grounded metal rod positioned high on a building to protect it from lightning.

light opera *n.* An operetta.

lights (lts) The lungs, especially of a slaughtered animal.

light-year *or* **light year** (ltyr) *n.* A measure equal to the distance light travels in one year, approximately 5.878 trillion miles.

lig-ne-ous (lign us) *adj.* Of or resembling wood; woody.

lig-ni-fy (lign f) *v.* To make or become woody or wood-like.

lig-nite (lignt) *n.* A brownish-black soft coal, especially one in which the texture of the original wood is distinct.

lig-ro-in (ligr in) *n.* A volatile, flammable fraction of petroleum used as a solvent.

like-mind-ed (lkmndid) *adj.* Of the same way of thinking.

lik-en (lkn) *v.* To describe as being like; to compare.

like-ness (lkns) *n.* Resemblance; a copy.

like-wise (lkwz) *adv.* In a similar way.

li-lac (llak) *n.* A shrub widely grown for its large, fragrant purplish or white flower cluster; a pale purple. **lilac** *adj.*

lilt (lĭlt) *n.* A light song; a rhythmical way of speaking.

lil-y (lĭl) *n. pl.* **-ies** Any of various plants bearing trumpet-shaped flowers; a plant similar or related to the lily, as the water lily.

lil-y--liv-ered (lĭl lĭvrd) *adj.* Timid; cowardly.

limb (lĭm) *n.* A large bough of a tree; an animal's appendage used for movement or grasping; an arm or leg.

lim-ber (lĭmbr) *adj.* Bending easily; pliable; moving easily; agile. *v.* To make or become limber. **limberly** *adv.* **limberness** *n.*

lime (lm) *n.* A tropical citrus tree with evergreen leaves, fragrant white flowers, and edible green fruit; calcium oxide.

lime-light (lmlt) *n.* A focus of public attention; the center of attention.

lim-er-ick (lĭmr ĭk) *n.* A humorous verse of five lines.

lime-stone (lmstn) *n.* A form of sedimentary rock composed mainly of calcium carbonate which is used in building and in making lime and cement.

lim-it (lĭmit) *n.* A boundary; a maximum or a minimum number or amount; a restriction on frequency or amount. *v.* To restrict; to establish bounds or boundaries. **-ation** *n.*

limn *v.* To describe; to depict by drawing.

li-mo-nite (lm∂ nt) *n.* A natural iron-oxide used as an ore of iron.

lim-ou-sine (lĭm∂ zn) *n.* A luxurious large vehicle; a small bus used to carry passengers to airports and hotels.

limp (lĭmp) *v.* To walk lamely. *adj.* Lacking or having lost rigidity; not firm or strong.

limply adv. **limpness** n.

lim-pet (limpit) n. Any of numerous marine gastropod mollusks having a conical shell and adhering to tidal rocks.

lim-pid (limpid) adj. Transparently clear.

limpidity n. **limpidly** adv.

linch-pin (linchpin) n. A locking pin inserted through a shaft to keep a wheel from slipping off.

lin-den (lindn) n. Any of various shade trees having heart-shaped leaves.

lin-e-age (lin ij) n. A direct line of descent from an ancestor.

lin-e-a-ment (lin a mnt) n. A contour, shape, or feature of the body and especially of the face.

lin-e-ar (lin r) adj. Of, pertaining to, or resembling a line; long and narrow.

linear perspective n. A technique in painting and drawing in which parallel lines converge to give the illusion of distance and depth.

lin-en (linn) n. Thread, yarn, or fabric made of flax; household articles, such as sheets and pillow cases, made of linen or a similar fabric. **linen** adj.

lin-er (lnr) n. A ship belonging to a ship line or an aircraft belonging to an airline; one that lines or serves as a lining.

line score n. In baseball, a statistical record of each inning of a game.

line-up (lnup) n. A line of persons formed for the purpose of inspection or identification; the members of a team who take part in a game; a group of television programs that are aired sequentially.

ling (ling) n. Any of various marine food fishes related to the cod.

lin-ger (linggr) v. To be slow in parting or reluctant to leave; to be slow in acting; to procrastinate. **lingerer** n. **lingeringly** adv.

lin-ge-rie (länzh r) n. Women's undergarments.

lingo (lingg) n. pl. **goes** Language that is unfamiliar; a specialized vocabulary.

lin-guist (linggwist) n. One who is fluent in more than one language; a person specializing in linguistics.

lin-i-ment (lin mnt) n. A liquid or semi-

liquid medicine applied to the skin.

lin-ing (lning) n. A material which is used to cover an inside surface.

link (lingk) n. One of the rings forming a chain; something in the form of a link; a tie or bond; a cuff link. v. To connect by or as if by a link or links.

link-age (linkij) n. The act or process of linking; a system of connecting structures.

links (lingks) n. pl. A golf course.

lin-net (linit) n. A small Old World finch.

li-no-le-um (li nl m) n. A floor covering consisting of a surface of hardened linseed oil and a filler, as wood or powdered cork, on a canvas or burlap backing.

lin-seed (linsd) n. The seed of flax, used in paints and varnishes.

lin-sey–wool-sey (linz wlz) n. A coarse, sturdy fabric of wool and linen or cotton.

lin-tel (lintl) n. A horizontal beam across the top of a door which supports the weight of the structure above it.

li-on (lən) n. A large carnivorous mammal of the cat family, found in Africa and India, having a short, tawny coat and a long, heavy mane in the male; a person of great importance or prestige. **lioness** n.

li-on–heart-ed (lən härtid) adj. Very courageous.

li-on-ize (lə nz) v. To treat someone as a celebrity.

lip service n. An expression of acquiescence that is not acted upon.

liq-ue-fy / liq-ui-fy To make liquid. **liquefaction** n. **liquefier** n.

li-queur (li kr) n. A sweet alcoholic beverage; a cordial.

liq-ui-date (likwi dt) v. To settle a debt by payment or other settlement; to close a business by settling accounts and dividing up assets; to get rid of, especially to kill. **liquidation** n. **liquidator** n.

liq-uor (likr) n. A distilled alcoholic beverage; a liquid substance, as a watery solution of a drug.

lisle (ll) n. A fine, tightly twisted cotton thread.

lisp (lisp) n. A speech defect or mannerism marked by lisping. *v.* To mispronounce the s and z sounds, usually as th. **lisper** *n.*

lis-some (lisøm) *adj.* Nimble. **lissomely** *adv.* **lissomeness** *n.*

list (list) *n.* A series of numbers or words; a tilt to one side. **list** *v.*

list-less (listlis) *adj.* Lacking energy or enthusiasm. **listlessly** *adv.* **-ness** *n.*

lit *abbr.* Literary; literature.

lit-a-ny (litø n) *n. pl.* **-ies** A prayer in which phrases recited by a leader are alternated with answers from a congregation.

li-tchi *or* **li-chee** (lch) *n.* A Chinese tree, bearing edible fruit; the fruit of the tree.

lit-er-al (litr øl) *adj.* Conforming to the exact meaning of a word; concerned primarily with facts; without embellishment or exaggeration. **literally** *adv.* **literalistic** *adj.*

lit-er-al-ism (litr ø lizm) *n.* Adherence to the explicit sense of a given test; literal portrayal; realism. **-ist** *n.* **literalistic** *adj.*

lit-er-ar-y (lit rer) *adj.* Pertaining to literature; appropriate to or used in literature; of or relating to the knowledge of literature.

lit-er-ate (litr it) *adj.* Having the ability to read and write; showing skill in using words. **literacy** *n.* **literate** *n.*

lit-e-ra-ti (lit rät) *n. pl.* The educated class.

lit-er-a-ture (litrø chr) *n.* Printed material, as leaflets for a political campaign; written words of lasting excellence.

lithe (lth) *adj.* Bending easily; supple. **lithely** *adv.* **litheness** *n.*

lith-i-um (lith m) *n.* A silver-white, soft metallic element symbolized by Li.

li-thog-ra-phy (li thogrø f) *n.* A printing process in which a flat surface is treated so that the ink adheres only to the portions that are to be printed.

li-thol-o-gy (li tholø j) *n.* The microscopic study and classification of rocks. **-ist** *n.*

lit-i-gate (lit gt) *v.* To conduct a legal contest by judicial process. **litigant** *n.* **litigation** *n.*

lit-mus (litms) *n.* A blue powder

obtained from lichens which turns red in acid solutions and blue in alkaline solutions, used as an acid-base indicator.

litmus paper *n.* Unsized paper that is treated with litmus and used as an indicator.

lit-ter (litr) *n.* A covered and curtained couch, mounted on shafts and used to carry a single passenger; a stretcher used to carry a sick or injured person; material used as bedding for animals; the offspring at one birth of a multiparous animal; an accumulation of waste material. **litter** *v.* **litterer** *n.*

lit-ter-bug (litr bug) *n.* One who litters a public area.

Little Dipper *n.* Ursa Minor.

lit-to-ral (litr øl) *adj.* Relating to or existing on a shore. *n.* A shore.

lit-ur-gy (litr jj) *n. pl.* **-ies** A prescribed rite or body of rites for public worship. **liturgical** *adj.* **liturgically** *adv.*

live-li-hood (lvl hd) *n.* A means of support or subsistence.

live-ly (lvl) *adj.* Vigorous. **liveliness** *n.*

liv-er (livr) *n.* The large, very vascular, glandular organ of vertebrates which secretes bile.

liv-er-wurst (livr wrst) *n.* A kind of sausage made primarily of liver.

liv-er-y (liv r) *n. pl.* **-ies** A uniform worn by servants; the care and boarding of horses for pay; a concern offering horses and vehicles for rent.

liv-er-y-man (liv r man) *n.* A keeper or employee of a livery stable.

live-stock (lvstok) *n.* Farm animals raised for human use.

live wire *n. Slang* An energetic person.

liv-id (livid) *adj.* Discolored from a bruise; very angry.

liz-ard (lizrd) *n.* One of various reptiles, usually with an elongated scaly body, four legs, and a tapering tail.

lla-ma (lämø) *n.* A South American ruminant, related to the camel family and raised for its soft wool.

load (ld) *n.* A mass or weight that is lifted or supported; anything, as cargo, put in a ship, aircraft, or vehicle for conveyance; something that is a heavy responsibility; a burden. **loader** *n.* **loading** *n.* **load** *v.*

load-ed (ldid) *adj.* Intended to trick or trap. *Slang* Drunk; rich.

loaf (lf) *n. pl.* **loaves** A food, especially bread, that is shaped into a mass. To spend time in idleness. **loafer** *v.*

loam (lm) *n.* Soil that consists chiefly of sand, clay, and decayed plant matter.

loan (ln) *n.* Money lent with interest to be repaid; something borrowed for temporary use. *v.* To lend.

loan shark One who lends money to individuals at exorbitant rates of interest.

loath (lth) *adj.* Averse.

loathe (lth) *v.* To dislike intensely.

loath-ing (lthing) *n.* Intense dislike; abhorrence.

loath-some (lthsøm) *adj.* Arousing disgust.
loathsomely *adv.* **loathsomeness** *n.*

lob (lob) *v.* To hit or throw in a high arc.

lob-by (lob) *n. pl.* **-ies** A foyer, as in a hotel or theatre; a group of private persons trying to influence legislators.
lobbyist *n.*

lobe (lb) *n.* A curved or rounded projection or division, as the fleshy lower part of the ear. **lobar** *adj.* **lobed** *adj.*

lo-bo (lb) *n.* The gray wolf, as referred to by those who reside in the western United States.

lo-bot-o-my (l botø m) *n. pl.* **-mies** Surgical severance of nerve fibers by incision into the brain.

lob-ster (lobstr) *n.* Any of several large, edible marine crustaceans with five pairs of legs, the first pair being large and claw-like.

lob-ule (lobl) *n.* A small lobe; a subdivision of a lobe. **lobular** *adj.*

lo-cal (lkøl) *adj.* Pertaining to, being in, or serving a particular area or place.

lo-cale (l kal) *n.* A locality where a particular event takes place; the setting or scene, as of a novel.

lo-cal-i-ty (l kali t) *n. pl* **-ties** A specific neighborhood, place, or district.

lo-cate (lkt) *v.* To determine the place, position, or boundaries of; to look for and find; to establish or become established; to settle. **locator** *n.*

lo-ca-tion (l kshøn) *n.* The act or process of locating; a place where something is or can be located; a site

outside where a motion picture or television studio where a movie is shot.

loch (lok) *n.* *Scot.* A lake.

lock (lok) *n.* A device used, as on a door, to secure or fasten; a part of a waterway closed off with gates to allow the raising or lowering of boats by changing the level of the water; a strand or curl of hair. **lock** *v.*

lock-et (lokit) *n.* A small, ornamental case for a keepsake, often a picture, worn as a pendant on a necklace.

lock-smith (loksmith) *n.* A person who makes or repairs locks.

lo-co (lk) *adj.* *Slang* Insane.

lo-co-mo-tion (lkø mshøn) *n.* The act of moving; the power to move from place to place.

lo-co-mo-tive (lkø mtiv) *n.* A self-propelled vehicle that is generally electric or diesel-powered and is used for moving railroad cars.

lo-co-weed (lk wd) *n.* Any of several plants found throughout the western and central United States which are poisonous to livestock.

lo-cust (lkst) *n.* Any of numerous grasshoppers which often travel in swarms and damage vegetation; any of various hard- wooded leguminous trees, such as carob, black locust, or honey locust.

lode-star (ldstar) *n.* A star; the North Star, used as a reference point.

lodge (loj) *n.* A house, such as a cabin, used as a temporary or seasonal dwelling or shelter; an inn; the den of an animal, such as a beaver; a local chapter of a fraternal organization; the meeting hall of such a chapter.

loft *n.* One of the upper, generally unpartitioned floors of an industrial or commercial building, such as a warehouse; an attic; a gallery in a church or hall.

loge (lzh) *n.* A small compartment, especially a box in a theatre; a small partitioned area, as a separate forward section of a theatre mezzanine or balcony.

log-ger-head (logr hed) *n.* Any of various large marine turtles, especially the carnivorous turtle found in the warm waters of the western Atlantic. **loggerheads** In a state of contention; at odds.

log-gi-a (loja) *n.* A roofed but open arcade along the front of a building; an open balcony in a theatre.

log-ic (lojik) *n.* The science dealing with the principles of reasoning, especially of the method and validity of deductive reasoning; something that forces a decision apart from or in opposition to reason. **logician** *n.*

log-i-cal (loji kal) *adj.* Relating to; or in accordance with logic; something marked by consistency of reasoning. **logically** *adv.*

lo-gis-tics (l jistiks) *n. pl.* The methods of procuring, maintaining, and replacing material and personnel, as in a military operation. **logistic** *adj.*

lo-gy (lg) *adj.* Something , marked by sluggishness. **loginess** *n.*

loin (loin) *n.* The area of the body located between the ribs and pelvis; a cut of meat from an animal.

loins The thighs and groin; the reproductive organs.

loi-ter (loitr) *v.* To stay for no apparent reason; to dawdle or delay. **loiterer** *n.*

loll (lol) *v.* To move or act in a lax, lazy or indolent manner; to hang loosely or laxly.

lol-li-pop *or* **lol-ly-pop (lol pop)** *n.* A piece of flavored hard candy on a stick.

lol-ly-gag *v. Slang* To fool around.

lone (ln) *adj.* Single; isolated; sole; unfrequented.

lone-ly (lnl) *adj.* Being without companions; dejected from being alone.

lon-er *n.* A person who avoids the company of others.

lone-some (lnsøm) *adj.* Dejected because of the lack of companionship.

long *abbr.* Longitude.

long-bow (långb) *n.* A wooden bow that is approximately five to six feet in length.

lon-gev-i-ty (lon jevi t) *n.* Long life; long duration; seniority.

long-hair (långhâr) *n.* A lover of the arts, especially classical music; a person with long hair.

long-hand (långhand) *n.* Cursive handwriting.

lon-gi-tude (lonji töd) *n.* The angular distance that is east and west of the prime meridian at Greenwich, Eng-land.

lon-gi-tu-di-nal (lonji töd nal) *adj.* Of or relating to the length; relating to longitude.

long-shore-man (långshrman) *n.* A dockhand who loads and unloads cargo.

look (lk) *v.* To examine with the eyes; to see; to glance, gaze, or stare at *n.* The act of looking; the physical appearance of something or someone.

loom (löm) *v.* To come into view as a image; to seem to be threatening. *n.* A machine used for interweaving thread or yarn to produce cloth.

loop (löp) *n.* A circular length of line folded over and joined at the ends; a loop-shaped pattern, figure, or path. *v.* To form into a loop; to join, fasten, or encircle with a loop.

loop-hole (löphl) *n.* A means of escape; a legal way to circumvent the intent of a law.

loose (ls) *adj.* Not tightly fastened; not confined or fitting; free.

loot (löt) *n.* Goods, usually of significant value, taken in time of war; goods that have been stolen. *v.* To plunder; to steal.

lop (lop) *v.* To remove branches from; to trim; to cut off with a single blow.

lope (lp) *v.* To run with a steady gait.

lop-sid-ed (lopsdid) *adj.* Larger or heavier on one side than on the other; tilting to one side. **lopsidedly** *adv.* **lopsidedness** *n.*

lo-qua-cious (l kwshus) *adj.* Overly talkative. **loquaciously** *adv.* **-city** *n.*

Lord (lârd) *n.* God. A man having dominion and power over other people; the owner of a feudal estate.

lore (lr) *n.* Traditional fact; knowledge that has been gained through education or experience.

lorn (lârn) *n.* Forlorn.

lose (löz) *v.* To mislay; to fail to keep.

loss (lås) *n.* The suffering or damage used by losing; someone or something that is lost. **losses** *pl. n.* Killed, wounded, or captured soldiers; casualties.

lost (låst) *adj.* Unable to find one's way.

lot (lot) *n.* Fate; fortune; a parcel of land having boundaries; a plot.

lo-tion *n.* A liquid medicine for external

use on the hands and body.

lot·ter·y (lot r) *n. pl.* **-ies** A contest in which winners are selected by a random drawing.

lo·tus (lts) *n.* An aquatic plant having fragrant pinkish flowers and large leaves; any of several plants similar or related to the lotus.

lo·tus–eater (lts tr) *n.* One of a people represented in the Odyssey of Homer as eating the lotus fruit and living in the dreamy indolence it produced.

loud (loud) *adj.* Marked by intense sound and high volume. **loud** *adv.* **loudly** *adv.*

lounge (lounj) *v.* To move or act in a lazy, relaxed manner. A room, as in a hotel or theatre, where people may wait; a couch.

louse (lous) *n. pl.* **lice** A small, wingless biting or sucking insect which lives as a parasite on various animals and also on human beings. *Slang* A mean, contemptible person.

lous·y (louz) *adj.* Lice-infested. *Slang* Mean; poor; inferior; abundantly supplied.

lout (lout) *n.* An awkward, stupid person. *v.* To stoop, bow, or bend.

lou·ver or lou·vre (lövr) *n.* An opening in a wall fitted with movable, slanted slats which let air in, but keep precipitation out; one of the slats used in a louver.

love (luv) *n.* Intense affection for another arising out of kinship or personal ties; a strong feeling of attraction resulting from sexual desire; enthusiasm or fondness; a score of zero in tennis. **love** *v.* **lovable** *adj.*

love–bird (luvbrd) *n.* Any of various Old World parrots which show great affection for their mates.

love·ly (luvl) *adj.* Beautiful. **-liness** *n.*

lov·er (luvr) *n.* A person who loves another; a sexual partner.

low (l) *adj.* Not high; being below or under normal height, rank, or level; depressed. *v.* To moo, as a cow.

low beam *n.* A low-intensity headlight.

low–brow (lbrou) *n.* An uncultured person. **lowbrow** *adj.*

low–down (ldoun) *n.* The whole truth; all the facts *adj.* Despicable; mean;

depressed.

low·er–case (lr ks) *adj.* Having as its typical form a, b, c, or u, v, w rather than A, B, C, or U,V, W.

lower class *n.* The group in society that ranks below the middleclass in social and economic status.

lowest common denominator *n.* The least common multiple of the denominators of a set of fractions.

lowest common multiple *n.* Least common multiple.

low frequency *n.* A radio-wave frequency between 30 and 300 kilohertz.

low–key or low–keyed (lk) *adj.* Restrained.

low·land (land) *n.* Land that is low and level in relation to the surrounding countryside.

low·ly (ll) *adj.* Low in position or rank.

low profile *n.* A deliberately inconspicuous life style or posture.

low–rise *adj.* Having one or two stories and no elevator.

low–ten·sion (ltenshan) *adj.* Having a low voltage; built to be used at low voltage.

lox (loks) *n.* Smoked salmon usually eaten with cream cheese and a bagel.

loy·al (loial) *adj.* Faithful in allegiance to one's country and government; faithful to a person, cause, ideal, or custom. **loyalty** *n.*

loy·al·ist (loialist) *n.* One who is or remains loyal to political cause, party, government, or sovereign.

loz·enge (lozinj) *n.* Small medicated candy, normally having the shape of a lozenge.

lu·au (lõ ou) *n.* A traditional Hawaiian feast with native music and entertainment.

lub·ber (lubr) *n.* An awkward, clumsy or stupid person; an inexperienced sailor.

lu·bri·cant (lõbr kant) *n.* A material, as grease or oil, applied to moving parts to reduce friction.

lu·cid (lösid) *adj.* Easily understood; mentally clear; rational; shining. **lu·cidity** *n.* **lucidness** *n.* **lucidly** *adv.*

luck (luk) *n.* Good fortune; the force or power which controls odds and which brings good fortune or bad fortune.

Whatever happens as if by chance. lucky, **luckily** adv.

lu-cra-tive (lōkra tiv) adj. Producing profits or great wealth. **-tively** adv.

lu-cre (lōkr) n. Money; profit.

lu-cu-brate (lōk brt) v. To study or work laboriously.

lu-di-crous (lōd krus) adj. Amusing or laughable through obvious absurdity; ridiculous. **ludicrously** adv. **-ness** n.

luff (luf) v. To turn a sailing vessel toward the wind.

lug (lug) n. An ear-like handle or projection used as a hold; a tab. v. To carry with difficulty.

luge n. A small sled similar to a toboggan which is ridden in a supine position and used especially in competition.

lug-gage (lugij) n. Something that is lugged, especially suitcases or a traveler's baggage.

lu-gu-bri-ous (l gōbr us) adj. Mournful; dejected; especially exaggeratedly or affectedly so. **lugubriously** adv.

luke-warm (lōkwårm) adj. Mildly warm; tepid; unenthusiastic; soothing.

lull (lul) v. To cause to rest or sleep; to cause to have a false sense of security. n. A temporary period of quiet or rest.

lul-la-by (lula b) n. pl. **-bies** A song to lull a child to sleep.

lum-ba-go (lum bg) n. Painful rheumatic pain of the muscles and tendons of the lumbar region.

lum-bar (lumbr) adj. Part of the back and sides between the lowest ribs and the pelvis.

lum-ber (lumbr) n. Timber, sawed or split into boards. v. To walk clumsily.

lum-ber-yard (lumbr yärd) n. A business place where lumber and other building materials are sold.

lu-mi-nes-cence (lōm nesns) n. An emission of light without heat, as in fluorescence.

lu-mi-nous (lōm nus) adj. Emitting or reflecting light; bathed in steady light; illuminated; easily understood; clear.

lum-mox (lumks) n. A clumsy oaf.

lump (lump) n. A projection; a protuberance; a swelling, as from a bruise or infection. v. To group things together.

lu-na-cy (lōna s) n. pl. **-ies** Insanity;

conduct; law Any form of unsoundness of the mind, not to include idiocy.

lu-nar (lōnr) adj. Of, relating to, caused by the moon.

lunar eclipse n. An eclipse where the moon passes partially or wholly through the umbra of the earth's shadow.

lu-na-tic (lōna tik) n. A crazy person.

lunch-eon (lunchen) n. A lunch.

lung (lung) n. One of the two spongy organs that constitute the basic respiratory organ of air-breathing vertebrates.

lunge (lunj) n. A sudden forward movement.

lu-pus (lōps) n. A bacterial disease of the skin, resulting in lesions and mucous membranes.

lure (lr) n. A decoy; something appealing; an artificial bait to catch fish. v. To attract or entice with the prospect of reward or pleasure.

lurk (lrk) v. To lie in concealment, as in an ambush.

lus-cious (lushus) adj. Very pleasant to smell or taste; appealing to the senses. **lusciously** adv. **lusciousness** n.

lush (lush) adj. Producing luxuriant growth or vegetation. Slang An alcoholic; a person who drinks liquor to excess. **lushly** adv. **lushness** n.

lust (lust) n. Intense sexual desire; an intense longing; a craving. **lustful** adj.

lus-ter or **lus-tre** (lustr) n. A glow of reflected light; sheen; brilliance or radiance; brightness. **lustrous** adj.

lust-y (lust) adj. Vigorous; healthy; robust; lively. **lustily** adv. **lustiness** n.

lu-sus na-tu-rae n. A deformed person, ani mal, or plant.

lute (lōt) n. A medieval musical stringed instrument with a fretted finger-board, a pear-shaped body, and usually a bent neck; a claylike cement or sealing compound used for packing joints or waterproofing surfaces.

lu-te-in n. A orange or yellowish compound found in many plants, animal fat, in egg yolks; used in certain biochemical studies.

lu-te-ti-um or **lu-te-ci-um** (lō tsh m) n. A silvery rare-earth metallic element symbolized by Lu.

lux-u-ri-ant (lug zhr ant) adj. Growing

or producing abundantly; lush; plentiful. **luxuriance** n. **luxuriantly** adv.

lux-u-ri-ate (lug zhr t) v. To enjoy luxury or abundance; to grow abundantly.

lux-u-ry (luksha r) n. pl. **-ies** Something desirable but costly or hard to get; something which adds to one's comfort or pleasure but is not absolutely necessary; sumptuous surroundings or living.

ly-ce-um (l sm) n. A hall where public programs are presented; an organization which sponsors such programs as lectures and concerts.

lye (l) n. A powerful caustic solution yielded by leaching wood ashes; potassium hydroxide; sodium hydroxide.

ly-ing--in (ling in) n. Confinement in childbirth.

lymph node n. A roundish body of lymphoid tissue; lymph gland.

lynch (linch) v. To execute without authority or the due process of law.

lynx (lingks) n. A wildcat, inhabiting Asia, Europe, and North America having a short tail, and tufted ears; a bobcat. adj. Having acute eyesight.

lyre (lr) n. An ancient Greek stringed instrument related to the harp, consisting of a hollow body with two curing arms connected near the top by a crosspiece from which strings are stretched to the body.

lyr-ic (lirik) adj. Concerned with thoughts and feelings; romantic; appropriate for singing. n. A lyric poem. **lyrics** The words of a song.

lysin n. A class of substance acting as a antibodies and capable of causing the dissolution or destruction of bacteria, blood corpuscles, and other cellular elements.

ly-so-zyme n. An enzyme capable of destroying bacteria, it can be founded in the latex of some plants, tears, and mucus.

lyt-ta n. A wormlike cartilage in the tongues of dogs and other carnivorous animals.

M

M, m (em) The thirteenth letter of the English alphabet; the Roman numeral

for 1,000.

ma'am (mam) n. Madam.

ma-ca-bre (ma kab re) adj. Suggesting death and decay.

mac-ad-am (ma kad am) n. Pavement for roads consisting of layers of compacted, broken stone, usually cemented with asphalt and tar. **macadamize** v.

mac-a-ro-ni (mak a r n) n. Dried pasta made into short tubes and prepared as food.

mac-a-roon (mak a rön) n. A small cookie made of sugar, egg whites, coconut, and ground almonds.

ma-caw (ma ko) n. Any of various tropical American parrots with long tails, brilliant plumage, and harsh voices.

mace (ms) n. An aromatic spice made by grinding the cover of the nutmeg.

mac-er-ate (mas e rt) v. To make a solid substance soft by soaking in liquid; to cause to grow thin. **macerater** or **macerator** n.

ma-chet-e (ma shet) n. A large, heavy knife with a broad blade, used as a weapon.

mach-i-nate (mak i nt) v. To plot. **machination** n. **machinator** n.

ma-chine (ma shn) n. A device or system built to use energy to do work; a political organization. v. To produce precision tools.

machine language n. In Computer Science, the system of numbers or instructions for coding input data.

ma-chin-er-y (ma sh ne r) n. pl. **-ies** A collection of machines as a whole; the mechanism or operating parts of a machine.

ma-chin-ist (ma sh nist) n. One skilled in the operation or repair of machines.

ma-chis-mo n. An exaggerated sense of masculinity. Slang Exhibiting machismo.

mack-er-el (mak r el) n. A fish with dark, wavy bars on the back and a silvery belly, found in the Atlantic Ocean.

mac-ra-me (mak ra m) n. The craft or hobby of tying knots into a pattern.

mac-ro-bi-ot-ic adj. Relating to or being on an extremely restricted diet to promote longevity, consisting mainly of whole grain, vegetables and fish.

ma-cron (mǐ′kron) *n.* A mark (-) placed over a vowel to indicate a long sound.

mac-ro-scop-ic *or* **macroscopical** (mak′rǒ skop′ik) *adj.* Large enough to be seen by the naked eye.

mad (mad) *adj.* Angry; afflicted with a mental disorder; insane.

made (md) *v.* Past tense of make.

madetoorder *adj.* Custom made.

madeup (md′up′) *adj.* Fabricated; invented; having only makeup on.

mad-house (mad′hous′) *n.* Slang A place of confusion and disorder.

mad-ri-gal (mad′ri gal) *n., Music* An unaccompanied song, usually for four to six voices, developed during the early Renaissance.

mael-strom (ml′strom) *n.* Any irresistible or dangerous force.

maes-tro (mǐ′str) *n. pl.* **-tros** *or* **-tri** A person mastering any art, but especially a famous conductor of music.

mag-a-zine (mag′a zn′) *n.* A publication with a paper cover containing articles, stories, illustrations and advertising; the part of a gun which holds ammunition ready for feeding into the chamber.

ma-gen-ta (ma jen′ta) *n.* A purplish red color.

mag-got (mag′ot) *n.* The legless larva of any of various insects, as the housefly, often found in decaying matter.

mag-ic (maj′ik) *n.* The art which seemingly controls foresight of natural events and forces by means of supernatural agencies. **magic** *adj.* **magical** *adj.* **magically** *adv.*

mag-is-trate (maj′i strt′) *n.* A civil officer with the power to enforce the law.

mag-ma (mag′ma) *n. pl.* **-mata** *or* **-mas** *Geol.* The molten rock beneath the earth's surface from which igneous rocks are formed.

mag-nan-i-mous (mag nan′i mus) *adj.* Generous in forgiving insults or injuries.

mag-nate (mag′nt) *n.* A person notable or powerful, especially in business.

mag-ne-sia (mag n′zha) *n., Chem.* A light, white powder used in medicine as an antacid and laxative.

mag-ne-si-um (mag n′z um) *n.* A light, silvery metallic element which burns with a very hot, bright flame and is used in lightweight alloys, symbolized by Mg.

mag-net (mag′nit) *n.* A body having the property of attracting iron and other magnetic material. **magnetism** *n.*

mag-net-ic (mag net′ik) *adj.* Pertaining to magnetism or a magnet; capable of being attracted by a magnet; having the power or ability to attract.

magnetic field *n.* The area in the neighborhood of a magnet or of an electric current, marked by the existence of a detectable magnetic force in every part of the region.

mag-net-ite (mag′ni tt′) *n.* A black iron oxide in mineral form, which is an important iron ore.

mag-net-ize (mag′ni tz′) *v.* To have magnetic properties; to attract by personal charm or influence. **magnetizable** *adj.*

mag-ne-to (mag n′t) *n.* A small alternator which works by means of magnets that are permanently attached, inducing an electric current for the spark in some engines.

mag-ne-tom-e-ter (mag′ni tom′i tr) *n.* An instrument used for measuring the direction and intensity of magnetic forces.

mag-ne-to-sphere (mag n′to sfr′) *n., Physics* A region of the upper atmosphere extending from about 500 to several thousand km above the surface, forming a band of ionized particles trapped by the earth's magnetic field.

mag-nif-i-cent (mag nif′i sent) *adj.* Having an extraordinarily imposing appearance; beautiful; outstanding; exceptionally pleasing.

mag-ni-fy (mag′ni f′) *v.* To increase in size; to cause to seem more important or greater; to glorify or praise someone or something. **magnification** *n.* **magnifier** *n.*

mag-nil-o-quent (mag nil′o kwent) *adj.* Speaking or spoken in a lofty and extravagant manner. **magniloquence** *n.*

mag-ni-tude (mag′ni tōd) *n.* Greatness or importance in size or extent. *Astron.*

The relative brightness of a star expressed on a numerical scale, ranging from one for the brightest to six for those just visible.

mag-num (mag´num) n. A wine bottle holding about two quarts or approximately 2/5 gallon.

magnum o-pus. A great work of art; literary or artistic masterpiece; the greatest single work of an artist, writer, or other creative person.

ma-ha-ra-ja (mä´härä´ja) n. A king or prince who rules an Indian state.

ma-hat-ma (ma hät´ma) n. In some Asian religions, a person venerated for great knowledge; a title of respect.

ma-hog-a-ny (ma hog´a n) n. pl. -ies Any of various tropical trees having hard, reddish-brown wood, much used for cabinet work and furniture.

maid (md) n. A young unmarried woman or girl; a female servant. **maiden** n.

maiden name. A woman's family name before marriage.

maid of honor. An unmarried woman who is the main attendant of a bride at a wedding.

mail (ml) n. Letter, printed matter, or parcel handled by the postal system. **mailer** n.

mail order n. Goods which are ordered and sent by mail.

maim (mm) v. To disable or to deprive of the use of a bodily part; to impair.

main (mn) adj. Being the most important part of something. n. A large pipe used to carry water, oil, or gas. **-ly** adv.

main-land (mn´land´) n. The land part of a country as distinguished from an island.

main-stream (mn´strm´) n. A main direction or line of thought.

main-tain (mn tn´) v. To carry on or to keep in existence; to preserve in a desirable condition. **maintainable** adj.

maize (mz) n. Corn.

maj-es-ty (maj´i st) n. pl. -ies Stateliness; exalted dignity. **majestic** adj. **-ically** adv.

ma-jor-ette (m´jo ret´) n. A young woman or girl who marches and twirls a baton with a band.

ma-jor-i-ty (ma jor´i t) n. pl. -ies The

greater number of something; more than half; the age at which a person is considered to be an adult, usually 21 years old.

make (mk) v. To cause something to happen; to create; to provide, as time; to manufacture a line of goods. n. A brand name, as a make of a car. **with** To carry off. **hay** To take advantage of a given opportunity in the early stages. **bones** To perform unhesitating.

make--be-lieve (mk´bi lv´) n. A pretending to believe. v. To pretend.

mal-a-chite (mal´a kt´) n. A green basic copper carbonate, used as a common ore of copper and for decorating stoneware.

mal-a-droit (mal´a droit´) adj. Lacking skill; awkward; clumsy. **-ly** adv.

mal-a-dy (mal´a d) n. pl. -ies A chronic disease or sickness.

mal-aise (ma lz´) n. The vague discomfort sometimes indicating the beginning of an illness.

mal-a-prop-ism (mal´a prop iz´um) n. A foolish misuse of a word.

mal-ap-ro-pos (mal´ap ro p´) adj. Not appropriate. **malapropos** adv.

ma-lar-i-a (ma lâr´ a) n., Pathol. The infectious disease introduced into the blood by the bite of the infected female anopheles mosquito and characterized by cycles of fever, chills, and profuse sweating.

ma-lar-key (ma lär´k) n. Slang Foolish or insincere talk; nonsense.

mal-con-tent (mal´kon tent´) adj. Unhappy with existing conditions or affairs.

mal de mer n. Seasickness.

male (ml) adj. Of or belonging to the sex that has organs to produce sperm atozoa. Bot. A plant with stamens but no pistil. n. A male person or animal. **maleness** n.

mal-e-dic-tion (mal´i dik´shan) n. A curse; execration. **maledictory** adj.

mal-e-fac-tor (mal´e fak´ter) n. A person who commits a crime or an unlawful act; a criminal.

ma-lev-o-lent (ma lev´o lent) adj. Full of spite or ill will for another; malicious. **-lently** adv. **malevolence** n.

mal-func-tion (mal fungk′shan) n. Failure to function correctly. **malfunction** v.

mal-ice (mal′is) n. The direct intention or desire to harm others. Law The willfully formed design to injure another without just reason or cause.

ma-lign (ma ln′) v. To speak slander or evil of. **maligner** n.

ma-lig-nant (ma lig′nant) adj., Pathol. Of or relating to tumors and abnormal or rapid growth, and tending to metasta size; opposed to benign; causing death or great harm. **malignancy** n. **malignity** n. **-ly** adv.

mall (mol) n. A walk or other shaded public promenade; a street with shops, restaurants, and businesses which is closed to vehicles.

mal-lard (mal′rd) n. pl. **mallard** or **-ards**. A wild duck having brownish plumage, the male of which has a green head and neck.

mal-le-a-ble (mal′ a bl) adj. Able to be bent, shaped, or hammered without breaking; capable of being molded, altered, or influenced. **malleability** n. **malleableness** n. **malleably** adv.

mal-le-us (mal′ us) n. pl. **-lei** Anat. The club-shaped bone of the middle ear or the largest of three small bones; also called the hammer.

mal-nour-ished (mal′ner′isht) adj. Undernourished.

mal-nu-tri-tion (mal′nō trish′an) n. Insufficient nutrition.

mal-oc-clu-sion (mal′o klō′zhan) n. Improper alignment of the teeth.

mal-o-dor-ous (mal′dr us) adj. Having a disagreeable or foul odor. **-ly** adv.

mal-prac-tice (mal prak′tis) n. Improper treatment of a patient by his doctor during surgery or treatment which results in damage or injury; failure to perform a professional duty in a proper, careful, or correct fashion, resulting in injury, loss, or other problems.

malt (molt) n. Grain, usually barley, used chiefly in brewing and distilling; an alcoholic beverage.

mal-tose (mol′ts) n. A white, crystalline sugar found in malt.

mal-treat (mal trt′) v. To treat badly,

unkindly, or roughly. **maltreatment** n.

ma-ma (mam′a) n. Mother.

mam-ba (mäm′bä) n. A venomous snake found in the tropics and in southern Africa.

mam-bo (mäm′b) n. A dance resembling the rumba of Latin America.

mam-mal (mam′al) n. Any member of a class whose females secrete milk for nourishing their young, including man.

mam-ma-ry gland (mam′a r) n. The milk-producing organ of the female mammal, consisting of small cavity clusters with ducts ending in a nipple.

mam-mog-ra-phy n. An X-ray examination of the breast for early detection of cancer.

mam-moth (mam′oth) n. An extinct, early form of elephant whose tusks curved upwards and whose body was covered with long hair; anything of great or huge size.

man (man) n. pl. **men** An adult or fully grown male; the human race; any human being, regardless of sex. Husband; an expression of pleasure or surprise.

man-a-cle (man′a kl) n. A device for restraining the hands; handcuffs.

man-age (man′ij) v. To direct or control the affairs or use of; to organize. **manageability** n. **manageable** adj.

man-ag-er (man′i jer) n. One in charge of managing an enterprise or business. **managerial** adj. **managership** n.

man-a-tee (man′a t′) n. An aquatic mammal of the coastal waters of Florida, West Indies, and the Gulf of Mexico.

man-date (man′dt) n. An authoritative order or command. Law A judicial order issued by a higher court to a lower one.

man-da-to-ry (man′da tr′) adj. Required by, having the nature of, or relating to a mandate; obligatory.

man-di-ble (man′di bl) n. The lower jaw bone. Biol. Either part of the beak of a bird.

man-do-lin (man′do lin) n. A musical instrument having a pear-shaped body and a fretted neck.

man-drake (man′drk) n. A plant having purplish flowers and a branched root sometimes resembling the human form.

man-drel or mandril (man'drel) *n.* A spindle or shaft on which material is held for working on a lathe.

man-drill (man'dril) *n.* A large, fierce West African baboon.

mane (mn) *n.* The long hair growing on the neck of some animals, as the lion, and horse.

maneat-er (man'tr) *n.* An animal which feeds on human flesh, such as a shark or a tiger.

ma-nege (ma nezh') *n.* The art of training and riding horses; the performance of a horse so trained.

ma-neu-ver (ma nö'vr) *n., Milit.* A planned strategic movement or shift, as of warships, or troops; any planned, skillful, or calculated move. **maneuverability** *n.*

man Friday *n.* A person devoted to another as a servant, aide, or employee.

man-ful (man'ful) *adj.* Having a manly spirit. **manfully** *adv.* **manfulness** *n.*

man-ga-nese (mang'ga ns') *n.* A hard, brittle, gray-white metallic element which forms an important component of steel alloys, symbolized by Mn.

mange (mnj) *n.* A contagious skin disease of dogs and other domestic animals caused by parasitic mites and marked by itching and hair loss. **mangy** *adj.*

man-gle (mang'gl) *v.* To disfigure or mutilate by bruising, battering, or crushing; to spoil. **mangler** *n.*

man-go (mang'g) *n. pl.* **-goes** *or* **-gos** A tropical evergreen tree that produces a fruit having a slightly acid taste.

man-han-dle (man'han'dl) *v.* To handle very roughly.

man-hole (man'hl) *n.* A circular hole, opening usually in a street, through which one may enter a sewer, drain, or conduit.

man-hood (man'hed) *n.* The state of being an adult male.

manhour (man'our') *n.* The amount of work that one person can complete in one hour.

ma-ni-a (m'n a) *n.* An extraordinary

enthusiasm or craving for something; intense excitement and physical over-activity, often a symptom of manicdepressive psychosis.

-mania suffix. Unreasonable or intense desire or infatuation with.

ma-ni-ac (m'n ak') *n.* A violently insane person. **maniac** *adj.* **-al** *adj.*

man-ic--de-pres-sive (man'ik di pres'iv) *adj.* Of a mental disorder characterized by alternating periods of manic excitation and depression. **manicdepressive** *n.*

man-i-cot-ti *n.* Pasta shaped like a tube, filled with meat or ricotta cheese and served with hot tomato sauce.

man-i-cure (man'i kr) *n.* The cosmetic care of the hands and fingernails.

man-i-fest (man'i fest') *adj.* Clearly apparent; obvious. *v.* To display, reveal or show. *n.* A list of cargo or passengers.

man-i-fes-ta-tion (man'i fe st'shan) *n.* The act or state of being manifest.

man-i-fes-to (man'i fes't) *n. pl.* **-toes** *or* **-tos** A public or formal explanation of principles or intentions, usually of a political nature.

man-i-kin or mannikin (man'i kin) *n.* A little man; a dwarf; a mannequin.

ma-nip-u-late (ma nip' lt') *v.* To handle or manage shrewdly and deviously for one's own profit. **manipulation** *n.*

man-kind (man'knd') *n.* The human race; men collectively, as opposed to women.

man-ly (man'l) *adj.* Pertaining to or having qualities which are traditionally attributed to a man. **manly** *adv.* **manliness** *n.*

manmade (man'md) *adj.* Made by human beings and not developed by nature.

man-na (man'a) *n.* The food which was miraculously given to the Israelites in the wilderness on their flight from Egypt; anything of value that one receives unexpectedly.

manned (mand) *adj.* Operated by a human being.

man-ne-quin (man'e kin) *n.* A life-sized model of a human figure, used to fit or display clothes; a woman who models clothes.

man-ner (man′r) *n.* The way in which something happens or is done; an action or style of speech; one's social conduct and etiquette.

man-ner-ism (man′e riz′um) *n.* A person's distinctive behavioral trait or traits. **mannerist** *n.* **manneristic** *adj.*

man-ner-ly (man′r lē) *adj.* Well-behaved; polite. **manner** *n.* **liness** *n.*

ma-nom-e-ter (ma nom′i tr) *n.* An instrument used to measure pressure, of gases or liquids. **manometric** *adj.* **-ial** *adj.*

man-or (man′r) *n.* A landed estate; the house or hall of an estate. **-ial** *adj.*

man pow-er (man′pou′r) *n.* The force of human physical power; the number of men whose strength and skill are readily available to a nation, army, project, or other venture.

man-que *adj.* Lacking fulfillment; frustrated.

man-sard (man′särd) *n. Archit.* A curved roof with the lower slope almost vertical and the upper almost horizontal.

manse (mans) *n.* The house of a clergyman.

man-sion (man′shan) *n.* A very large, impressive house.

mansize *or* **mansized** (man′sīzd′) *Slang* Quite large.

man-ta (man′ta) *n.* A rough-textured cotton fabric; any of several very large fishes having large, very flat bodies with winglike fins.

man-teau (man′tō) *n. pl.* **-teaus** *or* **-teaux** A robe or cloak.

man-tel *also* **mantle** A shelf over a fireplace; the ornamental brick or stone around a fireplace.

man-tis (man′tis) *n. pl.* **mantises** *or* **mantes** A tropical insect with a long body, large eyes, and swiveling head, which stands with its forelegs folded as if in prayer.

man-u-al (man′ al) *adj.* Used or operated by the hands. *n.* A small reference book which gives instructions on how to operate or work something. **manually** *adv.*

man-u-fac-ture (man′ fak′chr) *v.* To make a product; to invent or produce something.

ma-nure (ma ner′) *n.* The fertilizer used to fertilize land, obtained from animal dung.

man-u-script (man′ skript′) *n.* A typed or written material copy of an article, book, or document, which is being prepared for publication.

man-y (men′ē) *adj.* Amounting to a large or indefinite number or amount.

map (map) *n.* A plane surface representation of a region. *v.* To plan anything in detail. **mapmaker** *n.* **mapper** *n.*

maple sugar *n.* Sugar made from the sap of the maple tree.

mar *v.* To scratch or deface; to blemish; to ruin; to spoil.

mar-a-bou (mar′a bö) *n.* A stork of Africa, whose soft down is used for trimming women's garments.

ma-ra-ca (ma rä′ka) *n.* A percussion instrument made from gourds containing dried beans or pebbles.

mar-a-schi-no (mar′a sk′n) *n.* A cherry preserved in a cordial distilled from the fermented juice of the small wild cherry and flavored with cracked cherry pits.

mar-a-thon (mar′a thon′) *n.* A foot race of 26 miles, usually run on the streets of a city; any contest of endurance.

march (märch) *v.* To walk with measured, regular steps in a solemn or dignified manner. *Mus.* A musical composition.

mare (mâr) *n.* The female of the horse and other equine animals.

ma-re (mär′a) *n. pl., Astron.* Any of the dark areas on the surface of the moon.

mar-ga-rine (mär′jr in) *n.* A butter substitute made from vegetable oils and milk.

mar-gin (mär′jin) *n.* The edge or border of the body of written or printed text; the difference between the selling price and cost of an item.

mar-gi-na-li-a *n. pl.* The notes in the margin of a book.

ma-ri-a-chi *n.* A Mexican band; the music performed by a musician playing in a mariachi.

mar-i-gold (mar′i gld′) *n.* Any of a variety of plants having golden-yellow flowers.

mar-i-jua-na *or* **marihuana** (mär´i wä´na) Hemp; the dried flower tops and leaves of this plant, capable of producing disorienting or hallucinogenic effects when smoked in cigarettes or ingested.

ma-ri-na (ma r´na) *n.* A docking area for boats, furnishing moorings and supplies for small boats.

mar-i-nade (mar´i nd´) *n.* A brine made from vinegar or wine and oil with various herbs and spices for soaking meat, fowl, or fish before cooking.

mar-i-nate (mar´i nt´) *v.* To soak meat in a marinade.

ma-rine (ma rn´) *adj.* Of, pertaining to, existing in, or formed by the sea. *n.* A soldier trained for service on land and at sea. **Marine** A member of the Marine Corps.

mar-i-o-nette (mar´ o net´) *n.* A small jointed animal or human figure of wood which is manipulated from above by attached strings or wires.

mar-i-tal (mar´i tal) *adj.* Pertaining to marriage. **maritally** *adv.*

mar-i-time (mar´i tm´) *adj.* Located on or situated on or near the sea; pertaining to the sea and its navigation and commerce.

mark (märk) *n.* A visible impression, trace, dent, or stain; an identifying seal, inscription, or label.

mar-ket (mär´kit) *n.* The trade and commerce in a certain service or commodity; a public place for purchasing and selling merchandise; the possible consumers of a particular product. *v.* To sell. **-ability** *n.*

mar-ket-place (mär´kit pls´) *n.* A place, such as a public square, where ideas, opinions, and works are traded and tested.

marks-man (märks´man) *n.* A person skilled in firing a gun and hitting the mark.

mark-up *n.* The amount of increase in price from the cost to the selling price. *v.* To raise the price.

mar-lin (mär´lin) *n.* A large marine game fish of the Atlantic; the striped marlin found in the Pacific.

mar-line-spike (mär´lin spk´) *n., Naut.* A pointed tool used in splicing ropes.

ma-roon (ma rōn´) *v.* To put ashore and abandon on a desolate shore. *n.* A dull purplish red.

mar-que-try (mär´ki tr) *n.* Inlaid work of wood or ivory used for decorating furniture.

mar-quis (mär´kwis) *n.* The title of a nobleman ranking below a duke.

mar-qui-sette (mär´ki zet´) *n.* A fabric of cotton, silk, nylon, or a combination of these, used in curtains, clothing, and mosquito nets.

mar-riage (mar´ij) *n.* The state of being married; wedlock; the act of marrying or the ceremony entered into by a man and woman so as to live together as husband and wife.

mar-row (mar´) *n.* The soft, vascular tissue which fills bone cavities; the main part or essence of anything.

mar-ry (mar´) *v.* To take or join as husband or wife; to unite closely.

marsh (märsh) *n.* An area of low, wet land; a swamp. **marshy** *adj.*

marsh-mal-low (märsh´mel´) *n.* A soft, white confection made of sugar, corn syrup, starch, and gelatin and coated with powdered sugar.

mar-su-pi-al (mär sō´p al) *n.* An animal, such as a kangaroo, koala, or opossum, which has no placenta, but which in the female has an abdominal pouch with teats to feed and carry the off spring.

mart (märt) *n.* A trading market; a center.

mar-ten (mär´ten) *n.* A weasel-like-mammal of eastern North America with arboreal habits; the valuable brown fur of the marten.

mar-tial (mär´shal) *adj.* Of, pertaining to, or concerned with war or the military life.

martial arts *n. pl.* Oriental arts of self-defense, such as karate or judo, which are practiced as sports.

martial law *n.* Temporary rule by military forces over the citizens in an area where civil law and order no longer exist.

mar-ti-ni (mär t´n) *n. pl.* **-nis** A cocktail of gin and dry vermouth, served with an olive or lemon peel.

mar-tyr (mär´tr) *n.* A person who

would rather die than renounce his religious principles; one making great sacrifices to advance a cause, belief, or principle. **martyrdom** n.

mar-vel (mär'vel) n. Anything causing surprise, wonder, or astonishment.

mar-vel-ous or **marvellous** (mär've lus) Informal Excellent; very good

mar-zi-pan (mär'zi pan') n. A confection of grated almonds, sugar, and egg whites.

mas-car-a (ma skar'a) n. A cosmetic preparation used for coloring or darkening the eyelashes.

mas-cot (mas'kot) n. A person, animal, or object thought to bring good luck.

mas-cu-line (mas'k lin) adj. Of or pertaining to the male sex; male; the masculine gender.

ma-ser (m'zr) n., Physics One of several devices which are similar to the laser but which operate with microwaves rather than light.

mash (mash) n. A soft, pulpy mass or mixture used to distill alcohol or spirits. v. To crush into a soft, pulpy mass. **masher** n.

mask (mask) n. A covering used to conceal the face in order to disguise or protect. v. To hide or conceal.

ma-son (m'son) n. A person working with brick or stone.

ma-son-ic (ma son'ik) adj. Pertaining to or like Freemasonry or Freemasons.

mas-quer-ade (mas'ke rd') n. A costume party in which the guests are masked and dressed in fancy costumes. v. To disguise oneself. **masquerader** n.

mass (mas) n. A body of matter that does not have definite shape but is relatively large in size; physical volume; the measure of a body's resistance to acceleration.

mas-sa-cre (mas'a kr) n. The indiscriminate and savage killing of human beings in large numbers. **massacre** v.

mas-sage (ma säzh') n. The manual or mechanical manipulation of the skin to improve circulation and to relax muscles.

  mas-seur (ma ser') n. A man who gives massages.

mas-seuse (ma sös') n. A woman who gives massages.

mas-sive (mas'iv) adj. Of great intensity, degree, and size. **massively** adv. - **ness** n.

mast (mast) n. The upright pole or spar which supports the sails and running rigging of a sail boat.

mas-tec-to-my (ma stek'to m) n. pl. -**ies** The surgical removal of breast.

master key n. A key which will open many different locks whose keys are not the same.

mas-ter-mind (mas'tr mnd') n. A person who plans and directs at the highest levels of policy and strategy. v. To plan or direct an undertaking.

mas-ter-piece (mas'tr ps') n. Something having notable excellence; an unusually brilliant achievement which is considered the greatest achievement of its creator.

master plan n. A plan providing complete instructions.

mas-ti-cate (mas'ti kt') v. To chew.

mas-to-don (mas'to don') n. A large, extinct mammal which resembles an elephant.

mas-toid (mas'toid) n. Anat. The nipple shaped portion at the rear of the temporal bone behind the ear.

match (mach) n. Anything that is similar or identical to another; a short, thin piece of wood or cardboard with a specially treated tip which ignites as a result of friction. v. To equal; to oppose successfully. -**able** adj.

match-maker (mach'm'kr) n. A person who arranges a marriage.

mate (mt) n. A spouse; something matched, joined, or paired with another; in chess, a move which puts the opponent's king in jeopardy. Naval A petty officer. **mate** v.

ma-te-ri-al (ma tr' al) n. The substance from which anything is or may be composed or constructed of; anything that is used in creating, working up, or developing something.

ma-te-ri-al-ize (ma tr' alz') v. To give material or actual form to something; to assume material or visible appearance; to take form or shape. **materialization** n.

ma-te-ri-el (ma tr' el') n. The equipment and supplies of a military force, including guns and ammunition.

ma-ter-nal (ma ter´nal) *adj.* Relating to a mother or motherhood; inherited from one's mother.

ma-ter-ni-ty (ma ter´ni t) *n.* The state of being a mother; the qualities of a mother; the department in a hospital for the prenatal and postnatal care of babies and their mothers.

math (math) *n.* Mathematics.

math-e-mat-ics (math´e mat´iks) *n.* The study of form, arrangement, quantity, and magnitude of numbers and operational symbols. **mathematically** *adv.* **mathematician** *n.*

mat-i-nee (mat´i n´) *n.* An afternoon performance of a play, concert, movie, etc.

ma-tri-arch (m´tr ärk´) *n.* A woman ruler of a family, tribe, or clan. **matriarchal** *adj.*

mat-ri-cide (ma´tri sd´) *n.* The killing of one's own mother; one who kills his mother.

ma-tric-u-late (ma trik´ lt´) *v.* To enroll, or to be admitted into a college or university.

mat-ri-mo-ny (ma´tri m´n) *n.* The condition of being married; the act, sacrament, or ceremony of marriage. **matrimonial** *adj.*

ma-trix (m´triks) *n. pl.* **-rixes** *or* **-rices** Something within which something else develops, originates, or takes shape; a mold or die.

mat-ter (mat´r) *n.* Something that makes up the substance of anything; that which is material and physical, occupies space, and is perceived by the senses; something that is sent by mail; something that is written or printed.

mat-tock (mat´ok) *n.* A tool having a blade on one side and a pick on the other or one with a blade on each side.

mat-tress (ma´tris) *n.* A large cloth case filled with soft material and used on or as a bed.

mat-u-rate (mach´e rt´) *v.* To ripen or mature. **maturation** *n.*

ma-ture (ma ter´) *adj.* Completely developed; at full growth; something, as a bond at a bank, that is due and payable. **mature** *v.* **maturely** *adv.*

maturity *n.*

mat-zo (mät´sa) *n. pl.* **-zos** *or* **-zot** A large, flat piece of unleavened bread eaten during Passover.

maud-lin (mod´lin) *adj.* Overly sentimental; tearfully and overwhelmingly emotional.

maul (mol) *n.* A heavy hammer or mallet used to drive wedges, piles, and other materials. *v.* To handle roughly; to abuse.

maun-der (mon´dr) *v.* To wander or talk in an incoherent manner.

mau-so-le-um (mo´so l´um) *n. pl.* **-leums** *or* **-lea** A large and stately tomb.

mauve (mv) *n.* A purplish rose shade; a moderately reddish to gray purple.

mav-er-ick (mav´r ik) *n.* An unbranded or orphaned calf or colt. *Slang* A person who is unorthodox in his ideas or attitudes.

maw (mo) *n.* The jaws, mouth, or gullet of a hungry or ferocious animal; the stomach.

mawk-ish (mo´kish) *adj.* Disgustingly sentimental; sickening or insipid. **mawkishly** *adv.* **mawkishness** *n.*

max-i (mak´si) *n.* A floor-length garment, such as a skirt or coat.

max-il-la (mak sil´a) *n. pl.* **-lae** *or* **-las** The upper jaw or jawbone. **maxillary** *adj.*

max-im (mak´sim) *n.* A brief statement of truth, general principle, or rule of conduct.

max-i-mize (mak´si mz´) *v.* To increase as greatly as possible; to intensify to the maximum.

max-i-mum (mak´si mum) *n. pl.* **-mums** *or* **-ma** The greatest possible number, measure, degree, or quantity.

may (m) *v.* To be permitted or allowed; used to express a wish, purpose, desire, contingency, or result.

may-be (m´b) *adv.* Perhaps; possibly.

may-flow-er (m´flou´r) *n.* A wide variety of plants which blossom in May.

may-hem (m´hem) *n. Law* The offense of injuring a person's body; any situation brought on by violence, confusion, noise, or disorder.

may-o *n. Slang* Mayonnaise.

may-on-naise (m´o nz´) *n.* A dressing

for salads, made by beating raw egg yolk, oil, lemon juice, or vinegar and seasonings.

may-or (m´r) n. The chief magistrate of a town, borough, municipality, or city. **mayoral** adj. **mayoralty** n. **-ship** n.

may-pole (m´pl´) n. A decorated pole hung with streamers around which May Day dancing takes place.

maze (mz) n. A complicated, intricate network of passages or pathways; a labyrinth; a state of uncertainty, bewilderment, or perplexity.

me (m) The objective case of the pronoun I.

mead (md) n. An alcoholic beverage made from fermented honey and water with yeast and spices added.

mead-ow (med´) n. A tract of grassland used for grazing or growing hay.

mead-ow-lark (med´lärk´) n. A songbird of North America.

mea-ger or **mea-gre** (m´gr) adj. Thin; lean; deficient in quantity, richness, vigor, or fertility. **meagerly** adv. **meagerness** n.

meal (ml) n. The edible seeds of coarsely ground grain; any powdery material; the food served or eaten at one sitting at certain times during the day; the time or occasion of taking such food.

mean (mn) v. To have in mind as a purpose or intent; to be of a specified importance or significance. adj. Poor or inferior in ap pearance or quality. n. The medium point. **means** The method or instrument by which some end is or may be accomplished; the available resources.

me-an-der (m an´dr) v. To wander about without a certain course or a fixed direction.

mean-ing (m´ning) n. That which is meant or intended; the aim, end, or purpose; the significance; an interpretation. **meaningful** adj. **meaningfulness** adj.

mean-time (mn´tm´) n. The time or period between or during the intervening time.

mean-while (mn´hwl´) adv. At the same time.

mea-sles (m´zelz) n. A contagious viral disease usually occurring in children,

characterized by the eruption of red spots.

meas-ure (mezh´r) n. The range, dimension, extent, or capacity of anything. Mus. The group of beats marked off by regularly recurring primary accents; the notes and rests between two successive bars on a musical staff. v. To determine the range, dimension, extent, volume, or capacity of anything. **measurable** adj.

meas-ure-ment (mezh´r ment) n. The process or act of measuring.

meat (mt) n. The flesh of an animal which is used as food; the core or essential part of something. **meatiness** n. **meaty** adj.

mech abbr. Mechanical; mechanics.

me-chan-ic (me kan´ik) n. A person skilled in the making, operation, or repair of machines or tools.

me-chan-i-cal (me kan´i kal) adj. Involving or having to do with the construction, operation, or design of tools or machines; produced or operated by a machine. **-ly** adv.

mechanical drawing n. A drawing done with the aid of squares, compasses, or other instruments.

me-chan-ics (me kan´iks) n. pl. The scientific study and analysis of the action of forces and motion on material bodies.

mech-a-nism (mek´a niz´um) n. The arrangement or parts of a machine; the technique or process by which something works.

mech-a-nize (mek´a nz´) v. To make mechanical; to equip with tanks, trucks, mechanical and other equipment, as in the military. **mechanization** n.

med abbr. Medical.

med-al (med´al) n. A small piece of metal with a commemorative image or inscription which is presented as an award.

med-dle (med´l) v. To interfere or participate in another person's business or affairs.

me-di-a (m´d a) n. pl. The instruments of news communication, as radio, television, and newspapers.

me-di-an (m´d an) n. Something that is

halfway between two different parts. *adj.* Relating to or constituting the median of a set of numbers.

me-di-ate (m′d t′) *v.* To help settle or reconcile opposing sides in a dispute.

med-ic (med′ik) *n.* *Slang* A physician or intern; a medical student; in the armed forces, a corpsman or enlisted person trained to give first aid.

med-i-cal (med′i kal) *adj.* Relating to the study or practice of medicine.

medical examiner *n.* A physician who is authorized by a governmental body to ascertain causes of death.

med-i-cate (med′i kt′) *v.* To treat an injury or illness with medicine. **medication** *n.*

med-i-cine (med′i sin) *n.* Any agent or substance used in the treatment of disease or in the relief of pain; the science of diagnosing and treating disease; the profession of medicine.

medicine ball *n.* A large, heavy ball used for physical exercise.

medicine man *n.* In primitive cultures, a person believed to have supernatural powers for healing.

me-di-o-cre (m′d ′kr) *adj.* Common; fair; undistinguished.

med-i-tate (med′i tt′) *v.* To be in continuous, contemplative thought; to think about doing something. **meditative** *adj.* **meditation** *n.*

me-di-um (m′d um) *n.* *pl.* **-dia** *or* **-ums** Something which occupies a middle position between two extremes; the means of communicating information or ideas through publishing, radio, or television.

me-dul-la (mi dul′a) *n.* *pl.* **-las** *or* **-lae** *Anat.* The center of certain vertebrate structures, such as bone marrow.

medulla oblongata (mi dul′a ob′long gä′ta) *n.* The mass of nerve tissue found at the base of the brain, controlling bodily functions such as breathing and circulation.

meek (mk) *adj.* Showing patience and a gentle disposition; lacking spirit or backbone; submissive. **meekly** *adv.* **-ness** *n.*

meet (mt) *v.* To come upon; to encounter; to come into conjunction or contact with someone or something; to cope or deal with; to handle; to fulfill an obligation or need.

meg-a-hertz *n.* *pl.* **-hertz** *Physics.* One million cycles per second, used as a radio frequency unit.

meg-a-lo-ma-ni-a (meg′a l m′na) *n.*, *Psychiatry* A mental disorder marked by fantasies of power, wealth, or omnipotence. **megalomaniac** *n.*

meg-a-lop-o-lis (meg′a lop′o lis) *n.* A very large urban complex.

meg-a-ton (meg′a tun′) *n.* One million tons; the unit equal to the explosive power of one million tons of TNT.

meg-a-watt (meg′a wot′) *n.* A unit of electrical power equal to one million watts.

mei-o-sis (m′sis) *n.* *pl.* **-ses** *Biol.* The process by which undeveloped sex cells, sperm and ovum, mature by reduction division so that they contain only half of the full number of chromosomes. **meiotic** *adj.*

mel-an-cho-li-a (mel′an k′l a) *n.* *Psychiatry* A mental disorder of great depression of spirits and excessive brooding without apparent cause. **mel-an-chol-ic (mel′an kol′ik)** *adj.* Depressed; sad.

mel-an-chol-y (mel′an kol′) *adj.* Excessively gloomy or sad.

me-lange (m länzh′) *n.*, *French* A medley or mixture.

mel-a-nin (mel′a nin) *n.* *Biochem.* The brownish-black pigment which is contained in animal tissues, as the hair and skin.

mel-a-nism (mel′a niz′um) *n.* An abnormally dark pigmentation of the skin.

mel-a-no-ma (mel′a n′ma) *n.* *pl.* **-mas** *or* **-mata** A dark-colored tumor or malignant mole.

mel-io-rate (mel′ya rt′) *v* To cause to improve or to improve.

mel-lif-er-ous (me′ lif′r us) *adj.* Producing or making honey.

mel-lo *adj.* Sweet and soft; rich and full-flavored; rich and soft in quality, as in sounds or colors.

me-lo-di-ous (me l′d us) *adj.* Characterized by a melody; tuneful; pleasant to hear.

mel-o-dy (mel′o d) *n.* *pl.* **-ies** An

agreeable succession of pleasing sounds. **melodic** *adj.* **melodically** *adv.*

mel-on (mel′on) *n.* The large fruit of any of various plants of the gourd family, as the watermelon.

melt (melt) *v.* To change from a solid to a liquid as a result of pressure or heat.

melt-down *n.* The melting of a nuclear reactor core.

mem-ber (mem′br) *n.* A person who belongs to a society, party, club, or other organization. *Biol.* An organ or part of an animal or person's body, especially a limb.

mem-brane (mem′brn) *n.* A thin, pliable, sheet-like layer of tissue which covers body surfaces and separates or connects body parts.

me-men-to (me men′t) *n. pl.* **-tos** *or* **-toes** A keepsake.

mem-o (mem′) *n.* A memorandum.

mem-oir (mem′wär) *n.* Personal records or reminiscences; an autobiography.

mem-o-ra-ble (mem′r a bl) *adj.* Worth remembering or noting. **-bly** *adv.*

mem-o-ran-dum (mem′o ran′dum) *n. pl.* **-dums** *or* **-da** A brief, informal note written as a reminder.

me-mo-ri-al (me mr′ al) *n.* Something that serves to keep in remembrance, as a person or event. *adj.* Perpetuating remembrance.

mem-o-rize (mem′o rz′) *v.* To commit something to memory. **-ation** *n.*

mem-ory (mem′o r) *n. pl.* **-ries** The mental function or capacity of recalling or recognizing something that has been previously learned or experienced.

men *n. pl.* The plural of man.

men-ace (men′is) *n.* Something or someone who threatens; an annoying person. **menace** *v.* **menacingly** *adv.*

me-nar-che *n.* The beginning or the first occurrence of menstruation.

mend (mend) *v.* To fix; to repair; to correct.

men-da-cious (men d′shus) *adj.* Prone to lying; deceitful; untrue; false. **mendaciously** *adv.* **mendacity** *n.*

men-de-le-vi-um (men′de l′v um) *n.* A short-lived radioactive element of the actinide series, symbolized by Md.

me-ni-al (m′n al) *adj.* Relating to a household servant or household chores requiring little responsibility or skill.

men-in-gi-tis (men′in j′tis) *n., Pathol.* An inflammation of the membranes which enclose the brain and spinal cord.

me-ninx (m′ningks) *n. pl.* **meninges** The membrane which encloses the spinal cord and brain. **meningeal** *adj.*

men-ses (men′sz) *n. pl.* The blood and dead cell debris which are discharged from the uterus through the vagina by women who are not pregnant; menstruation, occurring at monthly intervals between puberty and menopause.

men-stru-a-tion (men′strō′shan) *n., Physiol.* The process, act, or periodical flow of bloody fluid from the uterus, also called period.

-ment *suffix* The result or product of achievement; action; process.

men-tal (men′tal) *adj.* Relating to or of the mind. **mentally** *adv.*

men-tal de-fi-cien-cy *n.* Subnormal intellectual development, marked by deficiencies ranging from impaired learning ability to social incompetence.

men-tal-i-ty (men tal′i t) *n. pl.* **-ies** Mental faculties or powers; mental activity; habit of mind.

men-tal re-tar-da-tion *n.* A mental deficiency.

men-thol (men′thl) *n. Chem.* The white, waxy crystalline alcohol which is obtained from and has the odor of peppermint oil.

men-tion (men′shan) *v.* To refer to incidentally, in passing, or briefly. **mentionable -er** *adj.*

men-tor (men′tr) *n.* A wise and trusted person.

men-u (men′) *n.* A list of food or dishes available at a restaurant; in computer science, a list of options displayed on the screen from which the operator may choose.

me-ow (m ou′) *n.* The cry of a cat.

me-phi-tis (me f′tis) *n.* A sickening or foul smell; a stench emitted from the earth.

mer-can-tile (mer′kan tl′) *adj.* Of or relating to merchants, trading, or commerce.

mer-cer-ize (mer´se rz´) v. To treat cotton yarn or thread with sodium hydroxide so as to give strength and receptiveness to dyes.

mer-chan-dise (mer´chan dz´) n. Commodities or goods that are bought and sold. v. To buy and sell.

mer-chant (mer´chant) n. A person who operates a retail business for profit.

mer-chant-man (mer´chant man) n. A ship used for commercial shipments.

mer-cu-ry (mer´k r) n. A silvery, metallic, liquid element used in thermometers and barometers, symbolized by Hg.

mer-cy (mer´s) n. pl. -ies Compassionate and kind treatment. -ciful adj.

mere (mr) adj. Absolute; no more than what is stated. **merest** adj. **merely** adv.

merge (merj) v. To unite or bring together as one; in computer science, to combine two or more files into one, retaining the internal order of both.

mer-it (mer´it) n. A characteristic act or trait which is worthy of praise. v. To earn; to be worthy of.

mer-i-toc-ra-cy (mer´i tr´a) n. pl. -ies A system which bases advancement on ability or achievement.

mer-i-to-ri-ous (mer´i tr´us) adj. Deserving honor, praise or reward.

mer-maid (mer´md´) n. An imaginary sea creature having the upper body of a woman and the tail of a fish. **mer-man** n.

mer-ry (mer´) adj. Delightful; gay; entertaining; festive; happy; joyous.

me-sa (m´sa) n. A flat-topped hill or small plateau with steep sides.

mes-mer-ize (mez´me rz´) v. To hypnotize or put into a trance.

mes-sen-ger (mes´en jr) n. A person who carries a message or does an errand for another person or company.

mess-y adj. Untidy; upset; dirty; lacking neatness. **messily** adv. **messiness** n.

met v. p.t. & p.p. Past tense of meet.

me-tab-o-lism (me tab´o liz´um) n. The chemical and physical changes in living cells which involve the maintenance of life.

meta-car-pus (met´a kär´pus) n. The part of the forefoot or hand which connects the bones of the toes or fingers to the ankle or wrist.

met-a-gal-ax-y (met´a gal´ak s) n. The universe; the entire system of galaxies.

metal (met´al) n. One of a category of opaque, fusible, ductile, and typically lustrous elements. **metallic** adj. **metallically** adv.

met-al-lur-gy (met´a ler´j) n. The technology and science which studies methods of extracting metals from their ores and of preparing them for use. **metallurgical** adj.

met-a-mor-pho-sis (met´a mor´fo sis) n. The transformation and change in the structure and habits of an animal during normal growth, as the metamorphosis of a tadpole into a frog.

met-a-phor (met´a for´) n. A figure of speech in which the context demands that a word or phrase not be taken literally, as the sun is smiling; a comparison which doesn't use like or as.

me-tas-ta-sis (me tas´ta sis) n. A spread of cancer cells from the original tumor to one or more additional sites within the body. **metastasize** v. **-tastatic** adj.

met-a-tar-sus (met´a tär´sus) n. pl. -si The part of the human foot which forms the instep and contains five bones between the ankle and the toes; the hind foot of four-legged animals.

me-te-or (m´t r) n. A moving particle in the solar system which appears as a trail or streak in the sky as it comes into contact with the atmosphere of the earth.

me-te-or-ic (m´t or´ik) adj. Of or relating to a meteor or meteors; resembling a meteor in speed, brilliance, or brevity.

me-te-or-ite (m´t o rt´) n. A stony or metallic mass of a meteor which reaches the earth after partially burning in the atmosphere.

me-te-or-ol-o-gy (m´t o rol´oj) n. The science concerned with the study of weather, weather conditions and weather forecasting. **meteorological** adj. **meteorologic** adj. **-gist** n.

me-ter (m´tr) n. The arrangement of words, syllables, or stanza as in verse or poetry; a measure equaling 39.37

inches.

meth-a-done (meth'a dn') *n.* A man-made narcotic used in the treatment of heroin addiction.

meth-ane (meth'n) *n.* A colorless, odorless flammable gas used as a fuel; a product of the decomposition of organic matter.

meth-a-nol (meth'a nl') *n.* A colorless, odorless flammable alcohol that is used as an antifreeze, as a fuel, and as a raw material in chemical synthesis.

me-thinks (mi thingks') *v.* It seems to me.

meth-od (meth'ŏd) *n.* A manner, a process, or the regular way of doing something; the orderly arrangement, development, or classification. **methodical** *adj.* **methodic** *adj.* **-ically** *adv.*

meth-yl (meth'il) *n.* An alkyl radical derived from methane which occurs in several organic compounds.

me-tic-u-lous (me tik' lus) *adj.* Very precise; careful; concerned with small details. **meticulously** *adv.* **meticulousness** *n.*

me-tis (m ts') *n.* A person of mixed blood, usually of French and Indian ancestry.

met-ric (me'trik) *adj.* Of or relating to the metric system.

metric system *n.* A decimal system of weights and measures based on the meter as a unit of length and the kilogram as a unit of mass, originated in France around 1790.

met-ri-fy (me'tri f') *v.* To adopt or convert to the metric system. **metrification** *n.*

met-ro (me'tr) *n.* A subway system for transportation.

met-ro-nome (me'tro nm') *n.* An instrument designed to mark times by means of a series of clicks at exact intervals.

me-trop-o-lis (me trop'o lis) *n.* A large or capital city of a state, region, or country.

mew (m) *n.* A hideaway; a secret place.

mez-za-nine (mez'a nn') *n.* A low story between two main stories of a building; the lowest balcony in a theatre.

mice *n. pl.* The plural of mouse.

mi-crobe (mi'krb) *n.* A germ, plant, or

animal so small that is can be seen only with the aid of a microscope.

mi-cro-bi-ol-o-gy (mi'kr b ol'oj) *n.* The scientific study of microorganisms. **microbiological** *adj.* **-biologist** *n.*

mi-cro-cir-cuit *n.* An electronic circuit composed of very small components.

mi-cro-com-put-er *n.* A computer which uses a microprocessor.

mi-cro-film (m'kro film') *n.* A film used to photograph printed matter at a greatly reduced size.

micro-or-gan-ism (m'kr or'ganiz'um) *n.* An organism too small to see without the aid of a microscope.

mi-cro-phone (m'kro fn') *n.* An instrument which converts acoustical waves into electrical signals and feeds them into a recorder, amplifier or broadcasting transmitter. **microphonic** *adj.*

mi-cro-proc-es-sor *n.* In Computer Science, a semiconduct or processing unit which is contained on an integrated circuit chip.

mi-cro-scope (m'kro skp') *n.* An optical instrument consisting of a lens or combination of lenses, used to produce magnified images of very small objects.

mi-cro-scop-ic (m'kro skop'ik) *adj.* Too small to be seen by the eye alone.

mi-cro-sur-ger-y *n.* Surgery performed by means of a microscope and laser beam.

mi-cro-wave (m'kr wv') *n.* A very short electromagnetic wave.

mid (mid) *adj.* In the middle or center; central.

mid-air *n.* A point in the air just above the ground surface.

mid-day (mid'd') *n.* Noon; the middle of the day.

mid-den *n.* A refuse heap or dunghill.

mid-dle (mid'l) *adj.* Being equally distant from extremes or limits; the central. *n.* Anything which occupies a middle position; the waist.

middle age *n.* A period of life from about 40 to 60 years.

middle class (mid'l klas') *n.* The social class of people between a high income and low income status.

middle ear *n.* A small membrane-lined cavity between the tympanic membrane and the inner ear through which sound waves are carried.

midg-et (mij´it) *n.* A very small person.

mid-i *n. Slang* A dress, skirt, or coat which extends to the calf.

mid-night (mid´nit) *n.* 12 o'clock p.m.; the middle of the night.

mid-point (mid´point) *n.* A point at or near the middle.

mid-riff (mid´rif) *n.* The midsection of the human torso; the diaphragm.

midst (midst) *n.* The central or middle part or position; a person positioned among others in a group.

mid-term (mid´term) *n.* The middle of an academic term.

mid-way (mid´wa´) *n.* The section of a carnival or fair where shows and rides are located.

mid-wife (mid´wf) *n.* A woman who gives assistance in the birth of a baby.

mid-year (mid´yr´) *n.* The middle of a calendar year; academic examinations which are given in the middle of the academic year.

miff (mif) *n.* Ill humor; displeasure. **miff** *v.*

might (mt) *n.* Force, power, or physical strength. *v.* To indicate a present condition contrary to fact; to ask permission politely.

might-y (m´t) *adj.* Showing or having great power.

mi-graine (m´grn) *n.* A condition of severe, recurring headaches often accompanied by nausea.

mi-grant (m´grant) *n.* A person who moves from one place to another to find work in the fields.

mi-grate (m´grt) *v.* To move from one place to another or from one climate to another. **migration** *n.* **-grational** *adj.*

mike (mk) *n. Slang* Microphone.

mil (mil) *n.* A unit of measure equal to 1/1000 of an inch, used in measuring wire.

milch (milch) *adj.* Giving milk.

mild (mild) *adj.* Gentle in manner, behavior, or disposition; not severe or extreme.

mil-dew (mil´dō´) *n.* A fungal growth which is usually white in color. **mildewy** *adj.*

mile (ml) *n.* A unit of measurement equaling 5,280 feet.

mile-age (m´lij) *n.* The distance traveled or measured in miles; an allowance given for traveling expenses at a set rate per mile; the average distance of miles a vehicle will travel on a gallon of gas.

mil-i-tant (mil´i tant) *adj.* Engaged in warfare or combat; aggressive. **militancy** *n.*

mil-i-tar-y (mil´i ter´) *adj.* Of or related to arms, war, or soldiers. *n.* A nation's armed forces.

mi-li-tia (mi lish´a) *n.* A military service or armed forces called upon in case of an emergency.

mil-li-ner (mil´i nr) *n.* Someone who designs, sells, or makes women's hats.

mil-lion (mil´yon) *n.* A very large number equal to 1,000 x 1,000. **-th** *adj.*

mime (mm) *v.* To act a part or performance without using words. *n.* An actor who portrays a part, emotion, or situation using only gestures and body language. **mimer** *n.*

mim-e-o-graph (mim´ o graf´) *n.* A duplicating machine that makes duplicates of typed or drawn information from a stencil through which ink is pressed.

mim-ic (mim´ik) *v.* To imitate another person's behavior or speech.

mince (mins) *v.* To cut or chop something into small pieces.

mind (mnd) *n.* The element of a human being which controls perception, thought, feeling, memory, and imagination. *v.* To obey; to take care of; to bring; to remember; to object to.

mine (mn) *n.* A pit or underground excavation from which metals or coal can be uncovered and removed. The one that belongs to me.

min-er-al (min´r al) *n.* A solid inorganic substance, such as silver, diamond, or quartz, which is taken from the earth. **mineral** *adj.*

mi-ne-stro-ne (min´i str´n) *n.* A very thick vegetable soup that may contain pasta and beans.

min-gle (ming´gl) *v.* To mix or come together.

min-i-a-ture (min´ a chr) *n.* A copy or model of something that has been greatly reduced in size.

min-i-com-put-er *n.* In computer science, a computer designed on a very small scale.

mini-disk *n.* Computer Science The 5 1/4 inch floppy disk which is used for storing information.

min-i-mum (min'i mum) *n. pl.* **-ums** or **-uma** The least, smallest, or lowest amount, degree, number, or position.

min-is-ter (min'i str) *n.* The pastor of a Protestant church; a high officer of state who is in charge of a governmental division.

mink (mingk) *n. pl.* **mink** or **minks** A semi-aquatic animal of the weasel family whose thick, lustrous fur is used for making fur coats.

min-now (min') *n.* A small, fresh-water fish used as bait.

mi-nor (m'nr) *adj.* Not of legal age; lesser in degree, size or importance.

mi-nor-i-ty (mi nor'i t) *n. pl.* **-ies** The smaller in number of two groups constituting a whole; a part of the population that differs, as in race, sex, or religion.

min-ster (min'str) *n.* A large cathedral or church.

min-strel (min'strel) *n.* A medieval traveling musician or poet.

min-u-end (min' end') *n.* A number of quantity from which another is to be subtracted.

min-u-et (min' et') *n.* A slow, stately dance.

mi-nus-cule (min'u skl') *adj.* Rather dim, or small in size.

mi-nus (m'nus) *prep.* Reduced, by subtraction. o The minus sign (-); a negative number.

min-ute (min'it) *n.* The unit of time which equals 60 seconds.

mi-nute (m nöt') *adj.* Extremely small in size.

mir-a-cle (mir'a kl) *n.* A supernatural event or happening regarded as an act of God.

mi-rage (mi räzh') *n.* An optical illusion in which nonexistent bodies of water with reflections of objects are seen.

mire (mr) *n.* Soil or heavy mud.

mir-ror (mir'r) *n.* A surface of glass which reflects light, forming the image of an object.

mirth (merth) *n.* Merriment or joyousness expressed by laughter.

mis- *prefix* Wrong, bad, or ill.

mis-an-thrope (mis'an thrp') *n.* Someone who hates mankind.

mis-ap-pre-hend (mis'ap ri hend') *v.* To understand something incorrectly; to misunderstand. **misapprehension** *n.*

mis-ap-pro-pri-ate (mis'a pr'prt') *v.* To embezzle money; to use wrongly for one's own benefit. **misappropriation** *n.*

mis-car-riage (mis kar'ij) *n.* The premature birth of a fetus from the uterus.

mis-ce-ge-na-tion (mis'i je n'shan) *n.* The marriage between two people of different races.

mis-cel-la-ne-ous (mis'e l'n us) *adj.* Consisting of a mixed variety of parts, elements, or characteristics.

mis-chance (mis chans') *n.* Bad luck or mishap.

mis-chief (mis'chif) *n.* Behavior which causes harm, damage, or annoyance.

mis-chie-vous (mis'chi vus) *adj.* Tending to behave in a playfully annoying way.

mis-con-ceive (mis'kon sv') *v.* To misunderstand the meaning.

mis-con-duct (mis kon'dukt) *n.* Improper conduct or behavior; bad management.

mis-count (mis kount') *v.* To count incorrectly; to miscalculate.

mis-cre-ant (mis'kr ant) *n.* A person who is involved in criminal or evil acts; a heretic.

mis-cue (mis k') *n.* An error; a mistake.

mis-deed (mis dd') *n.* A wrong or improper act; an evil deed.

mis-de-mean-or (mis'di m'nr) *n., Law* A crime less serious than a felony.

mis-er (m'zr) *n.* A person who hoards money; a person who lives a meager life in order to hoard his money.

mis-er-a-ble (miz'r a bl) *adj.* Very uncomfortable or unhappy; causing misery. **-bleness** *n.* **miserably** *adv.*

mis-er-y (miz'e r'r) *n.* A state of great unhappiness, distress, or pain.

mis-feed *n.* In computer science, the

failure of paper or other media to pass
through a printer or other device properly.

mis-fire (mis fīr´) v. To fail to explode,
ignite, or fire. **misfire** n.

mis-fit (mis fit´) n. A person who is not
adjusted to his environment; anything
which does not fit correctly.

mis-for-tune (mis for´chan) n. Bad
luck or fortune.

mis-giv-ing (mis giv´ing) n. A feeling of
doubt.

mis-guide (mis gd´) v. To guide incorrectly; to misdirect. **misguidance** n.
-edly adv.

mis-han-dle (mis han´dl) v. To handle
clumsily; to manage inefficiently.

mis-hap (mis´hap) n. An unfortunate
accident; bad luck.

mish-mash (mish´mash´) n. A jumble
or hodgepodge.

mis-in-ter-pret (mis´in ter´prit) v. To
understand or explain incorrectly.

mis-judge (mis juj´) v. To make a mistake in judgment. **misjudgment** n.

mis-lay (mis lā´) v. To lose; to put something in a place and not remember
where.

mis-lead (mis lēd´) v. To lead in a wrong
direction; to deliberately deceive. **mis-
leader** n. **misleading** adj.

mis-no-mer (mis nō´mr) n. A wrong or
inappropriate name.

mis-pro-nounce (mis´pro nouns´) v. To
pronounce a word incorrectly.

mi-sog-a-my (mi sog a m) n. Hatred of
marriage.

mi-sog-y-ny (mi soj´i n) n. Hatred of
women.

mis-place (mis pls´) v. To mislay; to put
in a wrong place.

mis-read (mis rd´) v. To read or interpret incorrectly.

mis-rep-re-sent (mis´rep ri zent´) v. To
represent wrongly, misleadingly, or
falsely.

mis-shape (mis shp´) v. To deform; to
shape badly; to distort. **-shapen** adj.

mis-sile (mis´il) n. An object that is
thrown or shot at a target. **missilery** n.

mis-sion (mish´an) n. An instance of the
act of sending; an assignment or task
to be carried out.

mis-sion-ar-y (mish´a ner´) n. pl. **-ies**

A person sent to do religious or charitable work, usually in a foreign country.

mis-spell (mis spel´) v. To spell a word
incorrectly. **misspelling** n.

mis-take (mi stk´) n. A wrong statement, action, or decision. **mistaken**
adj. **mistakable** adj. **mistakably** adv.

mis-tle-toe (mis´l t´) n. A parasitic plant
with thick leaves, small yellowish
flowers and white berries.

mis-treat (mis trt´) v. To treat badly or
wrongly. **mistreatment** n.

mis-tress (mis´tris) n. A woman having
authority, ownership, or a position of
control; a woman having a sexual relationship with a man who is not her
husband.

mis-tri-al (mis tr´al) n. A trial that is
invalid because of an error during the
procedure.

mis-trust (mis trust´) v. To have doubt;
to lack trust in something or someone.
mistrust n. **mistrustful** adj.

mis-un-der-stand (mis´un dr stand´) v.
To interpret incorrectly; to fail to
understand.

mite (mt) n. A very small insect; a small
amount of money.

mi-ter (m´tr) n. A joint made by cutting
two pieces at an angle and then fitting
them together.

mit-i-gate (mit´i gt´) v. To make or
become less severe or painful.

mi-to-sis (m t´sis) n. pl. **mitoses** A
process of cell division in which chro-
matin divides into chromosomes.

mitt (mit) n. A women's glove that covers only the wrist and hand, leaving the
fingers exposed; in baseball, a glove
for a catcher or first baseman made in
the style of a mitten.

mix (miks) v. To blend or combine into
one; to come or bring together. **mix-
able** adj.

mixed number n. A number representing the sum of an integer and a fraction, such as 5 1/2.

mix-ture (miks´chr) n. The state of
being mixed; the process or act of mixing; a combination of two or two substances.

mix-up (miks´up´) n. An instance or
state of confusion.

moan (mn) *n.* A very low, dull sound indicative of pain or grief.

moat (mt) *n.* A deep and wide trench surrounding a castle, usually filled with water.

mob (mob) *n.* A large, unruly crowd. *v.* To overcrowd.

mo-bi-lize (m´bi lz´) *v.* To put into motion; to make ready. **-lization** *n.*

moc-ca-sin (mok´a sin) *n.* A shoe or slipper made of a soft leather.

mo-cha (m´ka) *n.* An Arabian coffee of superior quality; a flavoring with coffee, often used with chocolate.

mock (mok) *v.* To treat with contempt or scorn; to imitate a mannerism or sound closely; to mimic. *adv.* In an insincere manner. *n.* An imitation; a copy.

mock--he-ro-ic (mok´hi r´ik) *n.* A satirical imitation of the heroic manner or style.

mock-ing-bird (mok´ing berd´) *n.* A common bird that is remarkable for its exact imitations of the notes of other birds.

mock-up *or* **mockup** (mok´up´) *n.* A model of a structure used for study, testing, or demonstration.

mod *n.* A modern and unusual style of dress. *adj.* Modern.

mode (md) *n.* A way or method of doing something; a particular manner or form; the value or score that occurs most frequently in a set of data; the current fashion or style, as in dress.

mod-el (mod´el) *n.* A small representation of an object; a pattern that something will be based on; a design or type; one serving as an example; one who poses for an artist or photographer. *v.* **modeler** *n.*

mod-er-ate (mod´r it) *adj.* Not excessive; tending toward the mean or average extent or quality; opposed to extreme political views. **moderate** *v.* **moderation** *n.*

mod-ern (mod´rn) *adj.* Typical of the recent past or the present; advanced or up-to-date. **modernity** *n.* **-ly** *adv.*

mod-ern-ize (mod´r nz´) *v.* To make or become modern. **modernization** *n.*

mod-est (mod´ist) *adj.* Placing a moderate estimate on one's abilities or worth; retiring or reserved; limited in size or amount.

mod-i-cum (mod´i kum) *n.* A small amount.

mod-i-fy (mod´i f´) *v.* To alter; to make different in character or form; to change to less extreme; to moderate. **modified** *adj.* **modification** *n.*

mod-ish (m´dish) *adj.* Fashionable. **modishly** *adv.* **modishness** *n.*

mo-diste (m dst´) *n.* A person dealing in fashionable clothing for women.

mod-u-late (moj´u lt´) *v.* To soften; to temper; to vary the intensity of. *Music* To change from one key to another; to vary the tone or intensity of.

mod-ule (moj´öl) *n.* One of a series of standardized components which work together in a system. *Electr.* A self-contained subassembly of electronic components, as a computer stage; the self-contained area of a spacecraft for performing a particular task.

mod-us vi-ven-di (m´dus vi ven´d) *n.* A compromise which avoids difficulties.

mo-gul (m´gul) *n.* A very great or important person; a small hill or bump of ice and snow on a ski slope.

mo-hair (m´hâr´) *n.* The fabric or yarn made from the silky hair of the Angora goat.

moi-e-ty (moi´e t) *n. pl.* **-ies** A half; any portion; part or share.

moi-re (mwä r´) *n.* Fabric, especially silk or rayon having a wavy pattern.

moist (moist) *adj.* Slightly wet; damp; saturated with moisture or liquid. **-ly** *adv.* **-ness** *n.*

mois-ten (moi´sen) *v.* To make or become moist or slightly wet. **moistener** *n.*

mois-ture (mois´chr) *n.* Liquid diffused or condensed in a relatively small quantity; dampness. **moisturize** *v.* **moisturizer** *n.*

mo-lar (m´lr) *n.* A grinding tooth which has a broad surface for grinding food, located in the back of the mouth.

mold (mld) *n.* A superficial, often woolly growth produced on damp or decaying organic matter or on living organisms; a fungus that produces such a growth; crumbling, soft, friable earth suited to plant growth; distinctive nature or character; the frame on or around which an object is constructed; *n.* a cavity in which an object is shaped; general shape; form.

mold-board (mld´brd´) *n.* The curved blade of a plow.

mold-er (ml´dr) *v.* To crumble or decay gradually and turn to dust.

mole (ml) *n.* A pigmented spot or mark on the human skin; a small, insectivorous mammal that lives mostly underground and has a narrow snout, small eyes, and silky fur; a large wall of stone or masonry used as a breakwater or pier.

mo-lec-u-lar (m lek´ lr) *adj.* Of, relating to, or caused by molecules.

molecular biology *n.* The branch of biology dealing with the structure and development of biological systems which are studied in terms of their molecular constituents. **molecular biologist** *n.*

mol-e-cule (mol´e kl´) *n.* The simplest structural unit into which a substance can be divided and still retain its identity.

mo-lest (mo lest´) *v.* To bother, annoy, or persecute; to accost sexually. **molestation** *n.* **molester** *n.*

mol-li-fy (mol´i f) *v.* To make less angry; to soften; to make less intense or severe.

mol-lusk *or* **mol-lusc** (mol´usk) *n.* Any of various largely marine invertebrates, including the edible shellfish.

molt (mlt) *v.* To cast off or shed an external covering, as horns, feathers, or skin, which is periodically replaced by new growth.

mol-ten (ml´ten) *adj.* Transformed to liquid form by heat.

mo-lyb-de-num (mo lib´de num) *n.* A hard, gray metallic element used to harden steel alloys, symbolized by Mo.

mo-men-tar-i-ly (m´men târ´il) *adv.* For just a moment; soon; from moment to moment.

mo-men-tar-y (m´men ter´) *adj.* Lasting just a moment; occurring presently or at every moment.

mo-men-tous (m men´tus) *adj.* Of great importance or consequence; signifi-

cant. **momentously** *adv.* **momentous-ness** *n.*

mo-men-tum (m men´tum) *n. pl.* **-ta** *or* **-tums** A property of a moving body which determines the length of time required to bring it to rest when under the action of a constant force.

mon-arch (mon´ärk) *n.* A person who reigns over a kingdom or empire; a large orange and black butterfly. **monarchic** *adj.*

mon-ar-chy (mon´r k) *n. pl.* **-chies** Government by a monarch; sovereign control; a government or nation ruled by a monarch.

mon-as-ter-y (mon´a ster´) *n. pl.* **-ies** A house for persons under religious vows.

mo-nas-tic (mo nas´tik) *adj.* Of, relating to, or typical of monasteries, monks, or life in monasteries.

mo-nas-ti-cism (mo nas´ti siz´um) *n.* The monastic lifestyle or system.

mon-au-ral (mon är´al) *adj.* Of or relating to a system of transmitting or recording sound by techniques in which one or more sources are channeled into one carrier.

mon-e-tar-y (mon´i ter´) *adj.* Of or relating to money or how it is circulated.

mon-ey (mun´) *n.* Anything which has or is assigned value and is used as a medium of exchange.

mon-ey-lend-er *n.* Someone whose business is lending money to others with interest.

mon-ger (mung´gr) *n.* One who attempts to stir up or spread something that is undesirable; one who deals.

mon-grel (mung´grel) *n.* An animal or plant, especially a dog, produced by interbreeding.

mo-ni-tion (mo nish´an) *n.* A caution or warning, as for an impending danger.

mon-i-tor (mon´i tr) *n.* A student assigned to assist a teacher; a receiver used to view the picture being picked up by a television camera; the image being generated by a computer. **monitorial** *adj.*

mon-i-to-ry (mon´i tr´) *adj.* Giving a caution or conveying a warning.

monk's cloth n. A sturdy cotton cloth having a coarse basket weave.

monks·hood (mungks′hed′) n. A normally poisonous plant of the genus Aconitum, having variously colored hooded flowers.

mon·o n. Mononucleosis.

mon·o·chro·mat·ic (mon′o kr mat′ik) adj. Of, consisting of, or having one color.

mon·o·cle (mon′o kl) n. An eyeglass for one eye.

mon·o·cot·y·le·don (mon′o kot′ĭld′on) n. Any of various plants having a single embryonic seed leaf appearing at germination. **monocotyledonous** adj.

mo·noc·u·lar (mo nok′ lr) adj. Of, relating to, or having one eye.

mo·nog·a·my (mo nog′a m) n. Marriage or sexual relationship with only one person at a time. **monogamist** n. **monogamous** adj.

mon·o·gram (mon′o gram′) n. A design consisting of one or more initials.

mon·o·graph (mon′o graf′) n. A scholarly pamphlet or book on a particular and usually limited subject. **monographic** adj.

mon·o·lin·gual (mon′o ling′gwal) adj. Knowing only one language.

mon·o·lith (mon′o lith) n. A single block of stone, as one used in architecture or sculpture.

mon·o·ma·ni·a (mon′o m′n a) n. A pathological obsession or mental disorder in which a person is totally obsessed with a single idea. **monomaniac** n.

mo·no·mi·al (m n′m al) n. An algebraic expression consisting of only one term.

mon·o·nu·cle·ar (mon′o nŏ′kl r) adj. Having only one nucleus.

mon·o·nu·cle·o·sis (mon′o nŏ′kl′sis) n. An infectious disease marked by an abnormal increase of too many cells having one nucleus.

mon·o·nu·cle·o·tide n. A nucleotide containing one molecule each of a phosphoric acid, a pentose, and either a purine or pyrimidine base.

mon·o·phon·ic (mon′o fon′ik) adj. Having only one part; a solo voice with accompaniment, as a piano.

mon·o·plane (mon′o pln′) n. An aircraft with one wing or one set of wings.

mo·nop·o·ly (mo nop′o l) n. pl. -ies Exclusive ownership or control, as of a service or commodity, by a single group, person, or company; a group, person, or company having a monopoly; exclusive possession; a service or commodity controlled by a single group.

mon·o·rail (mon′o rl′) n. A single rail serving as a track on which a wheeled vehicle can travel; a vehicle that travels on such a rail.

mon·o·so·di·um glu·ta·mate (mon′o s′d um glō′ta mt′) n. Sodium glutamate used as a seasoning, abbreviated as MSG.

mon·o·syl·la·ble (mon′o sil′a bl) n. A word of one syllable.

mon·o·the·ism (mon′o th iz′um) n. The belief that there is just one God. **monotheist** n. **monotheistic** adj.

mon·o·tone (mon′o tn′) n. The utterance of sounds, syllables, or words in a single unvarying tone.

mo·not·o·nous (mo not′o nus) adj. Spoken in a monotone; lacking in variety.

mon·ox·ide (mon ok′sd) n. An oxide that contains one oxygen atom per molecule.

mon·soon (mon sŏn′) n. A periodic wind, especially in the Indian Ocean and southern Asia; the season of the monsoon in India and parts of Asia.

mon·ster (mon′str) n. An animal or plant having an abnormal form or structure; an animal, plant, or object having a frightening or deformed shape; one unusually large for its kind. **monstrosity** n. **monstrous** adj.

mon·tage (mon täzh′) n. A composite picture made by combining several separate pictures or parts of several pictures; a rapid succession of images in a motion picture, designed to illustrate an association of ideas.

month (munth) n. One of the twelve divisions of a calendar year.

month·ly (munth′l) adj. Occurring, done, or payable each month. n. A publication issued once a month. **monthly** *adv.*

mon-u-ment (mon´ ment) *n.* An object, such as a statue, built as a memorial to a person or an event; a burial vault; an area set aside for public use by a government because of its aesthetic, historical, or ecological significance.

mon-u-men-tal (mon´ men´ tal) *adj.* Serving as or similar to a monument; massive; extremely important. **monumentally** *adv.*

mooch (mōch) *v. Slang* To acquire by begging; to steal. **moocher** *n.*

moon (mōn) *n.* The earth's only natural satellite; a natural satellite which revolves around a planet. *v.* To dream.

moon-set (mōn´set´) *n.* The descent of the moon below the horizon; the time of the moon's setting.

moon-shine (mōn´shn´) *n.* Moonlight; empty talk; nonsense; intoxicating liquor, especially illegally distilled corn whiskey.

moor (mer) *v.* To make fast with cables, lines, or anchors. *n.* An expanse of open, rolling, infertile land.

moor-ing *n.* A place where a ship or aircraft can be secured; a stabilizing device.

moose (mōs) *n. pl.* **moose** A very large North American deer having a large broad muzzle.

moot (mōt) *v.* To bring up as for debate or discussion; to argue. *adj.* Open to debate; having no legal significance.

mope (mp) *v.* To be uncaring or dejected; to move in a leisurely manner. **moper** *n.*

mop-pet (mop´it) *n.* A child; a darling baby.

mopup *n.* The process of completing a task.

mo-raine (mo rn´) *n.* An accumulation of earth and stones carried and finally deposited by a glacier.

mor-al (mor´al) *adj.* Of or pertaining to conduct or character from the point of right and wrong; teaching a conception of right behavior. The lesson to be learned from a story, event, or teaching. **morals** Standards of right and wrong. **morally** *adv.*

mo-rale (mo ral´) *n.* An individual's state of mind with respect to the tasks he or she is expected to perform; esprit decorps.

mor-al-ist (mor´a list) *n.* Someone concerned with moral principles and questions; someone who practices morality. **moralism** *n.* **-ic** *adj.*

mo-ral-i-ty (mo ral´i t) *n. pl.* **-ies** The quality of being morally right; moral behavior.

mor-al-ize (mor´a lz´) *v.* To think, discuss, or judge in a moral sense. **moralization** *n.*

mo-rass (mo ras´) *n.* A marsh or bog; low-lying wet, soft ground; something which hinders or overwhelms.

mo-ray (mr´) *n.* Any of various marine eels found usually in tropical waters.

mor-bid (mor´bid) *adj.* Of, pertaining to, or affected by disease; suggesting an unhealthy mental state of being; gruesome. **morbidity** *n.* **morbidness** *n.* **morbidly** *adv.*

mor-da-cious (mor d´shus) *adj.* Violent in action; prone to biting. **-city** *n.*

mor-dant (mor´dant) *adj.* Biting and caustic in thought, manner, or style. **mordancy** *n.* **mordantly** *adv.*

more (mr) *adj.* Greater number, size, or degree; additional. *n.* An additional or greater number, degree, or amount. *adv.* To a greater extent or degree; in addition. *pron.* Additional things or persons.

mo-rel (mo rel´) *n.* An edible mushroom having a sponge-like cap or hood.

more-o-ver (mr ´vr) *adv.* Furthermore; besides.

mo-res (mr´z) *n. pl.* The moral customs and traditional customs of a social group.

morgue (morg) *n.* A place in which dead bodies are kept until claimed or identified; the reference file at a newspaper or magazine office.

mor-i-bund (mor´i bund´) *adj.* Approaching extinction; at the point of death.

morn-ing (mor´ning) *n.* The early part of the day; the time from midnight to noon.

mo-ron (mr´on) *n.* An adult exhibiting an intelligence equal to that of a seven to twelve year old child; a very stupid person. **moronic** *adj.* **-ically** *adv.*

mo-rose (mo rs´) *adj.* Having a sullen disposition; marked by gloom.

mor-pheme (mor´fm) *n.* A meaningful unit which cannot be divided into smaller meaningful parts. **-phemic** *adj.*

mor-phi-a (mor´f a) *n.* Morphine.

mor-phine (mor´fn) *n.* A highly addictive narcotic derived from opium which can be used as either a sedative or to dull pain.

mor-phol-o-gy (mor fol´o j) *n.* The study of the form and structure of living organisms, considered separate from function; the study and description of word formation in a language. **morphological** *adj.* **morphologically** *adj* **morphologist** *n.*

mor-ris (mor´is) *n.* An old English folk dance.

mor-row (mor´) *n.* The next day.

mor-sel (mor´sel) *n.* A small piece or quantity of food; a tasty dish.

mor-tal (mor´tal) *adj.* Having caused or about to cause death; fatal; subject to death; very tedious or prolonged; unrelentingly hostile; of, relating to, or connected with death. *n.* A human being. **-ly** *adv.*

mor-tal-i-ty (mor tal´i t) *n. pl.* **-ies** The state or condition of being mortal; the death rate; deaths.

mor-tar-board (mor´tr brd´) *n.* A square-board with a handle, for holding mortar; an academic cap topped by a stiff, flat square.

mort-gage (mor´gij) *n.* A temporary conveyance of property to a creditor as security for the repayment of a debt; a contract or deed defining the terms of a mortgage. *v.* To pledge or transfer by means of a mortgage.

mor-ti-cian (mor tish´an) *n.* An undertaker.

mor-ti-fy (mor´ti f´) *v.* To destroy the strength or functioning of; to subdue or deaden through pain or self-denial; to subject to severe humiliation; to become gangrenous. **mortification** *n.* **mortifyingly** *adv.*

mor-tise (mor´tis) *n.* A usually hollowed out rectangular hole in a piece of wood which receives a tenon of another piece to form a joint.

mor-tu-ar-y (mor´chŏ er´) *n. pl.* **-ies** A place in which dead bodies are temporarily held until burial or cremation.

mo-sa-ic (m z´ik) *n.* A decorative inlaid design of small pieces, as of colored glass or tile, in cement. **mosaic** *adj.*

mo-sey (m z´) *v. Slang* To move slowly; to shuffle along.

mosque (mosk) *n.* A Moslem house of worship.

mos-qui-to (mo sk´t) *n. pl.* **-toes** or **-tos** Any of various winged insects of which the females suck the blood of animals or humans.

mosquito net *n.* A fine net or screen to keep out mosquitos.

most (mst) *adj.* The majority of. *n.* The greatest amount. *pron.* The largest part or number. *adv.* In or to the highest degree.

most-ly (mst´l) *adv.* For the most part; principally.

mot (mt) *n.* A short, witty saying.

mote (mt) *n.* A particle, as of dust; a speck of dust.

mo-tet (m tet´) *n.* A polyphonic vocal composition, based on a religious text and usually sung without accompaniment.

moth-er (muth´r) *n.* A female parent; one who holds a maternal relationship toward another; an old or elderly woman; a woman in a position of authority. *adj.* Of, relating to, or being a mother. *v.* To give birth to; to care for or protect like a mother.

mo-tif (m tf´) *n.* An underlying main element or theme that recurs in a musical, artistic, or literary work.

mo-tile (mt´il) *adj.* Exhibiting or capable of movement.

mo-tion (m´shan) *n.* The act or process of changing position; a purposeful movement of the body or a bodily part; a formal proposal or suggestion that action be taken.

mo-ti-vate (m´ti vt´) *v.* Causing to act.

mo-tive (m´tiv) *n.* Something, as a need or desire, which causes a person to act; a musical motif. *adj.* Causing or having the power to cause motion.

mo-tor (m´tr) *n.* Any of various devices which develop energy or impart motion. *adj.* Imparting or producing motion; driven by or equipped with a motor; of, relating to or designed for motor vehicles; of, relating to, or involving muscular movement. *v.* To travel or transport by motor vehicle.

motor-bike (m´tr bk´) *n.* A small motorcycle.

mo-tor-car (m´tr kär´) *n.* An automobile.

mo-tor-cy-cle (m´tr s´kl) *n.* A two-wheeled automotive vehicle. **motorcyclist** *n.*

mo-tor-ize (m´to rz´) *v.* To equip with a motor; to supply with motor-propelled vehicles.

motor vehicle *n.* A motor-powered vehicle which travels freely without the need for rails.

mot-tle (mot´l) *v.* To mark or be marked with spots or streaks of different colors or shades; to blotch. *n.* A blotch.

mot-to (mot´) *n. pl.* **-toes** or **-tos** A sentence, phrase, or word expressing purpose, character, or conduct; an appropriate phrase inscribed on something.

mound (mound) *n.* A small hill of earth, sand, gravel or debris; the slightly elevated ground in the middle of a baseball diamond on which the pitcher stands.

moun-tain (moun´tin) *n.* A land mass that rises above its surroundings and is higher than a hill.

mountain lion *n.* A large wildcat; puma.

moun-tain-ous (moun´ta nus) *adj.* Of or relating to a region with many mountains.

moun-te-bank (moun´te bangk´) *n.* A quack doctor; a false and boastful pretender; a charlatan.

mount-ing (moun´ting) *n.* A supporting frame or structure of an article.

mourn (mrn) *v.* To express grief; to feel grief or sorrow; to follow the religious customs and rituals surrounding the death of a loved one.

mouse (mous) *n. pl.* **mice** A small rodent that frequents human habitations; a timid person.

mousse (mös) *n.* A light frozen dessert.

mouth (mouth) *n. pl.* **mouths** The bodily opening through which food is taken in. **mouth-off** To speak disre-

spectfully.

mouthtomouth (mouth´tö mouth´) *adj.* Pertaining to a method of artificial resuscitation.

mov-ie (mö´v) *n.* A motion picture; motion picture industry.

mow (m) *v.* To cut down, as with a machine. *n.* The part of the barn where hay or grain is stored. **mower** *n.*

moz-za-rel-la *n.* A soft white cheese with a mild flavor.

much (much) *adj.* In great amount, quantity, degree, or extent. *adv.* To a great extent. *n.* Something impressive.

mu-co-sa (m k´sa) *n.* A mucous membrane.

mu-cous (m´kus) *adj.* Of, pertaining to, or secreting mucus.

mucous membrane *n.* A membrane secreting mucus which lines bodily channels that come into contact with air.

mu-cus (m´kus) *n.* The viscous liquid secreted by glands by the mucous membrane.

mug (mug) *n.* A large drinking cup; a person's face; a photograph of someone's face. *v.* To make funny faces; to assault viciously, usually with the intent to rob. **mugger** *n.*

mulct (mulkt) *n.* A financial penalty or fine. *v.* To punish by fining; to obtain by fraud or theft.

mule (mul) *n.* A hybrid animal that is the offspring of a female horse and a male ass. *Slang* A stubborn person. **mulish** *adj.* **mulishly** *adv.* **-lishness** *n.*

mull (mul) *v.* To mix or grind thoroughly; to ponder; to think about. *n.* A soft sheer muslin; a thin fabric of rayon.

mul-lein (mul´en) *n.* A plant having yellow flowers and downy leaves.

mul-li-gan stew (mul´i gan) *n.* A stew made of various vegetables and meats.

multi- *prefix* Much, many, multiple; more than two.

mul-ti-dis-ci-pli-nar-y *adj.* Using or related to a combination of several disciplines for a common cause.

mul-ti-far-i-ous (mul´ti fär´us) *adj.* Having much diversity or variety. **mul-tifariously** *adv.*

mul-ti-form (mul´ti form´) *adj.* Having many appearances or forms. **multifor-**

mity *n.*

mul-ti-lane *adj.* Having several lanes.

mul-ti-lat-er-al (mul´ti lat´r al) *adj.* Having many sides; involving or participated in by more than two parties or nations.

mul-ti-lin-gual (mul´ti ling´gwal) *adj.* Expressed in several languages. *n.* The ability to use several languages. **-ism** *n.*

mul-ti-mil-lion-aire (mul´t mil´yanâr´) *n.* A person whose fortune is worth many millions of dollars.

mul-tip-a-rous *adj.* Producing more than one at a birth.

mul-ti-ple (mul´ti pl) *adj.* Relating to or consisting of more than one individual, part, or element. *Math.* A number into which another number can be divided with no remainders.

multiple sclerosis *n.* A degenerative condition marked by patches of hardened tissue in the spinal cord or the brain.

mul-ti-pli-ca-tion (mul´ti plĭk´shan) *n.* The mathematical operation by which a number indicates how many times another number is to be added to itself.

mul-ti-plic-i-ty (mul´ti plis´i t) *n. pl.* **-ies** A large number or variety.

mul-ti-ply (mul´ti pl) *v.* To increase in amount or number; to combine by multiplication.

mul-ti-sense *adj.* Having several meanings.

mul-ti-tude (mul´ti töd´) *n.* A very large amount or number. **multitudinous** *adj.*

mul-ti-vi-ta-min *n.* A pill containing several vitamins that are essential to health.

mum-mer (mum´r) *n.* A performer who acts in a pantomime.

mum-mi-fy (mum´i f´) *v.* To dry and embalm as a mummy; to cause to shrivel and dry up. **mummification** *n.*

mun-dane (mun dn´) *adj.* Pertaining to or relating to the world; characterized by the ordinary and practical. **mundanely** *adv.*

mu-nic-i-pal (m nis´i pal) *adj.* Relating to or typical of a municipality; having self- government in local affairs.

mu-ni-tions *pl. n.* Guns and ammunition.

mu-ral (mer´al) *n.* A painting created

on a wall.

murk (merk) *n.* Darkness; gloom. **murkily** *adv.* **murkiness** *n.* **-y** *adj.*

mur-rain (mer´in) *n.* A plague affecting plants or domestic animals.

mus-cle (mus´l) *n.* Bodily tissue which consists of long cells that contract when stimulated.

mus-cu-lar (mus´k lr) *adj.* Relating to or consisting of muscle; brawny; having well- developed muscles. **muscularity** *n.*

muscular dystrophy *n.* A noncontagious hereditary disease characterized by gradual but irreversible muscular deterioration.

mus-cu-la-ture (mus´k la chr) *n.* The muscles of an animal's body.

muse (mz) *n.* A state of deep thought.

mu-sette (m zet´) *n* A small bagpipe having a soft, sweet tone or sound; a small bag with a shoulder strap.

mu-sic (mu´zik) *n.* Organized tones in sequences and combinations which make up a continuous composition, involving pitch, harmony, and rhythm. **musical** *adj.*

mu-si-cal com-e-dy *n.* A play with a plot that has songs and dances.

mu-si-cian (m zish´an) *n.* A composer or performer of music; one who plays a musical instrument; skilled in music.

mu-si-col-o-gy (m´zi kol´o j) *n.* The scientific and historical study of music.

mus-ket (mus´kit) *n.* A heavy, large-caliber shoulder gun with a long barrel; first developed in the 16th century.

musk-mel-on (musk´mel´on) *n.* A sweet melon having a rough rind and juicy, edible flesh.

musk-rat (musk´rat´) *n.* A rodent of North America with brown fur and partially webbed hind feet, and secretes a musky odor.

muss (mus) *v.* To make messy or untidy. *Slang* A confused conflict.

mus-sel (mus´el) *n.* A freshwater bivalve mollusk.

must (must) *v.* To be forced to; to have to; to be obligated to something; to be necessary to do something. *n.* A requirement; absolute; something indispensable.

mus-tang (mus´tang) *n.* A wild horse of

the western plains.

mustn't *contr.* Must not.

mus-ty (mus´ti) *adj.* Moldy or stale in odor or taste. **mustily** *adv.* **-ness** *n.*

mu-ta-ble (m´ta bl) *adj.* Prone to or capable of change; inconstant in feeling or mind; subject to change. **mutability** *n.* **-ness** *n.*

mu-tant (mt´ant) *n.* An individual or organism which differs from the parental strain as a result of mutation.

mu-tate (m´tt) *v.* To undergo or cause to undergo mutation. **mutative** *adj.*

mute (mt) *adj.* Unable to speak. *n.* A person who cannot speak; to muffle the sound, as in a musical instrument; to soften the intensity.

mu-ti-ny (mt´i n) *n.* *pl.* **-ies** Open revolt against lawful authority. **mutineer** *n.*

mut-ter (mut´r) *v.* To speak or utter in a low voice; to grumble; to complain.

mut-ton (mut´on) *n.* The flesh of a fully grown sheep, used for food.

mu-tu-al (m´chö al) *adj.* Having the same relationship; received and directed in equal amounts; shared the same. **mutuality** *n.*

my (m) *adj.* Relating to or of myself or one. *interj.* Used to express surprise, dismay, or pleasure.

my-ce-li-um (m s´l um) *n.* *pl.* **-lia** A mass of interwoven filaments which form the main growing structure of a fungus.

my-col-o-gy (m kol´o je) *n.* A branch of botany; the scientific study of fungi.

my-co-sis (m k´sis) *n.* A fungus such as ringworm.

my-dri-a-sis (mi dr´a sis) *n.* Dilatation of the pupil of the eye, due to the result of drugs or disease.

my-na *or* **my-nah** (m´na) *n.* A dark brown, slightly crested bird of southeastern Asia.

myo-car-dio-graph (m´o kär´d ograf´) *n.* A recording tool which traces the action of the heart muscles.

my-o-pi-a *n.* A condition of the eyes, in which images are focused in front of the retina; objects seen clearly only when near to the eye; nearsightedness.

myr-i-a-pod (mir´a pod´) *n.* An arthropod, having a segmented body and

many legs.

myr-mi-don (mer´mi don´) *n.* A loyal follower; one who is willing to execute unscrupulous commands.

my-self (m self´) *pron.* The one identical with me; used reflexively; my normal, healthy state or condition.

mys-ter-y (mis´te r) *n.* *pl.* **-ies** Something not understood; something that is kept secret or remains unexplained or unknown; any thing, affair or person left unexplained; a problem or puzzle; an enigma; a Christian sacrament.

mys-ti-cism (mis´ti siz´um) *n.* The spiritual discipline of communion with God.

mys-ti-fy (mis´ti f) *v.* To perplex, to bewilder.

mys-tique (mi stk´) *n.* A body of beliefs connected with a group, person, idea, or thing.

myth (mith) *n.* A legend or fable covering the convictions of a people as to their gods or other divine persons, their own orgin and early history and their heroes connected with it, or the origin of the world, any story with something or someone having no exisistence.

my-thol-o-gize (mi thol´o jz) *n.* To explain myths. *v.* To interpret in relation to mythology; to explain a myth.

my-thol-o-gy (mi thol´o j) *n.* *pl.* **-ies** A body of myths dealing with gods and heroes.

N

N, n. (en) The fourteenth letter of the English alphabet.

nab (nab) *v.* *Slang* To seize; to arrest; to catch suddenly.

na-cho (na´ch)*n.* A tortilla, often small and triangular in shape, topped with cheese or chili sauce and baked.

nag (nag) *v.* To bother by scolding or constant complaining. **nag** *n.* A worthless horse.

nai-ad (n´ad) *n.*, *Mythol.* A nymph presiding over and living in springs, brooks, and fountains.

nail (nl) *n.* A thin pointed piece of metal for hammering into wood and other materials to hold pieces together.

na-ive (nä v´) *adj.* Simple and trusting; not sophisticated. **naively** *adv.*

na-ked (n´kid) *adj.* Without clothes on the body; nude; exposed; uncovered.

name (nm) *n.* A title or word by which something or someone is known. *v.* To give a name. **namable,** *n.*

name-less (nm´lis) *adj.* Having no name; anonymous.

name-sake (nm´sk´) *n.* A person named after someone with the same name.

nap (nap) *n.* A short rest or sleep, often during the day. *v.* The surface of a piece of leather or fabric.

nape (np) *n.* The back of the neck.

nap-kin (nap´kin) *n.* A cloth or soft paper, used at the dinner table for wiping the lips and fingers.

na-po-le-on (na p´l an) *n.* A pastry of several flaky layers filled with custard cream.

nar-cis-sus (när sis´us) *n.* A widely grown type of bulbous plant which includes the jonquil, narcissus, and daffodil.

nar-cot-ic (när kot´ik) *n.* A drug which dulls the senses, relieves pain, and induces a deep sleep; if abused, it can become habit-forming and cause convulsions or comas.

nar-rate (na´rrt) *v.* To tell a story or give a description in detail. **-ration** *n.*

nar-row (nar´) *adj.* Slender or small in width; of less than standard width.

narrowmind-ed (nar´ mn´did) *adj.* Lacking sympathy or tolerance.

nar-whal (när´wal) *n.* An aquatic mammal of the Arctic regions, closely related to the white whale, having a long, twisted, protruding tusk in the male.

na-sal (n´zal) *adj.* Of or pertaining to the nose; producing a nasal speech sound.

nas-ty (nas´t) *adj.* Dirty, filthy, or indecent; unpleasant. **nastily** *adv.*

na-tion (n´shan) *n.* A group of people made up of one or more nationalities under one government.

na-tion-al-ism (nash´a na liz´um) *n.* Devotion to or concern for one's nation; a movement or desire for national independence.

na-tion-al-i-ty (nash´a nal´i t) *n.* The fact or condition of belonging to a nation.

na-tion-al-ize (nash´a na lz´) *v.* To place a nation's resources and industries under the control of the state.

na-tive (n´tiv) *n.* A person born in a country or place. *adj.* Belonging to one by nature or birth.

na-tiv-i-ty (na tiv´i t) *n.* Birth, circumstances, or conditions; the birth of Christ.

nat-u-ral (nach´r al) *adj.* Produced or existing by nature; not artificial. *Mus.* A note that is not sharp or flat. **ness** *n.*

natural childbirth *n.* Childbirth with little stress or pain; childbirth that requires training for the mother and father and medical supervision, but without the use of drugs, anesthesia, or surgery.

nat-u-ral-ize (nach´r a lz´) *v.* To confer the privileges and rights of full citizenship.

na-ture (n´chr) *n.* The universe and its phenomena; kind, sort, or type; one's own character or temperament. **natured** *adj.*

naught (not) *n.* Nothing; the number 0; zero.

naugh-ty (no´t) *adj.* Unruly; not proper; ill-behaved. **naughtily** *adv.*

nau-se-a (no´z a) *n.* An upset stomach with a feeling that one needs to vomit.

nau-ti-cal (no´ti kal) *adj.* Pertaining to ships or seamanship. **nautically** *adv.*

na-val (n´val) *adj.* Of or relating to ships; maritime.

na-vel (n´vel) *n.* A small mark or scar on the abdomen where the umbilical cord was attached.

nav-i-ga-ble (nav´i ga bl) *adj.* Sufficiently deep and wide enough to allow ships to pass.

nav-i-gate (nav´i gt´) *v.* To plan the course of a ship or aircraft; to steer a course. **navigation, navigator** *n.*

na-vy (n´v) *n.* One of a nation's organizations for defense; a nation's fleet of ships; a very dark blue.

near (nr) *adv.* At, to, or within a short time or distance. **near** *adj.* Closely or intimately related. **nearness** *n.*

near-by (nr´b´) *adj. & adv.* Close by; near at hand; adjacent.

near-sight-ed (nr´s´tid) adj. Able to see clearly at short distances only.

neat (nt) adj. Tidy and clean; free from disorder and dirt. Slang Great, fine, or wonderful. **neatly** adv. **neatness** n.

neb-u-lous (neb´ lus) adj. Confused or vague; hazy, cloudy, or misty.

nec-es-sar-y (nes´i ser´) adj. Unavoidable; required; essential; needed. **necessarily** adv.

ne-ces-si-tate (ne ses´i itt´) v. To make necessary; to oblige; to require; to force or be forced.

ne-ces-si-ty (ne ses´i t) n. pl.**necessities** The condition of being necessary; the condition making a particular course of action necessary; a requirement; something inevitable.

neck (nek) n. The part of the body which connects the head and trunk; a narrow part or projection, as of land, a stringed instrument, or bottle. **neck** v. To caress and kiss.

nec-tar (nek´tr) n. A good-tasting beverage; a sweet fluid in various flowers, gathered by bees to help make honey.

need (nd) n. The lack of something desirable, useful, or necessary; misfortune or poverty; a necessity.

nee-dle (nd´l) n. A slender, pointed steel implement which contains an eye through which thread is passed. v. To tease.

nee-dle-point (nd´l point´) n. Decorative stitching done on canvas in even stitches across counted threads.

need-n't (nd´ənt) contr. Need not.

ne-far-i-ous (ni fâr´ us) adj. Extremely wicked; despicable.

ne-gate (ni gt´) v. To nullify; to deny; to rule out. **negation** n.

neg-a-tive (neg´a tiv) adj. Expressing denial or disapproval; not positive. In photography, a negative photo.

neglect (ni glekt´) v. To ignore; to pay no attention to; to fail to perform. **neglectful** adj.

neg-li-gee (neg´li zh´) n. A woman's loosefitting dressing gown.

neg-li-gent (neg´li jənt) adj. To neglect what needs to be done; neglectful.

ne-go-ti-ate (ni g´sh t´) v. To confer with another person to reach an agreement; to accomplish successfully.

neigh-bor (n´br) n. One who lives near another; fellowman. **neighboring** adj.

neigh-bor-hood (n´br hed´) n. A section or small region that possesses a specific quality; the people living in such a region.

nei-ther (n´thr) adj. Not one or the other. **neither** pron. Not the one or the other. **neither** conj. Not either; also not.

neo prefix Recent; new.

neo-dym-i-um (n´ dim´ um) n. A metallic element of the rare-earth group, symbolized by Nd.

ne-on (n´on) n. An inert gaseous element used in lighting fixtures, symbolized by Ne.

ne-o-nate (no nt´) n. A newborn child less than a month old.

ne-o-na-tol-o-gy (n´o nt ol je) n. The medical study of the first 60 days of a baby's life.

ne-o-phyte (n´oft´) n. A novice; a beginner.

ne-o-plasm (n´o plaz´um) n. A tumor tissue serving no physiologic function.

neph-ew (nef´) n. The son of one's sister, brother, sister-in-law, or brother-in-law.

ne-phrit-ic (nef rit´ik) adj. Relating to the kidneys; afflicted with an inflammation of the kidneys.

nep-o-tism (nep´o tiz´um) n. The act of showing favoritism to relatives or friends in the work force. **nepotist** n.

nerve (nerv) n. The bundles of fibers which convey sensation and originate motion through the body. Slang Impudent.

nerv-ous (ner´vus) adj. Affecting the nerves or the nervous system; agitated; worried.

nervous system n., Physiol. The body system that coordinates, regulates, and controls the various internal functions and responses to stimuli.

nest (nest) n. A place, shelter, or home built by a bird to hold its eggs and young.

nes-tle (nes´l) v. To settle snugly; to lie close to. **nestler** n.

net (net) n. A meshed fabric made of cords, ropes, or threads knotted or woven together; the profit, weight, or price which remains after all additions, subtractions, or adjustments have been made.

neth-er (neth´r) *adj.* Situated below or beneath.

net-work (net´werk´) *n.* A system of interlacing tracks, channels, or lines; an interconnected system; a group of broadcasting stations.

neu-ral (ner´al) *adj.* Relating to a nerve or the nervous system.

neu-ral-gia (ne ral´ja) *n.* Pain that occurs along the course of a nerve.

neu-ri-tis (ne r´tis) *n.* An inflammation of a nerve which causes pain, the loss of reflexes, and muscular decline.

neu-rol-o-gy (ne rol´o j) *n.* The medical and scientific study of the nervous system and its disorders. **neurologist** *n.*

neu-ron *or* **neu-rone** (ner´ on) *n., Anat.* A granular cell nerve which is the main functional unit of the nervous system.

neu-ro-sis (ne r´sis) *n.* Any one of various functional disorders of the mind or emotions having no physical cause.

neu-ter (nö´tr) *adj.* Neither feminine nor masculine. **neuter** *n.* A castrated animal.

neu-tral (nö´tral) *adj.* Not supporting either side of a debate, quarrel, or party; a color which does not contain a decided hue. *Chem.* Neither alkaline nor acid.

neu-tral-ize (nö´tra lz´) *v.* To make or declare neutral.

neu-tron (nö´tron) *n.* An uncharged particle in the nucleus of an atom present in all atomic nuclei except the hydrogen nucleus.

nev-er (nev´r) *adv.* Not ever; absolutely not.

nev-er-the-less (nev´r the les´) *adv.* Nonetheless; however.

new (nö) *adj.* Not used before; unaccustomed; unfamiliar. **newness** *n.*

news (nöz) *n. pl.* Current information and happenings; matter considered newsworthy.

news-cast (nöz´kast´) *n.* A television or radio news broadcast.

news-pa-per (nöz´p´pr) *n.* A weekly or daily publication which contains recent news and information.

news-print (nöz´print´) *n.* An inexpen-

sive machine-finished paper made from wood pulp and used chiefly for newspapers and some paperback books.

next (nekst) *adj.* Immediately following or proceeding; nearest in space or position.

nib-ble (nib´l) *v.* To bite a little at a time; to take small bites. **nibble, nibbler** *n.*

nice (ns) *adj.* Pleasing; enjoyable; polite and courteous; refined. **nicely** *adv.* **niceness** *n.*

niche (nich) *n.* A recess or alcove in a wall, usually used for displays.

nick (nik) *n.* A small chip or cut on a surface; the final critical moment.

nick-el (nik´el) *n.* A hard, silver, metallic element used in alloys and symbolized by Ni; a United States coin worth five cents.

nick-el-o-de-on (nik´e l´d an) *n.* A movie theatre which charged five cents for admission; a coin-operated juke box.

nick-name (nik´nm´) *n.* The familiar form of a proper name, expressed in a shortened form. **nickname** *v.*

nic-o-tine *or* **nicotin** (nik´o tn´) *n.* A poisonous alkaloid found in tobacco and used in insecticides and medicine.

niece (ns) *n.* A daughter of one's sister or brother or one's sister-in-law or brother-in-law.

nigh (n) *adv.* Near in relationship, time, or space.

night (nt) *n.* The time between dusk and dawn or the hours of darkness.

night-cap (nt´kap´) *n.* An alcoholic drink usually taken before retiring for the night.

night-in-gale (nt´in gl´) *n.* A songbird with brownish plumage, noted for the sweet, nocturnal song of the male.

night-mare (nt´mâr´) *n.* A frightening and horrible dream.

nim-ble (nim´bl) *adj.* Marked by a quick, light movement; quick-witted. **nimbleness** *n.* **nimbly** *adv.*

nine (nn) *n.* The cardinal number that is equal to 8+1. **nine** *adj. & pron.*

ni-o-bi-um (n´b um) *n.* A gray, metallic element used in alloys, symbolized by Nb.

nip (nip) *v.* To pinch, bite, or grab something. *n.* A pinch, bite, or grab; a sharp, stinging feeling caused by cold temperatures.

nip-ple (nip´l) *n.* The small projection of a mammary gland through which milk passes; an artificial teat usually made from a type of rubber which a bottle-fed baby nurses.

ni-tro-gen (n´tro jen) *n.* A nonmetallic gaseous element which is essential to life, symbolized by N.

ni-tro-glyc-er-in (n´tro glis´r in) *n.* A highly flammable, explosive liquid, used to make dynamite and, in medicine, to dilate blood vessels.

no (n) *adv.* Used to express rejection, disagreement, or denial; not so; not at all.

no-bel-i-um (n b´l um) *n.* A radioactive element, symbolized by No.

no-bil-i-ty (n bil´i t) *n. pl.* **nobilities** The state or quality of being noble; the rank or status of a noble.

no-ble (n´bl) *adj.* Morally good; superior in character or nature. **noble** *n.* A person of rank or noble birth.

no-bod-y (n´bod´) Not anybody.

noc-tur-nal (nok ter´nal) *adj.* Pertaining to or occurring during the night; active at night and quiet during the daylight hours.

nod (nod) *n.* A quick downward motion of the head as one falls off to sleep; a downward motion of the head indicating acceptance or approval. **nod** *v.* To move the head down and then up again.

node (nd) *n.* A swollen or thickened enlargement.

no-el (n el´) *n.* A Christmas carol.

noise (noiz) *n.* A sound which is disagreeable or loud; in computer science, unwanted data in an electronic signal. **noisy** *adj.*

no-mad (n´mad) *n.* A member of a group of people who wander from place to place.

no-men-cla-ture (n´men kl´chr) *n.* The set of names used to describe the elements of art, science, and other fields.

nom-i-nal (nom´i nal) *adj.* Of or relating to something that is in name or form only.

nom-i-nate (nom´i nt´) *v.* To select a

candidate for an elective office; to appoint or designate to a position. **nomination** *n.*

nom-i-nee (nom´i n´) *n.* A person nominated for a position or office.

non- *prefix* Not.

non-a-ge-nar-i-an (non´a je när´an) *adj.* A person between 90 and 100 years of age.

non-cha-lant (non´sha länt´) *adj.* Giving an effect of casual unconcern.

non com-pos men-tis (non kom´pos men´ tis) *adj.* Mentally unbalanced; not of sound mind.

non-con-form-ist (non´kon for´mist) *n.* A person who does not feel compelled to follow or accept his community's customs or traditions.

none (nun) Not any; not one.

non-sec-tar-i-an (non´sek tär´an) *adj.* Not associated with or restricted to one religion, faction, or sect.

non-sense (non´sens) *n.* Something that seems senseless or foolish; something which is very unimportant.

non seq-ui-tur (non sek´wi tr) *n.* An inference that does not follow as the logical result of what has preceded it.

non-sex-ist *adj.* Not discriminating on the basis of gender.

noo-dle (nöd´l) *n.* A flat strip of dried dough made with eggs and flour. *Slang* The head.

noon (nön) *n.* The middle of the day; 12:00 o'clock.

noose (nös) *n.* A loop of rope secured by a slip knot, allowing it to decrease in size as the rope is pulled.

nor (nor) *conj.* Not either; or not.

norm (norm) *n.* A rule, model, or pattern typical for a particular group.

nor-mal (nor´mal) *adj.* Ordinary, average, usual; having average intelligence; standard. **normalcy, -mality** *n.*

north (north) *n.* The direction to a person's left while facing east.

nose (nz) *n.* The facial feature containing the nostrils; the sense of smell. **nose** *v.* To discover by smell.

nose-dive (nz´dv) *n.* A sudden plunge as made by an aircraft.

nos-tal-gia (no stal´ja) *n.* A yearning to return to the past. **nostalgic** *adj.*

nos-tril (nos´tril) *n.* The external openings of the nose.

nos-y or **nos-ey (nz)** *adj.* Snoopy; inquisitive; prying.

not (not) *adv.* In no manner; used to express refusal or denial.

no-ta-ble (n′ta bl) *adj.* Remarkable, distinguished.

notary public *n.* A person who is legally authorized as a public officer to witness and certify documents.

no-ta-tion (n t′shan) *n.* A process or system of figures or symbols used in specialized fields to represent quantities, numbers, or values. **-al** *adj.*

notch (noch) *n.* A v-shaped indentation or cut. **notch** *v.*

note (nt) *n.* A record or message in short form. *Mus.* A tone or written character.

not-ed (n′tid) *adj.* Famous; very well-known.

noth-ing (nuth′ing) *n.* Not any thing; no part or portion. **nothing** *adv.* In no way; not at all.

no-tice (n′tis) *n.* An announcement; a notification. *v.* To give notice; to become aware of. **noticeable** *adj.*

no-ti-fy (n′ti f′) *v.* To give notice of; to announce.

no-tion (n′shan) *n.* An opinion; a general concept; an idea. **notions** *n. pl.* Small useful articles, as thread or buttons.

no-to-ri-ous (n tr′ us) *adj.* Having a widely known and usually bad reputation.

noun (noun) *n.* A word which names a person, place, or thing.

nour-ish (ner′ish) *v.* To furnish with the nutriment and other substances needed for growth and life; to support.

nou-veau riche (nö′v rsh′) *n.* A person who has recently become rich.

nov-el (nov′el) *n.* An inventive narrative dealing with human experiences; a book.

nov-el-ty (nov′el t) *n. pl.* **novelties** Something unusual or new.

nov-ice (nov′is) *n.* A person who is new and unfamiliar with an activity or business.

now (nou) *adv.* At the present time; immediately.

no-where (n′hwâr′) *adv.* Not in or at any place.

noz-zle (noz′l) *n.* A projecting spout or vent of something.

nu-ance (nö′äns) *n.* A slight variation.

nub (nub) *n.* A knob; a small piece or lump.

nu-cle-ar (nö′kl r) *adj.* Pertaining to and resembling a nucleus; relating to atomic energy.

nu-cle-us (nö′kl us) *n. pl.* **nuclei** or **nucleuses** A central element around which other elements are grouped; the central core of an atom.

nude (nöd) *adj.* Unclothed; naked.

nudge (nuj) *v.* To poke or push gently.

nug-get (nug′it) *n.* A lump, as of precious metal.

nui-sance (nö′sans) *n.* A source of annoyance or inconvenience.

null (nul) *adj.* Invalid; having no value or consequence.

nul-li-fy (nul′i f′) *v.* To counteract.

numb (num) *adj.* Lacking physical sensation; paralyzed or stunned. **numb** *v.*

num-ber (num′br) *n.* A word or symbol which is used in counting or which indicates how many or which one in a series.

numberless *adj.* Too many to be counted; many

nu-mer-al (nö′mr al) *n.* A symbol, figure, letter, word, or a group of these which represents a number.

nu-mer-a-tor (nö′me r′tr) *n.* The term in mathematics indicating how many parts are to be taken; the number in a fraction which appears above the line.

nu-mer-ous (nö′mr us) *adj.* Consisting or made up of many units, things, or individuals.

nun (nun) *n.* A woman who has joined a religious group and has taken vows to give up worldly goods and never to marry.

nup-tial (nup′shal) *adj.* Of or pertaining to a wedding. **nuptials** *n. pl.* A wedding.

nurse (ners) *n.* A person who is trained to care for the disabled or sick. **nurse** *v.* To feed a baby from a mother's breast; to provide care to a sick or disabled person.

nurs-er-y (ners′se r) *n. pl.* **nurseries** A room reserved for the special use of infants or small children; a business or place where trees, shrubs, and flowers are raised and sold.

nur-ture (ner´chr) n. The upbringing, care, or training of a child. **nurture** v.

nut (nut) n. A hard-shelled fruit or seed which contains an inner, often edible kernal. *Slang* A person who does crazy or silly things.

nut-crack-er (nut´krak´r) n. A hinged tool for cracking nuts.

nut-meg (nut´meg) n. The hard seed of a tropical evergreen tree, which is grated and used as a spice.

nu-tri-ent (nō´tr ent) n. A substance which nourishes. **nutrient** adj.

nu-tri-tion (nō trish´an) n. The process by which a living being takes in food and uses it to live and grow. **nutritive** n.

nuts (nuts) adj. *Slang* Foolish, crazy.

nuz-zle (nuz´l) v. To gently rub against something with the nose; to cuddle as a person; to root dig or burrow with the nose, as an animal

nyc-ti-trop-ic (nik te´tr pik) adj. Certain plants, whose leaves assume different positions from day to night.

ny-lon (n´lon) n. A strong, elastic material; yarn or fabric made from nylon. **nylons** n. Pl. Stockings made of nylon.

nymph (nimf) n., *Gr. & Rom. Mythol.* Nature goddesses who lived in woods, rivers, and trees; various immature insects, especially the larva which undergoes incomplete metamorphosis. **nymphal** adj.

O

O, o (o) The 15th letter of the English alphabet.

oaf (f) n. A stupid or clumsy person. **oafish** adj. **oafishly** adv.

oak (k) n. A large tree of durable wood bearing acorns. **oaken** adj.

oar (or) n. A long pole, flat at one end, used in rowing a boat.

oasis (´sis) n. pl. **oases** A fertile section in the desert which contains water.

oat (ot) n. A cultivated cereal grass whose grain or seed is used as food.

oath (th) n. A solemn promise in the name of God or on a Bible that a person will speak only the truth.

oat-meal (t´ml´) n. A cooked cereal food made from rolled oats.

o-be-di-ent adj. Obeying or willing to do what one is told. **obedience** n.

o-bese (bs´) adj. Very fat. **obesity** n.

o-bit-u-ar-y (bich´ō er´) n. pl. **obituaries** A published announcement that a person has died, often containing a short biography of the person's life.

ob-ject (ob jekt´) v. To voice disapproval; to protest. n. Something that is visible or can be touched. *Gram.* A word in a sentence which explains who or what is acted upon.

ob-jec-tion (ob jek´shan) n. A feeling of opposition or disagreement; the reason for a disagreement.

ob-jec-tive (ob jek´tiv) adj. Pertaining to or dealing with material objects rather than mental concepts. **objective** n. Something that one works toward, a goal; a purpose.

ob-la-tion (o bl´shan) n. A religious act of sacrifice or offering; that which is offered.

ob-li-ga-tion (ob´li g´shan) n. A promise or feeling of duty; something one must do because one's conscience or the law demands it; a debt which must be repaid.

o-blige (o blj´) v. To constrain; to put in one's debt by a service or favor; to do a favor. **obliger** n. **obligingly** adv.

o-blique (o blk´) adj. Inclined; not level or straight up and down; slanting; indirect.

o-blit-er-ate (o blit´e rt´) v. To blot out or eliminate completely; to wipe out.

o-bliv-i-on (o bliv´ an) n. The condition of being utterly forgotten; the act of forgetting.

ob-liv-i-ous (o bliv´ us) adj. Not aware or conscious of what is happening.

ob-long (ob´long´) adj. Rectangular; longer in one direction than the other; normally, the horizontal dimension is the greater in length.

ob-nox-ious (ob nok´shus) adj. Very unpleasant; repugnant.

o-boe (´b) n. A double reed, tube-shaped woodwind instrument. **oboist** n.

ob-scene (ob sn´) adj. Indecent; disgusting.

ob-scure (ob skr´) *adj.* Remote; not clear; faint. **obscure** *v.* To make dim; to conceal by covering. **obscurely** *adv.* **obscurity** *n.*

ob-serve (ob zerv´) *v.* To pay attention; to watch. **-servable** *adj.* **-servant** *adj.*

ob-ser-va-tion (ob´zer v´shan) *n.* The act of observing something; that which is observed; a judgment or opinion. **observational** *adj.* **-tionally** *adv.*

ob-ser-va-to-ry (ob zer´vatr´) *n. pl.* **observatories** A building or station furnished with instruments used for studying the natural phenomena; a high tower affording a panoramic view.

ob-sess (ob ses´) *v.* To preoccupy the mind with an idea or emotion; to be abnormally preoccupied. **obsession** *n.*

ob-so-lete (ob´so lt´) *adj.* No longer in use; out-of-date. **obsolescence** *n.*

ob-sta-cle (ob´sta kl) *n.* An obstruction; anything which opposes or stands in the way of.

ob-ste-tri-cian (ob´sti trish an) *n.* A physician who specializes in the care of a woman during pregnancy and childbirth.

ob-stet-rics (ob ste´triks) *n.* The branch of medicine which deals with pregnancy and childbirth.

ob-sti-nate (ob´sti nit) *adj.* Stubbornly set to an opinion or course of action; difficult to control or manage; hard-headed. **obstinacy** *n.* **obstinately** *adv.*

ob-strep-er-ous (ob strep´r us) *adj.* Noisy, unruly, or boisterous in resistance to advice or control.

ob-struct (ob strukt´) *v.* To block, hinder or impede. **obstructor** *n.* **obstruction** *n.*

ob-tain (ob tn´) *v.* To acquire or gain possession of. **obtainable** *adj.*

ob-trude (ob trōd´) *v.* To thrust forward without request or warrant; to call attention to oneself.

ob-tuse (ob tōs´) *adj.* Lacking acuteness of feeling; insensitive; not distinct or clear to the senses, as pain or sound. *Bot.* Rounded or blunt at the end, as a petal or leaf.

ob-vi-ate (ob´v t´) *v.* To counter or prevent by effective measures; to provide for.

ob-vi-ous (ob´v us) *adj.* Easily seen, discovered, or understood.

oc-ca-sion (o k´zhan) *n.* The time an event occurs; the event itself; a celebration. **occasion** *v.* To bring about; to cause.

oc-ca-sion-al (o k´zha nal) *adj.* Appearing or occurring irregularly or now and then; intended, made, or suitable for a certain occasion; incidental.

oc-cip-i-tal bone (ok sip´i tal bn´) *n., Anat.* The bone which forms the back of the skull.

oc-cult (o kult´) *adj.* Concealed. **occult** *n.* The action or influence of supernatural agencies or secret knowledge of them.

oc-cu-pan-cy (ok´k pan s) *n.* The state or act of being occupied; the act of holding in possession; the time or term during which something is occupied.

oc-cu-pa-tion (ok´ p´shan) *n.* A job, profession, or vocation; a foreign military force which controls an area.

occupational therapy *n., Med.* The treatment of mental, nervous, or physical disabilities by means of work designed to promote recovery or readjustment.

oc-cu-py (ok´ p´) *v.* To take and retain possession of; to live in. **occupier** *n.*

oc-cur (o ker´) *v.* To suggest; to have something come to mind; to happen.

o-cean (´shan) *n.* An immense body of salt water which covers 3/4 of the earth's surface; one of the oceans. **oceanic** *adj.*

oc-ta-gon (ok´ta gon´) *n.* A polygon with eight angles and eight sides.

oc-tave (ok´tiv) *n., Music* A tone on the eighth degree above or below another tone.

oc-to-pus (ok´to pus) *n. pl.* **octopies** or **octopi** A cephalopod with a sac-like body and eight tentacles containing double rows of suckers.

oc-u-lar (ok´ lr) *adj.* Of or relating to the eye; perceived or done by the eye.

odd (od) *adj.* Unusual; strange; singular; left over; not even. **oddly** *adv.* **oddness** *n.*

odds (odz) *n.* An equalizing advantage given to a weaker opponent; a ratio between the probability against and the probability for something happening or being true.

odds and ends n. Miscellaneous things; remnants; scraps.

ode (d) n. A lyric poem usually honoring a person or event.

o-dor ('dr) n. A smell; a sensation which occurs when the sense of smell is stimulated.

od-ys-sey (od´i s) n. A long voyage marked by many changes of fortune; a spiritual quest.

of (uv) Proceeding; composed of; relating to.

off (of) adv. From a position or place; no longer connected or on. adj. Canceled. prep. Away from. interj. Go away.

of-fend (o fend´) v. To make angry; to arouse resentment; to break a law.

of-fense (o fens´) n. A violation of a duty, rule, or a propriety; the act of causing displeasure; the act of assaulting or attacking; in football and other sports, the team having possession of the ball.

of-fen-sive (o fen´siv) adj. Disagreeable or unpleasant; causing resentment; insulting.

of-fer (o´fr) v. To present for acceptance or rejection; to present as an act of worship; to make available; to present in order to satisfy a requirement.

of-fer-ing (o´fr ing) n. The act of one who offers; a contribution, as money, given to the support of a church.

off-hand (of´hand´) adj. & adv. Without preparation or premeditation.

of-fice (o´fis) n. A place where business or professional duties are conducted; an important job, duty, or position.

of-fi-cer (o´fi sr) n. A person who holds a title, position of authority, or office; a policeman.

of-fi-cial (o fish´al) adj. Something derived from proper authority. official n. One who holds a position or office; a person who referees a game such as football, basketball, or soccer. officialism n.

of-fi-ci-ate (o fish´at´) v. To carry out the duties and functions of a position or office.

of-fi-cious (o fish´us) adj. Offering

one's services or advice in an unduly forward manner. **officiously, officiousness** n.

off-spring (of´spring´) n. pl. offspring or offsprings The descendants of a person, plant, or animal.

of-ten (o´fen) adv. Frequently; many times.

oh () Used to express surprise, fear, or pain.

oil (oil) n. Any of various substances, usually thick, which can be burned or easily melted; a lubricant. **oil** v. To lubricate.

oil-cloth (oil´kloth´) n. A cloth treated with oil which therefore becomes waterproof.

oint-ment (oint´ment) n. An oily substance used on the skin as an aid to healing or to soften the skin.

ok-tane (ok´tn) n. Any of several hydrocarbon compounds which occur in petroleum.

old (ld) adj. Having lived or existed for a long time; of a certain age. **old** n. Former times.

old-en (l´den) adj. Of or relating to times long past; ancient.

old--fash-ioned (ld´fash´ond) adj. Pertaining to or characteristic of former times or old customs; not modern or up-to-date.

ol-fac-to-ry (ol fak´to r) adj. Pertaining to the sense of smell.

ol-ive (ol´iv) n. A small oval fruit from an evergreen tree with leathery leaves and yellow flowers, valuable as a source of oil.

om-e-let or **om-e-lette (om´e lit)** n. A dish made from eggs and other items, such as bacon, cheese, and ham, and cooked until set.

o-men (´men) n. A phenomenon which is thought of as a sign of something to come, whether good or bad.

om-i-nous (om´i nus) adj. Foreshadowed by an omen or by a presentiment of evil; threatening.

o-mis-sion (mish´an) n. The state or act of being omitted; anything neglected or left out.

o-mit (mit´) v. To neglect; to leave out; to overlook.

om-nis-cient (om nish´ent) adj.

Knowing all things; having universal or complete knowledge.

om-niv-or-ous (om niv´r us) adj. Feeding on both vegetable and animal substances; absorbing everything.

on (on) prep. Positioned upon; indicating proximity; indicating direction toward; with respect to; atop. **on** adv. In a position of covering; forward.

once (wuns) adv. A single time; at any one time. **once** conj. As soon as.

once-over (wuns´´vr) n. Slang A swift but comprehensive glance.

on-col-o-gy (on kol o j) n. The study of tumors. **oncological** n. **-gic** adj.

one (wun) adj. Single; undivided. **one** n. A single person; a unit; the first cardinal number (1). **oneself** pron. One's own self.

onesid-ed (wun´s´did) adj. Partial to one side; unjust. **one-sidedness** n.

on-ion (un´yon) n. An edible bulb plant having a pungent taste and odor.

online (on´ln) adj., Computer Science Controlled directly by a computer.

on-ly (n´l) adj. Sole; for one purpose alone. **only** adv. Without anyone or anything else.

on-shore (on´shr´) adj. Moving or coming near or onto the shore.

on-to (on´t) prep. To a position or place; aware of.

o-nus (´nus) n. A burden; a responsibility or duty which is difficult or unpleasant; the blame.

on-ward (on´wrd) adv. Moving forward in time or space. **onwards** adj.

on-yx (on´iks) n. A gemstone; a chalcedony in layers of different colors.

oo-dles (öd´lz) n. pl. Slang A great or large quantity.

ooze (öz) n. A soft deposit of slimy mud on the bottom of a body of water; muddy or marshy ground; a bog. **ooze** v. To flow or leak slowly; to disappear little by little.

o-pal (´pal) n. A translucent mineral composed of silicon, often marked with an iridescent play of colors. **opaline** adj.

o-paque (pk´) adj. Not transparent; dull; obscure. **opacity** n. **-ness** n.

o-pen (´pen) adj. Having no barrier; not sealed, locked, or fastened.

open n. A contest for both amateurs and professionals. **open** v. To begin or start.

op-er-a (´pr a) n. A drama having music as a dominant factor, an orchestral accompaniment, acting, and scenery.

op-er-ate (op´e rt) v. To function, act, or work effectively; to perform an operation, as surgery. **operative** adj.

op-er-a-tion (op´e r´shan) n. The process of operating; the system or method of operating; a series of acts to effect a certain purpose; a process; a procedure performed on the human body with surgical instruments to restore health; various mathematical or logical processes.

op-er-a-tor (op´e r´tr) n. A person who operates a machine; the owner or person in charge of a business.

oph-thal-mol-o-gy (of thal mol´o j) n. A branch of medical science dealing with diseases of the eye, its structure, and functions.

o-pin-ion (o pin´yan) n. A judgment held with confidence; a conclusion held without positive knowledge.

o-pi-um (´p um) n. A bitter, highly addictive drug; a narcotic.

o-pos-sum (o pos´um) n. pl. **opossum** or **opossums** A nocturnal animal which hangs by its tail and carries its young in a pouch.

op-po-nent (o p´nent) n. An adversary; one who opposes another.

op-por-tune (op´r tön´) adj. Occurring at the right or appropriate time.

op-por-tu-ni-ty (op´r tö´ni t) n. pl. **opportunities** A favorable position; a chance for advancement.

op-pose (o pz´) v. To be in direct contention with; to resist; to be against. **opposable** adj. **opposition** n.

op-po-site (op´o zot) adj. Situated or placed on opposing sides. **oppositeness** n.

op-press (o pres´) v. To worry or trouble the mind; to weigh down; to burden as in suffering. **-pression** n. **-pressor** n.

op-tic (op´tik) adj. Pertaining or referring to sight or the eye.

op-ti-cal (op´ti kal) adj. Pertaining to sight; constructed or designed to assist vision.

op-ti-cian (op tish´an) *n.* A person who makes eyeglasses and other optical articles.

op-ti-mism (op´ti miz´um) *n.* A doctrine emphasizing that everything is for the best.

op-ti-mum (op´ti mum) *n. pl.* **optima** The degree or condition producing the most favorable result. **optimum** *adj.* Conducive to the best results.

op-tion (op´shan) *n.* The act or the power of choosing; a choice.

op-tion-al *adj.* Left to one's decision; elective; not required. **optionally** *adv.*

op-tom-e-try (op tom´i tr) *n.* The occupation or profession of examining the eyes and prescribing corrective lenses.

op-u-lence (op´ lens) *n.* Wealth in abundance; affluence.

or (or) *conj.* A word used to connect the second of two choices or possibilities.

-or *suffix* Indicating a person or thing which does something.

or-a-cle (or´a kl) *n.* A seat of worship where ancient Romans and Greeks consulted the gods for answers; a person of unquestioned wisdom.

o-ral (r´al) *adj.* Spoken or uttered through the mouth; taken or administered through the mouth. **orally** *adv.*

or-ange (or´inj) *n.* A citrus fruit which is round and orange in color. **orange** *adj.* Yellowish red.

o-rang-u-tan (rang´e tan´) *n. pl.* **orangutans** A large anthropoid ape having brownish-red hair and very long arms.

o-rate (rt´) *v.* To speak in an elevated manner.

orb (orb) *n.* A globe or sphere.

or-bit (or´bit) *n.* The path of a celestial body or a man-made object. **orbit** *v.* To revolve or move in an orbit; to circle. **orbital** *adj.*

or-chard (or´chrd) *n.* Land that is devoted to the growing of fruit trees.

or-ches-tra (or´ki stra) *n.* A group of musicians performing together on various instruments. **orchestral** *adj.*

orchestra pit *n.* In theatres, the space reserved for musicians.

or-chid (or´kid) *n.* A plant found the world over having three petals in various colors.

or-dain (or dn´) *v.* To appoint as a minister, priest, or rabbi by a ceremony; to decree.

or-deal (or dl´) *n.* A painful or severe test of character or endurance.

or-der (or´dr) *n.* A condition where there is a logical arrangement or disposition of things; sequence or succession; method; an instruction for a person to follow; a request for certain objects. **order** *v.* To command; to demand.

orderly (or´dr l) *adj.* Neat, tidy.

or-di-nance (or´di nans) *n.* A command, rule, or order; a law issued by a municipal body.

or-di-nar-y (or´di ner´) *adj.* Normal; having no exceptional quality; common; average; plain.

ore (r) *n.* A natural underground substance, as a mineral or rock, from which valuable matter is extracted.

o-reg-a-no (o reg´a n´) *n.* A bushy perennial herb of the mint family, used as a seasoning for food.

or-gan (or´gan) *n.* A musical instrument of pipes, reeds, and keyboards which produces sound by means of compressed air; a part of an animal, human, or plant that performs a definite function, as the heart, a kidney, or a stamen.

or-gan-dy *or* **or-gan-die** (or´gan d) *n.* A translucent, stiff fabric of cotton or silk.

or-gan-ic (or gan´ik) *adj.* Effecting or pertaining to the organs of an animal or plant. **organically** *adv.*

or-gan-i-za-tion (or´ga ni z´shan) *n.* The state of being organized or the act of organizing; a group of people united for a particular purpose. **organizational** *adj.*

or-gan-ize (or´ga nz´) *v.* To assemble or arrange with an orderly manner; to arrange by planning. **organization** *n.*

or-gasm (or´gaz um) *n., Physiol.* Intensive emotional excitement; the culmination of a sexual act.

o-ri-ent (r´ ent) *v.* To determine the bearings or right direction with respect to another source.

or-i-gin (or´i jin) *n.* The cause or beginning of something; the source; a beginning place.

o·rig·i·nal (o rij´i nal) adj. Belonging to the first or beginning. **original** n. A new idea produced by one's own imagination; the first of a kind.

originality n.

or·i·ole (r´ l´) n. A songbird having brightly colored yellow and black plumage in the males.

or·na·ment (or´na ment) n. A decoration. **ornament** v. To adorn or beautify. **ornamental** adj. **ornamentally** adv.

or·nate (or nt´) adj. Excessively ornamental; showy, as a style of writing.

or·phan (or´fan) n. A child whose parents are deceased. **orphan** v. **orphanage** n.

or·ris (or´is) n. Any of several species having a fragrant root and used in medicine, perfumes, and cosmetics.

or·tho·dox (or´tho doks´) adj. Following established traditions and beliefs, especially in religion.

os·cil·late (os´i lt) v. To swing back and forth with regular motion, as a pendulum. **oscillation** n. **oscillator** n. **oscillatory** adj.

os·mi·um (oz´m um) n. A hard, but brittle metallic element symbolized as Os.

os·mo·sis (oz m´sis) n. The tendency of fluids separated by a semipermeable membrane to pass through it and become mixed and equal in strength. **osmotic** adj.

osteo– n. comb. form Bone; pertaining to the bones.

os·te·op·a·thy (os´t op´a th) n. A medical practice based on the theory that diseases are due chiefly to abnormalities of the body, which can be restored by manipulation of the parts by therapeutic measures.

os·te·o·po·ro·sis (os´t pe´r es) n. A disorder causing gradual deterioration of bone tissue, usually in older women.

os·tra·cize (os´tra sz´) v. To exile or exclude from a group; to shut out.

oth·er (uth´r) adj. Additional; alternate; different from what is implied or specified. **other** pron. A different person or thing.

oth·er·wise (uth´r wz´) adv. Under different conditions of circumstances.

ot·ter (ot´r) n. pl. otter or otters Webfooted aquatic mammals, related to the weasel.

ouch (ouch) n. & interj. An exclamation to express sudden pain.

ought (ot) v. Used to show or express a moral duty or obligation; to be advisable or correct.

ounce (ouns) n. A unit of weight which equals 1/16 of a pound.

our (our) adj. Of or relating to us ourselves. **our** pron. The possessive case of the pronoun we. **ourselves** Our own selves.

oust (oust) v. To eject; to remove with force.

out (out) adj. & adv. Away from the center or inside; away. **out** n. A means of escape. **out** prep. Through; forward from.

out·age (ou´tij) n. A loss of electricity.

out·break (out´brk´) n. A sudden outburst; an occurrence.

out·cast (out´kast´) n. A person who is excluded; a homeless person.

out·come (out´kum´) n. A consequence or result.

out·dated adj. Old-fashioned and obsolete.

out·do (out´dö´) v. To excel; achieve more.

out·land·ish (out lan´dish) adj. Extremely ridiculous, unusual, or strange.

out·law (out´lo´) n. A person who habitually breaks the law; a criminal. **outlaw** v. To ban; prohibit; to deprive of legal protection.

out·let (out´let) n. An exit.

out·line (out´ln´) n. A rough draft showing the main features of something.

out·look (out´lek´) n. A person's point of view; an area offering a view of something.

out·num·ber (out´num´br) v. To go over or exceed in number.

out·pa·tient (out´p´shent) n. A patient who visits a clinic or hospital for treatment but does not spend the night.

out·put (out´pet´) n. Production or yield during a given time.

out·rage (out´rj) n. An extremely violent act of violence or cruelty; the violent emotion such an act engenders.

out-right (out´rt´) *adj.* Free from reservations; complete; entire.

out-spo-ken (out´spo´ken) *adj.* Spoken without reserve; candid. **-kenly** *adv.*

out-stand-ing (out´stan´ding) *adj.* Excellent; prominent; unsettled, as a bill owed; projecting.

out-ward (out´wrd) *adj.* Pertaining to the outside or exterior; superficial.

out-wit (out´wit´) *v.* To trick, baffle, or outsmart with ingenuity.

o-val (´val) *adj.* Having the shape of an egg; an ellipse.

o-va-ry (´va r) *n. pl.* **ovaries** One of the pair of female reproductive glands.

o-va-tion (´shan) *n.* An enthusiastic display of approval for a person or a performance; applause.

ov-en (uv´en) *n.* An enclosed chamber used for baking, drying, or heating.

o-ver (´vr) *prep.* Above; across; upon. *adv.* Covering completely; thoroughly; again; repetition. **over** *adj.* Higher; upper. **over-** *prefix* Excessive, as over-do.

o-ver-act (´vr akt´) *v.* To act in an exaggerated way.

o-ver-all (´vr ol´) *adj.* Including or covering everything; from one side or end to another; generally. **overalls** *n. pl.* Pants with a bib and shoulder straps.

o-ver-arm (´vr ärm´) *adj.* Thrown or executed with the arms raised above the shoulders.

o-ver-board (´vr brd´) *adv.* Over the side of a boat or ship into the water.

o-ver-cast (´vr kast´) *adj.* Gloomy; obscured. *Meteor.* Clouds covering more than 9/10 of the sky.

o-ver-come (´vr kum´) *v.* To prevail; to conquer or defeat. **overcomer** *n.*

o-ver-con-fi-dence (´vr kon´fi dens) *n.* Extreme or excessive confidence.

o-ver-do (´vr dö´) *v.* To do anything excessively; to overcook.

o-ver-dose (´vr ds´) *n.* To take an excessive dose of medication.

o-ver-due (´vr dö´) *adj.* Past the time of return or payment.

o-ver-haul (´vr hol´) *v.* To make all needed repairs.

o-ver-head (´vr hed´) *n.* The operating expenses of a company, including utilities, rent, and upkeep. **overhead** *adj.* Situated above the level of one's head.

o-ver-look (´vr lek´) *v.* To disregard or fail to notice something purposely.

o-ver-night (´vr nt´) *adj.* Lasting the whole night; from dusk to dawn.

o-ver-pass (´vr pas´) *n.* A raised section of highway which crosses other lines of traffic. **overpass** *v.* To cross, pass over, or go through something; to overlook.

o-ver-ride (´vr rd´) *v.* To disregard; to take precedence over; to declare null and void.

o-ver-rule (´vr röl´) *v.* To put aside by virtue of higher authority.

o-ver-run (´vr run´) *v.* To spread out; to extend or run beyond.

o-ver-see (´vr s´) *v.* To supervise; to direct.

o-ver-shoe (o´vr shö´) *n.* A galosh worn over a shoe for protection from snow or water.

o-ver-sight (´vr st´) *n.* A mistake made inadvertently.

o-ver-size *or* **oversized** (´vr sz´) *adj.* Larger than the average size of something.

o-ver-step (´vr step´) *v.* To go beyond a limit or restriction.

o-ver-the-counter (´vr thekoun´tr) *adj.* Not traded on an organized security exchange; of or relating to medicine which can be purchased without a prescription.

o-ver-whelm (´vr hwelm´) *v.* To overcome completely; to make helpless.

ov-u-late (´v lt´) *v.* To discharge or produce eggs from an ovary.

o-vum (´vum) *n. pl.* **ova** The female reproductive cell.

owe ( ) *v.* To be in debt for a certain amount; to have a moral obligation.

owl (oul) *n.* A predatory nocturnal bird, having large eyes, a short-hooked bill, and long powerful claws. **owlish** *adj.*

own (n) *adj.* Belonging to oneself. **own** *v.* To possess; to confess; to admit.

ox (oks) *n. pl.* **oxen** A bovine animal used domestically in much the same way as a horse; an adult castrated bull.

ox-ford (oks´frd) *n.* A shoe which is laced and tied over the instep.

ox-ide (ok´sd) *n.* A compound of oxygen and another element.

ox-y-gen (ok´si jen) *n.* A colorless, odorless, tasteless gaseous element essential to life, symbolized by O.

oxygen mask *n.* A device worn over the mouth and nose through which a person can receive oxygen as an aid to breathing.

oys-ter (oi´str) *n.* An edible marine mollusk.

o-zone (´zn) *n.* A pale, bluish form of oxygen gas with an odor like chlorine, formed by an electrical discharge in the air. *Slang* Air.

P

P, p (p) The 16th letter of the English alphabet.

pace (ps) *n.* A person's step in walking or the length of a person's step; stride; the gait of a horse in which the legs on the same side are moved at the same time. **pacer** *n.*

Pa-cif-ic (pa sif´ik) *n.* The largest ocean on the earth, extending from North & South America westward to Asia and Australia.

pac-i-fy (pas´i f) *v.* To quiet or soothe anger or distress; to calm.

pack (pak) *n.* A bundle; a group or number of things tied or wrapped up; a full set of associated or like things, such as a pack of cards; a group of wolves or wild dogs that hunt together. **pack** *v.* To put things together in a trunk, box, or suitcase; to put away for storage. **send packing** To force to leave with haste and without ceremony.

package (pak´ij) *n.* Something tied up, wrapped or bound together.

pact (pakt) *n.* An agreement between groups, nations, or people.

pad (pad) *n.* Anything stuffed with soft material and used to protect against blows; a cushion; a drawing or writing tablet of paper gummed together at one edge; the cushion-like part of the foot on some animals, as the dog. *Slang* A person's home. **pad** *v.* To stuff, line, or protect with soft material; to extend or lengthen something by inserting unnecessary matter; to travel by foot in a soft and nearly inaudible way.

pad-dy wag-on *n. Slang* A police vehicle for transporting suspects.

pad-lock (pad´lok) *n.* A detachable lock, having a pivoted u-shaped hasp which can be inserted through a ring and then locked.

pa-dre (pa´dr) *n.* A title used in Spain and Italy for a priest.

pa-gan (pa´gan) *n.* A person who does not acknowledge God in any religion; a heathen. **pagan** *adj.* **paganism** *n.*

page (pj) *n.* A person hired to deliver messages or run errands; one side of the leaf of a book or letter. **page** *v.* To call or summon a person.

pag-eant (paj´ent) *n.* An elaborate exhibition or spectacular parade for public celebration.

pa-go-da (pa g´da) *n.* A sacred Buddhist tower built as a memorial or shrine.

paid *v.* Past tense of pay.

pail (pl) *n.* A cylindrical container usually having a handle; a bucket.

pain (pn) *n.* The unpleasant feeling resulting from injury or disease; any distress or suffering of the mind; sorrow. **pain** *v.* To cause or experience pain. **painful** *adj.* **painless** *adj.*

pair (pâr) *n.* Two things that are similar and used together; something made of two parts which are used together; two persons or animals which live or work together.

pa-ja-mas (pa jäm´az) *n.* A loose-fitting garment for sleeping, consisting of a jacket and pants.

pal-ace (pal´is) *n.* The royal residence of a sovereign, as of a king; a mansion.

pale (pl) *n.* The pointed stake of a fence; a picket; an area that is enclosed within bounds. **pale** *adj.* Having a whitish, or lighter than normal, complexion; pallid; weak.

pal-ette (pal´it) *n.* A thin oval board with a hole for the thumb, on which an artist lays and mixes colors.

pal-in-drome (pal´in drm´) *n.* A word, number, or sentence which reads the same backward or forward, such as toot or 1991.

pal-i-sade (pal´i sd´) *n.* A fence made of stakes for protection. **palisade** *v.*

pall-bear-er (pol´bâr´r) *n.* A person who assists in carrying a coffin at a funeral.

pal-let (pal´it) n. A wooden platform on which material for freight shipments can be moved or stored.

pal-lid (pal´id) adj. Deficient in color; lacking sparkle.

pal-lor (pal´r) n. Lacking color; paleness.

pal-sy (pol´z) n. pl. -ies Paralysis; the loss of ability to control one's movements.

pam-per (pam´pr) v. To treat with extreme care.

pam-phlet (pam´flit) n. A brief publication which is not permanently bound.

pan-a-ce-a (pan´a s´a) n. A remedy for all diseases, difficulties, or ills; a cure-all.

pan-cre-as (pan´kr as) n., Anat. An irregularly shaped, large gland situated behind the stomach which releases digestive enzymes and produces insulin. **pancreatic** adj.

pan-da (pan´da) n. A large bear-like animal of China and Tibet with black and white fur and rings around the eyes; a raccoon-like animal of the southeastern Himalayas with a ringed tail and reddish fur.

pan-de-mo-ni-um (pan´de m´n um) n. A place marked with disorder and wild confusion; disorder; confusion.

pan-der-er (pan´dr r) n. A go-between in sexual affairs; a pimp; one who profits from the base desires or passions of others. **pander** v. To act as a panderer for someone.

pan-ic (pan´ik) n. A sudden unreasonable fear which overpowers. **panic** v. To cause or to experience panic. **panicky** adj.

pan-o-ply (pan´o pl) n. pl. **panoplies** The complete equipment of a warrior, including his armor and weapons.

pan-o-ram-a (pan´o ram´a) n. An unlimited or complete view in all directions of what is visible.

pan-sy (pan´z) n. pl. **pansies** A flowering garden plant bearing blossoms in a variety of colors.

pant (pant) v. To breathe in rapid or short gasps; to yearn. **pant** n. A short breath.

pan-the-ism (pan´th iz´um) n. The belief that the laws and forces of nature are all manifestations of God.

pantheist n.

pan-ther (pan´thr) n. A black leopard in its unspotted form. **pantheress** n.

pan-to-mime (pan´to mm´) n. Voiceless communication done solely by means of facial and body gestures. **pantomime** v. To express or act in pantomime.

pan-try (pan´tr) n. pl. **pantries** A closet or room for the storage of food, dishes, and other kitchen items.

pants (pants) n. pl. Trousers; underpants.

pap (pap) n. A soft food for invalids or babies.

pa-pa-cy (p´pa s) n. pl. **papacies** A pope's term in office; the jurisdiction of a pope.

pa-per (p´pr) n. A substance made of pulp from wood and rags, formed into sheets for printing, wrapping and writing.

pa-poose (pa pös´) n. A North American Indian child or baby.

pa-pri-ka (pa pr´ka) n. A dark red seasoning powder made by grinding red peppers.

Pap test n. A test in which a smear of bodily secretion from the uterus is examined for the early detection of cancer.

par-a-ble (par´a bl) n. A short, fictitious story which illustrates a moral lesson.

par-a-chute (par´a shöt´) n. A folding umbrella- shaped apparatus made of light fabric used to make a safe landing after a free fall from an airplane. **parachutist** n.

pa-rade (pa rd´) n. An organized public procession; a march. **parader** n.

par-a-dise (par´a ds´) n. A state or place of beauty, bliss or delight; heaven. **paradisiac**. **paradisiacal** adj.

par-a-dox (par´a doks´) n. A statement which seems opposed to common sense or contradicts itself, but is perhaps true. **paradical** adj.

par-af-fin (par´a fin) n. A white, waxy substance derived from petroleum and used to make lubricants, candles, and sealing materials. **paraffin** v.

par-a-gon (par´a gon´) n. A pattern or model of excellence or perfection.

par-a-graph (par´a graf´) *n.* A section of a composition dealing with a single idea, containing one or more sentences with the first line usually indented.

par-a-keet (par´a ket´) *n.* A small parrot with a long, wedge-shaped tail.

par-al-lel (par´a lel´) *adj.* Moving in the same direction but separated by a distance, as railroad tracks. *n.* A parallel curve, line, or surface.

par-al-lel-o-gram (par´a lel´o gram´) *n.* A four-sided figure having parallel opposite sides which are equal.

pa-ral-y-sis (pa ral´i sis) *n. pl.* **-ses** Complete or partial loss of the ability to feel any sensation or to move.

par-a-lyze (par´a lz´) *v.* To cause to be powerless or inoperative.

par-a-med-ic (par´a med´ik) *n.* A person trained to give emergency medical treatment until a doctor is available.

par-a-mount (par´a mount´) *adj.* Superior to all others in rank, importance, and power.

par-a-noi-a (par´a noi´a) *n.* Mental insanity that is marked by systematic delusions of persecution or grandeur.

par-a-pher-na-lia (par´a fr nl´ya) *n.* Personal effects or belongings; the apparatus or articles used in some activities; equipment.

par-a-phrase (par´a frz´) *v.* To put something written or spoken into different words while retaining the same meaning.

par-a-site (par´a st´) *n.*, *Biol.* An organism which lives, grows, feeds, and takes shelter in or on another organism; a person depending entirely on another without providing something in return.

par-a-sol (par´a sol´) *n.* A small umbrella used as protection from the sun.

par-a-troops (par´ *n. pl.* Troops which are equipped and trained to parachute behind enemy lines.

par-boil (par´boil´) *v.* To precook something in boiling water.

par-cel (par´sel) *n.* A wrapped package; a bundle; a portion or plat of land.

parch (parch) *v.* To become very dry from intense heat; to become dry from thirst or the lack of water.

parch-ment (parch´ment) *n.* Goatskin or sheepskin prepared with a pumice stone and used as a material for writing or drawing.

par-don (par´don) *v.* To forgive someone for an offense; in law, to allow a convicted person freedom from the penalties of an office or crime. **pardonable** *adj.*

pare (par) *v.* To cut away or remove the outer surface gradually. **parer** *n.*

par-e-gor-ic (par´e gor´ik) *n.* A medication used to relieve stomach pains.

par-ent (par´ent) *n.* A mother or father; a forefather; an ancestor; a source; a cause. **parentage** *n.* **parenthood** *n.* **parental** *adj.*

pa-ren-the-sis (pa ren´thi sis) *n. pl.* **parentheses** One of a pair of curved lines ( ) used to enclose a qualifying or explanatory remark.

par-ish (par´ish) *n.* In association with the Roman Catholic Church, the district under the charge of a priest; the members of a parish.

park (park) *n.* A tract of land used for recreation. **park** *v.* To leave something temporarily in a stopping place or a garage or lot, as a car.

par-lia-ment (par´li ment) *n.* The assembly which constitutes the law-making body of various countries, as the United Kingdom.

pa-ro-chi-al (pa r´k al) *adj.* Belonging to a local parish; having to do with a parish.

pa-role (pa rl´) *n.* The conditional release of a prisoner before his sentence expires.

par-ox-ysm (par´ok siz´um) *n.* A violent attack or outburst; a spasm.

par-ri-cide (par´i sd´) *n.* A person who murders his mother or father; the crime of murdering one's parents. **-cidal** *adj.*

par-ry (par´) *v.* To avoid something; turn aside.

parse (pars) *v.* To identify the parts of speech in a sentence and to indicate their relationship to each other.

par-si-mo-ny (par´si m´n) *n.* Extreme reluctance to use one's resources or to spend money. **parsimonious** *adj.*

pars-ley (pars´l) *n.* An herb with curly leaves which is used for seasoning and garnishing.

par-son (pär´son) n. A pastor or clergyman.

parsonage (pär´so nij) n. The home provided by a church for its parson.

part (pärt) n. A segment, portion, or division of a whole; a component for a machine; the role of a character, as in a play.

par-take (pär tk´) v. To have a share or part; to take; to take a part in something.

par-tial (pär´shal) adj. Incomplete; inclined to favor one side more than the other.

par-tic-i-pate (pär tis´i pt´) v. To join in or share; to take part. **participant** n.

par-ti-cle (pär´ti kl) n. A very small piece of solid matter. *Gram.* A group of words, such as articles, prepositions, and conjunctions which convey very little meaning but help to connect, specify, or limit the meanings of other words.

par-tic-u-lar (pr tik´ lr) adj. Having to do with a specific person, group, thing, or category; noteworthy; precise.

part-ing (pär´ting) n. A division; a separation; the place where a division or separation occurs. adj. Done, given, or said on departing.

par-ti-tion (pär tish´an) n. A separation or division. **partition** v. To divide.

part-ner (pärt´nr) n. One who shares something with another.

part-ner-ship n. Two or more persons who run a business together and share in the profits and losses.

par-tridge (pär´trij) n. pl. **partridges** A plump or stout-bodied game bird.

pass (pas) v. To proceed; to move; to transfer; to go away or come to an end; to get through a course, trial or test; to approve; to vote for.

pas-sage (pas´ij) n. The act of going; proceeding, the enactment by a legislature of a bill into law; a small portion or part of a book or speech; something, as a path or channel, through or along which something else may pass.

pas-sen-ger (pas´en jr) n. One who travels in a vehicle, car, plane, boat, etc.

pas-sive (pas´iv) adj. Not working, acting, or operating; inactive; acted upon,

influenced, or affected by something external. *Gram.* Designating the verb form which indicates the subject is receiving the action.

Pass-o-ver (pas´´vr) n. The Jewish holiday which commemorates the Exodus from Egypt.

pass-port (pas´prt) n. An official permission issued to a person allowing him to travel out of this country and to return; a document of identification.

pass-word (pas´werd´) n. A secret word allowing a person to prove authorization to pass or enter.

past (past) adj. Having to do with or existing at a former time. **past** n. Before the present time; a person's history or background. **past** adv. To go by. **past** prep. After; beyond in time; beyond the power, reach, or influence.

pas-tel (pa stel´) n. A crayon made of ground pigments; a drawing made with these crayons. **pastel** adj. Pale and light in color or shade.

pas-teur-i-za-tion n. The process of killing disease-producing microorganisms by heating the liquid to a high temperature for a period of time.

pas-time (pas´tm´) n. Spending spare time in a pleasant way; a diversion.

pas-tor (pas´tr) n. A Christian clergyman in charge of a church or congregation.

pas-tor-al (pas´tr al) adj. Referring to the duties of a pastor; pertaining to life in the country; rural or rustic. **pastoral** n. A poem dealing with country life.

past participle n. A participle used with reference to actions and conditions in the past.

pas-try (p´strt) n. Food made with dough or having a crust made of dough, as pies, tarts, or other desserts.

pas-ture (pas´chr) n. An area for grazing of domestic animals.

pat (pat) v. To tap lightly with something flat. **pat** n. A soft, caressing stroke.

pat-ent (pat´ent) n. A governmental protection assuring an inventor the exclusive right of manufacturing, using, exploiting, and selling an invention. **patent** adj. Evident; obvious.

pa-ter-nal (pa ter´nal) adj. Relating to

or characteristic of a father; inherited from a father. **paternally** adv. **paternalism** n.

path (path) n. A track or course; a route; a course of action or life.

pa·thet·ic (pa thet´ik) adj. A rousing pity, tenderness, or sympathy. **pathetically** adv.

pa·thol·o·gy (pa thol´o j) n. The science that deals with facts about diseases, their nature and causes. **pathologic** adj.

pa·thos (p´thos) n. A quality in a person that evokes sadness or pity.

pa·tience (p´shens) n. The quality, state, or fact of being patient; the ability to be patient.

pa·tient (p´shent) adj. Demonstrating uncomplaining endurance under distress. **patient** n. A person under medical care. **patiently** adv.

pa·ti·o (pat´ ´) n. An area attached to a house, used for enjoyment and entertainment.

pa·tri·arch (p´tr ärk´) n. The leader of a tribe or family who rules by paternal right; a very old, revered man. **patriarchal** adj. **patriarchy** n.

pa·tri·ot (p´tr ot) n. A person who loves and defends his country. **patriotic** adj.

pa·trol (pa trl´) n. Walking around an area for the purpose of maintaining or observing security; a person or group carrying out this action. **patrol** v.

pa·tron (p´tron) n. A person who fosters, protects, or supports a person, enterprise, or thing; a regular customer.

pat·sy (pat´s) n. pl. patsies Slang A person who is taken advantage of.

pat·ty (pat´) n. pl. patties A small, flat piece of chopped meat.

pau·per (po´pr) n. A very poor person who depends on charity. **pauperism** n.

pause (poz) v. To linger, hesitate, or stop for a time. **pause** n.

pave (pv) v. To surface with gravel, concrete, asphalt, or other material.

pave·ment (pv´ment) n. A surface that has been paved.

pa·vil·ion (pa vil´yon) n. A large, roofed structure used for shelter.

paw (po) n. The foot of an animal. **paw** v. To handle clumsily or rudely.

pawn (pon) n. Something given as security for a loan; a hostage; a chessman of little value.

pawn-broker (pon´br´kr) n. A person who lends money on pledged personal property.

pay (p) v. To give a person what is due for a debt, purchase, or work completed; to compensate; to suffer the consequences.

pay·ment (p´ment) n. The act of paying.

pay-roll (p´rl´) n. The amount of money to be paid to a list of employees.

peace (ps) n. A state of physical or mental tranquillity; calm; serenity; the absence of war; the state of harmony between people. **peaceful** adj. **peaceably** adv.

pea·cock (p´kok´) n. A male bird with brilliant blue or green plumage and a long iridescent tail that fans out to approximately six feet.

peak (pk) n. A projecting edge or point; the summit of a mountain; the top. **peak** v. To bring to the maximum.

peal (pl) n. The ringing sound of bells; the long, loud sound of thunder or laughter. **peal** v. To ring.

pearl (perl) n. A smooth, rounded deposit formed around a grain of sand in the shell of various mollusks, especially the oyster; anything which is precious, rare, or fine.

peas·ant (pez´ant) n. A farmhand or rustic workman; an uneducated person of the lowest class. Slang Uneducated or uncouth.

peat (pt) n. The black substance formed when plants begin to decay in wet ground, as bogs.

peat moss n. A moss which grows in very wet areas, used as plant food and mulch.

peb·ble (peb´l) n. A small, smooth stone. **pebble** v. To treat, as to give a rough texture.

pe·can (pi kän´) n. A large tree of the central and southern United States with an edible oval, thin-shelled nut.

peck (pek) v. To strike with the beak; to eat without any appetite, taking small bites. **peck** n. A measure which equals 1/4 of a bushel.

pec-tin (pek´tin) *n.* A complex carbohydrate found in ripe fruits and used in making jelly.

pe-cu-liar (pi kl´yr) *adj.* Odd; strange.

ped-al (ped´al) *n.* A lever usually operated by the foot. **pedal** *v.*

ped-dle (ped´l) *v.* To travel around in an attempt to sell merchandise.

ped-es-tal (ped´i stal) *n.* A support or base for a statue. **to put on a pedestal** To hold something in high respect.

pe-des-tri-an (pe des´tr an) *n.* A person traveling by foot.

pe-di-at-rics (p´d a´triks) *n.* The branch of medicine dealing with the care of children and infants. **pediatric** *adj.* **pediatrician** *n.*

ped-i-cure (ped´i kr´) *n.* The cosmetic care of the toenails and feet. **pedicurist** *n.*

ped-i-gree (ped´i gr´) *n.* A line of ancestors, especially of an animal of pure breed.

ped-i-ment (ped´i ment) *n.* A broad, triangular architectural or decorative part above a door.

pe-dom-e-ter (pe dom´i tr) *n.* An instrument which indicates the number of miles one has walked.

pe-dun-cle (pi dung´kl) *n., Biol.* A stalk-like support in some plants and animals.

peek (pk) *v.* To look shyly or quickly from a place of hiding; to glance.

peel (pl) *n.* The natural rind or skin of a fruit. *v.* To pull or strip the skin or bark off; to remove in thin layers. *Slang* To undress.

peen (pn) *n.* The ball-shaped end of a hammer opposite the flat, striking surface.

peep (pp) *v.* To utter a very small and weak sound, as of a young bird.

peer (pr) *v.* To look searchingly; to come partially into one's view. *n.* An equal; a member of the British nobility, as a duke or earl.

peg (peg) *n.* A small pin, usually of wood or metal; a projecting pin on which something may be hung. *Slang* An artificial leg, often made of wood.

pei-gnoir (pn wär´) *n.* A woman's loose fitting dressing gown.

pe-koe (p´k) *n.* A superior black tea

made from young or small leaves.

pel-i-can (pel´i kan) *n.* A large, web-footed bird with a large pouch under the lower bill for the temporary storage of fish.

pel-let (pel´it) *n.* A small round ball made from paper or wax; a small bullet or shot.

pelt (pelt) *n.* The skin of an animal with the fur attached.

pel-vis (pel´vis) *n. pl.* **pelvises** *or* **pelves** The structure of the vertebrate skeleton which rests on the lower limbs, supporting the spinal column.

pen (pen) *n.* An instrument used for writing.

pe-nal (pn´al) *adj.* Of or pertaining to punishment or penalties.

pen-al-ty (pen´al t) *n. pl.* **penalties** The legal punishment for an offense or crime; something which is forfeited when a person fails to meet a commitment; in sports, a punishment or handicap imposed for breaking a rule.

pen-ance (pen´ans) *n.* A voluntary act to show sorrow or repentance for sin.

pen-cil (pen´sil) *n.* A writing or drawing implement made from graphite. **pencil** *v.* To make, write, or draw with a pencil.

pen-dant *or* **pen-dent** (pen´dant) *n.* Something suspended.

pend-ing (pen´ding) *adj.* Not yet decided; imminent. **pending** *prep.* During; until.

pen-du-lous (pen´ja lus) *adj.* Hanging downward so as to swing; wavering.

pen-du-lum (pen´ja lum) *n.* A suspended object free to swing back and forth.

pen-e-trate (pen´i trt´) *v.* To force a way through or into; to pierce; to enter; to pass through something. **-trable** *adj.*

pen-i-cil-lin (pen´i sil´in) *n.* A powerful antibiotic derived from mold and used to treat certain types of bacterial infections.

pen-in-su-la (pe nin´sa la) *n.* A piece of land projecting into water from a larger land mass.

pe-nis (p´nis) *n. pl.* **penises** *or* **penes** The male sex organ; the male organ through which urine leaves the body.

pen-i-tent (pen´i tent) *adj.* Having feelings of guilt and remorse for one's

misdeeds or sins; sorry. **penitence** *n.*
penitential *adj.*

pen-ny (pen´) *n. pl.* **pennies** A United
States coin worth one cent ($.01).

pen-sion (pen´shǝn) *n.* The amount of
money a person receives regularly
after retirement. **pensioner** *n.*

pen-sive (pen´siv) *adj.* Involved in serious, quiet reflection; causing melancholy thought. **pensively** *adv.* **pensive-
ness** *n.*

pen-ta-gon (pen´ta gon´) *n.* An object
or building having five sides and five
interior angles. **Pentagon** The five-
sided office building in Arlington, Va.
which houses the Defense Department.

pent-house (pent´hous) *n.* An apartment built on the roof of a building.

pe-on (p´on) *n.* A servant; a person
engaged in menial work. **peonage** *n.*

pe-o-ny (p´o n) *n. pl.* **peonies** A plant
with a large, fragrant red, white, or
pink flower.

peo-ple (p´pl) *n.* Human beings; a body
of persons living in the same country,
under the same government, and
speaking the same language; one's relatives or family.

pep-per (pep´r) *n.* A strong, aromatic
condiment. **pepper** *v.* To pelt or sprin-
kle.

pep-tic (pep´tik) *adj.* Pertaining to or
aiding digestion.

per an-num (pr an´um) *adv.* For, by, or
in each year; annually.

per-cale (pr kl´) *n.* A closely woven cotton fabric.

per cap-i-ta (pr kap´i ta) *adj. & adv.,
Latin* Of each individual.

per-ceive (pr sv´) *v.* To become aware of
by the senses; to understand; to feel or
observe. **-ceivable** *adj.* **-ceivably** *adv.*

per-cent-age (pr sen´tijj) *n.* The rate per
hundred; a part or proportion in relation to a whole. *Slang* Profit; advantage.

per-cept (per´sept) *n.* A mental impression of something perceived; the
immediate knowledge obtained from
perceiving.

per-cip-i-ent (pr sip´ent) *adj.* Having
the power of perception. **-ence** *n.*

per-co-late (per´ko lt´) *v.* To pass or
cause to pass through a porous sub-

stance; to filter. **percolation** *n.* **perco-
lator** *n.*

per-cus-sion (pr kush´an) *n.* The sharp
striking together of one body against
another; the striking of a cap in a
firearm. *Mus.* An instrument which
makes music when it is struck, as a
drum or a cymbal.

per-en-ni-al (pe ren´ al) *adj.* Lasting
from year to year; perpetual. *n.* A plant
which lives through the winter and
blooms again in the spring. **-ly** *adv.*

per-fect (per´fikt) *adj.* Having no defect
or fault; flawless; accurate; absolute.
perfect (per fekt´) *v.* To make perfect.
perfectly *adv.* **perfectness, -ion** *n.*

per-form (pr form´) *v.* To execute or
carry out an action; to act or function
in a certain way; to act; to give a performance or exhibition. **performable**
adj. **performer** *n.*

per-fume (per´fm) *n.* A fragrant substance which emits a pleasant scent;
one distilled from flowers. **perfume** *v.*

per-haps (pr haps´) *adv.* Possibly;
maybe; not sure.

per-i-gee (per´i j´) *n.* The point of an
orbit when a satellite of the earth is
closest to the earth; the lowest part of
an orbit.

per-il (per´l) *n.* A source of danger;
exposure to the chance of injury; danger. **perilous** *adj.*

pe-ri-od (pr´od) *n.* An interval of time
marked by certain conditions; an interval of time that is regarded as a phase
in development; menstruation; the
punctuation mark (.) which indicates
the end of a sentence or an abbrevia-
tion.

pe-riph-er-y (pe rif´e r) *n. pl.* **periph-
eries** The outer part, boundary, or surface. **peripheral** *adj.*

per-ish (per´ish) *v.* To ruin or spoil; to
suffer an untimely or violent death.

per-i-win-kle (per´i wing´kl) *n.* Any of
several edible marine snails; a trailing
evergreen plant with blue and sometimes white flowers.

per-jure (per´jr) *v.* To give false testimony while under oath. **perjury** *n.*

per-ma-nent (per´ma nent) *adj.*
Continuing in the same state; lasting
indefinitely; enduring.

per-me-ate (per´m t´) v. To spread through; to pervade; to pass through the pores. **permeation. -meable** adj.

per-mis-sion (pr mish´an) n. The act of permitting something; consent.

per-mit (pr mit´) v. To consent to; to allow. **permit** n. An official document giving permission for a specific activity.

per-ni-cious (pr nish´us) adj. Very harmful; malicious. **perniciously** adv.

per-ox-ide (pe rok´sd) n. Chem. Oxide containing the highest proportion of oxygen for a given series; a chemical used with other ingredients to bleach the hair.

per-pen-dic-u-lar (per´pen dik´ lr) adj. Being at right angles to the plane of the horizon. Math. Meeting a plane or given line at right angles. **perpendicular** n. **perpendicularity** n. **perpendicularly** adv.

per-pe-trate (per´pi trt´) v. To perform; to commit; to be guilty. **petration** n.

per-pet-u-al (pr pech´ö al) adj. Lasting or continuing forever or an unlimited time.

per-plex (pleks´) v. To confuse or be confused; to make complicated. **perplexing** adj. **perplexingly** adv.

per-se-cute (per´se kt´) v. To harass or annoy persistently; to oppress because of one's religion, beliefs, or race. **persecution** n. **persecutor** n. **-tive** adj.

per-se-vere (per´se vr´) v. To persist in any purpose or idea; to strive in spite of difficulties or obstacles. **perseverance** n.

per-sist (pr sist´) v. To continue firmly and despite obstacles; to endure.

per-son (per´son) n. A human being; an individual; the personality of a human being. Law Any human being, corporation, or other entity having legal rights and duties.

per-son-al (per´sö nal) adj. Belonging to a person or persons; of the body or person; relating to oneself; done by oneself.

per-son-i-fy (pr son´i f´) v. To think of or represent as having human qualities or life; to be a symbol of. **-fier** n.

per-son-nel (per´sö nel´) n. The body of people working for a business or service.

per-spec-tive (pr spek´tiv) n. A painting or drawing in which objects seem to have depth and distance.

per-spi-ra-tion (per ´spirshan) n. The salty fluid excreted from the body by the sweat glands.

per-spire (pr spr´) v. To give off perspiration.

per-suade (pr swd´) v. To cause to convince or believe by means of reasoning or argument. **-er** n. **persuasive** adj.

per-tain (pr tn´) v. To relate to; to refer to; to belong as a function, adjunct or quality; to be appropriate or fitting.

per-ti-na-cious (per´ti n´shus) adj. Adhering firmly to an opinion, belief, or purpose; stubbornly persistent. **pertinaciously** adv.

per-ti-nent (per´ti nent) adj. Relating to the matter being discussed.

per-turb (pr terb´) v. To disturb, make anxious, or make uneasy; to cause confusion.

per-vade (pr vd´) v. To spread through every part of something; to permeate.

per-ver-sion (pr ver´zhan) n. The act of being led away from the accepted course; a deviant form of sexual behavior.

per-vert (pr vert´) v. To lead away from the proper cause; to use in an improper way. **pervert** n. A person characterized by or practicing sexual perversion. **perverted** adj.

pes-si-mism (pes´i miz´um) n. The tendency to take a gloomy view of affairs or situations and to anticipate the worst. **pessimist** n.

pest (pest) n. A person or thing which is a nuisance; an annoying person or thing; a destructive insect, plant, or animal.

pes-ter (pes´tr) v. To harass with persistent annoyance; to bother.

pes-ti-cide (pes´ti sd´) n. A chemical substance used to destroy rodents, insects, and pests.

pes-ti-lence (pes´ti lens) n. A widespread and often fatal infectious disease, such as bubonic plague or cholera.

pet (pet) n. An animal, bird, or fish one keeps for companionship; any favorite or treasured thing. **pet** *adj.* Treated or tamed as a pet; favorite. **pet** *v.* To stroke or caress gently. *Slang* To make love by fondling and caressing.

pet-al (pet´al) *n., Bot.* One of the leaflike parts of a flower.

pe-tite (pe tt´) *adj.* Small in size; little.

pet-it four (pet´ fr´) *n. pl.* **petits fours** *or* **petit fours** A small decorated cake.

pe-ti-tion (pe tish´an) *n.* A solemn request or prayer; a formal written request addressed to a group or person in authority. **petitioner** *n.*

pet-ri-fy (pe´tri f´) *v.* To convert into a stony mass; to make fixed or immobilize, as in the face of danger or surprise. **petrification** *n.*

pe-tro-le-um (pe tr´l um) *n.* An oily, thick liquid which develops naturally below the ground surface, used in products such as gasoline, fuel oil, and kerosene.

pet-ti-coat (pet´ kt´) *n.* A woman's skirtlike garment worn as an underskirt.

pet-ty (pet´) *adj.* To have little importance or value; insignificant; trivial; having a low position or rank; minor; small minded.

petty cash *n.* The cash held on hand for minor bills or expenditures.

pe-tu-nia (pe tö´n a) *n.* A widely grown tropical plant having a funnel-shaped flower in various colors.

pew (p) *n.* A row of bench-like seats for seating people in church.

pew-ter (p´tr) *n.* An alloy of tin with copper, silver-gray in color, and used for tableware and kitchen utensils.

pfen-nig *n.* A small coin of Germany, equal to one hundredth of a Deutschemark.

phal-lus (fal´us) *n. pl.* **phalli** *or* **phalluses** A representation of the penis, often as a symbol of generative power. **phallic** *adj.*

phan-tom (fan´tom) *n.* Something which exists but has no physical reality; a ghost.

phar-ma-cy (fär´ma s) *n. pl.* **pharmacies** A place of business which specializes in preparing, identifying, and disbursing drugs; a drug store. **pharmaceutical** *adj.*

phar-ynx (far´ingks) *n. pl.* **pharynges**

or **pharynxes**. The part of the throat located between the palate and the esophagus, serving as a passage for air and food.

phase (fz) *n.* Any decisive stage in development or growth. *Astron.* One of the forms or appearances of a planet.

pheas-ant (fez´ant) *n.* A long-tailed game bird noted for the beautiful plumage of the male.

phe-nom-e-non (fi nom´e non´) *n. pl.* **phenomena** *or* **phenomenons** Something that can be observed or perceived; a rare occurrence. *Slang* An outstanding person with remarkable power, ability, or talent.

phi-lan-der (fi lan´dr) *v.* To make love without feeling or serious intentions.

phi-lat-e-ly (fi lat´e l) *n.* The collection and study of postage stamps and postmarked material. **philatelic** *adj.* **philatelist** *n.*

phil-har-mon-ic (fil´här mon´ik) *adj.* Relating to a symphony orchestra.

phi-los-o-phy (fi los´o f) *n. pl.* **philosophies** The logical study of the nature and source of human knowledge or human values; the set of values, opinions, and ideas of a group or individual.

pho-bi-a (f´b a) *n.* A compulsive fear of a specified situation or object.

phone (fn) *n.* A telephone. **phone** *v.* To call or communicate by telephone.

phon-ic (fon´ik) *adj.* Pertaining to sounds in speech; using the same symbol for each sound. **phonetically** *adv.* **phonetics** *n.*

pho-no-graph (f no graf´) *n.* A machine which uses a needle to reproduce sound from a grooved disc or record.

pho-ny (f´n) *adj. Informal* Counterfeit; fraudulent; not real or genuine.

phos-phate (fos´ft) *n., Chem.* A salt or phosphoric acid which contains mostly phosphorus and oxygen.

phos-pho-rus (fos´fr us) *n.* A highly flammable, poisonous, nonmetallic element used in safety matches, symbolized by P.

pho-to (f´t) *n. Slang* A photograph.

pho-to-cop-y (f´to kop´) *v.* To reproduce printed material using a photographic process.

pho-to-graph (f´to graf´) *n.* A picture or an image recorded by a camera and then reproduced on a photosensitive surface.

pho-to-stat (f´to stat´) *n.* A trademark for a camera designed to reproduce documents and graphic material.

pho-to-syn-the-sis (f´to sin´thi sis) *n.*, *Biochem.* The chemical process by which plants use light to change carbon dioxide and water into carbohydrates, releasing oxygen as a by-product. **photosynthesize** *v.*

phrase (frz) *n., Gram.* A brief expression which does not contain a predicate.

phre-nol-o-gy (fri nol´o j) *n.* The theory that the conformation of the human skull reveals the degree of intelligence and character; the study of the human skull.

phys-i-cal (fiz´i kal) *adj.* Relating to the human body, apart from the mind or emotions; pertaining to material rather than imaginary subjects. **physical** *n.* A medical exam to determine a person's physical condition.

phy-si-cian (fi zish´an) *n.* A person licensed to practice medicine.

phys-ics (fiz´iks) *n.* The scientific study which deals with energy, matter, motion, and related areas of science.

phys-i-ol-o-gy (fiz´ ol´o j) *n. pl.* **physiologies** The scientific study of living animals, plants, and their activities and functions; the vital functions and processes of an organism.

phys-i-o-ther-a-py (fiz´ ther´ap) *n.* The treatment of disease or physical defects by the use of heat and massage.

pi-an-o (pan´) *n.* A musical instrument with a manual keyboard and felt-covered hammers which produce musical tones when struck upon steel wires.

pi-az-za (p az´a) *n.* A public square or an open area in an Italian town or city.

pi-ca (p´ka) *n.* A printer's type size of 12 points, equal to about 1/6 inch; a typewriter type size with 10 characters to an inch.

pic-co-lo (pik´o´l) *n.* A small flute with a brilliant sound pitched an octave above the flute.

pick-pock-et (pik´ok´it) *n.* A person who steals from another's purse or pocket.

pic-nic (pik´nik) *n.* An outdoor social gathering where food is provided usually by the people attending. **picnic** usu. **picnicker** *v.*

pic-ture (pik´chr) *n.* A visual representation on a surface, which is printed, drawn or photographed; the mental image or impression of an event or situation. **picture** *v.*

piece (ps) *n.* An element, unit, or part of a whole; a musical or literary work. *Slang* A firearm.

piece-meal (ps´ml´) *adv.* Gradually, bit by bit.

pier (pr) *n.* A structure extending into the water, used to secure, protect, and provide access to vessels.

pierce (prs) *v.* To penetrate or make a hole in something; to force into or through.

pig (pig) *n.* A cloven- hoofed mammal with short legs, bristly hair, and a snout for rooting; the edible meat of a pig; pork. *Slang* A greedy or gross person.

pi-geon (pij´on) *n.* A bird with short legs, a sturdy body, and a small head.

pig-gy-back (pig´bak´) *adv.* Carried on the back and shoulders.

pig-head-ed (pig´hed´id) *adj.* Stubborn.

pig-ment (pig´ment) *n.* A material used as coloring matter, suitable for making paint. *Biol.* Any substance such as melanin and chlorophyll which imparts color to vegetable tissue or animals.

pike (pk) *n.* A long pole with a sharp, pointed steel head; a large edible freshwater fish with a long snout and slender body. *Slang* A turnpike or a major highway.

pile (pl) *n.* A quantity of anything thrown in a heap; a massive or very large building or a group of buildings.

pil-fer (pil´fr) *v.* To steal in little quantities; to steal items of little value. **pilferage** *n.*

pil-grim (pil´grim) *n.* A person who travels to a sacred place; a wanderer. **Pilgrims** The English Puritans who founded the Plymouth colony in New England in the year 1620.

pill (pil) *n.* A small tablet containing medicine which is taken by mouth; someone or something which is disagreeable but must be dealt with.

pil-lar (pil´r) *n.* A freestanding column which serves as a support.

pil-low (pil´) *n.* A cloth case filled with feathers or other soft material, used to cushion the head during sleep.

pi-lot (p´lot) *n.* A person who is licensed to operate an aircraft; someone who is trained and licensed to guide ships in and out of port. **pilot** *v.* To act or serve as a pilot.

pi-men-to (pi men´t) *n.* A sweet pepper used as a stuffing for olives or as a relish.

pim-ple (pim´pl) *n.* A small eruption of the skin, having an inflamed base.

pin-a-fore (pin´a fr´) *n.* A sleeveless apron-like garment.

pin-cer *n.* An implement having two handles and a pair of jaws working on a pivot, used to hold objects.

pinch (pinch) *v.* To squeeze between a finger and thumb causing pain or discomfort; to be miserly. **pinch** *n.* The small amount that can be held between the thumb and forefinger.

pine (pn) *n., Bot.* Any of various cone-bearing evergreen trees; the wood of such a tree.

pin-na-cle (pin´a kl) *n.* The highest peak; a sharp point; a pointed summit.

pi-noch-le *or* **pi-noc-le** (p´nuk l) *n.* A card game for two, three, or four people, played with a single or double deck of 48 cards.

pint (pnt) *n.* A liquid or dry measurement equal to half of a quart or two cups.

pin-to (pin´t) *n. pl.* **pintos** *or* **pintoes** A horse with spots; a spotted bean of the southwestern United States.

pin-worm (pin´werm´) *n.* A nematode parasite which infests the human intestines and rectum.

pi-o-neer (p´o nr´) *n.* One of the first settlers of a new region or country; the first developer or investigator in a new field of enterprise, research, or other endeavor.

pi-ous (p´us) *adj.* Reverently religious; devout.

pipe (pp) *n.* A hollow cylinder for conveying fluids; a small bowl with a hollow stem for smoking tobacco. *Mus.* A tubular flute.

pipe-line (pp´ln´) *n.* A pipe used to transfer gas or oil over long distances; a means for conveying information.

pique (pk) *n.* A feeling of resentment or irritation.

pi-rate (p´rat) *n.* A robber of the high seas. *Slang* Someone who uses or reproduces someone else's work without authorization.

pis-ta-chi-o (pi stash´´) *n.* A small tree of western Asia; the edible fruit from this tree.

pis-til (pis´til) *n.* The seed-producing female reproductive organ of a flower.

pis-tol (pis´tol) *n.* A small hand-held firearm.

pis-ton (pis´ton) *n. Mech.* A solid cylinder that is fitted into a larger cylinder, moving back and forth under liquid pressure.

pitch (pich) *n.* A thick, sticky, dark substance that is the residue of the distillation of petroleum or coal tar; the degree of slope of an incline; the property of a musical tone which makes it high or low. **pitch** *v.* To cover with pitch; to throw; to throw out; to slope.

pitch-er (pich´r) *n.* The person who throws the ball to the batter; a container for holding and pouring liquids.

pith (pith) *n., Bot.* The sponge-like soft tissue at the center of the branch or stem of many plants.

pit-i-ful (pit´i ful) *adj.* Evoking or meriting pity. **pitifully** *adv.*

pit-y (pit´) *n. pl.* **pities** A feeling of compassion or sorrow for another's misfortune.

piv-ot (piv´ot) *n.* A thing or person upon which development, direction, or effect depends. **pivot** *v.* To turn. **pivotal** *adj.*

piz-za (pt´sa) *n.* An Italian food consisting of a dough crust covered with tomato sauce, cheese, and other toppings and then baked.

place (pls) *n.* A region; an area; a building or location used for a special purpose; the position of something in a series or sequence. **place** *v.* To put in a

particular order or place.

place-ment (pls'ment) n. The act of being placed; a business or service which finds positions of employment for applicants.

pla-cen-ta (pla sen'ta) n. pl. **placentas** or **placentae** Anat. The vascular, membranous structure which supplies a fetus with nourishment before its birth.

plague (plg) n. Anything that is troublesome. Pathol. A highly contagious and often fatal epidemic disease, as the bubonic plague.

plaid (plad) n. A rectangular wool cloth or garment, usually worn by men and women, having a crisscross or checkered design.

plain (pln) adj. Level; flat; clear; open, as in view; not rich or luxurious; not highly gifted or cultivated. **plainly** adv. **plainness** n.

plain-tiff (pln'tif) n. A person who brings suit.

plan (plan) n. A scheme or method for achieving something; a drawing to show proportion and relationship to parts. **plan** v. To have in mind as an intention or purpose.

plane (pln) n. A tool for smoothing or leveling a wood surface. Geom. A surface as a straight line that joins any two points on it. Slang Airplane.

plan-et (plan'it) n., Astron. A celestial body which is illuminated by light from the star around which it revolves. **planetary** adj.

plan-e-tar-i-um (plan'i târ'um) n. A device for exhibiting celestial bodies as they exist at any time and for any place on earth.

plant (plant) n. A living organism belonging to the vegetable kingdom, having cellulose cell walls. **plant** v. To place a living organism in the ground for growing; to place so as to deceive or to spy.

plaque (plak) n. A flat piece, made from metal, porcelain, ivory, or other materials, engraved for mounting; the bacteria deposit which builds up on the teeth.

plas-ma (plaz'ma) n. The clear fluid part of blood, used for transfusions.

plas-tic (plas'tik) adj. Pliable; capable of being molded. n. A synthetically made material which is molded and then hardened into objects. **plasticity** n. **plasticize** v.

plastic surgery n. Surgery dealing with the restoration or repair of deformed or destroyed parts of the body or skin.

pla-teau (pla t') n. An extensive level expanse of elevated land; a period or stage of stability.

plat-form (plat'form) n. Any elevated or raised surface used by speakers, or by other performers or for display purposes; a formal declaration of principles or policy of a political party.

plat-i-num (plat'i num) n. A silverwhite, metallic element which is corrosive-resistant, used in jewelry; symbolized by Pt.

pla-toon (pla tön') n. A military unit subdivision commanded by a lieutenant.

plau-si-ble (plo'zi bl) adj. Seeming to be probable; appearing to be trustworthy or believable.

play (pl) v. To amuse or entertain oneself, as in recreation; to take part in a game; to perform in a dramatic role; to perform on a musical instrument; in fishing, to allow a hooked fish to tire itself out; to pretend to do something. **play** n. A dramatic presentation.

play-ful (pl'ful) adj. Lightly humorous; full of high spirits.

play-ground (pl'ground') n. The area set aside for children's recreation.

playoff n. A sports contest to break a tie; a series of games to decide the winner or championship.

pla-za (plä'za) n. An open-air marketplace or square; a shopping mall.

plea (pl) n. An urgent request; in law, an allegation made by either party in a law suit.

plead (pld) v. To argue for or against something in court; to ask earnestly.

pleas-ant (plez'ant) adj. Giving or promoting the feeling of pleasure; very agreeable.

please (plz) v. To make happy; to give pleasure; to be the will or wish of; to prefer.

pleas-ur-a-ble (plezh'r a bl) adj.

Pleasant; gratifying.

pleas·ure (plezh´r) *n.* A feeling of satisfaction or enjoyment; one's preference or wish.

pleat (plt) *n.* A fold in a cloth made by doubling the cloth back and fastening it down.

plebe (plb) *n.* A freshman or first year student at the United States Naval Academy.

pledge (plej) *n.* A solemn promise; a deposit of something as security for a loan; a person who is pledged to join a fraternity. **pledge** *v.* To promise or vow.

plen·ti·ful (plen´ti ful) *adj.* Having great abundance. **plentifully** *adv.*

plen·ty (plen´t) *n.* An ample amount; prosperity or abundance.

pli·a·ble (pl´a bl) *adj.* Flexible; easily controlled or persuaded. **pliability** *n.* **pliableness** *n.* **pliably** *adv.*

pli·ers *n.* **(pl´rz)** A pincers-like implement used for holding, bending, or cutting.

plight (plt) *n.* A distressing circumstance, situation, or condition.

plod (plod) *n.* To walk in a heavy, slow way.

plot (plot) *n.* A small piece of ground usually used for a special purpose; the main story line in a piece of fiction; a plan; an intrigue; a conspiracy. **plot** *v.* To represent something by using a map or chart; to scheme secretly.

plow (plou) *n.* An implement for breaking up or turning over the soil. **plow** *v.* To dig out.

pluck (pluk) *v.* To remove by pulling out or off; to pull and release the strings on a musical instrument. *Slang* To swindle.

plum·age (plö´mij) *n.* The feathers of a bird.

plumb (plum) *n.* A lead weight tied to the end of a string, used to test the exact perpendicular line of something.

plumb·er (plum´r) *n.* A person who repairs or installs plumbing in a home or business.

plume (plöm) *n.* A feather used as an ornament.

plun·der (plun´dr) *v.* To deprive of goods or property in a violent way.

plunderer *n.*

plunge (plunj) *v.* To thrust or cast something, as into water; to submerge; to descend sharply or steeply.

plunk (plungk) *v.* To put down or place suddenly; to pluck or strum a banjo.

plu·ral (pler´al) *adj.* Consisting of or containing more than one. **plural** *n.*

plus (plus) *prep. & adj.* Add; the symbol (+) which indicates addition; increase; extra quantity. **plus** *n.*

plu·to·ni·um (plö t´n um) *n.* A radioactive metallic element symbolized by Pu.

ply (pl) *v.* To mold, bend, or shape. **ply** *n.* A layer of thickness; the twisted strands of thread, yarn, or rope.

ply·wood (pl´wed´) *n.* A structural material consisting of thin layers of wood which have been glued and pressed together.

pneu·mo·nia (ne mn´ya) *n.* An inflammation caused by bacteria, virus of the lungs, or irritation.

poach (pch) *v.* To cook in a liquid just at the boiling point; to trespass on another's property with the intent of taking fish or wild game.

pock·et (pok´it) *n.* A pouch within a garment, having an open top and used for carrying items. **pocket** *v.* To put in or deposit in a pocket.

pod (pod) *n., Bot.* A seed vessel, as of a bean or pea. *Aeron* A separate and detachable compartment in a spacecraft.

po·di·a·try (pod ´atr) *n.* Professional care and treatment of the feet.

po·di·um (p´d um) *n. pl.* **podia** *or* **podiums** A small raised platform for an orchestra conductor or a speaker.

po·em (p´im) *n.* A composition in verse with language selected for its beauty and sound.

po·et (p´it) *n.* A person who writes poetry.

po·et·ry (p´i tr) *n.* The art of writing stories, poems, and thoughts into verse.

poin·set·ti·a (poin set´a) *n.* A tropical plant having large scarlet leaves.

poise (poiz) *v.* To bring into or hold one's balance. **poise.** *n.* Equilibrium; self-confidence; the ability to stay calm in social situations.

poi-son (poi´zon) *n.* A substance which kills, injures, or destroys.

poke (pk) *v.* To push or prod at something with a finger or other implement.

pok-er (p´kr) *n.* A card game, played by two or more people, in which the players bet on the cards dealt to them.

po-lar (p´lr) *adj.* Having to do with the poles of a magnet or sphere; relating to the geographical poles of the earth.

po-lar-ize (p´la rz´) *v.* To cause something to vibrate in an exact pattern; to break up into opposite groups. **polarization** *n.*

pole (pl) *n.* Either of the two ends of the axis of a sphere, as the earth; the two points called the North and South Poles, where the axis of the earth's rotation meets the surface; a long, slender rod.

pol-i-o-my-e-li-tis (p´l m´e l´tis) *n.* Inflammation of the spinal cord causing paralysis; also polio.

po-lice (po ls´) *n.* A division or department organized to maintain order; the members of such a department. **police** *v.* To patrol; to enforce the law and maintain order.

po-lice-man (po ls´man) *n.* A member of the police force. **policewoman** *n.*

pol-i-cy (pol´i s) *n. pl.* **policies** Any plan or principle which guides decision making.

pol-ish (pol´ish) *v.* To make lustrous and smooth by rubbing; to become refined or elegant.

po-lite (po lt´) *adj.* Refined, mannerly, and courteous.

po-lit-i-cal (po lit´i kal) *adj.* Concerned with or pertaining to government; involved in politics.

pol-i-ti-cian (pol´i tish´an) *n.* A person active in governmental affairs or politics.

pol-i-tics (pol´i tiks) *n.* The activities and methods of a political party.

poll (pl) *n.* The recording of votes in an election; a public survey taken on a given topic. **poll** *v.*

pol-len (pol´en) *n.* The yellow dust-like powder which contains the male reproductive cells of a flowering plant.

pol-lute (po lt´) *v.* To contaminate; to

make unclear or impure; to dirty. **pollution** *n.*

po-lo-ni-um (po l´n um) *n.* A radioactive metallic element symbolized by Po.

pol-ter-geist (pl´tr gst´) *n.* A mischievous ghost or spirit which makes much noise.

pol-y-es-ter (pol´ es´tr) *n.* A strong lightweight synthetic resin used in fibers.

pol-y-graph (pol´ graf´) *n.* A machine designed to record different signals given off by the body, as respiration, blood pressure, or heart beats, used to detect a person who may be lying.

pol-y-he-dron (pol´ h´dron) *n. pl.* **polyhedra** or **polyhedrons** *Geom.* A solid bounded by polygons.

pom-pa-dour (pom´pa dr´) *n.* A hairstyle which is puffed over the forehead.

pom-pous (pom´pus) *adj.* Showing or appearance of dignity or importance.

pond (pond) *n.* A body of still water, smaller in size than a lake.

pon-der (pon´dr) *v.* To weigh or think about very carefully; to meditate.

pon-der-ous (pon´dr us) *adj.* Massive; having great weight.

po-ny (p´n) *n. pl.* **ponies** A small horse.

pool (pl) *n.* A small body of water; the collective stake in gambling games.

poor (per) *adj.* Lacking possessions and money; not satisfactory; broke; needy; destitute.

pop (pop) *v.* To cause something to burst; to make a sharp, explosive sound. *Slang* Soda.

pop-corn (pop´korn´) *n.* A variety of corn which explodes when heated, forming white puffs.

pope (pp) *n.* The head of the Roman Catholic Church.

pop-lar (pop´lr) *n.* A rapid growing tree having a light, soft wood.

pop-u-lar (pop´ lr) *adj.* Approved of; widely liked; suited to the means of the people.

pop-u-la-tion (pop´ l´shan) *n.* The total number of people in a given area, country, or city.

por-ce-lain (pr´se lin) *n.* A hard, translucent ceramic which has been fired and glazed.

porch (prch) *n.* A covered structure forming the entrance to a house.

por-cu-pine (por´k pn´) *n.* A clumsy rodent covered with long sharp quills.

pore (pr) *v.* To ponder or meditate on something. *n.* A minute opening, as in the skin.

pork (prk) *n.* The edible flesh of swine. *Informal* Favors given by a government for political reasons and not public necessity.

por-nog-ra-phy (por nog´ra f) *n.* Pictures, films, or writing which deliberately arouse sexual excitement.

por-poise (por´pos) *n.* An aquatic mammal with a blunt, rounded snout.

port (prt) *n.* A city or town with a harbor for loading and unloading cargo from ships; the left side of a ship; a dark red, sweet, fortified wine.

port-a-ble (pr´ta bl) *adj.* Capable of being moved easily.

por-ter (pr´tr) *n.* A person hired to carry baggage.

port-fo-li-o (prt f´l´) *n.* A carrying case for holding papers, drawings, and other flat items.

port-hole (prt´hl´) *n.* A small opening in the side of a ship providing light and ventilation.

por-tion (por´shan) *n.* A section or part of a whole; a share. **portion** *v.* To allot; to assign.

por-tray (pr tr´) *v.* To represent by drawing, writing, or acting.

pose (pz) *v.* To place or assume a position, as for a picture.

po-si-tion (po zish´an) *n.* The manner in which something is placed; an attitude; a viewpoint; a job; employment. **position** *v.* To place in proper order.

pos-i-tive (poz´i tiv) *adj.* Containing, ex- pressing, or characterized by affirmation; very confident; absolutely certain; not negative. **positively** *adv.* **positiveness** *n.*

pos-se (pos´) *n.* A deputized group or squad.

pos-ses-sion (po zesh´an) *n.* The fact or act of possessing property; the state of being possessed, as by an evil spirit.

pos-ses-sive (po zes´iv) *adj.* Having a strong desire to possess; not wanting to

share. **possessive** *n.* The noun or pronoun case which indicates ownership.

pos-si-ble (pos´i bl) *adj.* Capable of happening, of being true, or of being accomplished.

post (pst) *n.* An upright piece of wood or metal support; a position or employment. **post** *v.* To put up information in a public place. **post** *prefix.* After; in order; or time; behind.

post-age (p´stij) *n.* The charge or fee for mailing something.

pos-te-ri-or (po str´ r) *adj.* Located in the back. **posterior** *n.* The buttocks.

post-mor-tem (pst mor´tem) *n.* The examination of a body after death; an autopsy.

post-op-er-a-tive *adj.* Following surgery.

post-pone (pst pn´) *v.* To put off; to delay or defer to a later time. **-able** *adj.*

post-script (pst´skript) *n.* A short message added at the end of a letter.

pos-ture (pos´chr) *n.* The carriage or position of the body.

po-tas-si-um (po tas´ um) *n.* A silvery-white, highly reactive metallic element, symbolized by K.

po-ta-to (po t´t) *n. pl.* potatoes A thick, edible, underground tuber plant native to America.

po-tent (pt´ent) *adj.* Having great strength or physical powers; having a great influence on the mind or morals; sexually competent.

po-ten-tial (po ten´shal) *adj.* Possible, but not yet actual; having the capacity to be developed. *Electr.* The potential energy of an electric charge that depends on its position in an electric field.

pot-pour-ri (p´pe r´) *n.* A mixture of sweet-smelling dried flower petals and spices, kept in an airtight jar.

pot-ter-y (pot´e r) *n. pl.* potteries Objects molded from clay and fired by intense heat.

pouch (pouch) *n.* A small bag or container for holding or carrying money, tobacco, and other small articles. *Zool.* The sac-like structure in which some animals carry their young.

poul-try (pl´tr) *n.* Domestic fowl as ducks and hens, which are raised for eggs or meat.

pound (pound) *n. pl.* **pound** A measure of weight equal to sixteen ounces; a public enclosure where stray animals are fed and housed. **pound** *v.* To strike repeatedly or with force; to throb or beat violently or rapidly.

pov-er-ty (pov´r t) *n.* The condition or state of being poor and needing money.

POW (p´´dub l´) *abbr.* Prisoner of war.

pow-er-ful (pou´r ful) *adj.* Possessing energy or great force; having authority.

power of attorney *n.* A legal document in which one person gives another the authority to act for him.

prac-ti-cal (prak´ti kal) *adj.* Serving an actual use or purpose; inclined to act instead of thinking or talking about something; useful.

prac-tice (prak´tis) *n.* A custom or habit of doing something. *v.* To work at a profession; to apply; to put into effect; to exercise or rehearse.

prai-rie (prâr´) *n.* A wide area of level or rolling land with grass and weeds but no trees.

praise (prz) *v.* To express approval; to glorify.

prank (prangk) *n.* A mischievous, playful action or trick. **prankster** *n.*

pray (pr) *v.* To address prayers to God; to ask or request.

prayer (prâr) *n.* A devout request; the act of praying; a formal or set group of words used in praying.

pre- *pref* Earlier or prior to something; in front.

preach (prch) *v.* To advocate; to proclaim; to deliver a sermon. **preacher** *n.* **preachment** *n.* **preachy** *adj.*

pre-am-ble (pr´am´bl) *n.* An introduction to something, as a law, which states the purpose and reasons for the matter which follows.

pre-cau-tion (pri ko´shan) *n.* A measure of caution or care taken in advance to guard against harm.

pre-cede (pri sd´) *v.* To be or go before in time, position, or rank. **-dence** *n.*

prec-e-dent (pres´i dent) *n.* An instance which may serve as a rule or example in the future.

pre-cept (pr´sept) *n.* A rule, order, or commandment meant to guide one's conduct.

pre-cinct (pr´singkt) *n.* An electoral district of a county, township, city, or town; an enclosure with definite boundaries.

pre-cious (presh´us) *adj.* Having great worth or value; beloved; cherished.

pre-cip-i-ta-tion (pri sip´i t´shan) *n.* Condensed water vapor which falls as snow, rain, sleet or hail. *Chem.* The act of causing crystals to separate and fall to the bottom of a liquid.

pre-cip-i-tous (pri sip´i tus) *adj.* Very steep; marked with very steep cliffs.

pre-cise (pri ss´) *adj.* Exact; definite; strictly following rules; very strict.

pre-ci-sion (pri sizh´an) *n.* Exactness; the quality of being precise; accuracy.

pre-clude (pri klöd´) *v.* To shut up; to make impossible; to prevent.

pre-con-ceive (pr´kon sv´) *v.* To form a notion or conception before knowing all the facts. **preconception** *n.*

pred-a-tor (pred´a tr) *n.* A person who lives or gains by stealing from another person; an animal that survives by killing and eating other animals.

pre-des-ti-na-tion (pri des´ti n´shan) *n.* Destiny; fate; the act by which God has predestined all events.

pred-i-ca-ble (pred´i ka bl) *adj.* Capable of being predicated to foretell.

pred-i-cate (pred´i kt) *n., Gram.* The word or words which say something about the subject of a clause or sentence; the part of a sentence which contains the verb. *v.* To establish.

pre-dict (pri dikt´) *v.* To tell beforehand; to foretell; to forecast. **predictability** *n.*

pre-dom-i-nant (pri dom´i nant) *adj.* Superior in strength, authority, number, or other qualities.

pree-mie *n. Slang* A baby born before the expected due date.

pre-empt (pr empt´) *v.* To get or take hold of before someone else; to take the place of; to do something before someone else has a chance to do it. **preemption** *n.*

pref-ace (pref´is) *n.* The introduction at the beginning of a book or speech.

pre-fect (pr´fekt) *n.* A high administrative official. **prefecture** *n.*

pre-fer (pri fer´) v. To select as being the favorite; to promote; to present.

pref-er-ence (pref´r ens) n. A choice; a special liking for anything over another.

pre-fix (pr fiks´) v. To put at the beginning; to put before.

preg-nant (preg´nant) adj. Carrying an unborn fetus; significant. **pregnancy** n.

pre-his-tor-i-cal (pr´hi stor´ik) adj. Of or related to the period before recorded history.

pre-judge (pr juj´) v. To judge before one knows all the facts. **-ment** n.

prej-u-dice (prej´a dis) n. A biased opinion based on emotion rather than reason; bias against a group, race, or creed.

pre-lim-i-nar-y (pri lim´i ner´) adj. Leading up to the main action. **preliminaries** n.

prel-ude (prel´d) n. An introductory action. *Music* The movement at the beginning of a piece of music.

pre-ma-ture (pr´ma ter´) adj. Occurring or born before the natural or proper time.

pre-med-i-tate (pri med´i tt´) v. To plan in advance or beforehand.

pre-mi-er (pri mr´) adj. First in rank or importance. n. The chief executive of a government. **premiership** n.

pre-mi-um (pr´m um) n. An object offered free as an inducement to buy; the fee or amount payable for insurance; an additional amount of money charged above the nominal value.

pre-na-tal (pr nt´al) adj. Existing prior to birth.

pre-oc-cu-py (pr ok´ p´) v. To engage the mind or attention completely.

prep (prep) *Slang* Preparatory school; preparation.

prep-a-ra-tion (prep´a r´shan) n. The process of preparing for something.

pre-pare (pri pâr´) v To make ready or qualified; to equip. **preparedly** n.

pre-pay (pr p´) v. To pay for in advance.

prep-o-si-tion (prep´o zish´an) n., *Gram.* A word placed in front of a noun or pronoun to show a connection with or to something or someone.

pre-pos-ter-ous (pri pos´tr us) adj. Absurd; ridiculous; beyond all reason.

prep-pie n. *Slang* A student attending a prep school; a young adult who behaves and dresses very traditionally.

pre-rog-a-tive (pri rog´a tiv) n. The unquestionable right belonging to a person.

pres-age (pres´ij) n. An omen or indication of something to come; a premonition.

pre-school (pr´skōl) adj. Of or for children usually between the ages of two and five.

pre-scribe (pri skrb´) v. To impose as a guide; to recommend.

pre-scrip-tion (pri skrip´shan) n., *Med.* A physician's written order for medicine.

pres-ence (prez´ens) n. The state of being present; the immediate area surrounding a person or thing; poise.

pres-ent (prez´ent) adj. Now going on; not past or future. *Gram.* Denoting a tense or verb form which expresses a current state or action. v. To bring into the acquaintance of another; to introduce; to make a gift of. n. A gift. adv. Currently.

pres-en-ta-tion (prez´en t´shan) n. A formal introduction of one person to another; to present something as an exhibition, show, or product.

pre-ser-va-tive (pri zer´va tiv) adj. Keeping something from decay or injury.

pre-serve (pri zerv´) v. To keep or save from destruction or injury; to prepare fruits or vegetables to prevent spoilage or decay. **preserves** Fruit which has been preserved with sugar.

pre-shrunk (pr shrungk´) adj. Material which has been washed during the manufacturing process to minimize shrinkage later.

pres-i-dent (prez´i dent) n. The chief executive officer of a government, corporation, or association. **presidency** n. **presidential** adj.

press (pres) v. To act upon or exert steady pressure or force; to squeeze out or extract by pressure; to smooth by heat and pressure; to iron clothes. n. A machine used to produce printed material. **presser** n.

pres-sure (presh´r) n. The act of or the

state of being pressed; a constraining moral force; any burden, force, painful feeling, or influence; the depressing effect of something hard to bear.

pres-tige (pres stzh´) *n.* Importance based on past reputation and achievements.

pres-to (pres´t) *adv., Music* Very fast and quick; at once.

pre-sume (pri zōm´) *v.* To take for granted; to take up on oneself without permission; to proceed overconfidently.

pre-sump-tion (pri zump´shan) *n.* Arrogant conductor speech; something that can be logically assumed true until disproved.

pre-tend (pri tend´) *v.* To make believe; to act in a false way. **pretender** *n.*

pre-tense (pri tens´) *n.* A deceptive and false action or appearance; a false purpose.

pre-ten-tions (pri ten´shan) *n.* Having or making claims to worth, excellence, etc.; showy.

pre-text (pr´tekst) *n.* A motive assumed in order to conceal the true purpose.

pret-ty (prit´) *adj.* Pleasant; attractive; characterized by gracefulness; pleasing to look at. **pretty** In a favorable position; good circumstances. **prettier** *adj.* **-iest** *adj.*

pre-vail (pri vl´) *v.* To succeed; to win control over something; to predominate. **prevailer** *n.* **prevailingly** *adv.*

pre-vent (pri vent´) *v.* To keep something from happening; to keep from doing something.

pre-ven-tive *or* **preventative** (pri ven´tiv) *adj.* Protecting or serving to ward off harm, disease, or other problems. **preventive** *n.*

pre-view *or* **prevue** (pr´v) *n.* An advance showing or viewing to invited guests.

pre-vi-ous (pr´v us) *adj.* Existing or occurring earlier. **previously** *adv.*

price (prs) *n.* The set amount of money expected or given for the sale of something.

prick (prik) *n.* A small hole made by a sharp point. *v.* To pierce something lightly.

pride (prd) *n.* A sense of personal digni-

ty; a feeling of pleasure because of something achieved, done, or owned.

priest (prst) *n.* A clergyman in the Catholic church who serves as mediator between God and His worshipers.

pri-ma-ry (pr´mer) *adj.* First in origin, time, series, or sequence; basic; fundamental.

prime (prm) *adj.* First in importance, time, or rank. *n.* A period of full vigor, success, or beauty. *v.* To make ready by putting something on before the final coat, as to prime wood before painting.

prim-i-tive (prim´i tiv) *adj.* Of or pertaining to the beginning or earliest time; resembling the style or manners of an earlier time.

prince (prins) *n.* The son of a king; a king.

prin-cess (prin´sis) *n.* The daughter of a king.

prin-ci-pal (prin´s pal) *adj.* Chief; most important. *n.* The headmaster or chief official of a school; a sum of money invested or owed which is separate from the interest.

prin-ci-ple (prin´si pl) *n.* The fundamental law or truth upon which others are based; a moral standard.

print (print) *n.* An impression or mark made with ink; the design or picture which is transferred from an engraved plate or other impression. *v.* To stamp designs; to publish something in print, as a book or magazine.

printer (print´tr) *n.* A person whose occupation is printing.

print-out (print´out´) *n., Computer Science* The output of a computer, printed on paper.

pri-or (pr´r) *adj.* Previous in order or time.

pri-or-i-ty (pr or´i t) *n.* Something which takes precedence; something which must be done or taken care of first.

prism (priz´um) *n.* A solid figure with triangular ends and rectangular sides, used to disperse light into a spectrum.

pris-on (priz´on) *n.* A place of confinement where people are kept while waiting for a trial or while serving time for breaking the law; jail. **prisoner** *n.*

pri-vate (pr´vit) *adj.* Secluded or

removed from the public view; secret; intimate; owned or controlled by a group or person rather than by the public or government. An enlisted person holding the lowest rank in military service.

priv-i-lege (priv´i lij) *n.* A special right or benefit granted to a person.

prize (prz) *n.* An award or something given to the winner of a contest; something exceptional or outstanding.

pro (pr) *n.* An argument in favor of or supporting something. *Slang* A professional or an expert in a given field.

prob-a-bil-i-ty (prob´a bil´i t) *n. pl. -ies* The state or quality of being probable; a mathematical statement or prediction of the odds of something happening or not happening.

prob-a-ble (prob´a bl) *adj.* Likely to become a reality, but not certain or proved.

pro-bate (pr´bt) *n.* The act of legally proving that a will is genuine.

pro-ba-tion (pr b´shan) *n.* A period used to test the qualifications and character of a new employee; the early release of law breakers who must be under supervision and must report as requested to a probation officer.

probe (prb) *n.* An instrument used for investigating an unknown environment; a careful investigation or examination.

prob-lem (prob´lem) *n.* A perplexing situation or question; a question presented for consideration, solution, or discussion.

pro-ce-dure (pro s´jr) *n.* A certain pattern or way of doing something; the normal methods or forms to be followed.

pro-ceed (pro sd´) *v.* To carry on or continue an action or process. *Law* To begin or institute legal action.

pro-ceeds (pr´sdz) *n. pl.* The profits received from a fund-raising venture.

proc-ess (pros´es) *n.* The course, steps, or methods toward a desired result. *Law* Any judicial request or order; in Computer Science, the sequence of operations which gives a desired result. *v.* To compile, compute, or assemble; data.

pro-ces-sion (pro sesh´an) *n.* A group which moves along in a formal manner; a parade.

pro-ces-sion-al (pro sesh´a nal) *n.* A hymn sung during a procession; *adj.* the opening of a church service; of or relating to a procession.

pro-ces-sor *n., Computer Science* The central unit of a computer which processes data.

pro-claim (pr klm´) *v.* To announce publicly.

proc-la-ma-tion (prok´la m´shan) *n.* An official public declaration or announcement.

pro-cras-ti-nate (pr kras´ti nt) *v.* To put off, defer, or postpone to a later time.

proc-tor (prok´tr) *n.* A person in a university or college whose job it is to see that order is maintained during exams.

pro-cure (pr kr´) *v.* To acquire; to accomplish.

prod (prod) *v.* To arouse mentally; to poke with a pointed instrument. *n.* A pointed implement used to prod or poke.

prod-i-gal (prod´i gal) *adj.* Wasteful expenditure of money, strength, or time; extravagance. *n.* One who is a spendthrift or is wasteful.

pro-duce (pro dōs´) *v.* To bear or bring forth by a natural process; to manufacture; to make; to present or bring into view.

pro-duct (prod´ukt) *n.* Something produced, manufactured, or obtained. *Math.* The answer obtained by multiplying.

pro-duc-tion (pro duk´shan) *n.* The process or act of producing; something produced, as a play.

pro-fane (pro fn´) *adj.* Manifesting disrespect toward sacred things; vulgar.

pro-fess (pro fes´) *v.* To admit or declare openly; to make an open vow.

pro-fes-sion-al (pro fesh´a nal) *adj.* Having to do with a job or profession; referring to or engaging in an occupation, usually a sport for money rather than for fun.

pro-fes-sor (pro fes´r) *n.* A faculty member of the highest rank in a college or university; a highly skilled teacher.

pro-fi-cient (pro fish´ent) adj. Highly skilled in a field of knowledge. **proficiency** n. **proficiently** adv.

pro-file (pro´fīl) n. The outline of a person's face or figure as seen from the side; a short biographical sketch indicating the most striking characteristics.

prof-it (prof´it) n. The financial return after all expenses have been accounted for. v. To gain an advantage or a financial reward.

pro-found (pro found´) adj. Deeply held or felt; intellectually penetrating.

pro-fuse (pro fūs´) adj. Extravagant; giving forth lavishly; overflowing. **profusely** adv. **profuseness** n.

prog-e-ny (proj´e ne) n. pl. **-ies** One's offspring, children, or descendants.

prog-no-sis (prog n´sis) n. pl. **-noses** A prediction of the outcome and course a disease may take.

pro-gram (pr´gram) n. Any prearranged plan or course; a show or performance, as one given at a scheduled time; in Computer Science, a sequence of commands which tell a computer how to perform a task or sequence of tasks. **program** v.

prog-ress (prog´res) n. Forward motion or advancement to a higher goal; an advance; steady improvement.

pro-hib-it (pr hib´it) v. To forbid legally; to prevent.

pro-ject (proj´ekt) n. A plan or course of action; a proposal; a large job. v. To give an estimation on something.

pro-jec-tile (pro jek´til) n. Anything hurled forward through the air.

pro-jec-tion (pro jek´shan) n. The act or state of being projected; the state or part that sticks out.

pro-lif-er-ate (pr lif e rt´) v. To grow or produce with great speed, as cells in tissue formation.

pro-logue (pr´log) n. An introductory statement at the beginning of a poem, song, or play.

pro-long (pro long´) v. To extend or lengthen in time.

prom-e-nade (prom´e nd´) n. An unhurried walk for exercise or amusement; a public place for such a walk, as the deck of a ship.

prom-i-nent (prom´i nent) adj. Jutting out; widely known; held in high esteem.

pro-mis-cu-ous (pro mis´k us) adj. Lacking selectivity or discrimination, especially in sexual relationships.

prom-ise (prom´is) n. An assurance given that one will or will not do something; a pledge. **promise** v.

pro-mote (pro mt´) v. To raise to a higher rank or position; to work on behalf of. **promotion** n. **promotional** adj.

prompt (prompt) adj. Arriving on time; punctual; immediate. v. To suggest or inspire.

prone (prn) adj. Lying flat; face down.

prong (prong) n. A pointed, projecting part, as the end of a sharp instrument or the end of an antler.

pro-noun (pr´noun´) n., Gram. A word which can be used in the place of a noun or noun phrase.

pro-nounce (pro nouns´) v. To deliver officially; to articulate the sounds. **pronounceable** adj. **pronunciation** n.

proof (prf) n. The establishment of a fact by evidence; the act of showing that something is true; a trial impression from the negative of a photograph. v. To proofread; to mark and make corrections.

proof-read (prf rd´) v. To read in order to detect and mark errors in a printer's proof.

prop (prop) n. A support to keep something upright. v. To sustain.

pro-pel (pro pel´) v. To thrust or cause to move forward; to motivate.

prop-er (prop´r) adj. Appropriate; especially adapted or suited; conforming to social convention; correct.

prop-er-ty (prop´r t) n. pl. **-ies** Any object of value owned or lawfully acquired, as real estate; a piece of land.

proph-e-cy (prof´i s) n. pl. **-ies** A prediction made under divine influence.

proph-et (prof´it) n. One who delivers divine messages; one who foretells the future.

pro-po-nent (pro p´nent) n. One who supports or advocates a cause.

pro-por-tion (pro pr´shan) n. The relation of one thing to another in size, degree, or amount. v. To adjust or

arrange with balance and harmony.
proportional *adj.* **proportion ate** *adj.*
proportionally *adv.*

pro-pose (pro pz´) *v.* To present or put forward for consideration or action; to suggest someone for an office or position; to make an offer; to offer marriage.

prop-o-si-tion (prop´o zish´an) *n.* A scheme or plan offered for consideration; a subject or idea to be proved or discussed. *v.* To make a sexual suggestion.

pro-pri-e-ty (pro pri´i t) *n. pl.* **-ies** The quality or state of being proper in accordance with recognized principles or usage.

pro-pul-sion (pro pul´shan) *n.* The act or process of propelling. **-sive** *adj.*

pro-rate (pr rt´) *v.* To distribute or divide proportionately. **proration** *n.*

pro-scribe (pr skrb´) *v.* To banish; to outlaw; to prohibit.

prose (prz) *n.* Ordinary language, speech, or writing which is not poetry.

pros-e-cute (pros´e kt´) *v.* To carry on. *Law* To bring suit against a person; to seek enforcement for legal process. **prosecution** *n.*

pros-pect (pros´pekt) *n.* Something that has the possibility of future success; a possible customer. *v.* To explore. **prospective** *adj.*

pros-per (pros´pr) *v.* To be successful; to achieve success. **prosperous** *adj.*

pros-tate (pros´tt) *n.* A small gland at the base of the male bladder.

pros-ti-tute (pros´ti tt´) *n.* One who sells the body for the purpose of sexual intercourse.

pros-trate (pros´trt) *adj.* Lying with the face down to the ground. *v.* To overcome; to adopt a submissive posture. **prostrative** *adj.* **prostrator** *n.*

prot-ac-tin-i-um (pr´tak tin´ um) *n.* A radioactive metallic element symbolized by Pa.

pro-tect (pro tekt´) *v.* To guard or shield from attack or injury; to shield. **protective** *adj.* **protectively** *adv.*

pro-tein (pr´tn) *n., Biochem.* Any of a very large group of highly complex nitrogenous compounds occurring in living matter and composed of amino

acids which are essential for tissue repair and growth.

pro-test (pro test´) *v.* To make a strong formal objection; to object to. *n.* The act of protesting. **protester** *n.*

pro-to-col (pr´to kol´) *n.* The code and rules of diplomatic and state etiquette.

pro-ton (pr´ton) *n.,* Physics A unit of positive charge equal in magnitude to an electron.

pro-tract (pr trakt´) *v.* To extend in space; to protrude.

pro-trude (pro tröd´) *v.* To project; to thrust outward. **protrusion** *n.*

proud (proud) *adj.* Showing or having a feeling that one is better than the others; having a feeling of satisfaction; having proper selfrespect or proper self-esteem.

prove (pröv) *v.* To show with valid evidence that something is true. **-able** *adj.*

pro-vide (pro vd´) *v.* To supply or furnish with what is needed.

pro-vi-sion (pro vizh´an) *n.* A supply of food or needed equipment.

pro-voke (pro vk´) *v.* To cause to be angry; to annoy. **provocation** *n.*

prox-i-mate (prok´si mit) *adj.* Immediate; direct; close.

prox-y (prok´s) *n. pl.* **-ies** The authority, usually written, to act for another.

pso-ri-a-sis (so r´a sis) *n., Pathol.* A non- contagious, chronic, inflammatory skin disease characterized by reddish patches and white scales.

psych *v. Slang* To prepare oneself emotionally or mentally; to outwit or outguess.

psy-chi-a-try (si k´a tr) *n.* The branch of medicine which deals with the diagnosis and treatment of mental disorders.

psy-chic (s´kik) *adj.* Cannot be explained by natural or physical laws. *n.* A person who communicates with the spirit world.

psy-chol-o-gy (s kol´o j) *n. pl.* **-ies** The science of emotions, behavior, and the mind. **psychological** *adj.* **-logist** *n.*

pu-ber-ty (p´br t) *n.* The stage of development in which sexual reproduction can first occur; the process of the body which culminates in sexual maturity.

pub-lic (pub´lik) *adj.* Pertaining to or

public domain *n.* Public property; a published work whose copyrights have expired.

pub·li·ca·tion (pub'li kā'shən) *n.* The business of publishing; any pamphlet, book, or magazine.

pub·lic·i·ty (pu blis'i t) *n.* The state of being known to the public; common knowledge.

pub·lish (pub'lish) *v.* To print and distribute a book, magazine, or any printed matter to the public. **publishable** *adj.* **publisher** *n.*

puck (puk) *n.* A hard rubber disk used in playing ice hockey.

pud·dle (pud'l) *n.* A small pool of water.

puff (puf) *n.* A brief discharge of air or smoke.

pull (pel) *v.* To apply force; to cause motion toward or in the same direction of; to remove from a fixed place; to stretch.

pulp (pulp) *n.* The soft juicy part of a fruit; a soft moist mass; inexpensive paper.

pul·pit (pel'pit) *n.* The elevated platform lectern used in a church from which a service is conducted.

pul·sate (pul'st) *v.* To beat rhythmically.

pulse (puls) *n., Physiol.* The rhythmical beating of the arteries caused by the action of the heart. **pulse** *v.*

pul·ver·ize (pul've rz') *v.* To be reduced to dust or powder by crushing.

pump (pump) *n.* A mechanical device for moving a gas or liquid. *v.* To raise with a pump; to obtain information through persistent questioning.

punch (punch) *n.* A tool used for perforating or piercing; a blow with the fist; a drink made of an alcoholic beverage and a fruit juice or other nonalcoholic beverage. *v.* To use a punch on something; to hit sharply with the hand or fist.

punc·tu·al (pungk'chŏ al) *adj.* Prompt; arriving on time.

punc·tu·ate (pungk'chŏ t') *v.* To mark words or written material with punctuation; to give or show emphasis.

punc·ture (pungk'chr) *v.* To prick or pierce with a pointed instrument. *n.*

The act or effect of puncturing.

pun·gent (pun'jent) *adj.* Sharp or acrid in smell or taste.

pun·ish (pun'ish) *v.* To subject a person to confinement or impose a penalty for a crime.

punishment (pun'ish ment) *n.* A penalty which is imposed for breaking the law or a rule.

punk (pungk) *n. Slang* A young, inexperienced boy. *adj.* Of or relating to a bizarre style of clothing; relating to punk rock bands.

punt (punt) *n.* A narrow, long, flat-bottomed boat; in football, a kick of a football dropped from the hands. *v.* To kick a football.

pup (pup) *n.* A puppy, young dog, or the young of other animals.

pu·pil (p'pĭl) *n.* A person who attends school and receives instruction by a teacher.

pup·pet (pup'it) *n.* A small figure of an animal or person which is manipulated by hand or by strings.

pur·chase (per'chas) *v.* To receive by paying money as an exchange. **purchaser** *n.*

pure (pr) *adj.* Free from anything that damages, weakens, or contaminates; innocent; clean.

purge (perj) *v.* To make clean; to free from guilt or sin; to rid of anything undesirable, as unwanted persons. *Med.* To cause or induce emptying of the bowels. **purge** *n.*

pu·ri·fy (pr'i f') *v.* To make clean or pure.

pu·ri·ty (pr'i t) *n.* The quality of being pure; freedom from guilt or sin.

pur·ple (per'pl) *n.* A color between red and violet **purplish** *adj.*

pur·port (per'prt) *v.* To give the appearance of intending; to imply, usually with the intent to deceive.

pur·pose (per'pos) *n.* A desired goal; an intention; the use for which something is intended. **purposeful** *adj.* **purposeless** *adj.*

purr (per) *n.* The low, murmuring sound characteristic of a cat. **purr** *v.*

purse (pers) *n.* A small pouch or bag for money; a handbag; a pocketbook; the sum of money offered as a prize.

purs·er (pûr´sr) *n.* An officer aboard a passenger ship charged with keeping the accounts and documents along with the service and care of all passengers.

pur·sue (pr sö´) *v.* To seek to achieve; to follow in an attempt to capture. **pursuer** *n.*

pur·suit (pr söt´) *n.* The act of pursuing an occupation; pursuing or following in order to take over.

pus (pus) *n.* A yellowish secretion formed in infected tissue which contains bacteria.

pus·tule (pus´chül) *n.* A pimple or blister, having an inflamed base and containing pus.

put (pet) *v.* To cause to be in a location; to move as a thing or person, as to get it into some place or position; to bring into a specific relation or state; to bring forward for debate or consideration, as to put up for. **down** To humiliate.

pu·tre·fy (p´tre f´) *v.* To cause to decay; to decay. **putrefaction** *n.* **-factive** *adj.*

putt (put) *n.* In golf, a light stroke made on a putting green to get the ball into the hole.

puz·zle (puz´l) *v.* To bewilder; to confuse. *n.* A toy, board game, or word game which tests one's patience and skills; to ponder over a problem.

pyg·my (pig´m) *n. pl.* **-ies** A very small person or animal; a dwarf; a race of dwarfs in ancient Greek literature or legend; something very small for its kind.

py·or·rhe·a (p´o r´a) *n., Pathol.* Inflammation of the gums and sockets of teeth.

pyr·a·mid (pir´a mid) *n.* A solid structure with a square base and sides which meet at a point; a ancient structure of this form built in different parts of the world, used as tombs especially Egypt. *v.* To use in or employ, as a stock, in a pyramiding series of transactions.

py·ro·ma·ni·a (p´ro m´n a) *n.* A compulsion to set fires.

py·ro·phyl·lite (po fil´t) *n.* Mineral consisting of hydrous silicate of aluminum, having a white or greenish color; one variety that is used to make slate pencils

py·ro·tech·nics (pro tek´niks) *n* The skill of making fireworks; the display of fireworks; something that resembles fireworks.

py·rox·y·lin (p rok´si lin) *n.* Any of a various cellulose nitrates used in making plastics and lacquers.

pyr·role (pi rl´) *n.* An oily organic compound, with an odor like chloroform, found in chlorophyll and bile pigments, and derived from coal tar.

py·thon (p´thon) *n.* A large non-venomous snake which crushes its prey; any of various related or similar snakes, as a boa.

py·u·ri·a (pi r´ a) *n.* Having pus in the urine.

pyx·ie (pik´s) *n.* A shrubby, evergreen, having numerous small blossoms.

pyx·is (pik´sis) *n.* A small box or vase, used in Roman and Greek days to hold jewelry.

Q

Q, q (k) The seventeenth letter of the English alphabet.

qt. *abbr.* Quart.

quack (kwak) *n.* The harsh, croaking cry of a duck; someone who pretends to be a doctor.

quad·rant (kwod´rant) *n.* A quarter section of a circle, subtending or enclosing a central angle of 90 degrees.

quad·ru·ped (kwod´re ped´) *n.* Any animal having four feet.

quad·ru·ple (kwo drö´pl) *adj.* Consisting of four parts; multiplied by four.

quail (kwl) *n. pl.* A small game bird.

quaint (kwnt) *adj.* Pleasing in an old-fashioned, unusual way.

quake (kwk) *v.* To shake or tremble violently.

quak·er (kw´kr) *n.* The religious sect called the Society of Friends.

qual·i·fy (kwol´i f´) *v.* To prove something able; restrict; limit; modify.

qual·i·ty (kwol´i t) *n. pl.* **ties** A distinguishing character which makes something such as it is; a high degree of excellence.

qualm (kwäm) n. A sudden feeling of sickness; sensation of uneasiness or doubt.

quan-ti-ty (kwon´ti t) n. Number; amount; bulk; weight; a portion; as a large amount.

quar-an-tine (kwor´an tn´) n. A period of enforced isolation for a specified period of time used to prevent the spread of a contagious disease.

quar-rel (kwor´el) n. An unfriendly or angry disagreement; a cause for dispute. **quarrel** v. To find fault with.

quar-ry (kwor´) n. pl. **quarries** An animal hunted for food; an open pit or excavation from which limestone or other material is being extracted.

quart (kwort) n. A unit of measurement equaling four cups.

quar-ter (kwor´tr) n. One of four equal parts into which anything may be divided; a place of lodging, as a barracks; a U.S. coin equal to 1/4 of a dollar.

quar-ter-back (kwor´tr bak´) n., *Football* The offensive player who directs the plays for his team.

quar-tet (kwor tet´) n. A musical composition for four voices or instruments; any group or set of four.

quartz (kworts) n. A hard, transparent crystallized mineral.

quea-sy (kw´z) adj. Nauseated; sick.

queen (kwn) n. The wife of a king; a woman sovereign or monarch; in chess, the most powerful piece on the board, which can move any number of squares in any direction; the fertile female in a colony of social insects.

quell (kwel) v. To put down with force; to quiet; to pacify.

quench (kwench) v. To extinguish or put out; to cool metal by thrusting into water; to drink to satisfy a thirst.

quest (kwest) n. A search; pursuit; an expedition to find something.

ques-tion (kwes´chan) n. An expression of inquiry which requires an answer; a problem; an unresolved matter; the act of inquiring or asking. v. To ask; to inquire.

question mark n. A mark of punctuation, (?), used in writing to indicate a question.

ques-tion-naire (kwes´cha nâr´) n. A written series of questions to gather statistical information often used for a survey.

queue (k) n., *Computer Science* A sequence of stored programs or data on hold for processing. v. To form a line; to stand in line.

quib-ble (kwib´l) v. To raise trivial objection. **quibble** n. **quibbler** n.

quiche (ksh) n. Unsweetened custard baked in a pastry shell, usually with vegetables or seafood.

quick (kwik) adj. Moving swiftly; occurring in a short time; responding, thinking, or understanding something rapidly and easily. **quickly** adv.

quick-sand (kwik´sand´) n. A bog of very fine, wet sand of considerable depth, that engulfs and sucks down objects, people, or animals.

quid (kwid) n. A small portion of tobacco; a cow's cud.

qui-et (kw´it) adj. Silent; making very little sound; still; tranquil; calm. v. To become or make quiet. n. The state of being quiet.

quill (kwil) n. A strong bird feather; a spine from a porcupine; a writing instrument made from a long stiff feather.

quilt (kwilt) n. A bed coverlet made of two layers of cloth with a soft substance between and held in place by lines of stitching. v. To sew or stitch together.

qui-nine (kw´nn) n., *Chem.* A very bitter, colorless, crystalline powder used in the treatment of malaria.

quin-tes-sence (kwin tes´ens) n. The most essential and purest form of anything.

quin-tet (kwin tet´) n. A musical composition written for five people; any group of five.

quin-til-lion (kwin til´yen) n. A thousand quadrillions, one followed by eighteen zeros.

quin-tu-ple (kwin tô´pl) adj. Increased five times; multiplied by five; consisting of five parts. v. To make five times larger.

quip (kwip) n. A sarcastic remark.

quirk (kwerk) n. A sudden, sharp bend

or twist; a personal mannerism.

quit (kwit) v. To cease; to give up; to depart; to abandon; to resign or leave a job or position.

quite (kwt) adv. To the fullest degree; really; actually; to a great extent.

quiz (kwiz) v. To question, as with an informal oral or written examination.

quo-ta (kw´ta) n. An allotment or proportional share.

quo-ta-tion (kw t´shan) n. The exact quoting of words as a passage.

quotation mark n. The marks of punctuation " " showing a direct quote.

quote (kwt) v. To repeat exactly what someone else has previously stated.

quo-tient (kw´shent) n., Math The amount or number which results when one number is divided by another.

R

R, r (är) The eighteenth letter of the English alphabet.

ra-ba-to (ra b´t) n. A wide lace-edged collar of the early 17th century.

rab-bet (rab´it) n. A recess or groove along the edge of a piece of wood cut to fit another piece to form a joint. **rabbeted** v.

rab-bi (rab´) n. An ordained leader of Jews; the leader and teacher of a Jewish congregation. **rabbinic** adj.

rab-bit (rab´it) n. A burrowing mammal related to but smaller than the hare.

rab-ble (rab´l) n. A disorderly crowd. **rabbling** v. **rabbled** v.

rab-id (rab´id) adj. Affected with rabies; mad; furious. **rabidly** adv. **rabidness** n.

ra-bies (r´bz) n. An acute, infectious viral disease of the central nervous system, often fatal, which is transmitted by the bite of an infected animal.

rac-coon (ra kön´) n. pl. **-coons, -coon** A nocturnal mammal with a black, mask-like face and a black-and-white ringed, bushy tail.

race (rs) n. The zoological division of the human population having common origin and other physical traits, such as hair form and pigmentation; a group of people having such common characteristics or appearances; people united

by a common nationality. n. A contest which is judged by speed; any contest, such as a race for an elective office.

rac-er (r´sr) n. A person who takes part in a race; one who runs in a race.

ra-chis (r´kis) n. A type of axial structure.

ra-cial (r´shal) adj. A characteristic of a race of people. **racially** adv.

rac-ism (r´siz um) n. A thought or belief that one race is better than another race. **-ist** n.

rack (rak) n. An open framework or stand for displaying or holding something; an instrument of torture used to stretch the body; a triangular frame used to arrange the balls on a pool table.

rack-et-eer (rak´i tr´) n. A person who engages in acts which are illegal.

rac-y (r´s) adj. Having a spirited or strongly marked quality; slightly improper or immodest. **racily, raciness** n.

ra-dar (r´där) n. A system which uses radio signals to detect the presence of an object or the speed the object is traveling.

ra-di-al (r´d al) adj. Pertaining to or resembling a ray or radius; developing from a center axis.

ra-di-ance (r´d ans) n. The quality of being shiny; the state of being radiant; relating or emitting to radiant heat.

ra-di-ant (r´d ant) adj. Emitting rays of heat or light; beaming with kindness or love; projecting a strong quality.

radiant heat n. Heat that is transmitted by radiation.

ra-di-ate (r´d t´) v. To move out in rays, such as heat moving through the air. - **radiately** adv.

ra-di-a-tion (r´d ´shan) n. An act of radiating; the process or action of radiating; the process of emitting radiant energy in the form of particles or waves. **-less** adj.

ra-di-a-tor (r´d ´tr) n. Something which radiates.

rad-i-cal (rad´i kal) adj. Proceeding from a foundation or root; drastic; making extreme changes in views, conditions, or habits; carrying convictions or theories to their fullest application. **radically ,**

rad-i-cate *v.* To take root.

rad-i-cle (rad´i kl) *n.* The lower part of a plant embryo or seedling.

radii *pl. of* Radius.

ra-di-o (r´d´) *n.* The technique of communicating by radio waves; the business of broadcasting programmed material to the public via radio waves. **radioing** *v.*

ra-di-o-ac-tive (r´d´ ak´tiv) *adj.* Exhibiting radioactivity.**radioactively** *adv.*

ra-di-o-fre-quen-cy (r´d fr´kwen´s) *n.* A frequency which is above 15,000 cycles per second that is used in radio transmission.

ra-di-o-gram (r´d gram´) *n.* A type of radiograph.

ra-di-ol-o-gy (r´d ol´o j) *n.* A science which deals with rays for a radioactive substance and use for medical diagnosis. **radiologist, radiological** *adj.*

rad-ish (rad´ish) *n.* The pungent, edible root of the radish plant.

ra-di-us (r´d us) *n. pl.* **-dii** or **-uses** A line from the center of a circle to its surface or circumference.

raff (raf) *n.* The rabble of a group or town.

raf-fi-a (raf´ a) *n.* A fiber from an African palm tree used for making baskets, hats, and other woven articles.

raf-fle (raf´l) *n.* A game of chance; a lottery in which one buys chances to win something.

raft (raft) *n.* A floating structure made from logs or planks and used for water transportation.

rag (rag) *n.* A cloth which is useless and sometimes used for cleaning purposes.

rag-a-muf-fin (rag´a muf´in) *n.* A child who is unkempt.

rag doll *n.* A child's doll that is usually made from scrap material and has a hand-painted face.

rage (rj) *n.* Violent anger; intense feelings. **raging** *adj.*

ragingly *adv.*

rag-ged (rag´id) *adj.* To be torn or ripped; unkempt. **raggedness** *n.* **raggedly** *adv.*

rag-lan (rag´lan) *n.* A loose fitting coat with extra wide sleeves.

raid (rd) *n.* A sudden invasion or

seizure.

rail (rl) *n.* A horizontal bar of metal, wood, or other strong material supported at both ends or at intervals; the steel bars used to support a track on a railroad.

rain (rn) *n.* The condensed water from at mospheric vapor, which falls to earth in the form of drops.

rain-bow (rn´b´) *n.* An arc that contains bands of colors of the spectrum and is formed opposite the sun and reflects the sun's rays, usually visible after a light rain shower.

rain-fall (rn´fol´) *n.* The amount of measurable precipitation.

rain for-est *n.* A tropical woodland that has an annual rainfall of at least 100 inches.

raise (rz) *v.* To cause to move upward; to build; to make greater in size, price, or amount; to increase the status; to grow; as plants; to rear as children; to stir ones emotions; to obtain or collect as funds or money.

rake (rk) *n.* A tool with a long handle at the end and a set of teeth at the other end used to gather leaves and other matter; a slope or incline, as the rake of an auditorium.

ral-ly (ral´) *v.* To call together for a purpose. *n.* A rapid recovery, as from depression, exhaustion, or any setback; in a meeting whose purpose is to rouse or create support; an automobile run over public roads at average speeds between checkpoints a route unfamiliar to the participants.

ram (ram) *n.* A male sheep; an implement used to drive or crush by impact; to cram or force into place.

RAM *abbr.* Random access memory.

ram-ble (ram´bl) *v.* To stroll or walk without a special destination in mind; to talk without sequence of ideas. ramble, **ramblingly** *adv.*

ram-bunc-tious (ram bungk´shus) *adj.* Rough or boisterous. **rambunctiousness** *n.*

ra-men-tum (ra men´tum) *n.* A type of scaly material that adheres to the leaves and the stems of certain ferns.

ra-mie (ram´) *n.* A perennial plant with strong fibers used in the manufacture of clothing.

ram-i-fy (ram´i f´) v. To send forth branches.

ramp (ramp) n. An incline which connects two different levels; movable staircase allows passengers to enter or leave an aircraft.

ram-page (ram pj´) n. A course of destruction or violent behavior. v. To storm about in a rampage. **rampageous, rampageously** adv.

ram-pan-cy (ram´pan s) n. The state or quality of being rampant.

ram-pant (ram´pant) adj. Exceeding or growing without control; wild in actions; standing on the hind legs and elevating both forelegs.

ram-part (ram´pärt) n. An embankment raised as a fortification or barrier.

ram-rod (ram´rod´) n. A metal rod used to drive or plunge the charge into a muzzle-loading gun or pistol; the rod used for cleaning the barrels of a rifle or other firearm.

ram-u-lose (ram´ya ls´) adj. To have small branches.

ranch (ranch) n. A large establishment for raising cattle, sheep, or other livestock; a large farm that specializes in a certain crop or animals. **rancher** n.

ran-cho (ranch) n. A small Mexican ranch.

ran-cid (ran´sid) adj. Having a rank taste or smell. **rancidness** n.

ran-cor (rang´kr) n. Bitter ill will. **rancorous, rancorousness** n.

ran-dom (ran´dom) adj. Done or made in a way that has no specific pattern or purpose; to select from a group whose members all had an even chance of being chosen.

range (rnj) n. An area over which anything moves; an area of activity; a tract of land over which animals such as cattle and horses graze; an extended line or row especially of mountains; an open area for shooting at a target; large cooking stove with burners and oven n., v. To arrange in a certain order; to extend or proceed in a particular direction.

range finder n. Instrument that is used in gunnery to determine the distance of a target.

rank (rank) n. A degree of official position or status. v. To place in order, class, or rank. adj. A strong and disagreeable odor, smell, or taste. **-ly** adv. **-ness** n. **-ness**

ran-sack (ran´sak) v. To search or plunder through every part of something.

ran-som (ran´som) n. The price demanded or paid for the release of a kidnaped person; the payment for the release of a person or property detained. **ransom** v.

rant (rant) v. To talk in a wild, excited loud way. **ranter** n.

ran-u-la (ran´la) n. A type of cyst that can occur under the tongue due to a blockage in a duct.

rap (rap) v. To talk with people with similar interest and problems.

rap-id (rap´id) adj. Having great speed; completed quickly or in a short time. **rapidity** n. **rapidness** n.

ra-pi-er (r´p r) n. A long, slender, straight sword with two edges.

rap-ine (rap´in) n. The forcible taking of another's property.

rap-pee (ra p´) n. A snuff made from dark tobacco leaves.

rap-pel (ra pel´) n. A descent from a cliff using a rope under one thigh, across the back and over the opposite shoulder.

rap-port (ra pr´) n. A harmonious relationship.

rapt (rapt) adj. Deeply absorbed or carried away with something and not to noticing anything else; engrossed. **raptness, raptly** adv.

rap-tor (rap tr) n. A bird of prey.

rap-ture (rap´chr) n. An experience of being carried away by emotion.

ras-bo-ra (raz br´a) n. A breed of brightly colored fish often kept in tropical aquariums.

ras-cal (ras´kal) n. A person full of mischief; a person who is not honest. **rascally** adj.

rash (rash) adj. Acting without consideration or caution. n. A skin irritation or eruption caused by an allergic reaction.

ra-so-ri-al (ra sr´al) adj. Pertaining to birds who have the caracteristics of scratching the ground in search of food.

rasp-y (ras´p) *adj.* Grating; irritable.

rat (rat) *n.* A rodent similar to the mouse, but having a longer tail. *Slang* A despicable person who betrays his friends or his associates.

rat-a-fia (rat´a f´a) *n.* A liqueur flavored with kernels of fruit and almonds.

rat-a-tat (rat´a tat´) *n.* A sharp tapping, or repeated knocking.

ratch-et (rach´it) *n.* A mechanism consisting of a pawl that allows a wheel or bar to move in one direction only.

rate (rt) *n.* The measure of something to a fixed unit; the degree of price or value; a fixed ratio or amount. *v.* To appraise.

ra-tel (rt´el) *n.* An African nocturnal carnivorous mammal resembling a badger.

rathe (rth) *adj.* To be before the normal time.

rath-er (rath´r) *adv.* Preferably; with more reason or justice; more accurate or precise.

rat-i-fy (rat´i f´) *v.* To approve something in an official way. **ratification** *n.*

ra-ti-ne (rat´i n´) *n.* A nubby ply yarn made by twisting a thick and a thin yarn under pressure.

rat-ing (r´ting) *n.* A relative evaluation or estimate of something.

ra-tio (r´sh) *n. pl.* **-tios** The relationship between two things in amount, size, degree, expressed as a proportion.

ra-tion (rash´an) *n.* A fixed portion or share. *v.* To provide or allot in rations. **rationing** *n.* **rationed** *v.*

ra-tion-al (rash´a nal) *adj.* Having the faculty of reasoning; being of sound mind. **rationality** *n.* **rationally** *adv.* **-ness** *n.*

ra-toon (ra tön´) *v.* To grow or sprout up from the root.

rat-tan (ra tan´) *n.* An Asian palm whose strong stems are used to make wicker-works.

rat-tle (rat´l) *v.* To make a series of rapid, sharp noises in quick succession; to talk rapidly; chatter. *n.* A baby's toy made to rattle when shaken.

rat-ty (rat´) *adj.* Shabby; unkempt.

rau-cous (ro´kus) *adj.* Loud and rowdy;

having a rough hoarse sound; disorderly. **raucously, raucousness** *n.*

rav-age (rav´ij) *v.* To bring on heavy destruction; devastate.

rave (rv) *v.* To speak incoherently; to speak with enthusiasm. *n.* The act of raving.

rav-el (rav´el) *v.* To separate fibers or threads; to unravel.

ra-ven (r´ven) *n.* A large bird, with shiny black feathers. *adj.* Of or relating to the glossy sheen or color of the raven.

rav-in *n.* Something seized as prey.

rav-i-o-li (rav´ l) *n.* A small piece of dough filled with meat or cheese served in a tomato sauce.

raw (ro) *adj.* Uncooked; in natural condition; not processed; inexperienced; damp, sharp, or chilly. **rawly , -ness** *n.*

raw-hide (ro´hd´) *n.* The untanned hide of cattle.

ray (r) *n.* A thin line of radiation or light; a small trace or amount; one of several lines emerging from a point.

ray-on (r´on) *n.* A synthetic cellulose yarn; any fabric made from such yarn.

raze (rz) *v.* To destroy or demolish.

ra-zor (r´zr) *n.* A sharp cutting instrument used especially for shaving.

razz (raz) *v. Slang* To heckle; to tease.

raz-zledaz-zle (raz´l daz´l) *n.* A state of complete confusion.

re- *prefix* Again, a new or reverse action.

reach (rch) *v.* To stretch out; to be able to grasp. *n.* The act of stretching out. **reachable, reacher** *n.*

re-act (r akt´) *v.* To act in response to. *Chem.* To undergo a chemical change; to experience a chemical reaction; to move in a reverse direction; to cause to react.

re-ac-tant (r ak´tant) *n.* Substance which enters into and alters the course of a chemical reaction.

re-ac-tion (r ak´shan) *n.* The mental or bodily response to an activity; the process or act or reacting; the action that is induced by vital resistance to another action; exhaustion caused by excessive exertion of stimulation; a emotional disorder forming a person's response to his life; the force that a body exerts when forced from another body in the opposite direction; a chemical change; the state resulting from an interaction of chemical entities. **reactional, reactionally** *adv.*

re-ac-tor (r ak´tr) *n.* A person, object, device, or substance which reacts to something.

read (rd) *v.* To visually go over something, as a book, and to understand its meaning; to learn or be informed; to perceive something in a meaning which may or may not actually be there; to become acquainted with or look at the contents; to recognize the nature of *v.* By observing outward expression or signs.

read-able (r´da bl) *adj.* Able to be read with ease. **readability** *adv.* **-ably** *adv.*

readi-ly (red´i l) *adj.* Without hesitation; without a lot of difficulty.

read-out (rd´out´) *n.* In computer science, the process of removing information from a computer and displaying it in an understandable form; the process of reading something; the radio transmission of pictures or information from a space vehicle either immediately upon acquisition or by tape recording playback. **readiness** *n.*

ready-y (red´) *adj.* Prepared for use or action; quick or prompt; willing.

re-a-gent (r ´jent) *n.* Any substance which causes a chemical reaction.

re-al (r´al) *adj.* Something which is existing, genuine, true, or authentic. *Law* Property which is regarded as permanent, fixed, or immovable; not illusory, artificial, or fraudulent.

re-al-ism (r´a liz´um) *n.* Concern or interest with actual facts and things as they really are. **realist, realistic** *adj.* -**ically** *adv.*

re-al-i-ty (r al´i t) *n. pl.* The fact or state of being real or genuine; an actual situation or real event; something that is neither dependent nor derivative but exists necessarily.

re-al-ize (r´a lz´) *v.* To understand correctly; to make real; to make or cause to seem real. **realizer** *n*

re-al-ly (r´a l) *adv.* Actually; truly; indeed; unquestionably.

realm (relm) *n.* A scope or field of any

power or influence.

ream (rm) *n.* A quantity of paper containing 500 sheets; *v.* To widen the opening of something.

reap (rp) *v.* To harvest a crop with a sickle or other implement; to cut with a scythe, sickle, or other harvesting machine.

reap-er (r´pr) *n.* A machine used to reap grain.

rear (rr) *n.* The back. *adj.* Of or at the rear. *v.* To raise upon the hind legs; to raise as an animal or child; to erect by building something. **rearer** *n.*

re-arm (r ärm´) *v.* To supply with new or better weapons. **rearmament** *n.*

rear-most (rr´mst´) *adj.* Being farthest in the rear.

rea-son (r´zon) *n.* A statement given to confirm or justify a belief, promise, or excuse; the ability to decide things, to obtain ideas, to think clearly, and to make logical and rational choices and decisions. *v.* To discuss something logically. **reasoning, reasoner** *n.*

rea-son-a-ble (r´zo na bl) *adj.* Moderate; rational; not excessive or extreme. **reasonableness, reasonably** *adv.*

rea-son-ing (r´zo ning) *n.* Conclusions drawn through the use of reason.

re-as-sur-ance (r) *n.* The act of reassuring; reinsurance.

re-as-sure (r´a sher´) *v.* To restore confidence. **reassuringly** *adv.*

reave *v.* To carry away. **reaver** *n.*

re-bate (r´bt) *n.* A deduction allowed on items sold; a discount; money which is returned to the purchaser from the original payment. *v.* To return part of the payment.

re-bel (ri bel´) *v.* To refuse allegiance; to resist any authority; to react with violence; to take arms against a government.

re-bel-lion (ri bel´yon) *n.* An organized uprising to change or overthrow an existing authority.

re-birth (r berth´) *n.* A revival or renaissance; reincarnation; spiritual regeneration.

re-bound (ri bound´) *v.* To spring back; to recover from a setback or frustration; to gain possession of a rebound ball in basketball. *n.* recoil.

re-bound-er n. A basketball player skilled at rebounding the ball.

re-broad-cast (r brod´kast´) v. To repeat or broadcast again at a later time or date. **rebroadcaster** n.

re-buff (ri buf´) v. To refuse abruptly; to snub.

re-build (r bild´) v. To restore or make extensive changes to a building; to reconstruct; remodel.

re-but (ri but´) v. To try and prove someone wrong by argument or evidence; to contradict by formal argument. **rebuttal** n. **-able** adj.

re-cal-cu-late (r kal´k lt´) v. To calculate again to discover an error or formulate new conclusions. **recalculation** n.

re-call (ri kol´) v. To order or summon to return to ask for something to be returned; so that defects can be fixed or repaired; to remember; to recollect.

re-cant (ri kant´) v. To formally admit that a previously held belief was wrong by making public confession; to withdraw; renounce.

re-cap (r´kap´) v. To restore an old tire; to review or summarize something.

re-cast (r kast´) v. To cast new people in a play; to cast once again.

re-cede (ri sd´) v. To move back; as floodwater; to withdraw from an agreement; to grow less or smaller.

re-ceipt (ri st´) n. The written acknowledgment of something received. pl., **receipts** The amount of money received.

re-ceive (ri sv´) v. To take or get something; to greet customers or guests; to accept as true or correct; to assimilate through senses.

re-cen-sion (ri sen´shan) n. A revision of a text.

re-cent (r´sent) adj. Happening at a time just before the present; relating to a short time ago. **-ly, recentness** n.

re-cep-ta-cle (ri sep´ta kl) n. Anything which holds something; an electrical outlet designed to receive a plug.

re-cep-tion (ri sep´shan) n. The act or manner of receiving something; a formal entertainment of guests, as a wedding reception.

re-cep-tion-ist (ri sep´sha nist) n. An employee who greets callers and answers the telephone for a business.

re-cep-tive (ri sep´tiv) adj. Able to receive; open and responsive to ideas.

re-cep-tor (ri sep´tr) n. A group of cells that receive stimuli.

re-cess (ri ses´) n. A break in the normal routine of something; a depression or niche in a smooth surface.

re-ces-sion (ri sesh´an) n. The act of receding; withdrawal; a period or time of reduced economic activity.

rec-i-pe (res´i p´) n. The directions and a list of ingredients for preparing food.

re-cip-i-ent (ri sip´ ent) n. A person who receives something.

re-cip-ro-cal (ri sip´ro kal) adj. To return the same way.

re-cit-al (ri st´al) n. A performance given by an individual musician or dancer.

re-cite (ri st´) v. To repeat something from memory; give an account of something in detail. **reciter** n.

reck-less (rek´lis) adj. State of being careless and rash when doing something. **recklessness, recklessly** adv.

reck-on (rek´on) v. To calculate; to compute; to estimate; to consider; to assume. **with** Take into consideration.

reck-on-ing (rek´o ning) n. The act of calculation or counting.

re-claim (ri klm´) v. To redeem; to reform; to recall; to change to a more desirable condition or state. **reclaimable** adj.

rec-la-ma-tion (rek´la m´shan) n. The state of being reclaimed.

re-cline (ri kln´) v. To assume a prone position.

rec-luse (rek´lōs) n. A person who chooses to live in seclusion.

rec-og-ni-tion (rek´og nish´an) n. An acknowledgment which is formal; the action of recognizing something; special attention or notice.

re-cog-ni-zance (ri kog´ni zans) n. An amount of money which will be forfeited for a nonperformance of an obligation.

rec-og-nize (rek´og nz´) v. To experience or identify something or someone as having been known previously; to be appreciative.

re-coil (ri koil´) v. To fall back or to rebound; to spring back under pressure.

rec-ol-lect (rek´o lekt´) v. To remember or recall to the mind.

rec-om-pense (rek´om pens´) v. To reward with something for a service.

re-com-pose (r´kom pz´) v. To restore the composure of. **recomposition** n.

rec-on-cile (rek´on sl´) v. To restore a friendship after an estrangement.

rec-on-dite (rek´on dt´) adj. Being obscure. **reconditely, reconditeness** n.

re-con-di-tion (r´kon dish´an) v. To return to a good condition.

re-con-firm (r´kon ferm´) v. Confirm something again. **reconfirmation** n.

re-con-nais-sance (ri kon´i sans) n. An observation of territory such as that of the enemy.

re-con-noi-ter (r´ko noi´tr) v. To survey a region. **reconnoitering** v.

re-con-sid-er (r´kon sid´r) v. To think about again with a view to changing a previous action or decision. **reconsideration** n.

re-con-struc-tion (r´kon struk´shan) n. Something which has been reconstructed or rebuilt.

re-cord (ri kord´) v. To write down for future use or permanent reference; to preserve sound on a tape or disk for replay; a phonograph record. n. Information which is recorded and kept permanently.

re-cord-er (ri kor´dr) n. A person who records things such as official transactions.

re-cord-ing (ri kor´ding) n. The act of making a transcription of sounds.

rec-ord play-er n. The machine which is used to play recordings.

re-count (r kount´) v. To tell the facts; narrate or describe in detail; to count again. n. A second count to check the results of the first count. **recounter** n.

re-coup (ri köp´) v. To be reimbursed; to recover. **-able** adj. **recoupment** n.

re-course (r´krs) n. A turning to or an appeal for help; a source of help.

re-cov-er (ri kuv´r) v. To regain something which was lost; to be restored to good health. Law. To obtain a judgment for damages. **recoverability** adj.

-able adj. **recoverer** n.

re-cov-er-y (ri kuv´e r´) n. The power to regain something.

rec-re-ant (rek´r ant) adj. Cowardly; unfaithful.

re-cre-ate (r´kr t´) v. To create again, to form in the imagination. **recreative** adj. **recreatable** adj. **recreative** adj.

rec-re-a-tion (rek´r´ shan) n. Refreshment of body and mind; a pleasurable occupation or exercise. **-al** adj.

re-cru-desce (r´krö des´) v. To break out; become raw again. **-cence** n.

re-cruit (ri krót´) v. To enlist someone for military or naval purposes; to look for someone as for a service or employment. n. A newly enlisted person.

rec-tal (rek´tal) adj. Referring to the rectum of the body. **rectally** adv.

rec-tan-gle (rek´tang´ gl) n. A parallelogram with all right angles. **rectangular, rectangularity** n.

rec-ti-fi-er (rek´ti f´r) n. That which rectifies something.

rec-ti-fy (rek´ti f´) v. To make correct. Chem. To purify by repeated distillations. Electr. To make an alternating current a direct current. **-ication** n.

rec-ti-lin-ear (rek´ti lin´ r) adj. Made up of or indicated by straight lines; bounded by straight lines. **rectilinearly** adv.

rec-ti-tude (rek´ti töd´) n. Rightness in principles and conduct; correctness.

rec-to (rek´t) n. The right-hand page of a book.

rec-tor (rek´tr) n. A member of the clergy in charge of a parish; a priest in charge of a congregation, church, or parish; the principal or head of a school or of a college. **rectorate** n. **rectorial** adj. **rectorship** n.

rec-to-ry (rek´to r) n. The rector's residence.

rec-tum (rek´tum) n. pl. **-tums, -ta** Anat. The lower terminal portion of the large intestine connecting the colon and anus.

re-cum-bent (ri kum´bent) adj. Lying down or reclining. **recumbently** adv.

re-cu-per-ate (ri kö´pe rt´) v. To regain strength or to regain one's health; to recover from a financial loss.

re-cur (ri ker´) v. To happen, to return, or to appear again. **recurrence** adj. **recurrent** adj.

re-cy-cle v. To return to an earlier usable condition. **recyclable** adj.

re-dact (ri dakt´) v. To adapt for publication. **redactional** adj.

rede (rd) v. To advise or counsel.

re-dec-o-rate (r dek´o rt´) v. To change in appearance; to refurbish.

re-deem (ri dm´) v. To buy back; to pay off; to turn something in, as coupons or rain checks and receive something in exchange. **redeemable** adj. **-er** n.

re-demp-tion (ri demp´shan) n. The act of redeeming; rescue; ransom; that which redeems; salvation. **redemptional** adj.

re-demp-tive (ri demp´tiv) adj. Relating to redemption.

re-de-ploy (r´di ploi´) v. To move men and equipment from one location to another.

re-de-scribe (rd skrb) v. To give a more updated version of something.

re-de-sign (r´di zn´) v. To change or revise the appearance or function of something.

re-de-vel-op-ment n. The renovation of a rundown area.

red-in-gote (red´ing gt´) n. A fitted double- breasted coat with wide flat cuffs and collar worn by men in the 18th century.

red-in-te-grate (red in´te grt´) v. To restore to a former sound state.

re-di-rect (r´di rekt´) v. To change the course of something. **redirection** n.

re-dis-trib-ute (r´di strib´t) v. To spread to different areas. **redistributive** adj.

re-doubt (ri dout´) n. A small enclosed fortification.

re-dound (ri dound´) v. To have an effect on something.

re-dress (ri dres´) v. To put something right; to remedy. **redresser** n.

re-duce (ri dös´) v. To decrease; lessen in number, degree, or amount; to put into order; to lower in rank; to lose weight by dieting. **reducer** n. **reducible** adj.

re-duc-tion (ri duk´shan) n. The state of being reduced. **reductional** adj.

re-dun-dant (ri dun´dant) adj. Exceeding what is necessary; repetitive. **redundancy** n.

redundantly adv. **redundancy** n.

re-du-pli-cate (ri dö´pli kt´) v. To repeat something.

reed (rd) n. Tall grass with a slender stem, which grows in wet areas; a thin tongue of wood, metal, cane, or plastic; placed in the mouthpiece of an instrument to produce sounds by vibrating.

reef (rf) n. A chain of rocks, coral, or sand at or near the surface of the water.

reek (rk) v. To emit vapor or smoke; to give off a strong offensive odor.

reel (rl) n. A device which revolves on an axis and is used for winding up or letting out fishing line, rope, or other string-like material; a lively and fast dance; a bobbin for sewing thread.

re-em-ploy (r´em ploi´) v. To rehire someone who previously worked for you.

re-en-act (r´en akt´) v. To perform again; to repeat the actions of a previous event.

re-en-ter (r en´tr) v. To enter a room or area again.

re-ex-am-ine (r´ig zam´in) v. Examine something or someone another time or again. **reexamination** n.

re-fer (ri fer´) v. To direct for treatment, information, or help; to classify within a general category or cause.

ref-er-ence (ref´r ens) n. The act of referring someone to someplace or to something.

ref-er-en-dum (ref´e ren´dum) n. A public vote on an item for final approval or for rejection.

ref-er-ent (ref´r ent) n. What is referred to, such as a person; the thing that a word or sign stand for. **referent** adj.

re-fill (r fil´) v. To fill something with an item again. **refillable** adj.

re-fine (ri fn´) v. To purify by removing unwanted substances or material; to improve. **refined** adj. **refinement** n.

re-fit (r fit´) v. To repair something.

re-flex (r´fleks) adj. Turning, casting, or bending backward. n. An involuntary reaction of the nervous system to a stimulus.

re-flex-ive (ri flek´siv) adj. A relation

that exists between an entity and itself.
reflexiveness n. **reflexivity** n.

re-flex-ol-gy (r fleks´) n. The science of behavior of simple and complex reflexes.

re-flow v. To flow back again.

re-fo-cus (r f´kus) v. To change the direction of.

re-form (ri form´) v. To reconstruct, make over, or change something for the better; improve; to abandon or give up evil ways. **-er** n. **reformed** adj.

re-fract (ri frakt´) v. The deflecting something, such as a ray of light.

re-frain (ri frn´) v. To hold back; to keep oneself from following a passing impulse. n. A recurring phrase at the end of each stanza of a poem or song.

re-fresh (ri fresh´) v. To freshen something again; to restore strength. **refreshingly, refreshing** adj. **-er** n.

re-frig-er-ant (ri frij´r ant) n. An agent which cools something.

ref-u-gee (ref´ j´) n. A person who flees to find safety. **refugeeism** n.

re-ful-gent (ri ful´jent) adj. State of being radiant or putting off a bright light.

re-fund (ri fund´) v. To return or pay back; to reimburse **refund** n. **refundability** n.

re-fuse (ri fz´) v. To decline; to reject; to deny.

re-fute (ri ft´) v. To overthrow or to disprove with the use of evidence.

re-gain (ri gn´) v. To recover; to reach again.

re-gale (ri gl´) v. To entertain or delight; to give pleasure.

re-gard (ri gärd´) v. To look upon closely; to consider; to have great affection for. n. Careful attention or thought; esteem or affection. **regards** Greetings of good wishes.

re-gen-cy (r´jen s) n. pl. **-ies** The jurisdiction or office of a regent.

re-gent (r´jent) n. One who rules and acts as a ruler during the absence of a sovereign, or when the ruler is underage.

re-gime (re zhem´) n. An administration.

reg-i-men (rej´i men´) n. Government control; therapy; a systematic plan to improve the health.

re-gion (r´jan) n. An administrative, political, social, or geographical area.

reg-is-ter (rej´i str) n. Something which contains occurrences; a book of public records.

reg-is-tered (rej´i strd) adj. Recorded with the owner's name; recorded on the basis of pedigree of an animal.

reg-let (reg´lit) n. A narrow strip of molding.

re-gret (ri gret´) v. To feel disappointed or distressed about; to be sorry for. n. A sense of loss or expression of grief; a feeling of sorrow. **regretably** adv.

re-group (r grp´) v. To reorganize after a setback in an activity.

reg-u-late (reg´ya lt´) v. To adjust to a specification or requirement; to bring order or authority.

reg-u-lus (reg´a lus) n. A star in the constellation Leo.

re-hash (r hash´) v. To rework or go over old material; to discuss again.

re-hu-man-ize v. To restore to a full life; restore human rights and dignity.

reign (rn) n. The period in time when the monarch rules over an area.

re-im-burse (r´im bers´) v. To repay; to make restitution. **reimbursement** n.

rein (rn) n. One of a pair of narrow, leather straps attached to the bit of a bridle and used to control a horse.

re-in-force (r´in frs´) v. To support; to strengthen with additional people or equipment. **reinforcement** n.

re-in-vent (r´in vent´) v. To remake something that has already been invented.

re-in-vest (r´in vest´) v. To invest money in additional securities.

re-is-sue (r ish´ö) v. To make available again.

re-ject (ri jekt´) v. To refuse; to discard as useless. **reject** n. **rejection** n.

re-ju-ve-nate (ri jö´ve nt´) v. To restore to youthful appearance or vigor. **-ion** n.

re-late (ri lt´) v. To tell the events of; to narrate; to bring into natural association. **relater, relatable** adj.

rel-a-tiv-i-ty (rel´a tiv´i t) n. A condition or state of being relative.

re-lay (r´l) n. A race in which a fresh team replaces another. v. To pass from one group to another.

rel-e-gate (rel´e gt´) v. To banish someone or something. **relegation** n.

re-lent (ri lent´) v. To soften in temper, attitude, or determination; to slacken. **relentless, relentlessness** adj.

rel-e-vant (rel´e vant) adj. Related to matters at hand. **relevantly** adv.

re-li-a-ble (ri lī´a bl) adj. Dependable; capable of being relied upon. **-ness** n.

re-li-ant (ri lī´ant) adj. State of being confident or having reliance.

rel-ic (rel´ik) n. Something which is very old; a keepsake; an object whose cultural environment has disappeared.

re-lin-quish (ri ling´kwish) v. To release something or someone; withdraw from; to give up. **-ment** n.

rel-i-quary (rel´i kwer´) n. A shrine in which sacred relics are kept.

re-luct (ri lukt´) v. To revolt; to feel opposition.

re-lume (ri lōm´) v. To light again.

re-ly (ri lī´) v. To trust or depend; to have confidence in someone.

re-main (ri mān´) v. To continue without change; to stay after the departure of others.

re-make v. To revise an old movie, etc.

re-mand (ri mand´) v. To order back; to send to another court or agency for further action; to return to custody pending trial.

re-mark (ri märk´) n. A brief expression or comment; to take notice; to observe; to comment.

re-match (r´mach) n. A second contest between the same contestants or teams.

re-me-di-al (ri mē´d al) adj. Concerned with the correction of study habits.

rem-e-dy (rem´i d) n. pl. **-ies** A therapy or medicine which relieves pain; something which corrects an error or fault. v. To cure or relieve a disease; to rectify.

re-mex (r´meks) n. A quill feather in the wing of a bird. **remigial** adj.

re-mind (ri mīnd´) v. To cause or help to remember. **reminder** n.

rem-i-nisce (rem´i nis´) v. To recall the past things which have happened.

re-mint v. To make old coins into new coins by melting down the old coins.

re-mise (ri mīz´) v. To release a claim to.

re-mit (ri mit´) v. To send money as

payment for goods; to forgive, as a crime or sin; to slacken, make less violent, or less intense. **remittance, remitter** n.

rem-nant (rem´nant) n. A small piece or a scrap of something.

re-mon-e-tize (r mon´i tz´) v. To restore to use as legal tender. **-ation** n.

rem-o-ra (rem´ā a) n. Any of several fishes that have anterior dorsal fin converted into a disk on the head thereby allowing them to cling to other fishes or ships.

re-morse (ri mors´) n. Deep moral regret for past misdeeds.

re-mount (r mount´) v. To mount something again.

re-mu-da (ri mö´da) n. A herd of horses from which they chose the horses to be used for the day.

re-mu-ner-ate (ri m´ne rt´) v. Pay an equivalent for a service; to reward.

re-nas-cence (ri nas´ens) n. A revival or a rebirth.

re-na-ture v. To restore to an original condition.

rend (rend) v. To remove from with violence; to split. **renderable** adj.

re-nege (ri nig´) v. To fail to keep one's word. **reneger** n.

re-new (ri nö´) v. To make new or nearly new by restoring; to resume.

re-ni-tent (ri nt´ent) adj. Resisting pressure; opposed.

re-nom-i-nate (r nom´i nt) v. To nominate for a succeeding term.

ren-o-vate (ren´o vt´) v. To return or to restore to a good condition; to make new. **renovation, renovator** n.

re-or-gan-i-za-tion (r or ga niz´shan) n. The process of reorganizing something.

re-pair (ri pâr´) v. To restore to good or usable condition; to renew; refresh.

re-pand (ri pand´) adj. Having a slightly wavy margin.

re-par-a-tive (ri par´a tiv) adj. Able to make amends.

re-past (ri past´) n. Something taken as food; food which comprises a meal.

re-peat (ri pt´) v. To utter something again; to do an action again.

re-pel (ri pel´) v. To discourage; to force away; to create a version.

re-pent (ri pent´) v. To feel regret for something which has occurred; to change one's sinful way. **repentance** n. **repentant** adj.

rep-e-ti-tion (rep´i tish´an) n. The act of doing something over and over again; the act of repeating.

re-plen-ish (ri plen´ish) v. To add to something to replace what has gone or been used. **replenisher** n. **replenishment** n.

rep-li-ca (rep´li ka) n. A reproduction or copy of something. **replicate** v.

re-pos-al (ri p´zal) n. An act or action of reposing.

re-pose (ri pz´) n. The act of being at rest. v. To lie at rest. **reposeful** adj.

re-pos-sess (r´po zes´) v. To restore ownership of something.

rep-re-hend (rep´ri hend´) v. To show or express disapproval of.

re-press (ri pres´) v. To restrain; hold back; to remove from the conscious mind.

re-prieve (ri prv´) v. To postpone punishment; to provide temporary relief; a temporary suspension of an execution.

re-prise (ri prz´) v. To take back by force.

rep-ro-bate (rep´ro bt´) adj. The state of being morally depraved. v. To condemn as unacceptable or evil.

re-pro-duce (r´pro dõs´) v. To produce an image or copy. Biol. To produce an offspring; to recreate or produce again.

re-prove (ri prõv´) v. To tell or express a disapproval of something.

re-pu-di-ate (ri p´d t´) v. To cast away; to refuse to pay something.

re-pugn (ri pn´) v. To offer resistance.

re-pulse (ri puls´) v. To repel or drive back; to repel or reject rudely; to disgust or be disgusted with. **repulsion** n.

re-pul-sive (ri pul´siv) adj. State of causing aversion. **repulsively** adv.

re-qui-em (rek´w em) n. The Roman Catholic mass for a deceased person.

req-ui-site (rek´wi zit) adj. Absolutely needed; necessary.

re-quite (ri kwt´) v. To reward; to repay someone. **requiter** n.

re-scind (ri sind´) v. To repeal; to void. **rescinder** n. **recindment** n.

re-send v. To send back.

re-sent (ri zent´) v. To feel angry about.

re-serve (ri zerv´) v. To save for a special reason; to set apart; to retain; to put off. n. Something that is saved for a future point in time; the portion of a country's fighting force kept inactive until called upon.

res-er-voir (rez´r vwär´) n. A body of water stored for the future; large reserve; a supply.

re-shape (r shp´) v. To give new form to.

re-side (ri zd´) v. To dwell permanently; to exist as a quality or attribute. **residence** n.

res-i-due (rez´i dö´) n. Matter remaining after treatment or removal of a part; something which remains.

re-sil-ience (ri zil´yens) n. The ability to recover from a shock without permanent after effects.

re-sist (ri zist´) v. To work against or actively oppose; to withstand.

res-o-lute (rez´o löt´) adj. Coming from or characterized by determination. **resolutely, resolution** n.

re-solve (ri zolv´) v. To make a firm decision on something; to find a solution.

res-o-na-tor (rez´o n´tr) n. A device for increasing sounds of a musical instrument.

re-sound (ri zound´) v. To be filled with echoing sounds; to ring or sound loudly. **resounding, resoundingly** adv.

re-spect (ri spekt´) v. To show consideration or esteem for; to relate to. n. Courtesy or considerate treatment. **fully** adv. **-ful** adj. **respectability** n.

re-spire (ri spr´) v. To inhale and exhale air; take in oxygen.

res-pite (res´pit) n. A temporary postponement.

re-splen-dent (ri splen´dent) adj. Having a shining appearance. **resplendently** adj.

re-spond (ri spond´) v. To answer or reply; to act when prompted by something or someone.

re-sponse (ri spons´) n. A reply; the act of replying. **responsive** adj.

rest (rest) n. A cessation of all work, activity, or motion. Mus. An interval of silence equal in time to a note of same value. v. To stop work; to place or lay.

res-ti-tu-tion (res´ti tö´shan) *n.* The act of restoring something to its rightful owner; compensation for injury, loss, or damage.

res-tive (res´tiv) *adj.* Nervous or impatient because of a delay; resisting control. **restively, restiveness** *n.*

re-store (ri str´) *v.* To bring back to a former condition or original state; to make restitution of. **restoration** *n.*

re-strain (ri strn´) *v.* To hold back or be held back; to control, limit, or restrict. **restrainer** *n.* **restraint** *n.*

re-strict (ri strikt´) *v.* To confine within limits. **restriction, restrictive , ly** *adv.*

re-sult (ri zult´) *v.* To happen or exist in a particular way. *n.* The consequence of an action, course, or operation.

res-u-me (rez´e m´) *n.* A summary of one's personal history, background, work, and education.

re-su-pi-nate (ri sö´pi nt´) *adj.* To bend backward to an inverted position.

re-sus-ci-tate (ri sus´i tt) *v.* To return to life; to revive; give mouth-to-mouth breathing technique to help a person to start breathing again. **resuscitation** *n.*

re-tain (ri tn´) *v.* To hold in one's possession; to remember; to employ someone, as for his services.

re-tal-i-ate (ri tal´´) *v.* To seek revenge against someone. **retaliation** *n.*

re-tard (ri tärd´) *v.* To delay or slow the progress of.

re-ten-tion (ri ten´shan) *n.* The act or condition of being retained.

ret-i-cent (ret´i sent) *adj.* Being uncommunicative in speech; reserved.

re-tic-u-late (ri tik´ya lit) *v.* To divide or construct as to form a network.

ret-i-na (ret´i na) *n. pl.* **-nas, nae** The light sensitive membrane lining the inner eyeball connected by the optic nerve to the brain.

re-tire (ri tr´) *v.* To depart for rest; to remove oneself from the daily routine of working. *Baseball* To put a batter out. **retirement, retired , retiree** *n.*

re-tort (ri tort´) *v.* A witty or cutting reply to another person.

re-tract (ri trakt´) *v.* To draw back or to take back something that has been said. **retractable** *adj.* **retraction** *n.*

re-tread (r tred´) *v.* To replace the tread of a worn tire. **retread** *n.*

ret-ri-bu-tion (re´tri b´shun) *n.* An act of getting revenge against another person. **retributively** *adv.* **retributive** *adj.*

re-trieve (ri trv´) *v.* To regain; to find something and carry it back. **retrievable, retrieval** *n.*

ret-ro-grade (re´tro grd´) *adj.* Moving backward; contrary to normal order.

ret-ro-spect (re´tro spekt´) *n.* A review of things in the past.

re-un-ion (r n´yan) *n.* A reuniting; the coming together of a group which has been separated for a period of time.

re-us-able (r´za bl) *adj.* Capable of using something over and over again.

re-val-u-ate (r val´t´) *v.* To increase the value of something.

re-val-ue (r val´) *v.* To reappraise something as jewelry.

re-vamp (r vamp´) *v.* Patch or reconstruct something again.

re-veal (ri vl´) *v.* To disclose or make known; to expose or bring into view.

rev-eil-le (rev´e l) *n.* The sounding of a bugle used to awaken soldiers in the morning.

rev-el (rev´el) *v.* To take great delight in.

rev-e-la-tion (rev´e l´shan) *n.* An act of or something revealed; a manifestation of divine truth. **Revelation** The last book in the New Testament.

re-venge (ri venj´) *v.* To impose injury in return for injury received.

rev-e-nue (rev´en´) *n.* Income returned by an investment.

revenue stamp *n.* A stamp which serves as evidence of payment of a tax.

re-verb (ri verb´) *n.* An echo effect produced electronically in recorded music.

re-vere (ri vr´) *v.* To honor and respect.

re-ver-sal (ri ver´sal) *n.* An act of over throwing a legal proceeding or judgment.

re-verse (ri vers´) *adj.* Turned backward in position. *n.* The opposite of something; a change in fortune usually from better to worse; change or turn to the opposite direction; to transpose or exchange the positions of. *Law* To revoke a decision.

re-vert (ri vert´) *v.* To return to a former practice or belief. **reversion** *n.*

re-view (ri v´) v. To study or look over something again; to give a report on it. A reexamination; a study which gives a critical estimate of something.

re-vile (ri vīl´) v. To use verbal abuse.

re-vise (ri vīz´) v. To look over something again with the intention of improving or correcting it. **reviser**, **revision** n.

re-vi-tal-ize (r vt´a lz´) v. To give new life or energy to. **revitalization** n.

re-viv-al (ri v´val) n. The act or condition of reviving; the return of a film or play which was formerly presented; a meeting whose purpose is religious reawakening.

re-vive (ri vv´) v. To restore, refresh, or recall; to return to consciousness or life.

re-voke (ri vk´) v. To nullify or make void by recalling. **revocation** n.

re-volt (ri vlt´) v. To try to overthrow authority; to fill with disgust.

rev-o-lu-tion (rev´o lö´shan) n. The act or state of orbital motion around a point; the abrupt overthrow of a government; a sudden change in a system.

re-volve (ri volv´) v. To move around a central point; to spin; to rotate.

re-vue (ri v´) n. A musical show consisting of songs, dances, skits, and other similar entertainment.

re-ward (ri word´) n. Something given for a special service. v. To give a reward.

rhab-do-man-cy (rab´do man´s) n. The discovery of things that are concealed in the ground by the use of a divining rod.

rham-na-ceous (ram n´shus) adj. To be pertaining to or belonging to the buckthorn family of plants.

rhap-sod-ic (rap sod´ik) adj. To have the characteristics of a rhapsody.

rhap-so-dy (rap´so d) n. pl. -ies An excessive display of enthusiasm.

rhat-a-ny (rat´a n) n. A type of South American shrub whose roots are used as an astringent.

rhea (r´a) n. A large flightless South American bird that resembles the African ostrich and has three toes, but smaller.

rhe-ni-um (r´n um) n. A metallic element symbolized by Re.

rhe-ol-o-gy (r ol´o j) n. The study of the behavior of a liquid matter. **-ical** adj.

rhe-om-e-ter (r om´i tr) n. A type of device that is used for measuring the flow of liquids.

rhe-sus (r´sus) n. A light-brown monkey that is used for laboratory tests.

rhet-o-ric (ret´r ik) n. Effective expression in writing or speech; language which is not sincere.

rhe-tor-i-cal (ri tor´i kal) adj. To be involving rhetoric. **rhetoricalness** n.

rhe-tor-i-cal ques-tion n. A kind of question that is used for an effect and no answer is expected.

rhet-o-ri-cian (ret´o rish´an) n. A person who writes elaborate prose.

rheum (röm) n. A fluid that is discharged from the mucus glands of the body.

rheu-mat-ic fe-ver n. A severe infectious disease that is characterized by the swelling of the heart lining and the heart valves.

rheu-ma-tism (rö´ma tiz´um) n. A kind of inflammation that affects the joints and muscles of the body and can be very painful.

Rh fac-tor n. A substance found in the red blood cells of 85% of all humans; the presence of this factor is referred to as PH positive; the absence as PH negative.

rhi-nal (rn´al) adj. To be referring to the nose.

rhine-stone n. An artificial gem made of paste or glass.

rhi-ni-tis (r n´tis) n. An inflammation that occurs in the nose or the membranes of the nose.

rhi-zan-thous (r zan´thus) adj. To be bearing very short stemmed flowers.

rhi-zo-bi-um (r z b´um) n. A type of bacteria that is important in maintaining the soil's fertility.

rhi-zo-ceph-a-lan (r´z sef´a lan) n. A kind of crustacean that lives off a host and causes the host to lose its ability to reproduce.

rhi-zoid (r´zoid) n. The hair-like structure that provides a root for ferns and mosses.

rhi-zome (r´zm) n. A subterranean plant

stem thickened by deposits of reserve food material which produces shoots above and roots below.

rhi-zo-mor-phous (r´z mor´fus) *adj.* To be shaped like a rhizome.

rhi-zo-pus (r´z pus) *n.* A type of mold fungus.

rho-da-mine (r´da mn´) *n.* A red dye.

rho-di-um (r´d um) *n.* A metallic element symbolized by Rh.

rho-do-chro-site (r´do kr´st) *n.* A kind of mineral that is made of manganese carbonate and is pink in color.

rhom-boid (rom´boid) *n.* A parallelogram where the angles are oblique and adjacent sides are unequal. **-bic** *adj.*

rhom-bus (rom´bus) *n.* A four sided figure whose sides are equal in length.

rhon-chus (rong´kus) *n.* A type of rale that occurs in the bronchial tubes of the airway.

rhu-barb (rö´bärb) *n.* A garden plant with large leaves and edible stalks used for pies.

rhy-thm (rĭth´um) *n.* Music, speech, or movements which are characterized by equal or regularly alternating beats.

rhyth-mics (rĭth´miks) *n.* The science of rhythms.

ri-ant (r´ant) *adj.* To be smiling.

rib (rib) *n.* One of a series of curved bones enclosed in the chest of man and animals. *Slang* To tease. **ribber** *n.*

rib-ald (rĭb´ald) *adj.* To be using indecent humor.

rib-band (rĭb´band´) *n.* A narrow strip used in ship building to hold frames in position during construction.

rib-bon (rĭb´on) *n.* A narrow band or strip of fabric, such as satin, used for trimming.

rib-bon fish (rĭb´on fish´) *n.* A kind of marine fish that has a long and flat body.

ri-bo-fla-vin (r´b fl´vin) *n.* A B complex vitamin that is found in milk, leafy vegetables, and liver.

rib-wort (rĭb´wrt´) *n.* A type of weed having a flower head and three-ribbed leaves.

rice (rs) *n.* A cereal grass grown extensively in warm climates.

rich (rich) *adj.* Having great wealth; of great value; satisfying and pleasing in voice, color, tone, or other qualities; extremely productive; as soil or land.

rich-es (rich´iz) *n.* One's wealth.

rich-ly (rich´l) *adv.* To be done in a rich manner or way.

Rich-ter scale *n.* An instrument which measures a seismic disturbance such as an earthquake with 1.5 being the smallest and 8.5 being a very devastating earthquake.

ri-cin (r´sin) *n.* A white powder that is poisonous and is used to cause the agglutination of the red corpuscles.

rick-ets (rik´its) *n.* A childhood disease which is caused by lack of inadequate sunlight or vitamin D resulting in severely deformed bones.

rick-ett-si-a (ri ket´s a) *adj.* A microorganism that is passed from arthropods to humans.

rick-et-y (rik´i t) *adj.* To be ready to fall apart or fall down. **ricketiness** *n.*

rick-rack (rikrak) *n.* A zigzag braid used in trimming.

rick-sha (rik´sho´) *n.* A small 2-wheeled vehicle that is pulled by one man and that originated in Japan.

ric-o-chet (rik´o sh´) *n.* A glancing blow off a flat surface.

ri-cot-ta *n.* A white whey cheese of Italy resembling cottage cheese.

ric-tus (rik´tus) *n.* An opening.

rid (rid) *v.* To make free from anything objectionable. **ridable** *adj.*

rid-dance (rid´ans) *n.* The getting rid of something or someone that is unwanted.

rid-dle (rid´l) *v.* To perforate with numerous holes. *n.* A puzzling problem or question which requires a clever solution. **-ed** *v.* **-ing** *v.*

ride (rd) *v.* To travel in a vehicle or on an animal; to sit on and drive, as a motorcycle. **fall** To flirt with danger. **high** To experience great success. **over** To treat with abuse.

rid-er (r´dr) *n.* One who rides as a passenger; a clause, usually having little relevance, which is added to a document.

ridge (rij) *n.* A long, narrow crest; a horizontal line formed where two sloping surfaces meet. **ridge** *v.*

ridge-pole (rij´pl´) *n.* Timber located at

the top of a roof which is horizontal.

rid-i-cule (rid´i kl´) n. Actions or words intended to make a person or thing the object of mockery. **ridiculer** n.

rid-ing (rīding) n. An action of a person who rides.

ri-dot-to n. A place of entertainment in masquerade popular in the 18th century England.

rife (rf) adj. State of being abundant or abounding. **rifely** adv.

rif-fle (rif´l) n. Ripply water which is caused by a ridge.

rif-fler n. A small scraping tool.

riff-raff (rif´raf´) n. The rabble; low persons in society; a disreputable person.

ri-fle (rˈfl) n. A firearm having a grooved bore designed to be fired from the shoulder.

ri-fle-man (rˈfl man) n. A person skilled in the shooting of a rifle.

ri-fling (rˈfling) n. The act of putting or cutting spiral grooves in the barrel of a gun.

rift (rift) n. A fault; disagreement; a lack of harmony; a shallow place in a stream.

rig (rig) v. To outfit with necessary equipment. n. The arrangement of sails, masts, and other equipment on a ship; the apparatus used for drilling water or oil wells.

rig-a-to-ni (rig´a t´n) n. A curved macaroni with fluted edges.

rig-ger (rig´r) n. A long pointed paintbrush; a ship with special rigs.

rig-ging (rig´ing) n. The lines used aboard a ship in working sails and supporting masts and spars; ropes, etc. used to support and manipulate scenery in the theatre.

right (rt) adj. In accordance with or conformable to law, justice, or morality; proper and fitting; properly adjusted, disposed, or placed; orderly; sound in body or mind. n. The right side, hand, or direction; the direction opposite left. adv. Immediately; completely; according to justice, morality, or law.

right angle n., Geom. An angle of 90 degrees; an angle with two sides perpendicular to each other.

right away adv. Immediately, without

hesitation.

right-eous (r´chus) adj. Free from guilt; morally right; acting in accordance with moral or divine law.

right-ful (rt´ful) adj. Having a legal claim.

right-hand-ed (rt´hand´did) adj. Using the right hand more easily than the left; designed to be used with the right.

right-ly (rt´l) adv. To be done suitably.

right triangle n. A type of triangle where one angle is 90 degrees.

rig-id (rij´id) adj. Not bending; inflexible; severe; stern. **rigidity** n. **rigidness** n.

ri-gid-i-fy (ri jid´i f´) v. To make something rigid. **rigidification** n.

rig-ma-role (rig´ma rl´) n. A meanless or complex procedure.

rig-or (rig´r) n. The condition of being rigid or stiff; stiffness of temper; harshness. **rigorous, rigorously** adv.

rig-or mor-tis (rig´r mor´tis) n. The rigidity of muscles occurring after death.

rile (rl) v. To make angry.

rill-et (ril´it) n. A small brook.

rim (rim) n. The outer edge or border of something; the outer part of a wheel joined to the hub on a car. **-less** adj.

rime (rm) n. An accumulation of granular ice on the windward sides of exposed objects formed from supercooled fog or clouds.

ri-mose (r´ms) adj. To be filled with fissures. **rimosity** n. **rimosely** adv.

rind (rnd) n. A tough outer layer which may be baken or peeled off.

rin-der-pest (rin´dr pest´) n. A kind of contagious disease that affects the ruminant animals.

ring (ring) n. A circular mark, line, or object; a small circular band worn on a finger; a group of persons acting together; especially in an illegal way. v. To make a clear resonant sound, as a bell when struck. n. The sound made by a bell.

ring-bone (ring´bn´) n. The callus growth that occurs on the pastern bones of a horse.

ring-er (ring´r) n. A person who sounds bells by ringing; in the game of horseshoes, a shoe that encircles the peg.

ring-lead-er (ring´lī´dr) n. The person who is the leader of a group, usually one that will violate the law.

ring-let (ring´lit) n. A small curl of hair.

ring-mas-ter (ring´mas´tr) n. The person in charge of performances in the circus.

ring-side (ring´sd´) n. A section or area that is located right around the ring, such as in a boxing match.

ring-worm (ring´werm´) n., Pathol. A contagious skin disease caused by fungi and marked by discolored, ring-shaped, scaly patches on the skin.

rink (ringk) n. A smooth area covered with ice used for hockey or ice-skating; a smooth wooden surface for roller-skating.

rinse (rins) v. To wash lightly with water. n. The act of rinsing; a hair coloring or conditioning solution. **-er, rinsed** v.

rin-sing (rin´sing) n. The action or act of a person who rinses.

ri-ot (rī´ot) n. A wild and turbulent public disturbance. Slang An irresistibly amusing person. **riotous** adj. **rioter** n.

rip (rip) v. To tear apart violently; to move violently or quickly. n. A torn place. **rip-off** To steal.

ri-par-i-an (ri pâr´ an) adj. To be located on the bank by water, such as a lake.

rip cord A cord which, when pulled, releases a parachute from its pack.

rip cur-rent n. A strong surface current flowing outward from shore which results from the return flow of waves.

ripe (rp) adj. Fully developed or aged; mature. **ripeness** n.

rip-en (r´pen) v. To age; to develop to maturity.

rip-per (rip´r) n. A machine used to break up rock, ore, etc.

rip-ping (rip´ing) adj. To be pertaining to the tearing of something.

rip-ple (rip´l) v. To cause to form small waves on the surface of water; to waver gently.

rip rap (rip´rap´) n. A foundation wall of stones thrown together in random fashion.

riproar-ing adj. To be noisy and loud.

rip saw (rip´so´) n. A coarse-toothed saw used to cut wood in the direction of the grain.

rip tide (rip´td´) n. Water made rough by the meeting of opposite tides and currents.

rise (rz) v. To move from a lower position to a higher one; to extend upward; to meet a challenge or demand. n. The act of going up or rising; an elevation in condition or rank.

ris-er (r´zr) n. A person who rises; the upright part of a stairway.

ris-i-bil-i-ty (riz´i bil´i t) n. The ability to laugh.

ris-i-ble (riz´i bl) adj. Being inclined to or causing laughter.

ris-ing (r´zing) adj. To be growing in height; to be more active.

risk (risk) n. A chance of suffering or encountering harm or loss; danger; a person who is a hazard to an insurer.

risk-y (ris´k) adj. To be hazardous or full of risk. **riskiness** n.

ri-sot-to (ri so´t) n. Rice cooked in meat stock, seasoned with cheese.

rite (rt) n. A formal religious ceremony; any formal custom or practice.

rit-u-al (rich´ö al) n. A prescribed method for performing a religious ceremony. adj. Pertaining to or practiced as a rite.

ritzy (rit´s) adj. To be fashionable; having a high fashion.

ri-val (r´val) n. One who strives to compete with another; one who equals or almost equals another.

ri-val-ry (r´val r) n. Competition.

rive (rv) v. To tear or to rip. **river** n.

riv-er (riv´r) n. A relatively large natural stream of water, usually fed by another body of water.

riv-er-bed (riv´r bed´) n. The channel thru which the river flows.

riv-er-ine (riv´e rn´) adj. To be caused or formed by a river.

riv-et (riv´it) n. A metal bolt that is used to secure two or more objects.

riv-u-let (riv´ lit) n. A small stream.

roach (rch) n. A European freshwater fish; cockroach. Slang The butt of a marijuana cigarette.

roach back n. A back that is curved.

road (rd) n. A public highway used for vehicles, people, and animals; a path or course; a course toward the achieve-

ment of something.

road-a-bil-i-ty (r´da bil´i t) n. In reference to a car, its ability to ride over all types of roads.

road met-al n. The material, such as stones, that is used for repairing a road.

road-ster (rd´str) n. The early kind of car that has a single seat for two people and a rumble seat in the rear.

road test n. The test for a car to know how it will handle on the road in normal conditions.

road-way (rd´w´) n. The land the road passes through.

roam (rm) v. To travel aimlessly or without a purpose. **roamer** n.

roan (rn) n. The color of a horse; a sheepskin tanned with sumac.

roar (rr) v. To utter a deep prolonged sound of excitement; to laugh loudly; a boisterous outcry. **roar** n. **roarer** n.

roar-ing (rr´ing) n. A loud sound or cry that is given off by something.

roast (rst) v. To cook meat by using dry heat in an oven. n. A cut of meat.

roast-er (r´str) n. A person that roasts.

rob (rob) v. To take property unlawfully from another person. **robber** n. **robbery** n.

rob-a-lo (rob´a l´) n. A type of marine fish that is found in the West Indian waters.

ro-band n. A piece of woven yarn used to fasten the sail to a spar.

rob-ber (rob´r) n. A person who steals for others.

rob-ber-y (rob´e r) n. The act of larceny from a person by violence or threat.

robe (rb) n. A long loose garment usually worn over night clothes; a long flowing garment worn on ceremonial occasions.

rob-in (rob´in) n. A large North American bird with a black head and reddish breast.

ro-ble (r´bl) n. Type of white oak tree that is found mainly in California.

ro-bot (r´bot) n. A machine capable of performing human duties.

ro-bot-ize (r´bo tz´) v. To make something automatic. **robotization** n.

ro-bust (r bust´) adj. Full of strength and health; rich; vigorous. **robustly - ness** n.

ro-bus-tious (r bus´chus) adj. To be sturdy or strong. **robustiousness** n.

roc-am-bole (rok´am bl´) n. One type of garlic that is cultivated.

rock (rok) n. A hard naturally formed material. *Slang* One who is dependable.

rock candy n. Candy made from boiling sugar and water and crystallized on string.

rock-er (rok´r) n. A curved piece, usually of wood, on which a cradle or chair rocks.

rock-et (rok´it) n. A device propelled with the thrust from a gaseous combustion. v. To move rapidly.

rock-et-ry (rok´i tr) n. The study of rockets.

rock-fish (rok´fish´) n. The striped bass.

rock-ling (rok´ling) n. A little codfish.

rock-oon (rok´ön) n. A research rocket carried by a balloon to a high altitude and then fired.

rockribbed (rok´ribd´) adj. Being firm and unyielding.

rock-rose (rok´rz´) n. Type of flowering shrub.

rock salt n. Salt that is artificially prepared in large crystals, sometimes used in the preparation of ice cream made at home.

rock-weed (rok´wd´) n. Type of seaweed that can be found on rocks during the low tide.

rock wool n. A mineral wool made by blowing steam through molten rock and used for heat and sound insulation.

rock-y (rok´) adj. Unsteady or unstable; full of rocks. **rockiness** n.

rod (rod) n. A straight stick growing from a tree or bush; a pole with a line attached for fishing. **rodlike** adj.

rode (v.) Past tense of ride.

ro-dent (rd´ent) n. A mammal, such as a rat, mouse, or beaver having large incisors used for gnawing.

ro-den-ti-cide (r den´ti sd´) n. A material that is used to destroy rodents.

ro-de-o (r´d´)´ n. A public show, contest, or demonstration of ranching skills, as riding and roping.

rod-man (rod´man) n. A surveyor's assistant.

rod-o-mon-tade (r´do mon td´) n.

Boasting that is vain.

roe (r) *n.* The eggs of a female fish.

roent-gen-o-gram (rent´ge no gram´) *n.* Type of photograph which is made with the use of X-rays. **roentgenographic** *adj.*

roent-gen-o-ther-a-py (rent´ge n ther´ap) *n.* Kind of medical treatment using X-rays.

rogue (rg) *n.* A scoundrel or dishonest person; an innocently or playful person. **roguishness** *n.* **roguishly** *adv.*

rogue el-e-phant *n.* The elephant that has been excluded from the herd.

roil (roil) *v.* To make one angry.

role (rl) *n.* The position or character that an actor or actress plays.

roll (rl) *v.* To move in any direction by turning over and over; to sway or rock from side to side, as a ship; to make a deep prolonged sound as thunder. *n.* A list of names. *Slang* A large amount of money.

roll call *n.* The act of calling out the names on a list in order to determine who is present.

roll-er (r´lr) *n.* A cylinder for crushing, smoothing or rolling something; any of a number of various cylindrical devices.

rol-lick (rol´ik) *v.* To frolic about.

roll-ing mill *n.* A type of mill where metal is rolled into sheets.

roll-ing pin *n.* A long cylinder having two handles and is rolled over dough in order to flatten it out.

roll up *v.* To collect items together.

ro-maine (r mn´) *n.* Type of lettuce that has narrow leaves.

ro-mance (r mans´) *n.* A love affair, usually of the young, characterized by ideals of devotion and purity; a fictitious story filled with extravagant adventures. **romancer** *n.*

Roman numeral *n.* The letter or letters of the Roman system of numbering still used in formal contexts, as V=5, X=10, L=50, C=100, D=500, M=1000.

ro-man-tic (r man´tik) *adj.* Very amorous; referring to romance.

romp (romp) *v.* To run, play, or frolic in a carefree way.

romp-er (rom´pr) *n.* A person who

romps around.

ron-dure (ron´jr) *n.* A form that is gracefully curved.

rood (rōd) *n.* A measurement of land which equals 1/4 acre.

roof (rōf) *n.* The top or covering of a house or other building keeping the elements of weather out. **rooflike** *adj.*

roof gar-den *n.* The garden that can be found on top of a building.

roof-ing (rō´fing) *n.* The supplies and material that are used to cover a roof.

rook-ie (rek´ n. An untrained person; a novice or inexperienced person.

room (rōm) *n.* A section or area of a building set off by partitions or walls. *v.* To occupy or live in a room.

rroom-mate (rōm´mt´) *n.* A person who will share or live in the same room with another.

room-y (rō´m) *adj.* To be spacious.

roost (rōst) *n.* A place or perch on which birds sleep or rest; a piece of meat which has been or is to be roasted.

roost-er (rō´str) *n.* The male chicken.

root (rōt) *n.* The part of a plant which grows in the ground. *Math* A number which, when multiplied by itself, will produce a given quantity. *v.* To search or rummage for something; to turn up the earth with the snout, as a hog. **rootlike, rootless** *adj.*

root-age (rō´tij) *n.* The action of taking root into.

root beer *n.* A nonalcholic beverage that is flavored with extracts of herbs and roots.

root crop *n.* A crop that is grown for its enlarged roots.

root-less (rōt´lis) *adj.* Having no roots at all.

root-let (rōt´lit) *n.* A small root.

root out *v.* To discover something.

root rot *n.* A plant disease which is recognized by the decaying of it's roots.

root-y (rō´t) *adj.* To have a lot of roots.

rope (rp) *n.* A heavy cord of twisted fiber. Know the ropes. To be familiar with all of the conditions at hand.

rope-walk (rp´wok´) *n.* A long building, or room where ropes are made.

rope yarn *n.* The strands of hemp that makes up a rope.

ro-que-laure *n.* A knee-length coat that

was worn in the 18th and 19th centuries.

ror-qual (ror´kwal) n. Large whale.

ro-sa-ry (r´za r) n. pl. **-ies** A string of beads for counting prayers; a series of prayers.

rose (rz) n. A shrub or climbing vine having sharp prickly stems and variously colored fragrant flowers.

ro-se-ate (r´z it) adj. To be of a deep pink color. **roseately** adv.

rose-bay (rz´b´) n. A flowering shrub.

rose-bud (rz´bud´) n. The state of the rose just before it blooms.

rosecol-ored (rz´kul´rd) adj. To be optimistic and bright.

rose fever n. The allergy that is associated to rose pollen.

ro-se-o-la (r z´o la) n. A rash that is rose colored and appearing on the skin.

ro-sette (r zet´) n. An ornament gathered to resemble a rose and made of silk or ribbon.

rose water n. A fragrant product made from rose petals, steeped in water, and used in cosmetics.

Rosh Ha-sha-nah (rsh´ ha shä´na) n. The Jewish New Year.

ros-i-ly (r´zi l) adv. In a cheerful manner; with a rosy color.

ros-ter (ros´tr) n. A list of names.

ros-y (r´z) adj. To be pink, like the color of roses. **rosiness** n.

rot (rot) v. To break down or decompose.

ro-ta-ry (r´ta r) adj. Turning or designed to turn; of or relating to axial rotation.

ro-tate (r´tt) v. To turn on an axis; to alternate something in sequence. **rotatable** adj., **rotation** n. **rotator** n.

rote (rt) n. Repetition of sounds.

ro-te-none (rt´e nn´) n. Type of compound that is used as an insecticide.

ro-tis-ser-ie (r tis´e r) n. A rotation device with spits for roasting food.

ro-tor (r´tr) n. A rotating part of a mechanical device.

rot-ten (rot´en) adj. Decomposed; morally corrupt; very bad.

rot-ten-stone (rot´en stn´) n. Type of soft stone that is used for polishing brass.

rot-ter (rot´r) n. A person who is really bad.

ro-tund (r tund´) adj. Plump; rounded.

ro-tun-da (r tun´da) n. A building that is round and having a domed roof.

rouge (Rözh) n. A cosmetic coloring for the cheeks.

rough (ruf) adj. Having an uneven surface; violent or harsh. n. The part of a golf course with tall grass. v. To treat roughly. adv. In a very rude manner. **roughly** adv.

rough-age (ruf´ij) n. Material that is coarse in texture.

rough-en (ruf´en) v. To cause something to become rough.

rou-leau (rö l´) n. A trimming for hats that is rolled.

rou-lette (rö let´) n. A gambling game in which players bet on which slot a small ball will land in.

round (round) adj. Curved; circular; spherical. v. To become round; to surround. adv. Throughout; prescribed duties, places, or actions. **roundness** n.

round-a-bout (round´a bout´) adj. To be going round something.

rouse (rouz) v. To awaken or stir up.

rout (rout) v. To dig something up, such as a root.

route (röt) n. A course of travel. v. To send in a certain direction.

rou-tine (rö tn´) n. Activities done regularly. adj. Ordinary.

rove (rv) v. To wander over a wide area.

rover , roving n.

rove bee-tle n. A beetle that has slender body and is able to run quickly.

row (r) n. A number of things positioned next to each other; a continuous line. v. To propel a boat with oars.

row-an tree (r´an tr) n. Type of smooth- barked tree that has clusters of red berries.

row-dy (rou´d) n. A person who is disorderly. **rowdily** adv. **rowdiness** n.

roy-al (roi´al) adj. Relating to a king or queen.

roy-al-ist (roi´a list) n. A person who supports the king.

rub (rub) v. To move over a surface with friction and pressure; to cause to become worn or frayed.

rub-ber (rub´r) n. A resinous elastic material obtained from the coagulated and processed sap of tropical plants or produced synthetically. **rubbery** *adj*.

rubber cement *n*. A type of adhesive that is liquid and made of rubber.

rub-ber-ize (rub'e rz') *v*. Coat or cover something with rubber.

rub-ber-neck (rub'r nek') *v*. To turn the head in order to see something.

rubber plant *n*. Type of plant that is found in East India and yields rubber.

rubber stamp *n*. A type of rubber plate which is coated with ink and used for the purpose of leaving prints on paper or other objects.

rub-bing (rub'ing) *n*. The action or act of a person or thing that rubs.

rub-bish (rub'ish) *n*. Worthless trash; nonsense.

rub-ble (rub'l) *n*. The pieces of broken material or stones.

rub-down (rub'doun') *n*. A type of quick and brisk massage.

ru-be-fa-cient (rö be f'shent) *n*. A type of substance which will turn the area of skin it is applied to red.

ru-bel-la (rö bel'a) *n*. The German measles.

ru-bel-lite (rö bel't) *n*. A red gem stone.

ru-be-o-la (rö b'o la) *n*. The German measles. **rubeoloid** *adj*. **rubeolar** *adj*.

ru-bi-cund (rö'bi kund') *adj*. State of being of a red color or hue. **rubicundi-ty** *n*.

ru-bid-i-um (rö bid'um) *n*. Symbol A silvery, highly reactive element symbolized by Rb.

ru-bi-ous (rö'b us) *adj*. Being red in color.

ru-bric (rö'brik) *n*. A heading, title, or initial letter of a manuscript which appears in red.
rubrically *adv*. **rubrical** *adj*.

ru-bri-cate (rö'bri kt') *v*. To color something red. **rubricator** *n*. **rubrica-tion** *n*.

ru-by (rö'b) *n*. *pl*. **-ies** A deep-red precious stone. **rubylike** *adj*.

ruby glass *n*. Type of red glass.

ruby spinal *n*. A gemstone, red in color.

ruche (rösh) *n*. Piece of crimped fabric which is used to trim a woman's clothes.

ruck (ruk) *n*. Trash.

ruck-sack (ruk'sak') *n*. A knapsack

that is carried by hikers.

ruck-us *n*. *Slang* A noisy uproar, or commotion.

ruc-tion (ruk'shan) *n*. A quarrel.

rud-beck-i-a (rud bek'a) *n*. A type of North American herb with dark brown center disks.

rud-der (rud'r) *n*., *Naut*. A broad, flat, hinged device attached to the stern of a boat used for steering.

ru-di-ment (rö'di ment) *n*. A first step, element, skill, or principle. *Biol*. An undeveloped organ. **-ariness** *n*.

rue (rö) *v*. To repent.

rue-ful (rö'ful) *adj*. To be causing sorrow or remorse. **ruefully** *adv*.

ru-fes-cent (rö fes'ent) *adj*. To be red in color or tint. **rufescence** *n*.

ruff (ruf) *n*. A stiff collar which has pleats in it.

ruf-fi-an (ruf'an) *n*. A lawless, rowdy person. **ruffianly** *adj*. **ruffianism** *n*.

ruf-fle (ruf'l) *n*. A pleated strip or frill; a decorative band. *v*. To disturb or destroy the smoothness.

ru-fous (rö'fus) *adj*. To be red in color or tint.

rug (rug) *n*. A heavy textile fabric used to cover a floor.

ru-ga (rö'ga) *n*. A wrinkle or fold in something.

rug-ged (rug'id) *adj*. Strong; rough; having an uneven or rough surface. **ruggedness** *n*.

ru-gose (rö'gs) *adj*. To be filled with folds and wrinkles. **rugous** *adj*. **rugosely** *adv*.

ru-in (rö'in) *n*. Total destruction. *v*. To destroy. **rule (röl)** *n*. Controlling power; an authoritative direction or statement which regulates the method of doing something; a standard procedure. *v*. To have control over; to make a straight line using a ruler; to be in command.

rule out *v*. To omit something.

rul-er (rö'lr) *n*. A straight edge used for measuring; a person who rules as a sovereign.

rul-ing (rö'ling) *n*. A type of decision which is handed down by a judge in a trial.

rum (rum) *n*. A type of liquor made from molasses and is distilled.

rum-ba (rum´ba) *n.* A type of dance which has a complex rhythm.

rum-ble (rum´bl) *v.* To make a heavy, continuous sound. *n.* A long deep rolling sound.

rum-bly (rum´bl) *adj.* To be characterized by a rumble.

ru-men (rö´min) *n.* The first stomach of ruminant animals, such as a cow or goat.

ru-mi-nant (rö´mi nant) *n.* A cud-chewing animal; as a cow, deer, sheep, or giraffe; an animal which chews something which was swallowed. **ruminantly** *adv.*

ru-mi-nate (rö´mi nt´) *v.* To chew a cud; to ponder at length. **rumination, ruminative** *adj.* **ruminator** *n.*

rum-mage (rum´ij) *v.* To look or search thoroughly by digging or turning things over; to ransack.

rum-mage sale *n.* A sale of second-hand objects, conducted to make money.

rum-mer (rum´r) *n.* A type of drinking glass that is large in size.

rum-my (rum´) *n.* A card game in which each player tries to get rid of his hand in sequences of three cards or more of the same suit.

ru-mor (rö´mr) *n.* An uncertain truth which is circulated from one person to another; gossip. *v.* To speed by rumor.

ru-mor-mon-ger (rö´mr mung´gr) *n.* One who aids in the spreading of rumors.

rump (rump) *n.* The fleshy hind quarter of an animal; the human buttocks.

rum-ple (rum´pl) *v.* To form into creases or folds; to wrinkle.

rum-pus (rum´pus) *n.* A loud noise or disturbance.

rund-let (rund´lit) *n.* A type of barrel which is small in size.

rung (rung) *n.* A bar or board which forms a step of a ladder.

run-nel (run´el) *n.* A small stream.

run-ner (run´r) *n.* The person who runs in a race.

run-ning (run´ing) *adj.* State of moving fast or rapidly.

run-ny (run´) *adj.* To be tending to run.

run-off (run´of´) *n.* That which runs off of something; as rain which flows off of land or building; a final race or con-

test held after no winner was decided.

runt (runt) *n.* The smallest animal in a litter.

rup-ture (rup´chr) *n.* A state of being broken; the act of bursting. **-able** *adj.*

ru-ral (rer´al) *adj.* Pertaining to the country or country life and country people. **-ist** *n.*

ru-ral-ize (rer´a lz´) *v.* The act of moving to or living in the country or the rural area.

ruse (röz) *n.* A type of trick.

rush (rush) *v.* To move quickly; to hurry; to be in a hurry. **rushy** *adj.*

rusk (rusk) *n.* A piece of toasted and sweet bread.

rus-set (rus´it) *n.* A reddish or yellow-ish brown color

rust (rust) *n.* Ferric oxide which forms a coating on iron material exposed to moisture and oxygen; deterioration through neglect. *v.* To form rust.

rus-tic (rus´tik) *adj.* Pertaing to or having the characteristic of country life; simple, unsophisticated, or rude *n.* A simple or unsophisticated person. **rus-tically** *adv.*

rus-ti-cate (rus´ti kt´) *v.* Living and staying in the country or rural area; to go to the country. **rusticator** *n.*

rus-tic-i-ty (ru stis´i t) *n.* The quality or state of being rustic.

rus-tle (rus´l) *v.* To move making soft sounds, such as those made by leaves of a tree; or parts rubbing gentle one on another.

rus-tler (rus´lr) *n.* A person who steals cattle.

rust-proof (rust´pröf´) *adj.* Being unable to rust.

rust-y (rus´t) *adj.* To be covered by rust; impaired by time and wear; out of practice. **rustiness** *n.* **rustily** *adv.*

rut (rut) *n.* An indented track made by the wheels of vehicles worn into the surface by repeated useage; a habitual form or pattern of behavior.

ru-ta-ba-ga (rö´ta b´ga) *n.* A vegetable of the mustard family which makes an underground white tuber.

ruth (röth) *n.* Grief; sorrowful for another.

ruth-ful (röth´ful) *adj.* To be mournful; sorrowful or compassionate.

ruth-less (rŏth´lis) *adj.* Merciless; having no pity; cruel.

ru-ti-lant (rōt´lənt) *adj.* To have a glow that is reddish in color.

rut-ty (rut´) *adj.* A state of having many ruts. **Rx** *n.* A prescription for medicine.

rye (r) *n.* A cultivated cereal grass used to make flour and whiskey.

S

S, s (es) The nineteenth letter of the English alphabet.

sa-ber (s´br) *n.* A lightweight sword.

sa-ble (s´bl) *n.* A carnivorous mammal having soft, black or dark fur.

sab-o-tage (sab´o täzh´) *n.* An act of malicious destruction, intended to obstruct production of war material by the opposing side.

sac (sak) *n., Biol.* A membranous pouch in an animal or plant, containing a liquid.

sac-cha-rin (sak´ra rin) *n.* A white, crystal-like powder used as a noncaloric sugar substitute.

sa-chet (sa sh´) *n.* A small bag of a sweet- smelling powder used to scent clothes.

sack (sak) *n.* A strong bag for holding articles. *Slang* Dismissal from a position or job; sleeping bag or bed.

sac-ra-ment (sak´ra ment) *n., Eccl.* A formal Christian rite performed in a church, as a baptism. **Sacrament** The consecrated bread and wine of the Eucharist; the Lord's Supper.

sa-cred (s´krid) *adj.* Dedicated to worship; holy. **sacredly** *adv.* **sacredness** *n.*

sac-ri-fice (sak´ri fs´) *n.* The practice of offering something, as an animal's life, to a deity. *v.* To give up something of value for something else. **-ficial** *adj.*

sad (sad) *adj.* Marked by sorrow; unhappy; causing sorrow; deplorable. **sadly** *adv.*

sad-dle (sad´l) *n.* A seat for a rider, as on the back of a horse or bicycle; a cut of meat which includes the backbone. *v.* To put a saddle on; to load down; to burden.

sa-dism (sad´iz um) *n., Psychol.* A condition in which sexual gratification comes from inflicting pain on others;

cruelty. **sadist** *n.* **sadistic** *adj.* **sadistically** *adv.*

sa-fa-ri (sa fär´) *n. pl.* **-ris.** A trip or journey; a hunting expedition in Africa.

safe (sf) *adj.* Secure from danger, harm, or evil; unharmed; not likely to cause harm. *n.* A strong metal container used to protect and store important documents or money. **sag** *v.* To droop; to sink from pressure or weight; to lose strength; decline in amount.

sa-ga (sä´ga) *n.* A long heroic story.

sage (sj) *n.* A person recognized for judgment and wisdom. **sage** *adj.*

said (sed) *v.* Past tense of say.

sail (sl) *n.* A strong fabric used to catch the wind and cause a ship to move; a trip on a sailing vessel or boat. *v.* To travel on a sailing vessel.

saint (snt) *n.* A person of great purity who has been officially recognized as such by the Roman Catholic Church; a person who has died and is in heaven. **sainted** *adj.*

sake (sk) *n.* Motive or reason for doing something.

sal-ad (sal´ad) *n.* A dish usually made of green vegetables, fruit, or meat tossed with dressing.

sal-a-man-der (sal´a man´dr) *n.* A lizard- like amphibian with porous, scaleless skin.

sa-la-mi (sa lä´m) *n.* A spiced sausage made of beef and pork.

sa-la-ry (sal´a r) *n. pl.* **-ies** A set compensation paid on a regular basis for services rendered. **salaried** *adj.*

sale (sl) *n.* An exchange of goods for a price; disposal of items at reduced prices.

sa-li-ent (s´l ent) *adj.* Projecting beyond a line; conspicuous.

sa-li-va (sa l´va) *n.* Tasteless fluid secreted in the mouth which aids in digestion.

Salk vaccine (salk´ vak sn´) *n.* A vaccine used to immunize against polio.

salm-on (sam´on) *n. pl.* **-on** or **-ons** A large game fish with pinkish flesh.

sa-lon (sa lon´) *n.* A large drawing room; a business establishment pertaining to fashion.

sa-loon (sa lön´) *n.* A place where alco-

holic drinks are sold; a bar room.
salt-pe-ter (solt´p´tr) n. Potassium nitrate.
sal-u-tar-y (sal´ ter´) adj. Wholesome; healthful; beneficial.
sal-u-ta-tion (sal´ t shən) n. An expression; a greeting of good will, as used to open a letter.
sal-vage (sal´vij) v. The act of rescuing a ship, its cargo, or its crew; property which has been saved. v. To save from destruction; to rescue.
salve (sav) n. A medicated ointment used to soothe the pain of a burn or wound.
sal-vo (sal´v) n. pl. -vos or -voes The discharge of a number of guns at the same time.
same (sm) adj. Identical; exactly alike; similar; not changing. pron. The very same one or thing. **sameness** n.
sam-ple (sam´pl) n. A portion which represents the whole. v. To try a little.
san-a-to-ri-um (san´a tr´ um) n. pl. -ums An institution for treating chronic diseases.
sanc-ti-fy (sangk´ti f´) v. To make holy.
sanc-tion (sangk´shən) n. Permission from a person of authority; a penalty to ensure compliance. v. To officially approve an action.
sanc-tu-ar-y (sangk´chö er´) n. pl. -ies. A sacred, holy place, as the part of a church, where services are held; a safe place; a refuge.
san-dal (san´dal) n. A shoe which is fastened to the foot by straps attached to the sole; a low shoe or slipper with an ankle strap.
sane (sn) adj. Having a healthy, sound mind; showing good judgment.
san-i-tar-y (san´i ter´) adj. Free from bacteria or filth which endanger health.
san-i-tize (san´i tz) v. To make sanitary; to make clean or free of germs.
sank v. Past tense of sink.
sap (sap) n. The liquid which flows or circulates through plants and trees. v. To weaken or wear away gradually. Slang A gullible person; fool.
sa-pi-ent (s´p ent) adj. Wise.
sap-phire (saf´r) n. A clear, deep-blue gem, used in jewelry.

sar-casm (sär´kaz um) n. An insulting or mocking statement or remark. **sar-castic, sarcastically** adj.
sar-dine (sär dn´) n. A small edible fish of the herring family, often canned in oil.
sar-don-ic (sär don´ik) adj. Scornful; mockingly cynical.
sar-sa-pa-ril-la (sas´pa ril´a) n. The dried root of a tropical American plant, which is used as flavoring.
sash (sash) n. A band worn over the shoulder or around the waist.
sass (sas) n. Slang Rudeness; a disrespectful manner of speech. v. To talk with disrespect.
sas-sa-fras (sas´a fras´) n. The dried root of a North American tree, used as flavoring.
Sa-tan (st´an) n. The devil.
sat-el-lite (sat´e lt´) n. A natural or man-made object which orbits a celestial body.
sat-in (sat´in) n. A smooth, shiny fabric made of silk, nylon, or rayon, having a glossy face and dull back.
sat-ire (sat´ r) n. The use of mockery, sarcasm, or humor in a literary work to ridicule or attack human vice.
sat-is-fac-tion (sat´is fak´shən) n. Anything which brings about a happy feeling; the fulfillment of a need, appetite, or desire; a source of gratification.
sat-u-rate (sach´a rt´) v. To make completely wet; to soak or load to capacity.
sauce (sos) n. A liquid or dressing served as an accompaniment to food. **saucing** v.
sau-cer (so´sr) n. A small shallow dish for holding a cup.
sau-na (sou´nä) n. A steam bath in which one is subjected to heat produced by water poured over heated rocks.
sau-sage (so´sij) n. Chopped meat, usually pork, which is highly seasoned, stuffed into a casing and cooked.
sav-age (sav´ij) adj. Wild; not domesticated; uncivilized; brutal. n. A vicious or crude person. **savagely** adv. **savagery** n.
save (sv) v. To rescue from danger, loss, or harm; to prevent loss or waste; to

keep for another time in the future; to be delivered from sin. **saver** n.

sav-ior--faire (sav´yr) n. One who saves. Christ Savior.

sa-voir--faire (sav´wär fãr´) n. Social skill; the ability to say and do the right thing.

sa-vor (s´vr) n. The taste or smell of something. v. To have a particular smell; to truly enjoy. **savory** adj.

saw (so) n. A tool with a sharp metal blade edged with teeth-like points for cutting. v. Past tense of see; to cut with a saw.

sax-o-phone (sak´so fn´) n. A brass wind instrument having finger keys and a reed mouthpiece. **saxophonist** n.

say (s) v. To speak aloud; to express oneself in words; to indicate; to show. n. The chance to speak; the right to make a decision.

scab (skab) n. The stiff, crusty covering which forms over a healing wound. Slang A person who continues to work while others are on strike.

sca-bies (sk´bz) n. A contagious skin disease characterized by severe itching, caused by a mite under the skin.

scal-a-wag (skal´a wag´) n. Slang A rascal.

scald (skold) v. To burn with steam or a hot liquid; to heat a liquid to a temperature just under boiling.

scale (skl) n. A flat plate which covers certain animals, especially fish and reptiles; a device for weighing; a series of marks indicating the relationship between a map or model and the actual dimensions. Music A sequence of eight musical notes in accordance. With a specified scheme of intervals. **scaly** adj.

scal-lop (skol´op) n. A marine shellfish with a fan-shaped, fluted bivalve shell; the fleshy edible muscle of the scallop.

scalp (skalp) n. The skin which covers the top of the human head where hair normally grows.

scal-pel (skal´pel) n. A small, straight knife with a narrow, pointed blade, used in surgery.

scamp (skamp) n. A scheming or tricky person.

scan (skan) v. To examine all parts closely; to look at quickly the rhythm of a poem. Elec... move a beam of radar in search o... target. **scanner** n.

scan-dal (skan´dal) n. Something which brings disgrace when exposed to the public; gossip.

scan-di-um (skan´d um) n. A metallic element symbolized by Sc.

scant (skant) adj. Not plentiful or abundant; inadequate. **scantly** adv. **scantness** n.

scant-ling (skant´ling) n. The dimensions of material used in building, as wood and brick.

scap-u-la (skap læ) n. pl. -lae One pair of large, flat, triangular bones which form the back of the shoulder. **scapular** adj.

scar (skär) n. A permanent mark which remains on the skin after a sore or injury has healed.

scarce (skârs) adj. Not common or plentiful; rare. **scarceness** n.

scarf (skärf) n. A wide piece of cloth worn around the head, neck, and shoulders for warmth.

scar-la-ti-na (skär´la t´na) n. A mild form of scarlet fever.

scar-let (skär´lit) n. A bright or vivid red.

scarlet fever n. A communicable disease caused by streptococcus and characterized by a sore throat, vomiting, high fever, and a rash.

scat-ter (skat´r) v. To spread around; to distribute in different directions.

scav-en-ger (skav´in jr) n. An animal, as a vulture, which feeds on decaying or dead animals or plant matter.

sce-nar-i-o (si när´) n. A synopsis of a dramatic plot.

scene (sn) n. A view; the time and place where an event occurs; a public display of temper; a part of a play.

scent (sent) n. A smell; an odor. v. To smell; to give something a scent.

scep-ter (sep´tr) n. A rod or staff carried by a king as a sign of authority.

sched-ule (skej´öl) n. A list or written chart which shows the times at which events will happen, including a plan given for work and specified deadlines.

scheme (skm) *n.* A plan of action; an orderly combination of related parts; a secret plot.

schol-ar (skol´r) *n.* A student with a strong interest in learning. **-ly** *adj.*

school (skōl) *n.* A place for teaching and learning; a group of persons devoted to similar principles.

schoon-er (skō´nr) *n.* A sailing vessel with two or more masts.

sci-ence (s´ens) *n.* The study and theoretical explanation of natural phenomena in an orderly way; knowledge acquired through experience. **scientific** *adj.* **scientist** *n.*

scis-sors (siz´rz) *n. pl.* A cutting tool consisting of two blades joined and pivoted so that the edges are close to each other.

scle-ro-sis (skli r´sis) *n. pl.* **-ses** A hardening of a part of the body, as an artery.

scold (skld) *v.* To accuse or reprimand harshly.

sconce (skons) *n.* A wall bracket for holding candles.

scoop (skōp) *n.* A small, shovel-like tool. *v.* To lift up or out. *Slang* An exclusive news report.

scoot (skōt) *v.* To go suddenly and quickly.

scope (skp) *n.* The range or extent of one's actions; the space to function or operate in.

-scope *suff.* A device for seeing or discovering.

scorch (skorch) *v.* To burn slightly, changing the color and taste of something; to parch with heat.

scorcher (skor´chr) *n. Slang* A very hot day.

____ (skr) *n.* A numerical record of ____ ____oints won in a game or other ____ result of an examination; a ____wenty items; a written ____tion which indicates ____formed by each per- ____de with a pointed ____r win; to arrange a

____ disdain; ____adj. ____rachnid ____with a

poisonous sting.

scour (skour) *v.* To clean by rubbing with an abrasive agent; to clean thoroughly.

scowl (skoul) *v.* To make an angry look; to frown. **scowl** *n.*

scrab-ble (skrab´l) *v.* To scratch about frantically, as if searching for something. **scrabble** *n.* **scrabbler** *n.*

scrag-gly (skrag´l) *adj.* Messy; irregular.

scrap (skrap) *n.* A small section or piece. *v.* To throw away waste.

scrape (skrp) *v.* To rub a surface with a sharp object in order to clean. *Slang* An embarrassing situation.

scratch (skrach) *v.* To mark or make a slight cut on; to mark with the fingernails. *n.* The mark made by scratching; a harsh, unpleasant sound.

scrawl (skrol) *n.* To write or draw quickly and often illegibly. **scrawl** *n.*

scraw-ny (skro´n) *adj.* Very thin; skinny.

scream (skrm) *v.* To utter a long, sharp cry, as of fear or pain. *n.* A long piercing cry. *Slang* A very funny person.

screech (skrch) *v.* To make a shrill, harsh noise. **screech** *n.*

screen (skrn) *n.* A movable object used to keep something from view, to divide, or to decorate; a flat reflecting surface on which a picture is projected. *v.* To keep from view.

scribe (skrb) *n.* A person whose profession is to copy documents and manuscripts.

scrim-mage (skrim´ij) *n.* In football, a practice game. **scrimmage** *v.*

scrim-shaw (skrim´sho´) *n.* The art of carving designs on whale ivory or whalebone.

scrip-ture (skrip´chr) *n.* A sacred writing. **Scriptures** The Bible.

scroll (skrl) *n.* A roll of parchment or similar material used in place of paper.

scro-tum (skr´tum) *n. pl.* **-ta** The external sac of skin which encloses the testes.

scrub (skrub) *v.* To clean something by rubbing. *Slang* To cancel.

scrump-tious (skrump´shus) *adj. Slang* Delightful.

scru-ple (skrō´pl) *n.* A principle which

governs one's actions. **scrupulous** *adj.*

scu-ba (skō´bə) *n.* An apparatus used by divers for underwater breathing; from the initials for self-contained underwater breathing apparatus.

scuff (skuf) *v.* To drag or scrape the feet while walking. *n.* A roughspot.

scuf-fle (skuf´l) *v.* To struggle in a confused manner. **scuffle** *n.*

scull (skul) *n.* An oar mounted at the stern of a boat, which is moved back and forth to produce forward motion.

sculp-tor (skulp´tr) *n.* A person who creates statues from clay, marble, or other material.

scum (skum) *n.* A thin layer of waste matter floating on top of a liquid.

scurf (skerf) *n.* Flaky dry skin; dandruff.

scur-ry (sker´ē) *v.* To move quickly; to scamper.

scythe (sth) *n.* A tool with a long handle and curved, single-edged blade, used for cutting hay, grain and grass.

seal (sl) *n.* A device having a raised emblem, displaying word or symbol, used to certify a signature or the authenticity of a document; a tight closure which secures; a large aquatic mammal with a sleek body and large flippers; the fur or pelt of a seal. *v.* To hunt seals. **sealer** *n.* **sealant** *n.*

seam (sm) *n.* The line formed at the joint of two pieces of material.

sear (sr) *v.* To wither or dry up; to shrivel; to burn or scorch.

search (serch) *v.* To look over carefully; to find something; to probe. **-er** *n.*

seat (st) *n.* A place or spot, as a chair, stool, or bench, on which to sit; the part of the body used for sitting; the buttocks.

se-cede (si sd´) *v.* To withdraw from an organization or group. **secession** *n.*

se-clude (si klōd´) *v.* To isolate; to keep apart.

sec-ond (sek´ond) *n.* A unit of time equal to 1/60 of a minute; a very short period of time; an object which does not meet first class standards. *Math* A unit of measure equal to 1/60 of a minute of angular measurement.

sec-on-dar-y (sek´on der´ē) *adj.* Not being first in importance; inferior; pertaining to a secondary school; high

school.

se-cret (s´krit) *n.* Knowledge kept from others; a mystery. **secretly** *adv.*

sec-re-tary (sek´ri ter´) *n. pl.* **-ies** A person hired to write and keep records for an executive or an organization; the head of a government department.

se-crete (si krt´) *v.* To produce and give off; to release or discharge.

sec-tion (sek´shən) *n.* A part or division of something; a separate part. *v.* To divide or separate into sections.

sec-tor (sek´tr) *n.* An area or zone in which a military unit operates; the part of a circle bounded by two radii and the arc they cut. *Math v.* To divide.

sec-u-lar (sek´yə lr) *adj.* Relating to something worldly; not sacred or religious.

se-cure (si kr´) *adj.* Safe and free from doubt or fear; sturdy or strong; not likely to fail. *v.* To tie down, fasten, lock,or otherwise protect from risk or harm; to ensure.

se-cu-ri-ty (si kr´i t) *n. pl.* **-ies** The state of being safe and free from danger or risk; protection; an object given to assure the fulfillment of an obligation; in computer science, the prevention of unauthorized use of a device or program.

se-dan (si dan´) *n.* A closed, hard-top automobile with a front and back seat.

se-date (si dt´) *adj.* Serene and composed. *v.* To keep or be kept calm through the use of drugs. **sedative** *n.*

sed-i-ment (sed´i ment) *n.* Material which floats in or settles to the bottom of a liquid. **sedimentary** *adj.* **sedimentation** *n.*

se-duce (si dōs´) *v.* To tempt and draw away from proper conduct; to c̶   someone to have sexual int̶   **seductive** *adj.*

see (s) *v.* To have the po̶   understand; to experi̶   to predict. **red̶   angry.

seed (sd) *n.* A ferti̶   an embryo, a̶   offspring̶   the see̶

seek (sl̶   to att̶

seem (sm) v. To appear to be; to have the look of. **seeming** adj. **seemingly** adv.

seep (sp) v. To leak or pass through slowly. **seepage** n.

seer (s´r) n. A person who predicts the future.

see-saw (s´so´) n. A board supported in the center which allows children to alternate being up and down.

seg-ment (seg´ment) n. Any of the parts into which a thing is divided. v. To divide. **-al** adj. **segmentation** n.

seg-re-gate (seg´re gt´) v. To separate or isolate from others.

seg-re-ga-tion (seg´re g´shan) n. The act of separating people based on the color of their skin.

seine (sn) n. A fishing net with weights on one edge and floats on the other.

seize (sz) v. To grasp or take possession forcibly.

sel-dom (sel´dom) adv. Not often.

se-lect (si lekt´) v. To choose from a large group; to make a choice. **selection** n. **selector** n.

se-le-ni-um (se l´n um) n. An element symbolized by Se.

self (self) n. pl. **-selves** The complete and essential being of a person; personal interest, advantage or welfare.

selfde-fense (self´di fens´) n. To act of defending oneself or one's belongings.

sell (sel) v. To exchange a product or service for money; to offer for sale. **seller** n.

se-man-tics (si man´tiks) n. The study of word meanings and the relationships between symbols and signs.

sem-a-phore (sem´a fr´) n. A system for signaling by using flags, lights or arms in various positions. **semaphore** v.

se-men (s´men) n. The secretion of the male reproductive system, thick and whitish in color and containing sperm.

se-mes-ter (si mes´tr) n. One of two periods of time in which a school year is divided.

sem-i-an-nu-al (sem´ an´ al) adj. Occurring twice a year.

sem-i-co-lon (sem´i k´lon) n. A punctuation mark (;) having a degree of separation stronger than a comma but less than a period.

sem-i-nar (sem´i när´) n. A course of study for students engaged in advanced study of a particular subject.

sem-i-nar-y (sem´i ner´) n. pl. **-ies** A school that prepares ministers, rabbis, or priests for their religious careers.

sen-ate (sen´it) n. The upper house of a legislature, as the United States Senate.

send (send) v. To cause something to be conveyed from one place to another; to dispatch.

se-nile (s´nl) adj. Having a mental deterioration often associated with old age.

sen-ior (sn´yr) adj. Being the older of two; of higher office or rank; referring to the last year of high school or college. n. One who is older or of higher rank.

sen-ior-i-ty (sn yor´i t) n. Priority over others based on the length of time of service.

sen-sa-tion (sen s´shan) n. An awareness associated with a mental or bodily feeling; something that causes a condition of strong interest.

sense (sens) n. Sensation; feeling; the physical ability which allows a person to be aware of things around him; the five senses taste, smell, touch, sight, and hearing; an ethical or moral attitude; the meaning of a word; v. To feel through the senses; to have a feeling about.

sen-si-bil-i-ty (sen´si bil´i t) n. pl. **-ies** The ability to receive sensations.

sen-si-ble (sen´si bl) adj. Capable of being perceived through the senses; sensitive; having good judgment. **sensibly** adv.

sen-si-tive (sen´si tiv) adj. Capable of intense feelings; affected by the emotions or circumstances of others; tenderhearted; of or relating to secret affairs of state. **-ly** adv.

sensitivity n. **sensitiveness** n.

sen-sor (sen´sr) n. A device which responds to a signal.

sen-su-al (sen´shô al) adj. Preoccupied with the gratification of the senses. **sensually,sensualist** n. **sensuality** n. **sensuous** adj.

sent v. Past tense of send.

sen-tence (sen´tens) n. A series of words arranged to express a single complete thought; a prison term for a convicted person, determined by a judge or jury. *v.* To impose or set the terms of punishment.

sen-ti-ment (sĕn´tĭ mĕnt) *n.* Feelings of affection; an idea, opinion, thought, or attitude based on emotion rather than reason.

sen-ti-men-tal (sĕn´tĭ mĕn´tăl) *adj.* Emotional; affected by sentiment.

sen-ti-nel (sĕn´tĭ nĕl) *n.* One who guards.

se-pal (s´păl) *n.* One of the leaves which forms a calyx in a flower.

sep-a-rate (sĕp´a rt´) *v.* To divide or keep apart by placing a barrier between; to go in different directions; to set apart from others. *adj.* Single; individual.

sep-a-ra-tion (sĕp´a r´shăn) *n.* The process of separating or being separated; an interval which separates.

se-quel (s´kwĕl) *n.* A new story which follows or comes after an earlier one and which uses the same characters.

se-quence (s´kwĕns) *n.* A set arrangement; a number of connected events; the regular order; the order in which something is done. **sequential** *adj.* **sequentially** *adv.*

ser-e-nade (sĕr´ĕ nd´) *n.* Music performed as a romantic expression of love.

se-rene (sĕ rn´) *adj.* Calm; peaceful.

serf (sĕrf) *n.* A slave owned by a lord during the Middle Ages.

serge (sĕrj) *n.* A twilled, durable woolen cloth.

ser-geant (sär´jĕnt) *n.* A noncommissioned officer who ranks above a corporal but below a lieutenant.

se-ri-al (sr´ al) *adj.* Arranged in a series with one part presented at a time.

se-ries (sr´z) *n. pl.* A number of related items which follow one another.

se-ri-ous (sr´ us) *adj.* Sober; grave; not trivial; important. **seriously** *adv.*

ser-mon (sĕr´mŏn) *n.* A message or speech delivered by a clergyman during a religious service.

ser-pent (sĕr´pĕnt) *n.* A snake.

ser-rate (sĕr´it) *adj.* Having sharp teeth; having a notched edge. **-ion** *n.*

se-rum (sr´um) *n. pl.* **-rums** *or* **-ra**

The yellowish fluid part of the blood which remains after clotting; the fluid extracted from immunized animals and used for the prevention of disease.

ser-vant (sĕr´vănt) *n.* One employed to care for someone or his property.

serve (sĕrv) *v.* To take care of; to wait on; to prepare and supply; to complete a term of duty.

serv-ice (sĕr´vĭs) *n.* Help given to others; a religious gathering; the military; a set of dishes or utensils. *v.* To repair; to furnish a service to something or someone.

ses-a-me (sĕs´a m) *n.* A tropical plant and its edible seeds.

ses-sion (sĕsh´an) *n.* A meeting or series of meetings; a meeting set for a specific purpose; the period during which a meeting takes place.

set (sĕt) *v.* To put or place; to cause to do; to regulate; to adjust; to arrange; to place in a frame or mounting; to go below the horizon; to establish or fix. *n.* A group of things which belong together; a piece of equipment made up of many pieces; a young plant. *adj.* Established; ready.

set-tee (sĕt ´) *n.* A small couch or bench with arms and a back.

set-ting (sĕt´ĭng) *n.* The act of placing or putting something somewhere; the scenery for a show or other production; the place where a novel, play, or other fictional work takes place; a jewelry mounting.

set-tle (sĕt´l) *v.* To arrange or put in order; to restore calm or tranquility to; to come to an agreement on something; to resolve a problem or argument; to establish in a new home or business.

sev-en (sĕv´en) *n.* The cardinal number 7, after 6 and before 8. **seventh** *adv.* & *n.*

sev-er (sĕv´r) *v.* To cut off or separate.

sev-er-al (sĕv´r al) *adj.* Being more than one or two, but not many; separate.

sew (s) *v.* To fasten or fix; to make stitches with thread and needle.

sew-age (sö´ĭj) *n.* The solid waste material carried away by a sewer.

sew-er (sö´r) *n.* A conduit or drain pipe

used to carry away waste.

sex (seks) *n.* One of two divisions, male and female, into which most living things are grouped; sexual intercourse.

sex-tet (seks tet´) *n.* A group of six people or things; music written for six performers.

shab-by (shab´) *adj.* Worn-out; ragged.

shack (shak) *n.* A small, poorly built building.

shad-ow (shad´) *n.* An area from which light is blocked; a shaded area. *v.* To cast or throw a shadow on. **-y** *adj.*

shaft (shaft) *n.* A long, narrow part of something; a beam or ray of light; a long, narrow underground passage; a tunnel; a narrow, vertical opening in a building for an elevator.

shake (shk) *v.* To move or to cause a back and forth or up and down motion; to tremble; to clasp hands with another, as to welcome or say farewell; to upset or disturb.

shall (shal) *v. p.t.* Past tense of should; used with the pronouns I or we to express future tense; with other nouns or pronouns to indicate promise, determination or a command.

shal-low (shal´) *adj.* Not deep; lacking intellectual depth.

sham (sham) *n.* A person who is not genuine but pretends to be; a cover for pillows. *v.* To pretend to have or feel something.

sham-ble (sham´bl) *v.* To walk while dragging one's feet. **shambles** A scene or state of complete destruction.

shame (shm) *n.* A painful feeling of embarrassment or disgrace brought on by doing something wrong; dishonor; disgrace; a disappointment.

shank (shangk) *n.* The portion of the leg between the ankle and the knee; a cut of meat from the leg of an animal, such as a lamb.

shape (shp) *n.* The outline or configuration of something; the form of a human body; the condition of something; the finished form in which something may appear. *v.* To cause to take a particular form.

share (shâr) *n.* A part or portion given to or by one person; one of equal parts, as the capital stock in a corporation. *v.* To divide or distribute portions.

shark (shärk) *n.* A large marine fish which eats other fish and is dangerous to man; a greedy, craft, person.

sharp (shärp) *adj.* Having a thin edge or a fine point; capable of piercing or cutting; clever; quick-witted; intense; painful. *Slang* Nice looking. *n. Music* A note raised half a tone above a given tone.

shat-ter (shat´r) *v.* To burst suddenly into pieces.

shave (shv) *v.* To remove a thin layer; to cut body hair, as the beard, by using a razor; to come close to. *n.* The act of shaving.

shawl (shol) *n.* An oblong or square piece of fabric worn over the head or shoulders.

she (sh) *pron.* A female previously indicated by name.

shear (shr) *v.* To trim, cut, or remove the fleece or hair with a sharp instrument; to clip.

sheath (shth) *n.* A cover or case for a blade, as a sword.

sheen (shn) *n.* Luster.

sheep (shp) *n. pl.* **sheep** A cud-chewing thick-fleeced mammal, widely domesticated for meat and wool; a meek or timid person.

sheer (shr) *adj.* Very thin; almost transparent; complete; absolute; very steep, almost perpendicular.

sheet (sht) *n.* A large piece of cloth for covering a bed; a single piece of paper; a continuous, thin piece of anything.

shelf (shelf) *n. pl.* **shelves** A flat piece of wood, metal, plastic, or other rigid material attached to a wall or within another structure, used to hold or store things; something which resembles a shelf, as a ledge of rocks.

shel-lac (she lak´) *n.* A clear varnish used to give a smooth, shiny finish to furniture and floors. *Slang* To defeat.

shel-ter (shel´tr) *n.* Something which gives protection or cover. *v.* To give protection.

shelve (shelv) *v.* To put aside; to place on a shelf.

shep-herd (shep´rd) *n.* A person who takes care of a flock of sheep; a person who takes care of others.

sher-bet (sher´bit) *n.* A sweet frozen dessert made with fruit juices, milk or water, egg white, and gelatin.

sher-iff (sher´if) *n.* A high ranking law enforcement officer.

shield (shld) *n.* A piece of protective metal or wood held in front of the body; anything which serves to conceal or protect; a badge or emblem. **shield** *v.* **shielder** *n.*

shift (shift) *n.* A group of people who work together; a woman's loose-fitting dress. *v.* To change direction or place; to change or move the gears in an automobile.

shim-mer (shim´r) *v.* To shine with a faint sparkle. **shimmery** *adj.*

shin (shin) *n.* The front part of the leg from the knee to the ankle. *v.* To climb a rope or pole by gripping and pulling with the hands and legs.

shine (shn) *v.* To give off light; to direct light; to make bright or glossy; to polish shoes. *n.* Brightness.

shiner (sh´nr) *n.* A black eye.

shin-gle (shing´gl) *n.* A thin piece of material, as asbestos, used to cover a roof or side of a house. *v.* To apply shingles to. **-er** *n.*

shin-gles (shing´glz) *n. pl., Pathol.* An acute, inflammatory viral infection, characterized by skin eruptions along a nerve path.

ship (ship) *n.* A large vessel for deep-water travel or transport. *v.* To send or transport.

ship-yard (ship´yärd´) *n.* A place where ships are built or repaired.

shirt (shert) *n.* A garment worn on the upper part of the body.

shiv-er (shiv´r) *v.* To tremble or shake with excitement or chill. **shiver, shivery** *adj.*

shock (shok) *n.* A sudden blow or violent impact; an unexpected, sudden upset of mental or emotional balance; a serious weakening of the body caused by the loss of blood pressure or sudden injury. *v.* To strike with great surprise, disgust, or outrage; to give an electric shock.

shone *v.* Past tense of shine.

shop (shop) *n.* A small business or small retail store; a place where certain goods are produced. *v.* To visit a store in order to examine or buy things.

shore (shr) *n.* The land bordering a body of water.

short order (short´or´dr) *n.* An order, usually for food, which can be quickly prepared and served.

shot (shot) *n.* The discharging of a gun, rocket, or other device; an attempt; a try; an injection; a photograph. *Slang* Useless; ruined.

should (shud) *v.* Past tense of shall, used to express obligation, duty, or expectation.

shoul-der (shl´dr) *n.* The part of the body located between the neck and upper arm; the side of the road. *v.* To use the shoulder to push or carry something; to take upon oneself.

should-n't (shed´ant) Should not.

shout (shout) *v.* To yell. *n.* A loud cry.

shov-el (shuv´el) *n.* A tool with a long handle and a scoop, used for picking up material or for digging. *v.* To move, dig, or scoop up with a shovel; to push or move large amounts rapidly.

show (sh) *v.* To put within sight; to point out; to explain; to put on display. *n.* A display; a movie, play or similar entertainment.

shrap-nel (shrap´nel) *n. pl.* **shrapnel** A large shell containing metal fragments; fragments of metal that are exploded with great force.

shrew (shrö) *n.* A small mouse-like mammal, having a narrow, pointed snout.

shriek (shrk) *n.* A loud, sharp scream or noise.

shrimp (shrimp) *n. pl.* **shrimp** or **shrimps** A small, edible shellfish. A small person.

shrine (shrn) *n.* A place for sacred relics; a place considered sacred because of an event or person associated with it.

shrink (shringk) *v.* To make or become less or smaller; to pull back from; to flinch. *Slang* A psychiatrist.

shroud (shroud) *n.* A cloth in which a body is wrapped for burial. *v.* To cover.

shrug (shrug) *v.* To raise the shoulders briefly to indicate doubt or indifference.

shuck (shuk) n. The outer husk that covers an ear of corn. **shuck** v.

shud-der (shud'r) v. To tremble uncontrol-lably, as from fear. **shudder** n.

shuf-fle (shuf'l) v. To drag or slide the feet; to mix together in a haphazard fashion; to rearrange or change the order of cards.

shun (shun) v. To avoid deliberately.

shut-tle (shut'l) n. A device used to move thread in weaving; a vehicle, as a train or plane, which travels back and forth from one location to another.

shy (sh) adj. Bashful; timid; easily frightened. v. To move suddenly from fear.

sib-ling (sib'ling) n. One of two or more children from the same parents.

sick (sik) adj. In poor health; ill; nauseated; morbid. **sickness** n.

sick-le (sik'l) n. A tool with a curved blade attached to a handle, used for cutting grass or grain.

side (sd) n. A surface between the front and back or top and bottom of an object.

SIDS abbr. n. Sudden infant death syndrome; an unexpected death of a seemingly healthy baby, occurring during sleep sometime in the first four months of life.

siege (sj) n. The action of surrounding a town or port in order to capture it; a prolonged sickness.

si-er-ra (s er'a) n. A rugged chain of mountains or hills.

si-es-ta (s es'ta) n. A rest or short nap.

sieve (siv) n. A meshed or perforated device which allows small particles to pass through but which holds back larger particles; a device for separating liquids from solids.

sift (sift) v. To separate coarse particles from small or fine ones by passing through a sieve. **through** To carefully examine. **sifter** n.

sigh (s) v. To exhale a long, deep breath, usually when tired, sad, or relieved.

sight (st) n. The ability to see with the eyes; the range or distance one can see; a view; a device mounted on a firearm used to guide the eye or aim.

sign (sn) n. A piece of paper, wood, metal, etc., with information written on it; a gesture that tells or means something. v. To write one's name on.

sig-nal (sig'nal) n. A sign which gives a warning; the image or sound sent by television or radio. v. To make or send a signal to.

sig-na-ture (sig'na chr) n. The name of a person, written by that person; a distinctive mark which indicates identity. Music A symbol indicating the time and key.

sig-nif-i-cance (sig nif'i kans) n. The quality of being important; the meaning of something which is considered important.

sig-ni-fy (sig'ni f') v. To express or make known by a sign; to indicate. -**ication**

sign language n. A means of communicating by using hand gestures; the language of deaf people.

si-lence (s'lens) n. The state or quality of being silent; quiet. v. To make quiet.

silent (s'lent) adj. Making no sound; not speaking; mute; unable to speak; an unpronounced letter, as the "g" in gnat.

sil-hou-ette (sil'ō et') n. The outline of something, as a human profile, filled in with a solid color, as black; the outline of an object. v. To make a silhouette.

sil-i-con (sil'i kon) n. The second most common chemical element, found only in combination with another substance, symbolized as Si.

silk (silk) n. A soft, thread-like fiber spun by silk-worms; thread or fabric made from silk.

sill (sil) n. The horizontal support that forms the bottom part of the frame of a window or door.

sil-ly (sil') adj. Foolish; lacking good sense, seriousness, or substance.

si-lo (s'l) n. A tall, cylindrical structure for storing food for farm animals; an underground shelter or storage for guided missiles.

sil-ver (sil'vr) n. A soft, white metallic element used in tableware, jewelry, and coins, symbolized by Ag. v. To coat with silver. adj. Of the color silver.

sim-i-lar (sim'i lr) adj. Almost the same, but not identical.

sim-mer (sim'r) v. To cook just below

boiling; to be near the point of breaking, as with emotion.

sim-ple (sim´pl) *adj.* Easy to do or understand; not complicated; ordinary; not showy; lacking intelligence or education.

sim-plic-i-ty (sim plis´i t) *n.* The state of being easy to understand; naturalness; sincerity.

sim-pli-fy (sim´pli f´) *v.* To make easy or simple. **simplification** *n.*

sim-u-late (sim´ lt´) *v.* To have the appearance, effect, or form of.

sin (sin) *n.* The breaking of a religious law or a law of God. To do something which is morally wrong. **sinless** *adj.* **sinner** *n.*

since (sins) *adv.* At a time before the present. *prep.* During the time later than; continuously from the time when something occurs.

sin-cere (sin sr´) *adj.* Honest; not deceitful; genuine; true. **sincerely** *adv.* **sincerity** *n.*

sing (sing) *v.* To use the voice to make musical tones; to make a humming or whistling sound.

singe (sinj) *v.* To slightly burn the surface of something; to remove feathers.

sin-gle (sing´gl) *adj.* Of or referring to only one, separate; individual; unmarried. *n.* A separate, individual person or item; a dollar bill; in baseball, a hit that allows the batter to progress to first base. **singly** *adv.*

sin-gu-lar (sing´g lr) *adj.* Separate; one; extraordinary; denoting a single unit, thing or person.

sink (singk) *v.* To submerge beneath a surface; to go down slowly; to become less forceful or weaker. *n.* A basin for holding water, attached to a wall and connected to a drain.

si-nus (s´nus) *n. pl.* **sinuses** *Anat.* A body cavity; one of eight air spaces in the bones of the face which drain into the nasal cavity.

sip (sip) *v.* To drink in small amounts.

si-phon (s´fon) *n.* A tube through which liquid from one container can be drawn into another by forced air pressure.

sir (ser) *n.* A respectful term used when addressing a man.

si-ren (s´ren) *n.* A whistle which makes a loud wailing noise, as a warning or signal; a seductive woman.

sis-ter (sis´tr) *n.* A female having the same parents as another; a woman in membership with others, as in a church group or society.

sit (sit) *v.* To rest the body with the weight on the buttocks; to cover eggs for hatching; to pose for a portrait.

six (siks) *n.* The cardinal number 6, after five and before seven.

size (sz) *n.* The measurement or dimensions of something; as tacky substance used to glaze walls, before applying wall paper. *v.* To arrange according to size.

skate (skt) *n.* A device with rollers which attaches to the shoe and allows one to glide over ice or roll over a wooden or cement surface; a shoe fitted with rollers. **skate** *v.*

skate-board (skt´bord) *n.* A narrow piece of wood with wheels attached.

skel-e-ton (skel´i ton) *n.* The framework of bones that protects and supports the soft tissues and organs.

skep-tic (skep´tik) *n.* A person who doubts or questions. **skepticism** *n.* **skeptical** *adj.*

sketch (skech) *n.* A rough drawing or outline; a brief literary composition. **sketchy** *adj.*

skew (sk) *v.* To turn or slant. *n.* A slant.

ski (sk) *n. pl.* **skis** One of a pair of long, narrow pieces of wood worn on the feet for gliding over snow or water. To travel on skis.

skid (skid) *v.* To slide to the side of the road; to slide along without rotating.

skill (skil) *n.* Ability gained through practice; expertise. **skilled** *adj.*

skim (skim) *v.* To remove the top layer; to remove floating matter; to read over material quickly; to travel over lightly and quickly. **-mer** *n.*

skimp (skimp) *v.* To economize; to hold back.

skin (skin) *n.* The tough, outside covering of man and some animals; the outside layer of a vegetable or fruit; the fur or pelt of an animal. **skinless** *adj.*

skip (skip) *v.* To move in light jumps or leaps; to go from one place to another, missing what is between. **skip** n.

skirt (skert) n. A piece of clothing that extends down from the waist. v. To extend along the boundary; to avoid the issue.

skull (skul) n. The bony part of the skeleton which protects the brain.

sky (sk) n. pl. **skies** The upper atmosphere above the earth; the celestial regions.

slab (slab) n. A thick piece or slice.

slack (slak) adj. Not taut or tense; sluggish; lacking in strength. v. To make slack. n. A part of something which hangs loose. **slacks;** Long pants or trousers.

slain v. Past tense of slay.

slam (slam) v. To shut with force; to strike with a loud impact. n. A loud noise produced by an impact.

slam-mer n. Slang Jail or prison.

slan-der (slan´dr) n. A false statement that deliberately does harm to another's reputation. **slanderous** adj.

slang (slang) n. Informal language that contains made-up words or common words used in a different or uncommon way.

slant (slant) v. To lie in an oblique position; to slope; to report on something giving only one side or viewpoint. n. An incline or slope.

slap (slap) n. A sharp blow with an open hand.

slash (slash) v. To cut with a fast sweeping stroke; to reduce or limit greatly. n. A long cut.

slate (slt) n. A fine grained rock that splits into thin layers, often used as a writing surface or roofing material.

slaugh-ter (slo´tr) v. To kill livestock for food; to kill in great numbers. Slang To soundly defeat. **slaughter** n.

slave (slv) n. A person held against his will and made to work for another.

sled (sled) n. A vehicle with runners, used to travel on snow or ice.

sleek (slk) adj. Smooth and shiny; neat and trim. **sleekly** adv. **sleekness** n.

sleep (slp) n. A natural state of rest for the mind and body. v. To rest in sleep.

sleet (slt) n. Rain that is partially frozen; a combination of snow and rain.

sleeve (slv) n. The part of a garment

which covers the arm; a case for something.

sleigh (sl) n. A vehicle mounted on runners, usually pulled over ice and snow by horses.

slen-der (slen´dr) adj. Slim; inadequate in amount. **-ly** adv. **slenderness** n.

slept v. Past tense of sleep.

slice (sls) n. A thin cut; a portion or share; in sports, a ball in flight that curves off to the right of its target. v. To cut into slices.

slick (slik) adj. Smooth and slippery; quick; smart; clever; attractive for the present time but without quality or depth. n. Water with a thin layer of oil floating on top.

slide (sld) v. To move smoothly across a surface without losing contact.

slight (slt) adj. Minor in degree; unimportant. v. To ignore. **slightly** adv.

slim (slim) adj. Slender; meager; not much.

slime (slm) n. A wet, slippery substance.

slip (slip) v. To move in a smooth, quiet way; to fall or lose one's balance. Slang To become less active, alert, or strong.

slith-er (slith´r) v. To slide or slip in an indirect manner; to move like a snake.

sliv-er (sliv´r) n. A thin, narrow piece of something that has been broken off.

slob-ber (slob´r) v. To dribble from the mouth. **slobber** n.

slo-gan (sl´gan) n. A phrase used to express the aims of a cause.

slope (slp) v. To slant upward or downward. n. An upward or downward incline, as a ski slope.

slosh (slosh) v. To splash in a liquid, as water.

slot (slot) n. A narrow, thin groove or opening. Slang A place or scheduled time for an event.

sloth (sloth) n. Laziness; a slow mammal found in South America.

slouch (slouch) n. A drooping or sagging posture; a lazy person. v. To sit or walk with poor posture.

slow (sl) adj. Moving at a low rate of speed; requiring more time than usual; not lively; sluggish; not interesting. adv. At less speed; in a slow manner. v. To make slower.

slug (slug) *n.* A slow animal related to the snail; a bullet or a lump of metal. *v.* To strike forcefully with the fist or a heavy object.

sluice (slōs) *n.* A man-made ditch used to move water; a sloping trough used for floating logs. *v.* To wash with flowing water.

slum (slum) *n.* A crowded urban neighborhood marked by poverty. **slum** *v.*

slum-ber (slum′br) *v.* To sleep; to doze. *n.* Sleep. **slumberer** *n.*

slump (slump) *v.* To fall or sink suddenly.

slung *v.* Past tense of sling.

slur (sler) *v.* To slide over without careful consideration; to pronounce unclearly. *n.* An insult. *Music* Two or more notes connected with a curved line to indicate they are to be slurred.

slush (slush) *n.* Melting snow; snow which is partially melted. **slushy** *adj.*

slut (slut) *n.* A woman of bad character; a prostitute. **sluttish** *adj.*

sly (sl) *adj.* Cunning; clever; sneaky.

small (smol) *adj.* Little in size, quantity, or extent; unimportant. *n.* The part that is less than the other. **smallness** *n.*

small-pox (smol′poks′) *n.* An acute, contagious disease marked by high fever and sores on the skin.

smart (smärt) *adj.* Intelligent; clever.

smash (smash) *v.* To break into small pieces; to move forward violently, as to shatter; to ruin. *n.* The act or sound of crashing. *adj.* Outstanding.

smear (smr) *v.* To spread or cover with a sticky, oily, or moist substance. *Slang* To discredit one's reputation. **smear** *n.*

smell (smel) *v.* To notice an odor by means of the olfactory sense organs. *n.* An odor; the ability to perceive an odor; the scent of something.

smelt (smelt) *v.* To heat metals or their ores to a high temperature in order to obtain pure metallic constituents.

smile (sml) *n.* A grin; a facial expression in which the corners of the mouth turn upward, indicating pleasure. **smile** *v.*

smirk (smerk) *v.* To smile in a conceited way. **smirk** *n.* **smirker** *n.*

smite (smt) *v.* To hit with great force using the hand.

smock (smok) *n.* A loose-fitting garment worn as a protection for one's clothes while working. *v.* To gather fabric into very small pleats or gathers.

smog (smog) *n.* A mixture of smoke and fog.

smoke (smk) *n.* A cloud of vapor released into the air when something is burning. *v.* To preserve or flavor meat by exposing it to smoke. **smokeless** *adj.* **smoky** *adj.*

smolder (sml′dr) *v.* To burn slowly without a flame and with little smoke.

smooth (smōth) *adj.* Not irregular; flat; without lumps, as in gravy; without obstructions or impediments. *adv.* Evenly. *v.* To make less difficult; to remove obstructions.

smor-gas-bord (smor′gas brd′) *n.* A buffet meal with a variety of foods to choose from.

smother (smuth′r) *n.* Failure to receive enough oxygen to survive. *v.* To conceal; to be overly protective. **-ery** *adj.*

smudge (smuj) *v.* To soil by smearing with dirt. *n.* A dirty mark or smear; a fire made to fill the air with smoke in order to protect fruit trees from frost.

smug (smug) *adj.* Complacent with oneself; self-satisfied. **-ly, smugness** *n.*

smug-gle (smug′l) *v.* To import or export goods illegally without paying duty fees.

snack (snak) *n.* A small amount of food taken between meals. **snack** *v.*

snag (snag) *n.* A stump or part of a tree that is partly hidden under the surface of water; a pull in a piece of fabric. *v.* To tear on a rough place. *Slang* To catch unexpectedly; to snatch.

snake (snk) *n.* Any of a large variety of scaly reptiles, having a long tapering body. *Slang* An untrustworthy person.

snap (snap) *v.* To break suddenly with a sharp, quick sound; to fly off under tension; to snatch something suddenly.

snare (snâr) *n.* Anything that entangles or entraps; a trap with a noose, used to catch small animals.

snarl (snärl) *v.* To speak in an angry way; to cause confusion; to tangle or be tangled. *n.* A growl.

snatch (snach) *v.* To seize or grasp something suddenly. *n.* The act of taking something; a brief or small part.

sneak (snk) *v.* To act or move in a quiet, sly way. *n.* A person who acts in a secret, underhanded way.

sneer (snr) *v.* To express scorn by the look on one's face.

sneeze (snz) *v.* To expel air from the nose suddenly and without control. **sneeze** *n.*

sniff (snif) *v.* To inhale through the nose in short breaths with a noise; to show scorn.

snip (snip) *v.* To cut off in small pieces and with quick strokes. *n.* A small piece.

snipe (snp) *n. pl.* **snipe** *or* **snipes** A bird with a long bill which lives in marshy places. To shoot at people from a hidden position.

snob (snob) *n.* A person who considers himself better than anyone else and who looks down on those he considers to be his inferiors.

snoop (snōōp) *v. Slang* To prowl or spy. *n.* One who snoops.

snore (snr) *v.* To breath with a harsh noise while sleeping. **snorer** *n.*

snor-kel (snor´kel) *n.* A tube that extends above the water, used for breathing while swimming face down.

snort (snort) *n.* To force air through the nostrils with a loud, harsh noise. *Slang* To inhale a narcotic through the nose.

snow (sn) *n.* Vapor that forms crystals in cold air and falls to the ground in white flakes. *Slang* To charm or overwhelm.

snub (snub) *v.* To treat with contempt or in an unfriendly way. **snub** *n.*

snug (snug) *adj.* Warm, pleasant, comfortable and safe.

so (s) *adv.* To a degree or extent as a result; likewise; also; indeed. *conj.* In order that; therefore.

soap (sp) *n.* A cleansing agent made of an alkali and a fat, and used for washing. *v.* To rub with soap.

soar (sr) *v.* To glide or fly high without any noticeable movement; to rise higher than usual.

sob (sob) *v.* To weep with short, quick gasps.

so-cia-ble (s´sha bl) *adj.* Capable of friendly social relations; enjoying the company of others. **sociably** *adv.*

so-cial (s´shal) *adj.* Having to do with

people living in groups; enjoying friendly companionship with others. *n.* An informal party or gathering.

socialism (s´sha liz´um) *n.* A system in which people as a whole, and not individuals, control and own all property.

so-ci-e-ty (so s´i t) *n. pl.* **-ies** People working together for a common purpose; companion ship.

so-ci-ol-o-gy (s´s ol´o j) *n.* The study of society and the development of human society. **sociologic** *adj.* **-logical** *adj.*

sock (sok) *n.* A short covering for the foot, ankle, and lower part of the leg; a hard blow. *Slang* To hit with force.

sock-et (sok´it) *n.* A hollow opening into which something is fitted.

Soc-ra-tes *n.* Greek philosopher.

so-da (s´da) *n.* Sodium carbonate; a flavored, carbonated drink.

sod-den (sod´en) *adj.* Completely saturated; very wet; lacking in expression.

so-di-um (s´d um) *n.* A metallic element symbolized by Na.

sod-om-y (sod´o m) *n.* Anal sexual intercourse.

so-fa (s´fa) *n.* An upholstered couch with arms and a back.

soft (soft) *adj.* Not stiff or hard; not glaring or harsh; mild or pleasant; gentle in sound.

soft-ware (soft´wâr´) *n.* In computer science, data, as routines, programs and languages, which is essential to the operation of computers.

sog-gy (sog´) *adj.* Saturated with a liquid or moisture.

sol-ace (sol´is) *n.* Comfort in a time of trouble, grief, or misfortune. **solacer** *n.*

so-lar (s´lr) *adj.* Relating to or connected with the sun; utilizing the sun for power or light; measured by the earth's movement around the sun.

so-lar-i-um (s lâr´um) *n. pl.* **-ia** *or* **-ums** A glassed in room exposed to the sun's rays.

solar system *n.* The sun and the planets, asteroids, and comets that orbit it.

sol-der (sod´r) *n.* Any alloy, as lead or tin, which is melted and used to mend or join other pieces of metal. *v.* To join or mend with solder.

soldier (sl´jr) *n.* An enlisted person who serves in the military.

sole (sl) n. The bottom of a foot or shoe; single, the only one; a flat fish very popular as seafood.

sol-emn (sol′em) adj. Very serious; characterized by dignity; sacred. **-ity** n. **solemnness** n.

so-lic-it (so lis′it) v. To try to obtain; to ask earnestly; to beg or entice a person persistently.

sol-id (sol′id) n. Having a definite firm shape and volume; having no crevices; not hollow; having height, weight and length; without interruption; reliable, sound and upstanding. n. A solid substance. **solidification** n. **solidness** n. **solidify** v.

sol-i-taire (sol′i târ′) n. A single gemstone set by itself; a card game played by one person.

sol-i-tude (sol′i töd′) n. The act of being alone or secluded; isolation.

so-lo (s′l) n. A musical composition written for and performed by one single person or played by one instrument.

sol-stice (sol′stis) n. Either of the two times in a twelve month period at which the sun reaches an extreme north or south position.

sol-u-ble (sol′ bl) adj. Capable of being dissolved; able to be solved or explained. **solubility** n. **solubly** adv.

solve (solv) v. To find the answer to.

som-ber (som′br) adj. Dark; gloomy; melancholy.

some (sum) adj. Being an indefinite number or quantity; unspecified. pron. An undetermined or indefinite quantity. adv. An approximate degree.

som-er-sault (sum′r solt′) n. The act or acrobatic stunt in which one rolls the body in a complete circle, with heels over head.

som-nam-bu-lism (som nam′bya liz′um) n. The act of walking during sleep.

son (sun) n. A male offspring.

so-na-ta (so nä′ta) n. An instrumental composition with movements contrasting in tempo and mood but related in key.

song (song) n. A piece of poetry put to music; the act or sound of singing.

son-ic (son′ik) adj. Pertaining to sound or the speed of sound.

son-net (son′it) n. A poem made up of fourteen lines.

soon (sön) adv. In a short time; in the near future; quickly.

soot (set) n. The black powder generated by incomplete combustion of a fuel, such as coal or wood.

soothe (söth) v. To make comfortable; to calm.

sop (sop) v. To soak up a liquid; to absorb. n. Anything softened by a liquid; something given as a conciliatory offering.

soph-o-more (sof′o mr′) n. A second year college or high school student.

so-pran-o (so pran′) n. pl. **-nos** or **-ni** The highest female singing voice.

sor-cery (sor′se r) n. The use of supernatural powers.

sor-did (sor′did) adj. Filthy, very dirty; morally corrupt.

sore (sr) adj. Tender or painful to the touch, as an injured part of the body; severe or extreme. n. A place on the body which has been bruised, inflamed, or injured in some way. **sorely** adv.

so-ror-i-ty (so ror′i t) n. pl. **-ies** A social organization for women.

sor-rel (sor′el) n. Any of several herbs with sour-tasting leaves, used in salads.

sor-row (sor′) n. Anguish; mental suffering; an expression of grief. **sorrowful** adj.

sor-ry (sor′) adj. Feeling or showing sympathy or regret; worthless.

sort (sort) n. A collection of things having common attributes or similar qualities. v. To arrange according to class, kind, or size.

sor-tie (sor′t) n., Mil. An attack on enemy forces; a combat mission flown by an aircraft.

SOS (es′′es′) n. A call for help; the international distress signal; a call made when a rescue is needed, especially by a ship or plane.

souf-fle (sö fl′) n. A fluffy dish made of egg yolks, whipped egg whites, and other ingredients, served as a main dish or sweetened as a dessert.

sought v. Past tense of seek.

soul (sl) n. The spirit in man that is believed to be separate from the body and is the source of a person's emotional, spiritual, and moral nature. *Slang* A spirit or attitude derived from Blacks and their culture.

sound (sound) n. A sensation received by the ears from air, water, noise, and other sources. v. To make a sound; to make noise. *adj.* Free from flaw, injury, disease, or damage.

soup (sp) n. A food made by boiling meat and or vegetables, in water.

sour (sour) adj. Sharp to the taste; acid; unpleasant; disagreeable. v. To become sour or spoiled. **sourly** adv.

source (srs) n. Any point of origin or beginning; the beginning or place of origin of a stream or river.

south (south) n. The direction opposite of north. adv. To or towards the south. adj. From the south. **southerly** adv. **southern** adj. **southward** adj.

south-paw (south´po´) n. A left-handed person.

South Pole n. The southern most part of the earth.

south-west (south´west´) n. The direction between south and west.

sou-ve-nir (sö´ve nr´) n. An item kept as a remembrance of something or someplace.

sov-er-eign (sov´rin) n. A ruler with supreme power; a monarch. adj. Possessing supreme jurisdiction or authority.

sow (s) v. To scatter or throw seeds on the ground for growth. n. A female pig.

space (sps) n. The unlimited area in all directions in which events occur and have relative direction; an interval of time; the area beyond the earth's atmosphere.

spade (spd) n. A tool with a flat blade used for digging, heavier than a shovel.

spa-ghet-ti (spa get´) n. Pasta made in long, thin pieces.

span (span) n. The extent of space from the end of the thumb to the end of the little finger of a spread hand; the section between two limits or supports. v. To extend across.

spank (spangk) v. To strike or slap the buttocks with an open hand as a means of punishment.

spare (spâr) v. To refrain from injuring, harming or destroying; to refrain from using; to do without. n. An extra, as a spare tire.

spark (spärk) n. A glowing or incandescent particle, as one released from a piece of burning wood or one produced by means of friction. v. To give off sparks.

spar-kle (spär´kl) v. To emit or reflect light.

spar-row (spar´) n. A small bird with grayish or brown plumage.

sparse (spärs) adj. Scant; thinly distributed. **sparsely** adv. **sparsity** n.

spasm (spaz´um) n. An involuntary muscle contraction.

spat-ter (spat´r) v. To scatter or splash a liquid.

spat-u-la (spach´a la) n. A kitchen utensil with a flexible blade for mixing soft substances.

spawn (spon) n. The eggs of fish or other water animals, as oysters or frogs. v. To lay eggs.

speak (spk) v. To utter words; to express a thought in words.

speak-er (sp´kr) n. A person who speaks, usually before an audience.

spear (spr) n. A weapon with a long shaft and a sharply pointed head. v. To strike, pierce, or stab with a spear.

spe-cial-ist (spesh´a list) n. A person, such as a doctor, who devotes his practice to one particular field.

spe-cial-ize (spesh´a lz´) v. To focus one's efforts or interests in one field of activity or study.

spec-i-men (spes´i men) n. A sample; a representative of a particular thing.

speck (spek) n. A small particle, mark, or spot.

spec-ta-cle (spek´ta kl) n. A public display of something unusual. pl. Eyeglasses.

spec-trum (spek´trum) n., *Physics* The band of colors produced when light is passed through a prism or other means, separating the light into different wave lengths.

spec-u-late (spek´ lt´) v. To reflect and

think deeply; to take a chance on a business venture in hopes of making a large profit.

speech (spch) *n.* The ability, manner, or act of speaking; a talk before the public.

speed (spd) *n.* Rate of action or movement; quickness; rapid motion. *Slang* A drug used strictly as a stimulant.

spell (spel) *v.* To say out loud or write in proper order the letters which make up a word; to relieve. *n.* The state of being controlled by magic; a short period of time; a time or period of illness; an attack. **spellbind** To fascinate or hold as if by magic.

spend (spend) *v.* To give out; to use up; to pay; to exhaust.

sperm (sperm) *n.* The male cell of reproduction; semen. **spermatic** *adj.*

sphere (sfr) *n.*, *Math* A round object with all points the same distance from a given point; globe, ball, or other rounded object. **spherical** *adj.* **spherically** *adv.*

sphinx (sfingks) *n.* *pl.* **sphinxes** or **sphinges** An ancient Egyptian figure having the head of a man, male sheep, or hawk and the body of a lion; a very mysterious person.

spice (sps) *n.* A pungently aromatic plant used as flavoring in food, as nutmeg, cinnamon, pepper, or curry. **spicy** *adj.*

spi-der (sp'dr) *n.* An eight-legged arachnid with a body divided into two parts spinning webs as a means of capturing and holding its prey.

spike (spk) *n.* A large, thick nail; a pointed metal piece on the sole of a shoe to prevent slipping, as on a sports shoe.

spill (spil) *v.* To allow or cause something to flow or run out of something. *Slang* A fall from a horse; to make known.

spin (spin) *v.* To draw out fibers and twist into thread; to run something around and around; to resolve. *Slang* A short drive or ride in an auto. **-er** *v.*

spin-dle (spin'dl) *n.* A rod with a slit in the top and a piece of wood at the other end, used to hold yarn or thread; a needle-like rod mounted on a base, used to hold papers.

spine (spn) *n.* The spinal column; the backbone; the back of a bound book, inscribed with the title.

spin-ster (spin'str) *n.* An unmarried woman; an old maid.

spir-it (spir'it) *n.* The vital essence of man, considered divine in origin; the part of a human being characterized by personality and self-consciousness; the mind; the Holy Ghost; the creative power of God; a supernatural being, as a ghost or angel.

spir-i-tual (spir'i chŏ al) *adj.* Of, like, or pertaining to the nature of spirit; relating to religion; sacred. *n.* A religious song originating among the Negroes of the southern United States. **spirituality** **-ize** *v.*

spite (spt) *n.* Hatred or malicious bitterness; a grudge; ill will. **spiteful** *adj.*

spitz (spits) *n.* A small dog with a tail which curls over its back.

splash (splash) *v.* To spatter a liquid; to wet or soil with liquid; to make a splash.

splash-down (splash'doun') *n.* The landing of a missile or spacecraft in the ocean.

spleen (spln) *n.*, *Anat.* A highly vascular, flattened organ which filters and stores blood, located below the diaphragm.

splen-did (splen'did) *adj.* Illustrious; mag- nificent.

splice (spls) *v.* To join together by wearing, overlapping, and binding the ends.

splint (splint) *n.* A device used to hold a fractured or injured limb in the proper position for healing. **splint** *v.*

splotch (sploch) *n.* A discolored and irregularly shaped spot.

splutter (splut'r) *v.* To make a slight, short spitting sound. **splutter** *n.*

spoil (spoil) *v.* To destroy the value, quality, or usefulness; to overindulge as to harm the character. **-s** *n.* **spoilage** *n.* **spoiler** *n.*

spoke (spk) *n.* One of the rods that serve to connect and support the rim of a wheel. *v.* Past tense of speak.

spokes-man (spks'man) *n.* One who speaks on behalf of another.

sponge (spunj) *n.* Any of a number of marine creatures with a soft, porous skeleton which soaks up liquid. *v.* To clean with a sponge.

spon-sor (spŏn´sr) *n.* A person who is re- sponsible for a debt or duty of another; a business that finances a television or radio program that in turn advertises its product.

spon-ta-ne-ous (spŏn t´n us) *adj.* Done from one's own impulse without apparent external cause. **sontaneity** *adv.*

spoof (spŏf) *n.* A deception; nonsense.

spook (spŏk) *n. Slang* A ghost. *v.* To scare or frighten. **spooky** *adj.*

spool (spŏl) *n.* A small cylinder for holding thread, tape or wire.

spoon (spŏn) *n.* An eating or cooking utensil; a shiny metallic fishing lure. *Slang* To make love, as by kissing or caressing. **spoonful** *n.*

spo-rad-ic (sp rad´ik) *adj.* Occurring occasionally or at irregular intervals.

spore (spr) *n., Bot.* The reproductive single- celled structure produced by nonflowering plants; any cell capable of developing into a new organism, seed, or germ.

sport (sprt) *n.* An interesting diversion; a particular game or physical activity with set rules; a person who leads a fast life. *Slang* To amuse and have a good time. *adj.* Relating or pertaining to sports. **sporting** *adj.*

sports-man-ship (sprts´man ship´) *n.* Fair play; the ability to win or lose graciously.

spot (spot) *n.* A small area that differs in size, portion, or color. *adj.* Delivered or made immediately. *Slang* A dangerous or difficult situation. **spotless** *adj.* **spotlessly** *adv.* **spotlessness** *n.*

spot-light (spot´lt´) *n.* A powerful light thrown directly at one area.

spouse (spous) *n.* One's husband or wife; a marriage partner.

spout (spout) *v.* To pour out forcibly, as under pressure; to cause to shoot forth. *Slang* To orate pompously; to declaim.

sprain (sprn) *n.* A wrenching or twisting of a muscle or joint.

sprawl (sprol) *v.* To sit or lie in an ungraceful manner; to develop haphazardly. **-er** *n.*

spray (spr) *n.* A liquid dispersed in a fine mist or droplets. *v.* To disperse or send forth in a spray. **sprayer** *n.*

spread (spred) *v.* To unfold or open fully; to apply or distribute over an area; to force apart; to extend or expand. **spread** *v.*

spree (spr) *n.* An excessive indulgence in an activity; a binge.

spright-ly (sprt´l) *adj.* Vivacious, lively.

sprin-kle (spring´kl) *v.* To scatter in small particles or drops; to rain in small drops.

sprint (sprint) *n.* A short, fast race.

sprock-et (sprok´it) *n., Mech.* A toothlike projection from the rim of a wheel.

spry (spr) *adj.* Quick; brisk; energetic.

spud (spud) *n: Slang* A potato.

spur (sper) *n.* A sharp, projecting device worn on a rider's boot, used to nudge a horse. *v.* To urge on.

sput-nik (spet´nik) *n.* An unmanned Soviet artificial satellite.

sput-ter (sput´r) *v.* To throw off small particles in short bursts; to speak in a confused or agitated manner.

spu-tum (sp´tum) *n. pl.* **-ta** Saliva or mucus that is expectorated.

spy (sp) *n. pl.* **spies** A secret agent who obtains information; one who watches other people secretly.

squab-ble (skwob´l) *v.* To engage in a petty argument. **squabble** *n.*

squad (skwod) *n.* A small group organized to perform a specific job.

squan-der (skwon´dr) *v.* To spend extravagantly or wastefully.

square (skwâr) *n.* A parallelogram with four equal sides; an implement having a T or L shape used to measure right angles. *Math.* To multiply a number by itself. *Slang* An unsophisticated person; a person who is not aware of the latest fads or trends.

square root *n.* A number which when multiplied by itself gives the given number.

squat (skwot) *v.* To sit on the heels; to crouch; to settle on a piece of land in order to obtain legal title. **squatter** *n.* **squatness** *n.*

squaw (skwo) *n.* An American Indian woman.

squeak (skwk) *v.* To utter a sharp, penetrating sound. **squeak** *n.* **squeaky** *adj.*

squea-mish (skw´mish) *adj.* Easily

squee-gee (skwē'j) n. A tool having a stout rubber blade across a wooden handle, used to wash windows.

squeeze (skwēz) v. To press together; to extract by using pressure. n. An instance of squeezing for pleasure; a hug.

squib (skwib) n. A firecracker that does not explode.

squint (skwint) v. To view something through partly closed eyes; to close the eyes in this manner. **squint** n.

squirm (skerm) n. To twist the body in a wiggling motion. **squirm** v.

squirt (skwert) v. To eject in a thin stream or jet; to wet with a squirt. n. The act of squirting.

sta-bi-lize (stā'bĭ lz') v. To make firm; to keep from changing.

sta-ble (stā'bl) n. A building for lodging and feeding horses or other farm animals. adj. Standing firm and resisting change.

stac-ca-to (sta kä't) adj. Music Marked by sharp emphasis. **staccato** n. & adv.

stack (stak) n. A large pile of straw or hay; any systematic heap or pile; a chimney. v. To fix cards so as to cheat.

sta-di-um (stā'd um) n. pl. **-dia** A large structure for holding athletic events or other large gatherings.

staff (staf) n. pl. **staffs** or **staves** A pole or rod used for a specific purpose; the people employed to assist in the day-to-day affairs of running a business, organization, or government. Mil. A group of people on an executive or advisory board. Music The horizontal lines on which notes are written.

stag-ger (stag'r) v. To walk unsteadily; to totter. adj. Strongly affected by defeat, misfortune, or loss of strength.

stag-nant (stag'nant) adj. Not flowing; standing still; foul from not moving; inactive.

stair (stâr) n. A step or a series of steps.

staircase (stâr'ks) n. A series or a flight of steps that connect one level to another.

stake (stk) n. A bet placed on a game of chance; a sharpened piece of wood for driving into the ground. **stake** v.

stale (stl) adj. Having lost freshness; deteriorated; lacking in interest; dull; inactive.

stale-mate (stl'mt') n. A position in chess when a player cannot move without placing his king in check.

stalk (stok) n. The main axis of a plant. v. To approach in a stealthily manner.

stall (stol) n. An enclosure in a barn, used as a place to feed and confine animals; a sudden loss of power in an engine; a booth used to display and sell. v. To try to put off doing something; to delay.

stal-lion (stal'yan) n. An uncastrated, fully grown male horse.

sta-men (st'men) n. pl. **stamens** Bot. The pollen-producing organs of a flower.

stam-i-na (stam'i na) n. Physical or moral endurance.

stam-mer (stam'r) v. To make involuntary halts or repetitions of a sound or syllable while speaking. **stammer** n. **stammerer** n.

stamp (stamp) v. To put the foot down with force; to imprint or impress with a die, mark, or design. n. The act of stamping; the impression or pattern made by a stamp; a postage stamp.

stam-pede (stam pd') n. A sudden rush of panic, as of a herd of horses or cattle. v. To cause a stampede.

stance (stans) n. The posture or position of a standing person or animal.

stand-ard (stan'drd) n. A model which stands for or is accepted as a basis for comparison.

stand-ing (stan'ding) n. A status, reputation, or accomplishment; a measure of esteem. adj. Unchanging; stationary; not moving.

sta-ple (stā'pl) n. A principle commodity grown in an area; a major element; a metal fastener designed to hold materials such as cloth or paper. **stapler** n.

star (stär) n., Astron. A self-luminous body that is a source of light; any of the celestial bodies that can be seen in the night sky; a symbol having five or six points and resembling a star.

star-board (stär'brd) n. The right side of a ship or boat. **starboard** & adv.

starch (stärch) *n.* Nutrient carbohydrates that are found in foods such as rice and potatoes. *v.* To stiffen clothing by using starch.

stare (stâr) *v.* To look with an intent, direct gaze. **stare** *n.* **starer** *n.*

stark (stärk) *adj.* Bare; total; complete; forbidding in appearance. **starkness** *n.*

star-ling (stär′ling) *n.* A common black or brown bird.

star-tle (stär′tl) *v.* To cause a sudden surprise; to shock. **startle** *n.*

starve (stärv) *v.* To suffer or die from not having food; to suffer from the need of food, love, or other necessities.

state (stt) *n.* A situation, mode, or condition of something; a nation; the governing power or authority of; one of the subdivisions or areas of a federal government, as the United States. *v.* To make known verbally.

stat-ic (stat′ik) *adj.* Not moving. *n.* A random noise heard on a radio. **statically** *adv.*

sta-tion (st′shɑn) *n.* The place where someone or something is directed to stand; a scheduled stopping place; the place from which radio and television programs are broadcast.

sta-tion-ar-y (st′shɑ ner′) *adj.* Not movable; unchanging.

sta-tis-tic (stɑ tis′tik) *n.* An estimate using an average or mean on the basis of a sample taken; numerical data.

stat-ue (stach′ö) *n.* A form sculpted from wood, clay, metal, or stone.

stave (stv) *n* A narrow piece of wood used in forming part of a container, as a barrel.

stay (st) *v.* To remain; to pause; to maintain a position; to halt or stop; to postpone or delay an execution. *n.* A short visit.

stead (sted) *n.* The position, place, or job of another.

stead-fast (sted′fast′) *adj.* Not changing or moving; firm in purpose; true; loyal. **steadfastly** *adv.* **steadfastness** *n.*

stead-y (sted′) *adj.* Firmly placed, fixed or set; not changing; constant; uninterrupted.

steal (stl) *v.* To take another person's property; to move in a sly way; to move secretly. *Baseball* To take a base

without the ball being hit. *Slang* A real bargain.

steel (stl) *n.* A various mixture of iron, carbon, and other elements; a strong material that can be shaped when heated.

ste-nog-ra-phy (stɑ nog′rɑ f) *n.* The skill of writing in shorthand. **stenographer** *n.*

ste-re-o (ster′′) *n.* A record player with stereophonic sound. **stereo** *adj.*

ste-re-o-phon-ic (ster′ ɑ fon′ik) *adj.* Relating to or giving a three-dimensional effect of auditory perspective.

ste-re-o-type (ster′ ɑ tp′) *n.* A conventional opinion or belief; a metal printing plate.

ster-ile (ster′il) *adj.* Free from microorganisms; sanitary; unable to reproduce.

ster-ling (ster′ling) *n.* An alloy of 92.5% silver and another metal, as copper.

stern (stern) *adj.* Inflexible; harsh. *n.* The rear of a boat or ship. **sternly** *adv.*

ster-num (ster′nɑm) *n. pl.* **-nums** or **-na** A long, flat bone located in the chest wall, connecting the collarbones and the cartilage of the first seven pairs of ribs. **sternal** *adj.*

steth-o-scope (steth′ɑ skp′) *n.* An instrument used to listen to the internal sounds of the body.

stew (stö) *v.* To cook slowly; to simmer; to boil. *n.* A dish of stewed meat and potatoes. *Slang* To worry.

stew-ard (stö′rd) *n.* A manager of another's financial affairs; a person responsible for maintaining household affairs; a male attendant on an airplane or ship.

stick (stik) *n.* A slender piece of wood; a club, rod, or walking stick. *v.* To put a hole in something; to pierce; to cling; to become jammed.

stiff (stif) *adj.* Not flexible; not easily bent; awkward. *n. Slang* A dead body.

sti-fle (st′fl) *v.* To suffocate; to cut off; to suppress; to keep back.

stig-ma (stig′mɑ) *n. pl.* **-mata** or **-mas** A mark of disgrace. **stigmata** The part of a flower where pollen is deposited at pollination; wounds resembling the crucifixion scars of

Jesus Christ. **stigmatic** *adj.*

still (stil) *adj.* Silent; calm; peaceful; until now or another time. *adv.* Nevertheless.

stillbirth (stil´berth´) *n.* The birth of a dead fetus.

stilt (stilt) *n.* One of a pair of long poles with foot supports, used for walking.

stim-u-lant (stim´ lant) *n.* An agent which arouses or accelerates physiological activity.

stim-u-late (stim´ lt´) *v.* To excite to a heightened activity; to quicken. **-ion** *n.*

stim-u-lus (stim´ lus) *n. pl.* **-li** Something that excites to action.

sting (sting) *v.* To prick with something sharp; to feel or cause to feel a smarting pain; to cause or feel sharp pain, either physical or mental. *n.* The act of stinging; the injury or pain caused by the stinger of a bee or wasp.

stin-gy (stin´j) *adj.* Not giving freely; cheap.

stink (stingk) *v.* To give off a foul odor that is highly offensive.

stip-u-late (stip´ lt´) *v.* To settle something by agreement; to establish conditions of agreement. **stipulation** *n.*

stir (ster) *v.* To mix a substance by moving round and round; to agitate or provoke.

stitch (stich) *n.* In sewing, a single loop formed by a needle and thread; the section of loop of thread, as in sewing. *v.* To join with a stitch.

stock-ade (sto kd´) *n.* A barrier placed around a fort for protection.

stock-ing (stok´ing) *n.* A knitted covering for the foot.

stock-y (stok´) *adj.* Short and plump; built sturdily.

stom-ach (stum´ak) *n., Anat.* The organ into which food passes from the esophagus; one of the primary organs of digestion. *v.* To tolerate or stand; to put up with.

stood *v.* Past tense of stand.

stool (stöl) *n.* A seat without a backrest and arms; a small version of this on which to rest the feet; a bowel movement.

stoop (stöp) *v.* To bend the body forward and downward from the waist. *n.* A porch attached to a house.

stop (stop) *v.* To cease; to halt; to refrain from moving, operating, or acting.

store (str) *n.* A business offering merchandise for sale; a supply to be used in the future. *v.* To supply; to accumulate.

stork (stork) *n.* A large, wading bird.

storm (storm) *n.* An atmospheric condition marked by strong winds with rain, sleet, hail, or snow. *v.* To charge or attack with a powerful force. **-y** *adj.*

sto-ry (str´) *n. pl.* **-ies** A narration of a fictional tale or account; a lie; a level in a building or house.

stout (stout) *adj.* Strong; sturdy; substantial; courageous. **stoutly** *adv.*

stove (stv) *n.* An apparatus in which oil, electricity, gas, or other fuels are consumed to provide the heat for cooking.

stow (st) *v.* To pack or put away.

strad-dle (strad´l) *v.* To sit or stand with the legs on either side of something; to favor both sides of an issue. **-er** *r.*

straight (strt) *adj.* Being without bends, angles, or curves; upright; erect; honest; undiluted; unmodified; heterosexual. *n.* In poker, a numerical sequence of five cards not of the same suit. **straightly, -ness** *n.*

strain (strn) *v.* To stretch beyond a proper limit; to injure by putting forth too much effort; to pass through a sieve to separate small particles from larger ones.

strait (strt) *n.* A narrow passageway which connects two bodies of water.

strand (strand) *n.* Land that borders a body of water; one of the threads that are twisted together to form a rope. *v.* To leave in a difficult situation.

strange (strnj) *adj.* Not previously known or experienced; odd; peculiar; inexperienced; alien. **strangely** *adv.*

stran-ger (strn´jr) *n.* A person unknown; a newcomer; an alien.

stran-gle (strang´gl) *v.* To kill by choking.

strap (strap) *n.* A long, narrow strip of leather or other material used to secure objects.

strat-e-gy (strat´i j) *n. pl.* **-ies** The skillful planning and managing of an activity. **strategic** *adj.* **strategist** *n.*

stra-tum (str´tum) *n. pl.* **-ta** *or* **-tums**

A horizontal layer, as of the earth's crust.

straw-ber-ry (strô´ber´) *n.* A low plant with white flowers and red fruit; the fruit of this plant.

stray (strā) *v.* To roam or wander. *n.* A lost or wandering animal or person. *adj.* Lost.

streak (strk) *n.* A narrow line or stripe that is different from the surrounding area; a run of good or bad luck. *v.* To rush or move rapidly; to make a streak. **streaky** *adj.*

stream (strm) *n.* A small body of flowing water; a steady or continuous succession or procession. *v.* To flow in or like a stream.

street (strt) *n.* A public thoroughfare in a town or city with buildings on either or both sides.

strength (strengkth) *n.* The quality of being strong; power in general; degree of concentration or potency.

strengthen (strengk´then) *v.* To grow strong or stronger.

stren-u-ous (stren´ us) *adj.* Necessitating or characterized by vigorous effort or exertion.

stress (stres) *n.* Special significance; an emphasis given to a specific syllable, word, action, or plan; strain or pressure. **-ful** *adj.*

stretch (strech) *v.* To extend fully; to extend forcibly beyond proper limits; to prolong. *n.* The state or act of stretching.

strew (strō) *v.* To scatter about.

strick-en (strik´en) *adj.* Suffering, as from an emotion, illness, or trouble.

strict (strikt) *adj.* Holding to or observing rules exactly; imposing absolute standards. **strictly** *adv.* **strictness** *n.*

stride (strd) *v.* To walk with a long, sweeping step. **stride** *n.*

strin-gent (strin´jent) *adj.* Of or relating to strict requirements; marked by obstructions or scarcity. **stringency** *n.* **stringently** *adv.*

stroll (strl) *v.* To walk in a slow, leisurely way. **stroll** *n.*

strong (strong) *adj.* Exerting or possessing physical power; durable; difficult to break.

stron-ti-um (stron´sh um) *n.* A metallic element symbolized by Sr.

struc-ture (struk´chr) *n.* A construction made up of a combination of related parts. **structure** *v.* **structural** *adj.*

strug-gle (strug´l) *v.* To put forth effort against opposition. **struggle** *n.* **struggler** *n.*

strych-nine (strik´nin) *n.* An extremely poisonous alkaloid derived from certain plants, used to kill rodents and as a neural stimulant.

stub (stub) *n.* A short, projecting part; the short end of something after the main part has been removed or used.

stub-born (stub´rn) *adj.* Inflexible; difficult to control, handle, or manage.

stuc-co (stuk´) *n. pl.* **-coes** *or* **-cos** Fine plaster used to coat exterior walls and to decorate interior walls.

stu-dent (stōd´ent) *n.* A person who studies at a school or college.

stu-di-o (stō´d ´) *n.* The place of work for an artist, photographer, or other creative person; a place for filming movies.

stud-y (stud´) *n. pl.* **-ies** The process of applying the mind to acquire knowledge.

stum-ble (stum´bl) *v.* To trip and nearly fall over something; to come upon unexpectedly.

stun (stun) *v.* To render senseless by or as if by a blow.

stu-pen-dous (stō pen´dus) *adj.* Astonishing or highly impressive. **stupendousness** *n.*

stu-pid (stō´pid) *adj.* Slow in apprehension or understanding. **stupidity** *n.*

stur-dy (ster´d) *adj.* Possessing robust strength and health. **sturdily** *adv.* **sturdiness** *n.*

stur-geon (ster´jen) *n.* A large freshwater fish highly valued as a source of caviar.

stut-ter (stut´r) *v.* To speak with involuntary repetitions of sound. **stutter** *n.*

sty (st) *n. pl.* **sties** An inflammation of the edge of an eyelid.

style (stl) *n.* A method, manner, or way of performing, speaking, or clothing; elegance, grace, or excellence in performance or appearance. **stylish** *adj.*

suave (swäv) *adj.* Ingratiating; smoothly

pleasant in manner.

sub- (sub) *prefix* Beneath, under, or below.

sub (sub) *abbr.* Substitute.

sub-con-scious (sub kon′shus) *adj.* Below the level of consciousness.

sub-due (sub dō′) *v.* To bring under control by influence, training, persuasion or force.

sub-ject (sub′jikt) *n.* The word in a sentence that defines a person or thing; a person who is under the control of another's governing power. *v.* To subdue or gain control over.

sub-jec-tive (sub jek′tiv) *adj.* Taking place within, relating to or preceding from an individual's emotions or mind. **subjectively** *adv.* **subjectivity** *n.*

sub-merge (sub merj′) *v.* To plunge under the surface of the water. **submergible** *adj.*

sub-mit (sub mit′) *v.* To give into or surrender to another's authority. **submission, submittal** *n.* **submissive** *adj.*

sub-or-di-nate (su bor′di nit) *adj.* Being of lower class or rank; minor; inferior. **subordinate** *v.* **subordination** *n.*

sub-poe-na (su p′na) *n.* A legal document requiring a person to appear in court for testimony.

sub-se-quent (sub′se kwent) *adj.* Following in time, place, or order. **subsequently** *adv.*

sub-side (sub sd′) *v.* To move to a lower level or sink; to become less intense.

sub-sid-i-ar-y (sub sid′er′) *adj.n. pl.-ies.* Providing assistance in a lesser capacity.

sub-si-dy (sub′si d) *n. pl.* **-dies.** Financial aid granted directly to a private commercial enterprise from the government.

sub-sist (sub sist′) *v.* To have continued existence.

sub-soil (sub′soil) *n.* The layer of earth that comes after the surface soil. **subsoiler** *n.*

sub-stance (sub′stans) *n.* Matter or material of which anything consists.

sub-sti-tute (sub′sti tōt′) *n.* Something or someone that takes the place of another.

sub-ten-ant (sub ten′ant) *n.* A person

who rents property from a tenant.

sub-ter-ra-ne-an (sub′te r′n an) *adj.* Located, situated, or operating underground.

sub-tract (sub trakt′) *v.* To deduct or take away from.

sub-trop-i-cal (sub trop′i kal) *adj.* Pertaining to regions adjacent to the tropics.

sub-urb (sub′erb) *n.* A residential community near a large city. **-ban** *adj.*

suc-ceed (suk sd′) *v.* To accomplish what is attempted; to come next or to follow.

suc-cess (suk ses′) *n.* Achievement of something intended or desired; attaining wealth, fame, or prosperity.

suc-ces-sive (suk ses′iv) *adj.* Following in order or sequence. **successively** *adv.*

suc-cu-lent (suk′u lent) *adj.* Juicy; full of juice or sap. **succulence** *n.* **-ly** *adv.*

such (such) *adj.* Of this or that kind or thing; a great degree or extent in quality. *pron.* Of a particular degree or kind; a person or thing of such.

su-crose (sō′krs) *n.* Sugar obtained from the sugar beet or sugar cane.

suc-tion (suk′shan) *n.* The process or act of sucking.

sud-den (sud′en) *adj.* Happening very quickly without warning or notice; sharp; abrupt; marked by haste. **suddenly** *adv.* **-ness** *n.*

suede (swd) *n.* Leather with a soft, napped finish.

su-et (sō′it) *n.* The hard fat around the kidney and loins of sheep.

suf-fer (suf′r) *v.* To feel pain or distress; to sustain injury, loss, or damage. **sufferer** *n.*

suf-fi-cient (su fish′ent) *adj.* As much that is needed or desired. **sufficiency** *n.* **-ly** *adv.*

suf-fix (suf′iks) *n.* A form affixed to the end of a word.

suf-fo-cate (suf′o kt′) *v.* To kill by depriving something or someone of oxygen.

sug-gest (sug jest′) *v.* To give an idea for action or consideration; to imply; hint or intimate.

sug-ges-tion (sug jes′chan) *n.* The act of suggesting; a slight insinuation; hint.

su-i-cide (sōō′i sd′) *n.* The act of taking one's own life. **suicidal** *adj.*

sul-len (sul′en) *adj.* Ill-humored, melancholy; gloomy; depressing.

sul-try (sul′tr) *adj.* Hot and humid; muggy.

sum (sum) *n.* The result obtained by adding; the whole amount, quantity, or number; summary.

sum-ma-ry (sum′a r) *n. pl.* -ries. Giving the sum or substance. *adj.* A statement covering the main points. **summarily** *adv.*

sum-mer (sum′r) *n.* The warmest of the four seasons, following spring and coming before autumn. **summery** *adj.*

sum-mit (sum′it) *n.* The top and highest point, degree, or level.

sum-mons (sum′onz) *n. pl.* -monses An order or command to perform a duty; a notice to appear at a certain place.

sun (sun) *n.* The star around which other planets of the solar system orbit; the energy, visible light, and heat, that is emitted by the sun; sunshine.

su-per (sōō′pr) *adj.* Exceeding a norm; in excessive intensity or degree; surpassing most others; superior in rank, status or position; excellent. *n. Slang* Superintendent of a building.

su-perb (se perb′) *adj.* Of first-rate quality.

su-per-fi-cial (sōō′pr fish′al) *adj.* Pertaining to a surface; concerned only with what is not necessarily real.

su-pe-ri-or (su pr′ r) *adj.* Of higher rank, grade, or dignity. *n.* A person who surpasses another in rank or excellence. **superiority** *n.* **-ly** *adv.*

su-per-la-tive (su per′la tiv) *adj.* Of the highest degree of excellence; pertaining to the degree of comparison of an adverb or adjective that shows extreme extent or level.

su-per-sede (sōō′pr sd′) *v.* To take the place of; to set aside.

su-per-son-ic (sōō′pr son′ik) *adj., Aero.* Characterized by a speed greater than that of sound.

su-per-sti-tion (sōō′pr stish′an) *n.* A belief founded, despite evidence that it is irrational; a belief, resulting from faith in magic or chance. **-ous** *adj.*

su-per-vise (sōō′pr vz′) *v.* To have charge in directing the work of other people.

sup-per (sup′r) *n.* The last or evening meal of the day.

sup-ple-ment (sup′le ment) *n.* A part that compensates for what is lacking. **supplementary** *adj.* **-al** *adj.*

sup-ply (su pli′) *v. n., pl.* -plies To provide with what is needed; to make available.

sup-port (su prt′) *v.* To bear or hold the weight of; to tolerate; to give assistance or approval. *n.* The act of supporting.

sup-pose (su pz′) *v.* To think or assume as true; to consider probable. **supposed** *adj.*

sup-pos-i-to-ry (su poz′i tr′) *n. pl.* -ries A medication, in solid form, that melts when inserted into the body cavity, as the rectum.

sup-press (su pres′) *v.* To put an end to something by force.

su-preme (su prm′) *adj.* Of the highest authority, rank, or power.

sur-charge (ser′chärj′) *n.* An extra fee added to the cost of something; to overcharge.

sure (sher) *adj.* Firm and sturdy; being impossible to doubt; inevitable; not liable to fail. **surer** *adj.* **surest** *adj.* **surely** *adv.*

sur-face (ser′fis) *n.* The exterior or outside boundary of something; outward appearance. *adj.* Situated on a surface.

surge (serj) *v.* To increase suddenly. *n.* A large swell of water.

sur-geon (ser′jon) *n.* A physician who practices surgery.

sur-ger-y (ser′je r) *n. pl.* -ies. The branch of medicine in which physical deformity or disease is treated by an operative procedure.

sur-mise (sr mz′) *v.* To guess; to conjecture.

sur-mount (sr mount′) *v.* To overcome; to be at the top.

sur-name (ser′nm′) *n.* A person's family's last name.

sur-pass (sr pas′) *v.* To go beyond the limits of; to be greater than. **surpassingly** *adv.*

sur-plus (ser′plus) *n.* An amount beyond what is needed.

sur-prise (sr prz´) v. To come upon unexpectedly or suddenly; to cause to feel amazed or astonished. **-ingly** adv.

sur-ren-der (su ren´dr) v. To give up or yield possession or power. n. The act of surrendering.

sur-rey (ser´) n. pl. **-reys.** A four-wheeled, horse-driven carriage.

sur-ro-gate (ser´o gt´) n. A person who puts himself in the place of another.

sur-round (su round´) v. To extend around all edges of something; to enclose or shut in.

sur-veil-lance (sr v´lns) n. Close observation kept over a suspect.

sur-vey (sr v´) v. n., pl. **-veys.** To examine in detail; to determine area, boundaries, or position and elevation of a section of the earth's surface. **sur-veyor** n.

sur-vive (sr vv´) v. To continue to exist; to outlast; to outlive. **survivor** n.

su-shi n. A Japanese dish of thin slices of fresh, raw fish.

sus-pect (su spekt´) v. To have doubt or distrust; to have a suspicion or inkling of someone or something. **suspect** n.

sus-pend (su spend´) v. To bar from a privilege for a certain time, as a means of punishment; to hang so as to allow free movement.

sus-pense (su spens´) n. The feeling of being insecure or undecided, resulting from uncertainty.

sus-pi-cion (su spish´an) n. The instance of suspecting something wrong without proof.

sus-tain (su stn´) v. To hold up and keep from falling; to suffer or undergo an injury.

su-ture (sō´chr) n. The stitching together or joining the edges of an incision or cut.

swab (swob) n. A small stick with a wad of cotton on both ends, used to apply medication. Slang A sailor.

swad-dle (swod´l) v. To wrap closely, using a long strip of flannel or linen.

swal-low (swol´) v. To cause food to pass from the mouth to the stomach; to retract or take back, as words spoken. n. The act of swallowing.

swap (swop) v. To trade something for something in return. **swap** n.

swarm (sworm) n. A large number of insects, as bees; a large group of persons or things. **swarm, swarmer** v.

swat (swot) v. To hit something with a sharp blow.

swatch (swoch) n. A strip of cloth cut off a larger piece, used as a sample.

swath (swoth) n. The area or width of grass cut by a machine. **swathe** v.

sway (sw) v. To move or swing from right to left or side by side; to exert influence or control. n. Dominating power.

swear (swâr) v. To make an affirmation under oath. **swearer** n.

sweat (swet) v. To excrete a salty moisture from the pores of the skin. Informal To work hard; to cause to sweat. Slang Being impatient; having anxiety.

sweat gland n. Anat. One of the tubular glands that secrete sweat externally through pores.

sweep (swp) v. To touch very lightly; to remove or clear away with a brush, broom, etc.; to move with an even action.

sweet (swt) adj. Having a sugary, agreeable flavor; arousing pleasant emotions; a beloved or dear person.

sweet sorghum n. Syrup or molasses.

swell (swel) v. To increase in size or bulk; to grow in volume.

swel-ter (swel-tr) v. To suffer from extreme heat.

swerve (swerv) v. To turn aside from the regular course.

swift (swift) adj. Moving with great speed; accomplished or occurring quickly.

swim (swim) v. To move oneself through water by moving parts of the body, as arms, head, and legs.

swin-dle (swin´dl) v. To cheat out of property or money; to practice fraud or deception in order to acquire illegally the assets of another. **swindle** n.

swine (swn) n. pl. **swine** A hoofed mammal with a snout, related to pigs and hogs; a low, despicable person.

swinge (swinj) v. To whip; to chastise.

swing shift n. Work shift from 4 p.m. until midnight.

swin-ish (swī´nĭsh) *adj.* Befitting or like swine; beastly.

swipe (swīp) *v.* To drive or strike with a great force; to strike with a sweeping blow. *n.* A strong glancing or sweeping blow.

swish (swĭsh) *v.* To move with or make a hissing sound.

switch (swĭch) *n.* A small, thin, flexible stick, twig or rod. *Electr.* A device for opening or closing an electric circuit; to shift to another train track by using a switch; to exchange.

swiv-el (swĭv´ĕl) *n.* A coupling device, ring, or pivot that allows attached parts to rotate or move freely. **swivel** *v.*

sword (srd) *n.* A weapon with a long, pointed cutting blade.

syc-a-more (sĭk´a mr´) *n.* A North American tree that is used widely for shade.

syl-la-ble (sĭl´a bl) *n. phonet.* A word or part of one that consists of a single vocal impulse, usually consisting of one or more vowels or consonants.

sym-bol (sĭm´bol) *n.* Something that stands for or represents something else.

sym-pa-thet-ic (sĭm´pa thĕt´ĭk) *adj.* Having or showing kindness or sympathy for others.

sym-pa-thy (sĭm´pa th) *n. pl.* **-thies** Mutual understanding or affection during a time of sadness or loss.

symp-tom (sĭmp´tom) *n.* A sign of change in a body's functions or appearance.

syn-a-gogue (sĭn´a gŏg´) *n.* A place for Jewish worship and prayer.

syn-chro-nize (sĭng´kro nz´) *v.* To operate or take place at the same time.

syn-di-cate (sĭn´dĭ kĭt) *n.* An organization set up to carry out business transactions; a company that sells materials for simultaneous publication at a number of different locations.

syn-drome (sĭn´drm) *n.* A set of concurrent symptoms that indicate or characterize a disorder or disease.

syn-o-nym (sĭn´o nĭm) *n.* A word that means the same or nearly the same as another.

syn-op-sis (sĭ nŏp´sĭs) *n. pl.* **-ses** A shortened statement or narrative.

sy-ringe (sĭ rĭnj´) *n.* A medical instrument used to inject or draw fluids from the body.

sys-tem (sĭs´tem) *n.* A method or way of doing something; the human body or related parts ofthebody that perform vital functions; an orderly arrangement.

systemic *adj.* Pertaining to a particular part or organs of the body; affecting the entire bodily system or body as a whole.

sys-to-le (sĭs´to l´) *n., Physiol.* The regular rhythmic contraction of the heart that pumps blood through the aorta and pulmonary artery.

sys-tyle *n.* Space between two columns, equal in length to two times the diameter of a column.

T

T, t The twentieth letter of the English alphabet. **tab** (tăb) *n.* A strip, flap, or small loop that projects from something. *Slang* A bill or total, as for a meal.

tab-er-na-cle (tăb´r nak´l) *n.* A portable shelter or structure used by the Jews during their journey out of Egypt; a place of worship.

ta-ble-spoon (t´bl spōn´) *n.* A unit of measure; a large spoon for serving food.

tab-let (tăb´lĭt) *n.* A pad used for writing; a thin, flat piece of stone or wood which is fit for or has an inscription.

tab-loid (tăb´loid) *n.* A small newspaper with news reported by means of pictures and concise reporting.

ta-boo (ta bŏ´) *n.* A custom or rule against doing, using, or mentioning something. *adj.* Forbidden by social authority, convention, or custom.

tab-u-lar (tăb´ lr) *adj.* Pertaining to or arranged in a table or list. **-ly** *adv.*

ta-chom-e-ter (ta kom´i tr) *n.* An instrument for measuring velocity and speed.

tac-it (tăs´ĭt) *adj.* Understood; expressed or implied nonverbally; implicit.

tack claw *n.* A small tool used to remove tacks.

tacki-ness n. The state of being tacky.

tacky (tak') adj. Slightly sticky; shabby; lacking style or good taste; flashy.

tact (takt) n. Having the ability to avoid what would disturb or offend someone.

tac-tic (tak'tik) n. A way or means of working toward a goal; the art of using strategy to gain military objectives or other goals.

tad (tad) n. A small boy; an insignificant degree or amount.

tag (tag) n. A piece of plastic, metal, paper, or other material that is attached to something in order to identify it; a children's game in which one child is "it" and tries to catch another child, who then becomes "it."

tail (tl) n. The posterior extremity, extending from the end or back of an animal.

tai-lor (tl'lr) n. One whose profession is making, mending, and altering clothing. v. To adapt for a specific purpose. **tailor** v.

taint (tnt) v. To spoil, contaminate, or pollute. n. A blemish or stain.

take (tk) v. To seize or capture; to get possession of; to receive, swallow, absorb, or accept willingly.

talc (talk) n. A soft, fine-grained, smooth mineral used in making talcum powder.

tale (tl) n. A story or recital of relating events that may or may not be true; a malicious or false story; gossip.

tal-ent (tal'ent) n. The aptitude, disposition, or characteristic ability of a person. **talented** adj. **talentless** adj.

talk (tok) v. To communicate by words or speech; to engage in chatter or gossip. n. A speech or lecture, usually given to a group of people. Slang To boast; to brag. **talkativeness**, **talkative**, **talker** adv.

tall (tol) adj. Of greater than average height; of a designated or specified height; imaginary, as a tall tale.

tal-low (tal') n. Hard fat rendered from sheep or cattle, used to make candles, lubricants, and soap. **tallow** adj.

tal-ly (tal') n. pl. -ies A record or counting of money, amounts, or scores. v. To agree with; to reckon on or figure a score; to count.

tal-on (tal'on) n. A long, curved claw found on birds or animals, used to kill or capture prey. **taloned** adj.

tam-bou-rine (tam'bo rn') n. A percussion instrument made of a small drum with jingling metal disks around the rim.

tame (tm) adj. Not wild or ferocious; domesticated or manageable. v. To make docile or calm.

tam-per (tam'pr) v. To change, meddle, or alter something; to use corrupt measures to scheme. **-proof** adj.

tan (tan) v. To cure a hide into leather by using chemicals. n. A brownish skin tone caused by exposure to the sun.

tan-dem (tan'dem) n. Any arrangement that involves two or more things, animals or persons arranged one behind the other.

tan-gent (tan'jent) n. A line that touches a curved line but does not intersect or cross it; a sudden change from one course to another.

tan-gi-ble (tan'ji bl) adj. Capable of being appreciated or felt by the sense of touch; capable of being realized.

tan-gle (tang'gl) v. To mix, twist, or unite in a confused manner making separation difficult. **tanglement** n.

tan-go (tang'g) n. A ballroom dance with long, gliding steps. **tango** v.

tank (tangk) n. A large container for holding or storing a gas or liquid. **tankful** n.

tank-ard (tang'krd) n. A large drinking mug, usually with a hinged top.

tan-ta-lize (tan'ta lz') v. To tease or tempt by holding or keeping something just out of one's reach. **-er** adv.

tan-trum (tan'trum) n. A fit; an outburst or a rage of bad temper.

tap (tap) v. To strike repeatedly, usually while making a small noise; to strike or touch gently; to make secret contact with something; in medicine, to remove fluids from the body.

tape (tp) n. A narrow strip of woven fabric; a string or ribbon stretched across the finish line of a race. **tape** v.

ta-per (t'pr) n. A very slender candle. v. To become gradually smaller or thinner at one end.

tap-es-try (tap'i str) n. pl. -ies A thick

fabric woven with designs and figures.

tap-i-o-ca (tap´ ´ka) n. A bead-like substance used for thickening and for puddings.

taps (taps) n. pl., Mil. A bugle call that signals lights out, also sounded at memorial and funeral services.

tar-dy (tär´d) adj. Late; not on time.
tardily, tardiness n.

tar-get (tär´git) n. An object marked to shoot at; an aim or goal.

tar-iff (tar´if) n. Duty or tax on merchandise coming into or going out of a country.

tar-nish (tär´nish) v. To become discolored or dull; to lose luster; to spoil.

tar-ot n. A set of 22 cards used for fortune telling, each card showing a virtue, an elemental force, or a vice.

tar-pau-lin (tär pa´lin) n. A sheet of waterproof canvas used as a protective covering.

tar-ry (tar´) v. To linger, delay, or hesitate.

tart (tärt) adj. Sharp; sour; cutting, biting in tone or meaning. **tartly, tartness** n.

tar-tan (tär´tan) n. A plaid fabric pattern of Scottish origin.

task (task) n. A bit of work, usually assigned by another; a job.

tas-sel n. An ornamental decoration made from a bunch of string or thread.

taste (tst) n. The ability to sense or determine flavor in the mouth; a personal liking or disliking. v. To test or sense flavors in the mouth.

tat-ter (tat´r) n. A torn scrap of cloth. v. To become or make ragged.

tat-tle (tat´l) v. To reveal the secrets of another by gossiping. **tattler** n.

tat-too (ta tö´) n. A permanent design or mark made on the skin by pricking and inserting an indelible dye. **-er** n.

taught v. Past tense of teach.

taut (tot) adj. Tight; emotionally strained.

tax (taks) n. A payment imposed and collected from individuals or businesses by the government. v. To strain. **taxable, taxation** n. **taxer** n. **-payer** n.

taxex-empt (taks´ig zempt) adj. Exempted from tax; bearing tax free interest on federal or state income.

tax-i (tak´s) v. To move along the ground or water surface on its own power before taking off.

taxi-cab (tak´s kab´) n. A vehicle for carrying passengers for money.

tax-i-der-my (tak´si dur´m) n. The art or profession of preparing, stuffing, and mounting animal skins. **taxidermist** n.

teach v. To communicate skill or knowledge; to give instruction or insight.

teach-er (t´chr) n. A person who teaches; one who instructs.

team (tm) n. Two or more players on one side in a game; a group of people trained or organized to work together; two or more animals harnessed to the same implement. v. To join or work together.

team-ster (tm´str) n. A person who drives a team of animals or a vehicle as an occupation.

tear (tär) v. To become divided into pieces; to separate; to rip into parts or pieces; to move fast; to rush. n. A rip or torn place. n. A fluid secreted by the eye to moisten and cleanse. v. To cry. **teary** adj.

tease (tz) v. To make fun of; to bother; to annoy; to tantalize. n. A person who teases. **teaser, teasingly** adv.

tech-ne-tium (tek´sh um) n. A metallic element symbolized by Tc.

tech-ni-cal (tek´ni kal) adj. Expert; derived or relating to technique; relating to industry or mechanics. **technically** adv.

tech-nique (tek nk´) n. A technical procedure or method of doing something.

tech-nol-o-gy (tek nol´o j) n. pl. **-ies** The application of scientific knowledge to serve man in industry, commerce, medicine and other fields.

te-di-ous (t´de us) adj. Boring; taking a long time. **tediously** adv.

tee (t) n. A peg used to hold a golf ball on the first stroke toward a hole or goal post; a peg used to support a football during a field goal attempt.

teem (tem) v. To abound; to be full of; to swarm or crowd.

teens (tnz) n. pl. The ages between 13 and 19

teeth n. pl. The plural of tooth.

tel-e-cast (tel´ kast´) *n.* A television broadcast. **telecast** *v.*

tel-e-gram (tel´e gram) *n.* A message sent or received by telegraph.

tel-e-graph (tel´e graf) *n.* A system for com- municating; a transmission sent by wire or radio. *v.* To send messages by electricity over wire. **telegraphist**, **telegrapher** *adj.*

te-lep-a-thy (te lep´a th) *n.* Communication by means of mental processes rather than ordinary means. **telepathic** *n.*

tel-e-phone (tel´e fn) *n.* A system or device for transmitting conversations by wire.

tel-e-pho-to (tel´ f´t) *adj.* Relating to a camera lens which produces a large image of a distant object. **telephotograph** *n.*

tel-e-scope (tel´i skp´) *n.* An instrument which contains a lens system which makes distant objects appear larger and near.

tel-e-thon (tel´e thon´) *n.* A long telecast used to raise money for a worthy cause.

tel-e-vi-sion (tel´e vizh´an) *n.* Reception and transmission of images on a screen with sound; the device that reproduces television sounds and images.

tel-ex *n.* Teletype communications by means of automatic exchanges.

tell (tel) *v.* To relate or describe; to command or order. **telling**, **-able** *n.* **-er** *n.*

tel-lu-ri-um (te lur´ um) *n.* An element symbolized by Te.

temp *abbr.* Temperature.

tem-per (tem´pr) *n.* The state of one's feelings. *v.* To modify something, making it flexible or hard. **temperable** *adj.*

tem-per-a-ment (tem´pr a ment) *n.* Personality; a characteristic way of thinking, reacting, or behaving. **temperamental** *adj.*

tem-per-ance (tem´pr ans) *n.* Moderation; restraint; moderation or abstinence from drinking alcoholic beverages.

tem-per-ate (tem´r it) *adj.* Avoiding extremes; moderate. **temperately** *adv.*

tem-per-a-ture (tem´pr a cher) *n.* A measure of heat or cold in relation to

the body or environment; an elevation in body temperature above the normal 98.6 degrees Fahrenheit.

tem-pest (tem´pist) *n.* A severe storm, usually with snow, hail, rain, or sleet.

tem-ple (tem´pl) *n.* A place of worship; the flat area on either side of the forehead.

tem-po (tem´po) *n. pl.* **-pos** *or* **-pi** *Mus.* The rate of speed at which a musical composition is to be played.

tem-po-rar-y (tem´po rer´) *adj.* Lasting for a limited amount of time; not permanent.

tempt (tempt) *n.* To encourage or draw into a foolish or wrong course of action; to lure. **temptation** *n.* **-er** *n.*

ten (ten) *n.* The cardinal number equal to 9 + 1; the number before eleven.

te-na-cious (te n´ shus) *adj.* Persistent; stubborn. **tenaciously**, **-ness** *n.*

ten-ant (ten´ant) *n.* A person who pays rent to occupy another's property.

Ten Commandments *n.* The ten rules of moral behavior which were given to Moses by God.

tend (tend) *v.* To be inclined or disposed; to be directed; to look after.

ten-den-cy (ten´den s) *n. pl.* **-ies** A disposition to act or behave in a particular way; a particular direction, mode, outcome, or direction.

ten-der-loin (ten´dr loin´) *n.* A cut of tender pork or beef.

ten-don (ten´dn) *n.* A band of tough, fibrous tissues that connect, a muscle and bone.

ten-dril (ten´dril) *n.* A thread- like part of a climbing plant which attaches itself to a support. **tendriled** *or* **tendrilled** *adj.*

ten-nis (ten´is) *n.* A sport played with a ball and racket by 2 or 4 people on a rectangular court.

ten-or (ten´r) *n.* An adult male singing voice, above a baritone.

tense (tens) *adj.* Taut or stretched tightly; nervous; under strain.

ten-sion (ten´shan) *n.* The condition of stretching or the state of being stretched.

tent (tent) *n.* A portable shelter made by stretching material over a supporting framework.

ten-ta-cle (ten´ta kl) *n.* A long, unjointed, flexible body part that projects from certain invertebrates, as the octopus. **tentacular** *adj.* **tentacled** *adj.*

ten-ta-tive (ten´tə tiv) *adj.* Experimental; subject to change; not definite. **tentatively** *adv.*

ten-ure (ten´yr) *n.* The right, state, or period of holding something, as an office or property. **tenurial, -ed** *adv.*

tep-id (tep´id) *adj.* Lukewarm. **-ly** *n.*

ter-bi-um (tür´b um) *n.* A metallic element of the rare-earth group symbolized by Tb.

ter-cen-ten-a-ry (tür sen´tə ner´) *n. pl.* **-ries**. The time span of 300 years; a 300th anniversary. **tercentenary** *adj.*

term *n.* A phrase or word; a limited time or duration; a phrase having a precise meaning. *Math* The quantity of two numbers either added together or subtracted.

ter-mi-nal (tür´mi nal) *adj.* Of, forming, or located at the end; final. *n.* A station at the end of a bus line, railway, or airline; in Computer Science, the instrument through which data enters or leaves a computer.

ter-mi-nate *v.* To bring to a conclusion or end; to finish; to fire someone from a job.

ter-mite (tüe´mt) *n.* The winged or wingless insect which lives in large colonies feeding on wood.

ter-race (ter´as) *n.* An open balcony or porch; a level piece of land that is higher than the surrounding area; a row of houses built on a sloping or raised site.

terra cotta *n.* A hard, baked clay used in ceramic pottery.

ter-rain (te rn´) *n.* The surface of an area, as land.

ter-ra-pin (ter´ə pin) *n.* An edible turtle of North America, living in both fresh and salt water.

ter-res-tri-al (te res´tr al) *adj.* Something earthly; not heavenly; growing or living on land.

ter-ri-ble (ter´i bl) *adj.* Causing fear or terror; intense; extreme; horrid; difficult.

ter-ri-er (ter´ r) *n.* A very active small dog, originally bred by hunters to dig for burrowing game, now kept as a

family pet.

ter-rif-ic (te rif´ik) *adj.* Terrifying. *Informal* Excellent; causing amazement.

ter-ri-fy (ter´i fi) *v.* To fill with fear or terror; to frighten; to menace. **-ied** *adj.* **terrifying** *adj.*

ter-ri-to-ry (ter´i tr) *n. pl.* **-ies** An area, usually of great size, which is controlled by a particular government; a district or area assigned to one person or group.

ter-ror (ter´r) *n.* Extreme fear; one who causes terror.

ter-ror-ism *n.* The state of being terrorized or the act of terrorizing; the use of intimidation to attain one's goals or to advance one's cause.

terse (türs) *adj.* Brief; using as few words as possible without loss of force or clearness.

test (test) *n.* An examination or evaluation of something or someone; an examination to determine one's knowledge, skill, intelligence or other qualities. **tester** *n.*

tes-ta-ment (tes´tə ment) *n.* A legal document which states how one's personal property is to be distributed upon his death. **Testament** One of the two sections of the Bible; the Old Testament and the New Testament.

tes-tate (tes´tt) *adj.* Having left a valid will.

tes-ti-fy (tes´ti f) *v.* To give evidence while under oath; to serve as proof. **testifier** *n.*

tes-ti-mo-ni-al (tes´ti m´n al) *n.* A formal statement; a gift, dinner, reception, or other sign of appreciation given to a person as a token of esteem.

tes-ti-mo-ny (tes´ti m´n) *n. pl.* **-ies** A solemn affirmation made under oath; an outward expression of a religious experience.

tes-tis (tes´tis) *n. pl.* **testes** The sperm producing gland of the male.

test tube *n.* A thin glass tube closed at one end, used in biology and chemistry.

tet-a-nus (tet´ə nus) *n., Pathol* An often fatal disease marked by muscular spasms, commonly known as lockjaw.

teth-er (teth´r) *n.* A rope or chain which

fastens an animal to something but allows limited freedom to wander within its range.

text (tekst) *n.* The actual wording of an author's work distinguished his from notes; the main part or body of a book. **-ual, textually** *adv.*

text-book (tekst´bŭk´) *n.* A book used by students to prepare their lessons.

tex-tile (teks´til) *n.* A cloth made by weaving; yarn or fiber for making cloth.

tex-ture (teks´chr) *n.* The look, surface, or feel of something; the basic makeup. **textural** *adj.* **texturally** *adv.*

thal-li-um (thal´ um) *n.* A metallic element resembling lead, symbolized by Tl.

than (than) *conj.* In comparison with or to something.

thank (thangk) *v.* To express one's gratitude; to credit.

thank-ful (thangk´ful) *adj.* Feeling or showing gratitude; grateful. **thankfully, -ness** *adj.*

that (that) *adj. pl.* **those** The person or thing present or being mentioned. Used to introduce a clause stating what is said.

thaw (tho) *v.* To change from a frozen state to a liquid or soft state; to grow warmer; to melt.

the *definite adj. or article* Used before nouns and noun phrases as a determiner, designating particular persons or things. *adv.* Used to modify words in the comparative degree; so much; by that much.

the-a-tre (the´a tr) *n.* A building adapted to present dramas, motion pictures, plays, or other performances; a performance.

the-at-ri-cal (th a´tri kal) *adj.* Extravagant; designed for show, display, or effect.

theft (theft) *n.* The act or crime of stealing; larceny.

their (thâr) *adj. & pron.* The possessive case of they; belonging to two or more things or beings previously named.

the-ism (th´iz um) *n.* The belief in the existence of God. **theist, theistic** *adj.*

them (them) The objective case of they.

theme (thm) *n.* The topic or subject of something. *Mus.* A short melody of a musical composition. **thematic** *adj.*

them-selves (them selvz´) *n.* or they; a form of the third person plural pronoun.

then (then) *adv.* At that time; soon or immediately. *adj.* Being or acting in or belonging to or at that time.

thence (thens) *adv.* From that place, event, fact, or origin.

the-oc-ra-cy (th ok´ra s) *n. pl.* **-ies** Government by God or by clergymen who think of themselves as representatives of God. **theocrat, theocratic** *adj.*

the-ol-o-gy (th ol o´ j) *n. pl.* **-ies** The religious study of the nature of God, beliefs, practices, and ideas. **theologian** *n.*

the-o-rize (th´o-rz) *v.* To analyze theories. **theoretician** *n.* **theorization** *n.* **theorizer** *n.*

the-o-ry (th´o r) *n. pl.* **-ies** A general principle or explanation which covers the known facts; an offered opinion which may possibly, but not positively, be true.

ther-a-peu-tics (ther´a p´tiks) *n.* The medical treatment of disease.

ther-a-py (ther´a p) *n. pl.* **-ies** The treatment of certain diseases; treatment intended to remedy an undesirable condition.

there (thâr) *adv.* In, at, or about that place; toward, into, orto. **thereabouts** *adv.* **thereafter** *adv.* **thereby** *adv.* **therefore** *adv.* **therefrom** *adv.* **-in** *adv.*

ther-mal (ther´mal) *adj.* Having to do with or producing heat.

ther-mom-e-ter (thr mom´i tr) *n.* A glass tube containing mercury which rises and falls with temperature changes. **-tric** *adj.*

ther-mo-plas-tic (ther´mo plas´tik) *adj.* Pliable and soft when heated or warm but hard when cooled.

ther-mo-stat (ther´mo stat´) *n.* A device that automatically responds to temperature changes and activates equipment such as air conditioners and furnaces to adjust the temperature to correspond with the setting on the device. **thermostatic** *adj.*

the-sau-rus (thi so´us) *n. pl.* **-ruses** or **-ri** A book which contains synonyms.

these *pron.* The plural of this.

the-sis (th′sis) *n. pl.* **-ses** A formal argument or idea; a paper written by a student that develops an idea or point of view.

they (th) *pron.* The two or more beings just mentioned.

they'd (thd) They had.

they'll (thl) They will.

they're (thr) They are.

they've (thv) They have.

thick (thik) *adj.* Having a heavy or dense consistency; having a considerable extent or depth from one surface to its opposite. *Slang* Excessive. **thickly** *adv.* **thicken** *n.*

thief (thf) *n. pl.* **thieves** A person who steals.

thieve (thv) *v.* To take by theft.

thigh (th) *n.* The part of the leg between the hip and the knee of man.

thimble (thim′bl) *n.* A small caplike protection for the finger, worn while sewing.

thin (thin) *adj.* Having very little depth or extent from one side or surface to the other; not fat; slender. *v.* To make or become thin. **thinly** *adv.* **thinness** *n.*

thing (thing) *n.* Something not recognized or named; an idea, conception, or utterance; a material or real object.

things *n. pl.* One's belongings.

think (thingk) *v.* To exercise thought; to use the mind; to reason and work out in the mind; to visualize. **-able** *adj.*

third (thûrd) *n.* Next to the second in time or place; the last in a series of three. *Mech.* The 3rd forward gear in an automobile, truck, tractor, or other vehicle.

thirst (thûrst) *n.* An uncomfortably dry feeling in the throat and mouth accompanied by an urgent desire for liquids. **thirsty** *adj.*

this (this) *pron. pl.* **these** The person or thing that is near, present, or just mentioned; the one under discussion.

this-tle (this′l) *n.* A prickly plant usually producing a purplish or yellowish flower.

thith-er (thith′r) *adv.* To that place; there; on the farthest side.

thong (thong) *n.* A narrow strip of leather used for binding.

tho-rax (thr′aks) *n. pl.* **-raxes** *or* **-races** The section or part of the human body between the neck and abdomen, supported by the ribs and breastbone. **thoracic** *adj.*

tho-ri-um (thr′ um) *n.* A radioactive metallic element symbolized by Th.

thorn (thorn) *n.* A sharp, pointed, woody projection on a plant stem. **thorniness** *n.*

thor-ough (thûr′) *adj.* Complete; intensive; accurate; very careful; absolute. **thoroughness** *n.* **thoroughly** *adv.*

thor-ough-bred (thûr′ bred′) *adj.* Being of a pure breed of stock.

thor-ough-fare (thûr′ fâr′) *n.* A public highway, road or street.

those *adj. & pron.* The plural of that.

though (th) *adv.* Nevertheless; in spite of.

thought (thot) *n.* The process, act, or power of thinking; a possibility; an idea. **thoughtful** *adj.* **thoughtless** *adj.*

thou-sand (thou′zand) *n.* The cardinal number equal to 10 X 100.

thrash (thrash) *v.* To beat or strike with a whip; to move violently about; to defeat.

thread (thred) *n.* A thin cord of cotton or other fiber; the ridge going around a bolt, nut or screw. *v.* To pass a thread through, as to thread a needle.

threads *n. pl. Slang* Clothes.

threat (thret) *n.* An expression or warning of intent to do harm; anything holding a possible source of danger. **threaten** *v.* **threatener** *n.* **-ingly** *adv.*

three (thr) *n.* The cardinal number equal to 2 + 1.

three-D *or* **3-D** (thr′d′) *n.* A three-dimensional form.

thresh (thresh) *v.* To separate seed from a harvested plant mechanically; to strike severely.

thresh-old (thresh′ld) *n.* A horizontal piece of wood or other material which forms a doorsill; a beginning point.

threw *v.* Past tense of throw.

thrice (thrs) *adv.* Three times.

thrift (thrift) *n.* The careful use of money and other resources. **thriftily** *adv.* **thriftiness** *n.* **thrifty** *adj.*

thrill (thril) *n.* A feeling of sudden intense excitement, fear, or joy.

thrilling adj.

thrive (thrv) v. To prosper; to be healthy; to do well in a position.

throat (thrt) n. The front section or part of the neck containing passages for food and air.

throb (throb) v. To beat, move, or vibrate in a pulsating way; to pulsate.

throm-bo-sis (throm b´sis) n. pl. -ses The development of a blood clot in a blood vessel or in the heart cavity.

throng (throng) n. A large group or crowd. v. To crowd around or into.

throt-tle (throt´l) n. The valve which controls the flow of fuel to an engine. v. To control the speed or fuel with a throttle.

through (thrö) prep. From the beginning to the end; in one side and out the opposite side. Slang Completed; finished.

through-out (thrö out´) adv. In every place; everywhere; at all times.

throw (thr) v. To toss or fling through the air with a motion of the arm; to hurl with force. Slang To entertain, as to throw a party. **up** To vomit. **out** To discard something.

thru (thrö) Through.

thrush (thrush) n. A small songbird having a brownish upper body and spotted breast.

thrust (thrust) v. To push; to shove with sudden or vigorous force. n. A sudden stab or push.

thru-way or **throughway** (thrö´w). A major highway; an expressway.

thud (thud) n. A heavy, dull thumping sound.

thug (thug) n. A tough or violent gangster.

thumb (thum) n. The short first digit of the hand; the part of the glove that fits over the thumb. v. To browse through something quickly. Slang To hitchhike.

thump (thump) n. A blow with something blunt or heavy. **thump** v.

thun-der (thun´dr) n. The loud explosive sound made as air is suddenly expanded by heat and then quickly contracted again.

thun-der-bolt (thun´dr klap´) n. A flash of lightning immediately followed by thunder.

thun-der-cloud (thun´dr kloud´) n. A dark cloud carrying an electric charge and producing lightning and thunder.

thun-der-show-er (thun´dr shou´r) n. A brief rainstorm with thunder and lightning.

thus (thus) adv. In this or that way; therefore.

thwack (thwak) v. To strike hard, using something flat.

thwart (thwort) v. To prevent from happening; to prevent from doing something. n. A seat positioned crosswise in a boat.

thy (th) adj. Pertaining to oneself; your.

thyme (tm) n. An aromatic mint herb whose leaves are used in cooking.

thy-roid (th´roid) adj., Anat. Pertaining to the thyroid gland. n. The gland in the neck of man which produces hormones which regulate food use and body growth.

thy-rox-ine (th rok´sn) n. A hormone secreted by the thyroid gland.

ti-ar-a (t ar´a) n. A bejeweled crown in the form of a half circle and worn by women at formal occasions.

tick (tik) n. One of a series of rhythmical tapping sounds made by a clock; a small bloodsucking parasite, many of which are carriers of disease.

tick-et (tik´it) n. A printed slip of paper or cardboard allowing its holder to enter a specified event or to enjoy a privilege; a list of candidates who represent a political party.

tick-le (tik´l) v. To stroke lightly so as to cause laughter; to amuse or delight.

tidal wave n. An enormous rise of destructive ocean water caused by a storm or earthquake.

tid-bit (tid´bit´) n. A choice bit of food, news, or gossip.

tide (td) n. The rise and fall of the surface level of the ocean which occurs twice a day due to the gravitational pull of the sun and moon on the earth.

tie (t) v. To secure or bind with a rope, line, cord or other similar material; to make secure or fasten with a rope; to make a bow or knot in; to match an opponent's score. n. A string, rope, cord or other material used to join parts or hold something in place; a necktie; a beam that gives structural support. **tie** A device, as timber, laid crosswise to support train tracks.

tier (tr) *n.* A layer or row placed one above the other. **tiered** *adj.*

ti-ger (t´gr) *n.* A large carnivorous cat having tawny fur with black stripes.

tight (tt) *adj.* Set closely together; bound or securely firm; not loose; taut; difficult. *adv.* Firmly. *Slang* Intoxicated.

tight-en (tt´en) *v.* To become or make tighter.

tile (tl) *n.* A thin, hard, flat piece of plastic, asphalt, baked clay, or stone used to cover walls, floors, and roofs. *v.* To cover with tile.

till (til) Until; unless or before. *v.* To cultivate; to plow. *n.* A small cash register or drawer for holding money.

till-er (til´r) *n.* A machine or person that tills land.

tilt (tilt) *v.* To tip, as by raising one end. *n.* The state of tilting or being tilted.

tim-ber (tim´br) *n.* Wood prepared for building; a finished piece of wood or plank.

timber line *n.* The height on a mountain beyond which trees cannot grow.

time (tm) *n.* A continuous period measured by clocks, watches, and calendars; the period or moment in which something happens or takes place. *adj.* Of or pertaining to time; pertaining to paying in installments. *Slang* A period of imprisonment.

tim-id (tim´id) *adj.* Lacking self-confidence; shy.

tin (tin) *n.* A white, soft, malleable metallic element, symbolized by Sn; a container made of tin. *adj.* Made of tin.

tinc-ture (tingk´chr) *n.* A tinge of color; an alcohol solution of some medicinal substance. *v.* To tint.

tin-der (tin´dr) *n.* A readily combustible substance or material used for kindling.

tin-der-box (tin´dr boks´) *n.* A portable metal box for holding tinder; a building which is a fire hazard; a situation which is about to explode with violence.

tine (tn) *n.* A narrow pointed spike or prong, as of a fork or antler.

tinge (tinj) *v.* To impart a faint trace of color; to tint. *n.* A slight trace of added color.

tin-gle (ting´gl) *v.* To feel a stinging or prickling sensation. **tingly** *adj.*

tink-er (ting´kr) *n.* A person who mends domestic household utensils; one who does repair work of any kind. *v.* To work as a tinker; to attempt to fix, mend, or repair something in a bumbling, unprofessional manner.

tin-kle (ting´kl) *v.* To produce a slight, sharp series of metallic ringing sounds.

tin-ny (tin´) *adj.* Pertaining to or composed of tin.

tin-sel (tin´sel) *n.* Thin strips of glittering material used for decorations.

tint (tint) *n.* A slight amount or trace of color. *v.* To color.

ti-ny (t´n) *adj.* Minute; very small.

tip (tip) *v.* To slant from the horizontal or vertical. *n.* Extra money given as an acknowledgment of a service; a gratuity; a helpful hint.

tip-ple (tip´l) *v.* To drink an alcoholic beverage to excess.

tip-sy (tip´s) *adj.* Partially intoxicated.

ti-rade (t´rd) *n.* A long, violent speech or outpouring, as of censure.

tire (tr) *v.* To become or make weary; to be fatigued; to become bored. *n.* The outer covering for a wheel, usually made of rubber, serving to absorb shock and to provide traction.

tire-less *adj.* Untiring. **tirelessly** *adv.*

tis-sue (tish´ö) *n., Biol.* Similar cells and their products developed by plants and animals; a soft, absorbent piece of paper, consisting of two layers.

ti-ta-ni-um (t t´n um) *n.* A metallic element symbolized by Ti.

tithe (tth) *n.* A tenth of one's income given voluntarily for the support of a church.

tit-il-late (tit´i lt´) *v.* To excite or stimulate in a pleasurable way. **-ing** *adj.*

ti-tle (tt´l) *n.* An identifying name of a book, poem, play, or other creative work; a name or mark of distinction indicating a rank or an office; in law, the evidence giving legal right of possession or control of something; in sports, a championship. *v.* To give a title or name to.

to (tō) *prep.* Toward, opposite or near; in contact with; as far as; used as a function word indicating an action, movement, or condition suggestive of movement; indicating correspondence, dissimilarity, similarity, or proportion; indicating the one for which something is done or exists. *adv.* In the state, direction, or condition.

toaster (t´str) *n.* A device for toasting bread.

to-bac-co (to bak´) *n.* A tropical American plant widely cultivated for its leaves, which are prepared in various ways, as for chewing or smoking.

to-day (to d´) *adv.* On or during the present day. *n.* The present time, period, or day.

tod-dle (tod´l) *v.* To walk unsteadily with short steps.

toddler *n.* A small child learning to walk.

toe (t) *n.* One of the extensions from the front part of a foot; the part of a stocking, boot or shoe that covers the toes. *v.* To kick, reach, or touch with the toe or toes.

tof-fee (to´f) *n.* A chewy candy made of butter and brown sugar.

to-geth-er (tü geth´r) *adv.* In or into one group, mass, or body; regarded jointly; in time with what is happening or going on.

toil (toil) *v.* To labor very hard and continuously. *n.* A difficult task.

toi-let (toi´lit) *n.* A porcelain apparatus with a flushing device, used as a means of disposing body wastes.

toi-lette (toi let´) *n.* The act of washing, dressing, or grooming oneself.

toilet water *n.* A liquid with a scent stronger than cologne and weaker than perfume.

to-ken (tk´en) *n.* A keepsake; a symbol of authority or identity; a piece of imprinted metal used in place of money. *adj.* Done as a pledge or indication.

tol-er-ate (tol´e rt´) *v.* To put up with; to recognize and respect the opinions and rights of others; to endure; to suffer. **toleration** *n.* **-ance** *adj.* **tolerant** *adj.*

toll (tl) *n.* A fixed charge for travel across a bridge or along a road. *v.* To sound a bell in repeated single, slow tones.

tom (tom) *n.* A male turkey or cat.

to-ma-to (to m´t) *n. pl.* **-toes** A garden plant cultivated for its edible fruit; the fruit of such a plant.

tomb (tōm) *n.* A vault for burying the dead; a grave.

tomb-stone (tōm´stn´) *n.* A stone used to mark agrave.

tom-cat (tom´kat´) *n.* A male cat.

to-mor-row (to mor´) *n.* The day after the present day. *adv.* On the day following today.

ton (tun) *n.* A measurement of weight equal to 2,000 pounds. *Slang* A large amount.

tone (tn) *n.* A vocal or musical sound that has a distinct pitch, loudness, quality, and duration; the condition of the body and muscles when at rest. *v.* To change or soften the color.

tongs (tongz) *n. pl.* An implement with two long arms joined at one end, used for picking up or lifting.

tongue (tung) *n.* The muscular organ attached to the floor of the mouth, used in tasting, chewing, and speaking; anything shaped like a tongue, as the material under the laces or buckles of a shoe.

ton-ic (ton´ik) *n.* A medicine or other agent used to restore health; in music, the first note of a scale. *Slang* Flavored carbonated soda.

to-night (to nt´) *n.* This night; the night of this day; the night that is coming. *adv.* On or during the present or coming night.

ton-sil (ton´sl) *n.* One of a pair of tissue similar to lymph nodes, found on either side of the throat.

ton-sil-lec-to-my (ton´sl lek´to m) *n.* The surgical removal of tonsils.

too (tō) *adv.* Also; as well; more than is needed.

tooth (tōth) *n. pl.* **teeth** One of the hard, white structures rooted in the jaw and used for chewing and biting; the small, notched, projecting part of any object, such as a gear, comb or saw. **toothed** *adj.* **toothless** *adj.*

to-paz (tō´paz) *n.* A gemstone, usually yellow in color.

top-coat (top´kt´) *n.* An outer coat.

top-ic (tăp-ik) *n.* The subject discussed in an essay, thesis, speech or other discourse; the theme.

top-most (top´mst´) *adj.* Uppermost.

to-pog-ra-phy (to pog´ra f) *n. pl.* **-ies** A detailed description of a region or place; a physical outline showing the features of a region or place.

top-ple (top´l) *v.* To fall; to overturn.

To-rah (tr´a) *n.* The body of law and wisdom contained in Jewish Scripture and oral tradition; a parchment scroll that contains the first five books of the Old Testament.

torch (torch) *n.* A stick of resinous wood which is burned to give light; any portable device which produces hot flame. *Slang* To set fire to.

tor-ment (tor´ment) *n.* Extreme mental anguish or physical pain; a source of trouble or pain. *v.* To cause terrible pain; to pester, harass, or annoy. **tormentingly** *adv.* **tormentor** *n.*

tor-na-do (tor n´d) *n. pl.* **-does** or **-dos** A whirling, violent windstorm accompanied by a funnel-shaped cloud that travels a narrow path over land; a whirlwind.

tor-pid (tor´pid) *adj.* Having lost the power of motion or feeling; dormant. **torpidity** *n.* **torpidly** *adv.*

tor-rent (tor´ent) *n.* A swift, violent stream; a raging flood. **torrential** *adj.*

tor-rid (tor´id) *adj.* Parched and dried by the heat. **torridly** *adv.*

tor-sion (tor´shan) *n.* The act or result of twisting; the stress produced when one end is held fast and the other turned. **-al** *adj.*

tor-so (tor´s) *n. pl.* **-sos** or **-si** The trunk of the human body.

tort (tort) *n., Law* A wrongful act requiring compensation for damages.

tor-toise (tor´tos) *n.* A turtle that lives on the land; a person or thing regarded as slow.

tor-tu-ous (tor´chö us) *adj.* Marked by repeated bends, turns, or twists; devious.

tor-ture (tor´chr) *n.* The infliction of intense pain as punishment; something causing anguish or pain. *v.* To subject or cause intense suffering; to wrench or twist out of shape. **torturer** *n.* **torturously** *adv.*

tot (tot) *n.* A young child; a toddler.

to-tal (tt´al) *n.* The whole amount or sum; the entire quantity. *adj.* Absolute; complete.

tote (tt) *v.* To carry something on one's arm or back. *n.* A load.

to-tem (t´tem) *n.* An animal or plant regarded as having a close relationship to some family clan or group; a representation or symbol.

tough (tuf) *adj.* Resilient and strong enough to withstand great strain without breaking or tearing; strong; hardy; very difficult; difficult to cut or chew. *n.* An unruly person; a thug. **toughly** *adv.* **toughness** *n.*

tou-pee (tö p) *n.* A wig worn to cover a bald spot on one's head.

tour (tür) *n.* A trip with visits to points of interest; a journey; a period or length of service at a single place or job. **tourism** *n.* **-ist** *n.*

tour-na-ment (tür´na ment) *n.* A contest involving a number of competitors for a title or championship.

tour-ni-quet (tür´nl kit) *n.* A device used to temporarily stop the flow of blood through an artery.

tou-sle (tou´zl) *v.* To mess up; to disarrange.

tout (tout) *v.* To solicit customers. *Slang* In horse racing, a person who obtains information on race horses and sells it to bettors.

to-ward or **to-wards** (trd) *prep.* In the direction of; just before; somewhat before; regarding; with respect to.

tow-el (tou´el) *n.* An absorbent piece of cloth used for drying or wiping.

town (toun) *n.* A collection of houses and other buildings larger than a village and smaller than a city.

tox-e-mi-a (tok´s´m a) *n. Pathol.* Blood poisoning; a condition in which the blood contains toxins.

tox-ic (tok´sik) *adj.* Relating to a toxin; destructive, deadly, or harmful.

tox-in (tok´sin) *n.* A poisonous substance produced by chemical changes in plant and animal tissue.

trace (trs) *n.* A visible mark or sign of a thing, person, or event; something left by some past agent or event. v. To follow the course or track of; to copy by drawing over the lines visible through a sheet of transparent paper.

tract (trakt) n. An extended area, as a stretch of land. *Anat.* An extensive region of the body, one comprising body organs and tissues that together perform a specialized function.

trade (trd) n. A business or occupation; skilled labor; a craft; an instance of selling or buying; a swap. **-able** adj.

trade-mark (trd´märk´) n. A brand name which is legally the possession of one company and cannot be used by another.

tra-di-tion (tra dish´an) n. The doctrines, knowledge, practices, and customs passed down from one generation to another. **traditional, -ally** adv.

tra-duce (tra dös´) v. To betray.

trag-e-dy (traj´i d) n. pl. **-ies** An extremely sad or fatal event or course of events; a story, play, or other literary work which arouses terror or pity by a series of misfortunes or sad events.

trait (trt) n. A quality or distinguishing feature, such as one's character.

trai-tor (tr´tr) n. A person who betrays his country, a cause, or another's confidence.

tra-jec-to-ry (tra jek´to ry) n. pl. **-ies** The curved line or path of a moving object.

tram-mel (tram´el) n. A long, large net used to catch birds or fish; something that impedes movement. **trammeler** n.

tram-ple (tram´pl) v. To tread heavily; to stomp; to inflict injury, pain, or loss by heartless or brutal treatment.

tram-po-line (tram´po ln´) n. A canvas device on which an athlete or acrobat may perform. **trampolinist** n.

trance (trans) n. A stupor, daze, mental state, or condition, such as produced by drugs or hypnosis.

tran-quil (trang´kwil) adj. Very calm, quiet, and free from disturbance. **tranquilly, tranquillity** n. **tranquilize** v.

trans-act (trans sakt´) v. To perform, carry out, conduct, or manage business in someway. **transaction** n. **-or** n.

tran-scend (tran send´) v. To pass beyond; to exceed; to surpass. **tran-scendent** adj.

tran-scribe (tran skrb´) v. To make copies of something; to adopt or arrange.

tran-script (tran´skript) n. A written copy.

trans-crip-tion (tran skrip´shan) n. The process or act of transcribing.

trans-fer (trans für´) v. To remove, shift, or carry from one position to another. **transferable, transferer** n.

trans-fig-ure (trans fig´yr) v. To change the outward appearance or form; to exalt; to glorify. **transfiguration** n.

trans-fix (trans fiks´) v. To pierce; to hold motionless, as with terror, awe or amazement.

trans-form (trans form´) v. To change or alter completely in nature, form or function.

trans-fuse (trans fz´) v. To transfer liquid by pouring from one place to another. *Med.* To pass blood from the blood vessels of one person into the vessels of another. **transfusion** n. **transfuser** n.

trans-gress (trans gres´) v. To go beyond the limit or boundaries; to sin against or violate.

tran-sient (tran´shent) adj. Not staying or lasting very long; moving from one location to another. **transient** n.

trans-late (trans lt´) v. To change from one language to another while retaining the original meaning; to explain.

tran-som (tran´som) n. A small, hinged window over a doorway; the horizontal crossbar in a window.

tran-spire (tran spr´) v. To give off waste products through plant or animal pores in the form of vapor; to happen; to take place.

trau-ma (trou´ma) n. pl. **-mas** or **-mata** A severe wound caused by a sudden physical injury; an emotional shock causing lasting and substantial damage to a person's psychological development.

tra-vail (tra vl´) n. Strenuous mental or physical exertion; labor in childbirth. v. To undergo the sudden sharp pain of childbirth.

trav-el (trav´el) v. To journey or move from one place to another. n. The process or act of traveling. **traveler** n.

tra-verse (trav´rs) v. To pass over, across, or through. n. A path or route across; something that lies across something else. **traversable** adj. **traversal** n. **traverser** n.

trawl (trol) n. A strong fishing net which is dragged through water.

tray (tr) n. A flat container having a low rim, used for carrying, holding, or displaying something.

treach-er-ous (trech´r us) adj. Disloyal; deceptive; unreliable. **treacherously** adv.

treas-ure (trezh´r) n. Hidden riches; something regarded as valuable. v. To save and accumulate for future use; to value.

treasurer (trezh´r r) n. A person having charge and responsibilities for funds.

treat-ment (trt´ment) n. The manner or act of treating; medical care.

treb-le (treb´l) adj. Multiplied by three; having three. Mus. Performing or having the highest range, part, or voice. v. A high-pitched sound or voice.

tre-foil (tr´foil) n. Any of various plants having three leaflets with red, purple, yellow, or pink flowers.

trek (trek) v. To make a slow and arduous journey. **trek** n. **trekker** n.

trem-ble (trem´bl) v. To shake involuntarily, as with fear or from cold; to express or feel anxiety. **tremble** n. **trembler** n.

tre-men-dous (tri men´dus) adj. Extremely huge, large, or vast. Slang Wonderful.

trem-or (trem´r) n. A quick, shaking movement; any continued and involuntary trembling or quavering of the body.

tres-pass (tres´pas) v. To infringe upon another's property; in law, to invade the rights, property, or privacy of another without consent or knowledge.

tribe (trb) n. A group of people composed of several villages, districts, or other groups which share a common language, culture, and name.

trib-u-la-tion (trib´l shan) n. Great distress or suffering caused by oppression.

trib-un-al (tr bn´al) n. A decision mak-

ing body.

tri-ceps (tr´seps) n., Anat. The large muscle at the back of the upper arm.

trick (trik) n. An action meant to fool, as a scheme; a prank; a feat of magic. v. To deceive or cheat. **tricky** adj.

trick-er-y (trik´e r) n. Deception.

trick-le (trik´l) v. To flow in droplets or a small stream. **trickle** n.

tri-col-or (tr´kul´r) n. The French color in the flag. **tricolored** adj.

tri-cy-cle (tr´si kl) n. A small vehicle having three wheels, propelled by pedals.

tried (trd) adj. Tested and proven reliable or useful.

tri-en-ni-al (tr en´al) adj. Happening every third year; lasting for a time period of three years. **triennial** n. **triennially** adv.

tri-fle (tr´fl) n. Something of little value or importance; a dessert made with cake, jelly, wine, and custard. v. To use or treat without proper concern.

trill n. A tremulous utterance of successive tones. v. To utter with a fluttering sound.

tril-lion (tril´yon) n. The cardinal number equal to one thousand billion.

trim (trim) v. To clip or cut off small amounts in order to make neater; to decorate. adj. Neat.

trin-ket (tring´kit) n. A small piece of jewelry.

tri-o (tr´) n. A set or group of three.

trip (trip) n. Travel from one place to another; a journey; a loss of balance. v. To stumble. Slang A hallucinatory effect induced by drugs.

tripe (trp) n. The stomach lining of oxen or similar animals, used as food. Slang Nonsense.

trip-le (trip´l) adj. Having three parts. v. To multiply by three; in baseball, a three-base hit.

trip-li-cate (trip´li kt´) n. A group of three identical things. **triplicate** v.

tri-pod (tr´pod) n. A three-legged stand or frame.

trite (trt) adj. Used too often; common.

tri-umph (tr´umf) v. To be victorious. n. A victory. **triumphant** adj.

triv-i-al (triv´al) adj. Insignificant; of little value or importance; ordinary.

troll (trl) v. To fish by pulling a baited line slowly behind a boat; to sing with a loud, full voice. n. The act of trolling for fish; a dwarf or elf.

troop (trōp) n. A group or assembly of people or animals; a group of Boy Scouts or Girl Scouts having an adult leader; a military unit. **trooper** n.

tro-phy (trʹf) n. pl. **-ies** A prize or object, such as a plaque, awarded to someone for his success, victory, or achievement.

trop-ic (tropʹik) n. Either of two imaginary parallel lines which constitute the Torrid Zone. **Tropics** The very warm region of the earth's surface between the Tropic of Cancer and the Tropic of Capricorn.

troth (troth) n. Good faith; the act of pledging one's fidelity. **troth** v.

trou-ble (trubʹl) n. Danger; affliction; need; distress; an effort; physical pain, disease or malfunction. v. To bother; to worry; to be bothered; to be worried.

trough (trof) n. A long, narrow, shallow container, especially one that holds food or water for animals.

trounce (trouns) v. To whip or beat; to defeat decisively.

trou-sers (trouʹzrz) n. pl. An outer garment that covers the body from the waist down.

trout (trout) n. A freshwater game or food fish.

trowel (trouʹel) n. A flat-bladed garden tool with a pointed blade, used for digging.

truce (trōs) n. An agreement to stop fighting; a cease fire.

trudge (truj) v. To walk heavily; to plod.

true (trō) adj. In accordance with reality or fact; not false; real; loyal; faithful. **-ly** adv.

trump (trump) n. In cards, a suit of any cards which outrank all other cards for a selected period of time.

trust (trust) n. Confidence or faith in a person or thing; care or charge. Law The confidence or arrangement by which property is managed and held for the good or benefit of another person. v. To have confidence or faith in; to believe; to expect; to entrust; to depend on.

truth (trōth) n. pl. **truths** The facts cor responding with actual events or happenings; sincerity or honesty.

try (tr) v. To make an attempt; to make an effort; to strain; to hear or conduct a trial; to place on trial. **-ing** adj. **-out** n.

tryst (trist) n. A meeting between lovers; a prearranged meeting.

tsp abbr. Teaspoon.

tsu-na-mi (tse näʹm) n. An extensive and destructive ocean wave caused by an underwater earthquake.

tub (tub) n. A round, low, flat-bottomed, vessel with handles on the side, as one used for washing.

tu-ba (tōʹba) n. A large, brass wind instrument having a low range.

tube (tōb) n. A hollow cylinder, made of metal, rubber, glass or other material, used to pass or convey something through.

tu-ber (tōʹbr) n. The underground stem of certain plants, as the potato, with buds from which new plants arise.

tuft (tuft) n. A small cluster of feathers, threads, hair, or other material fastened or growing closely together.

tug (tug) v. To strain and pull vigorously. n. A hard pull; a strong force.

tu-i-tion (tō ishʹan) n. Payment for instruc tion, as at a private school or college.

tu-lip (tōʹlip) n. A bulb-bearing plant, having upright cup-like blossoms.

tum-ble-down (tumʹbl dounʹ) adj. Ramshackle; in need of repair.

tu-mor (tōʹmr) n., Pathol. A swelling on or in any part of the body; an abnormal growth which may be malignant or benign.

tu-mult (tōʹmult) n. The confusion and noise of a crowd; a riot; any violent commotion.

tu-na (tōʹna) n. pl. **-na** or **-nas** Any of several large marine food fish.

tune (tōn) n. A melody which is simple and easy to remember; agreement; harmony. v. To adjust. **-able**, **tunably** adv.

tun-nel (tunʹel) n. An underground or underwater passageway. **tunnel** v.

tur-bine (terʹbin) n. A motor having one or more rotary units mounted on a shaft, which are turned by the force of gas or a liquid.

tur-bu-lent (ter´bya lent) *adj.* Marked by a violent disturbance. **turbulence** *n.*

tu-reen (te rn´) *n.* A large dish, often having a cover, used to serve soup or stew.

turf (terf) *n.* A layer of earth with its dense growth of grass and matted roots. *Slang* Home territory or ground.

tur-key (ter´k) *n.* A large game bird of North America, having a bare head and extensible tail; the meat of this bird. *Slang* A failure.

tur-moil (ter´moil) *n.* A state of confusion or commotion.

turn (tern) *v.* To move or cause to move around a center point; to revolve or rotate; to transform or change.

turn-down (tern´doun´) *n. Slang* A rejection or refusal.

tur-quoise (ter´koiz) *n.* A blue-green gemstone; a light bluish-green color.

tus-sle (tus´l) *n.* A hard fight or struggle with a problem or person. **tussle** *v.*

tu-tor (tö´tr) *n.* A person who teaches another person privately. *v.* To teach, coach, or instruct privately.

tu-tu (tö´tö) *n.* A very short ballet skirt.

tux-e-do (tuk s´d) *n.* A semiformal dress suit worn by men.

twain (twn) *n.* Two.

tweak (twk) *v.* To pinch and twist sharply.

tweez-ers (tw´zrz) *n. p.* A small, pincer- like implement used to grasp or pluck small objects.

twelve (twelv) *n.* The cardinal number equal to 11 + 1. **twelve** & *pron.*

twen-ty (twen´t) *n.* The cardinal number equal to 19 + 1 or 2 X 10. **twenty** & *pron.*

twice (tws) *adv.* Double; two times; on two occasions; in twofold degree or quantity; twice as much.

twig (twig) *n.* A small branch which grows from a larger branch on a tree or other plant; small offshoot.

twi-light (tw´lt´) *n.* The soft light of the sky between sunset and complete darkness.

twill (twil) *n.* A weave that produces the parallel rib on the surface of a fabric.

twine (twn) *v.* To weave or twist together. *n.* A strong cord or thread made by twisting many threads together.

twinge (twinj) *n.* A sudden, sharp pain; a brief emotional or mental pang.

twin-kle (twing´kl) *v.* To gleam or shine with quick flashes; to sparkle.

twirl (twerl) *v.* To rotate or cause to turn around and around. **twirl** *n.*

twist (twist) *v.* To wind two or more pieces of thread, twine, or other materials together to make a single strand; to curve; to bend; to distort or change the meaning of; to injure and wrench. *n.* The act of twisting.

twit (twit) *v.* To tease about a mistake. *n.* A taunting reproach.

twitch (twich) *v.* To move or cause to move with a jerky movement. *n.* A sudden tug.

two (tö) *n.* The cardinal number of 1 + 1; the second in a sequence.

ty-coon (t kön´) *n. Slang* A business person of exceptional wealth and power.

tyke (tk) *n.* A small child.

tym-bal (tim´bal) *n.* A kettledrum.

type-face (tp´fs´) *n.* A style or design of printing type.

type-set-ter (tp´set´r) *n.* A person who arranges or sets type. **typesetting** *n.*

ty-phoid (t´foid) *n. path.* An acute, infectious disease caused by germs in drink or food, resulting in high fever and intestinal hemorrhaging.

ty-phoon (t fön´) *n.* A tropical hurricane, especially one in the western part of the Pacific Ocean during the summer and fall.

typ-i-cal (tip´i-kal) *adj.* Conforming to some type; characteristic; serving as a representative of something.

typ-i-fy (tip´i f´) *v.* To be characteristic or typical of; to show all the traits or qualities of; to represent by a particular symbol or type; to exemplify.

typ-ist (t´pist) *n.* The operator of a typewriter.

tyr-an-ny (tir´a n) *n.* Harsh, absolute, and unfair rule by a king or other ruler

U

U, u The twenty-first letter of the English alphabet.

ud-der (ud´er) *n.* The milk-producing organ pouch of some female animals, having two or more teats.

ugh (ŏch) Used to express disgust or horror.

ug-ly (ug´l) *adj.* Offensive; unpleasant to look at.

uh *interj.* To express hesitation.

uhf *abbr.* Ultra high frequency.

u-ku-le-le (´ka l´l) *n.* A small, four-stringed musical instrument, originally from Hawaii.

ul-cer (ul´sr) *n.* A festering, inflamed sore on a mucous membrane or on the skin that results in the destruction of the tissue.

ul-na (ul´na) *n., Anat.* One of the two bones of the forearm.

ul-ti-mate (ul´ti mit) *adj.* Final; ending; most extreme; maximum; most. **ultimately** *adv.*

ul-ti-ma-tum (ul´ti m´tum) *n. pl.* -**tums, -ta** A final demand, proposal, or choice, as in negotiating.

ultra- (ul´tra) *prefix* Beyond the scope, range, or limit of something.

ul-tra-son-ic (ul´tra son´ik) *adj.* Relating to sound frequencies inaudible to humans.

ul-tra-vi-o-let (ul´tra v´o lit) *adj.* Producing radiation having wave lengths just shorter than those of visible light and longer than those of X-rays. **ultraviolet** *n.*

umbilical cord *n.* The structure by which a fetus is attached to its mother, serving to supply food and dispose of waste.

um-brel-la (um brel´a) *n.* A collapsible frame covered with plastic or cloth.

um-pire (um´p r) *n.* In sports, the person who rules on plays in a game.

un- *prefix* The reverse or opposite of an act; removal or release from.

un-able (un ´bl) *adj.* Not having the mental capabilities.

un-ac-com-pa-nied (un´a kum´pa nd) *adj.* Alone; without a companion. *Mus.* Solo.

un-ac-cus-tomed (un´a kus´tomd) *adj.* Not used to or in the habit of; not ordinary.

u-nan-i-mous (nan´i mus) *adj.* Agreed to completely; based on the agreement of all.

un-armed (un ormd´) *adj.* Lacking

means for protection.

un-as-sum-ing (un´a sö´ming) *adj.* Modest and not showy.

un-at-tach-ed (un´a tacht´) *adj.* Not engaged, going steady, or married.

un-a-void-a-ble (un´a void´a bl) *adj.* Inevitable; unstoppable. **-ably** *adv.*

un-a-ware (un´a wâr´) *adj.* Not realizing.

un-bear-a-ble (un bâr´a bl) *adj.* Not possible to endure; intolerable.

un-be-com-ing (un´bi kum´ing) *adj.* Unattractive; not pleasing; not proper, polite or suitable for the situation or occasion.

un-be-liev-a-ble (un´bi lv´a bl) *adj.* Incredible; hard to accept; not to be believed.

un-called for (un kold´for´) *adj.* Not necessary or needed; not requested.

un-can-ny (un kan´) *adj.* Strange, odd, or mysterious; exceptional. **-ily** *adv.*

un-cer-tain (un ser´tan) *adj.* Doubtful; not sure; not known; hard to predict.

un-changed (un changd´) *adj.* Having nothing new or different.

un-civ-i-lized (un siv´i lzd) *adj.* Without culture or refinement; without an established cultural and social way of living.

un-cle (ung´kl) *n.* The brother of one's mother or father; the husband of an aunt.

un-clean (un kln´) *adj.* Immoral; dirty; not decent.

un-com-fort-a-ble (un kumf´ta bl) *adj.* Disturbed; not at ease physically or mentally; causing discomfort. **-ly** *adv.*

un-com-mon (un kom´on) *adj.* Rare; odd; unusual; extraordinary. **uncommonly** *adv.*

un-con-cern (un´kon sern´) *n.* Lack of interest; disinterest; indifference.

un-con-di-tion-al (un´kon dish´a nal) *adj.* Without conditions or limits.

un-con-scious (un kon´shus) *adj.* Not mentally aware; done without thought; not on purpose.

un-cov-er (un kuv´r) *v.* To remove the cover from something; to disclose.

un-de-cid-ed (un´di s´did) *adj.* Unsettled; having made no firm decision; open to change. **undecidedly** *adv.*

un-der (un´dr) *prep.* Below, in place

or position; in a place lower than another; less in degree, number, or other quality.

un-der-de-vel-oped (un´dr di vel´∂pt) *adj.* Not fully mature or grown; lacking modern communications and industry.

un-der-go (un´dr g´) *v.* To have the experience of; to be subjected to.

un-der-grad-u-ate (un´dr graj´ō it) *n.* A college or university student studying for a bachelor's degree.

un-der-hand (un´dr hand´) *adj.* Done deceitfully and secretly; sly; sneaky.

un-der-line (un´dr ln´) *v.* To draw a line directly under something. **underline** *n.*

un-der-mine (un´dr mn´) *v.* To weaken; to make less strong.

un-der-neath (un´dr nth´) *adv.* Beneath or below; on the underside; lower. *prep.* Under; below.

un-der-pass (un´dr pas´) *n.* A road or walk that goes under another.

un-der-priv-i-leged (un´dr priv´i lijd) *adj.* Deprived of economic and social advantages.

un-der-rate (un´dr rt´) *v.* To rate or value below the true worth.

un-der-side (un´dr sd´) *n.* The side or part on the bottom.

un-der-stand (un´dr stand´) *v.* To comprehend; to realize; to know the feelings and thoughts of.

un-der-state (un´dr stt´) *v.* To make too little of the actual situation.

un-der-stood (un´dr sted´) *adj.* Agreed upon by all.

un-der-stud-y (un´dr stud´) *v.* To learn another person's part or role in order to be able to replace him if necessary.

un-der-take (un´dr tk´) *v.* To set about to do a task; to pledge oneself to a certain job; to attempt. **undertaking** *n.*

un-der-tak-er (un´dr t´kr) *n.* A person who prepares the dead for burial.

un-der-tone (un´dr tn´) *n.* A low, quiet voice; a pale or subdued color visible through other colors.

un-der-write (un´dr rt´) *v.* To sign or write at the end of something; to finance; to assume a risk by means of insurance.

un-de-sir-a-ble (un´dj z´r a bl) *adj.* Offensive; not wanted. **undesirably** *adv.*

un-do (un dō´) *v.* To cancel; to reverse; to loosen or unfasten; to open a package.

un-done *adj.* Not finished; unfastened; ruined.

un-dy-ing (un d´ing) *adj.* Without end.

un-earth (un erth´) *v.* To dig up from the earth; to find or discover.

un-eas-y (un ´z) *adj.* Feeling or causing distress or discomfort; embarrassed.

un-em-ployed (un´em ploid´) *adj.* Without a job; without work. **unemployment** *n.*

un-e-qual (un ´kwal) *adj.* Not even; not fair; not of the same size or time; lacking sufficient ability.

un-e-ven (un ´ven) *adj.* Not equal; varying inconsistency or form; not balanced.

un-e-vent-ful (un´i vent´ful) *adj.* Lacking insignificance; calm.

un-expect-ed (un´ik spek´tid) *adj.* Surprising; happening without warning. -**ly** *adv.*

un-fail-ing (un f´ling) *adj.* Constant, unchanging.

un-fair (un fâr´) *adj.* Not honest; marked by a lack of justice. **unfairly** *adv.* -**ness** *n.*

un-faith-ful (un fth´ful) *adj.* Breaking a promise or agreement; without loyalty; guilty of adultery.

un-fa-mil-iar (un´fa mil´yr) *adj.* Not knowing; strange; foreign. **unfavorable** (un f´vr a bl) *adj.* Harmful; unpleasant. **unfamiliarity** *n.*

un-fit (un fit´) *adj.* Not suitable; not qualified; in poor body or mental health.

un-fold (un fld´) *v.* To open up the folds of and lay flat; to reveal gradually.

un-fore-seen (un´fr sn´) *adj.* Not anticipated or expected.

un-for-get-ta-ble (un´fr get´a bl) *adj.* Impossible or hard to forget; memorable.

un-for-tu-nate (un for´cha nit) *adj.* Causing or having bad luck, damage, or harm. *n.* A person who has no luck.

un-found-ed (un foun´did) *adj.* Not founded or based on fact; groundless; lacking a factual basis.

un-friend-ly (un frend´l) *adj.* Showing a lack of kindness; not friendly; not

un-grate-ful (un grt´ful) adj. Not thankful; showing no appreciation. **un-´grate-ly** (ung´gwent) n. A healing or soothing salve; ointment.

un-happy (un hap´) adj. Sad; without laughter or joy; not satisfied or pleased.

un-heard (un herd´) adj. Not heard; not listened to.

u-ni-corn (´ni korn´) n. A mythical animal resembling a horse, with a horn in the center of its forehead.

u-ni-cy-cle (´ni s´kl) n. A one wheeled vehicle with pedals.

u-ni-form (´ni form´) n. Identical clothing worn by the members of a group to distinguish them from the general population.

u-ni-fy (´ni f´) v. To come together as one; to unite.

un-in-hab-it-ed (un in hib et ed) adj. Not lived in; empty.

un-in-ter-est-ed (un in´tr i stid) adj. Having no interest or concern in; not interested.

un-ion (n´yon) n. The act of joining together of two or more groups or things; a group of countries or states joined under one government; a marriage.

u-nique (nk´) adj. Unlike any other; sole.

u-ni-sex adj. Adaptable and appropriate for both sexes.

u-ni-son (´ni son) n. In music, the exact sameness of pitch, as of a tone; harmonious agreement.

u-nit (´nit) n. Any one of several parts regarded as a whole; an exact quantity that is used as a standard of measurement; a special section or part of a machine.

u-nite (nt´) v. To join or come together for a common purpose.

u-ni-ty (´ni t) n. pl. **-ies** The fact or state of being one; accord; agreement; harmony.

u-ni-valve (´ni valv´) n. A mollusk having a one piece shell, such as a snail.

u-ni-ver-sal (´ni ver´sal) adj. Having to do with the world or the universe in its entirety.

u-ni-verse (´ni vers´) n. The world,

stars, planets, space, and all that is contained.

u-ni-ver-si-ty (´ni ver´si t) n. pl. **-ies** An educational institution offering undergraduate and graduate degrees in a variety of academic areas.

un-just (un just´) adj. Not fair; lacking justice or fairness. **unjustly** adv.

un-kempt (un kempt´) adj. Poorly groomed; messy; untidy.

un-kind (un knd´) adj. Harsh; lacking in sympathy, concern, or understanding.

un-known (un nn´) adj. Strange; unidentified; not known; not familiar or famous.

un-like (un lk´) Dissimilar; not alike; not equal in strength or quantity; not usual for.

un-lim-it-ed (un lim´i tid) adj. Having no boundaries or limitations.

un-load (un ld´) v. To take or remove the load; to unburden; to dispose or get rid of by selling in volume.

un-lock (un lok´) v. To open, release, or unfasten a lock; open with a key.

un-loose (un ls´) v. To loosen or undo; to release.

un-manned (un mand´) adj. Designed to operate or be operated without a crew of people.

un-men-tion-a-ble (un men´sha na bl) adj. Improper or unsuitable.

un-mis-tak-a-ble (un´mi st´ka bl) adj. Very clear and evident; understood; obvious.

un-nec-es-sar-y (un nes´i ser´) adj. Not needed; not appropriate.

un-nerve (un nerv´) v. To frighten; to upset.

un-oc-cu-pied (un ok´ya pd´) adj. Empty; not occupied.

un-pack (un pak´) v. To remove articles out of trunks, suitcases, boxes, or other storage places.

un-pleas-ant (un plez´ant) adj. Not agreeable; not pleasant. **-ly** adv.

un-pop-u-lar (un pop´ya lr) adj. Not approved or liked. **unpopularity** n.

un-pre-dict-a-ble (un´pri dik´ta bl) adj. Not capable or being foretold; not reliable.

un-pre-pared (un´pri pârd´) adj. Not equipped or ready.

un-pro-fes-sion-al (un´pro fesh´a nal) *adj.* Contrary to the standards of a profession; having no professional status.

un-prof-it-a-ble (un profi´ta bl) *adj.* Showing or giving no profit; serving no purpose.

un-qual-i-fied (un kwol´i fd´) *adj.* Lacking the proper qualifications; unreserved.

un-rav-el (un rav´el) *v.* To separate threads; to solve; to clarify; to come apart.

un-re-al (un r´al) *adj.* Having no substance or reality.

un-rea-son-a-ble (un r´zo na bl) *adj.* Not according to reason; exceeding all reasonable limits.

un-re-li-a-ble (un´ri l´a bl) *adj.* Unable to betrusted; not dependable.

un-re-served (un´ri zervd´) *adj.* Done or given without reserve; unlimited.

un-re-strained (un´ri strnd´) *adj.* Not held back, forced, or affected.

un-ru-ly (un rö´l) *adj.* Disorderly; difficult to subdue or control.

un-sat-is-fac-to-ry (un´sat is fak´to r) *adj.* Unacceptable; not pleasing.

un-screw (un skrö´) *v.* To loosen or unfasten by removing screws from.

un-scru-pu-lous (un skrö´pya lus) *adj.* Without morals, guiding principles, or rules.

un-self-ish (un sel´fish) *adj.* Willing to share; thinking of another's well-being before one's own. **unselfishly** *adv.*

un-set-tle (un set´l) *v.* To cause to be upset or excited; to disturb. **-ed** *adj.*

un-sight-ly (un st´l) *adj.* Not pleasant to look at; ugly.

un-skilled (un skild´) *adj.* Having no skills or training in a given kind of work.

un-sound (un sound´) *adj.* Having defects; not solidly made; unhealthy in body or mind.

un-speak-a-ble (un sp´ka bl) *adj.* Of or relating to something which cannot be expressed or described. **-ably** *adv.*

un-sta-ble (un st´bl) *adj.* Not steady or firmly fixed; having the tendency to fluctuate or change.

un-stead-y (un sted´) *adj.* Not secure; unstable; variable. **unsteadily** *adv.*

un-sub-stan-tial (un´sub stan´shal)

adj. Lacking strength, weight, or solidity; unreal.

un-suit-a-ble (un sö´ta bl) *adj.* Unfitting; not suitable; not appropriate for a specific circumstance. **unsuitably** *adv.* **-ness** *n.*

un-tan-gle (un tang´gl) *v.* To free from snarls or entanglements.

un-thank-ful (un thangk´ful) *adj.* Ungrateful.

un-think-a-ble (un thing´ka bl) *adj.* Unimaginable.

un-ti-dy (un ti´d) *adj.* Messy; showing a lack of tidiness. **untidily** *adv.* **-iness** *n.*

un-tie (un t´) *v.* To unfasten or loosen; to free from a restraint or bond.

un-til (un til´) *prep.* Up to the time of. *conj.* To the time when; to the degree or place.

un-told (un tld´) *adj.* Not revealed; not told; inexpressible; cannot be described or revealed.

un-true (un trö) *adj.* Not true; contrary to the truth; not faithful; disloyal.

un-used (un zd´) *adj.* Not put to use; never having been used.

un-u-su-al (un ´zhö al) *adj.* Not usual; uncommon. **unusually** *adv.* **-ness** *n.*

un-veil (un vl´) *v.* To remove a veil from; to uncover; to reveal.

un-war-y (un wâr´) *adj.* Not cautious or careful; careless.

un-will-ing (un wil´ing) *adj.* Reluctant; not willing. **unwillingly** *adv.*

un-wor-thy (un wer´th) *adj.* Not deserving; not becoming or befitting; lacking merit or worth; shameful. **unworthiness** *n.*

up (up) *adv.* From a lower position to a higher one; on, in, or to a higher level, position, or place; to a greater degree.

up-beat (up´bt´) *n., Mus.* The relatively unaccented beat preceding the down beat. *adj.* Optimistic; happy.

up-bring-ing (upbringing) *n.* The process of teaching and rearing a child.

up-com-ing (up´kum´ing) *adj.* About to take place or appear.

up-date (up dt´) *v.* To revise or bring up- to-date; to modernize. **update** *n.*

up-grade (up´grd´) *v.* To increase the grade, rank, or standard of. *n.* An upward slope.

up-lift (up lift´) *v.* To raise or lift up; to

improve the social, economic, and moral level of a group or of a society.

up-on (*u pon´*) *prep. & adv.* On.

up-right (up´rt´) *adj.* Having a vertical direction or position; honest.

up-stage (up´stj´) *adj. & adv.* Toward or at the backpart of a stage. *Slang* To steal the show or scene from.

up-start (up´stärt´) *n.* One who has risen quickly to power or wealth, especially one who is conceited.

up-tight *adv.* Nervous, tense, or anxious.

up-ward (up´wrd) *adv.* Toward a high er place or position; toward a higher amount.

up-wind (up´wind´) *adv.* Toward or against the wind. Direction opposing that of the wind.

ur-ban (er´ban) *adj.* Pertaining to a city or having characteristics of a city; living or being in a city. **urbanite** *n.* **urbanize** *v.*

ur-chin (ur´chin) *n.* Mischievous child.

u-re-do (-r´d) *n., Pathol.* Skin disease characterized by itching and hives.

urge (erj) *v.* To encourage, push, or drive; to recommend persistently and strongly. *n.* An influence, impulse, or force.

ur-gen-cy (ur´jn-se) *n.* The quality of or fact of being urgent; an urgent need or request

ur-gent (er´jent) *adj.* Requiring immediate attention. **urgency** *n.* **-ly** *adv.*

u-ri-nate (ur´i-nt) *v.* To pass urine.

urine (r´in) *n.* In man and other mammals, the yellowish fluid waste produced by the kidneys.

urn (urn) *n.* A footed, large vessel or vase of various sizes and shapes, where the ashes of the dead are preserved; a closed container with a spigot used for brewing and serving hot drinks usually in large quantities.

u-rol-o-gy (-rol´o-j) *n.* The field of medicine relating to the study, diagnosis and treatment of the urinary tract.

us (us) *pron.* The objective case of we; used as an indirect object, direct object, or object of a preposition.

us-age (´sij) *n.* The way or act of using something; the way words are used.

use (z) *v.* To put into action; to employ for a special purpose; to employ on a

regular basis; to exploit for one's own advantage. *n.* The state or fact of being used; the act or way of using something; the reason or purpose for which something is used; the function of something; the occupation or utilization of property.

u-su-al (´zhō al) *adj.* Ordinary or common; regular; customary.

u-surp (serp´) *v.* To take over by force without authority.

u-ten-sil (ten´sil) *n.* A tool, implement, or container, especially one for the kitchen.

u-ter-us (´tr us) *n.* An organ of female mammals within which young develop and grow before birth. **uterine** *adj.*

u-til-i-ty (til´i t) *n. pl.* **-ies** The state or quality of being useful; a company which offers a public service, as water, heat, or electricity.

u-til-ize (t´i lz´) *v.* To make or put to use.

ut-most (ut´mst´) *adj.* Of the greatest amount, number, quantity or degree; most distant; the farest extremity or point.

u-to-pi-a (t´p a) *n.* A condition or place of perfection or complete harmony and peace.

ut-ter (ut´r) *v.* To say or express verbally; to speak.

u-vu-la (´vya la) *n.* The fleshy projection which hangs above the back of the tongue.

V

V, v (v) The twenty-second letter of the English alphabet; the Roman numeral for 5.

va-cant (v´kant) *adj.* Empty; not occupied; without expression or thought.

va-cate (v´kt) *v.* To leave; to cease to occupy; to give up or quit a position; to relinquish the possession or occupancy of.

va-ca-tion (v k´shan) *n.* A period of time away from work for pleasure, relaxation, or rest; freedom for one's regular activity. *v.* To take vacation.

vac-ci-nate (vak´si nt´) *v.* To inject with a vaccine so as to produce immunity to an infectious disease, as measles or smallpox.

vac-ci-na-tion (vak'si n'shan) n. The inoculation with a vaccine; the act of vaccinating.

vac-cine (vak sn') n. A solution of weakened or killed microorganisms, as bacteria or viruses, injected into the body to produce immunity to a disease.

vag-a-bond (vag'a bond') n. A homeless person who wanders from place to place; a tramp; a wanderer.

va-gar-y (va gâr') n. pl. -ies An eccentric or capricious action or idea.

va-gi-na (va j'na) n. pl., Anat. The canal or passage extending from the uterus to the external opening of the female reproductive system.

vag-i-ni-tis (vaj'i n'tis) n. An inflammation of the vagina.

va-grant (v'grant) n. A person who wanders from place to place. adj. Roaming from one area to another without a job.

vague (vg) adj. Not clearly expressed; not sharp or definite. **vaguely** adv.

vain (vn) adj. Conceited; lacking worth or substance; having too much pride in oneself.

val-ance (val'ans) n. A decorative drapery across the top of a window or hanging from a shelf or a bed frame.

vale (vl) n. A valley; low ground between hills.

val-e-dic-to-ri-an (val'i dik tr' an) n. The student ranking highest in a graduating class, who delivers a speech at the commencement.

val-en-tine (val'en tn') n. A card or gift sent to one's sweetheart on Valentine's Day, February 14th.

val-et (val'it) n. A man who takes care of another man's clothes and other personal needs; a hotel employee who attends to personal services for guests.

val-iant (val'yant) adj. Brave; exhibiting valor.

val-id (val'id) adj. Founded on facts or truth. Law Binding; having legal force. -ate n.

val-or (val'r) n. Bravery.

val-u-a-ble (val'a bl) adj. Of great value or importance; having a high monetary value.

val-ue (val) n. The quality or worth of something that makes it valuable; material worth; a principle regarded as worthwhile or desirable. Math A calculated numerical quantity. v. To estimate the value or worth of; to regard very highly; to rate according to importance, worth, or usefulness.

valve (valv) n. The movable mechanism which opens and closes to control the flow of a substance through a pipe or other passageway. Anat. A membranous structure in a vein or artery that prevents or slows the backward movement of fluid.

va-na-di-um (va n'd um) n. A metallic element symbolized by V.

van-dal-ism (van'da liz'um) n. The malicious defacement or destruction of private or public property.

vane (vn) n. A metal device that turns in the direction the wind is blowing; a thin rigid blade of an electric fan, propeller, or windmill.

van-ish (van'ish) v. To disappear suddenly; to drop out of sight; to go out of existence.

van-i-ty (van'i t) n. pl., -ies Conceit; extreme pride in one's ability, possessions, or appearance.

van-tage (van'tij) n. A superior position; an advantage.

va-por (v'pr) n. Moisture or smoke suspended in air, as mist or fog. **vaporish**, **vaporous** adj. **vaporize** v.

var-i-able (vâr' a bl) adj. Changeable; tending to vary; inconstant. n. A quantity or thing w hich can vary.

var-i-ance (vâr' ans) n. The state or act of varying; difference; conflict.

var-i-a-tion (vâr' 'shan) n. The result or process of varying; the degree or extent of varying. Mus. A different form or version of a given theme, with modifications in rhythm, key, or melody.

var-i-e-gat-ed (vâr' e gt'tid) adj. Having marks of different colors.

va-ri-e-ty (va r'i t) n. pl. -ies The state or character of being varied or various; a number of different kinds; an assortment.

var-i-ous (vâr' us) adj. Of different kinds.

var-mint (vär'mint) n. Slang A trou-

var-nish (vär´nish) n. A solution paint used to coat or cover a surface with a hard, transparent, shiny film. v. To put varnish on.

var-si-ty (vär´si t) n. pl. -ies The best team representing a college, university, or school.

var-y (vâr´) v. To change; to make or become different; to be different; to make of different kinds.

vas-cu-lar (vas´kya lr) adj. Biol. Having to do with vessels circulating fluids, as blood.

vast (vast) adj. Very large or great in size.

vault (volt) n. An arched structure that forms a ceiling or roof; a room for storage and safekeeping, as in a bank, usually made of steel; a burial chamber. v. To supply or construct with a vault; to jump or leap with the aid of a pole.

vb abbr. Verb; verbal.

veg-e-ta-ble (vej´ta bl) n. A plant, as the tomato, green beans, lettuce, raised for the edible part. adj. Resembling a vegetable in activity; passive; dull.

veg-e-tar-i-an (vej´i târ´ an) n. A person whose diet is limited to vegetables. adj. Consuming only plant products.

veg-e-ta-tion (vej´i t´shan) n. Plants or plant life which grow from the soil.

ve-hi-cle (v´i kl) n. A motorized device for transporting goods, equipment, or passengers; any means by which something is transferred, expressed, or applied.

veil (vl) n. A piece of transparent cloth worn on the head or face for concealment or protection; anything that conceals from view. v. To cover or conceal, as with a veil.

vein (vn) n., Anat. A vessel which transports blood back to the heart after passing through the body; one of the branc hing support tubes of an insect's wing; a long wavy, irregularly colored streak, as in marble, or wood.

ve-lour (ve ler´) n. A soft velvet-like woven cloth having a short, thick nap.

vel-vet (vel´vit) n. A fabric made of rayon, cotton, or silk, having a smooth, dense pile. **velvety** adj.

vend-er (vendr) A person who sells, as a peddler.

ven-det-ta (ven det´a) n. A fight or feud between blood-related persons, involving revenge killings.

ven-er-a-ble (ven´r a bl) adj. Meriting or worthy of respect by reason of dignity, position, or age.

venereal disease n. A contagious disease, as syphilis, or gonorrhea, which is typically acquired through sexual intercourse.

ven-i-son (ven´i son) n. The edible flesh of a deer.

ven-om (ven´om) n. A poisonous substance secreted by some animals, as scorpions or snakes, usually transmitted to their prey or an enemy through a bite or sting.

ve-nous (v´nus) adj. Of or relating to veins. Physiol. Returning blood to the heart after passing through the capillaries, supplying oxygen for the tissues, and becoming charged with carbondioxide. **venously** adv.

ven-ti-late (ven´ti lt´) v. To expose to a flow of fresh air for refreshing, curing, or purifying purposes; to cause fresh air to circulate through an area; to expose to public discussion or examination.

ven-ture (ven´chr) n. A course of action involving risk, chance, or danger, especially a business investment. v. To take a risk.

ven-ue (ven´ö) n. The place where a crime or other cause of legal action occurs; the locale of a gathering or public event.

verb (verb) n. The part of speech which expresses action, existence, or occurrence.

ver-bal (ver´bal) adj. Expressed in speech; expressed orally; not written; relating to or derived from a verb. n. An adjective, noun, or other word which is based on a verb and retains some characteristics of a verb.

ver-ba-tim (vr b´tim) adv. Word for word.

ver-be-na (vr b´na) n. An American garden plant having variously colored flower clusters.

verge (verj) n. The extreme edge or rim;

margin; the point beyond which something begins. *v.* To border on.

ver-min (ver'min) *n. pl.* **vermins** A destructive, annoying animal which is harmful to one's health.

ver-sa-tile (ver'sa til) *adj.* Having the capabilities of doing many different things; having many functions or uses.

verse (vers) *n.* Writing that has a rhyme; poetry; a subdivision of a chapter of the Bible. *v.* To make verse; to tell or celebrate in verse; to familiarize by close association or study.

ver-sion (ver'zhan) *n.* An account or description told from a particular point of view.

ver-so (ver's) *n. pl.* **-sos** The lefthand page.

ver-sus (ver'sus) *prep.* Against; in contrast to; as an alternative of.

ver-te-bra (ver'te bra) *n. pl.* **-brae, -bras** One of the bony or cartilaginous segments making up the spinal column. **-al** *adj.*

ver-tex (ver'teks) *n. pl.* **-es, -tices** The highest or topmost point; the pointed top of a triangle, opposite the base; the point at which two lines meet to form an angle.

ver-ti-cal (ver'ti kal) *adj.* In a straight up-and-down direction; being perpendicular to the plane of the horizon or to a primary axis; upright. **vertically** *adv.*

ver-y (ver') *adv.* To a high or great degree; truly; absolutely; exactly; actually; in actual fact.

ves-sel (ves'el) *n.* A hollow or concave utensil, as a bottle, kettle, container, or jar; a hollow craft designed for navigation on water, one larger than a rowboat. *Anat.* A tube or duct for circulating a bodily fluid.

vest (vest) *n.* A sleeveless garment open or fastening in front, worn over a shirt.

ves-tige (ves'tij) *n.* A trace or visible sign of something that no longer exists. **-ial** *adj.*

vet (vet) *n. Slang* A veterinarian; a veteran.

vet-er-an (vet'r an) *n.* A person with a long record or experience in a certain field; one who has served in the military.

vet-er-i-nar-i-an (vet'r i när'an) *n.*

One who is trained and authorized to give medical and surgical treatment to animals.

ve-to (v't) *n. pl.* **vetoes** The power of a government executive, as the President or a governor, to reject a bill passed by the legislature. *v.* To reject a bill passed by the legislature.

vex (veks) *v.* To bother, irritate, provoke or annoy. **vexation** *n.*

vi-a (v'a) *prep.* By way of; by means of as to travel by car, plane, bus etc.

vi-a-duct (v'a dukt) *n.* A bridge, resting on a series of arches, carrying a road or railroad.

vi-al (v'al) *n.* A small, closed container used especially for liquids.

vi-brate (v'brt) *v.* To move or make move back and forth or up and down.

vi-car-i-ous (v kâr'us) *adj.* Undergoing or serving in the place of someone or something else; experienced through sympathetic or imaginative participation in the experience of another.

vice (vs) *n.* An immoral habit or practice; evil conduct. *prefix* One who takes the place of another.

vi-ce ver-sa (v'se ver'sa) *adv.* With the order or meaning of something reversed.

vi-cin-i-ty (vi sin'i t) *n. pl.* **-ies** The surrounding area or district; the state of being near in relationship or space.

vi-cious (vish'us) *adj.* Dangerously aggressive; having the quality of immorality.

vic-tim (vik'tim) *n.* A person who is harmed or killed by another; a living creature which is slain and offered as sacrifice; one harmed by circumstance or condition.

vic-to-ri-ous (vik tr'us) *adj.* Being the winner in a contest. **victoriously** *adv.*

vic-to-ry (vik'to r) *n. pl.* **-ies** A defeat of those on the opposite side.

vid-e-o (vid'') *adj.* Being, related to, or used in the reception or transmission of television.

video disc *n.* A disc containing recorded images and sounds which may be played on a televi sion set.

video game *n.* A computerized game displaying on a display screen, controlled by a player or players.

video terminal n. Computer Science A computer device having a cathode-ray tube for displaying data on a screen.

vie (v) v. To strive for superiority.

view (v) n. The act of examining or seeing; a judgment or opinion; the range or extent of one's sight; something that is kept in sight. v. To watch or look at attentively; to consider.

vig-il (vij´il) n. A watch with prayers kept on the night before a religious feast; a period of surveillance.

vig-or (vig´r) n. Energy or physical strength; intensity of effect or action.

vile (vl) adj. Morally disgusting, miserable, and unpleasant. **-ly** adv. **-ness** n.

vil-la (vil´a) n. A luxurious home in the country; a country estate.

vil-lage (vil´ij) n. An incorporated settlement, usually smaller than a town.

vil-lain (vil´an) n. An evil or wicked person; a criminal; an uncouth person.

vin-ai-grette (vin´a gret´) n. A small orna mental bottle with a perforated top, used for holding an aromatic preparation such as smelling salts.

vin-di-cate (vin´di kt´) v. To clear of suspicion; to set free; to provide a defense or justification for. **vindication** n.

vin-dic-tive (vin dik´tiv) adj. Showing or possessing a desire for revenge; spiteful.

vine (vn) n. A plant whose stem needs support as it climbs or clings to a surface, as a wall or fence.

vin-e-gar (vin´e gr) n. A tart, sour liquid derived from cider or wine and used in flavoring and preserving food. **-y** adj.

vin-tage (vin´tij) n. The grapes or wine produced from a particular district in one season.

vi-nyl (v´nil) n. A variety of shiny plastics, similar to leather, often used for clothing and for covering furniture.

vi-o-la (v ´la) n. A stringed instrument, slightly larger and deeper in tone than a violin.

vi-o-late (v´o lt´) v. To break the law or a rule; to disrupt or disturb a person's privacy.

vi-o-lence (v´o lens) n. Physical force or activity used to cause harm, damage, or abuse.

vi-o-let (v´o lit) n. A small, low-growing plant with blue, purple, or white flowers; a purplish-blue color.

vi-o-lin (v´o ln´) n. A small stringed instrument, played with a bow.

VIP (v´´p´) abbr. Very important person.

vi-per (v´pr) n. A poisonous snake; an evil or treacherous person.

vir-gin (ver´jin) n. A person who has never had sexual intercourse. adj. In an unchanged or natural state.

vir-ile (vir´l) adj. Having the qualities and nature of a man; capable of sexual performance in the male. **virility** n.

vir-tu (vr t´) n. The love or knowledge of fine objects of art.

vir-tue (ver´ch) n. Morality, goodness or uprightness; a special type of goodness.

vi-rus (v´rus) n. Any of a variety of microscopic organisms which cause diseases.

vi-sa (v´za) n. An official authorization giving permission on a passport to enter a specific country.

vis-cid (vis´id) adj. Sticky; having an adhesive quality.

vise or (vs) n. A tool in carpentry and metal work having two jaws to hold things in position.

vis-i-bil-i-ty (viz´i bil´i t) n. pl. **-ies** The degree or state of being visible; the distance that one is able to see clearly.

vis-i-ble (viz´i bl) adj. Apparent; exposed to view.

vi-sion (vizh´an) n. The power of sight; the ability to see; an image created in the imagination; a supernatural appearance.

vis-it (viz´it) v. To journey to or come to see a person or place. n. A professional or social call. Slang To chat. **visitor, visitation** n.

vi-sor (v´zr) n. A brim on the front of a hat which protects the eyes from glare, the sun, wind, and rain.

vi-su-al (vizh´ al) adj. Visible; relating to seeing or sight.

vi-tal (vt´al) adj. Essential to life; very important. **vitally** adv.

vital signs n. pl., Med. The pulse rate, body temperature, blood pressure, and respiratory rate of a person.

vi-ta-min (vī´ta min) *n.* Any of various sub- stances which are found in foods and are essential to good health.

vit-ri-fy (vi´tri f´) *v.* To convert into glass or a substance similar to glass, by heat and fusion.

vi-va-cious (vi v´shus) *adj.* Filled with vitality or animation; lively. **-ly** *adv.*

viv-id (viv´id) *adj.* Bright; brilliant; intense.

vo-cab-u-lar-y (v kab´ya ler´) *n. pl.* A list or group of words and phrases, usually in alphabetical order; all the words that a person uses or understands.

vo-cal (v´kal) *adj.* Of or related to the voice; uttered by the voice; to speak freely and loudly. *n.* A vocal sound. **vocally** *adv.*

vocal cords *n. pl.* The lower of two folds or bands in the throat which produce sound when made tighter or loosened when air is breathed out while speaking or singing.

vo-ca-tion (v k´shзn) *n.* A career, occupation, trade, calling; a particular profession.

vo-cif-er-ate (v sif´e rt´) *v.* To utter or cry out loudly; to shout. **-tion** *n.*

vogue (vg) *n.* The leading style or fashion; popularity. **vogue** *adj.*

voice (vois) *n.* The sounds produced by speaking; the ability or power to produce musical tones. *v.* To express; to utter; to give voice.

void (void) *adj.* Containing nothing; empty; not inhabited; useless; vain; without legal force or effect; null. *n.* Empty space; the quality or state of being lonely. *v.* To make void; to discharge; to emit. A vacuum; any empty space.

void-ance (void´ans) The act of voiding, vacating, or ejecting.

void-ed (voi´did) *adj.* Pertaining to or being empty.

voile (voil) *n.* A fine, soft, sheer fabric of rayon and silk used for making light clothing and curtains.

vol-a-tile (vol´a-til) *adj.* Having the quality to pass off quickly by evaporation.

vol-can-ic (vol-kan´ik) *adj.* Pertaining to volcanoes; discharged from volca-

noes.

vol-ca-no (vol-k´n) *n.* A hole in the earth's surface through which molten rock, steam, ashes are expelled from, gradually forming a mountain.

volt-age (vl´tij) *n.* The amount of electrical power, given in terms and expressed in the number of volts.

vol-ume (vol´m) *n.* The capacity or amount of space or room; a book; a quantity; the loudness of a sound.

vol-un-tar-y (vol´an ter´) *adj.* Done cooperatively or willingly; from one's own choice.

vol-un-teer (vol´un tr´) *n.* One who offers himself for a service of his own free will. *adj.* Consisting of volunteers. *v.* To offer voluntarily for a service or purpose; to give freely.

vo-lup-tu-ous (vo lup´chŏ us) *adj.* Full of pleasure; delighting the senses; sensuous; luxury. **voluptuousness** *n.*

vom-it (vom´it) *v.* To eject contents of the stomach through the mouth. *n.* The food or matter ejected from the stomach by vomiting.

voo-doo (vŏ´dō) *n.* A religious cult derived from African ancestor worship.

vo-ra-cious (v r´shus) *adj.* Having a large appetite; insatiable. **-ly** *adv.*

vote (vt) *n.* The expression of one's choice by voice, by raising one's hand, or by secret ballot. *v.* To express one's views.

vouch (vouch) *v.* To verify or support as true; to guarantee.

vow (vou) *n.* A solemn pledge or promise, especially one made to God; a marriage vow. *v.* To make a vow.

vow-el (vou´el) *n.* A sound of speech made by voicing the flow of breath within the mouth; a letter representing a vowel, as a, e, i, o, u, and sometimes y.

voy-age (voi´ij) *n.* A long trip or journey.

vul-gar (vul´gr) *adj.* Showing poor manners; crude; improper; immoral or indecent.

vul-ner-a-ble (vul´nr a bl) *adj.* Open to physical injury or attack; capable of being hurt or wounded.

vul-ture (vul´chr) *n.* A large bird of the hawk family, living on dead animals; a greedy person; one who feeds on the mistakes or bad luck of others.

W

W, w (dub'l ') The twenty-third letter of the English alphabet.

wad (wod) *n.* A small crumpled mass or bundle; a soft plug used to hold shot or gunpowder charge in place. *Slang* A large roll of money.

wad-dle (wod'l) *v.* To walk with short steps and swing from side to side.

wade (wd) *v.* To walk through a substance as mud or water which hampers one's steps.

wa-fer (w'fr) *n.* A small, thin, crisp cracker, cookie, or candy.

waf-fle (wof'l) *n.* Pancake batter cooked in a waffle iron.

wag (wag) *v.* To move quickly from side to side or up and down. *n.* A playful, witty person. **waggish** *adj.*

wage (wj) *n.* A payment of money for labor or services. *v.* To conduct.

wa-ger (w'jr) *v.* To make a bet. **wager** *n.*

wail (wl) *v.* A loud, mournful cry or weep. *v.* To make such a sound.

waist (wst) *n.* The narrow part of the body between the thorax and hips; the middle part or section of something which is narrower than the rest.

wait (wt) *v.* To stay in one place in expectation of; to await; to put off until a later time or date; to be ready or prepared. *n.* A time of waiting.

waive (wv) *v.* To forfeit of one's own free will; to postpone or dispense with.

wake (wk) *v.* To come to consciousness, as from sleep. *n.* A vigil for a dead body; the surface turbulence caused by a vessel moving through water.

wall (wol) *n.* A vertical structure to separate or enclose an area. *v.* To provide or close up, as with a wall.

wal-let (wol'it) *n.* A flat folding case for carrying paper money.

wall-pa-per (wol'p'pr) *n.* Decorative paper for walls, usually having a colorful pattern.

wal-nut (wol'nut) *n.* An edible nut with a hard, light-brown shell; the tree on which this nut grows.

wal-rus (wol'rus) *n.* A large marine mammal of the seal family, having flippers, tusks, and a tough hide.

waltz (wolts) *n.* A ballroom dance in 3/4 time; music for a waltz. *v.* To dance a waltz; to advance successfully and easily.

wand (wond) *n.* A slender rod used by a magician.

wan-der (won'dr) *v.* To travel about aimlessly; to roam; to stray.

want (wont) *v.* To wish for or desire; to need; to lack; to fail to possess a required amount; to hunt in order to apprehend. *n.* The state of lacking a required or usual amount.

ware (wâr) *n.* Manufactured items of the same general kind; items or goods for sale.

ware-house (wâr'hous) *n.* A large building used to store merchandise.

warm (worm) *adj.* Moderate heat; neither hot or cold; comfortably established.

warn (worn) *v.* To give notice or inform beforehand; to call to one's attention.

war-rant (wor'ant) *n.* A written authorization giving the holder legal power to search, seize, or arrest.

war-ri-or (wor' r) *n.* One who fights in a war or battle.

wash (wosh) *v.* To cleanse by the use of water; to remove dirt; to move or deposit as if by the force of water.

was-n't (wuz'ant) Was not.

waste (wst) *v.* To be thrown away; to be available but not used completely. *n.* A barren region; the instance of wasting; useless material produced as a by-product. *Slang* To destroy or murder.

watch (woch) *v.* To view carefully; to guard; to keep informed. *n.* The act of staying awake to guard or protect; a small time piece worn on the wrist.

watch-ful (woch'ful) *adj.* Carefully observant or attentive. **watchfully** *adv.*

watch-man (woch'man) *n.* A person hired to keep watch; a guard.

wa-ter (wo'tr) *n.* The clear liquid making up oceans, lakes, and streams; the body fluids as tears or urine. *v.* To pour or spray water on something; to give water to drink.

wa-ter-proof (wo'tr prôf') *adj.* Capable of preventing water from penetrating.

v. To make or treat in order to make waterproof. *n.* A material or fabric which is waterproof.

wa·ter·way (wo´tr wā´) *n.* A navigable body of water; a channel for water.

watt (wot) *n.* A unit of electrical power represented by current of one ampere, produced by the electromotive force of one volt.

wave (wv) *v.* To move back and forth or up and down; to motion with the hand. *n.* A swell or moving ridge of water; a curve or curl, as in the hair.

wa·ver (w´vr) *v.* To sway unsteadily; to move back and forth; to weaken in force. **waver** *n.* **waveringly** *adv.*

wax (waks) *n.* A natural yellowish substance made by bees, solid when cold and easily melted or softened when heated. **waxy** *adj.*

way (w) *n.* A manner of doing something; a tendency or characteristic; a habit or customary manner of acting or living.

way·lay (w´l´) *v.* To attack by ambush.

we (w) Used to refer to the person speaking and one or more other people.

weak (wk) *adj.* Having little energy or strength; easily broken; having inadequate skills; not reasonable.

wealth (welth) *n.* An abundance of valuable possessions or property; all goods and resources having monetary value.

wean (wn) *v.* To accustom an infant or small child to food other than a mother's milk or bottle.

weap·on (wep´on) *n.* A device used in fighting a war; a device which can be used to harm another person.

wear (wâr) *v.* To have on or put something on the body; to display. *n.* The act of wearing out or using up; the act of wearing, as clothing. **wearable** *adj.*

wea·ry (wr´) *adj.* Exhausted; tired; feeling fatigued. *v.* To make or become tired; to become fatigued. **wearily** *adv.*

weath·er (weth´r) *n.* The condition of the air or atmosphere in terms of humidity, temperature, and similar features. *v.* To become worn by the actions of weather; to survive.

weave (wv) *v.* To make a basket, cloth, or other item by interlacing threads or

other strands of material. **weaver** *n.*

web (web) *n.* A cobweb; a piece of interlacing material which forms a woven structure; something constructed as an entanglement; a thin membrane that joins the toes of certain water birds.

wed (wed) *v.* To take as a spouse; to marry.

we'd (wd) We had; we should.

wed·ding (wed´ing) *n.* A marriage ceremony; an act of joining together in close association.

wedge (wej) *n.* A tapered, triangular piece of wood or metal used to split logs, to add leverage, and to hold something open or ajar. *v.* To force or make something fit tightly.

wed·lock (wed´lok) *n.* Marriage; the state of being married.

week (wk) *n.* A period of seven days, beginning with Sunday and ending with Saturday; the time or days normally spent at school or work.

week·day (wk´d´) *n.* Any day of the week except Saturday or Sunday.

week·ly (wk´l) *adv.* Every week; once a week. *adj.* Taking place or done every week of or relating to a week.

weep (wp) *v.* To shed tears; to express sorrow, joy, or emotion; by shedding tears; to cry.

wee·vil (w´vil) *n.* A small beetle having a downward curving snout, which damages plants.

weigh (w) *v.* To determine the heaviness of an object by using a scale; to consider carefully in one's mind; to be of a particular weight.

weight (wt) *n.* The amount that something weighs; heaviness; a heavy object used to hold or pull something down; an overpowering force; the quality of a garment for a particular season. *v.* To make heavy.

weird (wrd) *adj.* Having an extraordinary or strange character. **weirdly** *adv.*

wel·come (wel´kom) *v.* To extend warm hospitality; to accept gladly. *adj.* Received warmly. *n.* A greeting upon one's arrival.

weld (weld) *v.* To unite metallic parts by applying heat and sometimes pressure, allowing the metals to bond together. *n.* A joint formed by welding.

wel-fare (wel´fâr´) n. The state of doing well; governmental aid to help the disabled or disadvantaged.

well (wel) n. A hole in the ground which contains a supply of water; a shaft in the ground through which gas and oil are obtained. adj. Being in good health; in an agreeable state.

we'll (wl) We will; we shall.

wellbe-ing (wel´b´ing) n. The state of being healthy, happy, or prosperous.

welldone (wel´dun´) adj. Completely cooked; done properly.

wellgroomed (wel´grömd´) adj. Clean, neat, and properly cared for.

well-known (wel´nn´) adj. Widely known.

welt (welt) n. A strip between the sole and upper part of a shoe; a slight swelling on the body, usually caused by a blow to the area. v. To hit severly.

went v. Past tense of go.

wept v. Past tense of weep.

were (wer) v. Second person singular past plural of be.

we're (wr) We are.

were-n't (wernt) Were not.

whack (hwak) v. To strike with a hard blow, to slap. n. An attempt.

whale (hwl) n. A very large mammal resembling a fish which lives in salt water. Slang An outstanding or impressive example.

wharf (hworf) n. A pier or platform built at the edge of water so that ships can load and unload.

what (hwut) pron. Which one; which things; which type or kind. adv. In which way. adj. Which particular one.

what-ev-er (hwut ev´r) Everything or anything. adj. No matter what.

what's contr. What is.

wheat (hwt) n. A grain ground into flour, used to make breads and similar foods.

wheeze (hwz) v. To breathe with a hoarse whistling sound. n. A high whistling sound.

when (hwen) adv. At what time; at which time. pron. What or which time. conj. While; at the time that; although.

when-ev-er (hwen ev´r) adv. At any time; when. conj. At whatever time.

where (hwâr) adv. At or in what direc-tion or place; in what direction or place.

wher-ev-er adv. In any situation or place.

wheth-er (hweth´r) conj. Indicating a choice; alternative possibilities; either.

whet-stone (hwet´stn´) n. A stone used to sharpen scissors, knives, and other implements.

whey (hw) n. The clear, water-like part of milk that separates from the curd.

which (hwich) pron. What one or ones; the one previously; whatever one or ones; which ever. adj. What one; any one of.

which-ev-er (hwich ev´r) pron., adj. Any; no matter which or what.

whiff (hwif) n. A slight puff; a light cur-rent of air; a slight breath or odor.

while (hwl) n. A length or period of time. conj. During the time that; even though; at the same time; although.

whim (hwim) n. A sudden desire.

whim-per (hwim´pr) v. To make a weak, soft crying sound. whimper n.

whim-si-cal (hwim´zi kal) adj. Impulsive; erratic; light and sponta-neous.

whine (hwn) v. To make a squealing, plaintive sound; to complain in an irri-tating, childish fashion.

whip-lash (hwip´lash´) n. An injury to the spine or neck caused by a sudden jerking motion of the head.

whirl (hwerl) v. To rotate or move in circles; to twirl; to move, drive, or go very fast. n. A rapid whirling motion.

whisk (hwisk) v. To move with a sweep-ing motion; to move quickly or lightly. n. A sweeping movement; a utensil used in cooking; to stir.

whis-per (hwis´pr) v. To speak in a very low tone; to tell in secret. n. A low rustling sound; the act of whispering.

white (hwt) n. The color opposite of black; the part of something that is white or light in color, as an egg or the eyeball; a member of the Caucasian group of people. adj. Having a light color; pale; pure; blameless; without sin.

who (hö) pron. Which or what certain individual, person, or group; referring to a person previously mentioned.

who'd *contr.* Who would; who had.

who-ev-er (hō ev´r) *pron.* Whatever person; all or any persons.

whole (hl) *adj.* Complete; having nothing missing; not divided or in pieces; a complete system or unity; everything considered. *Math* Not a fraction.

who'll *contr.* Who shall; who will.

whom (hōm) *pron.* The form of who used as the direct object of a verb or the object of the preposition.

whom-ev-er (hōm ev´r) *pron.* The form of whoever used as the object of a preposition or the direct object of a verb.

who's *contr.* Who is; who has.

whose (hōz) *pron.* Belonging to or having to do with one's belongings. *adj.* Relating to *which* or *whom*.

why (hw) *adv.* For what reason or purpose. *conj.* The cause, purpose, or reason for which. *interj.* Expressing surprise or disagreement.

whither (with´r) v. To dry up or wilt from a lack of moisture; to lose freshness or vigor.

wick (wik) *n.* The soft strand of fibers which extends from a candle or lamp and draws up the fuel for burning.

wick-er (wik´r) *n.* A thin, pliable twig used to make furniture and baskets.

wide (wd) *adj.* Broad; covering a large area; completely extended or open. *adv.* Over a large area; full extent.

wide-spread (wd´spred´) *adj.* Fully spread out; over a broad area.

wid-ow (wid´) *n.* A woman whose husband is no longer living.

wid-ow-er (wid´ r) *n.* A man whose wife is no longer living.

width (width) *n.* The distance or extent of something from side to side.

wield (wld) *v.* To use or handle something skillfully; to employ power effectively.

wife (wf) *n.* A married female.

wig (wig) *n.* Artificial or human hair woven together to cover baldness or a bald spot on the head.

wig-gle (wig´l) *v.* To squirm; to move with rapid side-to-side motions.

wig-wam (wig´wom) *n.* An Indian dwelling place.

wild (wld) *adj.* Living in a natural, untamed state; not occupied by man; not civilized; strange and unusual. *adv.* Out of control. *n.* A wilderness region not cultivated or settled by man.

will (wil) *n.* The mental ability to decide or choose for oneself; strong desire or determination; a legal document stating how one's property is to be distributed after death. *v.* To bring about by an act of a will; to decide as by decree; to give or bequeath something in a will.

wilt (wilt) *v.* To cause or to become limp; to lose force; to deprive of courage or energy.

win (win) *v.* To defeat others; to gain victory in a contest; to receive. *n.* Victory; the act of winning. **winner** *n.*

wind (wnd) *n.* A natural movement of air. *v.* To become short of breath. *v.* To wrap around and around something; to turn, to crank. *n.* A turning or twisting.

win-dow (win´d) *n.* An opening built in a wall for light and air; a pane of glass.

win-ter (win´tr) *n.* The coldest season, coming between autumn and spring. *adj.* Relating to or typically of winter.

wipe (wp) *v.* To clean by rubbing; to take off by rubbing. *n.* The act or instance of wiping.

wis-dom (wiz´dom) *n.* The ability to understand what is right, true, or enduring; good judgment; knowledge.

wise (wz) *adj.* Having superior intelligence; having great learning; having a capacity for sound judgment marked by deep understanding. **-ly** *adv.*

wish (wish) *v.* To desire or long for something; to command or request. *n.* A longing or desire.

wish-bone (wish´bn´) *n.* The bone of a bird, which, according to the superstition, when broken brings good luck to the person who has the longer end.

wish-ful (wish´ful) *adj.* Having or expressing a wish; hopeful. **-fully** *adv.*

wisp (wisp) *n.* A tuft or small bundle of hay, straw, or hair; a thin piece. **-y** *adj.*

wit (wit) *n.* The ability to use words in a clever way; a sense of humor.

witch (wich) *n.* A person believed to have magical powers; a mean, ugly, old woman.

with (with) *prep.* In the company of;

wit-ness (wit'nis) *n.* A person who has seen, experienced, or heard something; something serving as proof or evidence. *v.* To see or hear something; to give proof or evidence of; to give testimony.

wiz-ard (wiz'rd) *n.* A very clever person; a person thought to have magical powers. *Slang* One with amazing skill.

wob-ble (wob'l) *v.* To move unsteadily from side to side, as a rocking motion.

woe (w) *n.* Great sorrow or grief.

wok *n.* A convex metal cooker for stir-frying food.

woke *v.* Past tense of wake.

wom-an (wem'an) *n.* The mature adult human female; a person who has feminine qualities.

womb (wōm) *n.* The uterus; the place where development occurs.

won-der (wun'dr) *n.* A feeling of amazement or admiration. *v.* To feel admiration; to feel uncertainty. **wonderful** *adj.*

won't (wnt) Will not.

word (werd) *n.* A meaningful sound which stands for an idea; a comment; a brief talk; an order or command. *v.* To express orally.

word processing *n.* A system which produces typewritten documents with automated type and editing equipment.

work (werk) *n.* The action or labor required to accomplish something; employment; a job.

work-er (wer'kr) *n.* A person who works for wages; an employee.

work-ing (wer'king) *adj.* Adequate to permit work to be done.

world (werld) *n.* The planet Earth; the universe; the human race.

world-ly (werld'l) *adj.* Interested in pleasure rather than religious or spiritual matters.

worn (wrn) *adj.* Made weak or thin from use; exhausted.

wor-ry (wer') *v.* To be concerned or troubled; to tug at repeatedly; to annoy; to irritate. *n.* Distress or mental anxiety.

wor-ship (wer'ship) *n.* Reverence for a sacred object; high esteem or devotion

for a person. *v.* To attend a religious service.

worst (werst) *adj.* Bad; most inferior; most disagreeable. *adv.* In the worst degree.

worth (werth) *n.* The quality or value of something; personal merit; the quantity that can be purchased for a certain amount of money.

wor-thy (wer'th) *adj.* Valuable or useful; deserving admiration or honor.

would-n't (wed'nt) Would not.

wound (wōnd) *n.* A laceration of the skin. *v.* To injure by tearing, cutting, or piercing the skin.

wran-gle (rang'gl) *v.* To quarrel noisily.

wrath (rath) *n.* Violent anger or fury.

wreak (rk) *v.* To inflict punishment upon another person.

wreath (rth) *n.* A decorative ring-like form of intertwined flowers, bows, and other articles.

wreck (rek) *v.* To ruin or damage by accident or deliberately; to spoil. *n.* Destruction; the remains of something wrecked or ruined.

wrench (rench) *n.* A tool used to grip, turn, or twist an object as a bolt or nut. *v.* To turn or twist violently; to give emotional pain.

wrest (rest) *v.* To twist or pull away in a violent way. *n.* A forcible twist.

wres-tle (res'l) *v.* To struggle with an opponent in order to pin him down. *n.* The instance of wrestling. **wrestler** *n.*

wretch (rech) *n.* An extremely unhappy person; a miserable person. **-ed** *adj.*

wrig-gle (rig'l) *v.* To squirm; to move by turning and twisting.

wring (ring) *v.* To squeeze and twist by hand or machine; to press together.

wrist (rist) *n.*, *Anat.* The joint of the body between the hand and forearm.

writ (rit) *n.*, *Law* A written court document directed to a public official or individual ordering a specific action.

write (rt) *v.* To form symbols or letters; to form words on a surface; to communicate by writing; to earn a living by writing books.

writ-ing (r'ting) *n.* A book or other written work; handwriting; the process of forming letters into words.

wrong (rong) *adj.* Incorrect; against

moral standards; not suitable; immoral; unsuitable; inappropriate. *n.* An act which is wicked or immoral. *v.* To do wrong; to injure or hurt.

wrought (rot) *adj.* Fashioned; formed; beatened or hammered into shape.

X

X, x (eks) The twenty-fourth letter of the English alphabet.

X chro-mo-some (eks´kr´mo sm) *n.* The sex chromosome, associated with female characteristics; occurs paired in the female and single in the male chromosome pair.

xe-non (z´non) *n.* The colorless, odorless gaseous element found in small quantities in the air, symbolized by Xe.

xen-o-phobe (zen´o fb´) *n.* A person who dislikes, fears, and mistrusts for eigners or anything strange. **-bia** *n.*

xe-roph-thal mi-a *n.* A itching soreness of the eyes that is caused by an insufficient amount of vitamin A.

xe-ro-phyte *n.* A plant that can live in a surrounding of extreme heat and drought. **xerophytic** *adj.* **-tism** *n.*

X-mas (eks´mas) *abbr. n.* Christmas.

XRa-di-a-tion *n.* Treatment with X-rays.

X ray (eks´r´) *n.* Energy that is radiated with a shortwave length and high penetrating power; a black and white negative image or picture of the interior of the body.

xsec-tion *n.* Cross section of something.

xy-lo-phone (z´lo fn´) *n.* A musical instrument consisting of mounted wooden bars which produce a ringing musical sound when struck with two small wooden hammers. **-ist** *n.*

xy-lose *n.* A crystalline aldose sugar.

xy-lot-o-mous *adj.* Capable of cutting or boring wood. **xylotomic** *adj.*

Y

Y, y (w) The twenty-fifth letter of the English alphabet.

yacht (yot) *n.* A small sailing vessel powdered by wind or motor, used for pleasure cruises. **yacht** *n.*

yak (yak) *n.* A longhaired ox of Tibet and the mountains of central Asia.

yam (yam) *n.* An edible root; a variety of the sweet potato.

yap (yap) *v.* To bark in a high pitched, sharp way. *Slang* To talk in a relentless, loud, or stupid manner.

yard (yärd) *n.* A unit of measure that equals 36 inches or 3 feet; the ground around or near a house or building.

yard-stick (yärd´stik´) *n.* A graduated measuring stick that equals 1 yard or 36 inches.

yarn (yärn) *n.* Twisted fibers, as of wool, used in knitting or weaving.

yawn (yon) *v.* To inhale a deep breath with the mouth open wide. **yawner** *n.*

Y-Chro-mo-some (w´kr´mo sm) *n.* The sex chromosome associated with male charac-teristics.

ye (y) You, used especially in religious contexts, as hymns.

yeah *adv. Slang* Yes.

year (yr) *n.* A period of time starting on January 1st and continuing through December 31st, consisting of 365 days or 366 days in a leap year.

yearn (yern) *v.* To feel a strong craving.

yeast (yst) *n.* Fungi or plant cells used to make baked goods rise or fruit juices ferment.

yell (yel) *v.* To cry out loudly. *n.* A loud cry; a cheer to show support for an athletic team.

yellow fever *n.* An acute infectious disease of the tropics, spread by the bite of a mosquito.

yes (yes) *adv.* To express agreement.

yes-ter-day (yes´tr d) *n.* The day before today; a former or recent time. *adv.* On the day before the present day.

yet (yet) *adv.* Up to now; at this time; even now; more so. *conj.* Nevertheless; but.

yew () *n.* An evergreen tree having poisonous flat, dark-green needles and poisonous red berries.

Yid-dish (yid´ish) *n.* A language spoken by Jews combining German and Hebrew; spoken by Jews. **Yiddish** *adj.*

yield (yld) *v.* To bear or bring forward; to give up the possession of something; to give way to. *n.* An amount that is produced.

yo-ga (y´ga) *n.* A system of exercises which helps the mind and the body in order to achieve tranquillity and spiritual insight.

yo-gurt (y´grt) *n.* A thick custard-like food made from curdled milk and often mixed with fruit.

yoke (yk) *n.* A wooden bar used to join together two oxen or other animals working together; the section of a garment fitting closely around the shoulders. *v.* To join with a yoke.

yolk (yk) *n.* The yellow nutritive part of an egg.

Yom Kip-pur (yom kip´r) *n.* The Jewish holiday observed with fasting and prayer for the forgiveness of sins.

you () *pron.* The person or persons addressed.

you'd (d) You had; you would.

you'll (l) You will; you shall.

young (yung) *adj.* Of or relating to the early stage of life.

your (yer) *adj.* Belonging to you or yourself or the person spoken to.

you're (r) You are.

your-self (yer self´) *pron.* A form of you for emphasis when the object of a verb and the subject is the same.

youth (th) *n.* The appearance or state of being young; the time of life when one is not considered an adult; a young person.

you've (v) You have.

yowl (youl) *v.* To make a loud, long cry or howl.

yo--yo (y´y) *n.* A grooved spool toy with a string wrapped around the spool so it can be spun or moved up and down.

yt-ter-bi-um (i ter´b um) *n.* A metallic element of the rare-earth group symbolized by Yb.

yt-tri-um (i´tr um) *n.* A metallic element symbolized by Y.

yule (l) *n.* Christmas.

yule-tide (l´td´) *n.* The Christmas season.

Z

Z, z (z) The twenty-sixth letter of the English alphabet.

za-ny (z´n) *n. pl.* **-nies** A clown; a person who acts silly or foolish. *adj.* Typical of being clownish. **zaniness** *n.* **zannily** *adv.*

zap *v. Slang* To destroy; to do away with.

zeal (zl) *n.* Great interest or eagerness.

zeal-ot (zel´ot) *n.* A fanatical person; a fanatic.

zeal-ous (zel´us) *adj.* Full of interest; eager; passionate. **zealously** *adv.*

zeph-yr (zef´r) *n.* A gentle breeze.

ze-ro (zr´) *n. pl.* **-ros, -roes** The number or symbol "0"; nothing; the point from which degrees or measurements on a scale begin; the lowest point. *v.* To aim, point at, or close in on. *adj.* Pertaining to zero; nonexisting.

zest (zest) *n.* Enthusiasm; a keen quality.

zinc (zingk) *n.* A bluish-white crystalline metallic element, used as a protective coating for steel and iron, symbolized by Zn.

zip (zip) *n.* To act or move with vigor or speed. **zip** *v.* To move with energy, speed, or facility; to open or close with a zipper. *Slang* Energy; zero; nothing.

zip code *n.* A five digit number, plus four to each postal delivery location in the United States.

zip-per (zip´r) *n.* A fastener consisting of two rows of plastic or metal teeth that are interlocked by means of sliding a tab.

zo-di-ac (z´d ak´) *n.* The celestial sphere; the unseen path followed through the heavens by the moon, sun, and most planets; this area divided into twelve parts or twelve astrological signs, each bearing the name of a constellation.

zone (zn) *n.* An area or region set apart from its surroundings by some characteristic.

zoo (zö) *n.* A public display or collection of living animals.

zo-ol-o-gy (z ol´o j) *n.* The science that deals with animals, animal life, and the animal kingdom. **zoologist** *n.*

zoom (zöm) *v.* To move with a continuous, loud, buzzing sound; to move upward sharply; to move toward a subject with great speed.

zy-gote (z´gt) *n.* The cell formed by the uniting of two gametes.

zy-mur-gy (z´mer j) *n.* The chemistry that deals with the fermentation processes, especially applied to distilling.